STANDARD GUIDE TO
AMERICAN
MUSCLE CARS

A SUPERCAR SOURCE BOOK 1960-2000

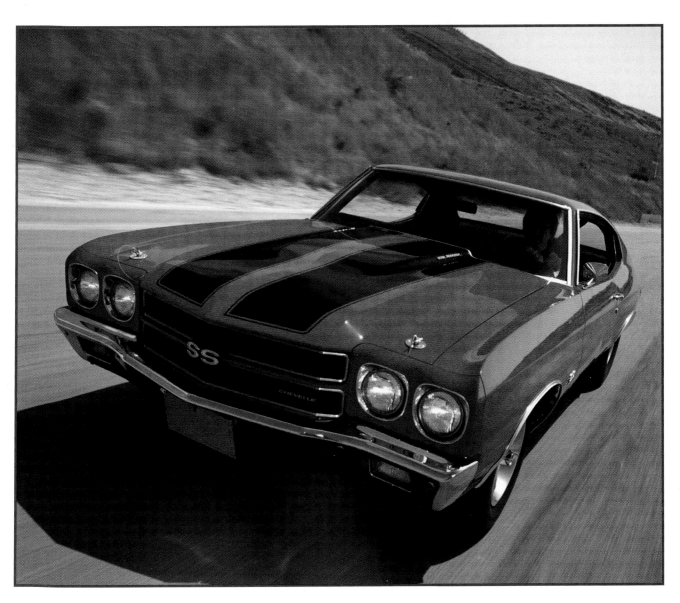

Edited by John Gunnell

Published by

**krause
publications**

700 East State Street • Iola, WI 54990-0001
715/445-2214 • FAX: 715/445-4087   www.krause.com

Please call or write for our free catalog of publications. Our toll-free number to place an order or obtain a free catalog is 800-258-0929 or please use our regular business telephone 715-445-2214.

Library of Congress Catalog Number 92-74075
ISBN 0-87349-262-5

Dedication

Your editor's interest in muscle cars began in the late 1960s, when I spent hour upon hour reading car enthusiast publications originally purchased by my father, Albert A. Gunnell. Those magazines were filled with stories and photos about the rare muscle cars that we collect now. Forward thinkers like *Motor Trend* columnist Mike Lamm were telling us, even way back then, that the real muscle cars were very rare and would be desirable to *future* collectors. Now, the future has come!

Credits & Acknowledgements

It would have been impossible to compile *Standard Guide to American Muscle Cars* without the help of many people who helped gather facts and photos for the book.

Bob Ackerson, Tom Brownell, John Gunnell, Phil Hall, Jerry Heasley, John Lee, Jim Lenzke and Terry Parkhurst are responsible for the muscle car histories. The majority of the color photos—which are new to this edition—were contributed by Jerry Heasley, a Texas photographer who has specialized in capturing America's "supercars" on film for nearly three decades. Other photos were supplied by individual car owners who responded to advertisements in *Old Car Weekly* soliciting photo contributions. The rest of the photos are from the giant *Old Cars Weekly* photo archives.

As for general encouragement, enthusiasm and spreading of knowledge about muscle cars, we greatly appreciate the support of Bill Bartels of Supercar Showdown, Reeves Callaway, Chevrolet Motor Div., The Chrysler Historical Foundation, Richie Clyne of the Imperial Palace, Rick Cole of Rick Cole Auctions, Walter E. Cunny, Jr., Dodge Div. of Chrysler Motors, Helen Early (Oldsmobile Historical), Gary Esse of Madison Classics, Ford Motor Co., Alex Gabbard, GM Media Archives, Jesse Gunnell, Phil Hall, Jerry Heasley, Craig Jackson of Barrett-Jackson, Gary F. Jole, Glenn Klobuchar, Ron Kowalke, John Lee, Jim Mattison of Pontiac Historic services, George McNeilus, Johnathan K. Meyers, Chip and Bill Miller of Carlisle Productions, Jack Miller, Joe Molina Public Relations (JMPR), Drew Phillips, Pontiac Motor Div., Ed Reavie of Nostalgia Productions, Vince Rufolo, John Sawruk, Marty Schorr, Carroll-Shelby Bill Siuru, Gordon Van Vechten, Robbie J. Wadzinski, Jim Wangers and Don Williams of Blackhawk.

We think this book will be successful as a reflection of the ever-growing interest in muscle car collecting and invite everyone who reads it to submit additional information and photos to make future editions bigger and better.

Table of Contents

OLDSMOBILE

PLYMOUTH

PONTIAC

SHELBY

STUDEBAKER

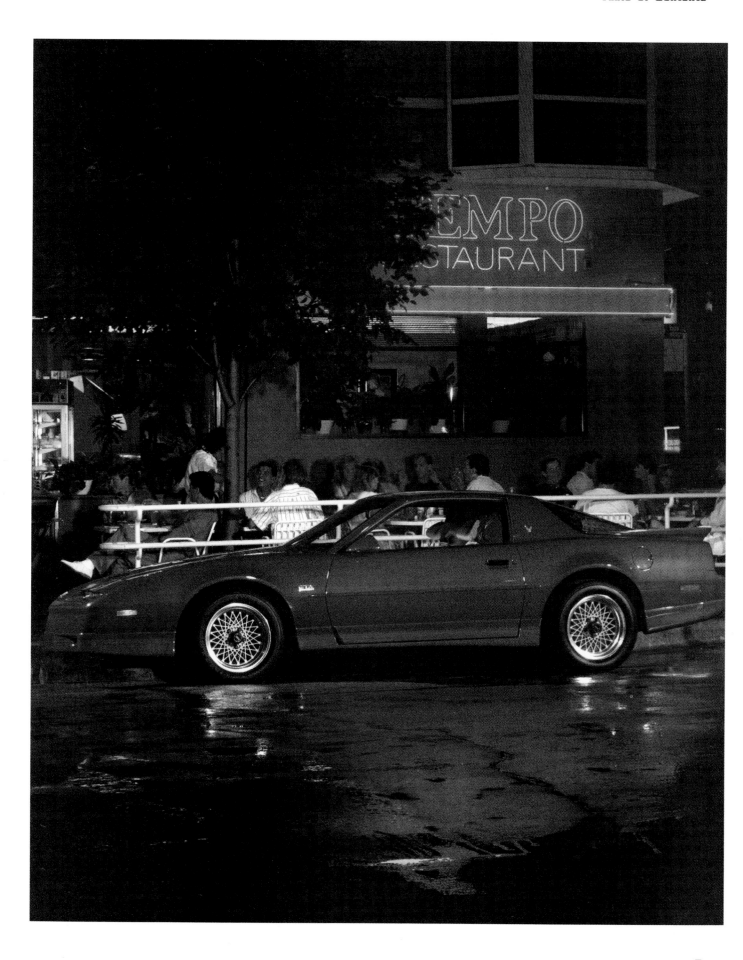

Introduction

Automotive historians have pulled out their hair trying to define what a muscle car is. Some will say the 1949 Olds 88 was the first muscle car. Others will give that honor to the 1955 Chrysler C-300. Purists of the bucket seat, four-speed and fat-tire sect insist that the GTO-optioned 1964 Pontiac Tempest was the original muscle car.

Some will say the "muscle car era" started in the early 1960s and ended in 1972, when federal anti-pollution laws and rising insurance rates curtailed muscle car production. However, the owners of powerful late-model cars will be quick to point out that some of them are faster than the quickest cars of the '60s. So this edition of the *Standard Guide to American Muscle Cars* will cover hot-charging cars built between 1960 and 2001.

We are now covering American-made cars only. Captive imports and trucks are gone. Some of the cars we are spotlighting are small, some are mid-sized and others are large. They have different kinds of engines. They are made by Chevrolet, Ford and Chrysler as well as by AMC and Studebaker. The rule we used is this: If it's U.S.-built, production-related and formidable in oval track racing, road racing or drag racing, it can be called a muscle car.

It's true that the "classic" muscle car is considered a GTO-like model, although it can be made by any American automaker. But, did you know that the term muscle car wasn't heard much back when these vehicles were first hitting the market? In those days, the enthusiast magazines favored the term supercar.

"Supercar" seems to be derived from Super-Stock drag racing terminology. Early supercars had solid-color vinyl interiors, hood scoops, consoles, mag wheels, floor shifters and red-stripe tires. Many had massively big power plants in a small body, which made them great for drag racing.

A few years later, the same big motors were shoehorned into even smaller cars: compacts, senior compacts and sports compacts (or pony cars). These were also drag raced. Then, people noticed that certain muscle cars were well suited for sedan races in the Sports Car Club of America's (SCCA) Trans-Am Challenge series.

There were also some huge cars that proved to be quite fast when big engines were stuffed into them: Thunderbirds, Marlins, Pontiac 2+2s and Chrysler Letter Cars come to mind. These machines were muscular, too, but they weren't the same as supercars like the GTO.

Eventually, the term "supercar" disappeared. "Muscle car" took its place and stuck like an F60-14 RWL tire on hot asphalt. Nowadays, collectors use it to refer to just about any of the types of cars mentioned above.

After 1982, genuine muscle cars started returning to the market. These smaller-sized, lower-weight, higher-tech performance machines were far different from '60s supercars, except that they also went fast. Now, we have four-cylinder rockets that can outrun yesterday's hottest factory hot rods.

The Standard Guide to American Muscle Cars is a book that covers the entire spectrum of muscle from "south-of-the-border" Lincolns to viscous Vipers. Rolling out research done for *Old Cars Weekly* and *Old Cars Price Guide*, this book fills in many of the gaps and presents approximately 400 muscle cars representing over 40 years worth of race-ready road warriors.

We hope you enjoy this book. Send us a nice picture of your muscle car and you might see it in future editions of *The Standard Guide to American Muscle Cars*.

John Gunnell, editor

AMERICAN MOTORS

1965 AMERICAN MOTORS RAMBLER MARLIN

Trying to slot the 1965 1/2 Rambler Marlin into a clear-cut category in the midst of the muscle car era is not an easy task. By design, Ramblers were not at the forefront of the performance armada, yet the semi-fastback two-door hardtop did have eye-catching lines that were right in fashion with the fastback trend that was prevalent in the mid-'60s.

It is well recorded that the original appearance of the Marlin roof was on the 1964 Tarpon show car that utilized the compact Rambler American's 106-inch wheelbase. Also, it is likely that, had the Tarpon been put into production, it would have fared better against the 1964 Plymouth Valiant-based Barracuda and 1965 Ford Mustang 2+2. However, the powers at American Motors transferred Dick Teague's styling to the intermediate 112-inch wheelbase Rambler Classic chassis and, from the beltline down, body.

The Rambler Classic was restyled for 1965 and grew about 5 inches in length. It was now made more distinct from the more luxurious Ambassador, which got 4 additional inches of wheelbase and more individual styling.

Instead of aiming at the performance-seeking customer, the Marlin stressed comfort and room. It featured an Ambassador instrument panel and could be had with individually reclining front seats or slim bucket-type seats with a center console or center cushion.

Standard in the Marlin Rambler—as in the Ambassador—was the new 232-cid Torque Command six with a two-barrel carburetor and a rating of 155 hp. Optional were a pair of first generation AMC V-8s, a mild 198-hp 287-cid version and the top 327-cid engine, which was rated at 270 hp, as it had been since the 1958 Ambassador days.

In the transmission department, a three-speed standard shift came as the base unit. On cars without buckets, overdrive or three-speed Flash-O-Matic was optional. Those with the console and buckets had an interesting option called Twin-Stick overdrive, which boasted five forward speeds. You could also get Shift-Command Flash-O-Matic, which could be shifted manually if preferred.

The chassis still utilized the dated torque tube drive with an enclosed drive shaft and coil springs in the rear. However, power disc front brakes and flanged rear drums were standard.

Not a screamer, the 327 Marlin was capable of average intermediate performance. *Mechanix Illustrated's* Tom McCahill found such a Marlin, with automatic transmission, capable of 0 to 60 mph in 9.7 seconds.

The factory base price for the Marlin was $3,100. There was sufficient curiosity in it to draw 10,327 orders in the short first-year run that followed its February 1965 introduction. That would be a high water mark, so to speak, as the 1966 Marlin, minus the Rambler nameplate, some previously standard equipment and with the addition of an optional four-speed manual gearbox, found only 4,547 customers. It was in that model year that the 1966 1/2 Dodge Charger was introduced. It used the same formula with a fastback body on an intermediate chassis and sold better.

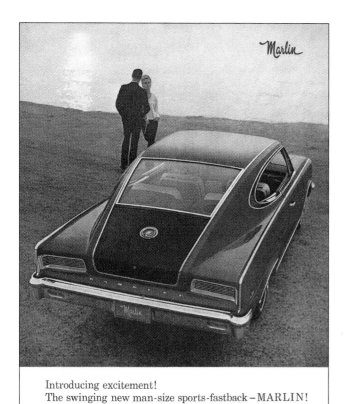

Introducing excitement!
The swinging new man-size sports-fastback – MARLIN!

The 1965 AMC Rambler Marlin had a unique fastback roofline.

Marlin BY RAMBLER – Newest of the Sensible Spectaculars

AMC called the 1965 Rambler Marlin "the most exciting Rambler ever built."

1966 AMERICAN MOTORS RAMBLER ROGUE V-8

The 1966 AMC Rambler Rogue was the first V-8 AMC compact.

The earth didn't move (well, maybe a little in Kenosha, Wisconsin) when American Motors introduced the Rambler Rogue Typhoon V-8 on April 7, 1966. After all, V-8 powered compacts had become common years before.

Of minor significance was that it offered the first factory V-8 installation in the 106-inch wheelbase Rambler American. More importantly, it was the first production role for the newly designed AMC V-8, which would be a standard bearer in the coming years for the independent auto manufacturer.

The old AMC V-8, which was not installed in Americans, first appeared in 1956 and didn't have much room to grow. It was somewhat heavy and generally didn't take well to attempts to extract more than 270 hp from the 327-cid version carried from 1958-1966. The new "Typhoon" V-8, in its initial form, displaced 290 cid from a bore of 3.75 inches and a stroke of 3.28. It had plenty of room to grow. It was rated at 200 hp with a two-barrel carburetor and 225 hp with a four-barrel. Before it was over, 304-, 343-, 360-, 390- and 401-cid engines came out of the same thin-wall-casting design. This engine gave both satisfactory service on the road and a good accounting of itself in racing and street performance. It was used in some of the interesting AMC muscle cars made after 1966.

The 290-cid V-8 was initially supposed to be installed in 1,500 special Rogue two-door hardtops with black tops and rear decks and Sungold lower bodies. For $2,961.60 you got the choice of Shift Command automatic or the American's first four-speed manual gear box—a Borg-Warner unit. Also included were spinner wheel covers, a blacked-out grille, V-badges on the rear fenders, power steering and power brakes.

Fewer than 1,500 Rogue V-8s were made. Since the option came in other Rambler Americans, there were leftover Rogue Typhoon pieces that went on six-cylinder cars and this doesn't help those finding or restoring these cars today.

Since any size V-8 would now fit in an American, they were used a couple of times for performance models. The 1969 SC/Rambler was the ultimate example and arrived just before AMC produced the last domestic car to carry the Rambler name.

1967 AMERICAN MOTORS MARLIN "343"

The 1967 AMC Marlin fastback coupe is hard to find today.

The big-engined 1967 AMC Marlin was a Walter Mitty kind of muscle car. It gave Mr. Average Family Man the opportunity to purchase a sporty two-door fastback with a 5-liter V-8 for just a shade above $3,000.

The new American Motors 343-cid V-8 was a bored-out version of the company's 290-cid block and cost just $91 extra in the Marlin. It had a single four-barrel carburetor and generated 280 hp at 4800 rpm. Its torque rating was 365 ft. lbs. at 3000 rpm. While it wasn't the hottest car-and-engine combination on the American roads, the power was up from that offered in the previous year's 327-cid V-8.

Hot Rod magazine test drove a Marlin with this engine, in a comparison against a Dodge Charger. The car turned in a 0-to-60 mph time of 9.6 seconds and a 17.6-second quarter mile at 82 mph. The writer compared this to the performance of a Charger with the base 383-cid two-barrel V-8. The same article mentioned a 343-cid, 320-hp heavy-duty equipment option for the Marlin, indicating a hairier engine was available on special order. Undoubtedly, any cars that were equipped this way are extremely difficult to find today.

The last Marlin's extra horsepower was handicapped by the fact that the size and weight of the car went up. For 1967, the "fish model" gained 6 inches in wheelbase and spanned 118 inches. Overall length got a 6 1/2-inch stretch. This added approximately 350 lbs. and did little for the power-to-weight ratio.

Styling-wise, the '67 model was cleaner and smoother looking. A new front-end treatment incorporated rally lights into a horizontal grille. The rear fenders had a "Coke bottle" shape characteristic of other muscle cars of the period.

Unlike the Mustangs, Barracudas and Chargers that it competed with, the Marlin did not come standard with bucket seats. They were $177 extra. A center console, priced at $113, was mandatory when the reclining buckets were ordered. Even vinyl upholstery was optional at $25. By the time a Marlin was all dressed up, the price tag was in the $3,500 range.

Perhaps it was predictable that AMC would run into problems marketing such a big car to anyone, let alone muscle car buffs. The company had firmly established the image of being an expert in the small-car field. So the Marlin actually represented a double leap—one into muscle and the other into the large-car market. When the jump was first made, the Marlin got off to a good start. Over 10,000 were delivered in 1965. But, the wind went out of its sails quickly. In 1966, production tapered off to just over 4,500. It bottomed out at 2,545 units for 1967, the nameplate's third and final year.

AMC would eventually tap the high-performance market with smaller models, such as the SC/Rambler and AMX, that better fit the AMC compact car image. For a time, things looked promising. It was not too little, just too late.

While the Marlin 343 wasn't a commercial success, it became a unique and rare automobile. Total production of cars with the optional "big" engine was counted in the low hundreds. That makes

The 1967 model gained 350 lbs. and 6 1/2 inches.

The 1967 Marlin's frontal styling was new.

survivors desirable to AMC muscle car fans wanting to preserve models that reflect the company's high-performance history.

1968 AMERICAN MOTORS AMX "390"

The AMX was a hot new 1968 model from AMC, with a sticker price at under $3,500.

Craig Breedlove broke many speed records in a '68 AMX, proving AMC had plenty of muscle in its muscle cars.

The 1968 AMX "390" has a lot going for it as a muscle car to buy. It is powerful and unique and the company that built it no longer exists. The AMX designation stood for "American Motors Experimental." The car that carried it was the second step in a program to revitalize American Motors Corporation's image to attract youthful high-performance car buyers. It was the first steel-bodied, two-seat American production model since the 1957 Ford Thunderbird.

From its inception as a prototype show car in 1966 through its 2 1/2-year production run to its ever-rising status as a collector muscle car, the two-passenger AMX has always blazed new trails for its seldom-respected corporate parent, American Motors. The initial non-running fiberglass AMX showed auto show attendees that ultra-conservative AMC could design a car with pizzazz. A later running model had a "Ramble Seat" in place of the rear deck.

AMC's belated entrant in the pony car sweepstakes—the Javelin—bowed in the fall of 1967 as a 1968 model, but the best was yet to come. The two-place AMX—which was a foot shorter in wheelbase and length—came out as a 1968 1/2 model that bowed to the press at Daytona Beach, Florida and the Chicago Auto Show on February 24, 1968. Along with it came the 390-cid version of the second-generation AMC V-8, which was rated at 315 hp.

Naturally, the short 97-inch wheelbase cut the 390-powered

AMX's curb weight to 3,205 lbs. That gave the little coupe a 10.8 pounds-per-horsepower ratio when equipped with the 315-hp version of the 390-cid V-8. *Car and Driver* found this combination good for a 6.6 second 0-to-60 mph time. It did the standing-start quarter mile in 14.8 seconds at 95 mph. Top speed was an estimated 122 mph.

Reclining bucket seats, carpeting, wood-grain interior trim and E70 x 14 Goodyear Polyglas tires were standard. Also included were a four-speed gearbox and heavy-duty suspension. Many buyers were happy with the performance of the standard 290-cid 225-hp V-8 or the one-step-up 343-cid 280-hp V-8, but the "390" was the most muscular version.

The '68 AMX was base-priced at $3,245, but *Road & Track* estimated the price of the 390-cid version at $3,500. Each AMX built in calendar year 1968 had a metal dashboard plate bearing a special serial number from 000001 to 006175. However, the first 550 cars, which were assembled in 1967, did not have this feature, so total production was 6,725 units.

In February 1968, on a test track in Texas, race driver Craig Breedlove established 106 world speed records with an AMX. Around 50 special red, white and blue "Craig Breedlove" editions were then built. They had 290-cid V-8s and a four-speed manual transmission.

1968 AMERICAN MOTORS JAVELIN SST "390"

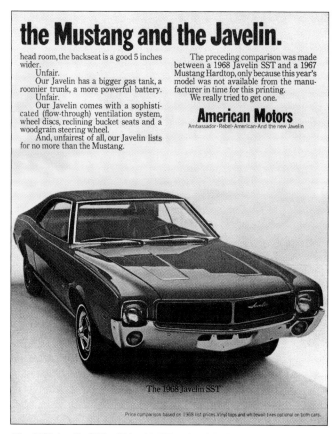

the Mustang and the Javelin.

head room, the backseat is a good 5 inches wider.
Unfair.
Our Javelin has a bigger gas tank, a roomier trunk, a more powerful battery.
Unfair.
Our Javelin comes with a sophisticated (flow-through) ventilation system, wheel discs, reclining bucket seats and a woodgrain steering wheel.
And, unfairest of all, our Javelin lists for no more than the Mustang.

The preceding comparison was made between a 1968 Javelin SST and a 1967 Mustang Hardtop, only because this year's model was not available from the manufacturer in time for this printing. We really tried to get one.

American Motors
Ambassador • Rebel • American • And the new Javelin

The 1968 Javelin SST

Price comparison based on 1968 list prices. Vinyl tops and whitewall tires optional on both cars.

The 1968 Javelin SST sold for $2,587 and weighed 2,836 lbs.

The Javelin SST was AMC designer Dick Teague's strikingly handsome answer to the Mustang and Camaro. It was about the same size as a Mercury Cougar, but had more rear leg room than that "Super Sized" Mustang, so AMC promoted it as a "full four-passenger car." However, with the proper engine option, the late-in-the-year Javelin SST could be turned into a *real* muscle car.

Upon the SST's introduction, AMC's Vic Raviolo told *Motor Trend* of plans to "homologate" a version of the Javelin for Sports Car Club of America Group 2 sedan racing. For drag racers there was a selection of hot cams. As usual, the "whompiest" versions were available only on a dealer-installed basis. Then, the big news hit after the AMX "390" arrived at the Chicago Auto Show in February.

American Motors' 390-cid V-8 had the same outside dimensions as the AMC 290- and 343-cid V-8s and fit very easily into the Javelin's engine bay. According to AMC expert Larry G. Mitchell, after the AMX came out, the 390-cid V-8 was made available in Javelins, too. "This engine doesn't show up in Javelin factory literature because it came out so late, but it makes sense," Mitchell says. "After all, it was just a question of taking the engine from this pile or that pile."

Car and Driver magazine got its hands on the original Javelin

"390" and used it in a comparison test printed in its March 1968 issue. "Our Javelin was the first 390 ever built," the magazine said. "But its long suit was its handling. It felt very much like a British sports car." Out of the six cars tested—Javelin SST, Camaro SS, Mustang 2+2 GT, Cougar XR-7, Barracuda Formula S and Firebird 400 HO—the SST was the favorite of everyone on the test crew as far as handling.

Car and Driver noted that the engine option was so new that "AMC hasn't had any time to play with the 390, at least officially, so we didn't expect the car to tear up the pavement." This proved to be an accurate assessment, as it was the slowest of the six pony cars with a 15.2 second quarter mile at 92 mph. Part of the blame fell to AMC for limiting early 390s, like the *Car and Driver* test car, to only a three-speed manual transmission supplied by Borg-Warner. For comparison, a "Go-Package" Javelin with the 343-cid 280-hp and four-speed gearbox (that *Motor Trend* said was one of the best production units around) was good for an 8.1 second 0-to-60 time and a 15.4 second quarter mile.

The '68 Javelin SST tested by *Car and Driver* had a manufacturer's suggested retail price of $3,943 with the 390 Go-Package. Its curb weight was 3,560 lbs. Other Javelin performance extras included front disc brakes, a special handling suspension (with a larger diameter sway bar and heavy-duty springs and shocks), 5 1/2-inch-wide wheels, traction bars and quick-ratio power steering.

While Pontiac's GTO was selected as *Motor Trend* "Car of the Year," the magazine offered category awards in 1968. It picked the Javelin as the winner in the sports-personal category saying that it exemplified "the most significant achievement for an all-new car and is the most notable new entry in (its) class."

Motor Trend liked the Javelin so much that it carried out a "Light-ning" project in a car that it called the Javelin SL (for Super Light). As the name implied, the editors started with a stock, off-the-showroom-floor Javelin and turned it into a completely modified, lightweight bomb that any enthusiast could duplicate without much difficulty. By removing accessories they cut 306 lbs. from the car, which was then fitted with a stock 390-cid V-8. In the "1/2-mile drags" the car covered the distance in 23.96 seconds and had a top speed of 102.22 mph.

With an Offenhauser aluminum intake and hood scoop, along with some chassis modifications, the Javelin SL did half-mile runs at 118.26 mph in 23.35 seconds. Later, at the Orange County Raceway, with its headers uncorked, the car did the quarter mile in 13.97 seconds at 104.25 mph! Only one Javelin SL was built. Production of other versions included 29,097 Javelins and 26,027 SSTs.

AMC did start racing Javelins during 1968. AMC hired Corvette racer Jim Jeffords to head a racing effort in SCCA competition. Drivers Peter Revson and George Follmer joined the team. A pair of the cars came in second and fourth in their second Trans-Am race at War Bonnet Raceway early in the season. Later, they broke the track record for sedan racers at Mid-Ohio Raceway. Although no all-out victories were registered that first season, the Javelins showed that they were at least competitive. Doug Thorley, one of the biggest names in drag racing, also campaigned a Javelin funny car. In addition, there was a privately sponsored Javelin that ran in NASCAR's GT races of that era.

1969 AMERICAN MOTORS AMX

The 1968 AMX created nearly instant respect for AMC and a bevy of speed records set by Craig Breedlove and his wife Lee were thrown in for good measure. The 1969 version had few changes. However, with a full model year to sell them, American Motors Corporation turned out 8,293 examples. It would be the two-passenger model's best year.

Power train availability in the 1969 AMX was the same as 1968, with the 290-cid four-barrel V-8 rated at 225 hp as standard

equipment. Adding $45 to the $3,297 base price bought a 343-cid, 280-hp V-8. The 315-hp engine was also back, at a reasonable $123 additional. The desirable "Go Package" cost $233 on the 343s and $311 on the 390s and included E70 red line tires on 6-inch rims, a handling package, power disc brakes, Twin-Grip differential and the visually identifying over-the-top stripes.

At midyear, several "Big Bad" option packages were introduced in wild (at least for AMC) colors. A Hurst Competition Plus

The 1969 AMX had few changes from 1968, but with a full year to sell them, AMC turned out 8,293 copies.

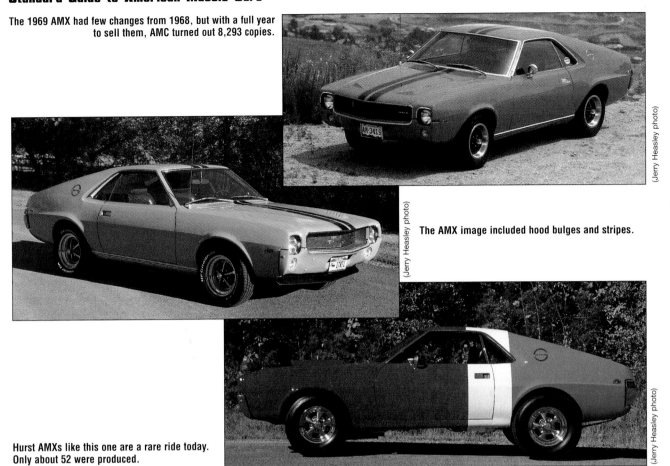

(Jerry Heasley photo)

The AMX image included hood bulges and stripes.

(Jerry Heasley photo)

Hurst AMXs like this one are a rare ride today. Only about 52 were produced.

(Jerry Heasley photo)

shifter for the Borg-Warner four-speed manual transmission was added to the options list at the same time at $205 extra. Javelins also got midyear Big Bad options.

Though the AMX Big Bad option was only $34, sales were limited, with 284 orange, 283 green and 195 blue copies being made. The most interesting and sought after AMX of all was the AMX SS. Only 52—or by some reports 53—AMX SS examples were sent to Hurst for "legalization" as drag racing cars. The AMX SS 390 was topped by a pair of 650-cfm Holley four-barrels on an Edelbrock aluminum cross-ram intake. Doug's Headers and other modifications resulted in a conservative advertised output of 340 hp. The suggested retail price of $5,994 seems a steal today, but was nearly twice the regular sticker price in 1969.

The AMX SS models went to NHRA and AHRA competitors, with Shirley Shahan —known as the "Drag-On-Lady" — being perhaps the most famous.

Two-place AMX production ended with the 1970 model run, but the nameplate returned on Javelin, Hornet, Concord and (finally) Spirit models. It was finally put to rest at midyear in 1980.

The two-passenger AMXs were the first AMC muscle cars to be sought by collectors other than AMC purists. Prices continue to outpace those of other AMC machinery, with special editions—not counting the AMC SS—topping $20,000 in top condition. For the few fortunate enough to have an SS, their value continues to blaze new trails for cars that were made in Kenosha, Wisconsin.

1969 AMERICAN MOTORS JAVELIN 390

Basically, the '69 Javelin was unchanged from the previous year. Styling treatments were improved and a few mechanical features were upgraded to create a better product. A new twin venturi grille was used.

As in 1968, engines started with a 232-cid 145-hp six, but everything else available was a V-8. The 290-cid V-8 came again in 200- and 225-hp editions and the latter was offered with an optional Hurst-shifted four-speed. The four-speed could also be linked to the carryover 343-cid V-8. The "big muscle" on the American Motors options list was the 390-cid with 315 hp. It was available with dealer-installed factory high-performance parts, as well as "Isky," Edelbrock or Offenhauser speed equipment and a Doug's Headers exhaust system. AMC was careful to offer it with a choice of automatic or four-speed transmissions.

Javelin SST in Matador Red.

The '69 Javelin SST came in 232, 290, 343 or 390 versions. Twin hood scoops were part of the Go Package.

Some people have a love then marry the Rebel.

Our Javelin is a beautiful machine with a beautiful body.

And our Rebel is a beautiful machine with a body. Which means you've got to get under its skin to see its beauty.

If you do, the Rebel may get under your skin.

You'll find beautiful little things like Molybdenum-filled #1 compression piston rings, not ordinary chrome-filled rings.

These expensive "Moly-Tops" help eliminate scuffing the cylinder walls, and could save you the expense of a ring job.

Your Rebel has a transistorized voltage regulator. It is solid state. No moving parts to break down, and give you the headache of costly repair bills.

Front shocks can go because of road dirt, grime and stones.

We put a stone and dirt shield on the Rebel's front shocks. This could save you from putting out a lot of money for replacing damaged shocks.

The Rebel has a coil resistor system.

AMC liked to brag about its subtle touches on the powerful '69 Javelin SST.

Javelin SSTs included special trim, reclining bucket seats and added chrome. The '69 SST was originally decorated with two more or less straight stripes on the beltline. On Jan. 9, these were changed to "C" stripes starting right behind the front wheel opening and running back along the mid-body feature.

The optional "C" rally stripe was also available on a new Big Bad Javelin introduced in the spring. This model came in Big Bad Orange, Big Bad Blue or Big Bad Green finish and included painted front and rear bumpers. A long list of options advertised for Big Bad Javelins included E70 x 14 Goodyear Polyglas Red Line tires; mag-style wheels; air conditioning; an "airless" spare tire; an 8-track stereo tape with AM radio; power disc brakes; a 140-mph speedometer and big-faced tachometer; Twin-Grip differential; Adjust-O-Tilt steering; a roof-mounted spoiler; a close-ratio four-speed with Hurst shifter and more.

Another option-created model was the Mod Javelin, which came in the same colors as the Big Bad Javelin and many Mod Javelins were also marketed with a Craig Breedlove package. It included a spoiler on the rear of the roof and simulated exhaust rocker mountings.

Offered again for the muscle car crowd was the Go-Package option, which included a 390-cid (or 343-cid) engine, heavy-duty springs and shocks, a thicker sway bar, wide wheel rims, Twin-Grip and other goodies. Traction bars could also be obtained as a factory-supplied dealer-installed item. As part of a performance package, buyers could install a pair of overlay fiberglass hood scoops on their Javelin, plus a new air cleaner that AMC claimed added 12 hp to the 390 due to better breathing.

Standard rear-end gears in the Javelin with a four-speed transmission were 3.54:1 and 3.15:1 gearing was a no-cost option. Serious enthusiasts could trot down to their AMC dealership and pay extra for 3.73:1, 3.91:1, 4.10:1 and 5.00:1 axle ratios, as well as a Twin-Grip differential.

Production totals for 1969 included 17,389 Javelins and 23,286 Javelin SSTs. American Motors built 17,147 of the 390-cid V-8s, but some were used in cars other than Javelin models.

1969 AMERICAN MOTORS SC/RAMBLER

Every muscle car lover knows the name Hurst. In 1969, American Motors hooked up with the performance parts company from Pennsylvania to surprise everyone with its SC/Rambler model (or "Scrambler" as some folks call it). Hurst actually thought up the idea and AMC bought it.

Based on the Rogue hardtop coupe, the SC/Rambler stressed the big engine-little car format. Below the hood went a 390-cid 325-hp V-8 linked to a Borg Warner four-speed with Hurst shifter. A 3.54:1 rear axle with Twin-Grip differential was included, too. With a curb weight of about 3,000 lbs., the hot little car had a power-to-weight ratio of 10.03 lbs. per horsepower. This made it eligible for drag racing in the National Hot Rod Association's F-stock class.

The factory estimated low 14-second quarter miles at 98 mph. *Road Test* magazine clocked 14.4 at 100.44 mph and managed to hit 109 mph without topping out. Modified SC/Ramblers have run the quarter mile in the 9-second bracket.

In addition to the power team, the SC/Rambler included a long list of goodies like a big hood scoop for Ram-Air induction, fat dual

This 1969 SC/Rambler has the "B" type trim with narrow stripes.

(Jerry Heasley photo)

exhaust pipes, a column-mounted Sun tachometer and Bendix front disc brakes. Blue-finished five-spoke mag-style wheels, 14 x 6-inch rims, trim rings and red-striped Goodyear tires were also standard. The interior was done in plain-looking gray vinyl, but had red-white-and-blue headrests. This color scheme was carried onto the body, in several variations. Full carpeting was another selling feature.

The first 500 cars built had red center body side panels and thick blue horizontal racing stripes on the hood, roof and deck. A blue arrow pointed towards the scoop, which had large letters spelling the word "AIR" and calling out the engine size. This was the "A" type graphic treatment.

When the cars sold quickly, another batch was made with new "B" type trim. These had a mostly white exterior with narrow red and blue stripes. Then, a third batch of cars was made, reverting to the type "A" trim, but lacking all of the elements. The A-finished cars seem to be the more common of the 1,512 built.

The '69 Hurst SC/Rambler was flashy and fast.

(Jerry Heasley photo)

1970 AMERICAN MOTORS AMX

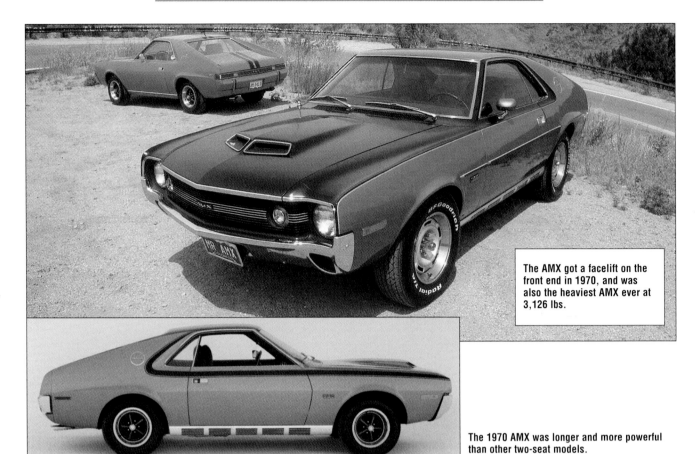

The AMX got a facelift on the front end in 1970, and was also the heaviest AMX ever at 3,126 lbs.

The 1970 AMX was longer and more powerful than other two-seat models.

"We made the AMX look tougher this year because it's tougher this year," heralded advertisements for the 1970 edition of American Motors' two-seat sports car. It came with a new 360-cid V-8 as standard equipment. This engine developed 290 hp—65 more than last season's 343-cid base engine. Other standard features included courtesy lights, a heavy-duty 60-amp battery, rear torque links (traction bars), a tachometer, a 140-mph speedometer, 14 x 6-inch styled steel wheels, fiberglass-belted Polyglas wide profile tires, an energy-absorbing anti-theft steering column, a Space-Saver spare tire, heavy-duty shocks and springs, an Autolite Model 4300 four-barrel carburetor and dual exhausts.

Base-priced at $3,395 (and advertised as "the only American sports car that costs less than $4,000") the new AMX had a production run of 4,116 units, which made it the rarest of the three two-seat editions—1968, 1969, 1970—that AMC offered. The height of the fastback coupe was reduced about 1 inch. While the wheelbase remained at 97 inches, the car's overall length grew about 2 inches to 179 inches. The increase gave it a longer nose and made it look more like its Mustang-Camaro-Firebird-Cougar-Barracuda-Challenger competitors, which should have helped sales, but didn't. It sold better when it was a totally distinct car. At 3,126 lbs., it was the heaviest AMX yet, but only by 29 lbs., so with the bigger engine the effect on performance was negligible.

On the outside, the AMX got new rear lamps and a completely restyled front end that was shared with Javelin performance models. The frontal treatment featured a grille that was flush with the hood and a redesigned bumper that housed the "mutant square" parking lamps. A horizontally divided, crosshatched grille insert with four very prominent, bright horizontal moldings was used. AMX lettering

filled a gap at the center of the second and third moldings. The grille also incorporated circular rally lights and the bumper included an air scoop system to cool the front brakes. The restyled hood had a large ram-induction scoop that took in cold air for the engine.

Inside the AMX cockpit were new contoured high-back bucket seats with integral head restraints and a completely redesigned instrument panel. An exclusive Corning safety windshield was also available.

An all-synchromesh "four-on-the-floor" transmission with a Hurst shifter was standard. Performance options included the AMX 390-cid V-8 with 325 hp and a close-ratio four-speed manual transmission. Very desirable today is the code 391-392 "Go Package," that was available on 360-powered AMXs for $299 and on 390-powered AMXs for $384. It included power front disc brakes, F70 x 14 raised-white-letter tires, a handling package, a heavy-duty cooling system and a functional Ram-Air hood scoop.

The metal dashboard plates affixed to 1970 models were numbered 014469 to 18584. This was the final year for the original type AMX. Although the nameplate was to be used again on Javelin- and Hornet-based models, the two-seater AMX was the true sports car and the real high-performance edition.

Eric Dahlquist wrote up the '70 AMX in the December 1969 edition of *Motor Trend* and summed it up as "one of the better constructed cars around." The test car had the optional 390-cid V-8 that produced 325 hp at 5000 rpm and 420 ft. lbs. of torque at 3000 rpm. It drove through the Borg-Warner four-speed gearbox to a 3.54:1 rear axle. Zero to 60 mph took 6.56 seconds and Dahlquist did the standing-start quarter mile in 14.68 seconds at 92 mph. Top speed in fourth gear was recorded as 109 mph.

1970 AMERICAN MOTORS JAVELIN SST

In 1970, race driver Mark Donahue put his mark on the Javelin. "Starting now, you can buy a Javelin with a spoiler designed by Mark Donahue," said an advertisement in the year's March issue of *Motor Trend* magazine.

Donahue and race-car builder Roger Penske, who teamed up to win the Trans-Am championships in 1968 and 1969, had recently signed a three-year contract with American Motors to drive Javelins in that road racing series. One of the modifications they made to their Trans-Am Javelin was Donahue's spoiler. To make this legal for racing, the spoiler had to be "homologated" through use on at least 2,500 cars that the public could buy.

In addition to the spoiler, these Javelin SSTs came standard with other extras, including dual exhausts, power front disc brakes, E70 x 14 white-letter wide-profile tires, 14 x 6-in. wheels, a handling package and a Ram-Air induction system that incorporated the AMX hood. The signature of Mark Donahue was seen on the right side of the spoiler. The "Mark Donahue Signature Edition" AMX was offered with the choice of a 360- or 390-cid V-8 and console-shift automatic transmission or four-speed manual transmission with a Hurst shifter. Actually, 2,501 cars were built this way.

The Trans-Am editions were also offered in 1970. These were replicas of Ronnie Kaplan's racing cars, with a red-white-and-blue paint scheme devised by Milwaukee, Wisconsin, industrial designer Brooks Stevens. Standard, in addition to SST equipment (minus sill moldings and paint stripes), were front and rear spoilers, black vinyl seats, the 390 "Go Package," a four-speed gearbox with Hurst shifter, a 140-mph speedometer, 14 x 6-inch wheels, a heavy-duty cooling system, a 3.91:1 rear axle and Twin-Grip differential and F70-14 glass-belted tires. The Trans-Am edition had a $3,995 sticker price. It weighed 3,340 pounds and only 100 copies were built, just enough to qualify for Trans-Am racing.

The 1970 Javelin SST with the 390-cid, 325-hp engine had only 10.4 lbs. per horsepower and could move pretty well. Zero to 60 mph took 7.6 seconds and the standing-start quarter mile could be done in 15.1 seconds. Total Javelin production for 1970 dropped down to 28,210 cars (a 31 percent decline), of which 19,714 were SSTs, including the Mark Donahue and Trans-Am special editions.

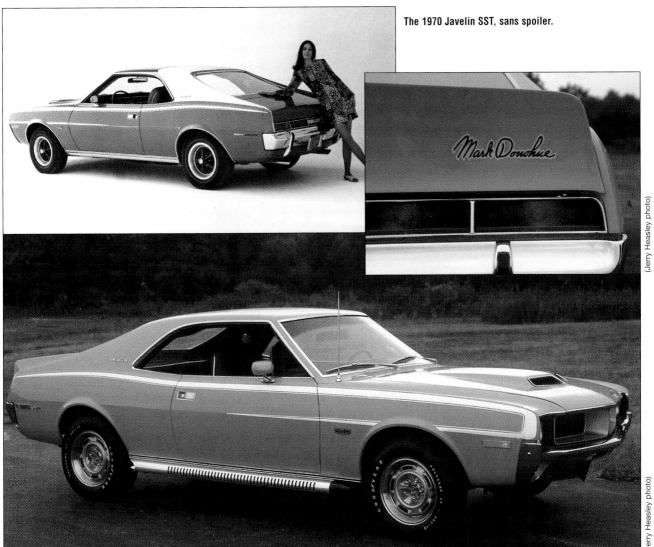

The 1970 Javelin SST, sans spoiler.

(Jerry Heasley photo)

(Jerry Heasley photo)

The '70 SST came with several engines, including a powerful 390-cid, 325-hp model.

1970 AMERICAN MOTORS REBEL "MACHINE"

Introducing the Rebel "Machine."

Standing before you is the car you've always wanted.

And, if you like everything about it, except for the paint job, which admittedly looks startling, you can order the car painted in the color of your choice.

You may be wondering why a company like American Motors would paint a car red, white and blue.

And that's what we keep asking ourselves: Why would a company like American Motors paint a car red, white and blue?

But we have nothing to be embarrassed about under the hood, which is all you should be concerned about.

The Machine has a 390 CID engine as standard equipment and develops a horsepower the equivalent of 340 horses all pulling in unison, which is no mean feat.

Next, and this will be particularly impressive to those people who have buried their heads in hot rod magazines since they were old enough to say "zoom . . . zoom . . . lookee it's a car," the Machine has a 4-speed

all-synchromesh close-ratio transmission with special Hurst shift linkage and a 3.54:1 standard rear axle ratio (or an optional 3.91:1).

To feed air to your engine, and it will be your engine once you buy the car, we have bolted on a ram-air hood scoop. And in the hood scoop, we mounted a tach that's lighted and registers 8000 rpm's.

Heavy-duty shocks and springs raise the rear end a bit and give the Machine, a raked, just mowed the lawn look.

And our dual exhaust system uses special low back pressure mufflers and larger exhaust pipes.

We will make the description of the rest of the Machine's features mercifully short. Front and rear sway bars, high-back bucket seats, 15 inch tires with raised white letters, mag styled steel wheels, power

disc brakes, and racing stripes that glow in the dark.

Incidentally, if you have delusions of entering the Daytona 500 with the Machine, or challenging people at random, the Machine is not that fast. You should know that.

For instance, it is not as fast on the getaway as a 427 Corvette, or a Hemi, but it is faster on the getaway than a Volkswagen, a slow freight train, and your old man's Cadillac.

In short, in order to fully make up your mind about

the Machine, you will have to see it in person at your American Motors dealer.

And when you're introduced to it, a simple "How do you do?," "Nice meeting you," or something friendly like "How are your pipes?," will suffice.

Up with The Rebel Machine

For a set of four "Up with the Rebel Machine" decals send 25¢ and your name and address to: Machine Decal Offer, American Motors Sales Corporation, 14250 Plymouth Road, Detroit, Michigan 48232.

The 1970 AMC Rebel "Machine" was an under-$3,500 high-performance model introduced at the NHRA World Championship drag races in October 1969.

"Standing before you is the car you've always wanted," AMC teased in a two-page advertisement introducing a new high-performance car to readers of *Hot Rod* magazine in December 1969. It showed the Rebel "Machine," a model that had debuted at the National Hot Rod Association World Championship drag races two months earlier.

In an unusual promotional technique, the advertising copy warned, "Incidentally, if you have delusions of entering the Daytona 500 with the Machine, or challenging people at random, the Machine is not that fast. You should know that. For instance, it is not as fast on the getaway as a 427 Corvette, or a Hemi, but it is faster on the getaway than a Volkswagen, a slow freight train, and your old man's Cadillac."

The Machine was fast enough, though. It had a 390-cid V-8 that was AMC's most powerful offering at that time. This engine produced 340-hp at 5100 rpm. Also on the "standard stuff" list was a four-speed, close-ratio synchromesh transmission; a Hurst shifter; a lighted 8000-rpm hood tachometer, a Ram-Air induction setup and choice of 3.54:1 or 3.91:1 rear axles; heavy-duty shocks and springs; a low-back-pressure dual exhaust system; front and rear sway bars; 15-inch raised white-letter tires; styled wheels; high-back bucket seats and power disc brakes.

All this came at a price of $3,475 in a car with a 114-inch wheelbase and curb weight of 3,640 lbs. This produced performance in the range of 14.4-second quarter miles at a 98-mph speed. It also produced sales of 2,326 cars.

The first 100 cars were delivered from the AMC factory in Kenosha, Wisconsin, finished in white. Hurst Performance Products did up the lower beltline stripes and hood in blue and then added red stripes on the upper body sides. At the rear, red-white-and-blue stripes ran across the fender tips and deck. Special "The Machine" emblems were tacked on the front fender sides and on the rear trim panel's right-hand side.

For buyers who didn't like the patriotic paint scheme, AMC advertised, "If you like everything about it except for the paint job, which admittedly looks startling, you can order the car painted in the color of your choice." When buyers did this, they got silver striping and a blacked-out hood. The original color scheme became a $75 option.

Although "The Machine" was a joint venture between AMC and Hurst, this association wasn't promoted to buyers. Customers were offered a chance to purchase "Up with the Rebel Machine" decals for 25 cents each. We wonder what those decals are worth now?

1971-1974 AMERICAN MOTORS JAVELIN-AMX "401"

From 1971 on, the Javelin and AMX shared the same body. It was longer in wheelbase and length and 3 inches wider, although it was slightly lower than before. The front tread was the same 59.7 inches that earlier models used, but rear tread was 3 inches wider.

Differentiating the four-seat AMX from the Javelin was a package including a rear-facing cowl-induction hood, add-on spoilers, AMX emblems and special trim pieces. *Hot Rod* magazine (October 1970) noted, "It's not really an AMX; it's a Javelin-AMX, taking over the top of the line in this series."

Standard V-8 engines, in 1971, were a 304-cid 210-hp two-barrel job for Javelins (except in special cases, like police cars) and a 360-cid 245-hp version two-barrel version for the Javelin-AMX. A 285-hp four-barrel 360 was extra in Javelin-AMXs, but the muscle-car mill for the high-performance model was a new 401-cid V-8 that grew from the 390. With 330 hp, it was the most powerful AMC engine ever offered.

In 1971, only 2,054 Javelin-AMXs were produced. In 1972, Javelin-AMX output rose to 3,220. In addition, the 1971 Javelin SST production total of 22,964 units included 100 Alabama State Police "Interceptors" with 401-cid V-8s.

Driver George Follmer took the Trans-Am racing title for American Motors in both 1971 and 1972 driving Javelins, so a special "Trans-Am Victory" package was offered for 1973 Javelins. It had a front fender decal pointing out that the model had won the SCCA race series in 1971 and 1972. Proving that racing helped sell cars, 1973 Javelin-AMX production rose to 5,707. The last year for the Javelin-AMX was 1974, when 4,980 were built.

The AMC 401-cid V-8 made the Javelin-AMX a real muscle car, despite its large four-place size and heavier weight. While the cars now had to move about 13 lbs. per horsepower, they were only a tad slower than the four-passenger Javelin 390s offered from 1968-1970.

The 401 had a 4.17 x 3.68-inch bore and stroke, a four-barrel carburetor and a 9.5:1 compression ratio. It developed 330 hp at 5200 rpm and 430 ft. lbs. of torque at 3300 rpm.

In 1972, a "401" Javelin-AMX was road tested. It moved from 0 to 60 mph in 8.3 seconds and did the quarter mile in 16.1 seconds. Although 50 lbs. heavier, a 1973 Javelin-AMX with the same engine required only 7.7 seconds for 0 to 60 and 15.5 seconds for the quarter mile.

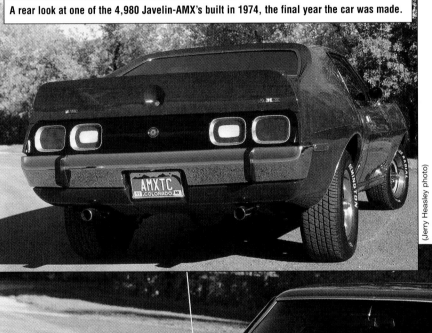

A rear look at one of the 4,980 Javelin-AMX's built in 1974, the final year the car was made.

(Jerry Heasley photo)

The AMC 401–cid V-8 made the 1974 Javelin-AMX a real muscle car.

(Jerry Heasley photo)

The 1971 AMX-Javelin offered a 401-cid 330-hp V-8.

(Jerry Heasley photo)

Besides being the most powerful engine ever offered in a Javelin, the 1971 version of the 401 was the last to require premium gas. In 1972, it was de-tuned to fall into the low-compression category and its output rating went to 255 nhp—or net horsepower.

A de-tuned 401-cid V-8 with 255 nhp was offered in 1973 Javelin-AMXs.

1971 AMERICAN MOTORS HORNET SC/360

American Motors thought that it was introducing a sensible alternative to the "money-squeezing, insurance-strangling muscle cars of America" when it advertised the all-new Hornet SC/360 in the December 1970 issue of *Hot Rod* magazine. Little did the company realize that it was also bringing out a rarity. Although it expected to make 4,000 of the cars and optimistically suggested that 10,000 sales might be possible, only 784 were ever made. That's what makes the SC/360 an especially interesting car. The model was never offered again, although a fairly mild version of the 360-cid V-8 was offered in other Hornets for a while.

The compact Hornet replaced the Rambler (formerly Rambler American) for 1970. It was efficiently sized with a 108-inch wheelbase and short 179.6-inch overall length. It was only 70.6 inches wide, despite having wheel wells that looked large enough to stuff in racing slicks. The largest engine at first was a 304-cid V-8, but that changed when the '71 SC/360 was introduced.

A 360-cid V-8 with 245 hp was standard for the base price of $2,663, along with: a "four-on-the-floor" all-synchromesh transmission; a heavy-duty clutch; D70 x 14 Polyglas tires; 14 x 6-inch mag-style wheels; a Space Saver spare; rally stripes and individually reclining seats. For $199 more you got the Go-Package with an AM 4300 model 1RA4 four-barrel carburetor; the 285-hp power plant with dual exhaust; a functional flat-black Ram-Air hood scoop; a handling package; raised white letter tires and a big tachometer. A four-speed manual gearbox with Hurst shifter or a Borg-Warner Shift-Command automatic (for $237.85) and a choice of 3.15:1 (with automatic) or 3.54:1 and 3.91:1 rear axles with a Dana Twin-Grip differential were other options.

A *Hot Rod* road test of the SC/360 was printed in the December 1970 issue of the magazine. The virtually out-of-the-box car, fitted with the automatic, was put through its paces five times and turned in a top performance of 94.63 mph in the quarter mile with a 14.80-second elapsed time. Can-Am driver Steve Diulo then wrung it out on a road racing course and summed it up as a great little car with slow steering that was "really a lotta car for the money!" Two other advantages were that it avoided a 25 percent surcharge insurance companies were levying on other muscle cars and that it got fuel economy as high as 17 mpg in freeway driving.

(Jerry Heasley photo)

The 1971 SC/360 Hornet was a rare muscle car with total production of 784 units.

(Jerry Heasley photo)

The SC/360 Hornet was marketed as more of an economy muscle car, with a 108-inch wheelbase and short 179.6-inch overall length.

BUICK

1965 BUICK RIVIERA GRAN SPORT

When the head of General Motors Styling, William Mitchell, first produced the Buick Riviera in 1963, the rumor was that he'd wanted to create an American Jaguar. But it wasn't until the 1965 Riviera Gran Sport that this vision really saw fruition.

The Riviera Gran Sport was available with only one engine and one transmission. This stood in stark contrast to its cousin the Wildcat, which pursued the more typical approach at Buick, coming with dozens of engine and transmission options. So, right away it was apparent that Buick had a clear vision of what it wanted the Gran Sport to be.

The Riviera Gran Sport's engine was a 425-cid V-8 with 10.25:1 compression that produced 360 hp at 4400 rpm and 465 ft. lbs. of torque at 2800 rpm. This engine put out .84 hp per cubic inch. It was linked up to the latest three-speed automatic from General Motors' Hydra-Matic Division. This transmission was touted, in a review of the Gran Sport in *Car and Driver* (June 1965), as "without question, the best automatic transmission in the world."

Buick also offered a limited-slip differential with a 3.42:1 ratio. That, coupled with a 117-inch wheelbase, made for a relatively compact and balanced car.

The Gran Sport was further differentiated from its brethren at Buick by the fact that its engine had dual four-barrel Carter AFB carburetors, large-diameter dual exhausts and bright metal engine accents, including a large, plated air cleaner and polished, ribbed valve covers.

Exterior identification was via the use of Gran Sport full wheel covers and Gran Sport lettering below the Riviera script on the deck lid and on the front fenders.

A Motor Trend magazine acceleration run made on a prototype Riviera Gran Sport at Willow Springs Raceway in early 1965 yielded a quarter-mile run of 16.2 seconds with a terminal speed of 87 mph. More importantly for a grand touring-type car such as this was the observed top speed of 123 mph. *Car and Driver* reported a 7.2-second 0-to-60 time and a standing-start quarter mile of 15.5 seconds at 95 mph.

The Gran Sport package also included a heavier front anti-roll bar than the standard Riviera, stiffer shock absorbers and springs at all four wheels, stiffer bushings in the rear suspension and a higher capacity dual exhaust system designed to give less back pressure and eliminate exhaust noise. *Car and Driver* said it "had that stumbling, sort of Chris-Craft V-8 rumble, much beloved of small boys—and ex-small boys—all over these United States."

The real significance of this car was the fact that Bill Mitchell and the engineers at General Motors achieved the goal that Mitchell had set quite well. *Car and Driver* loved the car and called it, "indecent luxury, but nice."

A 360-hp Wildcat V-8 isn't all that's new with Riviera Gran Sport. But what a start.

You can easily spend a party or two talking enthusiastically about the engine in Buick's new Riviera Gran Sport. But after your friends have heard all there is to hear, you can start in on some of the Gran Sport's extra added attractions. A limited-slip differential. Power steering and brakes. If you specified them, the heavy-duty springs, shocks and stabilizer bar. Better than talking, though, is driving. You can start that at your Buick dealer's. After all, wouldn't you really rather have a Buick?

One of the new Gran Sports from Buick
You need not be a professional driver to qualify.

The Gran Sport version of the 1965 Riviera came with only one engine—a 425-cid V-8—that produced 360 hp with a three-speed automatic transmission.

1965 BUICK SKYLARK GS

The new-for-1965 Skylark GS was Buick's answer to the GTO. "There is mounting evidence that our engineers have turned into a bunch of performance enthusiasts," read one of the company's advertisements. "First they stuff the Wildcat full of engine. Then the Riviera Gran Sport. And now this, the Skylark GS, which is almost like having your own, personal-type nuclear deterrent."

With a 400-cid 325-hp V-8 with a four-barrel carburetor and 10.25:1 compression ratio, the GS version of the Skylark tested by *Motor Trend* in May 1965 cranked out .81 hp per cubic inch and fed it through a two-speed Super Turbine 300 automatic transmission with a floor-mounted shift lever. (A floor-mounted three-speed stick

shift was standard.) The magazine reported that its 3,720-lb. test car reached the 60-mph mark in a mere 7.8 seconds, the quarter mile in 16.6 seconds at 86 mph and had a top speed of 116 mph.

Buick's engineers said that the Skylark GS was completely different than the regular Specials because all three body styles—coupe, hardtop and convertible—used a beefed-up convertible-type frame that resisted torque flexing. (Naturally, it was fitted with heavy-duty shocks and springs and a stiffer anti-roll bar up front.) Buick's marketing people claimed that the Skylark GS was like "a howitzer with windshield wipers."

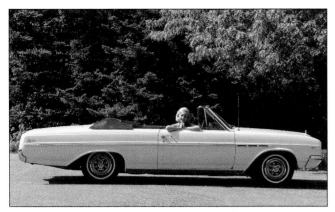

The 1965 Skylark Gran Sport convertible.

The 1965 Skylark GS hardtop was at home on the highway or a drag strip.

Other features of the first Skylark Gran Sport included heavy-duty upper control arm bushings, dual exhausts, 7.75 x 14 tires and a choice of 2.78:1, 3.08:1, 3.23:1, 3.36:1, 3.55:1 and 3.73:1 rear axle ratios. To show what a Skylark Gran Sport could do set up with 4.30 gears and cheater slicks, *Motor Trend* mentioned that Lenny Kennedy's race-prepped example clocked a 13.42-second, 104.46-mph quarter-mile run at the Winternational Drags.

"It seems to us that Buick has another winner in the Skylark Gran Sport," said Bob McVay, *Motor Trend's* assistant technical editor. "The point is that better cars are being built—and Buick is building them!"

1966 BUICK RIVIERA GRAN SPORT

The '66 Riviera Gran Sport had a new body and a more powerful V-8 with dual-quad carburetors available on a dealer-installed basis.

(Jerry Heasley photo)

For 1966, the Buick Riviera was treated to a major redo, sharing a new "E-body" with the Oldsmobile Toronado. "Though the details are different, they do have the same taut look," said *Road & Track* in its February 1966 road test. The Rivera had a smoother and cleaner look than the Toronado without its exaggerated wheel humps or cluttered hood.

The new Riviera's 119-inch wheelbase was 2 inches longer than before. It boosted overall length up to 211 inches and curb weight to 4,375 pounds. As a result, the Riviera engine was enlarged. The 425-cid V-8 had a bore and stroke of 4.31 x 3.64 inches. With the factory single-barrel carburetor and a 10.25:1 compression ratio it produced 340 hp at 4400 rpm and 465 ft. lbs. of torque at 2800 rpm. To turn the larger, heavier Riviera into a true muscle car, you really had to add a dealer-installed dual four-barrel carburetor setup.

Road & Track's test car had this option and others that raised the window sticker from the basic list price of $4,424 up to $5,940! The optional version produced 360 hp at 4400 rpm and 465 ft. lbs. of torque at 2800 rpm. That meant the Riviera Gran Sport was moving about 13.1 pounds for each unit of horsepower, and moving faster as well. It took 8.1 seconds to get up to 60 mph and 16.7 seconds to cover the quarter mile, with an 86.7-mph terminal speed. The magazine pointed out that while the Riviera seemed "too big," it was actually 2 inches shorter than a Chevy Impala and 10 inches under a Pontiac Bonneville.

Road & Track thought that the Gran Sport equipment package was a real bargain for its $176.82 installed price. The option included dual exhausts, a 3.23:1 ratio rear axle with Positraction, 8.45-15 red line or whitewall tires and a stiffer-than-stock suspension. "Considering everything you get in size, speed, power, comfort, luxury, prestige and, yes, even road manners, the Riviera Gran Sport has to be in a class by itself," said the magazine.

The Riviera had a big-car feel and a big enough motor to qualify it as a muscle car, especially with a four-barrel carburetor.

(Jerry Heasley photo)

1966 BUICK SKYLARK GRAN SPORT

Buick's Gran Sport package was introduced in December 1964 as a sporty option for the mid-size Special. It became a separate high-performance Skylark series in 1966 and moved Buick a step closer to a real muscle car image. The car was a surprise to enthusiast magazine road testers. "Now and then, we select a car to test which at the outset promises nothing spectacular, but by the conclusion of the testing program, has shown itself to be an automobile of many virtues and few vices," noted *Motor Trend's* Steve Kelly. "This is the story, in part, of the Buick Gran Sport." *Car and Driver* had sports car racer Masten Gregory wring out the Skylark Gran Sport at Bridgehampton Race Circuit. "I didn't like the car at first, because I thought it was too soft," he admitted. "But as I got used to it, I started liking it quite a bit."

The 1966 Gran Sport had most of the plusher features of the Skylark models, plus bright simulated air scoops, side paint stripes, a blacked-out grille, specific GS badges on the grille and deck and a black-finished rear beauty panel. It also featured a heavy-duty suspension, an all-vinyl interior with a standard notchback bench seat and optional bucket seats, carpeting and full wheel covers. Buyers could chose from whitewall or red line tires in size 7.75 x 14. Unlike other Skylarks, the GS-400 had no hood ornament.

The standard engine for the Gran Sport was the 325-hp 401 Wildcat V-8 with 10.25:1 compression and a four-barrel carburetor. It developed 445 ft. lbs. of torque at 2800 rpm. To placate the General Motors brass, the engine was advertised as a "400," which made it "legal" for use in an intermediate-sized GM car under corporate rules. In mid-season, a 340-hp engine option was released.

Three models were offered. The coupe listed for $2,956, weighed in at 3,479 lbs. and had a production run of 1,835 units. Tipping the scales at 3,428 lbs. was the sport coupe or hardtop, which sold for $3,019 and saw 9,934 assemblies. Convertibles sold for $3,167, weighed 3,532 lbs. and realized 2,047 assemblies.

Motor Trend actually tested two Skylark Gran Sport hardtops, both with Super Turbine automatic transmission. One was loaded with all power options and the other had no power options and several mild upgrades, such a 4.30:1 rear axle, racing slicks, headers, shimmed front springs and a transmission kick-down switch. The stock version weighed 3,660 pounds and retailed for $3,558.43. It did 0 to 60 mph in 7.6 seconds and covered the quarter mile in 15.47 seconds at 90.54 mph. The modified car did 0 to 60 in 5.7 seconds and the quarter mile in 14 seconds at 101 mph! *Car and Driver's* car—also a hardtop—had the 340-hp Wildcat 401 V-8, Super Turbine automatic and options that raised its price to $3,978.04. It covered the quarter mile in 14.92 seconds at 95.13 mph.

The 1966 Buick GS-400 was a nice combination of power and luxury.

1966 BUICK WILDCAT GRAN SPORT

Was the one-year-only 1966 Buick Wildcat Gran Sport a muscle car? In terms of character and specifications, we have to admit that the Wildcat GS doesn't seem to fit the muscle car label. However, when you consider its performance, this model looks like a genuine muscle machine. *Mechanix Illustrated* reported that it could move from 0 to 60 mph in just 7.5 seconds and had a 125-mph top speed. That compared to *Motor Trend's* 7.6 seconds for the smaller, lighter 325-hp Skylark Gran Sport and 8.6 seconds for the smaller Riviera GS with the same 340-hp V-8 and 3.23:1 rear axle as

the Wildcat. This, of course, seems to defy logic, unless *Motor Trend* editors were much better drivers.

Characteristically, the Wildcat was Buick's middle-priced, full-sized car. Specifications-wise, it had a 126-inch wheelbase and stretched more than 18 ft. long overall (the hardtop was 219.9 inches long and the convertible had 220.1 inches between its bumpers). Two-door versions tipped the scales at just under 4,100 lbs. The Gran Sport equipment package was available for either Wildcat or Wildcat Custom sport coupes or convertibles. Its ingredients inclu-

A mint-condition 1966 Buick Wildcat Gran Sport.

(Allen Pritchett photo)

ded a chrome air cleaner; cast aluminum rocker arm covers; dual exhausts; a heavy-duty suspension; Posi-traction and GS identification plates for the front and rear of the car.

Standard under the hood of the Wildcat GS was a 425-cid V-8 with a 4.31 x 3.64-inch bore and stroke. It had a single four-barrel Carter carburetor and 10.25:1 compression ratio. Buick rated it at 340 hp at 4400 rpm and 465 ft. lbs. of torque at 2800 rpm. It came only with a Super Turbine automatic transmission and a 3.23:1 ratio rear axle.

Prices for Wildcat GS models were $3,581 for the Sports Coupe and $3,735 for the convertible. The Wildcat Custom versions were $3,802 and $3,956, respectively.

1967 BUICK GRAN SPORT 340

It would be easy to dismiss the 1967 Buick Gran Sport 340 as a "pretend" muscle car if it had been introduced in a vacuum. However, it made a big-time debut at the Chicago Auto Show on February 25, 1967, as sort of a muscle car for the masses. Buick called it the "GS 400's running mate ... for people who look for a large measure of sporting flavor at a low price." Unlike the GS 400, though, the GS 340 came only as a Sport Coupe.

The 340-cid V-8 that was standard equipment in the GS 340 had a 3.750 x 3.850 inch bore and stroke with a single four-barrel carburetor and 10.25:1 compression ratio. It developed 260 hp at 4200 rpm and 365 ft. lbs. of torque at 2800 rpm, which was nothing to write home about. It was the same engine a buyer could order for any other intermediate-size Buick that year, including wagons. However, in the GS 340, it did come attached to a four-speed manual gearbox at no cost. Buick's two-speed Super Turbine automatic was extra.

Among other "GS 340" features touted at the Chicago Auto Show were red rallye stripes along the sides, red non-functional hood scoops, red rallye wheels and GS ornamentation. Even Buick's real high-performance car of the time—the Gran Sport 400 —didn't have the red decorative treatment. So, Buick offered its customers a choice between muscle-car image with the GS 340 or a genuine muscle-car motor in the GS 400. With a $2,845 window sticker— compared to $3,019 for a GS 400—price wasn't a major factor in selling a GS 340.

What probably made the GS-340 most interesting is that it came to market a half-year *before* the '68 Plymouth Road Runner. Buick and Plymouth both had the same idea of selling a high-performance car into the youth market for less than a top-line muscle car. The young buyers not only got image for less, but also saved on insurance premiums because of the lower horsepower rating. The Road Runner had more cubes and horses in standard form, but both cars came with plain bench seat interiors and a long list of good things on the options list.

GS 340 options included a Sport Pac suspension with heavy-duty underpinnings, a thick rear stabilizer bar and 15:1 steering. The list price was $2,850, but most carried enough extras to get over $3,000. Proving that the public pays attention to details, the GS 400 outsold the GS 340 darn near 4 to 1. Of course, the low production total of 3,692 units makes the GS 340 a lot scarcer and harder for today's collectors to find.

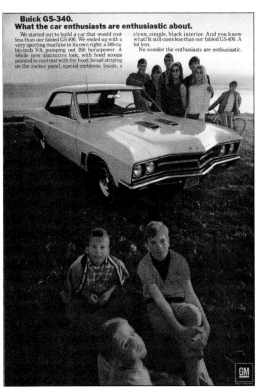

Buick GS-340.
What the car enthusiasts are enthusiastic about.

We started out to build a car that would cost less than our fabled GS 400. We ended up with a very sporting machine in its own right: a 340-cubic-inch V-8, pumping out 260 horsepower. A whole new distinctive look, with hood scoops painted to contrast with the hood, broad striping on the rocker panel, special emblems. Inside, a clean, simple, black interior. And you know what? It still costs less than our fabled GS 400. A lot less.

No wonder the enthusiasts are enthusiastic.

The 1967 Buick GS-340 hardtop coupe was available in either white or platinum mist with red accent stripes and red hood scoops.

1967 BUICK SKYLARK GRAN SPORT 400

The 1967 Buick GS 400 got high marks from enthusiast magazines.

"Before the wheels had made their first revolution we immediately noticed that the 1967 GS 400 was going to be an even far stronger performer than its 1966 counterpart—which itself was no slouch," said *Motor Trend* in its October 1966 report on the new Skylark muscle car.

Part of the reason that the '67 GS 400 generated positive reviews was an all-new 400-cid engine. It replaced the 1965-'66 "401" that had been derived from Buick's old pent-roof V-8 first seen in 1953. The new V-8 combined lightweight construction and better breathing characteristics to create a potent package.

This engine had a 4.040 x 3.900-inch bore and stroke, a single Rochester four-barrel carburetor and a 10.25:1 compression ratio. It produced 340 hp at 5000 rpm and 440 ft. lbs. of torque at 3200 rpm. It was also available with the variable-pitch-stator Super Turbine 400 transmission, a $236.82 option previously used only in big Buicks.

In April 1967, *Motor Trend's* Steve Kelly road tested a well-equipped GS 400 hardtop with automatic transmission and also drove a GS 400 with a four-speed manual transmission and fewer options. The automatic version did 0 to 60 mph in 4.6 seconds, which was 1 second slower than the four-speed car. Quarter-mile performance was 15.2 seconds for both cars, but the four-speed GS

400 was going 95 mph, as opposed to 93 mph for the car with the Super Turbine 400 gearbox.

This was the first year that the GS 400 was a separate series from regular Skylarks and Skylark GS 340s. The series contained a coupe with a $2,956 base price, a two-door hardtop with a $3,019 sticker and a convertible that listed for $3,167. With 10,659 assemblies, the hardtop or sport coupe sold the best, even though it wasn't exactly plentiful. Only 1,014 coupes were made, along with only 2,140 ragtops.

Special GS 400 equipment included a hood with twin simulated air scoops, a rallye stripe, GS ornamentation, all-vinyl seating with foam padded cushions, dual exhausts, white-stripe wide oval tires and a heavy-duty suspension. Desirable options include the four-speed manual transmission for $184.31; limited-slip differential for $42.13; front power disc brakes for $147; a tachometer for $47.39; a full console for $57.93 or a consolette for $36.86 and chrome-plated wheels for $90.58.

In addition to its acceleration and speed characteristics, *Motor Trend* said that the 1967 GS 400 had "the best road behavior of any car we've driven in quite a while." The editors credited this impressive muscle car with maintaining the Buick image of quality, while starting a new image for young, performance-minded buyers.

1967 BUICK RIVIERA GRAN SPORT

The 1967 Buick Riviera GS was the outstanding performer of five luxury specialty cars that *Motor Trend* tested in August 1967. It moved from 0 to 60 mph in only 7.8 seconds and completed its quarter-mile acceleration test in 15.9 seconds at 86 mph. It's true that calling the Riviera a "muscle car" seems like a stretch, but the performance of the car speaks for itself and it did have a larger, more powerful engine than its 1966 counterpart.

The new engine was a 430-cid V-8 with a 4.19 x 3.90-inch bore and stroke that produced 360 hp at 5000 rpm and 475 ft. lbs. of torque at 3200 rpm. It wore a four-barrel carburetor on its intake manifold and used a 10.25:1 compression ratio. A three-speed Super Turbine automatic (actually a Turbo-Hydra-Matic design) was standard with a gear shift on the steering column. Mounting the shifter on the console between the front bucket seats was a popular option

for buyers.

Ordering the GS package also gave you a heavy-duty dual-inlet air cleaner, stiffer-than-stock suspension, a Positraction rear axle, wide-oval tires with a choice of white or red stripes and GS monograms on the front fenders and instrument panel. A tilt steering wheel and dual exhausts were included on all 1967 Rivieras.

The Riviera sport coupe cost Buick dealers $3,210 and normally retailed for $4,469 with dealer mark-ups and federal excise tax. Dealers had to kick in an additional $98.30 for the RPO A9 Riviera Gran Sport Performance Group, but sold it for $137.88. It is not known how many Rivieras had this option. In *Motor Trend*, the manufacturer's suggested retail price of the Riviera GS was given as $4,791.88. That seems high, but there may have been a midyear price increase.

1968 BUICK SKYLARK GS 350 AND CALIFORNIA GS

In 1968, the Skylark GS 350 Sport Coupe replaced the Skylark GS 340. At $2,926, the new budget muscle car was slightly pricier, but more popular. Production ran to 8,317 units compared to just 3,692 of the 1967 GS 340 hardtops.

The GS 350 was based on the Skylark Custom, but had a more muscular exterior look. Finned, simulated air intakes decorated the front fenders and a paint stripe replaced chrome trim moldings on the lower edges of the body. Bright wheel lip moldings were used, but fender skirts were not. GS plaques decorated the grille, deck lid and rear fenders. All-vinyl seats were standard and bucket seats were available at extra cost. The hood had a scoop at the rear and concealed the windshield wipers.

Equipped with a mandatory-for-muscle-cars four-barrel carburetor—a GM Rochester Quadrajet—the 350-cid Buick V-8 had a 3.8 x 3.85 inch bore and stroke. In the Gran Sport model, it ran a 10.25:1 compression ratio and brake horsepower was 280 at 4600 rpm. The torque figure was 375 ft. lbs. at 3200 rpm. In basic form, the GS 350 came with a column-mounted three-speed manual transmission. Options included a two-speed Super Turbine automatic with column or console shifter or a choice of three- or four-speed manual gearboxes with a shifter on the column, floor or consolette. The only available axle ratio was 3.23:1, except on a special California GS model.

The California GS was a midyear addition to the Skylark line intended for California motorists. It was dressed up with a vinyl roof, extra chrome trim, styled wheels, a special steering wheel and GS California Buick emblems. The California GS used the same engine as the GS 350, but came only with the Super Turbine automatic transmission. Buyers could chose between a column or console mounted shifter and either a 3.42:1 or 2.93:1 rear axle. Buick manufactured 8,317 GS 350s, but there's no breakout of California GS sales.

The 1968 Buick California GS coupe came standard with a 350-cid V-8 and four-barrel carburetor.

The GS-350 sport coupe was based on the Skylark Custom.

1968 BUICK SKYLARK GRAN SPORT 400

Buick produced 2,454 of the 3,547-lb. convertible GS-400s in 1968.

GS-400 equipment was now available on only two models, a hardtop base priced at $3,127 and a ragtop with prices starting at $3,271. Buick built 10,743 of the 3,514-lb. hardtops and 2,454 of the 3,547-lb. convertibles. *Motor Trend* tested a convertible that weighed 4,300 lbs. with a bunch of options. Its top performance on the drag strip was 16.3 seconds at 88 mph. Zero-to-60 performance for a GS 400 hardtop was charted as a snappy 7.5 seconds.

Hot Rod magazine's Eric Dahlquist did a little bit better with a well-equipped hardtop he wrote about in January 1968. His car had an as-tested price of $4,505 and weighed 3,820 lbs. By using the hood scoop as part of a homemade cold-air package, Dahlquist got the car's quarter-mile performance down to 14.78 seconds and registered a terminal speed of 94 mph. He noted that beginning January 1, 1968, Buick would begin making two factory cold-air packages available. These Stage 1 and Stage 2 valve train packages were offered along with forged aluminum pistons, a special intake manifold gasket that blocked the heat riser; oversize rods, fully grooved main bearings, 6 percent richer carburetor metering rods, special spark plugs and headers.

Motor Trend found the '68 GS 400 to have "surprisingly good" performance and said it was "very tight and hard to excel." The magazine liked the construction, comfort and general quality of the car, but disliked the rear vision in coupes and the automatic shift lever. Dahlquist also had problems seeing out the back window past the high-back bucket seats, but liked just about everything else.

"Buick makes all kinds of cars because there are all kinds of people in the world," said a two-page color advertisement appearing in the fall of 1967. "So we thought we'd cater to the person who truly gets a thrill out of driving. The GS 400 is our contribution to his hobby."

The new Skylark had a 112-inch Skylark wheelbase that actually matched that of the compact 1961 Buick Special, although the '68 models were some 700 lbs. heavier. Styling revisions included an overall swoopier look with an S-shaped body side feature line. A huge air scoop was integrated into the trailing edge of the hood and chrome finned ornaments decorated the area immediately behind the front wheel openings. *Motor Trend* described the rear view as reminiscent of the limited-production 1954 Buick Skylark sport convertible and we agree.

The GS 400 again used the 400-cid 340-hp V-8 introduced in 1967 models. There were no changes in the horsepower or torque ratings. Standard equipment included a three-speed manual transmission and a 3.42:1 rear axle. A heavy-duty three-speed manual transmission was $84.26 extra and a four-speed manual gearbox was $184.31 extra. Cars with sticks had 3.64:1 and 3.91:1 rear axle options. Ordering the Turbo Hydra-Matic automatic transmission added $205.24 to the price. A 2.93:1 rear was standard with automatic and options were 3.42:1, 3.64:1 and 3.91:1.

The GS-400 had a base price of $3,127.

1969 BUICK SKYLARK GRAN SPORT 400

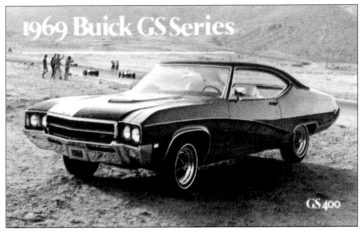

1969 Buick GS Series

GS 400

The Buick GS-400 sport coupe was the fastest car tested by *Car Life* magazine in 1969.

The 1969 Skylark GS 400 had minor styling revisions, but quite a few differences under the hood, which now carried a functional air scoop as standard equipment. As *Hot Rod* described this system, "Two 'muffs,' as they're called, reach up from twin air snorkels on the four-barrel air cleaner, compressing against the hood underside, directing only outside air to the fuel mixer." The cold air passed through chrome grilles on the car's more prominent air scoop. The grille also had a thick horizontal center bar.

The cold-air package was only the start of the good news that 1969 brought Buick fans. Although featured in *Hot Rod* magazine as early as January 1968 as part of a Super Performance package, the Stage I and Stage II engines options really came into their own this year. Both hi-po versions of the 400-cid V-8 offered drag strip-style performance enhancements, including the functional air scoop, for the serious muscle car lover. The calmer GS 400 Stage I was promoted in regular Buick ads, but the hairier Stage II hardware had to be ordered from a dealer's parts department and buyer-installed.

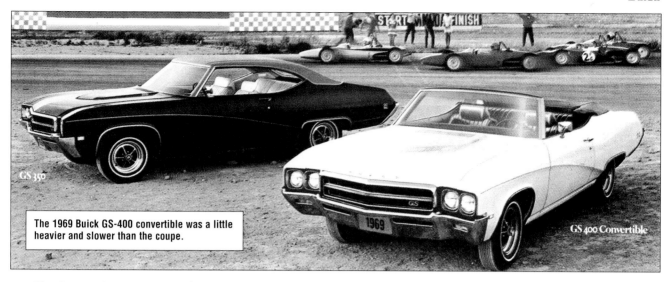

The 1969 Buick GS-400 convertible was a little heavier and slower than the coupe.

The Stage I "factory" package—designed for dealer installation—incorporated a high-lift camshaft, tubular push rods, heavy-duty valve springs and dampers and a high-output oil pump was rated for 345 hp at 4800 rpm. When it was ordered, the transmission was equipped with a 5200-rpm governor to protect against over-revving the engine and a 3.64:1 or 3.42:1 Positraction rear axle was used. Also included were dual exhausts with big 2 1/4-inch tailpipes and a modified quadrajet carburetor. A heavy-duty rallye suspension and front power disc brakes were available.

The Stage II option was an install-it-yourself package for all-out race cars and was not recommended for use on the street or on cars with mufflers. It included an even wilder cam and all the other goodies.

For the second year in a row in 1969, *Car Life* magazine found the GS 400 to be the fastest muscle car it tested. Its test car did 0 to 60 mph in 6.1 seconds. When *Motor Trend* tested a 3,706-lb. convertible with the standard 340-hp engine, it got the opposite result and concluded that the ragtop was the slowest of six muscle cars. It ran from 0 to 60 mph in 7.7 seconds and did the quarter mile in 15.9 seconds at 89 mph.

An interesting sidelight to 1969 GS 400 history was the fact that six of the cars were given away in a "Drive Like A Pro" contest jointly promoted by the Pit-Stop Co., Coca-Cola and Petersen Publishing Co. Doesn't it make you wonder if any of the cars survive today?

1970 BUICK GRAN SPORT 455

The 1970 Buick GS 455 coupe was a memorable muscle car.

pistons notched for valve clearance and an advanced-performance distributor. As in the past, the Stage I V-8 was available with either a special shift-governed automatic or a heavy-duty four-speed manual gearbox with a beefed-up clutch.

A Stage I GS 455 with automatic transmission could do 0 to 60 mph in 5.5 seconds and took only less than 14 seconds to zip down the quarter mile. One magazine did it in 13.39 seconds at 105.5 mph and Motor Trend clocked 13.79 seconds at 104.50 mph as it flew through

According to muscle car expert Phil Hall, the 1970 Buick GS 455 was one of the wildest of all Buicks on paper. Its 455-cid engine was derived from the earlier 430-cid V-8 and produced 350 hp at 4600 rpm. Torque output was a strong 510 ft. lbs. at 2800 rpm. It featured a 10.0:1 compression ratio and a Rochester four-barrel carburetor. This engine could push one of the approximately 3,800-lb. well-equipped Skylark bodies from 0 to 60 mph in about 6.5 seconds.

Available once again was the Stage I option. In fact, *Motor Trend* opined, "Buick's Stage I was interesting in 1969; now with the 455 mill it's an engineering tour de force." In addition, with a price of just $199.95, the engine option package was a bargain. It included extra-large nickel-chrome stellite steel valves; big-port cylinder heads with special machining and valve relieving; stronger valve springs; a high-lift cam; a carburetor with richer jetting; blueprinted

(Jerry Heasley photo)

The GS Stage 1 was "an engineering tour de force," according to *Motor Trend*.

Only 1,416 1970 Buick GS 455 Stage I convertibles were built.

(Jerry Heasley photo)

the traps. The stick-shifted version was just a little slower in reaching 60 mph from a standing start.

On top of its super performance, the GS 455 was a real handler and hugged the road even better when equipped with Rallye Ride package for $15.80 extra. It gave *Motor Trend's* press car extra stability at high speed. The test car had four-wheel manual drum brakes that could slow it from 60 mph in 139.1 ft. Senior editor Bill Sanders said of the brakes "they held up exquisitely without fade after repeated stops from over 100 mph."

The Gran Sport 455 option could be ordered for two body styles. The two-door hardtop cost $3,283 and 8,732 were put together. Buick built only 1,416 of the convertible version, which sold for $3,469 and up.

1970 SKYLARK GSX

The 1970 Buick GSX sport coupe in Saturn yellow.

"Buick's GSX. A limited edition," said the teaser headline on an advertisement that Buick Motor Division in the April 1970 issue of *Motor Trend* magazine. The automaker called it "another light-your-fire car from Buick." As things turned out, not too many people had their fires lit, but you have to admit that with a total production of 678 copies, the GSX is truly a limited-edition Buick muscle car.

Deep down inside, there wasn't too much of a difference between a 1970 GS 455 and a GSX of the same vintage. The latter carried a $1,200 ($1,196 to be exact) options package as standard equipment. According to the advertisement, the package included a 455-cid 350-hp four-barrel V-8; a hood-mounted tachometer; a special Rallye steering wheel; power front disc brakes; a four-speed manual transmission; a 3.42:1 ratio Positraction rear axle; G60-15 "billboard" Wide-Oval tires; a special front stabilizer bar; front and rear spoilers; black vinyl bucket seats; heavy-duty front and rear shocks; a rear stabilizer bar; rear control arms and bushings; Firm Ride rear springs and GSX ornamentation. The hood-mounted tach was specific to the GSX model and the four-speed gearbox had a

Hurst shifter, of course. The cars also carried a special graphics package with hood stripes and side panel stripes.

For 1970, the GSX came only in two exterior colors, called Saturn yellow and Apollo white. Buick built 491 of the Saturn yellow cars. The other 187 cars were Apollo White. Black vinyl interior trim, code 188, was used with both colors. Other special features included a distinctive padded steering wheel, a trunk tension bar designed to support the spoiler and a baffle incorporated into the rear spoiler. Of the 678 cars manufactured, 278 had standard 455-cid 315-hp V-8s and 400 had the 345-hp Stage 1 engine option. All of the cars were built between February and May of 1970, but the VIN numbering appears to be random.

According to the Buick GSX Registry at www.buickgsx.net, a GSX package was an option for 1971 and 1972 Buicks and could be ordered for any Skylark GSX from the GS 350 to the GS 455 Stage 1. These cars vary widely in color and came with an unlimited range of options. The registry stated that very little is known about them. Apparently, the option was added to 1224 cars in 1971 and 44 cars in 1972.

1971-1972 SKYLARK GSX

According to the Buick GSX Registry at www.buickgsx.net, a GSX package was a special option for 1971 and 1972 Buicks and could be ordered for any Skylark Gran Sport model from the GS 350 to the GS 455 Stage 1. To order a 1971 or 1972 GSX, customers had to get their Buick dealer to check off the Special Car Order or SCO section of the order form.

Like other 1971-1972 Buicks, the GSX editions used de-tuned engines, all of which had an 8.5:1 compression ratio and less horsepower and torque than in 1970. However, when equipped with Buick's potent 455 Stage 1 engine, the GSX was still one of the hottest muscle cars in town. In fact, Buick fans insist that the Stage 1s can run down the quarter mile faster than an LS6 big-block Chevelle.

In 1971 it was possible to put the GSX package on a car with the 350-cid 260-hp four-barrel V-8 that was standard in Grand Sports. This motor generated 360 ft. lbs. of torque at 3000 rpm. Another option was the standard 455-cid 315-hp V-8 with 450 ft. lbs. of torque at 2800 rpm. The 1971 version of the 455-cid Stage 1 engine produced 345 hp at 5000 rpm and 460 ft. lbs. of torque at 3000 rpm.

In 1972, the engines were further choked by government emissions rules and the output numbers looked even worse presented in SAE net horsepower (nhp) terms. The 350 produced 195 nhp at 4000 rpm and 290 ft. lbs. of torque at 2800 rpm. The base 455 produced 225 nhp at 4000 rpm and 360 ft. lbs. of torque at 2600 rpm. The 455 Stage 1 produced 270 hp at 4400 rpm and 390 ft. lbs. of torque at 3000 rpm. At the rear of the cars, 3.08:1 or 3.42:1 axles were standard, depending on the engine and transmission combination.

Both 1971 and 1972 GSXs used a special frame, a computer-designed rally-tuned-suspension and large-diameter sway bars. The use of side stripes and a rear spoiler was continued. These cars varied widely in color and came with an unlimited range of options and accessories. The GSX Registry stated that very little is known about them, except that the option was added to 124 cars in 1971 and 44 cars in 1972.

While nowhere near as muscular as 1970 editions, 1971 and 1972 Skylarks with the GSX package and the Stage 1 engine option are still tremendous performance cars and, since they were rare when new, they must be extremely hard to find today.

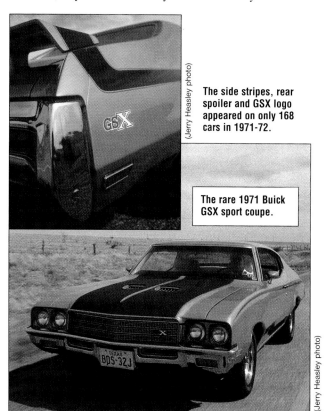

(Jerry Heasley photo)

The side stripes, rear spoiler and GSX logo appeared on only 168 cars in 1971-72.

The rare 1971 Buick GSX sport coupe.

(Jerry Heasley photo)

1971 BUICK GRAN SPORT 455

The 1971 Buick GS-455 sport coupe may not have been quite as fast as the 1970 model, but it was still a big seller.

Buick Gran Sport 455 Stage 1 cars accounted for better than 25 percent of Buick's sales in 1970. As a result, Buick worked hard to continue a good thing, albeit with modifications responding to government-mandated clean-air standards.

Buick combined the Gran Sport and the GS 455 into one series for 1971. This gentleman's muscle car—the Gran Sport Buick—was one of the few potent performance packages that was tractable in all kinds of driving. It could even be ordered with air-conditioning.

Gran Sport equipment included a blacked-out grille with bright trim, bright wheel house moldings and bright rocker panel moldings with red-filled accents. Dual, functional hood scoops sat in the center of the hood. GS monograms appeared on the front fenders, deck and grille. Cars equipped with the 455 or 455 Stage 1 options had additional emblems. Standard equipment was the same as the Skylark Custom, but bucket or notchback front seats in vinyl trim were optional.

For 1971, General Motors listed all its engines with SAE net horsepower ratings, along with gross horsepower ratings that reflected a reading without accessories. The SAE method was known as the "installed" output—the final output figure of the engine within a car carrying all necessary operating accessories. This may have been GM''s way of mollifying insurance companies that were starting to impinge on the salability of muscle cars.

The GS 455 cid V-8 had a gross rating of 330 hp and an installed rating of 265 hp. The 455-cid Stage 1 engine had a 275 SAE hp rating, but its gross output rating was 345 hp at 5000 rpm. This 345-hp rating was down from that of the 1970 Stage 1, which produced 360 hp at 4600 rpm. The reason was a lower 8.5:1 compression ratio, which was down from a 10.0:1 compression ratio in 1970. A functional Ram-Air induction system helped feed the engine cold air.

Buick's trademark—a high torque rating—was also down from 10 ft. lbs at 2800 rpm in 1970 to 460 ft. lbs. at 3000 rpm for 1971. Still, if one averaged all 1971 GS 455 road tests, the elapsed time for the quarter-mile was 14.25, which compares pretty favorably to an average ET of 14.02 for the 1970 cars.

The 455 cid V-8s used valve spring dampeners to reduce valve spring surging. Also, exhaust lobe profiles were longer to reduce valve opening acceleration and increase valve-opening overlap, which was 20 percent or more in the 455 cid V-8.

All exhaust valves were nickel-plated, due to GM's requirement that all 1971 engines be able to run no-lead fuel. The primary side of the venturi on the Quadrajet carburetor was 1/8 inch larger on the 455-cid engine. A problem with this was that the 1971 models had lower (higher number) axle ratios and gas mileage suffered.

Production figures show that 8,268 GS and GS 455 two-door hardtops were built. Of these, 801 had the Stage 1 option. Convertibles accounted for 902 total GS and GS 455 assemblies. A number of highly desirable options were offered, such as a Hurst-shifted Muncie M20 transmission and RPO E6 through-bumper exhaust extensions.

1972 BUICK SKYLARK GS 455 STAGE 1

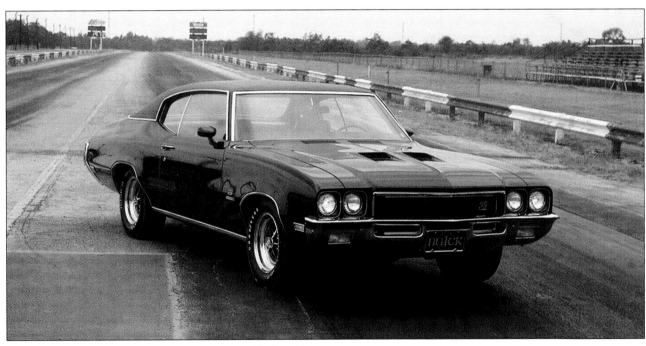

(Jerry Heasley photo)

The 1972 Buick GS 455 Stage 1 sport coupe was a star on the drag strip.

"Buick, it seems, has an indisputable knack for making singularly sneaky cars," said *Motor Trend* executive editor A. B. Shuman in his June 1972 report on the Buick GS Stage 1. The red GS he was driving had a white vinyl top and automatic transmission and looked for all the world like a typical grocery getter, except for the timing slips it had picked up at the National Hot Rod Association's "Winternationals" drag fest in Pomona, Calif.

The Buick Skylark-based muscle car had been the champion competitor in the Stock Eliminator category and then went on to beat all the other stock class winners to become overall category winner. In the hands of Shuman the car did 0 to 60 mph in 5.8 seconds and the quarter mile took 14.10 seconds with a 97 mph terminal speed. With open exhausts, fatter tires and a few "tweaks" allowed by NHRA rules, weekend drag racer Dave Benisek had set an elapsed time record of 13.38 seconds with the same machine at Pomona.

By coincidence, the 1970 GS 455 Stage 1 had also covered the quarter mile in 13.38 seconds, but that was because it had a higher compression ratio (10.0:1), more horsepower (360 at 4600 rpm) and a taller (numerically lower) 3.64:1 rear axle. By 1972, the no-lead version of the car ran an 8.5:1 compression ratio, produced 275 hp at 4400 rpm and came linked to a 4.30:1 rear axle. This, of course, made its performance numbers more impressive. "The amazing thing, considering all that's happened just in the area of emissions controls, is that a car that runs like the GS Stage 1 could still exist," noted Shuman. He called it "the best example of the Supercar genre extant."

Despite such a positive appraisal, Buick made only 7,723 GS hardtops and 852 GS convertibles in model year 1972 and that total included GS 350, GS 455 and Stage 1 production. In addition to a 350- 455- or 455-cid Stage 1 V-8, all 1972 Gran Sports had four-barrel carburetors, dual exhausts, functional hood scoops, and a heavy-duty suspension. GS monograms appeared on the front fenders and rear deck and bright moldings trimmed the rocker panels and wheel lips.

1982 BUICK REGAL GRAND NATIONAL

The first Buick Regal Grand National was introduced at Daytona International Speedway on February 10, 1982. This car marked a revival of the high-performance image that the Skylark Gran Sport models had fostered in the late '60s and early '70s. The GN kicked off a new series of real Buick muscle cars.

Buick had won NASCAR's manufacturer's trophy in Grand National stock car racing in 1981 and 1982. "The New Grand National Regal is a luxurious commemorative version of the winning Grand National Vehicle," said a dealer bulletin issued two days before the car's Daytona debut. "Buick designed this magnificent Regal to be a one-of-a-kind car. With its special GN styling treatment and appointments, it is a distinctive vehicle inside and out. Our objective in producing these Grand National Regals is to offer an attraction that will stimulate sales of all the 1982 Buicks. We also want to capitalize on the momentum being generated by the Grand National racing competition and take advantage of enthusiast's magazine coverage to increase Buick's penetration of the enthusiast market!"

The Grand Nationals were built on an off-line basis by Cars & Concepts of Auburn Hills, Michigan. The prototype car that appeared in Daytona was produced in December 1981. It was then shipped to Daytona the following February for the press introduction. Initially, a run of 100 units was planned, but production actually hit 216 cars, including the prototype. The Grand National package sold for $3,278, making it one of Buick's highest-priced options ever.

Buick sent stock Regals to Cars & Concepts for conversion into GNs. Factory parts used on the cars included the black-out style grille and headlight covers, the wheel center caps that say "GN," the horn button, body moldings and trim for the instrument panel and console. Cars & Concepts added the front spoiler, bucket seats made by Lear Siegler (the press kit says they were done in gray Branson cloth, but the color was actually silver), the rear airfoil, special seat covers, silver paint, GN decals, pin striping and door-pull appliqués. The stock clock was (usually) replaced with GN instrument panel inserts.

The press kit made it sound like all 1982 Grand Nationals were identical, but they were not. Regal coupes, Regal sport coupes and Regal Limited coupes were all used as the basis for some Grand Nationals. A small number of cars were made without the GN emblem in the dash and carried analog clocks in addition to the clock built into the ETR stereo.

Most of the 1982 Grand Nationals were powered by a normally aspirated 4.1-liter V-6 that made 125 hp at 4000 rpm and 205 ft. lbs. of torque at 2,000 rpm. This engine had a 3.965 x 3.400 bore and stroke and displaced 252 cid. It used a four-barrel carburetor and an 8.0:1 compression ratio.

About 10 to 15 of the first Grand Nationals had the 3.8-liter turbocharged V-6 that was used in the 1982 Regal sport coupe. This motor was not on the regular options sheet, but savvy buyers could get a Turbo Grand National by ordering a Regal sport coupe plus the Grand National package. The turbocharged V-6 had a 3.80 x 3.40-inch bore and stroke and 231 cid. With a four-barrel carburetor and 8.0:1 compression ratio it developed 175 hp at 4000 rpm and 275 ft. lbs. of torque at 2600 rpm.

The '82 is the only non-all-black Regal Grand National. Two-tone paint was featured with silver mist on the upper body and charcoal gray on the lower body. Red pin striping set off the two-tone finish. A sunroof was also included. While the '82 did not have the performance of later Grand Nationals, it is rare, unique and set the theme for the return of the Buick muscle car. The turbocharged versions are extremely rare today.

1982 BUICK REGAL SPORT COUPE

In the early '80s, Buick held proud memories of its muscle car heritage and models like the GS-400, the GS-455 and the GSX. Buick engineers became interested in creating a muscle car that could turn in amazing performance while meeting the more restrictive emissions and fuel-economy standards of the '80s. They dusted off the V-6 engine that had first appeared in the 1961 Buick Special and began experimenting with high-tech upgrades to boost its go-fast potential. They found that by fitting a turbocharger to the V-6 they could make it perform in the same neighborhood as a V-8.

By 1978, a turbo 3.8-liter V-6 with a four-barrel carburetor was made available for Regal and LeSabre sport coupes. It produced 165 hp, but the setup was far from perfected. It provided extra highway passing power, but little more. So, Buick set up a Turbo Engine Group dedicated to designing a V-6 with muscle-car-like performance. By 1982, the TEG had concocted a 3.8-liter turbocharged V-6 (RPO LC8)—still with a four-barrel carburetor—that generated 175 hp at 4000 rpm. It was available in a special model called the Regal sport coupe.

Improvements for 1982 V-6s included a re-sized Garrett AiResearch turbo unit with a smaller, more efficient housing that speeded up the time required for full turbo boost. The oil capacity of both the engine and the turbo unit was increased and hot air was used to warm the induction system, rather than hot water, as before. Buick engineers also relocated the knock sensor and linked it directly to the electronic control module (ECM). The diameter of the turbine outlet pipe was increased from 2 to 2 1/2 inches to nearly eliminate back pressure. Two other performance improvements were a Turbo Hydra-Matic (THM350c) automatic transmission with a lock-up torque converter and a lower 3.08:1 rear axle that improved acceleration, but not fuel economy.

The standard features of this car included its high-performance engine, sport mirrors, fast-ratio power steering, a voltmeter, a turbo boost gauge, a trip odometer, P205/70R14 steel-belted BSW tires, styled aluminum wheels and a Gran Touring suspension. To identify it as a modern muscle car, the 1982 Model K47 Regal sport coupe also had a special hood and black body accents. It had a base retail price of $9,738 and only 2,022 were made, including 10 to 15 with the special Regal Grand National package.

When it was completely warmed up, the turbo Regal could do 0 to 60 mph in 9.6 seconds and covered the quarter mile in 17.3 seconds at 81 mph. In the February 1982 *Motor Trend*, industry affairs editor Jim McGraw said of the turbo V-6, "Buick is leaning more toward V-8 performance and allowing the driver more motoring fun."

1983 BUICK REGAL TURBO T-TYPE

Buick introduced the Regal T-Type in the fall of 1982 as a 1983 model. At the same time, the Regal sport coupe disappeared. Also missing was the Grand National option, which would re-appear in 1984 and last through 1987. The Regal T-Type had the same sporty image as the sport coupe and a host of extra features. To make it into a real muscle car, Buick put a turbocharged V-6 under the hood.

Motor Trend feature editor Jim Hall bemoaned the fact that rear-wheel-drive models like the T-Type were scheduled to be discontinued soon, saying that it was "A pity, too, since the oldest (speaking from an engineering point) of the sporty Buicks offers the closest thing to '60s-style performance to come out of GM in a long while."

Speaking of the hood, it was of a special design with a "power" bulge at its rear end. Standard equipment on the T-Type included the AiResearch blown 3.8-liter V-6, a new THM 200-R4 four-speed overdrive automatic transmission, a 3.42:1 performamance rear axle,

sport mirrors, fast-ratio power steering, a turbo boost gauge, a temperature gauge, a trip odometer, P205/70R14 SBR tires, styled aluminum wheels, dual exhausts and a grand touring suspension.

The 3.8-liter turbo V-6 had cast-iron alloy cylinder head and engine block construction. It featured a 3.80 x 3.40-inch bore and stroke and displaced 231 cid. A four-barrel carburetor was used and it had an 8.0:1 compression ratio. The 1983 version put out 180 hp at 4000 rpm and 280 ft. lbs. of torque at 2400 rpm. New for the year was a computer-controlled EGR system that enhanced driveability. In addition, the "taller" top gear in the new overdrive transmission allowed a shorter axle to be used, thereby providing much better off-the-line performance.

According to the *Standard Catalog of Buick 1903-2000*, the T-Type listed for $10,366 in standard form. A total of 3,732 vehicles were built.

1984 BUICK REGAL GRAND NATIONAL

After showcasing its turbo-engine technology at the 1984 new-car shows, Buick brought out a new model it advertised as "the hottest Buick this side of a banked oval." This new Regal Grand National coupe was, according to Buick, "produced in limited numbers for those who demand a high level of performance." It's stated purpose was to give young and young-at-heart Buick buyers much of the feeling of a NASCAR racer and 2,000 copies were built.

The ad further stated, "A little chrome and a lot of power in basic black attire, that's what the Buick Regal Grand National coupe is all about." The cost of the option—$1,282—was quite modest considering all of the appearance and equipment extras it included. To begin with, Grand Nationals carried the 231-cid (3.8-liter) turbocharged V-6 with sequential fuel injection. This LM9 engine produced 200 hp at 4000 rpm and 300 ft. lbs. of torque at 2000 rpm. It came linked to a four-speed automatic transmission and 3.42:1 rear axle.

Ingredients of the GN option included black exterior finish on

the body; bumpers, bumper rub strips, bumper guards, front air dam, windshield wipers, rear deck lid spoiler, tail lamp bezels and aluminum wheels. The paint code was No. 19. Grand National identification was carried on the front fenders and the instrument panel. A sport steering wheel, a tachometer, a turbo-boost gauge, a 94-amp alternator; power brakes and steering, dual exhausts and a special hood with a turbo bulge were also included in the package. The code 995 Lear Siegler seats (sand gray cloth with charcoal leather inserts) were embroidered with the Grand National model's distinctive "6" (for V-6) logo.

Individual options available from Buick included a hatch top (RPO CC1); an Astroroof with silver glass (RPO CF5); a theft-deterrent system (RPO UA6); cruise control (RPO K34); electronic touch climate-control air conditioning (RPO C68); a rear window defogger (RPO C49); a remote trunk release (RPO A90); electronic instrumentation (RPO U52) and a lighted vanity mirror on the passenger-side sun visor.

1985 BUICK REGAL GRAND NATIONAL

The 1985 Buick Regal's forward-slanted nose carried a new grille. On the Grand National version it was finished in black, as was nearly everything else including the windshield wipers. Basically, the ultra-high-performance version of the Regal T-Type was the same as in 1984, but there were minor changes to the torque curve, the upholstery and the ornamentation.

The T-Type had a base retail price of $12,640, which included the 3.8-liter turbo, quick-ratio power steering, an instrumentation group, sport mirrors with left-hand remote control, a four-speed automatic transmission, air conditioning and P215/65R15 black sidewall tires. The Grand National package retailed for $675 additional.

Under the hood once again was the turbocharged 3.8-liter V-6 with sequential fuel injection. The system (introduced in 1984) provided more precise fuel delivery. Metered fuel was timed and injected into the individual combustion ports sequentially through six Bosch injectors. Each cylinder received one injection per every two revolutions, just prior to the intake valve opening.

A nine in the eighth position in the VIN number indicated the use of the 3.8-liter turbo, which carried option code RPO LM9, the same as in 1984. It was rated for 200 hp at 4000 rpm and 300 ft. lbs. of torque at a slightly higher 2400 rpm. The 1985 Regal Grand National wore its characteristic monotone black exterior treatment well and was identified by special exterior model badges.

Inside, something was different for 1985. A new two-tone cloth interior with front bucket seats carried code 583 soft trim. Underneath the car was a specific Gran Touring suspension. In addition, the following individual options could be added to a Grand National at extra cost: hatch roof (RPO CC1), Astroroof (RPO CF5), GM theft deterrent system (RPO UA6), electronic cruise control (RPO K34), electronic-touch climate control (RPO C68), rear window defogger (RPO C49), electronic instruments (RPO U52) and electric trunk lock release (RPO A90). Buick reported production of 2,102 Regal Grand Nationals in 1985.

The base price for the 1985 Buick Regal Grand National coupe was $12,940.

1986 BUICK REGAL AND LESABRE GRAND NATIONALS

The 1986 Buick Regal Grand National was dressed in all black and featured 3.8 turbo V-6 that produced 235 hp at 4400 rpm.

The 1986 Buick Regal Grand National package was a $558 option for the sporty T-Type, which itself listed for $13,714. The Grand National package included all Regal T-Type features, plus black (code 19) finish on the body, bumpers, bumper rub strips, bumper guards, rear spoiler and front air dam, Grand National and Intercooler identification trim, front bucket seats (trim code 583), a full-length-operation console and a performance-tuned suspension. Buyers had a choice of new standard chrome-plated steel wheels or new aluminum wheels. A high-mounted stop lamp became a part of the standard General Motors safety equipment package for 1986. Regal Grand National production climbed to 5,512 during the model run.

While overall appearance of the '86 Regal Grand National was very similar to the second (1984) and third (1985) Grand Nationals, but Ron Yuille and his Buick Turbo Engine Group worked out some significant engineering upgrades for 1986 models. They included the use of an intercooler that lowered the temperature of the air charge between the turbo and the intake manifold. Airflow was also improved over 1985 by using a two-piece aluminum intake manifold with an open-plenum chamber. This change alone was good for a 10-percent horsepower boost to 235 hp at 4400 rpm. Torque increased to 330 ft. lbs. at 2800 rpm. Another new-for-1986 item was an electric, temperature-controlled cooling fan.

A very different kind of Buick bearing the Grand National seal was introduced in conjunction with the 1986 Daytona 500. The 1986 1/2 LeSabre Grand National also featured monotone black finish, a front air dam, Buick's Level III suspension system, Electra T-Type wheels, Goodyear Eagle GT tires, unique rear quarter window trim and special GN badges. The LeSabre Grand National was built exclusively for promotional purposes only. It did not have a turbocharged V-6 or the performance of a Regal Grand National. Only 112 were made.

1987 BUICK GNX

(Jerry Heasley photo)

The 1987 Buick GNX by ASC/McLaren was the last of the Grand National series and one of the fastest American cars ever produced.

To commemorate the end of Grand National production in 1987, Buick joined with ASC/McLaren to build a high-performance car called the GNX. The concept behind the GNX was to merge basic high-performance techniques with the latest in electronics and turbocharging technology to create the ultimate production modern muscle car. It was to be the kind of car enthusiasts and collectors would want to own. Almost overnight, the GNX achieved a memorable spot in the "muscle car roll of honor."

Along with rear-wheel-drive Regals, the hot Grand National was to go out of production in June or July 1987. When enthusiasts realized these would be the last turbocharged, rear-wheel drive Buicks, orders picked up. The model got an extension on life and approximately 10,000 assemblies were scheduled between August 3, 1987 and December of that year. The 547 GNXs built were made as a part of this total.

Chief engineer Dave Sharpe dreamed up the idea of a special car to mark the series' farewell. Mike Doble, of Advanced Concepts & Specialty Vehicles, got the job and came up with an integrated high-performance machine that he saw as a modern-day GS-455/GSX Stage I. The car was outlined in an April 25, 1986, document detailing a plan to build the "quickest GM production supercar. Ever!"

ASC/McLaren (Short for Automobile Specialty Co./McLaren Engines) helped create the GNX in a joint venture with Buick after Buick General Manager Don Hackworth approved the program in July 1986. Brainstorming sessions helped develop two prototypes. A management change caused concern that a new general manager, Ed Mertz, might cancel the GNX. After a ride in a prototype, he gave it "thumbs up." Seven additional pilot cars were made from 1986 to 1987.

The heart of the GNX became a turbocharged and intercooled 3.8-liter SFI V-6 that developed 276 hp at 4400 rpm and 360 ft.-lbs of torque at 3000 rpm. It was blueprinted and fitted with such things as special bearings, shot-peened rods and a high rpm valvetrain. The Garrett AiResearch turbo was linked to a special intercooler. McLaren reworked the PROM (computer chip) to enhance fuel mix, spark control, boost characteristics and transmission functions. The Sequential Fuel Injection (SFI) system was designed by Buick.

A race-type chassis was developed for the GNX. It had features such as a longitudinal torque bar (bolted to special differential cover), a tubular steel Panhard rod, revised lower control arms and different size Gatorback tires front and rear. GNX program manager Lou Infante said, "The net result is a mid-13 second GNX that's at home on the drag strip, road course and interstate."

Outwardly, the GNX got a "high-intensity" image with glossy paint, low-gloss Vaalex fender louvers, cast aluminum wheels and flared fenders. The hood had a power bulge, the deck had an airfoil and the body had little identification—only two polished aluminum GNX badges on the grille and deck lid. A badge on the instrument panel showed a car's production number.

ASC/McLaren supplied the option package at a cost of $10,995, which gave the GNX an MSRP of $29,900. According to Buick, 0-to-60 performance was 5.5 seconds and the quarter mile took 13.43 seconds at 104 mph. Top speed was a claimed 124 mph. *Car & Driver* published test results of 4.7 seconds for 0 to 60 mph and 13.5 seconds for the quarter mile at 102 mph. The magazine reported top speed to be "120 mph limited by a cut-off."

(Jerry Heasley photo)

The option package jacked the GNX's price tag up over $29,000 in 1987.

1987 BUICK REGAL GRAND NATIONAL

There are two main differences between the 1987 Regal Grand National and the 1986 edition. The newer car has an all-black grille and the top section of the grille has no flat surface. Inside, the black vinyl door-pull straps of the 1986 edition were replaced by gray pull straps that matched the gray door panel in color. Under the hood of the '87 model, the turbocharged and intercooled V-6 was tweaked a bit to give 245 hp at 4400 rpm and 355 ft. lbs. of torque at 2000 rpm.

Standard equipment with the Gran National WE2 package was the same as in 1986 and again included a long list of appearance, convenience and performance features. Only five individual options were available: the RPO YF5 emissions equipment package; an RPO B88 body molding package; an RPO CC1 lockable hatch roof; an RPO WG1 driver's side six-way power seat and an RPO UA5 theft-deterrent system.

By the end of the summer of 1987, Grand National sales had practically doubled over those of the entire previous year. This was due largely to the massive publicity exposure the hot, high-performance model was receiving in enthusiast publications. Buick dealers then pressured the company to make more of the cars, since dealers were marking them up an additional $3,000 per unit.

Grand National production had originally been slated to halt in July 1987, when Buick was supposed to stop making rear-wheel-drive Regals. On August 3, company executive W.H. Lotts decided to extend production of only the Grand National model through December. By the end of the year, total production had risen to 20,193 cars.

All of the approximately 10,000 cars built after August 3 came with 17 required options. These included black exterior finish; gray interior trim code 583; the 3.8-liter turbocharged V-6; the Grand National equipment package; Soft-Ray tinted glass; door edge guards; two-speed wipers; an electric rear window defogger; a visor vanity mirror; remote-control mirrors; a limited-slip differential; a tilt steering column; tungsten halogen headlamps; headlight warning chimes; a heavy-duty battery; an RPO UM6 Delco radio and a front license plate mounting bracket. Buyers could add two option packages and five stand-alone options, but other regular Buick Regal options were unavailable.

The 1987 Grand Nationals were capable of doing 0 to 60 mph in the low six-second bracket. *Cars Illustrated* magazine published quarter-mile performance of 13.85 seconds and 99.22 mph. *Musclecars* magazine's test Buick was just a little slower, if you can call 13.90 seconds at 98.16 mph "slow." Collectors today like the superior performance of the 1987 Grand National model, even though the '86 is a whole lot rarer.

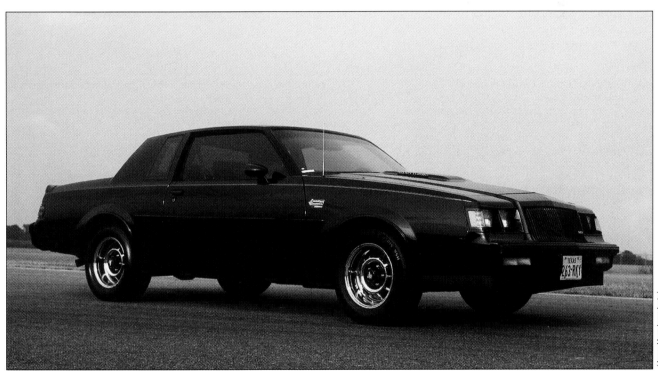

(Jerry Heasley photo)

More than 20,000 buyers brought home the super-fast 1987 Buick Regal Grand National.

CHEVROLET

1961 CHEVROLET IMPALA SS AND 409

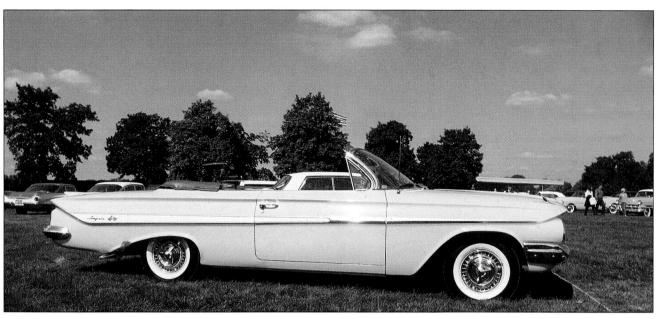

A 1961 Chevrolet Bel Air 409 convertible.

(Jerry Heasley photo)

The 1961 Chevrolet Impala SS sport coupe is plenty fast, but parts can be hard to find.

The first Super Sport is probably the purest of the "big" Chevy muscle cars, because the 1961 Impala was a downsized car. This added up to a small vehicle with a big engine and some super high-performance ability. For example, the SS two-door hardtop with a 409-cid 360-hp engine was good for 0 to 60 mph in 7.8 seconds and 15.8-second quarter miles.

This year, the SS option could be ordered for Impala two-door sedans, four-door sedans and hardtops. The package was strictly a dealer-installed extra, costing around $54 for the basics. These included "SS" emblems, padded dash, spinner wheel covers, power steering and brakes, heavy-duty springs and shocks, sintered metallic brake linings, a 7,000-rpm tachometer and 8.00 x 14 narrow whitewall tires, plus a dashboard grab bar and a chrome shift housing for the four-speed transmission with a floor-mounted shifter.

Two V-8 engines were available at prices between $344 and about $500. The Turbo-Thrust 348-cid big-block came with 11:25 compression in 340-hp (four-barrel carburetor) and 350-hp (three

two-barrel carburetor) versions. A new 409-cid Turbo-Fire engine was available with 360 hp (four-barrel), 380 hp (three two-barrel) or 409 hp (dual quad) options. It had 11:1 compression. A four-speed close-ratio transmission was $188 extra.

Some Chevy experts warn that the 1961 Impala SS is not the easiest car to restore. Only 456 Impalas were fitted with the "SS" package (including 142 with 409-cid engines), so parts are hard to find. This is something to consider if you have your heart set on becoming a Super Sport buyer. But take heart, because a 409-cid '61 Chevy without SS equipment is also a desirable muscle car.

According to the *Standard Catalog of Chevrolet 1912-1998*, a 1961 Bel Air sport coupe with the 409-cid 409-hp engine was reported to have done the quarter mile in 12.83 seconds. Don Nicholson was also Top Stock Eliminator at the 1961 National Hot Rod Association's Winternationals behind the wheel of a 409/409 Chevy.

1962 CHEVROLET BEL AIR 409 Z11

(Jerry Heasley photo)

The legendary 1962 Chevy "409" V-8 was a true American muscle car.

A close-ratio four-speed transmission made the 409 a terror at stoplight drags.

"She's so fine my 409!" Remember the song? "Gonna save my pennies and save my dimes. Gonna buy me a 409, 409, 409."

What yearning that Beach Boys pop hit lit in teenagers of the early 1960s. Save your pennies and save your dimes and buy yourself a 409, could it be true? Not really, but put in enough hours in the grocery store or as a pump jockey at the local Esso station, mow a few lawns on the side, get a little help from Dad on the down payment and maybe, just maybe. That is, if your dealer would sell a kid a 409. Most local dealers refused; they didn't want a kid getting killed in a car they had sold. A 409 was fast!

The 409 engine could be ordered in about anything Chevrolet built, even station wagons, but the heart-stopping combination was a 409 in a "bubble top" Bel Air two-door hardtop. This body style got its nickname from the vast sweeps of front and rear window glass and was a better pick than the imitation convertible Impala hardtop due to lighter weight. Fit the 409 with a close-ratio four-speed man-

ual transmission, and in the stoplight drags nobody else would even come close (unless you missed a shift or your contender had slipped a Chrysler Hemi into that chopped Ford coupe). Take that 409 to the Saturday night drags and you'd get your car's value, that and a documented race with some pretty impressive times—like 115 mph at the end of a standing-start quarter-mile.

A 409 would go! Its power rating? How about 409 hp for the dual four-barrel carburetor version. OK, so it's 1962 and you're not into drag racing. You're looking for a car to take out on the highway and eat up the miles. You'll stop a little more often to fill up the fuel tank, but a 409 fitted with tall gears, Chevrolet's optional heavy-duty suspension, and sintered metallic brakes would easily cruise with the top European sports sedans. On a long straight stretch you might even get the speedometer needle to nudge the 150 mph mark (the bubble-top body was fairly aerodynamic).

1962 CHEVROLET
CORVETTE FUEL-INJECTED
SEBRING 327

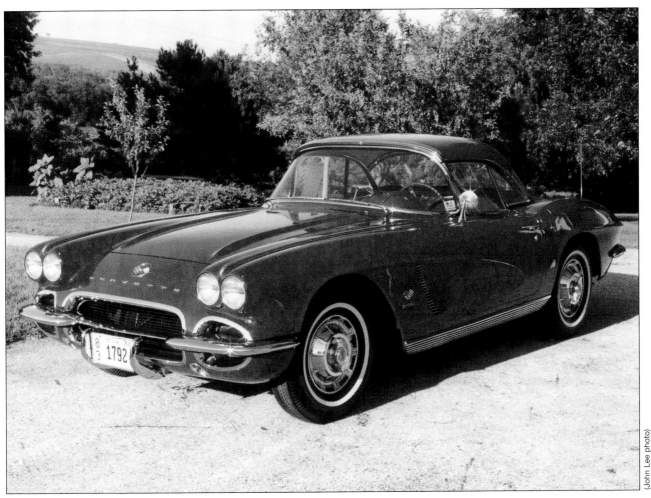

The Corvettes were plenty popular in 1962, but not many had the Sebring racing package that this red beauty had.

(John Lee photo)

The last of the straight-axle Corvettes was the first to offer a 327-cid small-block V-8. There were three versions of the engine and the hottest was part of a package nicknamed after the sports car races at Sebring, Fla. In this format, the Vette enthusiasts got the sole fuel-injected version of the new engine. But, that was cause for excitement. It churned out an unbelievable—for the time—360 hp!

Some say that the high-performance equipment offered for Corvettes of this era were related to the AMA racing ban of 1957 and its effect on Zora Arkus-Duntov. As the story goes, with these competition restrictions, the Corvette's "father" could no longer continue his racing with official factory backing. Therefore, he began to slip some serious racing equipment into the options bin. The story seems plausible, too, when you look at the 1962 Corvette options list. You could not get power steering, power brakes or air conditioning. However, you could add on hot "Duntov" camshafts, thermo-activated cooling fans and aluminum-cased transmissions.

Other competition-oriented Corvette "Sebring" extras included

15 x 5.5-inch wheels (no charge), a direct-flow exhaust system (no charge), a 24-gallon fuel tank ($118.40), a four-speed manual gearbox ($188.30), a Positraction rear axle ($43.05), sintered-metallic brake linings ($37.70) and heavy-duty suspension ($333.60). The 327-cid 360-hp Rochester fuel-injection engine was $484.20 by itself.

With a 3,080-lb. curb weight, the fuel-injected '62 Vette carried just 8.6 pounds-per-horsepower (the lowest ratio ever, up to that point) and could scat from 0 to 60 mph in just 5.9 seconds. It did the quarter mile in 14.9 seconds. Until the arrival of the Ford-powered Cobra in late 1962, Corvettes dominated B-production racing in Sports Car Club of America (SCCA) events. This period, in fact, has been called the first "Golden Age" of Corvette racing.

The high-performance image didn't hurt in the showroom. An all-time high of 14,531 Corvettes were manufactured in 1962. However, few had the ready-to-race Sebring package with all the competition-oriented options.

1962 CHEVROLET NOVA SS 327

With a front-mounted engine, rear-drive system and squared-off styling, the Chevy II achieved what it set out to do—serve as Chevrolet's counterpart to imported cars, Studebaker's Lark, Chrysler's Valiant/Lancer and Ford's Falcon. The original engine options for this economy compact were a ho-hum 90-hp four and slightly sprightlier 120-hp six. Someone at GM must have also remembered how the sporty Monza buoyed sagging Corvair sales and decided to put some sting under the Chevy II's bonnet—a dealer-installed V-8 engine option.

Around February 1962, GM announced that any Chevy II buyer wanting to transform the quiet little compact into a boulevard bombshell could do so by adding a dealer-installed Corvette V-8. Any of four Corvette engines—250-, 300-, 340- or 360-hp versions of the easy-breathing 327-cid V-8—could be selected. The conversion was not cheap, adding about $1,400 to the "economy" car's $2,200 base price, but what performance the Corvette engine produced!

Fitted with a fuel-injected 360-hp Corvette power plant, the little Chevy II was capable of a top speed in excess of 130 mph and leaped from 0-to-60 mph in just 7.3 seconds. A power transfusion of this magnitude presented two problems: keeping the rear tires from smoking with every blip of the acclerator and getting the car to go around corners. The Corvette V-8 and four-speed transmission outweighed the stock six and manual three-speed by 160 lbs.

Since almost all of this extra weight rested on the front wheels, heavy-duty front springs (included as part of the engine-swap kit) kept the Vette-powered Chevy II's nose at proper height. A front anti-roll bar helped with cornering. Other upgrades included heavy-duty (metallic) brake linings and rear traction arms. Surprisingly, the conversion kit did not include a beefier rear axle.

No external markings (except for the telltale dual exhausts) betrayed the beast lurking under a stock-looking Chevy II's hood, but sliding behind the steering wheel put you in front of a 200-mph speedometer and gave notice that this wasn't your typical shopping cart.

Because the Corvette engine was a dealer-installed option, figures aren't available on how many conversions were performed. But if you ever spot an early Chevy II with a V-8 wearing Corvette valve covers under the hood, chances are you're looking at a real factory-inspired hot rod.

1962 CHEVROLET IMPALA SUPER SPORT 409/409

(Jerry Heasley photo)

The 1962 Chevrolet Super Sport 409 didn't come with any real performance extras, but it was plenty fast without them.

Chevrolet's top models were in the Impala line in 1962 and the Super Sport option was available again, but only for sport coupes and convertibles this year. Selling for only $53.80 extra, the SS package was basically a group of special badges, hubcaps and trim items. It was identified as RPO 240 and included swirl-pattern body side moldings; "SS" rear fender emblems; an "SS" deck lid badge; specific Super Sport wheel discs with simulated knock-off spinners;

a locking center console and a passenger-assist bar.

The option really had nothing to do with high performance, although the SS name came from a hot drag-racing class and helped sell more cars to youthful buyers. Why, you could even get the SS goodies on an Impala hardtop or ragtop with a six-cylinder engine. If you wanted bucket seats, you had to add another $102.25 and you still didn't have a muscle car.

Things started to heat up if you were willing to part with an additional $428 for a 409-cid 380-hp V-8 with a four-barrel carburetor, dual exhausts, a high-lift camshaft and solid valve lifters. However, if you really wanted muscular performance, you had to move one step up to the 409-hp version of the big Turbo-Fire motor, which included a special lightweight valve train. Its price tag was $484, which sounds reasonable now, but represented a small fortune back in 1962.

A basic V-8-powered Super Sport hardtop listed for $2,776 and the convertible cost $2,919, but a well-optioned 409 version was probably $1,000 or more extra. Although a lighter-weight Bel Air Z11 is probably faster, a lot of today's muscle car collectors would rather have a brightly decorated Super Sport with the hottest 409. At least two car magazines printed road tests on sport coupes. The first car was an aluminum racing-type front-end version that weighed 3,500 pounds. It carried 8.6 lbs. per horsepower and did 0 to 60 in 4 seconds and the quarter mile in 12.2 seconds. The second car tipped the scales at 3,750 lbs., or 9.2 lbs. per horsepower. It needed 6.3 seconds to hit 60 mph from a standing start and did the quarter mile in 14.9 seconds.

1963 CHEVROLET NOVA 400 SS 327

Thrift like this is nothing new

sport like this is nothing new

Chevy II Nova Super Sport Converti

EC·4434

but both in one car...that is new

A happy combination? No doubt about it from the way these Chevy II Super Sports are catching on. □ Under the hood you've got a peppery 6-cylinder engine. Smooth, dependable, eager to do about everything but run through a gallon of gas. (From the way it nurses the stuff, in fact, you're likely to suspect that it goes around making its own.) □ With this goes our Super Sport package'—front bucket seats, all-vinyl trim, special instrument cluster, sports-minded styling accents and (with Power-

CHEVY II
SUPER SPORTS

CHEVROLET

THE MAKE MORE PEOPLE DEPEND ON

glide) transmission) a floor-mounted range selector. The package comes on either convertible or hardtop. Either way you've got a spruce easy-handling machine that gives you plenty of ginger—without a lot of needless gingerbread. Matter of fact, that pretty well describes our sedans, station wagons and the rest of the ten Chevy II models you've got to choose from, too. Drop down to your dealer's and take a long, close look. Chevrolet Division of General Motors, Detroit 2, Michigan. *(optional at extra cost)*

New owners of the 1963 Chevy II Nova could exchange the in-line six for any of the company's V-8s, but it wasn't cheap.

The Chevy II Nova SS Sport Coupe was a neat little car to drive in 1963. It combined excellent maneuverability, good operating economy, peppy performance and a luxurious interior in a compact-size car with a 110-inch wheelbase, 183-inch overall length and approximately 3,000-lb. curb weight.

The Nova featured unitary construction, which was catching on more and more in the early '60s. The integral, bolt-on front end supported the power plant. The front suspension relied on unequal-length upper 'A' arms, bottom control arms, coil springs and integral shocks (mounted above the 'A' arms). At the rear two single-leaf springs supported a rigid axle.

According to the *Standard Catalog of Chevrolet 1912-1998*, a 1963 Nova 400 SS Sport Coupe listed for $2,262 in standard format. Equipment that came as part of the $161.40 SS option package included a special gauge cluster (in place of "idiot" lights), front bucket seats, an all-vinyl interior, extra chrome trim inside and out, special wheel covers and a chrome transmission cover plate on models equipped with Powerglide.

Note the lack of a V-8 in the above list! An in-line six-cylinder mill was standard on Nova 400 models, even after the SS option was added. Still, as in 1962, Nova buyers could ask their local Chevy dealer to install any of the big Chevy V-8s in their new car. The Chevy II body was actually designed to accommodate V-8s from both the 283-cid and the 327-cid engine families.

This type of engine swap was not an inexpensive deal. *Motor Trend's* assistant technical editor, Bob McVay, took his Nova SS test car to a Los Angeles Chevrolet dealer. He was quoted a price of $1,555 for a "327" conversion, including a four-speed stick shift and a Positraction rear axle. The price did not cover the installation charges— only the hardware. McVay estimated that a Nova SS 327 would do 0 to 60 in 6.8 seconds, based on the magazine's 1962 test results.

1963 CHEVROLET IMPALA Z11 427/IMPALA SS 409

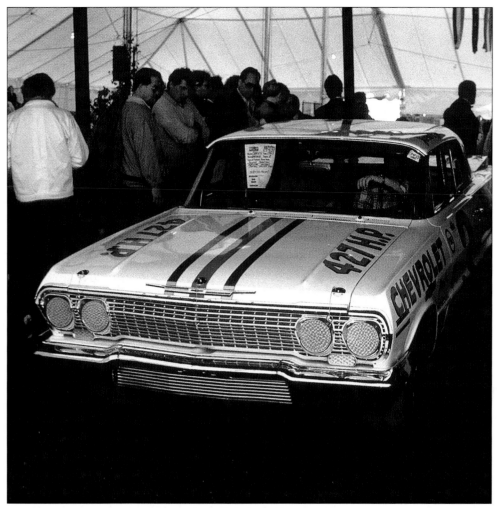

Baseball hall of famer Reggie Jackson made a 1963 Chevrolet Super Sport 409 part of his car collection.

Chevrolet dropped the Bel Air "bubbletop" in 1963. After that, the Impala coupe, with its squared-off roof, became the basis for the RPO Z11 drag-racing package. Only about 57 of these cars were built, specifically for Super/Stock drag-racing competition. Twenty-five Z11s were released by Chevrolet on December 1, 1962. An additional 25 were released on New Year's Day. Seven more were sold later.

The Z11 option included an aluminum hood, aluminum front fenders, aluminum fender brackets and other lightweight parts. The cars also had no center bumper backing and bracing. All extra insulation was deleted to cut total weight by about 112 pounds. Under the hood was a 427-cid 430-hp V-8 with dual four-barrel carburetors.

Also in 1963, Chevrolet built five Mark II NASCAR 427 "mystery" engines and used them in racing cars at Daytona Beach. The cars the engines went in won the two 100-mile preliminary races and set the track's new stock-car record. These engines were closely related to the Z11 engines and were also prototypes for the 1966 396-cid Chevy V-8. The cylinder block deck surfaces were angled to parallel the piston domes. The engines also used a staggered or "porcupine" valve layout. Early in the 1963 model year, General Motors ordered all of its divisions to halt factory support of racing and the mystery-engine project came to its close.

Since most Chevy buyers were not in the market for a Mark II "mystery" engine or a Z11 package, the best option for those interested in a muscular street car was the Impala SS with the extra-cost 409 V-8. The Super Sport equipment package, RPO Z03, was expanded to include all-vinyl bucket seats. All featured swirl-pattern side molding inserts, matching cove inserts, red-filled "SS" overlays for the Impala emblems on the rear fenders, specific full-wheel covers, a center console with a locking storage compartment (with optional Powerglide or four-speed manual transmissions), a dashboard trimmed with swirl-pattern inserts and an "SS" steering wheel center hub.

The package was again available for the Impala sport coupe ($2,774 with the base 283-cid V-8) and the Impala convertible ($3,024 with the base V-8). The Turbo-Fire 409 V-8 was available in three versions. The mild one had a single four-barrel carburetor and 10.0:1 compression; the middle one came with a single four-barrel carburetor, dual exhausts, a high-lift camshaft, solid valve lifters and an 11.0:1 compression ratio for $428, and the wilder 425-hp version, for $484 extra, had dual four-barrel carburetors, dual exhausts, a high-lift camshaft, solid valve lifters and an 11.0:1 compression ratio.

Motor Trend technical editor Jim Wright tested two versions of the Impala SS in the magazine's March 1963 issue. One had the 327-cid V-8. The other had the 409-cid 340-hp engine hooked to a Powerglide two-speed transmission. Even at that, it did 0 to 60 mph in 7.7 seconds and covered the quarter mile in 15.9 seconds at 88 mph. It was no Z11, but it was fast for 1963.

1963 CHEVROLET CORVETTE STING RAY Z06

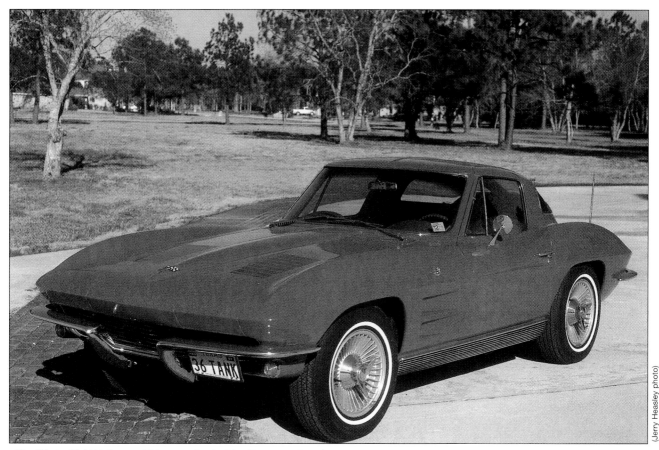

The "big-tank" 1963 Corvette Z06 was well suited for distance racing.

Chevrolet's all new Sting Ray for 1963 was hot. It had a glorious new body, broadened in scope with the first Corvette coupe. It had an independent rear suspension, fuel injection, even knock-off wheels. And it had a racing option Z06.

Z06 bore the mark of Zora Arkus-Duntov, but by no purposeful intent. In fact, Arkus-Duntov's intention was to keep the racing package nondescript because Chevrolet was supposedly out of racing.

The Z06 Corvette was impressive for its day and would possibly be as legendary as the L88 is today, except for the superiority of the Cobra, which unexpectedly destroyed Arkus-Duntov's 1963 Sting Ray party. Ready for sale in October of 1962— and available strictly on the coupe—the Z06 option consisted of a fuel-injected 327-cid engine, a 36.5-gallon fuel tank, heavy-duty brakes, heavy-duty suspension and knock-off wheels.

The heavy-duty brakes consisted of drums with sintered metallic linings, power assisted and backed by a dual circuit master cylinder. "Elephant ear" scoops rammed fresh air to the drums and cooling fans spun with the hub. Early in the 1963 calendar year, Z06 was expanded to include the really necessary racing part, the 36.5-gallon fuel tank, which fit the back of the coupe body like a pea in a pod. Coded N03, the "big tank" helped make the Corvette competitive in long-distance endurance racing events, such as Daytona.

Curiously, the knock-off wheels, which have become almost synonymous with the 1963 split-window Corvette, leaked due to the porosity of the aluminum and poor sealing at the rims, and no more than a dozen coupes and roadsters got them. Futhermore, only one Corvette has been documented original with original knock-offs. It was originally picked up at the factory by an independent racer. Edward Schlampp Jr. raced the car in the SCCA A-production class.

Later in the model year, N03 was not mandatory with Z06, so only about 60 of the 199 Z06 Corvettes ended up with the big tank. N03 Corvettes also came with their inner wheel well housings modified to fit larger-than-stock tires.

In 1963, no RPO option was hotter than Z06.

Only about 60 of the '63 Corvettes wound up with 36.5-gallon gas tanks.

1964 IMPALA SS 409

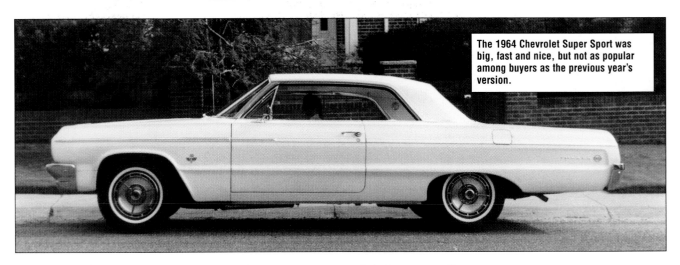

The 1964 Chevrolet Super Sport was big, fast and nice, but not as popular among buyers as the previous year's version.

Chevrolet's plushest and sportiest offerings became a separate Impala SS series in 1964. The list of standard equipment took off where regular Impala features left off. Super Sport buyers got leather-grained vinyl upholstery, individual front bucket seats and swirl-pattern dashboard and body molding inserts. They could also store their gloves or sunglasses in a locking center console. Naturally, there were red "SS" emblems all over the cars. In addition, the doors carried red reflectors and neat-looking wheel covers were included.

For 1964, due to the performance ban that GM brass put into effect the previous year, Chevrolet engine choices stayed about the same as in late 1963. Ban or no ban, that meant that the Impala SS 409 hardtop ($2,947) or convertible ($3,196) was still a big, fast car. The hardtop tested out at 7.5 seconds for 0 to 60 mph and 15.3 sec-

onds in the quarter mile.

The Turbo-Fire 409 V-8 was again available in three versions. The first had a single four-barrel carburetor and 10.0:1 compression; the second one came with a single four-barrel carburetor, dual exhausts, a high-lift camshaft, solid valve lifters and an 11.0:1 compression ratio for $428 and the third, a 425-hp version costing $484 extra, had dual four-barrel carburetors, dual exhausts, a high-lift camshaft, solid valve lifters and an 11.0:1 compression ratio.

In 1963, a total of 16,920 big Chevrolets left the factory with 409s under their hoods, but in 1964 the popularity of these engines dropped and only 8,684 were ordered. That makes the 1964 Impala SS 409 much harder to find than a 1963 edition. In both years, *most* 409-powered Chevys were Impala Super Sports.

1964 CHEVROLET CHEVELLE MALIBU SS 327

(Jerry Heasley photo)

These days, a cherry 1964 Malibu SS sport coupe will sell for many times its original $2,484 sticker price.

Life started out simple enough for the 1964 Chevrolet Chevelle. It was the lowest-priced of the four all-new A-body intermediates from General Motors that model year.

Inside and outside of the Chevrolet offices, comparisons were readily made to the late and already lamented 1955-1957 Chevrolets. The 115-inch wheelbase of the separate Chevelle frame was the same as the 1955 model's and other dimensions, except height, were close.

A variety of models were offered with the top-of-the-line Malibu two-door hardtop and convertible available with the $170 Super Sport option. This package included bucket seats, a console

and appropriate badging.

Initial power-plant offerings included the standard 194-cid six, an optional 230-cid six and a pair of old reliable 283-cid V-8s. In V-8 models, the 195-hp two-barrel version was standard. An L77 220-hp version with a four-barrel carburetor was $54 extra.

Nostalgia for the earlier models was fine, but when Pontiac shoved its big 389-cid 325-hp V-8 into GTO-optioned Tempests, the pressure was on to keep up. Oldsmobile answered quickly with a 330-cid 310-hp "police" option for its F-85, which soon evolved into the 4-4-2 in 400-cid form.

GM had just been through one of its soul-cleansing anti-

(Jerry Heasley photo)

A 327-cid V-8 gave the 1964 Malibu SS real muscle.

performance purges in 1963 and Chevrolet, at first, was turned down when it wanted the 327-cid small-block for the Chevelle.

GM brass relented and, in quick order, the 250-hp L30 and 300-hp L74 327 V-8s were added to the Chevelle options list at midyear. The former was only $95 over the base 283-cid V-8 and the latter added another $138. Chevy literature even advertised the 365-hp L76 out of the Corvette and some back-door drag racing specials most likely got them.

It seemed that Chevelle lived right, from its introduction through its value today as a collectible car. A Malibu two-door hardtop listed for $2,484 in base, V-8 form and the convertible at $2,587. Today, show condition convertibles sell for nearly 10 times their original price and the hardtops about six times. Models with four-speed manual gearboxes and SS trim do even better.

1964 CHEVROLET CORVETTE L84 "FUELIE"

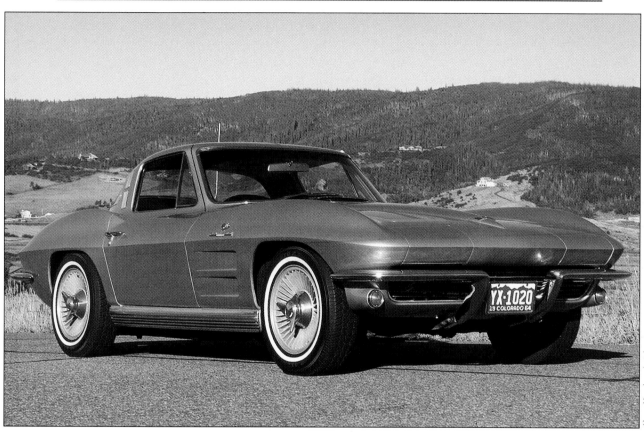

(Jerry Heasley photo)

The 1964 Sting Ray Corvette "fuelie" coupe started at a base price of $4,252.

The Corvette Sting Ray's styling was cleaned up a bit for 1964. On coupes, the previous year's distinctive rear window divider was replaced by a solid piece of glass. On all models, the fake hood vents were eliminated and the roof vents were restyled. A three-speed fan was available in the coupe to aid in ventilation.

Chevrolet made 8,304 fuel-injected Sting Ray coupes. They sold for $4,252 and up and weighed 2,945 lbs. The $4,037 convertible weighed in at 2,960 lbs. and had a 13,925-unit production run.

Seven exterior colors were available for 1964: tuxedo black; ermine white; Riverside red; satin silver; silver blue; Daytona blue and saddle tan. All body colors were available with a choice of black, white or beige soft tops.

All Corvettes built in 1964 had a 327-cid V-8 with a 4.00 x 3.25-inch bore and stroke. The base engine had a 10.5:1 compression ratio and developed 250 hp at 4400 rpm and 350 ft. lbs. of torque at 2800 rpm. It used a single Carter WCFB four-barrel carburetor.

The optional L75 V-8 ($53.80 extra) developed 300 hp at 5000 rpm and 360 ft. lbs. of torque at 3200 rpm. It had a Carter aluminum Type AFB four-barrel carburetor.

Next came Chevrolet's L76 V-8 with mechanical valve lifters, a high-lift camshaft and a Holley four-barrel carburetor. It had an 11.00:1 compression ratio and developed 365 hp at 6200 rpm and 350 ft. lbs. of torque at 4000 rpm.

Of course, real muscle car fans had to order the L84 option. This was basically the L75 V-8 fitted with Ram-Jet fuel injection. It was good for 375 hp at 6200 rpm and 350 ft. lbs. of torque at 4400 rpm.

Only 3.2 percent of 1964 Corvettes were sold with the standard three-speed manual transmission. Most—85.7 percent—were equipped with a four-speed manual transmission. An L84-powered 1964 Corvette could go from 0 to 60 mph in 6.3 seconds and from 0 to 100 mph in 14.7 seconds. It had a top speed of 138 mph.

1965 CHEVROLET CORVETTE STING RAY

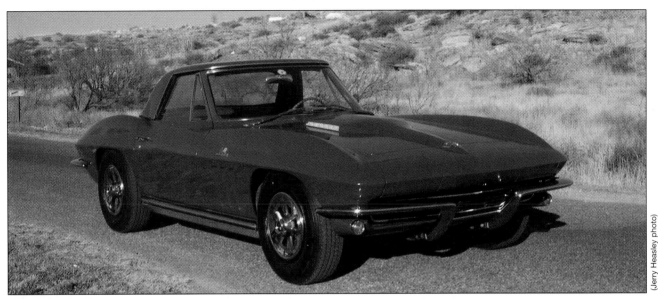

(Jerry Heasley photo)

The 1965 Corvette Sting Ray was the only Corvette to feature a 396-cid engine.

If the Sting Rays are the best of the Corvettes, quite possibly the 1965 model is the best of the Sting Rays. It is, most assuredly, a memorable Corvette.

Refinement was the key word again in 1965. The '64 Vette offered as improvements a higher horsepower "fuelie" engine option, smoother ride and better insulation. But the best was saved for 1965. The big news in '65 was the addition of four-wheel disc brakes as standard equipment. The small-block Vettes could always go. Now they could stop!

Styling changes were held to a minimum, although Corvette enthusiasts could immediately spot a new '65 by the functional front fender louvers, new wheel covers and restyled grille. With no depressions or trim, the 1965 hood was not interchangeable with the '63 or '64 units. The model range again included a choice of convertible or sleek fastback coupe. Sales reached a record 23,562, including 15,376 convertibles.

Corvette continued as Chevy's prestige leader and the inside story was a decidedly plush one in 1965. Newly styled bucket seats were offered and genuine leather seating surfaces were optional. Options few European sports cars could match included power steering, power brakes, power windows, air conditioning, AM-FM radio, telescopic steering column and a wood-rimmed steering wheel.

But the performance enthusiast was usually drawn first to the engine and power-train specifications sheet. Standard equipment—and meant for the boulevardiers—was Chevy's tried-and-true 327-cid 250-hp Turbofire V-8. The next step up was a 300-hp version of the 327 and new for '65 was the precursor to the famous LT1. This 327 developed an impressive 350 hp, combining "sizzle with calm, cool behavior." Up next was the most powerful carbureted 327, putting out 365 advertised horses.

A legend since 1957, Ram-Jet fuel injection made its final appearance in 1965. At $538,

fuel injection was an expensive option, but it made the 327-cid V-8 a 375-hp world-class stormer. It was the ultimate small block.

The introduction, in April 1965, of the 396-cid big-block V-8 marked the beginning of a new era for the Corvette. The 396 was introduced concurrently in the full-sized Chevrolet, in the Corvette and in the Chevelle. Rated at 425 hp and priced at only $292.70, the 396 made the fuel-injected Corvette seem superfluous in those days of cheap, high-octane gasoline.

The big-block Corvettes could be immediately identified by the "power bulge" on the hood. Introduced at the same time as the 396 were new side-mounted exhausts—a $134.50 option.

Although the fuel-injected Corvette remained through the end of the 1965 model year, it was not widely available and was quietly dropped when the '66s made their appearance. Interestingly, 1965 was also the only year of the 396-cid Corvette. In 1966, that engine was bored out to 427 awesome cubic inches.

Nineteen sixty-five was a vintage, memorable year for Corvette. It was the only year you could buy a fuel-injected, disc-braked Sting Ray. It was the first year for the big-block and side-mounted exhausts. And with prices starting at $4,106, the 1965 Corvette Sting Ray was also quite a bargain.

(Jerry Heasley photo)

The 1965 Sting Ray convertible was a lot of car for the money and one of the most memorable Vettes ever produced.

1965 CHEVROLET IMPALA SS 409

The 1965 Chevy Super Sport was available with a 400-hp engine, but the 340-hp model was more popular.

(Larry Mitchell photo)

Car and Driver (Dec. 1964) noted that things had changed, but stayed the same, since the early '60s, when the Beach Boys first sang "She's real fine, my 409." Engine displacements of over 400 cubes had been non-existent only half a decade earlier, but then 406-, 409-, 413- 425- and 426-cid motors had come along, consistently upping the ante for high-performance fans.

The 425 "porcupine-head" big block proved to be nearly a Chevy pipe dream, because after it put in a quick showing at Daytona in 1963, GM brass told all divisions to get out of racing and throw all their racing hardware away. Thus, the 425 became known as Chevrolet's "mystery engine."

As a result of this change, the 409 found its way to the top of the bow-tie options list again when the all-new '65 Chevys arrived. Chevrolet's full-size 1965 model was curvier and larger than its counterparts of 1963-1964. It gained nearly 4 inches of length, although on the same 119-inch wheelbase. Curb weights rose more than 125 lbs. over 1964 for most models. The fact that the new

Chevys were larger was a good reason for adding the 409 engine.

For the first time this year, Impala SS models were in their own separate series. The V-8 sport coupe sold for $2,947 and weighed 3,570 lbs. The counterpart convertible was priced at $3,212 and weighed 3,645 lbs.

The 409-cid V-8 came in 340- and 400-hp versions. The more powerful one was available with a Muncie four-speed manual transmission. It had an 11.0:1 compression ratio. However, the 340-hp engine was a better seller by far and is the one that *Car and Driver* tested. This engine featured a single four-throat Rochester carburetor and a 10.0:1 compression ratio. In the 4,200-lb. test car it provided 0.83 hp per pound.

Equipped with a Powerglide automatic transmission and 3.31:1 final gear ratio, the 340-hp Impala SS sport coupe did 0 to 60 in 8 seconds flat. It took all of 16.4 seconds to scoot down the quarter mile at 91 mph.

1965 CHEVROLET CHEVELLE Z16

In February of 1965, at the General Motors Proving Grounds in Mesa, Arizona, Chevrolet introduced its 396-cid 325-hp V-8 in the all-new Caprice luxury car, plus a 425-hp, solid lifter 396 for option status in the Corvette.

Chevelle went without a big-block once again—or so it seemed. However, through a "secret" program, Chevrolet did offer a 375-hp 396. The Chevelle Malibu SS-396 was the official name of this hot car. Chevrolet chose not to advertise it at first, because production would be extremely limited.

Why was production so limited, when the GTO was setting sales records and Chevy enthusiasts were wild for a 396-powered muscle Chevelle? Well, the new Malibu SS-396 (RPO Z16) was a hurry-up car that pushed the Chevelle into the big-block muscle car leagues. But, it was specially engineered at a high cost.

On the surface, the Z16 looked, quite simply, like a big-block Chevelle with the new porcupine-head 396 dropped in. In reality, the Z16 was much more. Underneath, it was a heavy-duty machine and much more like a big car than an intermediate model. Chevrolet

wasn't set to turn it out in mass quantities.

The closed car used a convertible frame filled with rear suspension reinforcements and two additional body mounts. Power-assisted brakes came from the larger cars, with 11-inch-diameter drums front and rear. Springs and shocks were stiffer. Ball joint studs were shot-peened and hubs were a sturdy Arma-steel design. The wheels were 6 inches wide, compared to the 5-inchers on the standard SS.

Every Z16 came out as a Chevelle Malibu SS sports coupe style No. 13837. All cars were coupes—there were no convertibles. The 375-hp 396 was the L37 engine option, with special left- and right-side exhaust manifolds to fit the engine bay. The engine was linked to a four-speed Muncie gearbox (no automatics were built) with a 2.56:1 first gear. The clutch conformed to big-car specs, too. It was 11 inches in diameter with pressure of 2,300-2,600 lbs. The regular 8.125-inch ring gear from the stock Chevelle wouldn't do, either. Chevrolet installed an 8.875-inch ring gear in its Z16.

Many other features were unique to the Z16, including the air

(Jerry Heasley photo)

The Chevelle Z16 option included a 396-cid 425-hp V-8.

cleaner (with crossed flags made of metal), "396 Turbo-jet" emblems on the front fenders, a special taillight board with an SS emblem and a unique ribbed molding with black paint. All Z16 Chevelles also had a 160-mph speedometer, an AM-FM Multiplex stereo with four speakers, an in-dash tachometer and a dash-mounted clock.

Exactly 201 of the Chevelle Z16s were built for 1965. In 1966, Chevrolet was "geared up" for regular production with an SS-396 Chevelle that was easier to order and available to the general public.

1966 CHEVROLET IMPALA SS 427

The 1965 Impala SS was the best-selling Super Sport ever and Chevrolet had no reason to mess with its success in 1966. A mild restyling gave the Chevrolets a slightly heavier look. The grille was slightly changed and, at the rear, horizontal taillights replaced the three round ones of a year earlier.

Anyone with muscle-car tendencies needed a V-8 and the hotter offerings started with a 327-cid 275-hp engine. That was mild compared to the Turbo-Fire 396 option, a 325-hp engine (RPO L35) that cost $158 above the base V-8. However, real muscle-car fanatics were sure not to settle for anything less than 427 cubic inches.

The new 427-cid V-8 grew out of the Chevrolet racing cars that Bill Thomas had whipped up for NASCAR competition. Big Chevrolets had not been competitive in circle-track racing since 1963, so Thomas took a 396 to his home garage, reworked it to 427 cid, got NASCAR to accept it and talked to the factory about his project. By November 1965, *Car Life* magazine reported that Chevy had enlarged the production 396 to 427.

Chevrolet decided to offer the so-called "Rat" motor in showroom cars in two editions. The RPO L36 version had a 10.25:1 compression ratio and generated 390 hp at 5200 rpm and 460 ft. lbs. of torque at 3600 rpm. With its higher 11.0:1 compression ratio and solid valve lifters, the RPO L72 "special purpose" version of the 427 was rated for 425 hp at 5600 rpm and 480 ft. lbs. of torque at 4000 rpm.

Fitted with a 390-hp 427, a big '66 Chevy carried about 10.8 lbs. per horsepower and could do 0 to 60 mph in 7.9 seconds or so. The quarter mile took about 15.5 seconds. According to Robert C. Ackerson's research for his book *Chevrolet High-Performance*, both versions of the 427 were relatively scarce in 1966. A total of 3,287 full-size Chevys carried the L36 and only 1,856 had the L72 installed.

Somehow Impala doesn't seem destined to be big with secret agents

Imagine nobody noticing you in a car that looks like this

After all, in a year when the lean, clean look is the thing, this Body by Fisher is bound to turn heads.

From the distinctive front styling to the smart new wraparound taillights, the Impala SS demands attention. Not a line's wasted.

The view from the inside is just as pleasing with wall-to-wall deep-twist carpeting and foam-cushioned Strato-bucket front seats standard on this model. It's all accented by touches of bright metal and brushed aluminum.

Of course the interiors are color-keyed to complement each Magic-Mirror finish. Nice? Naturally. Inconspicuous? Hardly.

STYLING THE CHEVROLET WAY

CHEVROLET GM

The 1966 Chevy Impala SS was available with the 427-cid big-block V-8.

1966 CHEVROLET CHEVY II
NOVA SS

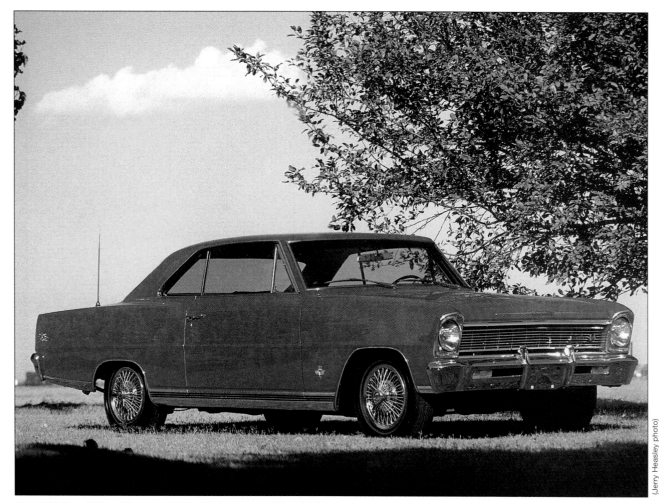

(Jerry Heasley photo)

The 1966 Chevy II Nova SS was available with the Corvette 327-cid V-8.

When it came to sales in the early '60s, Ford's Falcon was hot and Chevrolet's Nova was not. Therefore, by 1962, Chevrolet had its conventional Chevy II ready to take on the conventional Falcon.

By 1963, Chevrolet offered a Super Sport or SS option package for the Nova sport coupe and convertible. The Nova SS package included amenities such as a more complete instrument cluster, electric clock, deluxe steering wheel, bucket seats and wheel covers, plus special interior and exterior trim and emblems.

The Chevy II was significantly restyled for 1966 and the list of engines available for Nova Super Sports now included a 327-cid 350-hp V-8 with a staggering 11.0:1 compression ratio. In essence, this was a "factory hot rod." Race-car tuner Bill Thomas had constructed such a Nova, called the "Bad Bascomb," two years earlier. The production version did not have the Corvette independent rear suspension like Thomas' car did, but it was hot enough.

The 327-cid Chevy V-8 was a small-block engine derived from the 283-cid V-8. The 327 had a 4.00 x 3.35-inch bore and stroke. The 275-hp RPO L30 edition had a 10.51 compression ratio, hydraulic valve lifters and a single four-barrel carburetor. It generated 275 hp at 4800 rpm and 355 ft. lbs. of torque at 3200

rpm. The hotter RPO L79 version featured an 11.0:1 compression ratio and also had hydraulic lifters and a single four-barrel carburetor. It was good for 350 hp at 5200 rpm and 360 ft. lbs at 3600 rpm.

Car Life magazine (May 1966) tested the L79 Nova equipped in true muscle-car-era fashion with a four-speed manual gearbox, limited-slip differential, power steering and brakes, heavy-duty suspension, air conditioning, deluxe bucket seats, a console and full instrumentation. The Corvette engine and other options raised the price from $2,480 to $3,662.

The car did 0 to 60 mph in 7.2 seconds and handled the quarter mile in 15.1 seconds at 93 mph. The magazine criticized steering and braking, but not its all-out performance and top speed of 123 mph. In July 1966, *Motor Trend* test drove an L30 Nova with Powerglide automatic transmission. This car did the 0-to-60 run in 8.6 seconds and accomplished the quarter mile in 16.4 seconds with a terminal speed of 85.87 mph.

1966 CHEVROLET CHEVELLE SS 396

(Jerry Heasley photo)

The 1966 Chevy Chevelle SS was available with the 396-cid big-block V-8 with up to 375 hp.

The 1966 Chevelle had a new cigar-shaped body with forward-thrusting front fenders. It rode on a 115-inch wheelbase and had an overall length of 197 inches. Front and rear tread were both 58 inches. For muscle car fans, Chevrolet offered the Chevelle in the SS-396 series, which consisted of a $2,276 sport coupe and a $2,984 convertible. Together, the two body styles accounted for 72,272 cars.

Super Sport models had twin simulated hood air intakes, ribbed color-accented sill and rear fender lower moldings, a blackout style SS 396 grille and rear cove accents and "Super Sport" script plates on the rear fenders. Specific wheel covers were included, along with red-stripe tires. An all-vinyl bench seat interior was standard.

The 396-cid V-8 belonged to Chevy's big-block engine family. It was essentially a de-stroked 409 with a 4.09 x 3.76-inch bore and stroke. It was standard equipment in the muscular Chevelle model, but was offered in three configurations. The standard SS 396 engine was the RPO L35 version with 325 hp at 4800 rpm and 410 ft. lbs. at 3200 rpm. It had a 10.25:1 compression ratio and single exhausts.

Next up the rung was the RPO L34 version of the 396, which shared its cylinder head and compression ratio with the L35 version, but had certain upgrades such as a forged alloy crankshaft, dual exhausts, a higher-lift cam and chrome piston rings that helped to raise its output to 360 hp at 5200 rpm and 420 ft. lbs. of torque at 3600 rpm. The 360-hp SS 396 sport coupe could do 0 to 60 mph in 7.9 seconds and the quarter mile in 15.5 seconds.

Top option in the SS 396 was the RPO L78, a midyear release that was probably installed in less than 100 cars. It had an 11.0:1 compression ratio, fatter tailpipes, a hotter slide-lifter cam and other go-fast goodies that jacked its output number to 375 hp at 5600 rpm and 415 ft. lbs. at 3800 rpm. Cars with this engine could do 0 to 60 mph in about 6.5 seconds.

Any of the 396-cid engines could be ordered with the M20 wide-ratio four-speed manual transmission or the M-21 close-ratio four-speed. Also available was the M35 Powerglide automatic. Rear axle options included 3.31:1, 3.55:1, 3.73:1, 4.10:1, 4.56:1 and 4.88:1 depending upon the engine-transmission combination. You could get Positraction on all but the 3.31 and 3.55 axles.

1966 CHEVROLET CORVETTE 427

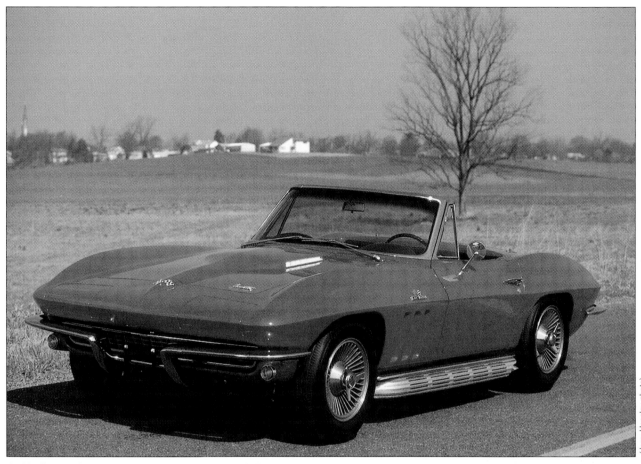

(Jerry Heasley photo)

A 1966 Corvette Sting Ray could be had with a hot 427-cid V-8.

When *Car Life* magazine did a comparison between two '67 Corvettes, it picked one car with a 327-cid V-8 and automatic and a second car with the 427-cid big-block V-8 and a four-speed manual gearbox. The latter vehicle was accurately described as, "a muscular, no-nonsense, do-it-right-now hustlecar." The editors added, "A drive in the 427 can convince anyone with a drop of sporting blood in his veins that an over-abundance of power can be controllable and greatly invigorating."

The basic format of the Corvette Sting Ray had been established by the classic 1963 model. For 1967, the overall appearance was cleaned up and the front fender had five functional, vertical air louvers that slanted forward towards their upper ends. The roof pillar air vents used on earlier fastback coupes were eliminated.

The new 427-cid V-8 came in 390- and 425-hp versions. *Car Life* tested the heftier version and found that it had power peak at a lower rpm and a wider range of torque delivery. This made the maximum muscle option more compatible to everyday driving, but didn't seem to hamper its quarter-mile capabilities. The 425-hp engine featured strong cam timing, special exhaust headers, a transistorized ignition system, solid lifters and a big four-barrel Holley carburetor. The 390-hp big-block initially came hooked to a mandatory wide-ratio four-speed manual gearbox and the 425-hp job came attached to a close-ratio four-speed stick. A modified Powerglide automatic was scheduled as a midyear option for the 390-hp engine only.

Car Life's 427/425 Corvette was a ragtop to boot. Its as-tested price tag of $5,401 included a Positraction rear axle, tinted windshield, transistor ignition, AM/FM radio, telescoping steering shaft, 7.75-15 UniRoyal Laredo gold stripe nylon tires, the close-ratio four-speed, power brakes, power steering and power windows. With a curb weight of 3,270 lbs. it had an 8.5:1 weight-to-power ratio. Zero to 60 mph came in just 5.7 seconds and the quarter mile was covered in 14 seconds with a terminal speed of 102 mph.

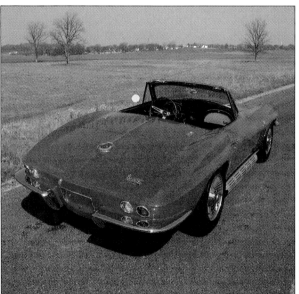

(Jerry Heasley photo)

Chevy made a few minor cosmetic changes to the Corvette one year after making a big splash with the '65 Vette.

1967 CHEVROLET CAMARO 427

Camaros fitted with big-block 427-cid Chevrolet V-8s were evaluated by Chevrolet's engineering department in early 1967, just a few months after the new model first hit the showrooms. At about that time, one of these creations was demonstrated to the press by Chevrolet technical projects manager Walter R. Mackenzie.

As you might guess, the experimental 427-powered Camaro topped the performance of even the hottest of the production versions of the car. Mackenzie's machine was able to accelerate down the quarter mile at times in the 13.5 to 13.90-second bracket. This car was actually a pilot model of the drag-racing-only machines that car builders would soon be constructing in various parts of the country.

These cars were constructed as "semi-factory-built" racing cars by a small number of high-volume Chevrolet dealerships that had close links to drag racing and Chevrolet Motor Division's Product Promotion Network. The managers and salesmen at such dealerships became key players in the development, sales and promotion of the 427 Camaros.

The specialized Chevrolet dealers involved in such programs included Don Yenko Chevrolet in Canonsburg, Pennsylvania; Baldwin Motion Chenrolet of Baldwin, Long Island, New York; Dana Chevrolet in South Gate, California; Nickey Chevrolet in Chicago, Illinois; and the Fred Gibb Agency of La Harpe, Illinois.

Don Yenko, Dana Chevrolet and Nicky Chevrolet all started selling Camaros fitted with L72 Corvette engines (the 427-cid, 425-hp V-8) in 1967. Dana's basic version listed for $3,995. In addition to the big motor, the package included a Muncie four-speed manual gearbox, a 3.55:1 Positraction axle, 14 x 6-inch wheels with D70-14 Firestone wide-oval nylon red line tires, metallic brake linings, headers and dual exhausts, heavy-duty clutch and pressure plate, a fat front stabilizer bar, heavy-duty shocks and a 17-quart radiator. *Motor Trend* tested a Dana 427 Camaro with a 3.73:1 axle and 9.00/9.50 x 14 tires. It did the quarter mile in 12.75 seconds at over 110 mph.

1967 CHEVROLET CAMARO INDY 500 PACE CAR

For its first year on the market, the 1967 Camaro was promoted with an aggressive sales campaign. To fend off competition like Ford's Mustang and Plymouth's Barracuda, there was a seemingly constant revision of first-year Camaro options and trim choices.

Initially, the Camaro line offered a base two-door hardtop or sport coupe and a convertible. You could add Rally Sport trim (including hidden headlights), as well as the SS 350, which added stripes around the nose, special badges and a 295-hp version of Chevy's new 350-cid small-block V-8.

Since the 350 Camaro didn't seem to be enough to pull many customers away from Ford's new 390-cid Mustang or Plymouth's 383-cid Formula S Barracuda, Chevrolet added its Mark IV big-block 396 to the Camaro options list shortly thereafter. This engine developed 325 hp in its L35 form. Additional power selections arrived when the L78 engine option was unleashed. It provided Camaro SS 396 buyers with a 375-hp option.

Chevrolet got the chance to show off its newest product at the Indy 500, where the Camaro paced the racing cars. However, marketing wasn't what it was to become in later years and the cars supplied were RS/SS 396 convertibles. Chevrolet employee and two-time 500 winner Mauri Rose (1947, 1948) drove the car and A.J. Foyt got to keep a Camaro for winning the event.

Instead of offering replicas to dealers, Chevrolet built only 104 of the Camaros and let Indianapolis Motor Speedway Corp. VIPs use them during the month of May. Most of these "Indy Pace Cars" were SS 350s with Powerglide automatics. The 396s used for track purposes had the new Turbo-Hydra-Matic installed. When the race was over, the replicas were sold through local dealers as used cars.

The first-year Camaro was a big success with 220,917 produced, but it did not quite beat Ford's Mustang. SS production for 1969 amounted to only 34,411 cars, making them rarer than thought by most who viewed all the Chevy SS promotions. The Camaro would be the Indy 500 pace car again in 1969 and that time around marketing was different.

(Jerry Heasley photo)

Only 104 of the 1967 Camaro RS/SS 396 Indy 500 Pace Cars were built (left), but there were many more to follow.

1967 CHEVROLET CAMARO SS 350/SS 396

In the mid-1960s the muscle car magazines were full of stories about a car called the Panther, which was being created as Chevrolet's version of the Mustang. When it bowed on Sept. 29, 1966, the bow-tie brand's version of a pony car had taken the name Camaro. Similar to the Mustang being based on the Falcon, the Camaro was based on the Chevy II Nova and that meant it could accommodate all kinds of muscular Chevy V-8s.

The initials "SS" meant performance in the Camaro's infancy. An extensive lineup of engines was offered for Chevy's late-breaking contender in the pony car market and the initial offering for muscle car maniacs was a hot new small-block RPO L48 V-8 with 350 cubic inches and 295 hp. You could order it only with the SS 350 package, which included a raised hood with non-functional finned louvers, "bumblebee" nose stripe, special ornamentation, fat red-stripe tires and a stiff suspension, all for $211.

A heavy-duty three-speed manual transmission was standard in the Super Sport and options included a two-speed powerglide auto-matic or a four-speed manual gearbox. There was also a wide variety of rear axle ratios including 2.73:1, 3.07:1, 3.31:1, 3.55:1, 3.73:1, 4.10:1, 4.56:1 and 4.88:1. *Car and Driver* tested an SS-350 at 0 to 60 mph in 7.8 seconds and the quarter mile in 16.1 seconds at 86.5 mph. *Motor Trend* needed 8 seconds to get to 60 mph, but did the quarter in 15.4 at 90 mph.

On Nov. 26, 1966, Chevy released a pair of 396-cid big-block V-8 options: The RPO L34 priced at $235 with the SS package produced 325 hp while the RPO L78 ($550 including the SS goodies) produced an advertised 375 hp. *Motor Trend* tested an L35 SS-396 Camaro with four-speed gearbox at 6 seconds for 0 to 60 mph and a 14.5-second quarter mile at 95 mph. *Car Life* (May 1967) drove a similar car with Powerglide and registered a 6.8-second 0-to-60 time and 15.1-second quarter mile at 91.8 mph. Since a total of 34,411 Super Sports were built and 29,270 were SS 350 models, that leaves 5,141 that were built as SS-396s.

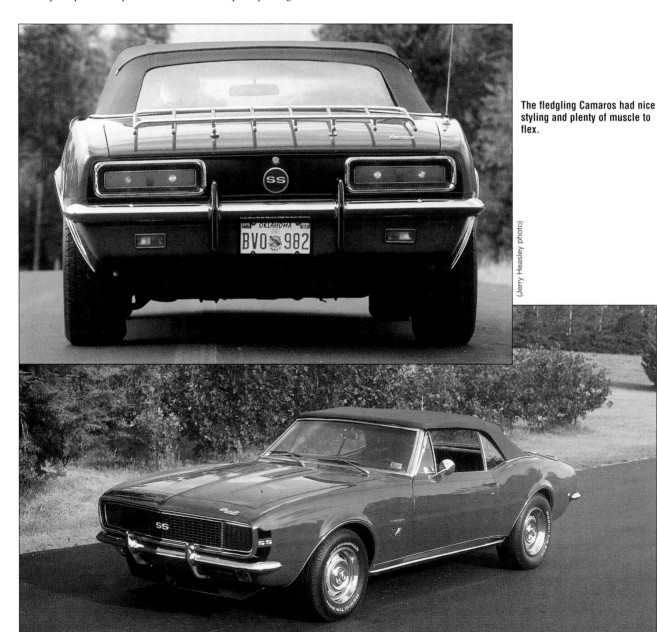

The fledgling Camaros had nice styling and plenty of muscle to flex.

(Jerry Heasley photo)

(Jerry Heasley photo)

The 1967 Camaro Super Sport came with a wide variety of engines and axle setups that produced up to 375 hp .

1967 CHEVROLET CAMARO Z/28

Chevy engineers were able to squeeze 350 hp out of the 302 V-8 in the 1967 Z/28.

As every muscle car fan knows, racing helps sell cars. In 1967, the preferred racing venue for pony cars like the Camaro was the Sports Car Club of America's new Trans-Am "sedan" racing series. In this form of racing, engine size was capped at 305 cid, so the automakers experimented to develop the most muscular motors they could that fit in this "formula." Chevy's production promotions manager Vince Piggins decided the answer was to create a Camaro powered by a maximum-performance version of the small-block V-8.

The Camaro Z/28 was the result of this effort. RPO Z/28 was a performance equipment package designed to make the Camaro a contender in SCCA Trans-Am competition. It was introduced on November 26, 1966, during the American Road Race of Champions at Riverside Raceway in California.

Chevrolet used a 283-cid V-8 in the pilot version of the new model, but that was too far below the 305-cid engine-displacement limit to be a winner. In the production car, Chevrolet combined the 327-cid block with the 283-cid crankshaft and came up with a 302-cid V-8. By playing with other high-performance parts like a giant four-barrel carb, an aluminum high-rise intake and L79 Corvette heads, they got this motor to crank out about 350 hp and 320 ft. lbs. of torque at 6200 rpm. However, to play it safe, the Z/28 was advertised at 290 hp at 5800 rpm and 290 ft. lbs. of torque at 4200 rpm.

The basic Z/28 package listed for $358, but other options were mandatory with the car and jacked the price up to where a typical Z/28 sold for at least $4,200. The price included a heater, but air conditioning was not available. And for those with serious racing in mind, even the heater could be deleted.

The Z/28 performed very well and, since it was designed for competitive road racing, it had terrific handling and braking to go with its impressive straight-line acceleration. The 1967 first-year model could move from 0 to 60 mph in 6.7 seconds and did the quarter mile in an amazing 14.9 seconds at 97 mph. Its top speed was 124 mph.

1967 CHEVROLET IMPALA SS 396

Everything new that could happen... *happened!*

in styling... in safety... and in all these things for your pure personal pleasure

'67 CHEVROLET

The 1967 Chevrolet Impala SS 396 was a big car with enough muscle to hold its own in the performance department.

After being at the center of the high-performance market when the 1960s began, full-sized muscle cars had a harder time attracting attention and buyers after mid-sized muscle cars caught on as the decade progressed. A good case in point was the Impala Super Sport. The Super Sport or SS package started life as a midyear option for the full-sized Chevrolet in 1961. One of the model's spotlight years was 1967, when the Impala SS offered a "no-excuses-sir" big-car alternative for the muscle car buyer.

This is not to say that all Impala Super Sports for 1967 were performance cars. Continuing a practice that started with the 1962 models, you could get either a two-door hardtop (sport coupe) or convertible with an SS designation and an incongruous six-cylinder engine. However, Chevy had a pair of Mark IV-based big-block V-8s that made the SS designation really mean something. The 396-cid 325-hp Turbo-Jet (L35) engine was a good option for starters.

The 396-cid Chevy motor had a 4.094 x 3.76-inch bore and stroke. With its one-barrel Holley carburetor and 10.25:1 compression ratio, the version used in the Impala SS cranked up 325 hp at 4800 rpm and 410 ft. lbs. of torque at 3200 rpm. The standard transmission used with this engine in the Impala SS was a fully synchronized three speed. Options included four-on-the-floor, a console-mounted two-speed Powerglide automatic or the three-speed Hydra-Matic.

The Impala was a big car in 1967. It rode a 119-inch wheelbase and was 213.2 inches long overall. The front tread was 62.5 inches, the rear was 62.4 inches. Regular equipment included 8.25 x 15 tires or 8.15 x 15 tires if the optional disk brakes were ordered. The V-8 powered hardtop listed for $3,003 and weighed 3,615 lbs. The convertible with a base V-8 had a $3,535 list price and weighed in at 3,650 lbs. Nevertheless, these cars could move from 0 to 60 mph in about 8.5 seconds and did the quarter mile in around 16.3 seconds.

While not a huge sales success, the 1967 Impala SS collected 66,510 orders for the hardtop and 9,545 for the convertible and most were SS 396s. The big Impala SS models returned to extra-cost-option status after 1967.

1967 CHEVROLET IMPALA SS 427

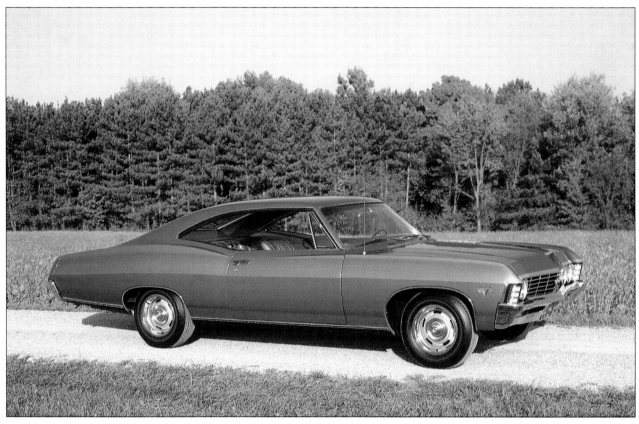

(Jerry Heasley photo)

The 1967 Chevrolet Impala SS 427 was plenty big, but it had many muscle-car options.

In 1967, with Chevelle sales soaring on the SS 396's muscle reputation, Chevrolet concluded that high performance could help to sell big cars. This led to the Impala SS 427.

To understand the SS 427's role in the product mix, it's important to remember that the Chevelle SS 396 was more than a Malibu with Super Sport trim. Malibus were not available with the big Turbo-Jet V-8, while SS 396s came only that way. That made the SS 396 exclusive. Its real job was establishing a high-performance identity that would spur sales of the less costly Chevelles it resembled.

Similarly, the Impala SS 427 was intended to be an "image" car, though one of larger proportions. While the 427-cid engine was made available in other Chevrolets, only the SS 427 came with a full assortment of muscle-car goodies. They included special badges and engine call-outs, a Corvette-inspired power dome hood, larger wheels, a stiffer suspension and standard red-stripe tires.

When first introduced, SS 427 features were optional for two body styles in the separate 1967 Impala SS series. Regular Super Sport equipment included vinyl-clad Strato bucket seats, black grille finish, wheelhouse moldings, black lower body and deck lid accents, badges and specific wheel covers. A second option, coded RPO L36, turned the SS into an SS 427. This $316 package included the SS 427 trim and a 385-hp 427 Turbo-Jet V-8.

Ordering this option required the buyer to add at least the heavier-duty M13 three-speed manual gearbox. For additional go-power, an M20 four-speed or Turbo-Hydra-Matic could be specified, as could a more powerful 425-hp engine. Out of a total run of 76,055 Impala Super Sports, only 2,124 were SS 427s.

Viewing any SS 427 as a muscle car depends on one's definition of the species. The '67 version was road tested at 8.4 seconds for 0 to 60 mph and 15.8 seconds for the quarter mile. That's just slightly slower than a 1970 SS 396 Chevelle with 350 hp, which isn't bad at all for a full-sized Chevy.

1967 CHEVROLET II NOVA SS

The Chevy II was still available with a 327-cid V-8 in 1967.

(Jerry Heasley photo)

Chevrolet made only modest changes to the Nova in the second year of its "second-generation" styling. There was a new anodized aluminum grille that had a distinct horizontal-bars motif with a Chevy II nameplate on the driver's side. The Super Sport, or SS, series continued to be available as an upper line in the Nova model range.

The Nova SS sport coupe had a suggested base price of $2,467 and weighed 2,690 lbs. Appearance items included with the SS ranged from a special black-accented grille and specific Super Sport full wheel covers to body and wheelhouse moldings. Naturally, there were SS badges in several locations. The interior featured all-vinyl trim with front Strato bucket seats, a three-spoke steering wheel and a floor shift trim plate.

This boxy, but neat-looking Chevy compact continued to make an excellent muscle car when equipped with the right extras, but as LeRoi "Tex" Smith noted in *Motor Trend* in January 1967, "The fattest parts catalog of all is authored by Chevrolet, but with it comes the sad tale of yanking power options from some of the lines, notably Corvair and Chevy II, to the extent that one wonders if Ralph Nader has been secretly elected to the board of directors."

Smith pointed out that the maximum output engine for the 1967 Nova SS was a 327-cid 275-hp V-8 that had 75 hp less than the top 1966 engine option. This four-barrel motor with 10.25:1 compression generated peak horsepower at 4800 rpm and put out 355 ft. lbs. of torque at 3200 rpm. Tex did point out, however, that the Nova SS retained all of its 1966 gearing selections and was "surprisingly alert" despite the changes Chevrolet had made.

The motivation for the power reduction was the new Camaro, which was actually based on the Chevy II/Nova. Chevrolet did not want a hot Corvette-engined Nova stealing muscle car fans away from the new pony car. In the end, the people spoke and a lot of parts managers were kept busy ordering Camaro bits for smart Nova owners. Total production of the Nova SS was 10,100 units.

1967 CHEVROLET CHEVELLE SS 396

Chevrolet's mid-size 1967 Chevelle continued on with a cigar-shaped body and forward-thrusting front fenders. The radiator grille had more prominent horizontal bars. The prices for the SS 396 coupe jumped to $2,825 and the SS 396 convertible's price increased by the same amount to $3,033. Annual production of Chevelle SS-396s fell a bit, with 63,006 being made.

Chevelle Super Sport models again had twin simulated hood air intakes, ribbed color-accented sill and rear fender lower moldings, a black-out style SS 396 grille and rear cove accents and "Super Sport" script plates on the rear fenders. Specific SS wheel covers were included, along with red-stripe tires. An all-vinyl bench seat interior was standard.

The 325-hp engine (RPO L35) was carried over as the base choice in 1967. The RPO L34 version was also offered again, but its horsepower rating dropped to 350 hp at 5200 rpm. The L78 375-hp version of the 396-cid V-8 was not listed on Chevy specifications sheets, but it was possible to purchase the components needed to "build" this option at your Chevy dealer's parts counter. The total cost of everything needed to upgrade a 350-hp engine to a 375-hp job was $475.80.

A 1967 Chevelle SS 396 with a 375-hp engine could be had new for about $3,300.

(Jerry Heasley photo)

SS-396 buyers could get the 325-hp engine with a standard heavy-duty three-speed manual transmission, a four-speed manual gearbox, Powerglide automatic (or later in the year, Turbo-Hydra-Matic). There was a choice of nine axle ratios from 3.07:1 to 4.10:1, but specific options depended upon transmission choice. The 350-hp engine came with the heavy-duty three-speed manual, wide- or close-ration four speeds or Powerglide. There were eight rear axle ratios from 3.07:1 to 4.88:1, but you could not get all of them with every engine and transmission setup.

The 1967 SS-396 sport coupe with 375 hp did 0 to 60 mph in 6.5 seconds and did the quarter mile in 14.9 seconds.

1967 CORVETTE 427

(Jerry Heasley photo)

The cool 1967 Corvette Sting Ray "427" coupe could run 13.8 seconds in the quarter mile.

After being at the center of the high-performance market when the 1960s began, full-sized muscle cars had a harder time attracting attention and buyers after mid-sized muscle cars caught on as the decade progressed. A good case in point was the Impala Super Sport.

The Super Sport or SS package started life as a midyear option for the full-sized Chevrolet in 1961. One of the model's spotlight years was 1967, when the Impala SS offered a "no-excuses-sir" big-car alternative for the muscle car buyer.

The Corvette "427," with its own funnel-shaped, power bulge on the hood, was introduced in 1966. The new engine was related to Chevrolet's 427-cid NASCAR "mystery" racing engine and the production-type Turbo-Jet 396. A 427-cid 435-hp 1967 Corvette convertible carried on 7.7 lbs. per horsepower. It could hit 60 mph in 5.5 seconds and do the quarter mile in 13.8 seconds. Three four-speed manual gearboxes—wide-ratio, close-ratio and heavy-duty close-ratio—were optional. A desirable extra was side-mounted exhaust pipes.

For 1967, the Corvette got additional engine cooling vents and cars with 427s got a different power bulge hood and more top horsepower (435) when fitted with three two-barrel carburetors. The new hood had a large, forward-facing air scoop, usually with engine call-outs on both sides.

There were four versions of the 427 in 1967. The regular L36 was about the same. Next came the L68, with 400 hp and then the Tri-Power L71 with 435 hp. Extremely rare (only 20 were built)—and off in a class by itself—was the aluminum-headed L88. This powerhouse was officially rated at only 430 hp, but in fact developed nearly 600 hp!

(Jerry Heasley photo)

The '67 Corvette "427" featured a telltale hood scoop.

1968 CHEVROLET CAMARO SS 396

(Jerry Heasley photo)

The 1968 Camaro Super Sport, which came in both coupe and convertible varieties, featured four different engine options.

Only minor changes were made in 1968 Camaros. The front end received subtle changes and ventless side windows were introduced. A new Astro-Ventilation system was relied on to bring fresh air into the cockpit. Rectangular parking lamps replaced the square ones of 1967 and side marker lamps, required by new federal laws, were added. The grille insert was finished in silver instead of black. Front and rear spoilers were now optional.

Chevrolet expanded the number of Camaro SS options to five. The SS 350 had the same hood as in 1967, but the SS 396s had a unique hood with four non-functional intake ports on either side. The SS-396 represented the ultimate Camaro production car for muscle car lovers and it came in four versions. The L35, which produced 325 hp at 4800 rpm and 410 ft. lbs. of torque at 3200 rpm, was the most popular with 6,752 installations. Second in popularity was the L78 edition, which 4,889 buyers ordered. It produced 375 hp at 5600 rpm and 415 ft. lbs. at 3600 rpm. The L34 version, which generated 350 hp at 5200 rpm and 415 ft. lbs. of torque at 3600 rpm

went into 2,018 cars. Rarest was the L89 version with aluminum heads. It was conservatively rated for 375 hp at 5600 rpm and 415 ft. lbs. at 3600 rpm, but due to its high $896 price tag drew only 311 orders.

In 1968, the L35 option cost $63.20 over the base 350-cid Camaro SS engine. The L34 was $184.35 extra and the L78 was $316 extra. Other desirable SS options included the M20 and M21 four-speed manual gearboxes, both for $195.40; the M22 heavy-duty four-speed manual gearbox for $322.10; M40 Turbo-Hydra-Matic transmission for $221.80; a ZL2 cowl-induction hood for $79; a JL8 four-wheel disc brakes package for $500.30; a U16 tachometer for $52.70; U17 special instrumentation for $94.80 and G80 Positraction for $42.15.

Car Life magazine road tested a 375-hp SS 396 with cold-air induction and other muscle car hardware. It did 0 to 60 mph in 6.8 seconds and the quarter mile in 14.77 seconds at 98.72 mph. Its top speed was 126 mph.

1968 CAMARO Z/28

Even though only 602 copies were made, the Chevrolet Camaro Z/28 made a strong impact on muscle car fans in 1967, especially considering that it was made primarily for road racing and had only half of a selling season in the marketplace. While it did not catch the Ford Mustang in sales, the Camaro was not that far behind the original, four-year-old pony car in racing results and that's something that rapidly enhanced the Z/28's appeal to enthusiasts.

In the hard-fought Trans-Am racing series, Roger Penske's Camaros had taken the checkered flag at Marlboro, Las Vegas and

Kent, Washington, earning driver Mark Donohue some much-deserved recognition. The Camaro Z/28's image was mostly associated with this form of competition and the Z/28 was specifically designed to fit the Sports Car Club of America's small-cubic-inches formula.

As in its first year, the 1968 Z/28 came only as a sport coupe. You could not order it with air conditioning or with an automatic transmission. In fact, you had to order a four-speed manual transmission, as well as optional power-assisted front disc brakes.

The 1968 Camaro Z/28 came only as a hardtop coupe.

(Jerry Heasley photo)

Below its hood, the Z/28 featured the same hot 302-cid Chevy small-block V-8 that had been used in 1967. This engine had an easy-to-remember 4.0 x 3.0-inch bore and stroke. It carried a single 800-cfm Holley four-barrel carburetor on top of a special intake manifold and had 11.0:1 compression pistons. Maxium horsepower was 290 at 5800 rpm and it generated 290 ft. lbs. of torque at 4200 rpm.

In addition to the standard Muncie four-speed, a Muncie close-ratio four-speed gearbox was the only option. A 3.73:1 rear axle was standard and six other ratios were optional: 3.07:1, 3.31:1, 3.55:1, 4.10:1, 4.56:1 and 4.88:1.

Z/28 sales started to take off this year, and Chevrolet put together 7,199 examples of its Camaro road racer.

1968 CHEVROLET IMPALA SS 427

(Jerry Heasley photo)

Only 1,778 1968 Impala sport coupes had the SS 427 package.

When it returned in 1968, the SS 427 reflected both styling and marketing changes. Chevrolet adopted a new technique of sculpting bodies by stretching cloth over a wire frame and blowing it out to create "fluid" shapes. The result was a smoother, softer appearance. Chevrolet also dropped the Impala SS series, replacing it with a new Z03 Super Sport option. Priced at $179.05, it included the same extras that cars in the 1967 Impala SS series had. Another marketing change involved making the performance option available for three Impala models instead of just two. You could order it for the $2,968 sport coupe, the $3,021 custom coupe or the $3,197 convertible.

Making the SS an option made the SS 427 package an option for an option. Coded RPO Z24, it had all of the basic SS features, plus a special hood, red-stripe tires, 15-inch wheels and the RPO L36 427-cid Turbo-Jet engine for $358.10. This "standard" version of the 427 had a 10.25:1 compression ratio. It developed 385 hp at 5200 rpm and 460 ft. lbs. of torque at 3400 rpm.

Chevrolet buyers could also spend $542.45 to get a second SS-427 package featuring the L72 version of the engine with 11.0:1 compression. It was good for 425 hp at 5600 rpm and the same 460 ft. lbs. of torque at a higher 4000 rpm.

Unfortunately, the 1968 Impala SS 427 proved ineffective in boosting big-car sales to enthusiasts. Total production of Impalas with Super Sport equipment took a big drop to 38,210 units. A mere 1,778 had the SS 427 option. Experts say the 1968s are the more desirable to collectors, but they also represent the easiest SS-427 model to fake.

In September 1968, *Hot Rod* magazine published an article entitled "600-Plus Horsepower from Chevy's 427" that covered some 427-cid racing modifications that could produce 600 hp. It also talked about the availability of a "triple two-barrel" option. According to editor Eric Rickman, this setup used primary No. 3925517 and secondary No. 3902353 in conjunction with the 1967 intake manifold No. 3904574. While perhaps not strictly stock, a 600-hp SS-427 would be a helluva muscle car.

1968 CHEVROLET NOVA SS 396

Restyled to resemble a small Chevelle, the second-generation Nova rode on a 111-inch wheelbase and stretched 183.3 inches bumper to bumper. It was 72.4 inches wide, 52.6 inches high and weighed 2,850 lbs.

The new Nova appeared to be anything but a real muscle car when it bowed in the fall of 1967. Only two models were offered and SS equipment was now an option. However, the car's new stub frame came from the Camaro and, by January 1968, this brought some exciting big-block engine options.

The milder 327-cid V-8 with 275 hp was carried over from the last two years, along with two additional and hotter small-block options. These were the new 350-cid 295-hp V-8 with a 10.25:1 compression ratio and a 325-hp version of the 327 with 11.0:1 compression. However, the really big news was the 396-cid V-8 that was now being offered for serious muscle-car lovers.

Sharing 4.094 x 3.76-inch bore and stroke dimensions and single four-barrel carburetion, the 396-cid big-blocks came two ways. The first version had a 10.25:1 compression ratio and generated 350 hp at 5200 rpm and 415 ft. lbs. of torque at 3200 rpm. The second version had an 11:1 compression ratio and delivered 375 hp at 5600 rpm and 415 ft. lbs. of torque at 3600 rpm. Chevrolet didn't advertise this engine, which provided 6-second 0-60 mph performance and was good for 14-second quarter-mile runs.

The Nova's standard transmission was a column mounted three-speed. Options included a three-speed with floor shifter, a four-speed stick (commonly ordered by muscle car fans) and Powerglide automatic.

The Nova SS had a base price of about $2,995. Chevrolet built a total of just 5,571 cars carrying the Nova SS package this year. Of those, only 234 had the milder 396-cid engine and 667 had the 396-cid 375-hp option

1968 CHEVELLE SS 396

The '68 Chevelle had a wide range of axle and transmission options and V-8 engines that put out between 325 and 375 hp.

A new body with a "wrap-over" front end characterized 1968 Chevelles. It had the long nose, short rear deck styling that was popular in this era. Starting in 1968, GM mid-size cars came with two wheelbases, 112 inches for two-door models and 116 inches for four-door models. The SS 396 was a separate series in 1968. It included a sport coupe base-priced at $2,899 and a convertible priced at $3,102. Both had the short wheelbase.

Overall length, at 197.1 inches, was just a tad longer than in 1967, even though the wheelbase was cut by 3 inches. Front and rear tread width was also up an inch to 59 inches, and it was nearly an inch taller at 52.7 inches.

The SS 396 models were made even more distinctive by the use of matte black finish around the full lower perimeter of the bodies, except when the cars were finished in a dark color. Other SS features included F70 x 14 wide-oval red-stripe tires, body accent stripes, a special twin-domed hood with simulated air intakes, "SS" badges, vinyl upholstery and a heavy-duty three-speed transmission with floor shifter.

The standard engine was the RPO L35 version of the 396-cid V-8, which had an advertised 325 hp. The RPO L34 version with 350 hp was $105 extra and was the only option early in the year. That situation didn't last long, as competitors like the 375-hp Dodge Charger R/T and 350-hp Olds 4-4-2 were stealing sales away from Chevrolet based on horsepower alone. At midyear, Chevy re-released the RPO L78 version of the 396 with 375 hp. This option

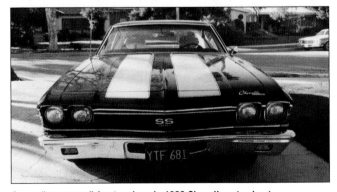

A new "wrap-over" front end made 1968 Chevelles stand out.

cost $237 more than a base V-8. A '68 SS 396 with this engine and the close-ratio four-speed manual gearbox was road tested from 0 to 60 mph in 6.6 seconds and did the quarter mile in 14.8 seconds at 98.8 mph.

As in the past, Chevrolet continued to offer the SS 396 with a wide range of transmission and rear axle options. Also standard were finned front brake drums and new bonded brake linings all around. About 57,600 Chevelle SS 396s were made and this total included 4,751 with the L78 engine and 4,082 with the L34 option.

1968 CHEVY II SS 427

Not a factory item, the 427-powered 1968 Chevy II was still an awesome combination.

(Jerry Heasley photo)

Chevrolet's senior-sized compact underwent a basic styling change in 1968. The new body was longer and wider and featured a Chevelle-inspired semi-fastback roofline with wide, flaring sail panels. However, the new Chevy II was actually more of a five-passenger version of the Camaro and both cars shared the same platform floor, forward subframe, front suspension and staggered-shocks rear suspension. This meant that all engines that fit in a Camaro could also be stuffed into a Chevy II.

Based on a 1-inch longer 111-inch wheelbase, the new Chevy II was 187.7 inches long and 54.1 inches wide. When the car first arrived, it continued to use an in-line six as its basic (and most-ordered) engine. But V-8s up to a 350-cid, 295-hp version were available. A midyear, the 327-cid 325-hp V-8 was added. Cars with this engine were capable of doing the quarter mile in under 16 seconds at around 90 mph. Since this didn't quite cut the mustard during the muscle-car era, it wasn't long before the 396-cid Turbo-Jet

V-8 with a choice of 350- or 375-hp was also offered.

It didn't take long for drag racers like Dickie Harrell and high-performance dealers (like Don Yenko Chevrolet and Nickey Chevrolet) to realize that the Chevy II's Camaro-type engine bay could also accommodate a 427-cid Chevrolet big-block V-8 and a small number of such cars were constructed, mainly with drag racing in mind.

Since 427-powered Camaros were not a factory-issued item, it's hard to pin down concrete information about cost, performance or rarity. When installed in Camaros, the 427 was made available in 410- and 450-hp versions and it's likely the output was roughly the same in the Chevy II. Such a Camaro sold for just under $4,000 in 1968, so a 427-powered Chevy II would have cost a bit less. Performance of both cars was probably in the same general bracket, which was around 13 seconds for the quarter mile at a bit over 100 mph.

1968 CHEVROLET CORVETTE 427

(John Kefalonitis photo)

The restyled 1968 Corvette "427" had a more aerodynamic front end than previous models.

Corvette's first major restyling since 1963 occurred in 1968. As the sales brochure read, "Corvette '68 . . . all different all over." The fastback was replaced by a tunneled-roof coupe. It featured a removable back window and a two-piece detachable roof section or T-top. The convertible's optional hardtop had a glass rear window.

The front end was more aerodynamic than those on previous Corvettes. As before, the headlights were hidden. Now they were vacuum-operated, rather than electrical. The wipers also disappeared when not in use. Except for the rocker panels, the sides were devoid of chrome. Conventional door handles were eliminated and in their place were push buttons. The blunt rear deck contained four round taillights with the word Corvette printed in chrome in the space between them. The wraparound, wing-like rear bumper and license-

plate holder treatment resembled that used on the 1967 models.

Buyers had a choice of 10 exterior colors: tuxedo black, polar white, Corvette bronze, LeMans blue, international blue, Cordovan maroon, rally red, silverstone silver, British green and safari yellow. All convertibles came with a choice of black, white or beige soft tops. Interior colors were: black, red, medium blue, dark blue, dark orange, tobacco and gunmetal.

Chevrolet's big-block 427-cid V-8 with a 4.251 x 3.76-inch bore and stroke was available in the Corvette in four different muscular versions. The least powerful was RPO L36. It had hydraulic valve lifters, a 10:25:1 compression ratio and a single Holley four-barrel carburetor. Its output was 390 hp at 5400 rpm and 460 ft. lbs. of torque at 3600 rpm.

The second-most powerful 427 was the L68 version which featured a 10.25:1 compression ratio and three Holley two-barrel carburetors. It produced 400 hp at 5400 rpm and 460 ft. lbs. of torque at 4000 rpm. *Car and Driver* tested one of these cars with a four-speed manual gearbox and 3.70:1 rear axle in its May 1968 issue. It did 0 to 60 mph in 5.7 seconds and the standing-start quarter mile in 14.1 seconds at 102 mph. Its top speed was estimated to be 119 mph.

Next came RPO L71, which was a step up the performance ladder with its special-performance, solid-lifter camshaft, three Holley two-barrels and an 11.0:1 compression ratio. It was good for 435 hp at 5800 rpm and 460 ft. lbs. of torque at 4000 rpm. The L71-powered Corvette could go from 0 to 30 mph in 3.0 seconds; from 0 to 50 in 5.3 seconds and from 0 to 60 in 6.5 seconds. An L71 with a four-speed manual transmission and 3.55:1 rear axle was tested by *Car Life* in June 1968. It did the quarter mile in 13.41 seconds at 109.5 mph. Its top speed was 142 mph.

The ultimate option was the super-powerful RPO L88 aluminum-head V-8, a $947 option intended primarily for racing. The L88 had mechanical valve lifters, a special ultra-high-performance camshaft with .5365-inch intake and a single Holley 850CFM four-barrel. With a 12.50:1 compression ratio it produced an advertised 430 hp at 5200 rpm. However, some said its actual output was 560 hp at 6400 rpm. Advertised torque was 450 ft. lbs. at 4400 rpm.

The L88 package also included a "power blister" hood. In addition, four heavy-duty options were required: RPO J56 heavy-duty brakes at $384.45; RPO F41 heavy-duty suspension at $36.90; RPO K66 transistor ignition at $73.75 and RPO G81 Positraction at $46.35. With a special high-performance Turbo Hydra-Matic transmission ($290.40 extra) the L88 convertible sold for $6,562. With a 3.36:1 rear axle it did the quarter mile in 13.56 seconds at 111.10 mph. "The tall gear in back made 13.56 seconds at 111 mph seem respectable," said *Hot Rod* in 1969. "But we know it's about two seconds from where it should be."

1968 CHEVROLET YENKO SUPER CAMARO 427

A 1968 Chevrolet SYC 427 Camaro did nearly 115 mph in the quarter mile.

(Jerry Heasley photo)

One of the first Chevrolet dealers to turn Camaros into hot rods was Don Yenko, of Canonsburg, Pennsylvania. During the early 1960s, Yenko had turned out race-modified Corvettes and Corvairs. Starting in 1967, his Yenko Sportscars facility began dropping L72 427-cid "rat" motors into the all-new bow-tie brand pony car —the Camaro.

Yenko offered his 427-powered Camaros with two choices of horsepower ratings, 435 or 450. After having the mechanics at his dealership put together a few cars, he then helped to establish a distributorship called Span, Inc., which was based in Chicago, Illinois. This company was created to market the muscular Camaros nationally.

The 1967 original Yenko Super Camaro was actually the brainchild of drag racer Dickie Harrell, who had previously worked for another Chevy dealer who specialized in performance modifications —Nickey Chevrolet of Chicago. It is likely that many of the cars were actually modified in Chicago. When they were shipped to his

dealership, Yenko added decals, badges and other special features. To help sell the cars, Yenko even sent sales literature out to other performance-minded dealers like Fred Gibbs Chevrolet.

The 1968 Yenko Camaro COPO 9561 was a stripper version of the Chevy pony that Yenko built with a 427-cid V-8, with additional features added to satisfy each individual customer. The rarest Yenko Camaro is a 1968 model built under COPO 8008.

In 1968, Don Yenko and his father visited Chevrolet to talk about getting cars with factory-installed 427s, since his mechanics couldn't keep up with orders for conversions. It was decided to use the COPO ordering system to provide 100 such 1969 Camaros to Yenko Sportscars. Later, about 100 additional units were built for Yenko. These cars had factory-installed 140-mph speedometers and Z/28 suspensions. They could be ordered with a close-ratio four-speed manual transmission or an M40 four-speed automatic transmission.

1969 CHEVROLET CAMARO COPO/427

Costing around $4,000 new, some COPO Camaros are worth six-figure prices today.

(Jerry Heasley photo)

During 1967 and 1968, Chevrolet dealers such as Fred Gibb of LeHarpe, Illinois, Don Yenko of Canonsburg, Pennsylvania, and Nickey Chevrolet of Chicago were putting 427-cid "big-block" V-8s into Camaros for drag-racing enthusiasts. Late in June of 1968, Yenko sat down with Chevrolet executives to ask them about the possibility of building a factory-version 427-powered Camaro. Some dealers wanted this because the Camaro was really catching on with drag buffs and the dealers could no longer handle the heavier demand for doing engine swaps.

Chevrolet came up with the idea of dealers employing the seldom-used Central Office Production Order system to provide such cars through factory channels. These vehicles began life as L78 Camaros with a 396-cid 325-hp engine. They then had about 14 modifications done to them in terms of hardware, trim and badges. Yenko Chevrolet ordered the first 100 COPO cars and later took about 100 more. It is believed that about 1,015 cars were built in all—822 with four-speed manual transmissions and 193 with automatics.

The COPO cars were made at the Norwood, Ohio, and Van Nuys, California, assembly plants. Prices ranged from about $3,500 at the low end to $4,500, depending on what regular Camaro options were also ordered.

Although Yenko inspired the production of COPO units, they were technically available through any Chevrolet dealer. Berger Chevrolet, of Grand Rapids, Michigan, also ordered 40 to 50 COPO Camaros for its high-performance department. A few more COPO cars were sold by Fred Gibb, the dealer best known for playing a role in developing the ZL-1 Camaro. Dana Chevrolet, of South Gate, California, was another dealership that handled COPO cars.

Nickey Chevrolet continued to do many of its own 427 transplants in 1969. It was advertised nationally in *Hot Rod* magazine. Motion Performance, of Baldwin (Long Island), New York also did its own 427 conversions. In 1969, the company offered the 427-cid 450-hp SS 427 "Baldwin-Motion" Camaro for $3,895 and the 427-cid 500-hp Phase III SS 427 Camaro for $4,999.

1969 CHEVROLET CAMARO RS/SS 396 INDY 500 PACE CAR

The 1969 Camaro Indy Pace Cars had RS/SS 396 options.

(Jerry Heasley photo)

Although not the hottest muscle Camaro of 1969, (some 427-powered COPO cars were also factory built) the 396-powered Indy Pace Car is one of the most collected.

After making a hit at the "Brickyard" in 1967, Chevy was invited to bring the Camaro back for a repeat performance. This time the company took better advantage of sales promotional opportunities by releasing a pace car replica option package.

The genuine Indianapolis 500 Pace Cars were 375-hp SS 396 convertibles with "hugger" orange racing stripes, rear spoilers and black and orange hound's-tooth upholstery. About 100 were built to pace the race and transport dignitaries and members of the press around Indianapolis.

Chevrolet then released the Indy Pace Car replica option (RPO Z11) and sold 3,674 copycat cars to the general public. The Z11 was

actually just a $37 striping package for convertibles only. But other extras, such as the $296 Super Sport option and the special interior, were also required. Buyers could order the pace car treatment on either RS/SS 350 or RS/SS 396 ragtops. The 350-powered versions are much more common, but only had 300 hp.

To qualify as a collectible muscle car, a pace car replica has to have the big-block, which came in four variations. These were the L35 ($63) with 325 hp, the L34 ($184) with 350 hp, the L78 ($316) with 375 hp and the L89 ($711) with aluminum heads and 375 hp. It isn't hard to guess which is rarest and most valuable.

The 375 hp ragtops were good for 7-second 0-to-60 acceleration and could do the quarter mile in just about 15 seconds, so they have some real muscle to go with their good looks.

1969 CHEVROLET CAMARO Z/28

With blueprinting the 1969 Camaro Z/28 could make 450 hp.

(Jerry Heasley photo)

Chevrolet Motor Division built 602 Camaros with the Z/28 package in the first year of the option—1967. The Z/28 package was popular from the start and sales leaped to 7,199 cars in 1968. But even divisional brass weren't ready for 1969's larger increase to 20,302 assemblies of Camaros with the Z/28 Special Performance Package.

The restyled 1969 Camaro body featured more defined sculpturing and a squarish, race-car-like look. It was the perfect repository for the Z/28's redesigned high-output, small-block V-8. This 302-cid engine was created with Trans-Am racing in mind. It featured a 4.002 x 3.005-inch bore and stroke, big-valve heads, forged steel crank, new four-bolt-mains block with larger webbing, nodular iron main bearing caps, new pistons, 30/30 solid-lifter camshaft, 11.0:1 compression ratio and numerous other performance goodies.

The Z/28 package was offered only for the Camaro coupe. Some sources say that it came in a basic version priced at $458 and a version with dealer-installed headers for $758. However, there were actually at least six variations. The basic package released September 26, 1967, included the 302 V-8, dual exhausts with deep-tone mufflers, special front and rear suspensions, rear bumper guards, a heavy-duty radiator with a temperature controlled fan, quick-ratio power steering, 15 x 7 rally wheels, E70 x 15 special white-lettered tires, a 3.73:1 rear axle and special hood and trunk stripes. Chevrolet mandated a four-speed manual transmission and power disc brakes and recommended a Positraction rear axle.

On October 18, bright engine accents and Z/28 emblems for the grille, front fender and rear panel were added and rally wheels were no longer specified, but wheel trim rings were added. The price remained at $458. On January 2, 1969, a tachometer or special instrumentation was made mandatory and the price rose to $474. On April 1, the specs were changed to read "dual exhausts" only, wheel center caps were specified along with a front valance panel and rear deck-lid spoiler. The price increased to $507.

The 1969 model had an extended model-year run and on September 18, 1969, the package was revised again, with the price going to $522. New ingredients included bright exhaust tips. The final documented changes came on November 3, 1969, and were very minor.

There are many variations between Z/28s, as well as between original cars and the written factory specifications. For example, very-early-in-the-run cars were manufactured with the 1968-style stripes and 15 x 6-inch rally wheels. Buyers ordering a spoiler on the early cars got the 1967-1968 style. And these cars were the only ones to carry the chambered dual exhaust system.

A typical, well-equipped Z/28 set up for racing could be purchased for under $4,000. *Hot Rod Magazine* drove a stock Z/28 through the quarter mile in 14.34 seconds at 101.35 mph. The editors then bolted on some aftermarket hardware and did it in 13.11 seconds at 106.76 mph.

1969 CHEVROLET CAMARO ZL1

(Jerry Heasley photo)

Chevrolet dealer Fred Gibb came up with the idea that led to development of the ZL1. The ZL1 Camaro has been called the "ultimate muscle car."

In 1968, Chevrolet dealer Fred Gibb was well-known to drag racing enthusiasts for his support of their hobby. Gibb talked to Chevrolet high-performance legend Vince Piggins about constructing the ultimate muscle car using and all-aluminum 427-cid V-8 in a Camaro to create a Super Stock racing car. National Hot Rod

Association (NHRA) rules said that a minimum of 50 cars had to be built to qualify the super-hot Camaro for competition. Chevrolet general manager Pete Estes gave Fred Gibbs his word that Chevrolet would build the first ZL1s before the end of the year, if the dealer would take 50 of them at a proposed price of $4,900.

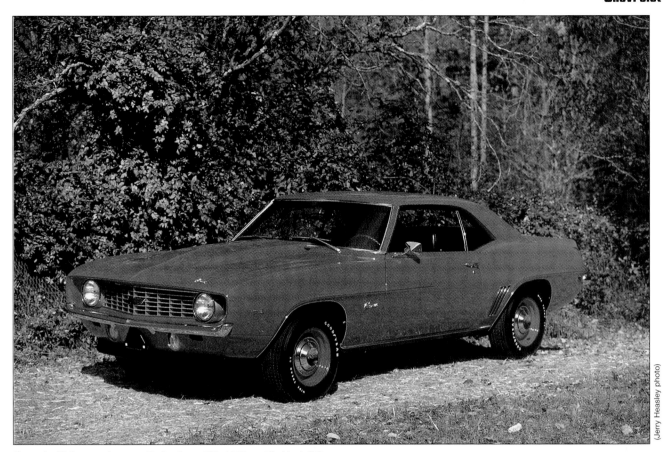

(Jerry Heasley photo)

Power for ZL1s came from an all-aluminum 427-cid Chevy big-block V-8.

Gibbs accepted and the Central Office Production Order system was utilized to order the cars. The first ZL1s built were a pair of dusk blue cars made at the Norwood, Ohio, assembly plant on December 30, 1968. They arrived at the LeHarpe, Illinois, dealership the next day, covered with snow. Unfortunately, the factory invoice price had climbed to $7,269!

All 50 cars shipped to Gibbs were virtually identical, except for the choice of color and transmission. They had the COPO #9560 option with the aluminum 427. Nineteen additional cars were also built for other dealers. Equipment on all 69 cars included the Z22 Rally Sport package; J50 power brakes; N40 power steering; V10 tachometer; racing style rearview mirrors; exhaust resonators; dual exhausts with tailpipe extensions; a special steering wheel; F70-15 black sidewall tires with raised gold letters; special lug nuts; special wheel center caps; special identification decals on the hood, grille and rear panel; a special instrument cluster and an extra-wide front valance panel.

According to the February 1969 issue of *Super Stock* magazine, the ZL-1 Camaro in racing trim could cover the quarter mile in as little as 10.41 seconds at 128.10 mph with a stock Holley 850-cfm carburetor. Dickie Harrell, who raced for the Fred Gibbs dealership, traveled around the country campaigning a ZL1. He took four wins and registered a best performance of 10.05 seconds at 139 mph.

1969 CHEVROLET SUPER YENKO CAMARO 427

In 1968, Don Yenko Chevrolet of Canonsburg, Pa., decided to expand his high-performance car operation by making SYC (Super Yenko Camaro) models available to enthusiasts through a small number of selected factory dealers.

The plan was to base these cars on 1969 Camaros ordered from Chevrolet via a COPO (Central Office Production Order) arrangement. This type of purchase allowed dealers to order special equipment on a Chevrolet as long as building the car did not upset the normal stream of output at the factory. Yenko's cars were produced under order number 9561 and were fitted with 427-cid, 425-hp L72 V-8 engines; M21 or M22 four-speed gear boxes (or an M40 Turbo Hydra-Matic); front disc brakes; a special Zl2 ducted hood; a heavy-duty radiator; a special suspension; a 4.10:1 positraction rear axle and a rear spoiler.

Originally, Yenko had planned to take all of the COPO 9561 cars, but other dealers wanted a piece of the same action and also placed orders. As a result, about 100 cars were sold. However, Yenko also ordered a batch of COPOI 9737 Camaros, which had 15-inch wheels, Goodyear Wide Tread GT tires, a 140-mph speedometer and a beefy one-inch front stabilizer bar. So, in the end, between 100 and 201 Yenko SYC Camaros were made, depending upon which source you refer to.

A 1969 Chevrolet Super Yenko Camaro 427 did nearly 115 mph in the quarter mile.

Yenko's SYC Camaros came only in seven colors: hugger orange; LeMans blue; fathom green; Daytona yellow; rally green and Olympic gold. The cars had a base price of $3,895, including shipping. Available options included front and rear bumper guards ($25); front and rear floor mats ($12); an AM-FM push-button radio ($134); heavy-duty Air Lift shocks ($45); traction bars ($50) and chromes exhaust extensions ($38).

On April 19, 1969 a Yenko Camaro with factory-installed headers and racing slicks, driven by a man named Ed Hedrick, did the quarter mile at a drag strip in York, Pennsylvania, in 11.94 seconds at 114.5 mph.

1969 CHEVROLET BALDWIN-MOTION CORVETTE

There's been a re-emergence of special muscle cars that have been termed "Street Rats." Some of these are Chevrolet products with Motion Performance Co. equipment packages. This specialty speed shop, from Baldwin (Long Island), New York, did post assembly-line customizing and re-engineering.

There are few "Baldwin-Motion" modified cars in existence. The most desirable to muscle car collectors are Baldwin-Motion Corvettes. These cars hold a magnetic force over Corvette enthusiasts. They embody nostalgia, speed and individuality. They also make a good investment, since they can't be duplicated. The 1969 Sting Ray with the Baldwin-Motion treatment included high-performance engine and chassis features, plus body modifications.

Each Baldwin-Motion Corvette was different. Many utilized 427-cid Chevy big-block V-8s with three two-barrel carburetors. When equipped with a four-speed manual transmission and fueled with high-octane racing gas, they could really fly down a drag strip.

Factory colors, such as LeMans Blue, were often retained. Wide racing stripes were added for distinction. An SS-427 emblem decorated the Baldwin-Motion designed hood scoop. Options included headers, side pipes, special racing mirrors, a competition gas cap and styled rims, such as the S-200 prototype wheels used on some cars.

Other Baldwin-Motion cars included Novas, Camaros, Chevelles and Monte Carlos. A key characteristic of these packages was suitability for street racing. They were also built with serious quarter-mile running in mind and had enough power to make any challenger take notice. The thrill that came with controlling more power than any other local driver came with such vehicles.

To own the fastest car in town was the aim of Motion Performance customers and the cars delivered great potential towards such a goal. They earned an unequalled reputation for cars and drivers alike.

Baldwin-Motion cars first became famous on the East Coast. Changes were made in accordance with an individual owner's desires and price range. There were no standard catalog specs and no dealer invoices, only plenty of action and attention.

1969 CHEVROLET CORVETTE ZL1

Perhaps the wildest, most exotic, highest-performance muscle engine ever offered to the public was the ZL1. It was an all-aluminum, 427-cid, Chevy "Rat" engine. Just 69 engines were installed in 1969 Camaros and two in 1969 Corvettes. That was it!

Use in Camaros was explained by the need to homologate the engine for National Hot Rod Association competition. A minimum of 50 had to be built for it to be considered stock and eligible for class drag racing. But, in the Corvette, the ZL1 wasn't homologated.

It was more a case of optioning the ultimate high-performance Chevrolet with the ultimate high-performance big-block.

You might say it was a matter of pride. In any event, there were 10 to 12 engineering test Corvette "mules" built with the ZL1. They were used in magazine road tests, engineering and track evaluations and driven by the likes of Zora Arkus-Duntov and GM VIPs. Of course, these ZL1 evaluation vehicles had to be destroyed—eventually.

In the process, two Vettes went out the door as RPO ZL1s. They included a Canary Yellow car with side pipes and a Can-Am white T-top coupe with black ZLl side stripes.

In 1989, the yellow car, also a T-top, was confiscated by the U.S. government. It had been in the possession of a convicted cocaine dealer now serving a life sentence (with no parole) in an Alabama prison. The owner paid $225,000 for the excellent ZL1 (55,317 original miles) some years ago. The government estimated its value at around $500,000 but sold it for the minimum reserve bid of $300,000.

Greg Joseph, a Ph.D of history at Long Beach College, in California, researched ZL1 history. This led him to *Hot Rod* magazine (December 1968), with a cover story on Chevy's new all-aluminum 427. The article told of a "painted-block ZL1" engine in a test Corvette driven by the automotive press. A parenthetical statement added: "And all those guys at the '69 Chevy preview thought it was an L88. Forgot your pocket magnets, right, guys?"

Chevrolet had painted the ZL1s, possibly to hide them from the press, as had been the case with one of the test cars spotlighted in *Hot Rod.*

To the journalists, the ZL1 (a $3,010 assortment of aluminum cylinder block and heads) was a $1,032.15 RPO L88 package. The L88 engine itself was a race option, but in ZL1 metal, it featured thicker walls and main webbing, along with dry-sump lubrication provisions.

The bottom end had four-bolt main bearings, with a forged steel crank and rods with 7/16-inch bolts, spiralock washers and full floating pins. Pistons were even higher domed than the L88's, yielding a titanic compression ratio of 12.5:1. The cylinder heads were also aluminum and featured open combustion chambers, round exhaust ports and 2.19-inch/1.88-inch valves (a configuration adopted by the L88 in mid-1969). The aluminum dual-plane intake was topped by an 850-cfm Holley "double-pumper" four-barrel carburetor featuring mechanical secondaries. The ZL1's solid-lifter camshaft was radical, so the engine could live in the upper revs.

It's hard to believe there was a step above the L88 in the muscle-car era, but the ZL1 filled the bill. It still ranks, today, as the wildest RPO engine option ever offered to the public.

1969 CHEVROLET IMPALA SS 427

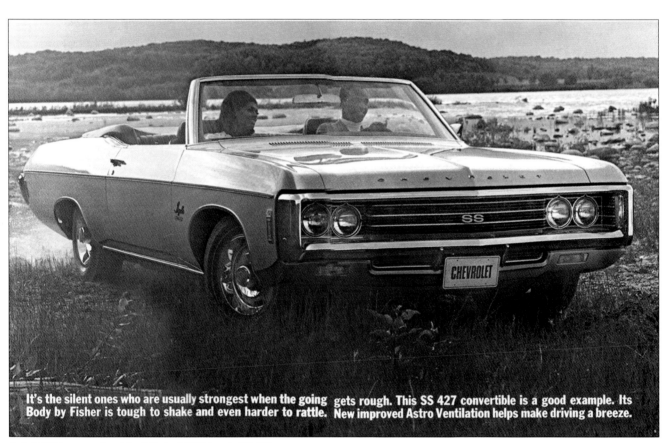

It's the silent ones who are usually strongest when the going gets rough. This SS 427 convertible is a good example. Its Body by Fisher is tough to shake and even harder to rattle. New improved Astro Ventilation helps make driving a breeze.

Only 2,455 buyers ordered the full-sized 1967 Impala SS 427.

The Impala SS 427 was merchandised differently in each of three years it was offered: 1967, 1968 and 1969. The high-performance package became a little more distinctive as it aged. In fact, the final version—offered in 1969—was the purest expression of the super-sized Supercar's reason for existing.

When Chevrolet Motor Division introduced its 1969 model, the regular Impala Super Sport was gone. There was neither an SS series, nor a straight SS option. The only way that a buyer could get his or her hands on a Super Sport was to order the SS 427 package.

In other words, if you wanted to get a full-sized Chevy with a muscle car image, you had to go all the way!

The Z24 code was again used to identify the option. It could be ordered for three Impalas: The $3,085 custom coupe, the $3,033 sport coupe (with V-8) or the $3,261 convertible. The SS option package retailed for $422.35. The SS package included power disc brakes, a special three-speed transmission, special ornamentation, chassis and suspension upgrades, 15-inch wheels, red-stripe tires and the 427-cid V-8.

This year the regular 427 with a single four-barrel carburetor and 10.25:1 compression ratio had a little more muscle. It carried ratings of 390 hp at 5400 rpm and 460 foot-pounds of torque at 3600 rpm. It had a Rochester four-barrel carburetor. There was also a special COPO (Central Office Production Option) version that featured an 11.0:1 compression ratio and an 800-cfm Holley carburetor. It put out 425 hp at 5600 rpm and 460 ft. lbs. of torque at 4000 rpm. The

'69 SS-427 was the most similar to the SS-396 Chevelle, since it was all-inclusive. If you wanted SS badges, you had to order an SS-427. Only 2,455 buyers did.

The '67 version was road tested at 8.4 seconds for 0-60 mph and 15.8 seconds for the quarter mile. That's just slightly slower than a 1970 SS-396 with 350 hp, but not bad at all for a full-sized Chevy.

1969 CHEVROLET NOVA SS 396

The Nova nameplate replaced the Chevy II in 1969, and became a popular muscle car with up to 396-hp straight from the factory.

The Chevy II name was officially replaced by the Nova name for the 1969 model year. Due to this change, a Chevrolet emblem was placed at the center of the upper grille bar in place of the previous Chevy II grille badge. Vertical louvers were featured on the sides of the cowl, behind the front wheel openings. The front side marker lights were enlarged and moved closer to the body corners.

Nova Super Sport models still had "SS" emblems decorating the front and rear of the body, but the "Super Sport" lettering that had previously appeared on the front fenders where the new cowl louvers were added had to be relocated elsewhere.

In 1969, the 327-cid small-block V-8 engines disappeared from the Nova's options list, but three hot options remained. They started with the 350-cid small-block V-8, which came from the Camaro SS and had five more horses (300 at 4800 rpm) than in 1968. It produced 380 ft. lbs. of torque at 3200 rpm. The 396-cid big-block V-8 was available once more and came in the same power options

offered in 1968, which were 350 hp at 5200 rpm and 375 hp at 5600 rpm.

The standard transmission for 1969 Novas was a special three-speed manual gearbox with a floor shifter. A four-speed Muncie gearbox with a floor shift was optional and was available with a center console. Buyers could also get a two-speed Powerglide or a three-speed Turbo Hydra-Matic transmission with column- or console-mounted shifters. Standard rear axle ratios were 3.31:1 with manual transmissions or 3.08 with automatic. Options included 3.55:1 and 3.07:1 with manual transmission and 2.73:1 or 3.36:1 with automatic transmissions.

This season Chevy cranked out 17,654 Nova SS models, compared to only 5,571 the year before. Of those, 5,262, or 30 percent, had the 396-cid 375-hp V-8 and 1,947, or 11 percent, had the 350-hp version.

1969 CHEVELLE SS 396/SS 427

Chevy stuck with what worked in the 1969 Chevelle SS 396.

Except for the manner in which the SS 396 was merchandised, Chevrolet made no basic change in the design or configuration of its mid-size muscle car in 1969. There was no separate SS 396 series this year. The Super Sport equipment package became the Z25 option, which was ordered for 86,307 cars.

The popular option package included the 396-cid 325-hp engine, dual exhausts with oval tailpipes and bright tips, a black-painted grille, bright wheel opening and roof drip moldings, a black-painted cove panel, Malibu-style rear quarter end caps, taillights and taillight bezels, a twin power dome hood, special "SS 396" emblems on the grille, front fenders and rear deck lid and 14 x 7-inch Super Sport wheels with F70 x 14 white-letter tires. The interior featured a black steering wheel and column; a steering wheel shroud with a black-accented center area and horn-blowing tab, an "SS" steering wheel center emblem, an SS 396 nameplate on the instrument panel, a black-accented instrument panel and SS 396 emblems on the door

sidewalls. The price of the option was about $440.

Three optional engines were available: the L34 with 350 hp ($121), the L78 with 375 hp ($253) and the new L78/89 with 375 hp. This engine had special aluminum cylinder heads for higher performance, despite its conservative advertised horsepower rating.

An extremely rare 1969 engine was a 427-cid V-8 available on a special Central Office Production Order (COPO) basis from GM's Tonawanda, New York, factory. Only 358 of these engines were assembled and most, or all, of them went to dealer Don Yenko, who had them custom installed in cars sold at his Yenko Sports Car dealership in Canonsburg, Pennsylvania.

A road test on the 969 SS 396 with 375 hp proved it to be a tad slower than earlier editions, probably due to a slight weight increase. The car moved from 0 to 60 mph in 7.6 seconds and covered the quarter mile in 15.4 seconds.

1969 CHEVROLET CORVETTE 427

After a year's absence, the Stingray name (now spelled as one word) re-appeared on the front fenders in 1968. The back-up lights were integrated into the center taillights. The ignition was now on the steering column and the door depression button used in 1968 was eliminated and a key lock put in its place.

Front and rear disc brakes, headlight washers, a center console, wheel trim rings, carpeting and all-vinyl upholstery were now standard Corvette equipment. Buyers had their choice of 10 exterior col-

ors: tuxedo black, can-am white, Monza red, LeMans blue, Monaco orange, fathom green, Daytona yellow, Cortez silver, burgundy and riverside gold. Convertibles came with a choice of black, white or beige soft tops. Interior colors were black, bright blue, green, red, gunmetal and saddle.

The 427-cid 390-hp RPO L36 V-8 was again the starting-point engine for muscle car enthusiasts. Then came RPO L68 for $326.55 extra. It was the same 10.25:1 compression V-8 fitted with three

A 1969 Corvette Stingray L88 could blitz the quarter mile in well under 14 seconds.

The L89 version of the 1969 Corvette had aluminum cylinder heads and could produce 435 hp.

two-barrel carburetors, which upped its output to 400 hp. The 427-cid 435-hp RPO L71 Tri-Power engine also returned in much the same form as 1968. Its price tag was $437.10.

Three ultra-high-performing options began with the RPO L88 V-8. It again included a "power blister" hood. *Hot Rod* magazine tested an L88 and described it as a "street machine with soul." This year the basic package was $1,032.15 and also required heavy-duty brakes and suspension, transistor ignition and Positraction. The test car—a Stingray convertible—was base priced at $4,583.45, but went out the door at $6,562 as an L88 with a beefy Turbo Hydra-Matic and 3.36:1 rear axle. It did the quarter mile in 13.56 seconds at 111.10 mph.

There was also the RPO L89 V-8 for $832.05. This was a solid-lifter version of the 427 with aluminum cylinder heads on the L71 block. It had a 12.0:1 compression ratio, a 435 hp at 5800 rpm rat-ing and produced 460 ft. lbs. of torque at 4000 rpm.

The ultimate 1969 power option was the aluminum block and aluminum heads RPO ZL1 V-8, which is listed separately. Other 1969 Corvette muscle options included an RPO M20 four-speed manual transmission for $184.80, an RPO M21 four-speed close-ratio manual transmission for $184.80, an RPO M22 heavy-duty close-ratio four-speed manual transmission for $290.40 and an RPO M40 Turbo Hydra-Matic automatic transmission for $221.80. And of course, what muscle Corvette fan would be caught dead without an RPO N14 side-mount exhaust system, which sold for $147.45 in 1969?

For the top engines listed here, the L71 and the L88 were the closest in performance. The L71 made the trip down the quarter mile in 13.94 seconds at 105.63 mph and the L88 did it in 14.10 seconds at 106.89 mph. The L88 had a top speed of 151 mph.

1969 CHEVROLET YENKO "SYC 427" NOVA

On paper, the SYC 427 Nova, built by Don Yenko Chevrolet in Canonsburg, Pennsylvania, is one of the most outrageous muscle cars to ever hit the highway and be street legal. It was a compact Nova with Chevrolet's monster 427-cid 425-hp V-8 stuffed into it. This RPO L72 solid-lifter big-block engine was made famous in the 1966 Corvette. In 1969, it was offered as a COPO (Central Office Production Order) option in the Chevelle and Camaro.

If a mid-sized Chevy 427 was a terror on the street, then a lighter 427 Camaro would have an even better power-to-weight ratio, second only to the Corvette. That's how things were until the absolutely wicked 427 Nova was produced. Don Yenko once said in an interview that his 427 Nova was "a beast, almost lethal." That is precisely why the insurance companies stepped in and virtually ended its production. They didn't want to insure it and, after 30 were converted at Yenko's Chevrolet agency, the other seven that had been slated to get 427s remained SS-396 Novas with 4.10:1 Positraction rear ends.

SYC Novas supposedly started out as SS-396s, although at least one was a base Nova without SS equipment. The stock L78-optioned 396 engine, less heads, intake, carburetor, water pump and other top end components, was pulled and replaced with a crate-type 427 short-block. That's how easy the swap was, which is why it was so popular in the '60s. Many dealerships did these conversions for customers, but only certain dealers did them when the cars were brand new. In fact, Yenko went one step further and gave these cars special names. Every car—whether Camaro, Chevelle or Nova—was an SYC. The initials stood for "Yenko Super Cars." The center letter "Y" appeared larger than the other two letters on the badge.

A stripe kit—including SYC decals and Yenko badges—was installed, along with a unique tachometer atop the steering column. Each car was supposed to have had four options—a radio, Rally

The 1969 "SYC 427" Nova was the creation of performance dealer Don Yenko (Joe Maggio photo).

wheels, a vinyl roof and power steering. However, at least one car came minus each of these options and its history has been researched back to the original owner.

Greg Joseph, ex-curator of the former Otis Chandler muscle car collection in Oxnard, California, also believes that some of these Novas could have been COPO 427 cars with the larger engine installed at the factory. This is a distinct possibility, but the rarity of the vehicles is the reason that no broadcast sheets or original engines (with engine production code suffixes) or Protect-O-Plates (also showing a production code suffix) have yet been located.

Whether or not a Yenko SYC was COPO or not, it was still a 427 Nova and among just 30 built. Zero-to-60 mph times for such cars fell in the under-four-second bracket, according to Don Yenko, and the quarter-mile elapsed times were radical, too.

1970 CHEVROLET CAMARO RS/SS 396

The 1970 Camaro RS/SS 396 featured all-new styling and an engine that produced up to 350 hp.

Due to slow sales of 1969 Camaros, no new design was introduced for this series at the 1970 model introduction time in the fall of 1969. Chevrolet dealers continued to sell leftover 1969s until supplies ran out. The true 1970 models (often called 1970 1/2 Camaros) did not go on sale until Feb. 26, 1970.

The new Camaro had completely revamped styling with high-intensity headlamps, a semi-fastback roof line, a snout-style grille

carrying and "egg crate" insert and a much smoother looking rear end. The convertible was gone and the only available body style was the sport coupe. Standard equipment included all GM safety features, Starto-Bucket front seats, an all-vinyl interior, carpeting; an Astro-Ventilation system, a left-hand outside rear view mirror, side marker lights and E78-14 bias-belted blackwall tires. The base V-8 was a 307-cid small block.

RPO Z27 was the Camaro SS option package. It included a 350-cid 300-hp V-8, bright engine accents, power brakes, special ornamentation, hood insulation, F70-14 white-lettered tires, 14 x 7-inch diameter wheels, a black-painted grille, hide-away wipers with black arms and Super Sport "SS" emblems for $289.65 above the V-8 coupe's base price of $2,839.

RPO Z22 was the Rally Sport option package. It included a black-painted grille with a rubber-tipped vertical center bar and resilient body-color grille frame, independent left and right front bumpers, license plate bracket mounted below the right front bumper, parking lights with bright accents molded on the grille panel, hide-away headlamps, bright window, hood panel and body sill moldings, body-colored door handle inserts, RS emblems, nameplates, bright-accented tail lamps and bright-accented back-up lamps. It cost $188.35 and F78-14 or E70-14 tires were required.

The SS-396 Camaro substituted a big-block V-8 for the 350. The 396-cid engine had a 4.126 x 3.76-inch bore and stroke and actually displaced 402 cid, although Chevrolet promoted it as a "396." It had a 10.25:1 compression ratio and a single four-barrel carburetor. Advertised horsepower was 350 at 5200 rpm. The torque rating was 415 ft. lbs. at 3400 rpm.

1970 CHEVROLET CAMARO Z/28

(Jerry Heasley photo)

The 1970 Camaro Z/28 did the quarter mile in 14.5 seconds at 100.22 mph.

Styling, engineering, performance and quality in the 1970 Camaro Z/28 were all high. On the other hand, its production total of 8,733 units was low enough to make owning one an uncommon treat. A good indication of this car's stature was its selection as the winner of *Car Life* magazine's first "Showroom Trans-Am Championship."

In this comparison, the magazine pitted pure stock versions of four American sports compacts against each other in acceleration, braking and cornering, rating the comparative performance of each according to a point system such as the Sports Car Club of America (SCCA) used. The cars were then run in the "main event"—a challenging road course—to see which could go the distance the fastest.

Engines in the four cars ranged from a 302-cid Ford V-8 to a 400-cid Pontiac, but the acceleration test proved that cubic inches didn't have a direct influence on performance. In fact, the Z/28, with its new-for-1970 engine of 350 cid, was the quickest on the drag pad. It did the quarter mile in 14.50 seconds with a 100.22-mph terminal speed. This gave the Camaro five championship points.

Braking was the second performance aspect considered, with tests to measure stopping distances (from 80 mph) and fade. Credit for best braking went to the Mustang (which was third in acceleration). Coming in second gave the Camaro four more points, keeping it ahead of the pack, overall, with nine.

In the steady-rate-cornering category, a skid pad at a California test facility was used to rate lateral acceleration, handling characteristics and tire grip. General Motors' two pony cars exhibited virtually neutral handling and the AMC product oversteered. With its neutral cornering, the Mustang also proved the best in handling, but the Camaro was again a close second.

As might be anticipated, the characteristics that showed up in individual tests were again revealed on the road course. This meant that the Camaro and the Mustang often led the pack. Each had its strengths and weaknesses. Traction proved to be a problem for the Ford, when it was pushed to the max. The Camaro exhibited rear axle hop while screaming through the switchback.

When the dust cleared, honors for the fastest average over the tricky course actually belonged to the Pontiac Trans Am, giving it 15 total points. The Camaro's average course speed (1:02.6) was the next fastest, giving it second place in the main event and 17 total points. The Mustang averaged 1:04 and wound up with 16 points.

"The winner is the Camaro Z/28 with 17 points," the magazine concluded. "One first, three seconds. The fastest car, and the more consistent."

1970 CHEVROLET MONTE CARLO SS 454

(Jerry Heasley photo)

The 1970 Monte Carlo SS 454 combined luxury and muscle.

Chevrolet's all-new Monte Carlo was a luxury-personal-performance car based on the 116-inch-wheelbase Chevelle sedan. Even though the Monte Carlo had its own eight-inches-longer frame, many of its chassis parts were interchangeable with those of the Chevelle. The reason for the longer frame was the Monte Carlo's 6-foot-long hood, which was there to enhance its classic look more than anything else. The length wasn't needed to accommodate optional big-block V-8 engines, which fit easily in the new car's engine bay.

Due to the body and frame changes, the Monte Carlo had different weight distribution characteristics than the Chevelle and Chevrolet engineers had to beef up the springs and shocks and install heavier stabilizers. The front stabilizer bar was larger than the Chevelle's and the rear stabilizer bar was of a type available only as an option on the Chevelle SS 396. The SS 454 version of the Monte Carlo came standard with an automatic leveling control system in which the rear shocks had pressurized air bags that extended the shocks as more weight was added to the rear of the car. The Monte Carlo's 60.3-inch front track and 59.3-inch rear track were both wider than those of the Chevelle.

The Monte Carlo was sheer luxury inside with comfortable seats, an electric clock, assist straps and simulated elm-burl dash panel inlays. There was a full complement of gauges, although Motor Trend's tester complained that they were "rather small" and hard for the driver to see. Standard equipment included all features found on Chevelle Malibus, plus power front disc brakes and G78-15B tires. Chevrolet's new 454-cid version of the Turbo-Jet big-block V-8 was available with the SS-454 package only.

The new 454-cid engine had a 4.251 x 4.00-inch bore and stroke, a 10.25:1 compression ratio and a single Rochester 4MV carburetor. It developed 360 hp at 4400 rpm and 500 ft. lbs. of torque at 3200 rpm. *Motor Trend's* 3,575-lb. test car had a 3.31:1 axle and moved from 0 to 60 mph in 7.0 seconds flat. The standing-start quarter mile took 14.9 seconds at 92 mph. *Car Life's* test car was a bit slower, doing the quarter mile in 16.2 seconds at 90.1 mph.

With only 2.6 percent of the 1970 Monte Carlos built with the SS 454 option, total production for the year was a mere 3,823 copies of the muscle-car version. That's one reason why a 1970 SS 454 Monte Carlo is now almost worth its weight in gold.

1970 NOVA SS 396

The 1970 Nova had a new grille insert with squarer openings than the previous year's model. It continued to use the 111-inch wheelbase platform introduced two years earlier. The "Coke bottle" body shape had the popular long hood/short rear deck look and a trim overall length of 190 inches. Variable-ratio power steering was a new extra for 1970. Of course, it was also the era of General Motors' infamous in-the-windshield radio antenna, which helped

many youthful Nova owners tune in their favorite music while cruising the strip on Friday and Saturday night.

Chevrolet dealers had plenty of extra-cost options to sell Nova buyers to pump up the out-the-door price of the coupe model, which sold for $2,503 in the base V-8 series. Naturally, muscle car fans did not want the base 307-cid V-8 and much preferred moving up to the RPO Z26 Nova SS package. Its basic ingredients included a 350-cid

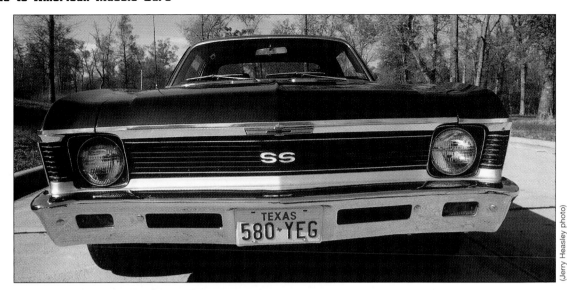

The '70 Nova featured a new grille and plenty of dealer options.

(Jerry Heasley photo)

For 1970, the Nova SS 396 coupe was still available.

(Jerry Heasley photo)

300-hp V-8, dual exhausts, power front disc brakes, a simulated air intake on the hood, simulated front fender louvers, bright accents, a black-finished radiator grille, a black-finished rear end panel, wide 14 x 7-inch wheels, E70 x 14 white-stripe tires, hood insulation and "SS" emblems. A four-speed manual or Turbo Hydra-Matic transmission was mandatory with the $290.70 Super Sport option.

Two optional Turbo-Jet V-8s were available for those who wanted to compete in the "stoplight grand prix" either at a drag strip or the downtown cruising strip. The first big-block package, coded RPO L34, came with the 396-cid (actually a 402) 350-hp engine and cost $184.35 extra. The second package, coded RPO L78, included the 396-cid 375-hp engine at $316 above the cost of the base 350-cid V-8. Nova packages were added to a grand total of 19,558 cars in 1970, of which 1,947 had the L34 engine and 5,262 had the L78 engine.

1970 YENKO DEUCE NOVA

Sometimes it seems like every car that left Don Yenko's Chevy dealership in Canonsburg, Pennsylvania, (southwest of Pittsburgh) carried a COPO Chevy 427-cid big-block V-8, but that's not quite true. A good example was the 1970 Yenko Duece, a rather busy-looking Nova two-door sedan that was powered by the LT/1 Corvette/Camaro engine.

The Yenko Deuce was based on the standard Nova, rather then the Super Sport edition, but it had enough bolt-on goodies and decals to make it look pretty special. The grille had a black-out appearance. Racing stripes running up either edge of the hood in "suspender" style carried LT/1 call-outs. A black-finished hood-mounted tachometer was attached on the driver's side, just ahead of the cowl vents. A "Deuce" decal decorated the nose of the hood.

Regular "350" engine badges sat atop the side marker lamps.

A "hockey stick" decal ran along the sides of the car, then over the rear deck. Where it grew wider at the rear the words "Yenko Deuce" were positioned. Spoked mag-style wheels and white-lettered tires rounded out the package.

The LT/1 V-8 was pirated from the Corvette and Camaro Z/28. It had a 4.0 x 3.48-inch bore and stroke. A single four-barrel 800-cfm Holley carburetor was mounted. Another performance enhancement was an 11.0:1 compression ratio. The LT/1 generated 360 hp at 6000 rpm and 380 ft. lbs. of torque at 4000 rpm. The Yenko Deuce cranked out a few more horses than the 350-hp RPO L34 Nova, but didn't quite match the 375-hp output of the factory's L78 version. However, it was a lot more distinctive and had much lower "production" numbers.

1970 CHEVELLE SS 396

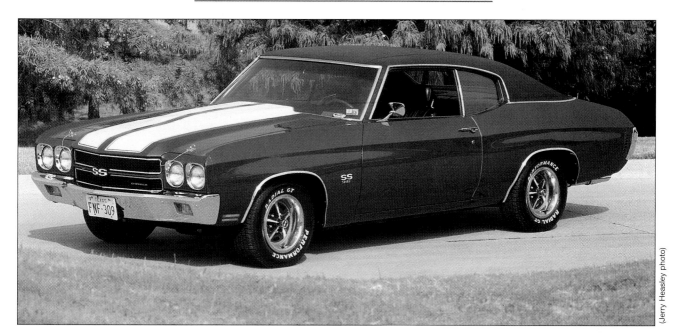

(Jerry Heasley photo)

Chevy gave the Chevelle SS 396 a modest facelift for 1970.

The 1970 Chevelle SS 396 convertible didn't lack for style or horse-power.

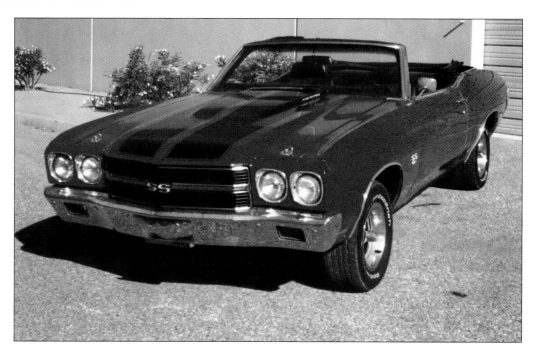

Chevelles had a fatter, more sculptured appearance for 1970. A horizontally split grille with "blended" dual headlamps was new. The SS 396 returned, but shortly after production of 1970 engines started, the bore size of the big-block V-8 was increased from 4.094-inches to 4.125 inches. This increased the engine's actual displacement to 402 cubic inches. In spite of this change, Chevrolet continued identifying the engine as the "Turbo-Jet 396."

The standard version of the "396" V-8 was coded RPO L34 and, despite its larger displacement, it carried the same advertised power ratings as 1969: 350 hp at 5,200 rpm and 415 ft. lbs. of torque at 3400 rpm. There was also the RPO L78 optional "396" engine with 375 hp at 5600 rpm and 415 ft. lbs. of torque at 3600 rpm.

A list of 13 items made up the content of the SS 396 package for 1970. In addition to the 350-hp engine they included: bright

engine accents, power front disc brakes, dual exhausts with bright tips, a black-accented grille, wheel opening moldings, a black resilient rear bumper panel, a special domed hood, the F41 heavy-duty suspension, special chassis features, SS identification (including SS emblems on the grille, fenders, rear bumper, steering wheel and door trim), 17 x 7-inch Rally wheels (RPO ZL7) and F70 x 14 raised-white-letter tires.

The base price of a 1970 Malibu sport coupe was $2,809 and the cost of the SS package was $445.55. If you added the L78 engine it was $210.65 extra. Chevrolet produced 49,826 of its 1970 Chevelle models with the SS-396 option. With a curb weight of 3,990 lbs., one of the 350-hp cars had to carry about 11.4 lbs. per horsepower. In road testing it was found that it could move from 0 to 60 in 8.1 seconds and cover the quarter mile in 15.5 seconds.

1970 CHEVROLET CHEVELLE SS 454

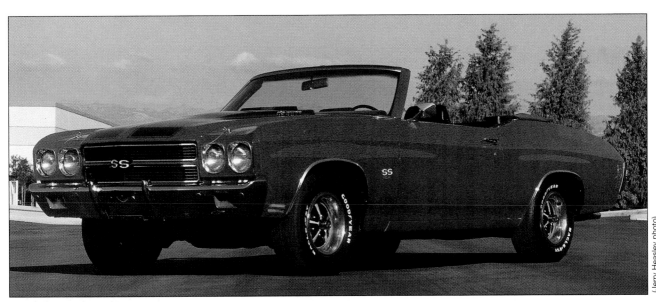

(Jerry Heasley photo)

A Chevelle SS 454 LS6 convertible is a rare find.

The 1970 Chevelle SS 454 sport coupe was considered by many enthusiasts to be the best of the Chevelle series.

(Jerry Heasley photo)

By 1970, the Chevelle SS 396 had been around since 1966 and was no longer the fastest muscle car in town. It was a snappy performer, but muscular newcomers from other automakers were proving to be a bunch faster on the streets and drag strips. To swing the balance back in Chevrolet's favor, the division decided to release a new 454-cid big-block V-8 for use in the Chevelle. The resulting model was called the SS 454 and is considered by many collectors to represent the pinnacle of the hot Chevelle SS series.

The 454-cid engine had a 4.250 x 4.00-inch bore and stroke and was made available in two different versions. The LS5 edition featured a 10.25:1 compression ratio and a 750-cfm Rochester Quadrajet carburetor. It was rated for 360 hp at 5400 rpm and 500 ft. lbs. of torque at 3200 rpm. This engine was included in the SS 454 option, which had a $503.45 package price. Even more awesome was the LS6 version, which used an 11.25:1 compression ratio and

a 780-cfm Holley four-barrel carburetor. It developed 450 hp at 5600 rpm and 500 ft. lbs. of torque at 3600 rpm. To get an LS6 you had to pay the SS 454 package price plus $263.30.

The LS6 was a super-high-performance engine featuring things like four-bolt main bearings, nodular iron bearing caps, heavy-duty connecting rods, big-diameter exhaust valves and a solid-lifter camshaft. A test car powered by the LS6 engine moved from 0 to 60 mph in 5.4 seconds and did the standing-start quarter mile in 13.81 seconds at 103.8 mph. That was with Turbo Hydra-Matic transmission and a 3.77:1 rear axle. You could also order either 454-cid engine with one of three available four-speed manual transmissions.

Only 3,773 of the SS sport coupes and convertibles built in 1970 had the 454-cid V-8s and only a relative handful were LS6 editions.

1970 CHEVROLET CORVETTE

The 1970 Corvette featured refinements on the basic styling used since 1968. There was a new ice-cube-tray design grille and matching side fender louvers, rectangular, amber-colored front signal lights, fender flares and square exhaust exits. The bucket seats and safety belt retractor containers were also improved.

Standard equipment included front and rear disc brakes, headlight washers, wheel trim rings, carpeting, a center console and all-vinyl upholstery (in either black, blue, green, saddle or red). Buyers had their choice of 10 exterior colors: Mulsanne blue, Bridgehampton blue, Donnybrooke green, Laguna gray, Marlboro maroon, Corvette bronze, Monza red, Cortez silver, classic white and Daytona yellow.

All Corvette convertibles came with a choice of black or white soft tops. Interior colors available were black, blue, green, red, brown and saddle. The 1970 sport coupe had a $5,192 base price and weighed 3,153 lbs. The convertible listed for a little less—$4,849—and weighed a little more at 3,167 lbs.

Chevrolet built 10,668 coupes and 6,648 ragtops. A total of 1,287 buyers interested in muscle-car-like performance separately checked off the LT-1 engine.

In addition, 25 Corvettes with a ZR1 option package carried the LT-1 engine.

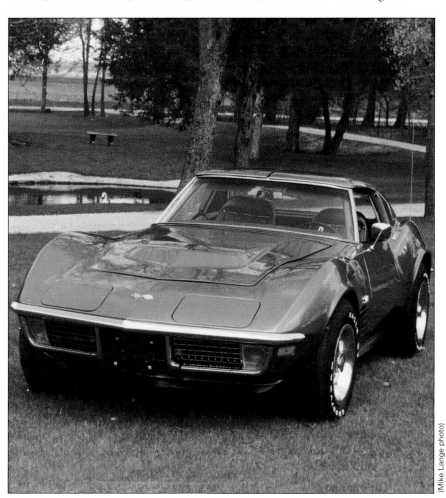

The 1970 Corvette Stingray received some styling refinements and carried a powerful 454 V-8 big block.

(Mike Lange photo)

RPO LS5—a new 454-cid big-block V-8—featured a: 4.251 x4.00-inch bore and stroke. It had a relatively mild 10:25:1 compression ratio, a high-performance hydraulic lifter camshaft and a single Rochester 750CFM Quadra-Jet four-barrel carburetor. The LS5 Corvette had an advertised 390 hp at 4800 rpm and 500 ft. lbs. of torque at 3400 rpm.

Another hot option was the RPO LT1 V-8, which was based on the 350-cid small-block V-8. This 4.00 x 3.48-inch bore and stroke motor had 11.0:1 compression, solid lifters and a four-barrel Holley carburetor on an aluminum intake manifold. It was good for 370 hp at 6000 rpm and 380 ft. lbs. of torque at 4000 rpm.

A 454-cid 465-hp RPO LS7 V-8 was listed in some early 1970 Corvette sales literature, but never made it to the showroom. It had solid valve lifters, a high-performance camshaft and a Holley 800CFM four-barrel carburetor. Only one car with the LS7 engine was ever built. *Sports Car Graphic* editor Paul Van Valkenburgh drove it 2,500 miles from a press conference at Riverside, California, to Detroit and raved about it. The car did the quarter mile in 13.8 seconds at 108 mph. However, GM's policies against ultra-high-performance cars at the time led to the option being dropped.

The LT1-powered 1970 Corvette could do 0 to 30 mph in 2.5 seconds, 0 to 60 mph in 5.7 seconds and 0 to 100 mph in 13.5 seconds. It covered the quarter mile in 14.17 seconds at 102.15 mph and had a top speed of 122 mph.

1970 CORVETTE "ULTIMATE" ZL1

When *Motor Trend's* editors went to the 1970 Chevrolet long lead press conference, they got to drive one of the hottest Corvettes that had ever been put together. The brilliant red T-top coupe was a prototype 1970 model with a power plant similar to the then current, all-aluminum ZL1 engine. The muscular four-bolt-mains motor had the same heads and camshaft as the ZL1, but featured a special induction system and a custom-made exhaust system. It was fitted with ZL1-like TRW forged pistons and was also completely blue-printed.

In addition to some minor re-working of the aluminum cylinder heads, Gib Hufstaders, Bob Clifts, Tom Langdons and Bob Keithman of Chevrolet's high-performance engines group deburred the exhaust ports and double cut the valves before carefully lapping them in. The result was a higher 11.45:1 compression ratio. The inlet manifold was shielded with a steel pan under it to keep hot oil off. The carburetion was also tweaked a bit with some machining to allow use of a Holley 4500 NASCAR carburetor with a flow rate between 1200 and 1400 cfm.

The Chevy engineers also built up a set of exotic-looking 180-degree exhaust headers and then modified the suspension drag racing by using a 2-inch spacer and 3-inch rubber to eliminate wheel hop. A set of 4.88:1 No. 4650 high-nickel alloy gears were installed in the differential.

When tested, the "Ultimate ZL1" had been re-converted to a standard "drag racing" type of exhaust set up with collectors. Performance was in the same bracket with both setups and *Motor Trend's* driver covered the quarter mile in 10.60 seconds at 132 mph.

1971 CHEVROLET CAMARO RS/SS 396

(Jerry Heasley photo)

The 1971 Camaro RS/SS 396 sport coupe received only minor changes from 1970.

Due to the late release of the "real" 1970 Camaro, no major design changes were made in 1971 models. The easiest way to spot a 1971 edition is to look for high-back bucket seats with integral headrests in the front compartment.

Standard equipment now included power front disc brakes and steel inner door guardrails, as well as all other GM safety features, all-vinyl upholstery, bucket-style rear seat cushions, carpeting; a cigar lighter, Astro-Ventilation, E78-14 bias-belted blackwall tires and a three-speed manual transmission with floor shifter. The base V-8 was a 307-cid small block.

The base Camaro SS package included a 350-cid 270-hp V-8, dual exhausts, bright engine accents, power brakes, special ornamentation, hood insulation, F70-14 white-lettered tires, 14 x 7-inch diameter wheels, a black-finished grille, hide-away wipers with black arms and Super Sport "SS" emblems. The Rally Sport option package added: a special black-finished grille with a rubber-tipped vertical center bar and resilient body-color grille frame; independent left and right front bumpers; license plate bracket mounted below

the right front bumper; parking lights with bright accents molded on the grille panel; hide-away headlamps; bright window, hood panel and body sill moldings; body-colored door handle inserts; RS emblems (deleted when the SS package was also installed); an RS steering wheel medallion; bright-accented tail lamps and bright-accented back-up lamps.

An M20 wide-ratio four-speed manual transmission with floor shifter was standard with the 396-cid V-8 and could be hooked to 3.73:1 or 4.10:1 rear axles. The M21 close-ratio four-speed was another possibility with the same axles. Two automatic transmission options were both based on the three-speed M40 Turbo Hydra-Matic automatic transmission, which came with either a steering-column-mounted gear shifter or a floor shift.

The 1971 version of the 396-cid engine (actually 402 cubic inches) had a high-lift camshaft, hydraulic valve lifters, dual exhausts, an 8.5:1 compression ratio and a single Rochester four-barrel carburetor. Advertised horsepower was 300 at 4800 rpm. The torque rating was 400 ft. lbs. at 3200 rpm.

1971 CHEVROLET MONTE CARLO SS 454

Chevrolet Motor Division made few changes in the Monte Carlo during its second year in the market. Well, it's true that the automaker did take the never-actually-made convertible out of its sales brochure. It also replaced the round 1970 front parking lamps with rectangular units and substituted a grille with an insert having a finer texture. Returning from the grave, so to speak, was the hood ornament, which was now designed with a spring-loaded attachment to avoid impaling pedestrians.

A touch of greater distinction was added to the Monte Carlo Super Sport option, which now featured a blackout-style rear beauty panel and "SS 454" identification on the lower front fenders. There was also an "SS" badge on the rear beauty panel. The best news was that muscle car lovers could now order two versions of the 454-cid V-8 in the Monte Carlo and both provided more horsepower, at least on paper. The standard version had a lower 8.5:1 compression ratio, but a higher 365 hp at 4800 rating (this doesn't make sense until you realize that, in 1970, Chevy actually rated the 454 at

390 hp in full-size cars). Torque was down a bit to 465 ft.lbs. at 3200 rpm. The LS6 version of the 454 was a new option. It was de-tuned to a 425 advertised horsepower rating from the 450-hp rating it carried in 1970 Chevelles.

Monte Carlo SS 454s came standard with a three-speed Turbo Hydra-Matic automatic transmission. The only option was a fully synchronized four-speed manual with floor shifter, and this option was a special-order item only. The Monte Carlo SS 454 sold for $3,901 and weighed 3,488 lbs.

The 1971 SS 454 package included all of the same goodies it featured in 1970, such as heavy-duty front and rear springs, heavy-duty shocks with automatic level control and heavy front and rear stabilizer bars. Of course, with the government and the insurance industry breathing down its neck, Chevrolet didn't promote the Monte Carlo SS very heavily and production for the model year dropped nearly 50 percent to only 1,919 cars.

1971 CHEVELLE "HEAVY CHEVY"

The 1971 Chevelle "Heavy Chevy" coupe was a snappier version of the Malibu.

(Jerry Heasley photo)

Clouds were aplenty for the surviving muscle cars of 1971. High insurance rates for young drivers in fast cars ravaged the market. At the same time, emission standards imposed by the federal government cut output and compression for the top high-performance engines. American automakers were rapidly losing their enthusiasm due to the shrinking demand for muscle cars and rising manufacturing costs that evolved through satisfying an armada of coming federal safety and emission standards.

As the big-horsepower machines of the 1960s fell by the wayside, they were replaced by a growing number of "visual" muscle cars that looked much the same as real muscle cars, but were far tamer under the hood. Chevrolet announced a pair of these in March of 1971. They were called the Rally Nova and the Heavy Chevy.

The RPO YF3 Heavy Chevy option-created-model was a ver-

sion of the $2,980 Malibu V-8 two-door hardtop. The package added side striping, a blacked-out grille, base Rally wheels and appropriate front fender decals that read "Heavy Chevy." An air induction hood—complete with hood pins—was an option.

How "heavy" your Heavy Chevy got was up to you. Under the hood, options started with the standard 307-cid 200-hp small-block V-8 engine. You could check other boxes for the RPO L65 power plant, which was a 350-cid V-8 with a two-barrel carburetor and 245 hp. If you needed more than that, you could opt for a 270-hp four-barrel RPO L48 version of the 350-cid engine or go all the way up to the 300-hp 402-cid big-block. However, if you wanted the gang-buster 454-cid V-8, you had to go the Super Sport route. Production figures of the Heavy Chevy option came to 6,727 units, but very few of these cars still survive today.

1971 CHEVROLET CHEVELLE SS 454

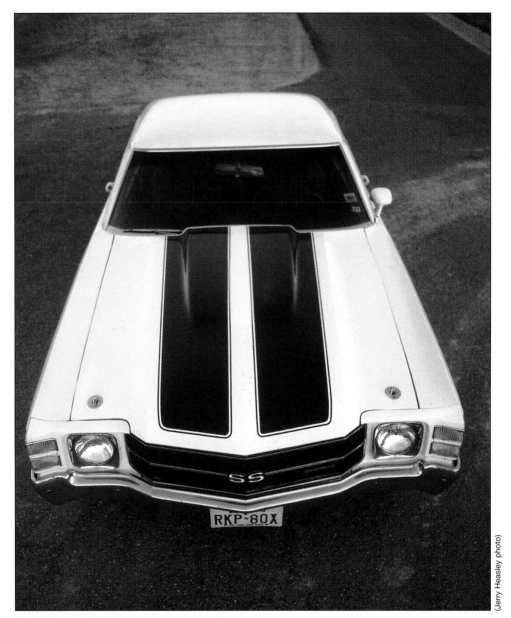

(Jerry Heasley photo)

The '71 Chevelle SS 396 received some noticeable changes to the front end.

Chevelle models received changes to the front end in 1971. A new twin-level grille was divided by a bright horizontal bar. The front parking lights were moved from the bumper into the fender tips. "Don't panic," says a 1971 Chevrolet sales brochure. Although the muscle car era was in decline, there were still some hot options left. "There's still an SS-454. Any car that was named the best of its kind in *Car and Driver's* reader's choice (the 1970 Chevelle SS 454) is sure to stay around."

There were changes, however. The early '70s was the era of low-cost muscle cars and "lick-'em-stick-'em" muscle cars that had the decals, but not the big-cube engines, of the recent past. Chevrolet set things up so buyers could order all of the Super Sport goodies on any Malibu sport coupe or convertible as long as it had a 350-, 400- or 454-cid V-8.

With a V-8 engine, the Malibu sport coupe sold for $2,980 and weighed 3,342 lbs. The convertible, which came only with a V-8, was base priced at $3,260 and weighed some 3,390 lbs. Only 5,089 Chevelle convertibles were built in 1971.

The RPO Z15 SS package sold for $357. It included: power brakes with disc brakes up front, a black-accented grille, a special suspension, a special domed hood with functional hood lock pins, SS identification for the hood, rear deck and fenders, a driver's side remote-control sports mirror, gray-finished 15 x 7-inch five-spoke sport wheels, F60 x 14 white-lettered tires, a black-accented steering column, and a steering wheel with SS nameplate.

If you wanted a 1971 SS 454 Chevelle, you had to order one of the two big-block engines as an add-on option. This year Chevrolet listed the net horsepower rating and gross horsepower rating for both engines. The LS5 version produced 285 net hp and 365 gross hp. The LS6 version generated 325 nhp and 425 ghp. Both came with a choice of a four-speed manual transmission or a three-speed Turbo-Hydra-Matic transmission.

Chevrolet put together an estimated 80,000 cars that carried the SS option this year. Of those units, 19,292 were equipped with 454-cid V-8s.

1971 CORVETTE

(Jerry Heasley photo)

Aside from a few small exterior changes and slightly less engine compression, the 1971 Stingray "454" coupe was the same as the '70 model.

If you liked the 1970 Corvette, you liked the 1971 version. They were virtually the same car, at least on the outside. A new resin process (that supposedly improved the body) and a different interior were the major changes. Under the hood, the compression ratios were dropped a bit to enable Corvette engines to run on lower-octane fuel.

Standard equipment included all-vinyl upholstery; a dual-exhaust system, an outside rearview mirror, carpeting, a center console, wheel trim rings, an electric clock, a tachometer, a heavy-duty battery, front and rear disc brakes with a warning light and tinted glass.

Corvette buyers had their choice of 10 exterior colors: Mulsanne blue, Bridgehampton blue, brands hatch green, steel cities gray, Ontario orange, Millie Miglia red, Nevada silver, classic white, sunflower yellow and war bonnet yellow. All convertibles came with a choice of black or white soft tops. The interior colors were black, dark blue, dark green, red and saddle.

High-performance engine options included the RPO LS5 V-8. This $295 extra version of the 454-cid big-block now had an 8.5:1 compression ratio. It was rated for 365 hp at 4800 rpm and 465 ft. lbs. of torque at 3200 rpm. It featured hydraulic valve lifters, a high-performance camshaft and a Rochester 750CFM Quadra-Jet four-barrel carburetor.

Corvette buyers willing to part with $1,221 could add the RPO LS6 V-8. It also had hydraulic lifters, a high-performance cam, an 8.5:1 compression ratio and a four-barrel carburetor. However, the LS6 carb was a big 880-cfm Holley model. The motor was rated 425 hp at 5600 rpm and 475 ft. lbs. of torque at 4000 rpm.

Another hot option available again to Corvette fans was the small block-based RPO LT1 V-8. This 350-cid engine had a 9.0:1 compression ratio. It generated 330 hp at 5600 rpm and torque was 360 ft. lbs. at 4000 rpm.

A 1971 Corvette with the LS5 engine could go 0 to 60 mph in 5.7 seconds, 0 to 100 mph in 14.1 seconds and do the standing-start quarter mile in 14.2 seconds at 100.33 mph. A 1971 Corvette with the LS6 engine and 3.36:1 rear axle was tested by *Car and Driver* magazine in June 1971. It moved from 0 to 60 mph in 5.3 seconds, from 0 to 80 mph in 8.5 seconds and from 0 to 100 mph in 12.7 seconds. The same car did the quarter mile in 13.8 seconds at 104.65 mph.

An LT1-powered Vette with the M-21 four-speed manual transmission and a 3.70:1 rear axle was also tested by *Car and Driver* magazine in June 1971. It moved from 0 to 40 mph in 3.4 seconds, 0 to 60 mph in 6.0 seconds and from 0 to 100 mph in 14.5 seconds. The car did the quarter mile in 14.57 seconds at 100.55 mph and its top speed was 137 mph.

Production for 1971 increased to 14,680 sport coupes and 7,121 convertibles. A total of 1,949 buyers separately checked off the LT1 engine option in 1971. In addition, eight ZR1 Corvettes carried the LT1 engine.

1972 CHEVROLET CAMARO RS/SS 396

The Camaro for 1972 had a slightly different grille mesh and new high-back bucket seats. The fate of the muscular "pony car" was said to be in danger, since a strike at the Camaro assembly plant in Lordstown, Ohio, turned into a disaster. The walkout stranded thousands of Camaro and Firebird bodies on the assembly line and, by the time it was ended, these cars were unfit for sale under new federal safety standards. General Motors was forced to scrap them and almost did the same with the entire F-car program. Chevrolet engineer Alex C. Mair fought for the survival of the Camaro, which ultimately went on to achieve higher sales.

Standard equipment again included power front disc brakes and steel inner-door guardrails, as well as all other GM safety features: all-vinyl upholstery, bucket-style rear seat cushions, carpeting, a cigar lighter, Astro-Ventilation, E78-14 bias-belted blackwall tires and a three-speed manual transmission with floor shifter. The base engine was a 307-cid small-block V-8 with a 170-hp rating.

The Camaro SS package included: a 350-cid 200-hp V-8, dual exhausts, bright engine accents, power brakes, special ornamentation, hood insulation, F70-14 white-lettered tires, 14 x 7-inch diameter wheels, a black-finished grille, hide-away wipers with black arms and Super Sport "SS" emblems and was priced at $306. The Rally Sport option package added a special black-finished grille with a rubber-tipped vertical center bar and resilient body-color grille frame; independent left and right front bumpers; license plate bracket mounted below the right front bumper; parking lights with bright accents molded on the grille panel; hide-away headlamps; bright window, hood panel and body sill moldings; body-colored door handle inserts; RS emblems (deleted when the SS package was also installed); an RS steering wheel medallion; bright-accented tail lamps and bright-accented back-up lamps. It was priced at $116.

The 1972 version of the "396" (402-cid) engine had 240 hp at 4400 rpm. The torque rating was 345 ft. lbs. at 3200 rpm. Chevrolet built 6,522 cars with the SS option.

1972 CHEVELLE "HEAVY CHEVY"

Changes made to the mid-sized Chevelles were of a very minor nature in model year 1972. The updated grille had a new texture and it was divided horizontally by two even-spaced moldings. This gave the front end a three-tier look. As in 1971, the front parking lamps were found in the fender caps, but they now had a larger, one-piece plastic lens with a square shape. The lenses wrapped around the body corners to serve extra duty as side marker lamps.

The basic Chevelle hardtop coupe came in six- and eight-cylinder series. Prices for V-8-powered hardtop models started at $2,759 and they weighed only 3300 lbs., making them the lightest of all of Chevrolet's mid-size offerings. The RPO YF3 Heavy Chevy option-created-model returned to the line up again as a "muscle-car-image" version of the $2,923 Malibu V-8 two-door hardtop.

As it had in 1971, the RPO YF3/YF8 Heavy Chevy package added special side striping (in a choice of black or white colors), a black-accented radiator grille, Heavy Chevy decals, a special domed hood with hood locking pins, 4 x 6-inch Rally-type wheels with bright lug nuts and special Rally wheel center caps. The package had a wholesale price of $107.64 and a retail price of $138. With that kind or mark-up, it's no wonder that dealers didn't push them out the door. A ZL2/YF8 cowl-induction hood package was a $154 extra-cost option.

The standard Chevelle V-8 in 1972 was the 307-cid job with a rating of 130 SAE net horsepower (nhp) at 4400 rpm. You could order a Heavy Chevy with it or any other options up to the "400." The next step up from the 307 was the RPO L65 350-cid V-8 with 165-nhp rating. Then came another RPO L48 version of the 350 with a four-barrel carburetor and 175-nhp rating. The new 400-cid V-8 was available in only one version for Chevelles. It carried a 240-hp rating.

1972 CHEVROLET CHEVELLE SS 454

There were very few differences between 1972 Chevelles and the models of the previous year. What stood out most were the single-unit front turn signals and side markers. In 1971, there had been multiple lenses "stacked" on one another, but this year there was a one-piece lens with horizontal lines molded on it.

Chevrolet buyers could again order all of the Super Sport goodies on any Malibu sport coupe or convertible as long as it had a V-8. That's right, you could even get an "SS-307" based on a base Malibu sport coupe this year. The 307-powered Malibu sport coupe cost $2,922.70. If you wanted a Super Sport convertible, a base V-8 was already figured in, since you could not get a Malibu ragtop with Chevy's in-line six-cylinder engine. The least expensive version of the open model retailed for $3,186.70.

The RPO Z15 Super Sport package included power front disc–rear drum brakes, a black-finished grille, a special domed hood with locking pins, a left-hand remote-control sport rearview mirror, Super Sport "SS" emblems, a sport suspension, 15 x 7-inch wheels with bright lug nuts, special wheel center caps, wheel trim rings and F60-15 white-lettered tires. The package listed for $350.15 for both body styles and required the optional V-8 engine and an optional transmission. The exact transmission used varied by engine.

If you wanted an SS-454 you got the LS5 version. It cost $272 and the SS equipment package and a heavy-duty battery were required. The battery was a $15 option. The 1972 version of the 454 had an 8.5:1 compression ratio and a single Rochester 4MV carburetor. It was rated for 270 SAE nhp at 4000 rpm and 390 ft. lbs. of torque at 3200 rpm. Standard transmission with the 454 was a special four-on-the-floor manual with Turbo Hydra-Matic optional at $231 extra. Chevrolet built 5,333 cars with the SS-454 setup this year.

1973 CHEVROLET CHEVELLE SS 454

Totally new "Colonnade" styling was seen on 1973 General Motors A-body cars, including Chevelles. Designed to meet federal rollover safety standard, the new construction featured a body with inner and outer shells, guard beams inside the doors and better isolated fuel tanks. The windows and roof pillars had a limousine-like character. The styling looked best on two-door models and supported different rear quarter window treatments from opera windows to louver vents.

On Chevelles, general styling highlights included cross-hatched grilles with a "flat" look that continued beneath the single headlamps. The tail lamps were circular units recessed into a back panel that was "veed" horizontally along its center line. The Chevelle Malibu SS package was a $243 option this year. It included SS emblems for the grille, fenders and area above the rear bumper, accent striping on the lower body, color-keyed wheel cutouts and dual sport mirrors. Super Sports also featured heavy-duty front and rear stabilizers and a special instrument panel. For the first (and only) time, you could order the SS package for a Malibu station wagon.

With the change to Colonnade styling, the convertible body style was dropped. There was also no true hardtop or sport coupe. The Colonnade SS coupe listed for about $3,253, not including the big-block V-8. The price on the Chevelle SS station wagon, also without the 454, was about $3,318.

If you wanted an SS-454 you got a de-tuned version of the LS5 engine. It cost $235. The 1972 version of the 454 continued with the 8.5:1 compression ratio and a single Rochester 4MV carburetor. It was rated for 245 SAE net horsepower (nhp) at 4000 rpm and 375 ft. lbs. of torque at 2800 rpm. Standard transmission with the 454 was a close-ratio four-speed manual gearbox with floor-mounted gear shifter. Turbo Hydra-Matic was optional at $210 extra.

Chevrolet built 2,500 cars with the SS 454 setup for 1973. While they were not the hottest examples of the big-block Chevelle, they were different and rare and relatively few are seen today—especially the station wagons.

1977 CHEVROLET CAMARO Z/28

One of the early signs that there could be a performance specialty car market after a so-called energy crisis came in February of 1977 when Chevrolet brought back the Z/28 option for the Camaro. The once popular Z/28 had been one of the many casualties in the 1974 wake of our first energy crisis. It was dropped after that model run.

The official return came February 18, 1977, at Daytona International Speedway, where Camaros were being raced in the International Race of Champions (IROC) series opener. It was noted by Robert D. Lund, Chevrolet general manager, that unprecedented demand for the Camaro and recent changes in the market made the decision to reactivate the Z/28 obvious to Chevrolet planners months before.

While compared to previous Z/28s the 1977 1/2 was rather tame, it was a revelation in its time. Standard was the four-barrel carbureted 350-cid V-8 with a mild rating of 170 nhp. Also standard, except in California, was the Borg-Warner T-10 four-speed along with 3.73:1 rear end gearing. California residents had to make do with automatic transmissions.

Dual exhaust with resonators replacing mufflers, front and rear stabililizer bars, 14:1 steering, GR70x15 white letter tires and body-colored styled steel wheels came standard. Visuals, of course, were part of the deal as body-colored bumpers, blackout trim, front and rear spoilers, sport mirrors and appropriate decal badging came along with it.

The Z/28 price came to $5,170 compared to $4,223 for the base V-8 Camaro. Production, which started February 1, was set at an annual rate of 20,000-25,000. For its half year, the Z/28 lived up to expectations with 14,349 being produced. It continued to be offered as the image leader of the Camaro line for many years to come.

1985 CHEVROLET CAMARO 5.0-LITER IROC-Z

The 1985 Chevrolet Camaro IROC-Z was inspired by a racing series that originated in 1973. The first IROC-Z could be purchased with a beefed-up 5.0-liter engine that produced 215 hp.

One of the most highly publicized forms of racing that Camaros took part in was the International Race of Champions, or IROC, race series. It originated in 1973, when drivers competed in 15 identically prepared Porshe Carreras. For several reasons, including a desire to expand the series to include oval track drivers, Camaros replaced Porsches in 1974.

The IROC series ran through 1980, with Roman numerals identifying each year. After the IROC VII competition in 1980, the series was dropped, but it returned in 1984 when the IROC VIII title was taken by NASCAR driver Cale Yarborough.

Thanks to television, the IROC series earned wide exposure and a strong link was created between the Camaro name and the IROC name. By 1985, this was strengthened even further by the release of a hot production version of the Chevy pony car called the IROC Z/28—more popularly called the "IROC-Z."

The IROC-Z was actually a sports equipment package (RPO B4Z). The standard engine was Chevy's LG4 190-hp version of the 305-cid (5.0-liter) V-8. This engine used a four-barrel carburetor and developed 240 ft. lbs. of torque at 3200 rpm. A more muscular engine was available as the optional LB9 version of the 5.0-liter V-8, with electronic fuel injection and a tuned aluminum intake plenum with individual intake runners for each cylinder. This was dubbed "tuned port injection" and was good for 215 hp at 4800 rpm and 275 ft. lbs. of torque at 3200 rpm.

The 5.0-liter H.O. engine also featured a hotter camshaft and a larger-diameter exhaust system. It came only with four-speed manual transmission attachments for 1985. A 3.42:1 rear axle was standard. Other IROC-Z equipment included a lower stance and center of gravity, re-valved Delco front struts, a faster spring jounce rate, front stabilizer bar, re-calibrated performance power steering, Bilstein rear gas shocks, fatter-than-normal rear anti-roll bar and unidirectional 245/50VR16 Goodyear Eagle tires mounted on 8 x 16-inch wheels.

In road tests, *Motor Trend* reported a 6.87-second 0-to-60 time and a 15.32-second quarter-mile run at 89.6 mph. *Popular Hot Rodding* took a little longer (7 seconds) to get up to 60 mph, but ran the quarter mile in 14.94 seconds at 92.60 mph.

1986 CHEVROLET MONTE CARLO SS AEROCOUPE

Chevrolet fans have NASCAR racing driver Bill Elliott to thank for the sharpest Monte Carlo SS of them all—the Aerocoupe—which was introduced in the middle of the 1986 model year. During the 1985 NASCAR Winston Cup season, Elliott drove a Ford Thunderbird. His car captured a record 11 superspeedway wins and Elliott took a much publicized $1 million bonus.

This happened even though Junior Johnson's Monte Carlo SS driver Darrell Waltrip took the driving championship and even though Chevrolet—which tied Ford (with 14 wins apiece)—claimed the manufacturer's title for the third year in a row. Despite taking the championship, the bow-tie brand drivers complained that they could not catch the T-birds on the big tracks. To make matters worse, Ford redesigned the Thunderbird for 1986 and it came out being sleeker than ever.

With no new model of the Monte Carlo in the works, Chevrolet did the next best thing and improvised a solution to the problem. To keep costs to a minimum, Chevy extended the back window glass on the Monte Carlo SS. On December 18, 1985, the Aerocoupe option (B5T) was announced. It dropped the drag coefficient from .375 to .365. To accommodate the 25-degree slope of the glass, a smaller trunk lid was used.

Kits to turn the Monte Carlo SS race cars into Aerocoupes were readily available, but production models were not that common and only 200 Monte Carlo SS Aerocoupes were built for 1986. The SS option, which technically was an extra-cost package, came out in the middle of 1983 and was an immediate hit in the showroom and on the racetrack. The standard engine was a 180-nhp version of the 305-cid small-block V-8. The car's sloping nose, which was developed in a wind tunnel, was a key part of its high-performance image.

1987 CHEVROLET CAMARO 5.7-LITER IROC-Z

(Jerry Heasley photo)

American Sunroof Corp. turned a limited number of 1987 Chevrolet Camaro IROC-Zs into muscle car convertibles.

The 5.7-liter Camaro IROC-Z model arrived on schedule for 1987. Chevrolet advertised the availability of the new engine by promoting the car as "a mean hombre in '87 with the arrival of the 5.7-liter TPI V-8 power plant roaring under the hood of the hot IROC-Z."

With the earlier 5.0-liter IROC-Z already accounting for nearly 25 percent of Camaro Z/28 sales (which in turn represented 47 percent of all Camaros sold) the 5.7-liter version was expected to have a strong influence on overall business. A potential impediment, the unavailability of air conditioning on the 5.7-liter IROC-Z, was only temporary, since it was slated for production beginning in October 1986.

Except for its Camaro LB9 accessory drive belts, exhaust system and electronic control module, the new L98 IROC-Z V-8 was identical to the Corvette 5.7-liter TPI engine. Its power ratings were 220 hp at 4200 rpm and 320 ft. lbs. of torque at 3200 rpm. With the exception of its 3.27:1 geared 7.75-inch Australian-built Borg-Warner rear axle, the 5.7-liter IROC-Z shared its running gear with the 5.0-liter version. All IROC-Z models had slightly revised suspensions for 1987.

The price of this engine, identified as RPO B2L, was $1,045 over the $13,488 cost of an IROC-Z with the base LG4 engine. Chevrolet required the purchase of a number of mandatory options. These included RPO MX4, a special version of the four-speed 700R4 automatic transmission with an upgraded torque converter; RPO B80, a limited-slip differential; RPO J85, four-wheel disc brakes and the RPO KC4 engine oil cooler. The cost of these features raised the price of the 5.7-liter engine to $1,924, which contrasted with the $707 list price of RPO LB9, the tunnel-port-injected 305 cid V-8.

The cost of the 5.7-liter IROC-Z paled before its exceptional performance. *Hot Rod* magazine, in its January 1987 issue, suggested that "it could be the closest facsimile to a full-bore road racing car you'll ever drive." Chevrolet's acceleration data underscored this perspective. Chevrolet test drivers achieved a 0 to 60-mph time of 6.2 seconds and a standing-start quarter-mile time of 14.5 seconds. Subsequent road tests essentially duplicated these figures.

Also available in limited numbers as a 1987 model was an IROC-Z Camaro convertible conversion done by the American Sunroof Corp. (ASC) of Livonia, Michigan.

1987 CHEVROLET MONTE CARLO SS AEROCOUPE

The 1987 Monte Carlo SS Aerocoupe produced a modest 180 net horsepower, but it still sparkled on the track.

(Jerry Heasley photo)

For 1987, the Chevrolet Monte Carlo coupe, model 1G, came in LS and SS versions. A V-6 was standard in the LS and the V-8 version listed for $11,746 or $440 more than the V-6. The V-8-only Monte Carlo SS (RPO Z37/Z65) had a base price of $13,463. A new SS feature for 1987 was aerodynamic composite headlamps.

Also returning for the 1987 was the Monte Carlo SS Aerocoupe package, which was technically an option (RPO Z37/Z16). Its big, slanting back window reduced the high-performance model's coefficient of drag from 0.375 to 0.365, but it also added $1,395 to the price of the Monte Carlo SS coupe. That brought the sticker on a production-type Aerocoupe to $14,838 without any add-on extras.

Powering the 3,528-lb. Aerocoupe was the high-output Super Sport version of the 5.0-liter (305-cid) small-block V-8, which produced 180 nhp. It came attached to a four-speed overdrive automat-

ic transmission.

For its second season, the Monte Carlo SS Aerocoupe was made more readily available and Chevrolet wound up producing 6,052 copies. The main change between the original version and the 1987 edition was the placement of decals on the front doors.

Monte Carlo Aerocoupe production continued until December 11, 1987. When the short-run 1988 models were introduced, the Aerocoupe was no longer on the option list.

The Aerocoupe worked so well that Chevrolet drivers gave the factory manufacturer's championships in 1987 and 1988, along with a solid lead in May of 1989, when the stock car racing program switched over to the Chevy Lumina body.

Aerocoupes are still being raced successfully today on other racing circuits.

1990 CHEVROLET CORVETTE ZR1

(Jerry Heasley photo)

The 1990 ZR1 was fast and cool, and carried a hefty $60,000-plus sticker price.

Could it be that Chevrolet Motor Division decided to launch an effort to compete in the space race? The 1990 Corvette ZR1 was a rocketship that might give that impression. Another impression that the ZR1 imparted was that this built-for-speed bow-tie creation would become an instant collecter car.

The collectibility of the 1990 ZR1 went beyond initial demand for the car, which far outpaced supply. Subtle styling changes that set it apart from the 1990 Corvette coupe, along with low production

numbers in its first year, marked the ZR1 as a car collector's target. Estimates from Chevrolet had only 2,000 ZR1 Corvettes being produced for 1990.

The ZR1, at first glance, looked similar to the Corvette coupe, but it was stretched 1 inch and was 3 inches wider to accommodate an increased rear tread width. The telltale difference between the base Corvette and the ZR1 was the high-performance model's revised rectangular tail lamps.

What really put a stamp of uniqueness on the ZR1 was the drive train. The ZR1's all-aluminum 350-cid LT5 V-8 produced enough thrust to launch the Corvette from 0 to 60 mph in 4.3 seconds. The LT5 was rated at 375 hp and was constructed by boat-engine specialists at Mercury Marine. An AZF six-speed manual transmission was mated to the ZR1's power plant. This transmission was offered as optional equipment on 1989 Corvette coupes. The ZR1 did not have an automatic transmission option.

The first 1990 Corvette ZR1 to orbit public roads was purchased by Glenn Ross of Marietta, Ga. His car was the 114th ZR1 produced and the first delivered to a dealership. "The ZR1 is head and shoulders above the Ferraris and Lamborghinis," Ross said. "It drives like it's on silk." He added that he placed the order for his ZR1 14 months prior to its arrival in September 1989. Ninety-five percent of the cars were pre-ordered by March 1988.

The factory list price of a ZR1, as shipped with both the automatic climate control and one-piece removable top options, was $62,675. This was compared to the 1990 Corvette coupe's asking price of $37,900. But, because of the great demand for ZR1s, dealers asked for—and got—prices that were out of this world.

1991 CHEVROLET CORVETTE ZR1

After the launch of the first ZR1 Corvette the previous year, the 1991 model had very few changes. The "super Vette" again had a convex rear fascia and two rectangular tail lamps on either side of the car, but standard Corvettes were restyled at the rear to more closely resemble the hi-po model.

A new front end with wrap-around parking lamps was used on both models, along with new side-panel louvers and wider body-color body side moldings. Although more like the standard 1971 Corvette in a visual sense, the ZR1 again had different doors and a wider rear end to accommodate its 11-inch-wide rear wheels. Also, the high-mounted stop lamp went on the roof of the ZR1, instead of on the rear fascia as on other Corvettes.

All ZR1s were again equipped with ABS II-S anti-lock braking and a driver's side airbag, as well as a standard anti-theft system. The ZR1 was again powered by a 32-valve DOHC 5.7-liter V-8 matched with a six-speed transaxle. Its "valet" power access system was offered again, but it was changed in that it now defaulted to normal power on each ignition cycle. The "full power" light was relocated next to the valet key.

On ZR1s, the fourth and fifth symbols in the vehicle identification number were YZ. The last six symbols indicate the sequential production number starting with 800001 for the ZR1, which came only as a hatchback coupe. The 1991 ZR1 listed for $64,138 and Chevrolet built 2,044 of them.

The ZR1's RPO LT5 Tuned-Port-Injected engine was a 90-degree overhead valve V-8 with four valves per cylinder and four overhead camshafts. The 350-cid (5.7-liter) engine utilized a cast-iron block and aluminum cylinder head. It had hydraulic lifters, an 11.0:1 compression ratio, 375 hp at 5800 rpm and 370 ft. lbs. of torque at 5600 rpm.

1992 CHEVROLET CORVETTE ZR1

(Jerry Heasley photo)

Only 502 1992 Corvette ZR1s were built.

The year 1992 was another of little change in the makeup of the Corvette line. The ZR1 was basically a carry-over from the year previous with new model badges above the rear fender vents. It was again powered by the 32-valve DOHC 5.7-liter V-8 producing 375 hp at 5,800 rpm. The engine was matched with a six-speed transaxle.

Both the ZR1 and the regular Corvette had new rectangular exhausts. A new all-black dash treatment, a relocated digital speedometer and improved instrument graphics were adopted. A Traction Control system became standard equipment along with new Goodyear GS-C tires. The standard tires were Goodyear Eagle GTS, size P275/40ZR17 up front and P315/35ZR17 in the rear.

The 1992 Corvettes came in white, yellow, black, bright aqua metallic, polo green II metallic, black rose metallic, dark red metallic, quasar blue metallic and bright red. Interiors came in blue, beige, black, light beige, light gray, red and white. The price for the ZR1 rose to $65,318. It weighed in at 3,465 lbs., but sales were light weight with only 502 of the muscle Corvettes built.

On August 28, 1992, Chevrolet Motor Division announced that David McLellan would be retiring as Corvette chief engineer. McLellan had taken over the Corvette program after the retirement of Zora Arkus-Duntov in 1975. Chevy's assistant manager of public relations Tom Hoxie said in 1992, "During McLellan's 18-year tenure he transformed the Corvette from an American muscle car into an internationally acclaimed, high-performance sports car that runs rings around a host of more expensive European and Japanese models." Said McLellan, "I can't think of a better time for me to be leaving. No manufacturer has ever built 1 million sports cars and at the age of 40 the Corvette is stronger than it's ever been. Our all-new car is a few years old and it's time to let someone else put their stamp on it."

1993 CHEVROLET CAMARO Z/28

The 1993 Chevrolet Camaro Z/28 could do the quarter mile in 14 seconds flat with its 275-hp, 350-cid V-8.

By 1993, muscle cars like the Z/28 had come a long way with interior creature comforts.

Despite the softening of the old pony car market, Chevrolet didn't look for any easy way out when it introduced its fourth-generation Camaro a few months into the 1993 model run. It featured an all-new body, reworked chassis and a Z/28 that came only one way—fast.

While the 1982-1992 Camaro (and its close relative the Pontiac Firebird) stuck to rear-wheel drive and solid V-8 power in a changing automotive world of front drive and less cylinders, it still left room for improvement, mainly in handling and structural tightness. The new 1993 Camaro (and Firebird) improved on performance, handling and even comfort.

For the 1993 model year, only a hatchback coupe was offered. It came two ways, in a base model priced at $13,889 with a 3.4-liter, 160-hp V-6, and as a Z/28 priced at $17,269.

The body, while much sleeker than the old style, featured a 68-degree raked windshield and steel structure to which composite (plastic) panels were attached. Only the rear quarters and hood were steel. Optional removable glass roof panels retailed for $895.

A new short-and-long arm coil spring front suspension and power rack-and-pinion steering replaced the old struts and re-circulating ball setup. The rear continued with coils with multi-link bars.

By checking the Z/28 box on the order form you got a LT1 350-cid V-8 with aluminum heads. It was rated at 275 hp (up 30 from

1992). You also got a standard Borg-Warner T-56 six-speed manual transmission, four-wheel antilock disc brakes, 16 x 8-inch aluminum wheels and Goodyear GA P235/55R16 rubber. Z-rated GS-C Goodyears were optional at $144.

If you kept the standard tires, you also got a governed top speed of 108 mph, which you could hit in fourth, fifth or sixth gear. Going for the Z-rated doughnuts meant the Z/28 could do what it wanted, which several magazines found exceeded 150 mph.

The 1993 Camaro sat on the same 101.1-inch wheelbase as in the past. Length was up .6 of an inch to 193.2 inches while the car's width ballooned by 1.7 inches to 74.1 inches. Height was up nearly an inch to 51.3 inches.

Optional on the Z/28 at $595 was the Turbo Hydra-Matic 4L60 automatic. Like the LT1 engine, the transmission had seen service on the Corvette.

The no-excuses Z/28 was an immediate hit with the car magazines. *Car & Driver* pitted it against the Ford Mustang Cobra and declared the Z-28 the fastest with a 0-60 in 5.3 seconds and a quarter-mile romp of 14 seconds flat at 100 mph. *Motor Trend* tested several performance cars and noted that the Camaro—with a top speed of 151 mph—represented the "biggest bang for the buck" of the bunch.

1993 CHEVROLET CAMARO INDY PACE CAR

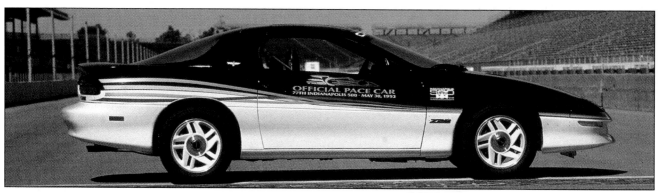

Pacing the Indianapolis 500 in 1993 was a Camaro Z/28.

The 1993 through 1995 Chevrolet Camaro Z/28 models are essentially the same cars. They differ mainly in details, such as what type of fuel-injection system they use, control of each of the transmissions, axle ratios, colors of the numbers on the dash and so forth. However, if you want one of these modern muscle cars that really stands out in looks, history and value, then grab yourself a 1993 Indianapolis 500 Pace Car replica.

A new Camaro paced the Indianapolis 500-mile race for the fourth time that year (the previous years for Camaro pace cars were 1967, 1969 and 1982). Chevrolet provided the Indianapolis Motor Speedway with three "Official Pace Cars" and another 125 replicas for track officials. In addition, dealers were to get 500 copies, with another 20 reserved for Canada. The tally puts the 1993 Camaro Indy Pace Car replica squarely in the limited-production class, at least as far as Chevrolets go.

Only the Camaro hatchback coupe was available for 1993. The replica came with a special black-and-white exterior and multi-colored accents. Interiors featured the same color combination with a new 3D knitting process for the seats and door panels. A gold hood emblem topped it all off. Mechanically, nothing special was needed, as the 350-cid 275-hp LT1 Corvette V-8 met Indianapolis Motor Speedway's performance requirements without modification. "Performance-wise, every 1993 Camaro Z/28 is capable of pacing Indy," said Jim Perkins, Chevrolet general manager and driver of the pace car for the 500.

Camaro Indy Pace Cars were fitted with automatic transmissions. Chevrolet installed the 4L60 Hydra-Matic with a .70 fourth gear. The rest of the Z/28 driveline and underpinnings were just fine for track duty. Camaro Z/28s equipped with the optional six-speed manual transmission were clocked in the 155-mph range by magazines in 1993.

1993 CORVETTE LT1

(Jerry Heasley photo)

The 1993 Corvette LT1 convertible boasted a 300-hp engine and $41,000-plus price tag.

First released as a 1984 model, the C4 Corvette picked up the trick ZR1 option for 1990 and a second-generation small-block LT1 base engine for 1992. This LT1 engine was so good that it reduced demand for the much more expensive ZR1. It came connected to a four-speed overdrive automatic transmission. A six-speed manual gearbox was optional.

The LT1 was a 90-degree overhead-valve engine with an aluminum cylinder head. The 350-cid (5.7-liter) hydraulic-lifter V-8 had a bore and stroke of 4.00 x 3.48 inches, a 10.5:1 compression ratio and multi-port fuel injection. It produced 300 hp at 5000 rpm and 340 ft. lbs. of torque at 3600 rpm. The 1993 LT1-powered Corvette did 0 to 60 mph in 5.4 seconds.

For 1993, a great deal of interest was focused on the Corvette's 40th anniversary. To mark the occasion, a 40th Anniversary Appearance Package was offered for the $34,145 coupe or $41,745 convertible. Coughing over another $1,455 for the package got you Ruby Red paint, Ruby Red leather seats with special embroidery and appropriate badges. You did have to kick in $305 more for a power seat mechanism, whether you really wanted it or not.

Vehicle identification numbers for LT1-powered Corvettes ran from 1G1YY[ ]3PXP5100001 to 1G1YY[ ]3PXP5121142. The first symbol 1 indicated U.S. built. The G indicated General Motors product. The second 1 indicated Chevrolet. The fourth and fifth symbols were YY for a base Corvette. The sixth symbol was 2 for a coupe or

3 for a convertible. The seventh symbol indicated the type of passenger-restraint system. The eighth symbol indicated the engine and was a P in the case of the LT1 5.7-liter MPFI V-8. The ninth symbol was a check digit that varied. The 10th symbol indicated the model year, P for 1993. The 11th symbol indicated the assembly plant, 5 for Bowling Green, Kentucky. The last six symbols indicated the sequential production number starting with 100001 for LT1s. The LT1 engine code suffixes were ZVA with automatic transmission and ZVB with manual transmission.

The Sport Coupe sold for $34,595, weighed 3,333 lbs. and had a production run of 15,898 units. The convertible was priced at $41,195. It tipped the scales at 3,383 lbs. and 5,712 were built. Total model-year production was 21,590 cars. The RPO Z25 40th Anniversary Package was added to 6,749 cars with no body style breakout available.

1993 CHEVROLET CORVETTE ZR1

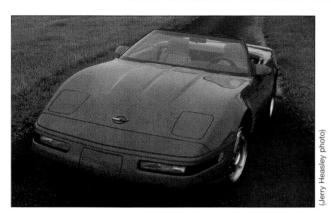

(Jerry Heasley photo)

The 1993 Corvette ZR1 was clocked at 178 mph by *Road and Track* magazine.

The ZR1's 5.7-liter LT-5 V-8 was upgraded this year and featured significant power and torque increases. Improvements in the LT5 engine's cylinder head and valve train included "blending" the valve heads and creating three-angle valve inserts, plus the use of a sleeve spacer to help maintain port alignment of the injector manifold. These added up to a 30-hp increase and higher torque rating. In addition, the LT-5 was now equipped with four-bolt main bearings, platinum-tipped spark plugs and an electrical linear exhaust gas recirculating (EGR) system. Improved air flow from the cylinder head improvements and valve train refinements boosted its rating from 375 hp to 405 hp!

A special 40th anniversary appearance package that included an exclusive "ruby red" exterior and interior with color-keyed wheel centers, headrest embroidery and bright emblems on the hood, deck and side gills was optional equipment on all models, including ZR1s. The 1993 Corvette also introduced GM's first Passive Keyless Entry system whereby simply leaving or approaching the Corvette automatically unlocked or locked the appropriate doors. The 1993 Corvette was also the first North American automobile to use recycled sheet-molded-compound body panels.

The ZR-1 again used a six-speed transaxle. Arctic white, black, bright aqua metallic, polo green II metallic, competition yellow, ruby red, torch red, black rose metallic, dark red metallic and quasar blue metallic were the colors offered this year. Interiors came in beige, black, light beige, light gray, red, ruby red and white.

ZR1s were identified by a YZ in the vehicle identification number. The last six symbols indicate the sequential production number starting with 800001 for ZR1s. The engine code suffix ZVC identified the 350-cid 405-hp RPO LT5 V-8 used in the ZR1 model only.

The 1991 ZR1 Special Performance Package was actually a $31,683 option for the hatchback coupe and brought its base price up to $66,278. In standard trim, the ZR1-optioned hatchback weighed 3,503 lbs. Only 448 cars were built with the ZR1 option this year.

Motor Trend tested a 1993 Corvette ZR1 and found it could do 0 to 60 mph in 4.9 seconds. Quarter-mile performances were 13.1 seconds and 109.6 mph for the ZR. As for top speed, *Road and Track* did 178 mph in another ZR1.

1994 CHEVROLET CAMARO Z/28

The 1994 Chevrolet Camaro Z/28 was considered by *Car & Driver* to easily be the best in its class.

(Jerry Heasley photo)

When the 1994s came out, there was mixed news for Camaro fans. A new convertible was added, being built in-house for the first time since the 1969 models. It listed for $22,565, compared to $19,235 for the coupe. At first, it lacked some of the heavier suspension parts of the coupe and was governed to 104 mph.

Other 1994 changes included a new electronically controlled automatic and a Computer Aided Gear Selection device for the six-speed that, similar to the Corvette, hit you with a first to fourth shift if you were not engaged in hard acceleration. Back to the good side, the LT1 got sequential port fuel injection, an improvement over multi-port.

All 1994 Camaros were equipped with improved brakes and the Z/28 included four-wheel disc brakes. Ordering the 1LE special performance suspension package was simplified, as it now appeared as a regular production option (RPO) on the order form.

The Camaro interior had modest changes. High-contrast black knobs and white graphics were used in place of the gray knobs and yellow graphics of 1993. Camaro Z/28s with optional speed-rated Goodyear tires had 150-mph speedometers substituted for the stock 115-mph type. Also new were sun visors with storage provisions, flood light door illumination and a new optional keyless entry system. Flame red was a new color of fabric available.

Highlights of the Camaro's standard equipment list included driver and passenger air bags, ABS VI anti-lock brakes, intermittent windshield wipers, a tilt steering wheel, left- and right-hand covered visor mirrors, side-window defoggers, a PASS-Key II theft-deterrent system, cup holders, in-door storage pockets, a lighted console and a locking glove box. Two new exterior colors were dark bright teal and polo green metallic.

The newly bodied 1994 Mustang GT and Cobra were natural comparisons for the year old Camaro Z/28, which had little trouble holding its class crown. *Car & Driver* pointed to the Camaro's top speed of 156 mph versus 137 mph for the Mustang, among other numbers, in noting the Mustang got "hammered."

Chevrolet built a total of 112,539 Camaro coupes and 7,260 Camaro convertibles in 1994, but it is not known how many had the Z/28 package.

1994 CHEVROLET IMPALA SS

The 1994 Chevrolet Impala SS sedan was a throwback in many ways and a definite collector car.

From a 1960s perspective, the 1994 Chevrolet Impala SS is an odd duck. It's a four-door sedan, it's big and it caters to comfort as much as performance. However, putting the SS back in context, it ranks as one of the last remnants of the old big-horsepower era. It combines a large-for-its-time V-8 with ample horsepower, rear-wheel drive and full-frame construction.

The last Impala SS had been the 1969 model. As domestic automakers converted to front-wheel drive, smaller engines and smaller bodies, big high-performance cars disappeared. Chevrolet continued offering a full-size, rear-wheel-drive car with V-8 power, but downsized it in 1977. The Caprice name was usually attached, but a few low-buck Impala models were produced through the 1985 model year.

There was a controversial restyling for 1991, utilizing basically the same chassis. The Caprice was popular with the police and taxi segments of the market, but "civilian" buyers tended to be on the senior side. All that changed in November of 1992 when Chevrolet tricked up a Caprice sedan for the Specialty Equipment Market Association (SEMA) show in Las Vegas. It had an LT1 350-cid V-8, 17-inch aluminum wheels, 50-series tires, full rear-wheel cutouts, slightly modified rear quarter windows and a blackout-style paint job.

Chevy went to its retired name farm and revived the Impala SS tag and reaction at the SEMA show and other previews that followed was the same: "Build it!" This is just what Chevrolet Motor Division general manager Jim Perkins wanted to hear and on Valentine's Day of 1994 the first of the new Impala SS models rolled off an assembly line in the GM Assembly Plant in Arlington, Texas.

Unlike some production versions of show cars, the SS was not a watered-down, whimped-out version. The 260-hp version of the 350-cid LT1 came standard and was attached to a 4L60-E automatic transmission. The wheels were special 17 x 8.5-inch units like those on the show car. They were wrapped with P255/50ZR17 tires.

Four-wheel ventilated disc brakes were used at all four corners, as were stiffer coil springs and DeCarbon shocks similar to those on the Camaro Z/28. The result was a 20 percent stiffer suspension, much better handling and a still comfortable ride. From the police car parts bin came front and rear anti-roll bars and other hardware aimed at going fast on straight or curved roads.

On the outside was the same rear spoiler, altered rear quarter windows, black-on-black badging and blacked-out grille and body moldings. Inside, bucket-type front seats were part of the gray leather interior, which was trimmed with black satin pieces. "We already have 5,000 dealer orders," said Jeff Hulbert, Chevrolet's general marketing manager, when the first Impala SS was made.

It is true, you could get the same LT1 V-8 in a Chevy Caprice Classic wagon, Buick Roadmaster or Cadillac Fleetwood, but those cars just weren't in the same ballpark as the Impala SS, which carried a delivered price of $22,495. That was about $2,700 over a base Caprice Classic sedan. Compared to the V-8-powered competition from Europe and Japan, the Impala SS cost about half as much.

Chevrolet listed a 0 to 60-mph time of 7.1 seconds, but a spirited *Car & Driver* crew got a 6.5-second run and a quarter-mile of 15 seconds with a 92 mph trap speed. A couple of SS examples were even quicker. GM put a 502 big-block in a test car and got 0 to 60 mph in 6.0 seconds and a 14.5 quarter mile at 98.2 mph. Horsepower was claimed to be 385. Reeves Callaway converted customers' Impalas into the SuperNatural SS with a 383-cid small-block with 404 horses. *Motor Trend* performance figures were 0 to 60 mph in 5.9 seconds and for the quarter mile 14.0 seconds at 100.3 mph!

The late-model Impala SS turned out to be a small-volume niche car in the GM scheme of things. For the model's first year, 6,303 units were built. Of course, instant collector status was assured for the Impala SS. We may not see anything like it again, at least from General Motors.

1994 CHEVROLET CORVETTE LT1

The 1994 Corvette LT1 had a few goodies the '93 version didn't, including standard leather seats.

Several refinements that focused on safety and smoother operation were the order for 1994 Corvettes. A passenger-side airbag was added and all Corvettes now offered dual airbags. In addition, other interior changes included new carpeting, new door-trim panels, new seats, a new steering wheel, a redesigned instrument panel and a restyled console. Other new equipment included an optional rear-axle ratio, revised spring rates, a convertible backlight with heated glass and new exterior colors.

The 1994 Corvettes came in Arctic white, admiral blue, black, bright aqua metallic, polo green metallic, competition yellow, copper metallic, torch red, black rose metallic and dark red metallic. Interiors came in beige, black, light beige, light gray, red and white. Standard features included a removable body-color roof panel for hatchbacks or a convertible top. All Corvette convertibles except those with polo green metallic finish could be ordered with one of three top colors: beige, black or white cloth top. The white convertible top was not available for polo green metallic cars. Leather seats became standard upholstery.

The vehicle identification numbering system was basically unchanged for 1994. LT1 Corvettess were numbered 1G1YY[2/3]2P9R5100001 to 1G1YY[2/3]2P9R5122882. The 10th symbol indicating model year changed to R. The 1994 LT1 engine suffixes were ZWA for the cars with automatic transmission and ZWB for those with the optional six-speed manual gearbox.

The hatchback sport coupe was $36,185 this year and weighed in at 3,317 lbs. The $42,960 convertible was a tad heavier at 3,358 lbs. Chevrolet built 17,984 coupes and 5,320 ragtops. Total model-year production including ZR1s was 23,330 units.

Carryover specifications included a 96.2-inch wheelbase, a 178.5-inch overall length and a height of 46.3 inches for the coupe and 47.3 inches for the convertible with its top raised. The width was 70.7 inches and the front and rear tracks were 57.7 and 59.1 inches, respectively. Standard tires were P255/45ZR15 Goodyear Eagle GTs up front with P285/40ZR17 Goodyear Eagle GTs at the rear.

1994 CHEVROLET CORVETTE ZR1

Several refinements that focused on safety and smoother operation were the order for all 1994 Corvettes. A passenger-side airbag was added and all Corvettes now offered dual airbags. In addition, other interior changes included new carpeting, new door-trim panels, new seats, a new steering wheel, a redesigned instrument panel and a restyled console. The ZR1 also received new non-directional wheels for 1994.

The ZR1 again used the LT5 5.7-liter V-8. It was fitted with a six-speed manual transmission. Arctic white, admiral blue, black, bright aqua metallic, polo green metallic, competition yellow, copper metallic, torch red, black rose metallic and dark red metallic were the 1994 colors. Interiors came in beige, black, light beige, light gray, red and white.

As with the LT1, the 1994 Corvette ZR1 received only subtle changes from the previous year.

Vehicle identification numbers were visible through the windshield on the driver's side and the ZR1 numbers were 1G1YZ22J9R5800001 to 1G1YZ22J9R5800448. The first symbol 1 indicates U.S. Built. The second symbol G indicates General Motors product. The third symbol 1 indicates Chevrolet Motor Division vehicle. The fourth and fifth symbols were YZ for all Corvette ZR1s and the sixth symbol was 2 for the hatchback. The seventh symbol indicates the restraint code: 1 = Active manual belts, 2 = Active manual belts with driver and passenger inflatable restraint system, 3 = Active manual belts with driver-inflatable restraint system, 4 = Passive automatic belts, 5 = Passive automatic belts with driver inflatable restraint system and 6 = Passive automatic belts with driver and passenger inflatable restraint system. The eighth symbol indicates engine with J used for the RPO LT5 5.7-liter MFI V-8. The ninth symbol is a check digit that varies. The 10th symbol indicates model year (R for 1994). The 11th symbol 5 identified the Bowling Green, Kentucky assembly plant. The last six symbols indicate the sequential production number. Engine code suffixes for 1994 Corvette ZR1s were ZWC for the 350-cid 405-hp RPO LT5 V-8 with 11.0:1 compression and manual transmission.

The ZR1 option package actually saw a slight price reduction to $31,258 in 1994, but the cost of the base Corvette hatchback rose to $36,185. This made the total cost of the ZR1 higher at $67,443. The curb weight this year was 3,503 lbs. Production was, once again, 448 cars with the option.

1995 CHEVROLET CAMARO Z/28

The 1995 Chevrolet Camaro Z-28 convertible could be had for about $23,000.

Camaro returned with a coupe and convertible in 1995. Each body style was offered in base and Z/28 trim levels. The Z/28 rag-top listed for $23,095 and weighed 3,480 lbs. The 3,390-lb. Z/28 coupe was a bit more of a bargain at $17,915.

New-for-1995 features included body-colored outside dual sport mirrors on all models and an optional monochromatic roof treatment for the Z/28 with T-tops. Chrome-plated wheel covers and aluminum wheels were also optional and, on Z/28s, could be shod with optional Goodyear speed-rated tires (including a 150-mph speedometer). Also optional was an acceleration-slip regulation system.

The Z/28 again featured the 5.7-liter LT-1 V-8 engine which had a 4.00 x 3.48-inch bore and stroke, 10.5:1 compression ratio, four-barrel carburetor and 275 hp at 5000 rpm. It came hooked to a Borg-Warner T-56 six-speed manual transmission. A four-speed automatic was optional in Z/28s.

Road and Track held a competition in 1995 for the fastest cars in America and a nearly new 1995 Camaro did 155.3 mph. It was *driven* to the test, while its competitors were mostly trailered.

1995 CHEVROLET IMPALA SS

The Impala SS four-door sedan returned for its second appearance in 1995. It was again a specialty entry in the Chevrolet's Series 1B Caprice Classic lineup. The Impala SS was coded as the L19/BL5 model. This year it had a base price of $22,910 and tipped the scales at 4,036 lbs. That was about $1,000 more and 200 lbs. less than in the previous season.

As in 1994, the Impala SS featured a host of special equipment as part of its standard price. The assortment included five-spoke 17 x 8.5-inch aluminum wheels, 17-inch B.F. Goodrich Comp T/A tires, quick-ratio power steering; air conditioning with CFC-free refrigerant, a unique grille, a rear deck lid spoiler, Impala SS emblems, reshaped rear quarter windows with inserts, four-wheel disc brakes, an anti-lock braking system, a center console, a leather-wrapped steering wheel, dual air bags, black satin-finished trim, gray cloth upholstery, an electronic tachometer, and a special ride and handling suspension system with DeCarbon shock absorbers.

Gray leather upholstery trim was optional.

The Impala SS was powered by the 5.7-liter (350-cid) LT1 Corvette V-8 engine with platinum-tipped spark plugs and a stainless-steel exhaust system, which produced 260 hp. It was linked to a 4L60-E electronic automatic transmission with a floor-mounted gear shifter. Performance was in the same bracket as with the 1994 model. Different sources listed times between 6.5 and 7.1 seconds for 0 to 60-mph runs. (The 7.1-second figure was the official one from Chevrolet Motor Division). A typical quarter-mile trial was done in 15 seconds at 92 mph.

Several new colors were introduced and added to the original monotone black color scheme in 1995. Black, however, remained the most popular with 9,858 cars being finished in that shade. Dark cherry was the second most popular Impala SS color and was put on 7,134 cars. Another 4,442 Impala SS sedans were done in dark gray green, another new-for-1995 color.

1995 CHEVROLET CORVETTE LT1

The 1995 Corvette LT1 coupe was the Indy Pace Car.

Changes on the 1995 LT1-powered Corvette included the addition of heavy-duty brakes with larger front rotors as standard equipment, along with new low-rate springs. De Carbon gas-charged shock absorbers were used for improved ride quality.

In addition to exterior color changes, Corvettes featured a new "gill" panel behind the front wheel openings to help quickly distinguish the 1995 models from predecessors. Other improvements included reinforced interior stitching and a quieter cooling fan. Engine and transmission offerings remained unchanged from the year previous.

The year's colors were dark purple metallic, dark purple metallic and Arctic white, Arctic white, admiral blue, black, bright aqua metallic, polo green metallic, competition yellow, torch red and dark red metallic. Interiors came in beige, black, light beige, light gray, red and white. Standard features included a removable body-color roof panel for hatchbacks or a convertible top.

All Corvette convertibles except those with dark purple metallic and Arctic white or polo green metallic finish could be ordered with one of three top colors: beige, black or white. The dark purple metallic and Arctic white combination was available only with a white convertible top, which was again not available for polo green metallic cars. Leather seats were standard equipment.

For 1995, the LT1 VIN range was 1G1YY[2/3]P7S5100001 to 1G1YY[2/3]P7S5120294. S was the 10th symbol, indicating 1995. Engine code suffixes were: ZUC with automatic and ZUD with manual transmission. The coupe sold for $36,785 and the convertible for $43,665. Weights for the two models were 3,203 and 3,360 lbs., respectively. Chevy built 15,771 coupes and 4,971 convertibles.

The 1995 Corvette LT1 was selected to serve as the official pace car for the Indy 500. An RPO Z4Z Indy 500 Pace Car replica option was released for convertibles only and had a $2,816 price tag. It was the third time (1978 and 1986 were the previous years) that a Corvette paced the race at the famed Brickyard. The dark purple metallic over Arctic white Corvette Official Pace Car was driven by 1960 Indy 500 winner Jim Rathmann. Chevrolet built a total of 527 Corvettes in 1995 with the RPO Z4Z Indy 500 Pace Car replica package.

(Jerry Heasley photo)

Chevy built almost 5,000 Corvette LT1 convertibles in 1994. They carried a price tag of $43,665.

1995 CHEVROLET CORVETTE ZR1

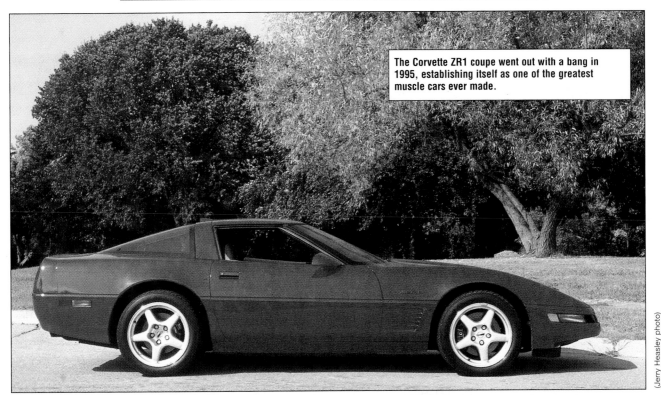

The Corvette ZR1 coupe went out with a bang in 1995, establishing itself as one of the greatest muscle cars ever made.

(Jerry Heasley photo)

The 1995 Corvette ZR1 was cool from all angles, but carried a sticker price of more than $68,000.

(Jerry Heasley photo)

The big news of 1995 for Corvette fans was the final appearance of the ZR1 performance coupe after several years of availability. The last of these hot Corvettes was built on April 28, 1995, in the Corvette assembly plant in Bowling Green, Kentucky. It was then driven across the street to the National Corvette Museum, where it was put on exhibition.

Was the ZR1 a bad car? Absolutely not! It was easily the best Corvette ever made. It was also the most expensive production Corvette Chevrolet ever made. ZR1 owners are extremely loyal and point out the advantages of the car's docile driving personality, as much as its all-out performance. Unfortunately, not enough loyal buyers could be found to support the ZR1.

Part of Chevrolet's motivation for dropping the car was that there was simply not much difference between the regular LT1 Corvette and the costlier ZR1. Commenting in *Car & Driver*,

Chevrolet general manager Jim Perkins said, "It began to set in that there was no differentiation between the two cars except for the engine option."

The 1995 Corvettes came in dark purple metallic, dark purple metallic and Arctic white, Arctic white, admiral blue, black, bright aqua metallic, polo green metallic, competition yellow, torch red and dark red metallic. Beige, black, light beige, light gray, red and white interiors were offered. Leather seats were standard equipment.

The Vehicle numbering system was the same as 1995 with new ZR1s numbered from 1G1YZ22JOS5800001 to 1G1YZ22JOS 5800448. ZUF was the engine code for the 350-cid 405-hp RPO LT5 V-8 with 11.0:1 compression and manual transmission that was used in the ZR1 model only. This year the base Corvette sport coupe retailed for $36,785 and the ZR1 option price was unchanged, so it cost a minimum of $68,043 to buy one of the 448 made.

1996 CHEVROLET CAMARO SS

The 1996 Chevrolet Camaro SS could run the quarter mile in 13.8 seconds with the help of a slick air-induction system.

(Jerry Heasley photo)

Ed Hamburger first got involved in the high-performance field by drag racing Mopars in the 1960s. Later, in the 1980s, he created SLP Engineering, of Red Bank, New Jersey—a company that converted Pontiac Firebirds and Chevrolet Camaros into "street-legal performance" machines. His 1992 Firehawk version of the Firebird was a successful venture for SLP, as well as for the Pontiac dealers who sold the SLP package.

In 1996, Hamburger started working in conjunction with Chevrolet Motor Division to produce a Camaro muscle car that could be sold by Chevrolet dealers as a high-priced, factory-approved option package.

The secret of the 1996 Camaro SS was a special air-induction system which, when combined with an optional low-restriction exhaust system, boosted horsepower of the 10.4:1 compression 350-cid LT1 V-8 to 305 at 5000 rpm and torque to 325 ft. lbs. at 2400 rpm. The engine had a cast-iron block and aluminum cylinder heads.

It came with a sequential port fuel injection system and was hooked up to a six-speed manual transmission.

Like any *real* muscle car, the 1996 Camaro SS needed an image and a "feel" to suit its higher-than-standard performance capabilities. Therefore, the SS package also included a special composite hood with an "ant eater" air scoop, 17 x 9.0-inch Corvette ZR1-style wheels, BF Goodrich Comp T/A tires and special SS badges. It also featured a Torsen limited-slip differential, Bilstein shock absorbers, progressive-rate springs and performance-altered lower rear control arms.

The Camaro SS was a roughly $28,000 package. It weighed in at 3,565 lbs. and, while that didn't exactly make it a lightweight, it could accelerate from 0 to 60 mph in 5.3 seconds. It handled the quarter mile in 13.8 seconds at 101.4 mph. Speaking of handling, it could brake from 60 mph in 117 feet and registered 0.88 gs in lateral acceleration testing.

1996 CHEVROLET IMPALA SS

When the original Chevrolet Super Sport debuted in the mid-'60s "four on the floor" and a chrome-plated tachometer were the hallmarks of a cool car. Both were back on the 1996 Impala SS, but with a high-tech twist. The Impala SS had a new floor-mounted shifter to control its sophisticated four-speed automatic transmission. A new analog tachometer kept tabs on its powerful LT1 V8.

The heart of the Impala SS was again the Corvette-derived 5.7-liter LT1 V-8 with sequential fuel injection (SFI) recalibrated to deliver 260 hp at 5000 rpm and 330 ft. lbs. of torque at 2400 rpm. It came mated to the GM electronically controlled 4L60-E four-speed automatic transmission, which harnessed the LT1's potent performance with smooth and precise shift points. A 3.08:1 final-drive ratio and a limited-slip differential helped provide quick acceleration.

The 1996 Impala SS was more than just a one-dimensional stop-light sensation. A special ride and handling suspension derived from the Chevrolet law enforcement package, coupled with quick-ratio power steering (12.7:1 vs. the standard 15.3:1 ratio), added an impressive level of agility for such a spacious sedan.

Specially tuned de Carbon gas-pressure shocks—a luxury normally found only on Europe's finest cars—provided impressive dampening to maintain critical road feel. Tuned front and rear stabilizer bars were also fitted to help flatten cornering.

The Impala SS again wore aggressive P255/50ZR-17 speed-rated tires, along with lightweight 17 x 8.5-inch, five-spoke cast-alloy wheels. Standard four-wheel, ventilated disc brakes (12-inch diameter front and rear) and a four-wheel anti-lock brake system (ABS) allowed the Impala SS to stop as confidently as it went.

The 1996 Impala SS continued with the three monochromatic paint schemes of 1995 and production included 19,085 Black cars, 12,180 Dark Cherry cars and 10,676 Dark Gray Green cars. Body-color front and rear fascias, rocker moldings, door handles, key locks, tail amp moldings and an antenna base were used. To add to its svelte style, body-side moldings, rear deck-lid moldings and external ornamentation were deleted. The Impala SS also sported a body-color grille, body-color 3-D Impala SS scripts along its flanks, a unique rear deck-lid spoiler and "stylish" Impala emblems on the sail panels and rear deck lid.

The interior was designed for driving enthusiasts. Deeply contoured front bucket seats were outfitted with gray leather seating surfaces, as was the full-width rear seat. A center console with cup holders, a thick, leather-wrapped steering wheel and map pockets were standard in every Impala SS. Black satin finish was featured on the instrument panel and door trim panels.

The 1996 Impala SS incorporated a rugged steel safety cage that surrounded the entire passenger compartment, along with front and rear crush zones. It complied with 1997 federal side-impact standards. Standard safety features included driver and front-passenger air bags and child security rear door locks.

Impala SS filled a unique market niche for an affordable, full-size, highly styled performance sedan. Unfortunately, although the 1996 model enjoyed a nice sales boost, General Motors management decided to end production of rear-wheel-drive sedans at the end of the 1996 model year. The last Impala SS was purchased by Chevrolet collector Pinky Randall of Houghton Lake, Michigan.

1996 CHEVROLET CORVETTE GRAND SPORT/ COLLECTOR EDITION

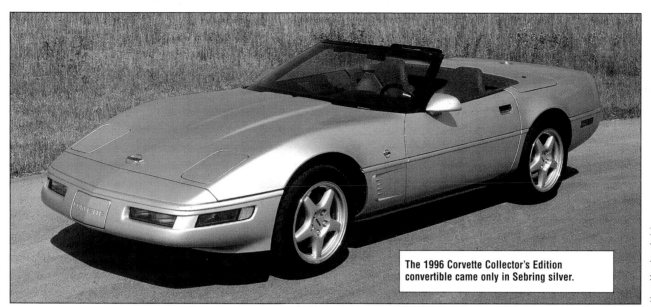

The 1996 Corvette Collector's Edition convertible came only in Sebring silver.

(Jerry Heasley photo)

The 1996 Corvette Grand Sport coupe was unmistakable.

(Jerry Heasley photo)

Nineteen ninety-six was a landmark year for Corvette enthusiasts. With the demise of the ZR1, Chevrolet offset the void by introducing two new special edition Corvettes—the Grand Sport and Collector Edition models. The Grand Sport evoked memories of its 1962-1963 racing predecessors, sporting admiral blue metallic paint, a white stripe, red "hash" marks on the left front fender and black five-spoke aluminum wheels. Powering the Grand Sport and optional in all other Corvettes was a 330-hp 5.7-liter LT4 V-8 featuring a specially prepared crankshaft, steel camshaft and water pump gears driven by a roller chain. The LT4 was available only with the six-speed manual transmission.

The Collector Edition Corvette was produced as a tribute to the final year of production of the fourth-generation Corvette (the fifth-generation model was to debut the following year). The 1996 Collector Edition Corvette featured exclusive Sebring silver paint, Collector Edition emblems, silver five-spoke aluminum wheels and a 5.7-liter LT1 V-8 fitted with a four-speed automatic transmission. The LT4 V-8 and six-speed manual transmission were both optional if you wanted to turn your Collector Edition into a muscle Corvette.

A Selective Real Time Damping system that employed sensors at each wheel to measure movement was new for 1996. Data retrieved from each wheel and the Powertrain Control Module was processed by an electronic controller that calculated the damping mode to provide optimum control. The Sebring silver metallic (code 13) cars came only with black cloth tops. Admiral blue (code 28) Grand Sports came only with white cloth tops.

The 5.7-liter (350-cid) LT4 was a 90-degree overhead valve with four valves per cylinder and four overhead camshafts. It had a cast-iron block and aluminum cylinder head. With sequential multiport fuel injection and a 10.8:1 compression ratio, it developed 330 hp at 5800 rpm and 340 ft. lbs. at 4500 rpm. According to manufacturer's test data, the LT4-powered Grand Sport did 0 to 60 mph in 4.7 seconds and the quarter mile in 13.3 seconds at 109.7 mph.

The Z15 Collector's Edition was a $1,250 option and was installed on 5,412 cars. The Z16 Grand Sport Package option, which cost $2,880 to $3,250 depending body style, was installed on 1,000 cars.

1997 CHEVROLET CAMARO Z/28 SS AND 30TH ANNIVERSARY EDITION

(Jerry Heasley photo)

The 1997 Camaro Z/28 came with either a 285-hp 350-cid engine, or a 305-hp Corvette LT1 V-8.

The Camaro observed its 30th anniversary in 1997 and Chevrolet marked the occasion by offering a 30th Anniversary Package for the Z/28 models. The $575 option consisted of Artic white paint with Hugger Orange stripes, a combination patterned after the collectible 1969 Camaro Indy Pace car. Also included in the package were white door handles, white five-spoke aluminum wheels and a white front fascia air intake. The seats inside the 30th Anniversary Camaro were trimmed in Artic White with black-and-white houndstooth cloth inserts. The floor mats and headrests had five-color embroidery.

The Z/28 came in coupe and convertible models for 1997. The closed car sold for $20,115 and weighed 3,433 lbs. The open car had a base retail price of $25,520 and weighed 3,589 lbs. All Camaros came with daytime running lights, four-wheel ABS disc brakes, dual airbags, an electronically controlled AM/FM stereo with cassette player, steel side-door guard beams and a reinforced steel safety cage. The Z/28 included a 5.7-liter sequential fuel injected V-8 and six-speed manual transmission.

The 350-cid engine developed 285 hp at 5200 rpm and 325 ft. lbs. of torque at 2400 rpm. Also available as an option was the Camaro SS Z/28, which was powered by a 305-hp Corvette LT1 V-8. It featured a hood scoop, a high-performance exhaust system, a Hurst gear shifter and a sport suspension package with Bilstein shock absorbers.

The 30th Anniversary Camaros had black-and-white seat cloth and standard dual airbags.

(Jerry Heasley photo)

1997 CORVETTE C5

The 1997 Corvette C5 coupe was billed as the "fifth-generation" Vette.

(Jerry Heasley photo)

It was another landmark year for Corvette in that the 1997 C5 model was the first all-new Corvette in 13 years and only the fifth or sixth (depending upon your viewpoint) major change in the car's 44-year history. The "fifth-generation" Corvette was offered only as a coupe in its debut year. It was designed under the direction of John Cafaro.

Among the equipment featured for the C5 was a new, more compact, 5.7-liter LS1 V-8 that produced 350 hp and 345 ft. lbs. of torque. A rear-mounted transaxle opened up more interior space and helped maintain a near 50/50 front-to-rear weight distribution. An electronic throttle control system allowed engineers a limitless range of throttle progression.

The 1997 Corvette's underbody structure was the stiffest in the car's history and consisted of two full-length, hydro-formed perime-

ter frame rails coupled to a backbone tunnel. The rails consisted of a single piece of tubular steel, replacing the 14 parts used previously.

The cockpit of the all-new Corvette featured a twin-pod design reminiscent of the original 1953 Corvette. The instrument panel contained traditional backlit analog gauges and a digital "Driver Information Center" that comprised a display of 12 individual readouts in four languages. The new-design blunt tail section allowed for smoother airflow and resulting 0.29 coefficient of drag.

The C5 Corvette was offered with a 4L60-E electronic four-speed overdrive automatic as the base transmission and a six-speed manual transmission was optional. Corvettes came in Arctic white, Sebring silver metallic, Nassau blue, black, light Carmine red metallic, torch red and fairway green metallic. Interiors came in black, light gray and firethorn red. Standard features included a removable body-color roof panel. Leather seats were standard equipment.

The C5 coupe sold for $37,495 and weighed 3,229 lbs. The car's SFI V-8 engine had a cast aluminum block and heads. Its displacement was 346 cu. in. or 5.7 liters. It had a 3.90 x 3.62-inch bore and stroke, a 10.1:1 compression ratio and 345 hp at 5600 rpm. Torque was 350 ft. lbs. at 4400 rpm. An automatic transmission with floor-mounted gear shifter was standard equipment.

The C5 rode a 104.5-inch wheelbase and had an overall length of 179.6 inches. It was 47.7 inches high and 73.6 inches wide with a 62.0-inch front tread and a 62.1-inch-wide rear tread. It rode on P245/45ZR17 tires up front and larger P275/40ZR18 tires in the rear. Chevrolet built only 9,092 of these cars.

The '97 Vette was sleek and plenty maneuverable with its compact 5.7-liter V-8.

1998 CAMARO Z/28 SS

Chevrolet did not let the Camaro rest on its laurels following its 30th birthday in 1997. The 1998 model was treated to significant changes, including the discontinuance of the Camaro RS coupe and convertible.

The Camaro Z/28 SS received some significant exterior changes in 1998, and was no longer available as an RS coupe or convertible.

(Jerry Heasley photo)

The Camaro exterior was restyled for 1998. Alterations included a redesigned hood, front fenders and front fascia, composite headlamps with reflector optics and optional fog lamps. A new four-wheel disc brake system was standard, along with an all-welded exhaust system.

The standard Camaro Z/28 was enhanced by making a "new-generation" 5.7-liter LS1 V-8 the base engine. The engine was the same aluminum block, 10.1:0 compression-ratio, sequential fuel-injected V-8 that came in Corvettes. It was rated for 305 hp at 5200 rpm and 335 ft. lbs. of torque at 4000 rpm.

Instead of the RS model, Chevrolet offered an optional Sport Appearance Package that was available on all models except the Z/28 SS. The SS was changed from a "factory-approved" aftermarket option installed by an outside "partner" company to an extra added right at the Chevrolet factory.

Cataloged as the WU8 SS Performance and Appearance Package, it included an upgrade to a 320-hp V-8, a forced-air-induction hood, a rear deck lid spoiler, 17-inch aluminum wheels, a high-performance ride and handling package and special SS badging. The option was available only for Z/28s. It retailed for $3,500. A six-speed manual gearbox was again used with V-8 engines.

1998 CHEVROLET CORVETTE C5

(Jerry Heasley photo)

The C5 convertible was back in 1998, including 1,163 Indy Pace Car versions.

In its 45th year, the Corvette returned to offering convertible and coupe models with the debut of a "topless" version of the C5 Corvette. The convertible's glass rear window was heated and the top had an "express-down" feature that released the tonneau cover and automatically lowered the windows part way at the touch of a button.

New for 1998 was a magnesium wheel option featuring light-weight wheels with a unique bronze tone. Standard features included a stainless steel exhaust system, tires capable of running for 200 miles with no air pressure, dual heated electric remote breakaway outside rearview mirrors, daytime running lamps and 5-mph front and rear bumpers.

For the fourth time (1978, 1986, 1995, 1998) a Corvette was selected to pace the Indianapolis 500. Indy 500 veteran Parnelli Jones drove the Purple and Yellow pace car.

The LS1 V-8 and four-speed automatic transmission were again the standard offering, with the T56 six-speed manual transmission optional. Corvettes were available in Artic white, Sebring silver metallic, Nassau blue metallic, black, light Carmine red metallic, torch red, magnetic red II clearcoat and fairway green metallic. Leather seats were standard and came in black, yellow, light oak,

light gray and firethorn red. Convertible tops came in black, light oak and white.

The 1998 Corvette C5 coupe retailed for $37,495 and tipped the scales at 3,245 lbs. It had a production run of 19,235 units. The convertible could be purchased for a minimum of $44,425. It weighed just a pound more than the coupe. Chevrolet built 11,849 ragtops and 1,163 had the Indy pace car package.

Some neat performance options were on the C5 Corvette's list. They included the RPO F45 Continuously Variable Real Time Damping system for $1,695; an RPO G92 performance axle ratio for $100 (not available with six-speed); an RPO JL4 Active-Handling system for $500; the RPO MN6 six-speed manual transmission for $815; the RPO Z4Z Indy Pace Car package for $5,039 with automatic transmission and $5,804 with manual transmission and the RPO Z51 Performance Handling package with Bilstein's adjustable ride-control system for $350.

Corvette made its long-awaited return to Trans-Am racing successfully by placing first in the 1998 season-opening event on the street circuit at Long Beach, California, in the AutoLink Corvette driven by veteran road racer Paul Gentilozzi.

The 1998 Corvette C5 coupe retailed for $37,495.

1999 CHEVROLET CAMARO Z/28 SS

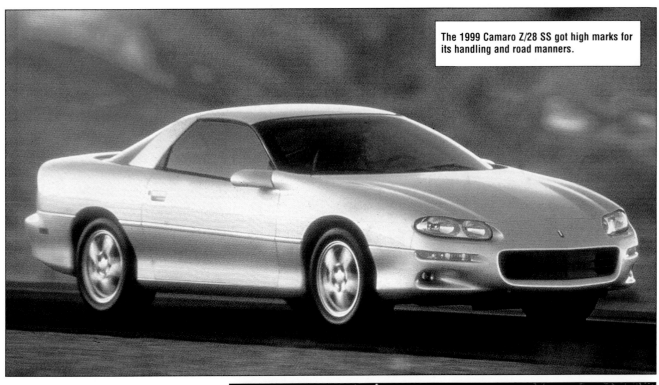

The 1999 Camaro Z/28 SS got high marks for its handling and road manners.

The Z/28 SS convertible could zip through the quarter mile in 13.9 seconds.

The 1999 Camaro Z/28 SS was the top dog in a comparison test that *Car and Driver* magazine conducted in August 1999. The face-off pitted the convertible version of Chevy's muscular pony car against counterpart ragtops wearing Pontiac Firebird Trans Am and Ford SVT Cobra Mustang badges.

Powering the Camaro Z/28 SS was a 346-cid 16-valve Chevrolet LS1 V-8 with an aluminum block and aluminum cylinder heads. It had General Motors' engine-control system with port fuel injection. This system generated 320 hp at 5200 rpm and 335 ft. lbs. of torque at 4000 rpm. The available factory transmission options included a six-speed manual gearbox or a four-speed automatic.

The $33,955 fully equipped Camaro Z/28 SS ragtop used in the road test did 0 to 60 mph in just 5.3 seconds; 0 to 100 mph in 12.8 seconds and 0 to 130 mph in 24.6 seconds. The quarter mile took all of 13.9 seconds with a trap speed of 103 mph. The car's top speed was recorded as 160 mph.

The Camaro Z/28 SS was not the fastest car in the *Car and Driver* test, but it was right up there and it really excelled where it came to roadability and handling. The original equipment P275/40ZR-17 Goodyear Eagle F1 GS tires were a big plus and it had a tight suspension, excellent steering and great brakes. The Camaro Z/28 SS could stop from 70 mph in just 175 ft. and turned 0.86 gs on a skidpad. It also turned in the best performance when a professional driver, Paul Gentilozzi, put it through its paces on a road course.

Car and Driver said that the Camaro Z/28 SS was the best car to drive on an everyday basis and suggested that ABS braking and traction control were important considerations when it came to daily driving in such a machine.

1999 CHEVROLET CORVETTE

Convertible fans were surely not disappointed in the '99 C5 Corvette.

The 1999 C5 Corvette was a star on the road and the track, capable of hitting top speeds of more than 170 mph.

(Jerry Heasley photo)

In its second year of production, the C5 Corvette made *Car and Drivers'* list of the 10 best cars. The magazine said that the car possessed "a stellar blend of value, performance, practicality and extroverted personality, as well as a few enhancements." The car was a bit on the large side, with a 104.5-inch wheelbase and 179.7-inch overall length, but it could really fly despite a weight range from 3,150 to 3,250 lbs., depending upon the body style.

The C5's pushrod aluminum engine was a masterpiece of production engineering. The 16-valve 5.7-liter V-8 had a 10:1:1 compression ratio and put out 345 hp at 5600 rpm. Buyers had a choice of hooking it to a six-speed manual transmission or a four-speed automatic. Typically, the C5 turned in 0 to 60-mph times between 4.8 seconds and 5.3 seconds depending upon the transmission and rear axle combination. It did the standing-start quarter mile in somewhere between 13.2 and 13.8 seconds. Top speed estimates recorded in various tests were from 162 to 175 mph.

A strong perimeter frame with a center backbone provided the C5 with a rigid platform that carried a host of innovative performance features including: ABS with four-wheel disc brakes, a rear-mounted transmission, a double wishbone suspension, lightweight aluminum alloy wheels, speed sensitive variable ratio steering, extended mobility tires and a choice of three different suspensions. The Corvette could brake from 70 mph in about 166 ft. and maintained .086 to 0.90 gs on a skidpad, reflecting its outstanding road-holding characteristics.

New for 1999 was the first fixed-roof Corvette to see the light of day since 1967. It was a bit less expensive to buy than the regular coupe and the convertible, but included a few high-performance extras that did not come as standard equipment with the other models. Overall, the Corvette price range was $39,361 to $46,154 in 1999.

1999 CHEVROLET LIGENFELTER TWIN-TURBO CORVETTE

The 1999 Ligenfelter Twin-Turbo Corvette was a 650-hp muscle car that *Motor Trend* (March 2000) described as "The fastest, meanest, street-legal car we've ever tested." Race driver and car builder John Ligenfelter "remanufactured" these cars in his shop in Decatur, Indiana.

For $43,995 and up, Ligenfelter Performance Engineering would convert a new Corvette into a car with nearly double the factory model's price and performance. The conversion process started with the blueprinting of the stock Corvette LS1 engine. Then Ligenfelter installed a forged steel crankshaft, billet steel connecting rods and forged aluminum pistons, ported the cylinder heads, fitted larger stainless steel valves, added a new roller-bearing camshaft and installed two Garrett turbos with up to 8.5 lbs. of boost pressure.

The 346-cid engine featured an aluminum block and heads, a 3.90 x 3.62-inch bore and stroke, a 9.5:1 compression ratio and sequential fuel injection. It produced 650 hp at 5800 rpm and 600 ft.

lbs. of torque at 5000 rpm. The engine was linked to a six-speed manual transmission.

Motor Trend tested the car with a 2.73:1 axle ratio for top speed and a 3.43:1 axle for acceleration runs. It also had some minor suspension changes like stiffer anti-roll bars, Penske adjustable shock absorbers, Baer brakes and thinner-than-stock Michelin Pilot Sport street tires (P235/235ZR18 up front and P275/235ZR18 in the rear) to improve its aerodynamics at 200-plus mph.

The Ligenfelter Twin-Turbo Corvette turned 0 to 60 mph in 3.3 seconds and went from 0 to 100 mph in 6.7 seconds (which would have been a great 0-to-60 time for any 1960s muscle car). The standing-start quarter mile was covered in 11.8 seconds at 132.1 mph with street tires. The test was then repeated with drag racing slicks and the car did the distance in 10.8 seconds at 133.5 mph. Its top speed was 226 mph!

2000 CHEVROLET SLP CAMARO RS

Over the years, Ed Hamburger's SLP Engineering had grown successful building "Bandit" Trans Ams and Firebird Firehawks for Pontiac dealers to sell as a factory option. The company had started out in Red Bank, New Jersey, with such Pontiacs, but by 2000 it was operating in Troy, Michigan, and had added Camaro conversions to its line.

The SLP package for the 2000 Camaro RS was merchandised as an $849 Chevrolet dealer option with code Y3B. Ingredients of the SLP package included the Camaro Z28 dual-slot exhaust system and black longitudinal racing stripes, plus "RS" badges on the fenders and dash. A second SLP package costing $699 added 8 x 16-inch

five-spoke alloy wheels.

The changes brought the price of the Camaro up to about $20,000 and added a little performance in addition to the appearance enhancements. Specifically, the 231-cid V-6 from the stock Camaro was tweaked to generate 205 hp at 5200 rpm and 225 ft. lbs. of torque at 4000 rpm. *Car and Driver* (December 2000) found that good enough to produce a 7.5-second 0 to 60-mph time and a 15.8-second quarter mile at 86 mph. The magazine pointed out that such performance wasn't likely to win any modern-day street races, but outdid the performance of the 350-cid V-8 used in the original "Bandit" Trans Ams that SLP created back in 1987.

2000 CHEVROLET CAMARO SS

The 2000 Camaro came in a price range from $17,500 to $35,000.

Chevrolet's Camaro entered the new millennium continuing to play its traditional role as one of the greatest values among modern muscle cars. The 2000 Camaro was offered in a choice of coupe and convertible body styles with prices ranging from a low of about $17,500 to a high of $35,000. Regardless of where you purchased on the Camaro price spectrum, you wound up with a lot of car for your hard-earned bucks.

The base model came with a 3.8-liter 200-hp V-6 that was plenty adequate for the general public. A few rungs up the ladder you got to the Z/28, which used a 305-hp version of the venerable 5.7-liter (350-hp) V-8. However, for muscle car lovers, the hot ticket was the SS, which came stuffed with a tweaked 5.7-liter motor that cranked

up 320 hp and promised 5.2-second 0 to 60-mph times, even with a 3,306-lb. curb weight.

Chevrolet offered a wide choice of convenience options and handling packages for the Camaro and those wanting to drive quick or fast were well advised to order the optional traction-control system and 1LE performance suspension.

2000 CORVETTE

The Corvette coupe, hardtop and convertible were all relatively affordable in 2000, and all featured a dandy 5.7-liter, 345-hp aluminum V-8.

Entering the new millennium, the Corvette represented a tremendous bargain in the muscle car market niche when you balanced what you got for each buck you spent and compared it to its international competitors. The base prices for the coupe, convertible and hardtop models ranged from $39,000 to $46,000 and bought you a world-class machine that could go from 0 to 60 mph in only 4.8 seconds.

The heart of the 2000 Corvette was a 5.7-liter 345-hp aluminum V-8 that rumbled like a '60s muscle car engine. It produced its peak power at 5600 rpm and could be had hooked to an RPO MN6 six-speed manual gearbox (for $815) or attached to Chevy's M30 four-speed automatic. A 2.73:1 axle was standard with the automatic transmission and a 3.15:1 performance axle was available for $500 extra. A 3.42:1 axle was standard on stick-shift cars. The 2000 Corvette took 13.2 seconds to cover the quarter mile and its top speed was in the 165-mph bracket.

Introduced as a budget performance car, the $38,900 hardtop (a.k.a. "fixed-roof coupe") came standard with the six-speed manual transmission, Goodyear Eagle F1 tires and Chevrolet's Z51 high-performance suspension kit. It wound up being a rare car, too, since Chevy made only 2,090 of them. The coupe listed for $39,475 and had a production run of 18,113 units, making it the first choice of Corvette buyers. The ragtop was base priced at $45,900 and 13,479 were built.

There were 10 colors for 2000 Corvettes and two of them were special at extra cost. The optional colors were millennium yellow and magnetic red metallic (the latter was not available for hardtops) and both finishes cost $500 above the price of a standard color. That was also the price of the optional Active Suspension System, which was ordered for 22,668 Corvettes this year. For $10 less (or $490), you could get the "Museum Delivery Package" option and pick up your new car at the National Corvette Museum in Bowling Green, Kentucky.

2001 CORVETTE Z06

The 2001 Z06 more than measured up to its Corvette predecessors.

Everyone has to have a goal in life and for Chevrolet Motor Division's Corvette engineers it was to make the already great C5 Corvette even better for 2001. As a result, we have the Z06 Corvette to lust after now. It takes the place of the previous model known as the hardtop, but it retains that body style as the sole platform for the Z06 model option. Basically, as compared to the 2000 hardtop, the Z06 gains 40 hp and loses 103 lbs. This adds up to an amazingly muscular super car. In fact, if performance terms the ZO6 can speed from 0 to 60 mph in just 4.7 seconds.

The new 346-cid LS6 small-block Chevy V-8 under the hood of this impressive car produces 385 hp at 6000 rpm and 385 ft. lbs. of torque at 4800 rpm. Its special features include modifications to the engine block casting to alleviate crankcase pressures, a special high-airflow intake manifold, a high-lift camshaft with increased duration, a 10.5:1 compression ratio and over-sized fuel injectors.

To lighten the cars, Chevrolet came up with a weight reduction of 6 lbs. for each tire and wheel, thinner glass in the windshield and backlight and a titanium exhaust system that is 17 lbs. lighter than a conventional steel exhaust system. The increased power combined with the weight reduction adds up to a car that carries just 8.09 lbs. per horsepower!

Other features of the $46,800 Corvette Z06 are a six-speed manual transmission, 12.6-inch-diameter vented disc brakes front and rear with ABS standard, forged aluminum wheels and Goodyear Eagle F1 SC tires size 265/40ZR18 up front and size 295/35ZR18 in the rear.

The interior of the Z06 includes black seats with red pleated inserts and matching door panels, but all-black door panels can be substituted. However, you can't get any other seats but the red and black ones.

CHRYSLER

1960 CHRYSLER 300-F "LETTER CAR"

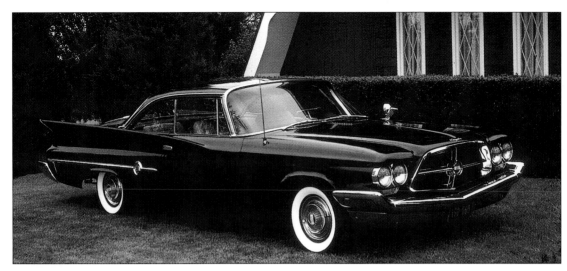

This 1960 Chrysler 300-F set a Flying Mile speed record at 144.9 mph.

When Chrysler took away the 300's Hemi in 1959, its performance image suffered. Even though the "Golden Lion" wedge-head V-8 was shown to be equally as potent (92 mph in the quarter mile), the loss of the Hemi created a vacuum.

In 1960, the vacuum was filled by providing the 300-F with a ram-inducted 413-cid V-8 good for 375 hp in standard form and 400 hp in optional form. Engine hardware common to both included a hot cam, heavy-duty valve springs, low-back-pressure exhaust system, dual-point distributor, low-restriction air cleaner, special plugs and dual quad carbs.

The carbs were mounted on a wild-looking cross-ram manifold that put one air cleaner on each side of the engine. The stacks were 30 inches long and had to be crisscrossed to fit under the hood. At low speeds, the "long" rams worked great, but they hurt performance above 4000 rpm. To solve the problem, engineers removed a section of the inner walls of the manifolds to create the optional 400 hp engine. On the outside, these "short" rams looked the same, but they were effectively 15 inches long.

This option was really intended only for Daytona-bound cars that competed in the Flying Mile there and about 15 "short" ram cars were built. The $800 option also included a rare four-speed gearbox made for the Facel Vega, a Chrysler-powered French luxury car. One of the 400-hp cars, driven by Greg Ziegler, set a Flying Mile record of 144.9 mph. In 1960, a total of 969 hardtops and 248 convertibles, all with ram manifolds, were made.

1961 CHRYSLER 300-G "LETTER CAR"

The Chrysler 300-G convertible had few peers when it came to engineering and performance in 1961.

(Robert Seroka photo)

Car Life called the Chrysler 300-G "the best road car on the market." Chrysler called it "the brand-new 1961 version of Chrysler's championship breed of rare motorcars. A limited-edition automobile, precision built for the connoisseur of careful craftsmanship and superb engineering."

The 300-G's suspension had front torsion bars that were approximately 33 percent stiffer than standard. The 60-inch leaf springs were 9 percent stiffer than stock. The 1.38-inch shock absorbers were considerably larger than units found on other Chryslers. The tires were 8.00 x 15 Goodyear Blue Streak Super Sport high-performance whitewalls.

The standard "Constant-Control" power steering had an overall ratio of 19.6:1. The steering was a quick 3.5 turns lock to lock. Center-lane power brakes with a total lining area of 251 sq. in. were standard. Brake cooling was aided by 15-inch wheels.

The 300-G continued to use Chrysler's 413-cid wedge V-8 with 375 hp at 5000 rpm and 495 ft lbs. of torque at 2800 rpm. This engine had 30-inch ram-induction tubes that increased torque up to 10 percent in the mid-engine range. Dual Carter four-barrel carbs were carried over. As with the 300-F, Chrysler offered a 400-hp option for the 300-G. This V-8 had solid lifters, "short" induction tubes, slightly larger carburetors and a longer-duration (284- to 268-degree) cam. The short rams reduced maximum torque to 465 ft. lbs. at 3600 rpm. The 300-G's standard axle ratio was 3.23:1. This change gave the G a slight top speed advantage over the F.

The standard transmission for the 300-G was a heavy-duty TorqueFlite with increased oil pressure and stronger internal components. With ratios of 2.45, 1.45 and 1.00:1 plus a maximum stall ratio of 2.2:1, this push-button-controlled transmission gave test results of: 0 to 30 mph: 3.2 seconds; 0 to 40 mph: 4.6 seconds; 0 to 50 mph: 6.1 seconds; 0 to 60 mph: 8.4 seconds; 0 to 70 mph: 10.6 seconds; 0 to 80 mph: 13.8 seconds and 0 to 100 mph: 21.2 seconds. The quarter mile took 16.2 seconds at 87.4 mph.

Top speed of the 300-G was reported by *Car Life* to be 131 mph. At Daytona, a 300-G running with the optional 2.93:1 axle ratio won the NASCAR Flying Mile Championship with a two-way average of 143.0 mph. A 300-G also won the NASCAR Standing Mile Championship with a speed of 90.7 mph.

Replacing the four-speed Pont-a-Mousson manual transmission as an alternative to TorqueFlite was a heavy-duty three-speed Chrysler-built gearbox. A manual transmission 300-G had almost identical acceleration times as the TorqueFlite version.

The appearance of the 300-G was altered by the use of an inverted grille shape and the relocation of the taillights from the fins to above the rear bumper. Other revisions included a redesign of the headlights, reshaping the canted tailfins and replacing the (optional) Imperial-like trunk lid with a ribbed unit. Interior revisions were highlighted by a speedometer that read from 0 to 150 mph in single-mph intervals, a black finish for the painted sections of the dash and changes in the design of the dash panel padding and seat perforation. Four exterior colors were offered: formal black, Alaskan white, Mardi Gras green and cinnamon.

Among the 300-Gs equipment features were chrome wheel covers, a "SilentFlite" fan drive, front and rear center armrests, windshield washers and an electric clock. Numerous options were available, such as air conditioning, remote-control exterior mirrors, six-way power seat, power door locks and a "Sure-Grip" differential.

Letter Car production was the highest since 1955. A total of 1,617 Chrysler 300-Gs—1,280 hardtops and 337 convertibles—were manufactured. Respective prices for the hardtop and convertible were $5,413 and $5,843.

1962 CHRYSLER 300-H "LETTER CAR"

The Chrysler Letter Car was a legend in its own time. But after eight years, its time was beginning to run out. For 1962, Highland Park (Chrysler headquarters) decided to cash in on the 300's high-performance reputation by offering a series of non-letter Sport 300s. These cars used a milder 383-cid two-barrel V-8 as standard equipment and shared their 122-inch wheelbase with Chrysler's low-priced Newport line.

A real Letter Car was still offered. It was based on the same, smaller platform to hold down production costs. This 300-H came in the traditional two-door hardtop and convertible models. The shorter wheelbase actually shaved about 300 lbs. off its curb weight and therefore increased the horsepower-per-pound factor. At the same time, the standard 413-cid V-8 was boosted to 380 hp, five more than the 1961 300-G offered.

The lighter weight and higher horsepower resulted in an excellent performing car. With just 10.6 lbs. to move with each unit of power, the H had the best power-to-weight ratio seen in any Letter Car. It did 0 to 60 mph in the same 7.7 seconds as the Hemi-motivated 1957 300-C. And it covered the quarter mile in 16 seconds. This tied the Ram-Tuned 1960 Chrysler 300-F for elapsed time.

Standard equipment for the 300-H didn't cut any corners, either. It included an interior with four bucket seats done in tan leather. Other colors of leather were available on special order. Two big four-barrel carburetors sat atop the base engine, continuing a long-standing Letter Car feature. And a 405-hp Ram-Tuned engine was an exclusive-to-the-300-H option.

Push-button TorqueFlite transmission was standard in the Letter Car. Although an outstanding performer, the 300-H lacked the apart-from-the-crowd image of earlier Letter Cars. Its smaller size and close similarity to non-letter cars held down buyer interest. Some potential customers may even have opted for a loaded version of the Sport 300. The list of extras available for these non-Letter Car models included most of the goodies that came standard in the H.

The 1962 Chrysler 300-H was the muscular version of the Sport 300.

An interesting item was mentioned in *Motor Trend's* "Spotlight on Detroit" column in the magazine's June 1962 issue. It read, "You can now order 426 cubic inches on any Chrysler 300 or 300-H. Factory 413-cubic-inch blocks bored .060 are available on special order, with component combinations including forged pistons of 12-to-1 compression, 292-degree-duration cam with solid lifters, big exhaust valves, streamlined exhaust headers, and the original dual-four-barrel ram manifolds with passages shortened to "tune" above 4000 rpm. This top engine is rated 421 hp at 5400 rpm. Chrysler Division isn't going in for any dragging like Dodge and Plymouth, but they will supply the hot stuff if you want it."

We don't know if any cars were really so equipped, but it seems possible! In any case, only 435 hardtops and 123 convertibles were made with 300-H trim. The hardtop sold for $5,090 and weighed 4,050 lbs. The convertible was $5,461 and 4,105 lbs.

Another big difference between the 300-H and earlier Letter Cars was its lack of tailfins. A management shake-up at Chrysler in the early 1960s inspired a move away from the design influences of stylist Virgil Exner, who was a big fan of fins. To make its purge complete, Chrysler simply shaved the rear end of the 1962 models.

Of course, no one single factor explained the low production of the 300-H. Rather, the combination of decreased size, less distinction and corporate changes in thinking teamed up to make the Chrysler 300-H a rare car.

Today, the same rarity works in the favor of collectors. Values for nicely restored 300-Hs seem to be climbing as high as they are for other Chrysler Letter Cars of similar body style. Anyone interested in a luxurious high-performance machine will find this model satisfying. In fact, the lack of tall tailfins could even become a plus as younger collectors enter the market.

1963 CHRYSLER 300-J "LETTER CAR"

Only 400 of the beautiful 1963 Chrysler 300-Js were produced.

All Chrysler 300 Letter Cars deserve recognition as "beautiful brutes," but the 300-J has the added distinction of also being a rare beautiful brute when new. Only 400 were produced, so a sighting nowadays is worth celebrating.

Like the original C-300 and 300-B models, the 300-J was available only as a two-door hardtop. Chrysler adopted new styling for 1963 that it said possessed a "crisp, clean and custom look." As applied to the 300-J, a more appropriate description would be "restrained elegance." It's true that the 300-J shared much of its styling with lesser Chryslers, but the 300-J's lack of extraneous trim, its muscular profile and marvelously distinctive grille that evoked memories of earlier 300 models all contributed to make the 300-J one of America's most handsome automobiles.

The 300-J was available in five colors: formal black, alabaster, Madison gray, oyster white and claret. Adding a touch of class were the two pin stripes (in a contrasting color) that ran the length of the body and 300-J medallions situated on the C-pillar and the rear deck. The interior featured the controversial square steering wheel that many drivers found uncomfortable, but the outstanding design of the front bucket seats (finished in claret red leather), plus vinyl door panel trimming, color-coordinated claret carpeting and a center console with a built-in tachometer served as at least partial redemptions for this lapse of judgment by Chrysler.

A feature unique to Chryslers that was found on the 300-J were windshield wiper blades fitted with airfoils to press the blade against the windshield at high speeds. A great deal of equipment was included in the 300-J's list price of $5,184. A partial list includes: power steering/brakes/windows, front seat belts, padded instrument panel, windshield washers, variable-speed wipers, electric clock, remote control exterior mirror, four-way driver side power seat, 7.60 x 15 Bluestreak tires mounted on 6-inch-wide rims, TorqueFlite transmission, viscous fan driver and a 150-mph speedometer. Several options were available, including air conditioning, Sure-Grip limited-slip differential and a manual three-speed transmission.

Only one engine was offered for the 300-J—Chrysler's 413-cid wedge-head V-8. This engine, with mechanical lifters and a compression ratio of 10.0:1, had ratings of 390 hp at 4800 rpm and 485 ft. lbs. of torque at 3600 rpm. Dual four-barrel AFB 3505S carburetors were used on a special cross-ram intake manifold. The dual-exhaust system was designed for maximum flow with minimum restriction.

The 300-J's suspension consisted of torsion bars up front and leaf springs at the rear. Power drum brakes were used all around with the periphery of the drums flared to aid cooling.

The 300-J's physical dimensions were consistent with those of earlier 300 models; Chrysler never built a down-sized 300! Its wheelbase was 122 inches, overall length was 215.5 inches and curb weight more than 4,400 lbs.

Performance of the 300-J paralleled or exceeded that of many smaller and lighter vehicles. *Motor Trend*, April 1963, reported a 0 to 60-mph time of 8.0 seconds and a quarter-mile time and speed of 15.8 seconds at 89 mph in a Torqueflite-equipped 300-J running with a 3.23:1 axle ratio. The true forte of the 300-J was its top speed, which was in excess of 142 mph.

The 300-J was a thoroughbred American grand touring car that maintained a tradition of excellence, which today gives it a status unique among performance automobiles. What a pity there aren't enough to go around!

1964 CHRYSLER 300-K "LETTER CAR"

(Bob Schwartz photo)

The Chrysler 300-K convertible could be had new in 1964 for about $4,500.

The 1964 Chrysler 300-K was the most popular of the Chrysler 300 Letter Cars that started as 1955 models and ended with the 300-L for 1965. While it can be argued that the later Letter Cars lacked the performance that the earlier models abounded in, they were still among the fastest-accelerating cars of their era, although the competition was getting hotter and would soon pull ahead.

The first Chrysler 300 had 300 hp and was a leader in that category at the time of its introduction. Each year an updated version came out and set the 300s apart from the Chrysler line. This was diluted starting in 1962, when the mid-priced Chrysler Windsor was replaced with the Sport 300 series, which shared most special appearance features with the 300-H. However, the Letter Cars still retained a high-performance edge with bigger, more powerful engines.

The 1963 Chrysler 300-J (there was no Chrysler 300-I to avoid confusing the "I" with a Roman numeral I) was completely restyled on a 122-inch wheelbase and came only as a hardtop. The 1964 Chrysler got only mild styling changes, but the Chrysler 300-K did get some much-needed attention.

A convertible returned and lower prices—$4,056 for the two-door hardtop and $4,522 for the convertible—did attract attention. This compared with regular 300 series models at $3,443 and $3,803, respectively. The 300-K's attractively styled interior also featured bucket-type seats and a console. Leather trim was now optional at just $93 extra.

The 300-K's standard engine was the 413-cid V-8 with a 360-hp rating, but for $375 you could order the 390-hp 413-cid power plant that featured twin Carter AFB four-barrel carbs on a short-ram intake manifold. TorqueFlite automatic was standard and a new four-speed manual transmission was optional.

When the counting of 300-K's was done at the end of the 1964 model year, 3,022 hardtops and 625 convertibles were turned out—a grand total of 3,647 units. That topped the 1957 Chrysler 300-C's record of 2,402.

1965 CHRYSLER 300-L "LETTER CAR"

The last of the legendary Chrysler 300 "Letter Cars" was the 1965 300-L. It closed 10 years of milestone Mopar performance history. Some automotive historians and enthusiasts feel that the 1955 Chrysler C-300 was the first real "muscle car." If so, the last Letter Car has to be considered a significant automobile for serious collectors.

As the last edition of Chrysler's "beautiful brute," the 300-L was perhaps a bit tamed by old age. Nevertheless, the 300 Letter Car series did end with a car that was a capable performer. The Chrysler 300-L, with its standard 413-cid 390-hp engine, could hurl its 4,660 pounds from 0 to 60 mph in 8.8 seconds. In the process, it coddled its passengers in beautiful vinyl front bucket seats and a notchback rear seat. The elegant dashboard used on all 1965 Chryslers was strewn prettily across the 300-L's interior and was complemented by a commanding center console between the bucket seats.

Aside from its massive, high-output power plant, the 300 L's only major distinction was a lighted medallion at the center of its silver crossbar grille. At night, the medallion glowed softly when the headlights were switched on.

Though lacking in individuality when compared to the standard Chrysler 300, the last of the Letter Cars moved just 11.8 lbs. per horsepower and could scat down the quarter mile in 17.3 seconds. That was slower than a 396-cid 325-hp Chevrolet Caprice, but faster than a 390-cid 300-hp T-Bird. It also managed to attract a good number of buyers, with 2,405 driving away in a 300-L hardtop and an additional 440 taking off in a rare 300-L convertible.

Even with such modest production totals, the Chrysler 300-L models were the second-best selling Letter Cars in history. Alas, this achievement went largely unnoticed and plans for the 1966 Chrysler 300-M were cancelled. A great Chrysler tradition had come to an end with the 300-L.

The 1965 Chrysler 300-L ended the Letter series on a high note.

1970 CHRYSLER HURST 300

The hulking 1970 Chrysler Hurst 300 had to have plenty of power to qualify it as a muscle car, and it did.

George Hurst was much like the King Midas of motor heads—everything that he touched with his hands turned to muscle—even big boats such as the 1970 Chrysler 300. The Chrysler 300 came as a two-door hardtop with a 124-inch wheelbase. Its 224.7 inches of length made it look like an aircraft carrier. Yet, George Hurst convinced Chrysler Corporation that he could remake the car in the image of the legendary Chrysler 300 Letter Cars.

The heart of the 1970 Chrysler 300-Hurst was a TNT engine displacing 440 cid. It generated 375 hp thanks to a special hydraulic-lifter cam and a low-restriction dual exhaust system. The Hurst 300 included a heavy-duty suspension, power front disc brakes and H60-15 raised-white-letter tires.

Appearance features started with special spinnaker white paint set off with gold accents. The fiberglass rear deck lid incorporated a recessed integral airfoil. There was also a power bulge hood, gold-accented road wheels with trim rings and fiberglass rear fender extensions. A brown leather interior was included. A TorqueFlite automatic was the only available transmission.

Hurst Performance Products Co. had one record indicating production of 650 cars, but another company document said that 501 were produced to the published specifications, plus one with a sunroof and one convertible. However, it has been discovered that two additional ragtops were possibly made, one by the factory and one by a dealer. One of these—the dealer-made car—was actually fitted with a 426-cid Hemi engine and appeared in *The Hurst Heritage* written by Bob Lichty and Terry Boyce. It even has Hemi hood emblems.

The normal Hurst 300 sold for $4,234. It could hit 60 mph in 7.1 seconds and did the quarter mile in 16.8 seconds at 87.3 mph. Not bad for a 4,125-lb. "aircraft carrier."

1999 CHRYSLER 300M

Some may not consider the 1999 Chrysler 300M a muscle car, but it did have a top speed of more than 145 mph.

(Jerry Heasley photo)

This is a car that is hard to define. It's a specialty vehicle and it's chock full of luxury, but is it really a muscle car? With a 0 to 60-mph time of 7.8 seconds, you have to admit it's no rapid-accelerating Camaro SS, Mustang Cobra R or Corvette C5, but then it's not intended to be. On the other side of the coin, it has a top speed in excess of 145 mph.

In a way, that places it squarely in the tradition of earlier Chrysler Letter Cars, which also needed 8 seconds to get from rest to 60 mph, but then kept *accelerating* when the needle swept past double zeros! If the earlier "beautiful brutes" are muscle cars—and we think they are—the current one seems to fit the same image.

The front-engined, front-wheel-drive 300M first bowed in 1999. It featured a single overhead camshaft, 24-valve, 3.5-liter, all-aluminum V-6 that made it scoot pretty good. In 1999, this engine produced 253 hp at 6400 rpm and 255 ft. lbs. of torque at 3950 rpm. It came linked to an AutoStick dual mode manual/automatic transmission that permitted driver control on winding roads. Differentiating the $29,445 300M from other Letter Cars was an extra set of doors. It was a sedan, while all earlier Letter Cars were two-door hardtops or convertibles.

The 1999 Chrysler 300M's standard equipment list included heated leather seats, 16-inch tires, a premium four-disc changer Infinity sound system and a black-and-white analog clock and gauge cluster. Also featured was Chrysler's "cab-forward styling," driver and passenger air bags and all-wheel ABS disc brakes. Options included a pair of specific suspension settings and two different steering and braking levels that aided high-performance operation.

2000 CHRYSLER 300M

The 2000 Chrysler 300M four-door sedan wasn't really a muscle car, but it should appeal to muscle car fans.

After its 1998 introduction, the modern-day Chrysler 300M made it to *Car and Driver* magazine's "10 best" list two times in a row. Unlike its predecessors, the 300M did not change its "letter"—even though it was not only a different year, but also a new millennium. While its V-6 engine and extra set of doors made it a bit different in character than the original Chrysler 300 Letter Cars, the 300M has earned a following among collectors of the early, Hemi-powered and wedge-powered Chrysler 300s and, for that reason alone, it deserves at least an honorary spot in this muscle car book.

The 2000 model had a base retail price of $29,295. For that you got a big, stealthy looking, cab-forward, front-engine, front-wheel-drive four-door sedan on a 113-inch wheelbase with an overall length of 197.8 inches and curb weight of 3,600 lbs.

Below the hood there was a single overhead cam, 24-valve V-6 with an aluminum block and heads and a Chrysler SBEC III engine-management system with port fuel injection. The 215-cid engine developed 253 hp at 6400 rpm and 255 ft. lbs. of torque at 3950 rpm. It came hooked to a four-speed automatic transmission with a lock-up torque converter.

In testing, the Chrysler 300M moved from 0 to 60 mph in 7.8 seconds and did the standing-start quarter mile in 15.9 seconds at 89 mph. It had a top speed of 139 mph. Was it a real muscle car? The answer is probably no, but it might be a great car for collectors of the original muscle car—the Chrysler 300 Letter Car—to use as an everyday driver

DODGE

1963 DODGE POLARA 500

With its 119-inch wheelbase and 3,985-lb. curb weight, it is a bit hard to think of the 1963 Dodge Polara 500 convertible as a muscle car, until you see the results that Jim Wright recorded when he test drove such a car for *Motor Trend* magazine. His ragtop was equipped with the 383-cid 330-hp V-8 and managed to get from 0 to 60 mph in a mere 7.7 seconds. The quarter mile took 15.8 seconds, by which time the big, open-top Dodge was moving at 92 mph. And we assume that a lighter coupe would have done even better.

With its 4.25 x 3.38-inch bore and stroke the 383 was considered a Chrysler big-block engine and it was one of the best for all-around driving. It used 10.0:1 aluminum pistons and the 330-hp version had a Carter four-barrel carburetor that let the engine breathe deeply and rev to a 5,500-rpm redline above its 4,600-rpm horsepower peak. The torque output was a strong 425 ft. lbs. at 2,800 rpm. Wright's combination attached the 383 to a Borg-Warner T-10 four-speed with a 2.20.0:1 low gear, which didn't hurt its drag-strip performance one bit.

"Barring the all-out drag-strip engines, there aren't many that can stay with the 330-hp "383" in acceleration," Wright wrote in his article. He noted that the car's times through various speeds and the quarter mile were "very impressive," especially considering that it used a 3.23.0:1 rear axle.

The 1963 Polara was considered the top trim level "Dodge" back in 1963, when the even fancier Custom 880 was thought of as, well, a Custom 880 instead of a Dodge. The basic Polara 500 convertible (which included four bucket seats) listed for just $3,196 and weighed 3,546 lbs. Wright's test car had some 340 lbs. of extras, including a Sure Grip differential, power steering, power brakes, electric windows, an AM/FM radio, a heater, a Sun tachometer and seat belts. The cost was $4,265.79

1966 DODGE CHARGER 383

The 1966 Dodge Charger became a muscle car with the 383-cid V-8.

Dodge called its 1966 Charger a "Sports Sedan," even though it was really a coupe. This was an attempt to widen its sales appeal beyond the youth market and to stress its cargo-carrying abilities. With a full-size 117-inch wheelbase and 203.6 inches of overall length, the Charger was certainly roomy. And its 75.3-inch width didn't hurt either. With seating for only four on its front and rear bucket seats, the Charger was not really sedan-like in the passenger-carrying category, either. Its real appeal was its sporty flavor.

Nevertheless, young-at-heart American dads canny enough to convince their better half that the Charger was really a "kind of station wagon" were likely to go for the base 318-cid 230-hp V-8 or the one-step-up 361-cid 265 hp option, both fitted with two-barrel carburetors. Once you got to the big-block 383 or the even heftier 426-cid "Street Hemi," you were talking "muscle car" when you talked about a Charger.

The 383-powered Charger was honestly not the ultimate muscle machine, but it was entirely adequate for many buyers. The 383-cid V-8 had a 4.25 x 3.38-inch bore and stroke, a 10.0:1 compression ratio and a single four-barrel Carter carburetor. This added up to a package delivering 325 hp at 4800 rpm and 425 ft. lbs. of torque at 2800 rpm.

A nicely outfitted Charger with power steering, power brakes, power steering, a limited-slip differential, a Rallye suspension, a few other goodies and the 383 hooked to a three-speed automatic transmission went out the door for just over $3,100. And two nice performance enhancements included at the regular price were dual exhausts and the well-known responsiveness of the Chrysler automatic gearbox.

On the test track, a '66 Charger 383 could move from 0 to 60 mph in 7.2 seconds and zip down a quarter-mile drag strip in 15.6 seconds at 89 mph. No one is saying that acceleration like that would win the NHRA Nationals, but the '66 Charger 383 was still a kind of "everyman's muscle car" that every man, woman or child could love back then.

1966 DODGE HEMI CORONET

(Jerry Heasley photo)

The Dodge Hemi Coronet was unmatched in 1966 when it came to raw power.

Introduced in 1965, the mid-sized Coronet became the centerpiece of Dodge muscle car history. An ad that ran that year asked "Why not drop a Hemi in the new Coronet 500?" However, the '65s came only with the 12.5:1 compression Race Hemi, which created more of a drag machine than a muscle car.

This was corrected by making the 426-cid 425-hp dual-quad Street Hemi available in 1966. Displacement-wise and power-wise, it matched the race version, but the big difference was a hydraulic lifter cam and a 10.5:1 compression ratio. It was the most powerful production car engine ever built, but was still well suited to street use. In addition, the optional Hemi engine was a good deal for less than $500.

The Coronet was restyled for model year 1966. While it retained the 117-inch wheelbase used previously, overall length was reduced 1 inch to 203 inches. The new styling featured crisp, well-defined character lines, but the cantilevered roof was retained. The top-of-the-line Coronet 500 model had Charger-like bucket seats with a choice of all-vinyl or vinyl-and-fabric upholstery. Dodge offered a selection of 15 exterior colors in acrylic enamel finish.

A "500" designation on the car indicated the model, but not the engine. In fact, you really had to open the hood to see if there was a Hemi lurking underneath. Hemi Coronets could hit 60 mph in 6.1 seconds and do the quarter mile in 14.5. Only 340 Coronet 500 hardtops (204 of them four-speeds) got the Hemi, along with just 21 convertibles (12 with four-speeds). Another 379 of the other Coronets also had this engine added to them.

1966 DODGE HEMI CHARGER

Fastback styling was back in vogue in the mid-1960s and the Dodge Charger was a participant in the "Dodge Rebellion" that featured a drastic version of such a roofline. The Charger was really a Coronet with a streamlined look and rich interior appointments and trimmings.

After the Charger arrived, most enthusiast magazines rushed to do a test drive and most of them tested the version with the 383-cid V-8 that cranked out 325 hp at 4800 rpm. This combination was actually quite fast, with *Car and Driver* registering a 7.8-second 0-to-60 time and doing the quarter mile in 16.2 seconds at 88 mph.

With the same engine and tranny, *Motor Trend* reported an 8.9-second 0-to-60 time and 16.3 seconds for the quarter mile at 85 mph. The Hemi could shave two seconds or more off of both times.

Though it looked mighty large and lush, the availability of an optional 426-cid Hemi V-8 engine made it a contender in the muscle car market. This 425-hp big-block V-8 featured dual four-barrel carburetors, extra-wide dual exhausts and all sorts of heavy-duty performance hardware. The Hemi package also included engine call-out badges, a heavy-duty suspension, larger brakes and 7.75 x 14 Blue Streak racing tires. The use of either a four-speed manual

(Jerry Heasley photo)

The 1966 Dodge Charger fastback coupe sported a 426 Hemi engine.

gearbox or a TorqueFlite automatic transmission was mandatory. Dodge specified that the Hemi's short 12-month or 12,000 miles warranty would be invalidated by "extreme operation" or driveline modifications.

Total production of 1966 Chargers hit 37,300 cars. Of these, only 468 had Hemis, of which a mere 218 featured TorqueFlite.

NASCAR drivers thought the fastback roof would enhance the Charger's aerodynamics in Grand National stock car racing. However, they actually tended to lift at the rear, a problem that the race car builders solved by adding a small rear deck lid spoiler. After that, the Chargers won 18 races.

1967 DODGE HEMI CORONET

Dodge production numbers show that only 283 Hemi Coronet L/Ts were built in 1967.

You could get the new-for-1966 Street Hemi in the 1966 Dodge Coronet 500, as well as in the Dodge 440 and base models. So when the 1967 pre-production publicity photos showed a couple of Coronet 500 hardtops with 426 Hemi badges, it led to a bit of confusion because press kits and literature said the Hemi engine would only be available as a limited-production option for the top-line Coronet R/T and also for the Charger fastback.

Production figures bear out the limited-production concept, since they show that only 283 Coronet R/Ts and 118 Chargers with Street Hemis were built and seem to indicate that you couldn't get a Street Hemi in any other Coronet. However, that's incorrect.

On January 23, 1967, Dodge announced that the Coronet 440 two-door hardtop was being built on a production basis to meet National Hot Rod Association's (NHRA) Super Stock B rules. The WO23 cars—as they are known—were the latest in the Mopar tradition of special lightweight models built for drag racing. A shipping weight of 3,686 lbs. was given for Dodge 440s with Street Hemi engines.

The lightweight body had standard sheet metal and the big fresh-air hood scoop that was common to earlier S/S Dodges. Sound deadeners and body sealers were deleted and the battery was mount-

ed in the trunk. The usual sway bar up front was also axed, since quick travel around corners was not in the job description for the S/S-B cars.

There were two versions of these drag-racing-only Dodges. One came with a modified TorqueFlite automatic using a 2,300 to 2,500-rpm-stall-speed torque converter and 4.86:1 Sure-Grip Chrysler-built 8 3/4-inch differential. The second had a four-speed manual transmission with Hurst linkage, reinforced gearing and clutch and an explosion-proof clutch housing. This second combo drew a 4.88 Sure-Grip Dana differential.

The S/S-B cars could be ordered through your friendly Dodge dealer, but if you wanted a five-year, 50,000-mile warranty he would become unfriendly in a hurry, since the cars came without a warranty of any kind.

To meet the rules, Dodge had to build at least 50 of the cars and when 55 went out the door, enough was enough. Plymouth was also allowed to build 55 similar Plymouth Belvedere II two-door hardtops (RO23).

At least the availability of S/S-B Dodge Coronets was of some consolation to those who missed the Coronet 500 and other lesser-model Hemis. Prices for nice survivors are in the stratosphere today.

1967 DODGE CORONET R/T

1967 Dodge Coronet R/T convertible listed for $3438, about $239 more than the hardtop.

The 1967 Dodge Coronet R/T came standard with a 440 Magnum V-8.

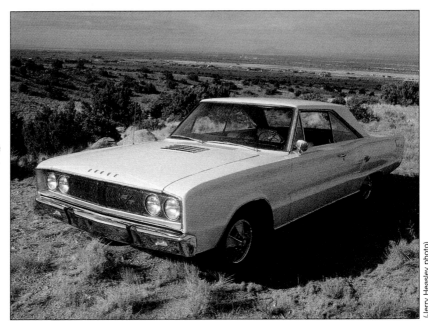

(Jerry Heasley photo)

Many "street" muscle cars were weekend racing cars in the 1960s and the R/T badge announced the road-and-track nature of such vehicles. A Charger-like grille distinguished the hot mid-size Dodge, although it lacked the fastback's retractable headlamps. Other features included simulated rear fender air vents and non-functional hood scoops.

Standard under the hood was the 440 Magnum V-8 linked to either a four-speed manual gearbox or TorqueFlite automatic transmission. The Magnum engine had a 4.32 x 3.75-inch bore and stroke, a 10.1:1 compression ratio and a single four-barrel carburetor. It developed 375 hp at 4600 rpm and 480 ft. lbs. of torque at 3200 rpm. One 440-powered R/T did 0 to 60 mph in 7.2 seconds and the quarter mile in 15.4 at 94 mph. *Motor Trend* drove the same car with racing slicks mounted and did the 0-to-60 test in 6.5 seconds. The fat-tired car required 14.7 seconds for the quarter mile with a 96-mph terminal speed.

The R/T hardtop listed for $3,199 and a convertible was $3,438. The package also included a stiff suspension, heavy-duty brakes and 7.75 x 14 Red Streak tires. Production amounted to 10,181 cars, including a mere 628 ragtops.

For $907.60, the Hemi V-8 could be special ordered for a Coronet R/T. This powerful V-8 had a 4.25 x 3.75-inch bore and stroke, a 10.25:1 compression ratio and two four-barrel carbs. It produced 425 hp at 5000 rpm and 490 ft. lbs. of torque at 4000 rpm. *Motor Trend's* stock-tired Hemi-powered Coronet went 0 to 60 in 6.8 seconds and ran the quarter mile in 15.0 seconds at 96 mph. When shod with racing slicks, it went 0 to 60 in 6.6 seconds and did the quarter mile in 14.8 seconds at 99 mph.

A total of 238 Coronet R/T coupes and convertibles carried the Hemi engine option in 1967 and 121 also had four-speed manual gearboxes.

1967 DODGE HEMI CHARGER

The Hemi engine could propel the big 1967 Dodge Charger fastback to 14.4 seconds in the quarter mile.

(Jerry Heasley photo)

As in 1966, the little-changed 1967 Dodge Charger was aimed at the sporty-car buyer who didn't want to give up room and comfort. The Charger also assumed that the type of man (or woman) interested in such a car would be willing to spring for a bit extra to get bigger and more powerful engines.

With its slant towards competition in NASCAR and USAC, Dodge wanted the Charger to reflect its racing image and again offered it with a nice selection of V-8s. The base engine was a 318-cid 230-hp job that pushed the Charger from 0 to 60 mph in 10.9 seconds and down the quarter mile in 18.6 seconds at 76 mph. The next step up was a 383-cid 326-hp big-block V-8 that took the Charger from 0 to 60 mph in 8.9 seconds and down the quarter mile in 16.5 seconds at 86.4 mph. There was also the 440-cid 375-hp engine good for 0 to 60 in 8 seconds and a 15.5-second quarter mile at 93 mph. But again, the top dog was the 426-cid 425-hp Hemi. With this engine the Charger went 0 to 60 mph in 7.6 seconds and did the quarter mile in 14.4 seconds at 100 mph!

The Hemi was an $877.55 option in the Charger, while the 383 cost $119.55 extra and the 440 was $313.60 extra. With either the 440 or the Hemi, the three-speed TorqueFlite automatic came with a high-upshift speed governor. If you ordered a four-speed manual transmission, the Sure-Grip no-slip rear axle was mandatory. A good idea for the Hemi Charger was 11-inch front disc brakes, which could slow the car down from 60 mph in an amazing 133 feet.

The 1967 Chargers were much rarer than '66s and only 15,788 were built. This included 118 cars with the Hemi, of which half were four-speeds. If you're considering buying a 1967 Hemi Charger today, you might appreciate knowing that it got 11.7 mpg in city driving and about 14.4 mpg on the open highway. Don't tell that to the people who set CAFE standards. One of them might have a heart attack!

1968 DODGE CHARGER R/T

What's striped for action   …built for comfort   …and has a lot of dash?

Charger R/T…the only car that looks as good as it goes.

No wonder Charger sales are up more than 250% over last year's. Where else can you get a shape you can tell a block away, hidden headlights, deep foam buckets in luxurious deep-pleated vinyl, and that great-looking dash with the readable dials? Not to mention an electric clock that really works, a racing gas cap, and handy door pockets for maps and things. Plus that combination of agility and comfort that's hard to match.

The car shown above is an R/T—in our new spring color, Charger Green Metallic. In Dodge lingo, R/T means you get a 440 Magnum V8, special rallye suspension, over-sized police-type brakes, and your choice of shiftable three-speed automatic or four-on-the-floor, all at no extra cost. Which, all added up, means just about the greatest piece of machinery on four wheels. About the bumblebee stripes. Whether or not they

go on your R/T is up to you. Options? Air conditioning, 8-track stereo tape player, Auto Pilot speed control, rear window defogger—the works. But you'll still pay less for a car equipped the way you want because more of the things you want are standard equipment.

Satisfied with a 250% sales increase? Good heavens, sir! We haven't even warmed up yet.

It's your turn for Dodge fever

Dodge CHRYSLER

The 1968 Dodge Charger R/T fastback could again be had with a Hemi engine.

The Charger underwent a vast amount of change in 1968, giving up the flat, wide fastback roof of 1966-1967 that resembled a jumping ramp for Jake Kochman's Dodge-loving "Helldrivers." Dodge stylists did a great job of adopting the popular late-1960s "Coke bottle" look to the more smoothly rounded body. Neat details included an integral rear spoiler and a competition-type gas filler cap. The Charger retained its 117-inch wheelbase, but its rear track was widened from 58.5 inches to 59.2 inches.

The image of a car that was equally suited to street performance and drag racing was what Dodge's R/T designation implied. *Motor Trend* summed up the look of the R/T model as a Charger with a set of mags and wide ovals with a bumblebee stripe around its rear end. Also emphasizing the new model's dual-purpose character were suitable name badges, heavy-duty underpinnings and a 440-cid 375-hp Magnum V-8. This engine had a 4.32 x 3.75-inch bore and stroke, a 10.1:1 compression ratio and a single four-barrel carburetor.

Merchandised as a model with a base price of $3,480 (including TorqueFlite automatic transmission), the standard R/T could move from 0 to 60 mph in 6.5 seconds and zip down a drag strip in 15 seconds at 93 mph. This was the only Charger you could get a Hemi in during 1968. The engine option cost $604.75, which might explain why only 475 such cars were built. Of the total, 211 had the four-speed manual gearbox, which was a no cost option. Other available extras included a limited-slip differential for $42.35; a tachometer for $48.70; custom wheels for $97.30; a console for $52.85; power brakes for $41.75 and front disc brakes for $72.95. Bucket seats and high-performance tires were standard.

The most famous 1968 Charger was the one that Steve McQueen drove in the motion picture "Bullitt."

1968 DODGE CORONET R/T

The Dodge Coronet R/T was restyled for 1968 and praised for its comfort and roominess.

Coronets were completely restyled for 1968, when 10,456 coupes ($3,353) and convertibles ($3,613) were made. Equipment included bucket seats, dual exhausts, stiff suspension, heavy-duty brakes and other goodies, including a 150-mph speedometer. TorqueFlite automatic transmission was standard. Bumblebee stripes (or no-cost optional body side stripes) set off the 1968 model's appearance. Coronet R/Ts used the same interior as Coronet 500s, but had a special "power bulge" hood with simulated air vents.

In a *Motor Trend* comparison of eight 1968 super cars (Plymouth Road Runner, Dodge Charger R/T, Pontiac GTO, Buick GS 400, Chevelle SS 396, Olds 4-4-2, Ford Torino and Dodge Coronet R/T) the Coronet was said to have a "good engine" and "easily the best in comfort and in room." It's quality of construction was rated "surprisingly good" and the magazine liked its comfort, roominess, engine and boulevard ride.

The standard 440-cid Magnum V-8 was the same as in 1967 with its 4.32 x 3.75-inch bore and stroke, 10.1:1 compression ratio and single four-barrel. Horsepower (375 at 4600 rpm) and torque (480 ft. lbs. at 3200 rpm) remained unchanged. A four-speed manual or automatic transmission were also standard again. What did vary very slightly was the published performance numbers: 6.9 seconds for the 0 to 60-mph test and 15.1 seconds for the quarter mile at 94 mph. The bad news was the 440-motivated Coronet R/T got 9.6 to 12.1 mpg fuel economy (if you could call that economy).

High-performance options for the Coronet R/T included a limited-slip differential for $42.35, custom wheels for $97.30, front disc brakes for $72.95 and a console for $52.85. High-performance tires and bucket seats were standard. This season, the optional Street Hemi V-8 cost $604.75 and was ordered for 94 Coronet R/Ts with four-speeds and 136 with TorqueFlite automatic transmissions. Experts believe that one stick-shift car and eight automatics were convertibles. Hemi cars came with a special heavy-duty suspension, but air conditioning couldn't be ordered.

The 440 Magnum V-8 let the 1968 Coronet L/T pull a 15.1-second quarter mile, but the Coronet was no economy car when it came to gas mileage.

1968 DODGE CORONET SUPER BEE

The 1968 Dodge Coronet Super Bee two-door sedan could be bought for less than $3,500.

Budget-priced muscle cars were a Chrysler innovation in the late 1960s. Dodge's entry was the Coronet Super Bee, introduced in February 1968 with a price tag in the $3,395 range. It was based on the Coronet 440 two-door sedan, because a "post" coupe was needed to accommodate the non-lowering rear windows that swung open on hinges mounted to the center pillar.

Base engine was the big-block 383-cid V-8 in 335-hp format linked to a heavy-duty four-speed with Hurst's "Competition-Plus" floor shifter. Fat dual exhausts, fat F40 x 14 tires and a heavy-duty suspension with fat torsion bar were included. Everything was fat except the price tag.

Also part of the Super Bee look was a dummy hood "power bulge," bench seat interior, wide wheels and rear bumblebee striping with a bee inside a circular decal emblem. You couldn't get a vinyl roof, but for $712, you could add the Hemi.

A total of 166 Hemi Super Bees were produced—92 had four-speed transmissions and 74 had Torque Flite attachments.

Cars equipped with the standard engine went from 0 to 60 mph in 6.8 seconds while the Hemis made the same speed in 6.6. Quarter-mile times were 15 seconds and 14 seconds for the two engines, respectively.

The Super Bee was only slightly fancier than the Plymouth Road Runner, with which it competed for customers. The Super Bee included door-to-door carpeting, pleated vinyl seats and door panels and a Charger-type instrument panel. The wheel lips and the rear body panel were accented with thin bright moldings.

1968 DODGE DART GTS

The 1968 Dodge Dart GTS came standard with a 340-cid small block, but the 383 was also available.

The GTS label stood for GT Sport, but the new-for-1968 mini muscle car was more than a sporty compact. "Not to take the edge off the Road Runner, the GTS might be a more sensible package," said *Hot Rod's* Steve Kelly in the magazine's April 1968 issue. "The base price is higher, but you get things like carpet on the floor, fat tires, bucket seats and a few other niceties that can make Saturday night roaming more comfortable. The engine's smaller, but that could prove an advantage for drag racing classes."

Two hefty V-8s were available. A 340-cid small-block engine was standard. It was derived from the 273-318-cid Chrysler family of engines and had a 4.04 x 3.31-inch bore and stroke, a 10.5:1 compression ratio and a single four-barrel carburetor. The 340 cranked out 275 hp at 5000 rpm and 340 ft. lbs. of torque at 3200 rpm. A 383-cid big-block engine with a four-barrel carburetor and 300 hp was optional. The 383 added 89 lbs. to the car if you got a four-speed and 136 lbs. if you got an automatic. A standard 3.23:1 rear axle was supplied, but 3.55:1 and 3.91:1 ratio axles were options.

Other technical enhancements included a low-restriction exhaust system with chrome tips, a Rallye suspension, 14 x 5.5-inch wheels and E70-14 Red Streak tires. Although a column-shifted three-speed manual transmission was standard, most Dart GTS models had either a four-speed manual gearbox with a Hurst floor shifter or a competition-type TorqueFlite automatic transmission.

Also identifying the GTS were hood power bulges with air vents, body side racing stripes, special GTS emblems and simulated mag wheel covers. A rear-end bumblebee stripe was a no-cost option. Vinyl bucket seats were standard in the $2,611 hardtop and optional in the $3,383 convertible.

In 1968, the production of the GTS models was lumped into the total of 24,100 GT series V-8s produced. The 1968 Dart GTS hardtop with the 340-cid 270-hp power train tested out with a 0-to-60 time of 6 seconds. It did the quarter-mile in a "Scat Pack" time of 15.2 seconds. *Hot Rod* published even better numbers for its 340-cid TorqueFlite-equipped GTS, which did the quarter mile in 14.38 seconds at 97 mph.

1969 DODGE CHARGER 500

Dodge sold more than 96,000 of the Charger 500 fastbacks in 1969.

Beautiful new styling characterized the 1968 Dodge Charger and boosted its sales to 96,100 cars. Wind-tunnel testing showed that the good-looking body's recessed grille and tunneled-in rear window created turbulence on the high-speed NASCAR superspeedways. Dodge engineers figured out that a flush grille and flush-mounted glass could reduce its wind resistance. Some say the prototype with these changes (actually the first Charger 500) was really a 1968 model.

The production–type 1969 Charger 500 was a special model based on the style of the Charger 500 prototype. It was released to the public on September 1, 1968, but as a 1969 model. Chrysler literature said it was offered specifically for high-performance racing tracks and available only to qualified race drivers. In reality, that was a great promotion as muscle car lovers flocked to Dodge dealers trying to buy one of the cars.

The handcrafted body modifications were actually handled by Creative Industries, an aftermarket firm from Detroit. A minimum of 500 such cars had to be sold to authorize the changes and make the Charger legal for racing under NASCAR rules. The model designation was based on the number of cars that was supposed to be made.

Even though some books say Hemis were standard, 392 of these cars have been researched and only about 9 percent turned out to have Hemis. You did get heavy-duty suspension, a four-speed manual gearbox (or TorqueFlite automatic transmission), a rear bumblebee stripe, "500" model badges, a special shorter-than-stock deck lid and a custom-made package shelf.

Officially, 32 Hemi-powered cars were built, though experts have tracked down serial numbers for 35 such vehicles. About 15 cars had four-speed manual gearboxes. Charger 500s with automatics covered the quarter mile in 14.01 seconds at 100 mph. Cars with the optional four-speed manual transmissions were significantly faster. They did the quarter mile in 13.60 seconds at 107.44 mph.

1969 DODGE CHARGER DAYTONA

The 1969 Charger Daytona looked fast and the record books prove it was.

One of Chrysler's famous "winged warriors" was the Charger Daytona—the ultimate expression of the first Charger 500's built-for-racing inspiration. Shortly after the Dodge Charger 500 bowed in 1969, Ford Motor Co. launched the Torino Talladega and Mercury Cyclone Spoiler models. Both FoMoCo products had superior aerodynamics, which helped them to outrun the slippery Charger 500s in enough races to take the National Association of Stock Car Automobile Racing title. The 1969 Charger Daytona was designed to get the NASCAR championship back.

A fiberglass "nose cone," front fender-top scoops (for tire clearance) and a massive 2-foot-high rear spoiler distinguished Dodge's new rocketship race car. A company named Creative Industries received the contract to build 500 Daytonas to legalize the 200-mph body modifications for stock car competition.

(Jack Passey, Jr. photo)

The 1969 Dodge Charger Daytona came with a base 440 Magnum V-8, but Hemi V-8s were also available.

The first Charger Daytona was shipped to a Canadian Dodge dealer on June 27, 1969. A dealer in Lafayette, Indiana, received the last one on September 8 of the same year.

Bobby Isaac drove a Daytona sponsored by K & K Insurance Co. to a world closed-course speed record of 201.104 mph. Daytonas swept the first four places in the race they were named after—the Daytona 500—that season. At the Bonneville Salt Flats in Utah, Bobby Isaac also set an unlimited class speed record of 217 mph.

Experts say that total production of Daytonas was 503 units. Officially, 433 cars with base 375-hp 440 Magnum V-8s were built for the streets and 70 were turned out with Hemi V-8s under their snout. The breakout as to how many of the Hemi Daytonas had four-speed manual or automatic transmissions was 22 and 48, respectively. One yellow Daytona, with 5,000 original miles, has been documented to be a car with a dealer-installed 440 Six-Pack V-8. Dodge did not, however, offer this set up as a factory option.

1969 DODGE CHARGER R/T

(Don Bowser photo)

The 1969 Dodge Charger R/T fastback could turn the quarter mile in 13.9 seconds.

The 1969 Dodge Charger didn't change much from 1968. As *Motor Trend* magazine put it, "That brute Charger styling, that symbol of masculine virility, was still intact." (Of course, those were the good old days when you could say things like that in a national magazine!) For 1969, the Charger's grille was divided into two sections and the taillights were modified a bit. However, the fastback Dodge was basically the same good-looking beast as before on the outside.

The interior treatment, including the well-designed instrument panel, also had very few changes. There was a large-faced tachometer and the gauges were done in white on black to make them stand out very distinctly.

The R/T was the high-performance version of the Charger and came only as a hardtop coupe with a base price of $3,592. That included the 440-cid Magnum V-8, with a four-barrel carburetor, hooked to a three-speed TorqueFlite automatic transmission. Also

included as part of the R/T package were dual exhausts with chrome tips; heavy-duty manually adjusted brakes; F70-14 Red Line tires; the R/T handling package and bumblebee stripes.

With a 3.55:1 rear axle, the standard-equipped 440-powered model (with a column-mounted shift lever no less) was found to run the quarter mile in 13.9 seconds at 101.4 mph. The R/T was the only Charger available with the Hemi engine again this year. The 426-cid 425-hp powerhouse had a $648 price tag this year.

Charger R/T production leaped from the 1969 total of 17,582 units up to 20,057 units. A new option for Chargers that was also available on the R/T models was the SE (or Special Edition) interior with leather bucket seats, lots of extra lights and wood-grained trim pieces. Sinking in popularity to 400 production units was the Hemi Charger R/T. Around 192 of the Hemi-powered cars had four-speed manual transmissions in 1969.

1969 DODGE CORONET R/T

The 1969 Dodge Coronet R/T featured a "six-pack" carburetor that helped produce 390 hp.

In 1969, the Dodge Coronet R/T continued as the high-performance model in the Coronet series. It included all of the features of the Coronet 500 model, plus the Magnum 440-cid V-8, TorqueFlite automatic transmission, a light group option, body sill moldings and R/T bumblebee stripes across the trunk lid and down the fender sides. Two simulated hood scoops located on the rear fenders, just ahead of the rear wheel openings, were optional.

The Coronet two-door hardtop, model WS23, listed for $3,442 and weighed 3,601 lbs. Also available was the model WS27 convertible with a $3,660 base sticker price and weight of 3,721 lbs.

A "six-pack" of carburetors was the big news for the Coronet R/T in 1969. The triple two-barrel Holleys sat atop a 440 Magnum V-8 that harnessed 390 horses and 490 ft. lbs. of torque. A fiberglass performance hood covered the three carburetors. Also available was a Ramcharger fresh-air induction system (which was standard on Hemi-powered cars) with twin hood scoops that fed cold air into a fiberglass plenum bolted to the underside of the hood. There was also a wider choice of rear axle ratios. Standard equipment was a

3.23:1 unit but 3.54:1, 3.55:1, 3.91:1 and 4.10:1 performance axle packages were available.

Obviously, Dodge was placing additional emphasis on the "Track" portion of the Road and Track model designation by adding more performance to its Coronet muscle car. Overall styling was similar to 1968, except that the previous front fender medallion became a large decal that appeared as part of the rear bumblebee stripe. The four-barrel 440-cid was, of course, the standard motor.

A Hemi was an additional $418 option for 1969 Coronet R/Ts. Model year production totaled 7,238 hardtops and convertibles combined. This included 97 two-door hardtops (58 with a four-speed manual transmission) and 10 ragtops (six with TorqueFlite) fitted with 426 Hemis.

One magazine test-dragged a '69 six-pack R/T (complete with dummy rear fender scoops) to a 105.14-mph 13.65-second quarter-mile run. The Dodge's 0-to-60 time was a scant—or should we say "Scat"—6.6 seconds.

1969 DODGE CORONET SUPER BEE

A two-door hardtop with a $3,138 starting price joined the Coronet Super Bee line in 1969. The coupe returned with a $3,076 sticker. There were few changes in appearance or standard equipment. They included a single, wider rear bumblebee stripe and a Dodge "Scat Pack" badge on the grille and trunk, plus front fender engine call-outs.

Three two-barrel Holley carbs on an aluminum Edelbrock manifold were the heart of the new "six-pack" performance option. Cars so equipped generated 390 hp and 490 ft. lbs. of torque. The Six-Pack option included a flat black fiberglass hood that locked in place with four chrome pins so that it could be entirely removed for access to the engine.

There was also a new Ramcharger cold-air induction system (standard with cars having the optional Street Hemi V-8) that fea-

tured two large hood-mounted air scoops, an under hood air plenum and a switch to select between warm and cold air. The Super Bee Six-Pack came with a choice of a four-speed manual gearbox or a TorqueFlite automatic transmission linked to a 9 3/4-inch Dana 60 Sure-Grip axle with 4.10:1 gears. A total of 27,800 Super Bees were built. This included 166 Hemi-powered cars, 92 of them with four-speeds.

In a January 1969 comparison of six "econo-racers" *Car and Driver* magazine got its hands on a new Super Bee with: a 3.55:1 limited-slip differential ($102.15 extra); power disc brakes ($93.10); head restraints ($26.50); foam-padded seats ($8.60); automatic transmission ($40.40); a remote-adjustable mirror ($9.65); three-speed windshield wipers ($5.40); undercoating ($16.60); rear quarter air scoops ($35.80); rear bumper guards ($16); a tachometer and

(Don Bowser photo)

The 1969 Coronet Super Bee hardtop had plenty of goodies to make it go fast, including three two-barrel Holly carburetors.

clock ($50.15); cold air induction ($73.30); AM radio ($63.35); power steering ($97.65); styled wheels ($88.55); F70 x 14 tires and the base 383-cid 335-hp V-8.

The car, which listed for $3,858 fully equipped and weighed 3,765 lbs., could go from 0 to 60 in 5.6 seconds. It did the quarter mile in 14.04 seconds at 99.55 mph. However, the magazine found the car to have a dual-point distributor and large-diameter exhaust pipes, which seemed at first to be "stock" but later proved to be tweaks made by Chrysler. "We can't consider our test car's performance to be representative of a 383 Super Bee you would buy," said the editors. "From our experience, we would estimate a production car in good tune to run about 98.5 mph in the 14.20-second range." Even that's not too shabby!

1969 DODGE DART GTS

A 1969 Dodge Dart GTS hardtop with 340 cid V-8 was a hot little Mopar.

The GTS or GT Sport was one of nine different Dart models that Dodge buyers could select in 1969. It combined a dressy look and assortment of upscale equipment with a 340-cid base engine and a powerful new big-block option. This year the hardtop was base priced at $3,226 and the convertible was $3,419. Bucket seats were optional in the ragtop.

The 1969 version of the GTS sported a new black grille with a bright horizontal center bar. There was also a new blacked-out rear body panel. Also included were E70-14 Red Line tires, TorqueFlite automatic transmission, a three-spoke steering wheel, dual exhausts, carpeting and an engine dress-up kit.

The 1969 GTS 383 was a kind of "sleeper" in muscle car circles because the optional 383-cid V-8 was up-rated to 330 hp. It came standard with a 3.23:1 rear axle. Optional 3.55:1 and 3.91:1 rear axles were also available and at no extra cost when the Sure-Grip differential was ordered, too. Also new for the GTS was a rear bumblebee stripe with a separate lower section and the GT Sport name written on it.

As in 1968, the production of 1969 Dart GTS models was a part of the total of 20,900 GT series V-8s produced, but hardtops and convertibles together came to 6,700 cars with the GTS goodies.

1969 DODGE DART SWINGER 340

(DeWayne Behnke photo)

The 1969 Dodge Dart Swinger 340 hardtop originally listed for a modest $2,863.

Another member of the Dodge "Scat Pack" to proudly wear its bumblebee stripes was the 1969 Dodge Dart Swinger 340. Designed to give muscle car fans more bang for the buck by emphasizing performance over luxury, the Swinger fit right into the "budget muscle car" trend that produced cars like the Plymouth Road Runner and Pontiac GTO Judge. It was like a small-scale counterpart to such models.

"Play your cards right and three bills can put you in a whole lot of car this year," said an advertisement showing a red Swinger two-door hardtop with a black vinyl roof. "Dart Swinger 340. Newest member of the Dodge Scat Pack. You get 340 cubes of high-winding, 4-barrel V-8. A 4-speed Hurst shifter on the floor to keep things moving. All the other credentials are in order."

Standard equipment for 1969 included the 340-cid 275-hp V-8

engine, four-speed full-synchro manual transmission with Hurst shifter; a three-spoke steering wheel with a padded hub, a heavy-duty Rallye suspension, "Swinger" bumblebee stripes, D70 x 14 wide-tread tires, dual exhausts, a performance hood with die-cast louvers and fat 14-inch wheels. Seven colors were available for the car and four colors for vinyl roofs. All-vinyl upholstery (with full-carpeting on four-speed cars only) was included.

The Swinger 340 came only as a two-door hardtop for $2,836. Two axle options—a 3.55:1 and a 3.91:1—gave better drag strip performance.

A total of 20,000 were built. Even today, muscle car collectors can find bargains in the Swinger 340 market, since these cars don't look as flashy as a GTS, although they are equally fast.

1970 DODGE CHALLENGER R/T 440

(Jerry Heasley photo)

The 1970 Challenger came in three models, including a 375-hp version.

The Challenger was Dodge's answer to the Mustang and Camaro and was offered in three body styles: hardtop, formal coupe and convertible. Challengers featured a low, wide look with a full-width, scoop-like grille opening. The body sides had the familiar "Coke bottle" profile with raised rear fenders tapering down at the taillights. Two large, rectangular taillights nearly filled the rear beauty panel.

For high-performance buffs, Dodge offered all three models in the Challenger R/T series. The terminology suggested "road and track." The R/T package included everything on the base equipment list, plus a 383-cid V-8 with a four-barrel carburetor; an electric clock; a Rallye gauge cluster for the instrument panel; front and rear Rallye suspension hardware with a sway bar; heavy-duty drum brakes; F70-14 fiberglass-belted black sidewall tires with raised white letters; longitudinal tape or bumblebee stripes and special R/T

exterior ornamentation.

The 440-cid Magnum V-8 was an option for the R/T. The standard version of this overhead-valve V-8 was a $250 option. It featured a 4.32 x 3.75-inch bore and stroke, hydraulic valve lifters, five main bearings, a 10.0:1 compression ratio, a Carter AFB four-barrel carburetor and a 350 hp at 4000 rpm output rating. It produced 425 ft. lbs. of torque at 3400 rpm. A dual exhaust system with reverse-flow mufflers was standard. A 375-hp version with a hotter cam was $113 additional. There was also a "six-pack" version with three Holley two-barrel carburetors.

Dodge built a total of 14,889 Challenger R/T two-door hardtops, which had a base price of $3,266. The formal hardtop listed for $3,498 and 3,979 were built. Naturally, the convertible was the rarer model. The ragtop had a $3,535 window sticker and a mere 1,070 were made.

1970 DODGE CHALLENGER R/T HEMI

(Jerry Heasley photo)

The 1970 Dodge Challenger R/T was a head turner and listed for $3,266.

(Jerry Heasley photo)

The Challenger R/T Hemis were fast and rare in 1970.

The Challenger came as a beautifully styled hardtop and rag-top, plus a Special Edition (SE) formal-roofed hardtop in 1970.

All three Challenger body styles were offered in the high-performance, V-8-only R/T series. R/Ts included base Challenger features plus a 383-cid V-8 engine, four-barrel carburetor, electric clock, Rallye instrument cluster, front and rear Rallye suspension with sway bars, heavy-duty drum-type brakes, F70-14 fiberglass belted raised-white-letter tires, R/T emblems and bumblebee or longitudinal tape stripes.

The 1970 Challenger R/T hardtop listed for $3,266 and 14,889 were built. The convertible listed for $3,535 and had a 3,979-unit production run. Only 1,070 Challenger SEs, base priced at $3,498, left the factory.

Buyers could add a 375-hp 440-cid Magnum V-8 to the Challenger R/T for $130.55 or get a 390-hp version for $249.55 more. The Street Hemi was available for $778.75.

Hemi production included 287 hardtops (137 with four-speeds), 60 SE hardtops (23 with four-speeds) and nine convertibles (five with four-speeds). All Hemi Challengers were R/Ts. They could do the quarter mile in 14 seconds at 104 mph.

1970 DODGE CHALLENGER T/A

(Jerry Heasley photo)

To allow room for the dual exhaust and fatter tires, the 1970 Dodge Challenger T/As were jacked up in the back.

"Wild and woolly" is a good way to describe the 1970 Dodge Challenger T/A sport coupe. Chrysler Corporation's Dodge Division scheduled production of 2,500 copies to meet the requirements for racing its new Challenger "pony car" in the Sports Car Club of America's (SCCA) Trans-American Sedan Championship series.

The Trans-Am was a competitive venue for small-block-V-8-powered two-door hardtops and two-door sedans. Chrysler's Pete Hutchinson used a de-stroked 340-cid V-8 block as the basis for a competition coupe with only 305-cid, but 440 hp. Ray Caldwell—who worked for a company called Autodynamics—built the Challenger T/A that Sam Posey drove to fourth place in SCCA standings.

Street-ready T/As had the same snorkel-type hood scoop, side-exit exhausts and lock-pin-secured flat-black hood as the racing car. They had differences in the engine compartment, however. The special underhood goodies included a 340-cid six-pack engine and

choice of TorqueFlite automatic transmission or a four-speed gearbox.

A ducktail rear deck lid spoiler was part of the package, along with heavy-duty underpinnings. The package included a Sure-Grip differential. Performance axle ratios, semi-metallic front disc and rear drum brakes, a specific black body side tape stripe and mixed size tires (E60-15 tires were used up front with G60-15s mounted in the rear). To provide clearance for the pipes of the dual exhaust system with the fatter rear tires, the T/As were "jacked up" in the rear through the use of increased rear spring camber.

The 1970 Challenger T/As were good for 0-60 mph in a flat 6 seconds. They could hit 100 mph in 14 seconds and do the quarter mile in 14.5 seconds. An eight-page ad in *Hot Rod* magazine's October 1970 issue showed a yellow and black 1971 Challenger T/A. However, no production versions of the Challenger T/A was actually manufactured by Dodge Division that year.

1970 DODGE CHARGER 500 "383"

Naturally, the attention-getting Dodge Charger 500 that had been introduced in 1969 was back again in 1970. This year it did not have any aerodynamic enhancements like flush-mounted grille or flush rear window glass. It was available with a six-cylinder engine for $3,139 or with a 318-cid base V-8 for $3,246.

Neither of these models was a true muscle car and the 500 model in standard form was little more than a regular Charger with "500" badges. The main extras in the 500 package were new vinyl front bucket seats, an electric clock and wheel lip moldings. New options included a pistol-grip gear shifter and an electrically operated sunroof.

The biggest regular engine option for the 1970 Charger 500

was the 383-cid V-8. It came in a two-barrel E61 version for $69.70, but this had only modest appeal to enthusiasts. The E63 version, with a single four-barrel carburetor added $137.55 to the price. The 383-cid four-barrel V-8 was offered in 330-hp and 335-hp options and the latter was significantly different than the former. The more powerful version used the 375-hp 440-cid engine's Plymouth Commando/Dodge Magnum camshaft and freer flowing heads. It had a new cast-iron intake manifold that carried a Holley four-barrel carburetor rather than a Carter AVS carburetor.

The Charger R/T was available with 440 Six-Pack and Hemi V-8s, but these weren't listed as regular production options for the Charger 500.

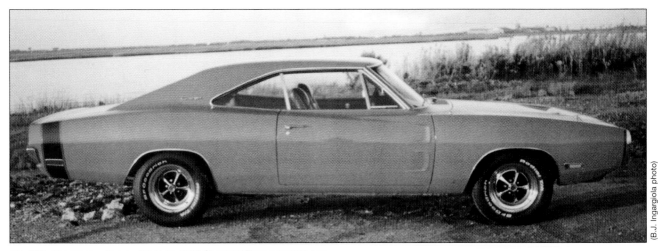

(B.J. Ingargiola photo)

The 383-cid engine option qualified the 1970 Charger 500 as a muscle car.

In addition to 13 standard exterior colors, buyers could special order plum crazy, sublime, go mango, Hemi orange and banana yellow paint.

None of the 1970 Charger 500s were made with Hemi engines.

This wasn't as much a muscle car as the '69 edition, but we felt that muscle car buyers should be aware of the big difference between the two years. Plus, there's the rare possibility that cars with special-order engine options were produced.

1970 DODGE CHARGER R/T

(Jerry Heasley photo)

A bright pink Dodge Charger R/T fastback would get you noticed in 1970.

The 1970 Dodge Charger continued to use the same body as in 1969 with minor trim changes. The R/T was again marketed as a higher-performance version. It had a new grille, a new loop-style front bumper, two hood scoops near the outside edges of the hood, big bolt-on scoops with R/T badges on the rear quarter panels and a choice of longitudinal or bumblebee racing stripes. A new interior and some wild exterior colors were offered.

The 440-cid Magnum V-8 engine was standard equipment, along with TorqueFlite automatic transmission, a heavy-duty 70-amp/hour battery, heavy-duty automatic-adjusting drum brakes, heavy-duty front and rear shock absorbers, an extra-heavy-duty suspension, three-speed windshield wipers, all-vinyl front bucket seats, carpeting, a cigar lighter and F70-14 fiberglass-belted white sidewall tires or black sidewall raised-white-letter tires. R/T model designations were also carried on the center of the rear escutcheon panel

below the Dodge name.

All Charger R/T models included blacked-out escutcheon panels and large bumblebee stripes running across the trunk lid and down the rear fender sides. A hefty jump to $3,711 was seen in the price of the basic 440 Magnum-powered Charger R/T for 1970. Total production this year dropped to 10,337 units, including a mere 42 cars with 426 Hemis.

Motor Trend did a comparison test between a 440-powered Charger R/T, a Mercury Cyclone GT and an Oldsmobile Cutlass SX in April 1970. The test car again had the stock 375 hp at 4600 rpm and 480 ft. lbs. of torque at 3200 rpm. It also had the 3.55:1 rear axle. The car did 0 to 60 mph in 6.4 seconds and covered the quarter mile in 14.9 seconds at 98 mph. It also averaged 14.9 to 15.7 mpg, much better than the two other cars. The magazine liked the Charger R/T's image and race-bred heritage.

1970 DODGE CORONET R/T

For 1970, new sheet metal graced the front of the R/T, adding a smooth split grille that tapered towards the center. Dummy rear fender scoops above and ahead of the front wheel openings were now standard. The air scoops wore R/T emblems (which were repeated on the nose and between the segmented, tapering tail lamps). A bumblebee stripe circled the rear end of the car.

The Coronet R/T hardtop was base priced at $3,569 and had a production run of 2,319 units. Only 296 Coronet R/T convertibles (base priced at $3,785) were made. It was the last year for the Coronet convertible body style and also the last year for the Coronet R/T model.

Standard R/T equipment included all Coronet 500 features plus the 440-cid Magnum V-8 engine, TorqueFlite automatic transmission, a heavy-duty 70-amp/hour battery, heavy-duty self-adjusting drum brakes, heavy-duty front and rear shock absorbers, extra-heavy-duty suspension, three-speed windshield wipers, all-vinyl front bucket seats, carpeting, a cigar lighter, F70-14 tires (whitewall or raised white letter) and twin hood air scoops. Buyer's could substitute a four-speed manual gearbox for the TorqueFlite if they preferred to shift for themselves.

Engines were essentially the same as before with the "440 Six-Pack" back for the second year with its triple two-barrel carburetors. The 426-cid 425-hp Hemi was priced at $718 and only 14 Hemi R/Ts—13 hardtops and one convertible—were built. The R/T continued to come in an outrageous assortment of colors, like plum crazy (purple), sublime (green), go-mango, Hemi orange and banana yellow. Optional vinyl roofs came in black, white, green or "gator grain."

Five Scat Pack options were available to muscle car fans who wanted to dress up their Coronet R/T a little bit. They included the Showboat engine dress-up kit, the Read-Out gauge package, the Kruncher axle and Hurst shifter combination, the Bee-Liever high-rise manifold and carb setup and the six-pack option with a fiberglass hood and other hi-po goodies.

1970 DODGE CORONET SUPER BEE

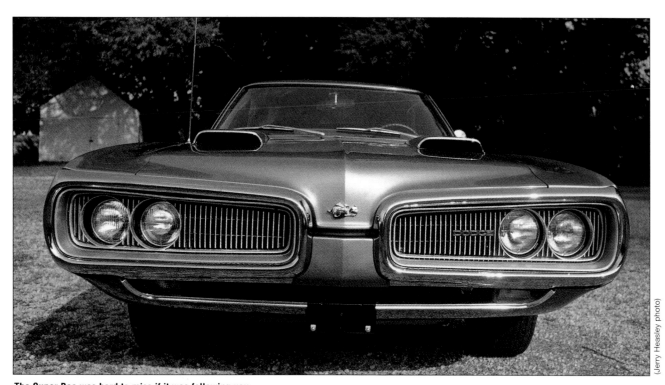

(Jerry Heasley photo)

The Super Bee was hard to miss if it was following you.

Restyled for 1970 along the lines of the Coronet R/T, the Super Bee did not get the dummy rear fender scoops as standard equipment. It also had horizontally divided (rather than individually segmented) tail lamps. New options included a hood tach and spoiler. Buyers could get the R/T-type bumblebee stripe or pipe-shaped upper and lower rear fender stripes with a circular Super Bee decal between them.

"Dodge introduces a new model Super Bee at a new lower price. $3,074," said an advertisement on the inside front cover of the April 1970 edition of *Motor Trend* magazine. According to the copy, that was $64 lower than the previous year's price. Actually, the base prices of both models were lowered $64 and more standard features were added at the same time.

"We've added as standard equipment a couple of last year's popular options like fiberglass-belted wide-tread tires," said the ad. "Then we put in what you couldn't get with last year's Super Bee: Lane-change signal; key-left-in-ignition buzzer; three-way ignition, steering and transmission lock."

Still standard ingredients were the 383-cid magnum V-8, a heavy-duty torsion-bar suspension and a three-speed manual transmission (last year's four-speed manual gear box was optional). Despite the price reduction, production dropped to 11,540 hardtops and 3,966 coupes. Hemis went into only 32 hardtops (21 with four-speed) and four coupes (all four-speeds). Wouldn't you love to own one today?

1970 DODGE DART SWINGER 340

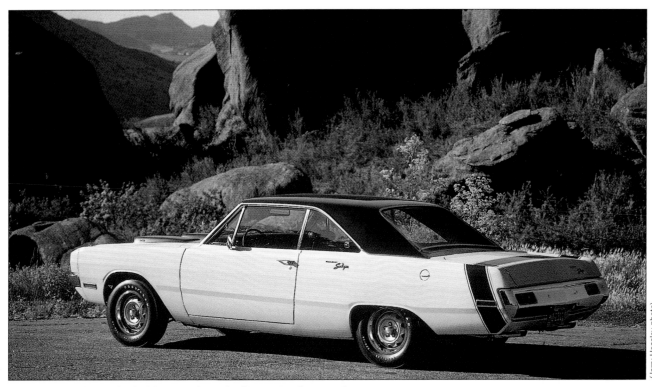

The Dart was perhaps undersized for a muscle car, but it was not underpowered.

Another member of the Dodge "Scat Pack" returning in 1969 was the Swinger 340 two-door hardtop. It had revised front and rear cosmetics and a slightly lower $2,808 price tag. A three-speed manual gearbox was on the standard equipment list. Instead of small power vents, the mini Mopar muscle machine now carried two long, narrow hood scoops.

Other standard Swinger 340 features included a 3.23:1 rear axle ratio, Firm Ride shock absorbers, a Rallye suspension, E78-14 fiberglass belted black sidewall tires and Dart 340 nameplates on the front fenders, just in back of the front wheel openings. Front disc brakes were also included.

Despite the introduction of the Challenger, the Swinger 340 remained popular enough to generate 13,785 assemblies. One reason for its popularity was that insurance companies considered it a "compact" car and charged lower premiums than other muscle cars required. Of course, it was also as fast as—or even slightly faster than—the 340 powered Dart GT Sport. It accomplished 0 to 60 mph in about 6.5 seconds and did the quarter mile in around 14.5 seconds. At 3,179 lbs., the '70 Swinger carried about 11.4 lbs. per horsepower and proved to be highly motivated by the 340's "herd" of 275 horses.

Even today, muscle car collectors can find bargains in the Swinger 340 market, since these cars don't look as flashy as a GTS, although they are equally as fast.

The 1970 Dodge Dart Swinger 340 hardtop featured two distinctive hood scoops.

1971 DODGE HEMI CHALLENGER

CHALLENGER T/A
End of the road for the Do-It-Yourself Kit.

This is one car where the list of standard equipment is longer than the list of options. Hey, man, this isn't the beginning of something great, it's the driving end.

Big bias-belted skins in front, bigger ones in back. The good shift, Hurst style. Power discs up front: drums, heavy-duty, in the rear. Dual exhausts with low restriction mufflers, chrome side exit megaphones.

Challenger T/A. Just the way you'd do it yourself. If you had the time. And the money. Yeah, the money. Frankly, it would probably cost you more to do it yourself. So why bother

with do-it-yourself dreams? Check out this bargain for the man who'd rather be moving than building.

Check out the Standard Equipment List carefully. You'll find that everything is in order. From engine to drive train, Dodge puts it all together for you.

STANDARD EQUIPMENT

340 4-bbl. V8 □ TorqueFlite automatic transmission or 4-on-the-floor fully synchronized manual transmission □ Fiber-glass hood with Fresh Air Pack □ Hood pins □ Special Rallye Suspension (includes rear sway bar, larger front sway bar, heavy-duty shock ab-

sorbers, increased camber of rear springs) □ Rear duck tail □ Low-restriction dual side exit exhaust with megaphones □ Tires: E60x15, front; G60x15, rear; raised white letters □ 15x7.0JJ wheels □ Power front disc brakes with special semimetallic pads; 10″ rear drums □ 3.55 axle ratio—8¾ ring gear □ Vinyl front bucket seats □ Deep-pile carpeting □ Simulated wood-grained door trim inserts □ Locking flip-top gas cap □ Flush outside door handles □ T/A body side tape stripes □ Grille and deck panel blackout.

The 1971 Dodge Hemi Challenger Sport Coupe was pure muscle.

Dodge scored a hit with its first pony car, the 1970 Challenger. Up until then, Dodge had relied on special mid-size Chargers and Coronets and compact Darts to uphold its performance image. With

the Plymouth Barracuda due for a total restyling in 1970, Dodge was handed the same package to create a 2 + 2 configuration to compete with Pontiac's Firebird and Mercury's Cougar.

The Challenger succeeded so well that it outsold the Barracuda 83,000 to 55,000 in its first year. The next season, though, sales fell off drastically and the Challenger sold 30,000 units. Still, the Barracuda's dropped to 19,000.

With the Challenger, Dodge was clearly selling performance in a package that looked the part. So it's not surprising that 93 percent of the 1971 model run was fitted with V-8 engines, even though the "Slant Six" was available. Nearly 17 percent were optional engines, ranging all the way up to the 425-hp Hemi.

Unfortunately, 1971 would be the last year for the 426-cid Hemi, as emissions, safety and insurance considerations put the horsepower race under a caution flag. However, in 1971, Dodge was definitely promoting power and performance.

The Street Hemi engine, a $790 option on the '71 Challenger, had continued unchanged after its introduction in 1966. It had a bore and stroke of 4.25 x 3.75 inches, a 10.25:1 compression ratio, hydraulic valve lifters and dual four-barrel Carter AFB carbs mounted inline.

On the Hemi Challengers, a flat-black finished air scoop was mounted to the carbs and poked through a hole in the hood. This was the impressive "shaker" hood, so named because you could watch the torque twist the engine as throttle was applied. Some cars also had chrome NASCAR-style hood hold-down pins.

The R/T (the initials stood for "road/track") was Dodge's high-performance car. The R/T package for the '71 Challenger included Rallye suspension, an instrument cluster with an 8,000-rpm tachometer and 150-mph speedometer, plus heavy-duty drum brakes, chrome exhaust tips and distinctive graphic stripes. On top of the R/T performance package, Dodge offered the SE (for Special Edition) trim package. It included a vinyl top and choice of leather or vinyl upholstery. Other extras included chrome wheel well and door edge moldings, twin outside rearview mirrors and an AM/FM/cassette stereo with rear speakers and a microphone.

For maximum visual impact, as well as an outward statement of purpose, many Hemi Challenger owners selected bright Hemi orange paint trimmed in white. After all, if you put the big engine under the hood, you might as well let the world know it.

1971 DODGE CHALLENGER R/T HEMI

(John Lee photo)

The 1971 Dodge Challenger R/Ts came with a standard 250-hp 383-cid Magnum V-8, but a few carried the optional 426-cid Street Hemi.

For 1971, the Dodge Challenger R/T sub-series had only one model left. This was the two-door hardtop. It listed for $3,273 and weighed 3,495 lbs. With the muscle car fervor winding down, this rare car found a mere 4,630 buyers. Styling changes in 1971 included a new grille, color-keyed bumpers and two dummy scoops in front of the rear wheel wells.

Standard equipment on all 1971 Challengers included Chrysler's Air Control system, front and rear side armrests, a front ash tray, a cigarette lighter (except in the base Challenger coupe), an evaporative emission control system, color-keyed carpeting, ventless side glass, a glove box with a rotary latch (lockable in convertibles), dual headlights, a heater and defroster, dual horns (except coupe), dome and parking-brake system warning lights, a manual left-hand outside mirror, an inside day-night mirror, roof drip moldings, wheel opening moldings (except Coupe), bucket seats with foam front cushions, a three-spoke steering wheel with simulated woodgrain and a padded hub and electric windshield wipers.

A 198-cid six or Chrysler's 318-cid V-8 were considered the 1971 Challenger's base engines. The R/T model also included heavy-duty drum brakes, bright exhaust tips, a Rallye instrument cluster with simulated wood grain trim, a Rallye suspension, body side tape stripes, variable-speed windshield wipers, F70 x 14 bias-

belted whitewall tires and a 383-cid four-barrel V-8. All of Chrysler's 1971 base engines had lower compression ratios. The Challenger R/T's standard 383-cid Magnum V-8 came with an 8.5:1 compression ratio and was rated for 250 nhp. However, the optional performance power plants were still available.

Only 71 of the Challenger R/Ts with the 426-cid Street Hemi V-8 were ordered this season. A dozen of these cars had TorqueFlite automatic transmission. The rest were equipped with a four-speed manual transmission. It was the last year for the Challenger R/T model.

1971 DODGE CHARGER R/T 440/440 SIX-PACK

(Jerry Heasley photo)

The Charger R/T 440 Six-Pack was Dodge Division's quintessential "street muscle" car.

The Dodge Charger started life in 1966 as a semi-limited-production specialty car, but it caught on and grew to become an important part of the Chrysler division's line. In 1969, more than 70,000 Chargers were sold. For 1971, management decided that it was time to give the Charger an image of its own—one quite separate from that of the mid-sized Coronet. The Charger name was applied to two-door hardtops that now had a 115-inch wheelbase, while the Coronet name was used on 118-inch-wheelbase four-door sedans.

The re-sized Charger was 2 inches shorter in wheelbase than the 1970 model and more than 3 inches shorter at 205.4 inches. However, it had nearly 3 more inches of front overhang and 3 1/2 inches more width. This made it the perfect size for a sporty performance car. The Charger R/T was the quintessential "muscle" model and technically represented a sub-series of the middle-priced Charger 500 series. It included all of the many features of the Charger 500, plus hot stuff like heavy-duty underpinnings and the 440-cid Magnum V-8.

This engine had the same 3.75-inch stroke as the 426-cid Hemi, but a larger 4.32-inch bore size. The base version, with a single four-barrel carburetor, produced 370 hp at 4600 rpm and 480 ft. lbs. of torque at 3200 rpm. It had a 9.1:1 compression ratio. In a four-Charger test in December 1970, *Motor Trend* drove a 370-hp 1971 Charger SE with automatic transmission and a 3.23:1 rear axle. It did 0 to 60 mph in a flat 7 seconds and covered the quarter mile in 14.93 seconds at 96.4 mph.

Also featured in the same test was a 1971 Charger Super Bee

with the 440 "Six-Pack" engine. This version added three two-barrel carburetors and a 10.3:1 compression ratio. The Six-Pack V-8 developed 385 hp at 4700 rpm and 490 ft. lbs. of torque at 3200 rpm. The car it was in also had an automatic transmission, but it was hooked to a 4.10:1 rear axle. This cut the 0 to-60 time to 6.9 seconds. The Super Bee did the quarter mile in 14.74 seconds at 97.3 mph.

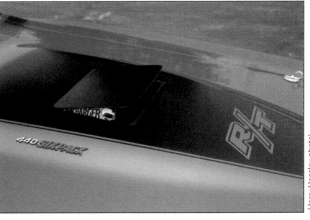

(Jerry Heasley photo)

The 440 Six-Pack needed breathing room and produced 390 hp.

1971 DODGE CHARGER SUPER BEE HEMI

A mere 22 1971 Dodge Hemi Charger Super Bees were built.

(Jerry Heasley photo)

The Hemi Charger Super Bee could fly down the quarter-mile drag strip in 13.7 seconds.

(Jerry Heasley photo)

The Charger was completely restyled for the 1971 model year. It had a semi-fastback roofline with a flush rear window and an integral rear deck lid spoiler. Dodge's one-year-only Charger Super Bee used the same body. It was aimed at the same market niche as the Coronet Super Bee and represented a low-cost, high-performance package.

Price-tagged at $3,271, the Charger Super Bee included a standard 383-cid 300-hp Magnum V-8, four-barrel carburetor, three-speed floor-mounted gear shifter, a "power bulge" hood with flat black finish, tape stripes, bumblebee decals and an interior similar to that of the Charger 500, but substituting a standard bench seat. The Rallye suspension components package was used. It included heavy-duty front torsion bars, heavy-duty rear springs, a front anti-sway bar, heavy-duty shock absorbers and heavy-duty brakes (11 x 3 inches up front and 11 x 2.5 inches in the rear). The tires were fat F70-14s and the optional equipment list was fat, too.

Available engines included the 440 Six-Pack or the 426-cid Street Hemi. Unlike the 8.7:1 compression base engine, these muscle car mills had high-test hardware and continued to offer 390 or 425 hp. Other neat extras were a first-for-the-Charger functional Ramcharger hood scoop, color-keyed bumpers, a Super Trak-Pack performance axle (with up to 4.10:1 gearing), a four-speed gearbox with Hurst "pistol grip" shifter, a dual-point distributor, heavy-duty cooling aids and bucket seats.

The 440 Six-Pack Charger Super Bee was advertised at 485 hp. It did 0 to 60 mph in 6.9 seconds and the quarter mile took 14.7. With a Hemi V-8, this 3,640-lb. machine moved into the same bracket as the original Charger 500, needing only 5.7 seconds to get up to 60 mph and a mere 13.7 to reach the traps at a drag strip!

Not too many 1971 Charger Hemi Super Bees were built. In fact, the total was 22 cars, of which nine had four-speeds and 13 came with TorqueFlite automatic transmissions.

1971 DODGE HEMI CHARGER

The Dodge Charger was given a complete restyling in 1971. This was done to make it look more distinct from the Coronet. A new 115-inch wheelbase chassis was used to carry semi-fastback coupe and hardtop bodies.

All models featured rear quarter window styling that swept up from the fender to meet the sloping upper rear window frame. A full-width bumper/grille was split by a large vertical divider and the rear end was set off with a small "lip" on the trunk lid that formed a short

spoiler.

The base Charger was offered with the choice of a 225-cid Slant Six engine for $2,707 or a 318-cid small-block V-8 for $2,802. The hotter Charger 500 series—which included the $3,271 Super Bee model and the $3,422 SE (special edition) model—came standard with a 383-cid "big-block" V-8. There was also a one-car R/T series. The Charger R/T listed for $3,777 and included a 70-amp-hour battery; heavy-duty brakes, heavy-duty shock absorbers, a

Only 63 of these Charger R/Ts were produced with the Hemi V-8.

(Jerry Heasley photo)

pedal dress-up kit, an extra-heavy-duty Rallye suspension, TorqueFlite automatic transmission (or a four-speed manual gear box), a 440-cid Magnum V-8 and R/T identification.

The 426-cid Hemi V-8 was available in Charger R/Ts for $707 extra and in Charger Super Bees for an additional $837. The "Street Hemi" had a 4.25 x 3.75-inch bore and stroke, a 10.25:1 compression ratio and twin Carter AFB four-barrel carburetors. It produced

425 hp at 5600 rpm! According to Mopar authority Galen V. Govier Hemi Charger production was extremely low. The big engine was bolted into 22 of the 1971 Charger Super Bees and 63 Charger R/Ts.

In December 1970, *Motor Trend* road tested a Hemi Super Bee with automatic transmission and a 4.10:1 ratio rear axle. The car did 0 to 60 mph in 5.7 seconds. The quarter mile was covered in an elapsed time of 13.73 seconds at 104 mph.

1971 DODGE DART DEMON 340

The quick and successful 1971 Dodge Dart "Demon 340" coupe was renamed the Dart Sport starting in 1973.

(Jerry Heasley photo)

After its runaway sales success as the 1970 Plymouth Valiant Duster, Dodge Division of Chrysler Corp. couldn't wait to get its hands on the 108-inch wheelbase coupe version for its compact Dart line. That chance came in the fall of 1970, when the Dart Demon was added to the 1971 lineup. It was the first Dart, since its inception as a long compact for 1963, to have less than a 111-inch wheelbase.

Like the Duster, the Demon came in two models. The base version had the 198-cid "Slant Six" and minimal equipment. It listed for $2,343, only $30 over the base Duster. More interesting was the Demon 340, which at $2,721 was a mere $18 upstream from the Duster 340. It came standard with a well-balanced 275-gross horsepower version of the 340-cid small-block V-8. A three-speed, fully synchronized floor shifter was standard along with a Rallye instrument cluster, heavy-duty suspension, E70-14 rubber, stripes and dual exhaust.

Playing the option list was the name of the game with domestic compacts and the 340 had some interesting extras. They included a dual-scoop hood complete with hood pins, rear spoiler and "Tuff" steering wheel. You could also order a four-speed manual

gearbox, TorqueFlite automatic transmission or an upgraded interior.

The 340 was a card-carrying member of the 1971 Dodge "Scat Pack," which boasted many performance cars. It would be the final year for the Scat Pack, however. At midyear, the Demon Sizzler option package became available. It was on the base Demon and started with the base six, but it added some of the 340's pieces and stripes to the base model. Demons also became the vehicles of choice for Pro Stock Dodge-mounted drag racers. Though the basic body was used, the cars were highly modified.

All the tricks worked and the Demon was a success, with 69,861 base models built and the 340 adding 10,098 more. While cousin Duster produced 173,592 base models, the 340 sales race was surprisingly close, as the Plymouth version came in at 12,886.

The Dodge Demon returned for 1972, but the name was scrapped after that, in part because the religious community less than thrilled by the name. Dart Sport nomenclature sufficed from 1973 models through the end of production after the 1976 model year.

1972 DODGE DEMON 340

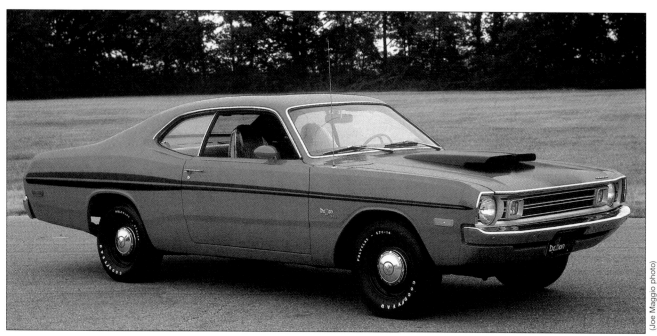

(Joe Maggio photo)

For 1972, the Dodge Demon got minor trim and taillight changes.

In January 1971, *Motor Trend* writer Jim Brokaw described the first Dodge Demon 340 as a "reasonable alternative" for buyers who wanted an insurable muscle car with just enough spice to make it interesting. The Demon was essentially a repainted and striped Plymouth Duster with a bit more styling flair and tougher quality control.

In the 1971 road test, the Demon was compared to the Mercury Comet GT, the Chevrolet Nova SS 350 and the AMC Hornet SC 360. Although it did not have the biggest engine of the pack, it was the top performer. The $2,721 car did the quarter mile in 14.49 seconds at 98.25 mph, and it went from a standing start to 60 mph in 6.5 seconds, which was also best among the four cars.

The 340-cid V-8 had a 4.04 x 3.31-inch bore and stroke. It developed 275 hp at 5000 rpm and 340 ft. lbs. of torque at 3200 rpm. It came as standard equipment in the Demon 340 with a single four-

barrel carburetor and 10.0:1 compression ratio. This mini Mopar muscle machine was the only one of the four cars tested to feature a four-speed manual transmission. The other came with three-speed stick shift, which was standard in the Demon 340. A 3.91:1 rear axle was used along with E70-14 tires. Curb weight was 3,360 lbs., making it the heaviest of the lot.

For 1972, the Dodge Demon received just minor trim and taillight changes. It remained on the same 108-inch wheelbase utilized the year before. It was 192.5 inches long, 71.6 inches wide and 52.8 inches high. Dodge used a 57.5-inch front track and a 55.5-inch rear track. If you ordered a 1972 Demon 340, Dodge would add heavy-duty shock absorbers front and rear, a front sway bar and heavy-duty torsion bars. The 1972 version of the 340-cid engine had a lower 8.5:1 compression ratio and carried an output rating of 240 nhp.

1992 DODGE DAYTONA IROC/RT

Dodge's performance selection, which already included two of the fastest production cars on the market, was expanded even more with the midyear introduction of the 1992 Daytona IROC/RT. This new entry fit between the Dodge Stealth sports car and the Dodge Spirit R/T four-door sports sedan. The initial appearance of the latter model, in 1991, struck a chord with auto enthusiasts.

At the heart of the Daytona IROC/RT was the same 2.2-liter, 16-valve, DOHC turbocharged four-cylinder engine that powered the Spirit R/T. This high-performance engine was exclusive to the IROC/RT model in the Daytona lineup.

While it shared the exterior refreshening applied to the entire line, the IROC/RT boasted a few aesthetic extras of its own. The suspension redesign introduced on the 1991 Daytona (and other Chryslers) in 1991 was re-tuned especially for the IROC/RT to accommodate its more aggressive character.

The IROC/RT 2.2 turbo engine, which included an intercooler and twin balance shafts, had the highest specific power output—

100 hp per liter—of any production engine ever developed by Chrysler Engineering. It produced 224 hp at 6000 rpm and 217 foot-pounds of torque at 2800 rpm with an engine redline of 6500 rpm.

Some of the front-end Dodge performance cues from the Stealth and the then-yet-to-be-introduced Dodger Viper were incorporated into the IROC/RT appearance. A new Daytona hood treatment continued forward into a redesigned front fascia that replaced the previous grille opening panel. In addition, aero-style headlamps displaced the former hidden headlamps. The IROC/RT sported fascia openings for fog lamps, as well as an aggressive front air dam configuration. This two-door hatchback, which seated four passengers, also had stylish application of body side cladding.

Specific performance re-tuning in the IROC/RT afforded a better balanced ride and more driver control. The spring rates were revised and stronger front struts and larger rear shock absorbers were employed.

1992 DODGE VIPER RT/10

It all started in a brainstorming session by Chrysler's president Bob Lutz, vice-president of design Tom Gale, vice president of vehicle engineering Francois Castaing and race car legend Carroll Shelby. They thought it was time for a successor to the great American sports cars of the 1960s. Shelby's famous Cobra was used as a benchmark.

They envisioned a car that brought back all the memories and emotions of the 1960s roadster, but with the technology and refinement of the 1990s. Their concepts laid out the pattern for the Dodge Viper.

All involved agreed that the new car had to have a smooth, sensuous shape that appealed to enthusiasts who fondly remember the great Cobras. It had to fit equally well in someone's driveway or at the racetrack. It had to be more stunning and more refined than the original Cobra. And all this had to be incorporated into a package selling for under $50,000.

Gale used the analogy of remembering a high school sweetheart. "In the mind's eye, looking back, we always remember her as absolutely perfect. She was gorgeous, intelligent, courteous. Everything a perfect person could be. That's how the Viper had to be. In our minds' eye, the Cobra was perfect. So, we had to design Viper as we remembered Cobra."

The shape recalled the roadsters of the mid-1960s and featured an integrated sport bar and side exhaust pipes. The full-width sport bar contained both head restraints and high-mounted stop lamp. The instrument panel provided large, driver-oriented analog gauges.

Recreating the Cobra's driving attributes and making them "perfect" for the modern world was Francois Castaing's job. "The Viper had to evoke all the emotions of driving the 1960s muscle car, but it had to be refined to today's engineering standards. The engine had to be powerful—and sound like it—but much more drivable and durable than yesterday's muscle car engines," Castaing said.

Power for the concept car came from an aluminum V-10 engine that produced 400 hp and 450 ft. lbs. of torque. It was mated to a six-speed transmission that featured a gated selector. The Viper rode on 17-inch wheels and tires.

The original Viper concept car made its debut at the North American International Auto Show in Detroit in January 1989. The reaction from both the press and the public was overwhelmingly positive. Letters started flowing into the Chrysler headquarters demanding that the car be developed for production. Enthusiastic customers mailed deposit checks directly to Chrysler Corporation for the car (the checks were returned).

Chrysler quickly formed a small task force to study the feasibility of producing such a vehicle for today's market. Chassis mules were built to study vehicle dynamics. Within a year, the first V-8 Viper prototype was completed. A second, this time powered by a V-10 engine, was completed by spring 1990.

In May 1990, Chrysler Chairman Lee Iacocca announced the official "go ahead" for the program. The task force grew to a team of 85 engineers, designers, finance experts, purchasing agents and manufacturing personnel representing every aspect of vehicle development. They worked side by side to bring Viper to market.

Iacocca challenged Team Viper to bring the Viper to production within three years from the time the first Viper Concept Car was shown in January 1989—a world-class development time.

Although some minor modifications were made between its debut at the Indianapolis 500 and final production, the Dodge Viper Pace Car was nearly identical to the showroom version of the car. It was seen and driven for the first time publicly at Indianapolis Motor Speedway that May. The Pace Car retained all the design and engineering integrity that made it such a popular concept car. The shape remained intact and the performance lived up to its promise. In fact, the Viper needed no power-train modifications to pace the race. It was only the third vehicle in the race's 75 years able to make that claim.

The fact that a Viper prototype paced the Indianapolis 500 was a testament to the program proceeding on schedule. A total of 285 Viper RT/10 roadsters were produced in 1992. They carried serial numbers 1B3BR65E( )NV100001 to 1B3BR65E( )NV100285 (the N indicated 1992 and the V indicated the New Mack Avenue assembly plant). All the cars were originally painted red. However, three Vipers used as factory development cars were repainted in three different colors: black, green and yellow. On one car, the standard grey interior was replaced with a black one.

The 1992 models had a retail price of $50,700, plus a $2,600 gas guzzler tax and a $2,280 luxury tax. The 488-cid (8.01-liters) V-10 engine had a bore and stroke of 4.00 x 3.88 inches. It produced 400 hp at 4600 rpm and 465 ft. lbs. of torque at 3600 rpm.

1993 DODGE VIPER RT/10

For 1993, the Dodge Viper RT/10 was scheduled to get several new colors. Black, green and yellow were announced, along with a special black-and-tan interior (instead of grey) that was to be combined with the green paint. In the end, however, only the black Viper became a reality. Green and dandelion (a new name for yellow) were held over to be new features for the 1994 Viper.

The 1993 Viper's wholesale price was $43,125 and the list price was $50,000. A $700 destination charge applied. Uncle Sam collected a gas guzzler tax of $2,100 and a $2,280 luxury tax. Power again came from the same 8-liter V-10 with 400 hp. It featured a 9.1:1 compression ratio, electronic direct ignition and sequential multipoint fuel injection.

Standard Viper equipment included: a tubular space frame with a center spine structure, a side-mounted stainless steel exhaust system, composite body panels with a reinforced skin. a four-wheel independent suspension with unequal-length upper and lower control arms and a coil-over-shocks design, double-acting Koni gas shocks with rebound adjustment, tubular design front and rear sway bars, rear-wheel drive with a limited-slip differential, air-conditioning prep (A/C wiring harness, adaptable instrument control panel and pre-set engine electronic control unit), power-assisted four-piston four-wheel vented disc brakes, aluminum directional three-spoke silver wheels with a six-bolt mounting flange (17 x 10-inch up front and 17 x 13-inch in the rear with a 16 x 4-inch eight-spoke spare), Michelin XGTZ speed-rated directional tires (P275/40ZR 17 front, P335/35ZR17 rear and T155/80D16 Michelin spare), aero polyellipsoid halogen headlamps, a leather-wrapped steering wheel and shifter knob, power-assisted rack-and-pinion steering, an energy-absorbing tilt steering column, a forward-hinged one-piece clamshell hood, two-way manual seat adjusters with linear recliners, fog lamps with removable lens covers, bold graphic white-faced analog gauges; a tonneau cover with a nylon center zipper; a folding top with a removable rear window and plastic zipper-windowed side curtains and a premium sound system with AM/FM cassette stereo.

1994 DODGE VIPER RT/10

The futuristic 1994 Dodge Viper RT/10 roadster retailed for a whopping $54,500.

(Joe Maggio photo)

The 1994 Viper had speed to match its looks. It could reach 165 mph.

(Joe Maggio photo)

Buying a 1994 model Dodge Viper RT/10 roadster was a more expensive proposition. The dealer wholesale price rose to $47,450 and the suggested retail price went up to $54,500. Many cars were sold for above sticker price. The destination charge remained $700 and the gas guzzler tax was again $2,100, but the luxury tax (based on 10 percent of the price in excess of $30,000) rose a bit to $2,520.

An antitheft security system became standard equipment and factory air conditioning was now a $1,200 option. All cars still came "wired for air." Other 1994 changes were minor, but they included a transmission reverse lockout function; mesh map pockets on the seats; a passenger-door grab handle and a Viper embossed heat shield and EMI protector attached to the underside of the hood. All cars built this year had a windshield mounted radio antenna and amplifier.

Production nearly tripled in the Viper's third year and Dodge produced 3,083 Viper RT/10 roadsters in the 1994 model year. They carried VINs 1B3BR65E ( ) RV100001 to 1B3BR65E( )RV103087. The first symbol 1 indicated U.S. manufacture; the second symbol B indicated a Dodge product; the third symbol 3 indicated a passenger car; the fourth symbol B indicated manual seat belts (used on all 1994 Vipers); the fifth symbol R indicated the Viper car line; the sixth symbol 6 indicated what Chrysler termed a "performance-image" series; the seventh symbol 5 indicated an open boy model; the eighth symbol E indicated the V-10 engine; the ninth symbol was a check digit; the 10th symbol R indicated 1994 and the 11 symbol V indicated the New Mack Avenue assembly plant. The remaining digits were the sequential production number.

The 1994 Viper RT/10 roadster accelerated from 0 to 60 mph in 4.6 seconds and did the quarter mile in 12.9 seconds at 113.8 mph. It had a top speed of 165 mph. Chrysler estimated that 2,189 of the 1994 models were finished in red, 678 were black, 133 were Viper emerald green pearl and 83 were viper bright yellow.

1995 DODGE VIPER RT/10

"New exterior design themes" was the terminology that Chrysler adapted in the fall of 1994 to promote the availability of several new color combinations for the 1995 Dodge Viper RT/10 roadster. In addition to basic Viper red, black, emerald green and Viper bright yellow with the standard cast-aluminum directional wheels and forged aluminum wheel caps, buyers could now opt for a red exterior with yellow five-spoke wheels, a black exterior with a silver center stripe or a white exterior with a blue center stripe.

The base price for a Viper remained at $54,500 and standard equipment again included the 8.0-liter V-10 engine, a six-speed manual transmission, four-wheel independent suspension, power-assisted rack-and-pinion steering; dual stainless-steel side exhausts and 17-inch wheels. There were now three options: air conditioning, California emissions and Massachusettes emissions.

Production dropped nearly in half this season with Dodge pro-ducing 1,577 Viper RT/10 roadsters during the 1995 model year. This included about 515 black cars, 458 red cars, 307 green cars and 298 yellow cars. Grey-and-black interiors were used in 1,005 cars and 572 Vipers had a tan-and-black interior.

Like the 1992 to 1994 models, the official performance figures for the 1995 Viper RT/10 roadster were 0 to 60 mph in 4.6 seconds and the quarter mile in 12.9 seconds at 113.8 mph. The top speed of 165 mph was also generally quoted again.

Although the 1995 model year didn't bring a great deal of exciting changes to the Viper line it did register a couple of histori-cal milestones. It was the last year that Vipers were produced in the New Mack Avenue assembly plant. It was also the year that the pilot model for the dramatic Dodge Viper GTS-R coupe was unveiled at the Pebble Beach Concours d'Elegance in Monterey, California.

1996 DODGE VIPER RT/10 ROADSTER

The 1996 Dodge Viper RT/10 roadster received several enhancements including a removable hardtop, sliding rigid plastic side windows, a more robust differential, stronger drive shafts, aluminum suspension control arms and revised spring and shock absorber rates.

The 488-cid (8.0-liter) V-10 engine continued to power the Viper. The 90-degree V-10 had a cast aluminum block with cast iron cylinder liners, aluminum cylinder heads and an aluminum crankcase. It had a 4.00-inch bore and a 3.88-inch stroke and a 9.1:1 compression ratio. It was attached to a six-speed manual, fully synchronized transmission with electronic 1-4 skip-shift and reverse-lockout mechanisms.

A new rear-exiting exhaust system replaced the side-mounted pipes used on 1992 to 1995 models. In addition to a cleaner look and quieter operation, this change was partly responsible for extra horsepower, too. New spark tuning and fuel calibration also helped boost the engine's output to 415 hp at 5200 rpm and 488 ft. lbs. of torque at 3600 rpm. *Motor Trend* (November 1995) reported a 0-to-60 time of 5 seconds and a standing-start quarter mile in 13.2 seconds at 113.4 mph. *Car and Driver* reported a 4.1-second 0-to-60 run and a 12.6-second quarter mile at 113 mph and a top speed of 173 mph!

The resin transfer-molded composite body was mounted on a tubular space frame chassis with a separate cowl structure. The Viper roadster weighed in at 3,445 lbs., with the weight distributed 50/50 front to rear. It had double-acting gas-charged hydraulic shock absorbers with adjustable rebound rates, 16.7:1 power rack-and-pinion steering and al-wheel vented disc brakes.

For the model year, Dodge manufactured 721 Viper RT/10 roadsters. About 231 of the roadsters were black, about 166 were red and about 324 were white. A Dodge Viper was entered in the 24 Hours of LeMans and took a 10th place finish in the GT-1 class.

Dodge turned out only 721 Viper RT/10 roadsters in 1996.

1996 DODGE VIPER GTS COUPE

The 1996 Dodge Viper GTS coupe acquired a few refinements that were previously missing in the Viper series.

(Jerry Heasley photo)

The original Dodge Viper RT/10 roadster had its roots in a visceral back-to-the-basics, uniquely American sports car, but the 1996 Dodge Viper GTS coupe reached into a new, more sophisticated arena, offering more in the way of comfort and amenities than its Roadster sibling.

Like the RT/10 before it, the GTS coupe first stole hearts when it was introduced as a concept car. That was at the 1993 North American Auto Show in Detroit. The GTS program was given the green light in May 1993 and just 34 months later the first GTS production car started down the line at the Connor Avenue Assembly Plant in Detroit.

In August, 1995, Dodge displayed a GTS coupe prototype at the second annual Dodge Viper Owner Invitational in Monterey, California, and made an exclusive offer to current owners—a voucher for the first GTS coupes produced. More than three-quarters of the 1996 calendar-year production of 1,700 was instantly spoken for. "We wanted to demonstrate a serious commitment to our owners," said Martin R. Levine, Dodge Division general manager. "Their response was overwhelming, but the fact is it's a fantastic car offered at a fantastic price."

The base manufacturer's suggested retail price (MSRP) of the first GTS coupe was $66,700, including destination charge. Additional gas and luxury taxes added approximately $6,330.

While the GTS continued the look of the original Viper roadster, more than 90 percent of the car was new. To start, there was a new body, a new interior and a modified V-10 engine with less weight and increased horsepower.

Horsepower in the GTS was increased to 450 from 415 in the 1996 roadster and torque was boosted 10 additional ft. lbs., bringing it to 490 at 3700 rpm. A NACA duct design on the hood of the car force-fed oxygen into the V-10's intake and E-type louvers above each of the front wheels prevented air pressure from building under the hood.

Enclosing the Viper necessitated a new weatherstrip system for the doors and glass. Cooling the closed body also required a more powerful air conditioning system. Other engineering challenges included packaging dropped glass in the doors and designing an innovative electronic entry system.

To improve the overall driving experience, the Viper team pioneered a unique adjustable pedal system that allowed the driver to move the clutch, brake and accelerator pedals up to four inches closer by simply turning a knob mounted under the steering column. This manual system, coupled with a tilt steering wheel and seat that allowed generous fore-and-aft adjustment, provided for an optimal driving position for a wide range of people.

The roof was made from a resin transfer-molding process, as

were most other body panels. The hood was made of sheet molding compound. The sweeping shape of the car resulted in improved aerodynamics, dropping the coefficient of drag to 0.39 from the roadster's 0.50. With the enclosed cockpit, the GTS had about 12 percent more torsional rigidity than the roadster.

Even with the addition of the roof, backlight and roll-up windows, the GTS was actually 60 lbs. lighter than that of the roadster. Team Viper's re-engineering of the frame, a lighter-weight aluminum suspension, new castings for the aluminum engine block and cylinder heads and new seats dropped the coupe's weight to 3,345 lbs.

Other significant features that differentiated the GTS coupe from the roadster included a rear storage compartment designed to stow a full-size Viper tire and increase cargo capacity; redesigned interior trim, dual airbags, a new instrument panel with revised gauge locations and—on the exterior—a racing-style fuel filler cover a twin-bubble roof line that provides ample headroom and a one-piece glass bonded hatch with a defroster.

Dodge built 1,166 of the GTS coupes at the Conner Avenue assembly plant in 1996. Blue finish was on 1,163 of them and three were done in white. Five cars had white wheels and the rest had polished alloy wheels.

1997 DODGE VIPER RT/10 ROADSTER

The "second generation" 1997 Dodge Viper RT/10 roadster that arrived in 1997 was powered by the same 488-cid V-10 engine originally engineered for the GTS coupe. It produced 450 hp at 5200 rpm and 490 ft. lbs. of torque at 3700 rpm. It had, by far, the highest output of any American production automobile. The power was channeled by a high-performance six-speed gearbox and transferred to the road via independent front and rear suspension system.

Braking was provided by power-assisted, four-piston, caliper front disc brakes and a single-piston rear disc design. The Viper R/T10 roadster came with high-performance Michelin Pilot SX MXX3 tires on 17-inch rims.

In addition to the soft top, the Viper RT/10 roadster also featured a removable body-color hardtop that has been redesigned for 1997 for increased headroom. The hard top was a "delete option," meaning owners could choose not to equip their Viper with the hardtop for a lower base price. Air conditioning was also a delete option for 1997.

Like the Viper GTS coupe, the Viper RT/10 roadster had a smooth exterior design that was free of add-ons. It offered an electronically assisted remote entry system, and, for the first time, standard power glass windows. A manual override system could be accessed through the rear window, which had key locks.

To improve the overall driving experience, Team Viper pio-

neered a unique adjustable pedal system that allowed the driver to move the clutch, brake and accelerator pedals up to 4 inches closer by simply turning a knob mounted under the steering column. That system was featured on all 1997 Viper RT/10 roadsters, along with a tilt steering wheel and a seat that allowed a generous fore-and-aft adjustment of 5.2 inches.

While the Viper's interior had evolved since 1989, it remained a simple, cleanly styled cockpit with an emphasis on function. The instrument panel featured full analog instrumentation with a 7,000-rpm tachometer, 200-mph speedometer, engine coolant gauge, oil pressure gauge; fuel gauge and a voltmeter. Safety items included standard driver and passenger air bags and three-point inboard-mounted seat belts.

For the first time, both the Dodge Viper RT/10 roadster and GTS coupe were available in either blue with white painted stripes, or solid red. Silver wheels were standard on the RT/10 roadster in blue, while red RT/10 roadsters featured standard gold wheels. Also available as options were additional wheel choice colors and special badging.

Only 117 RT/10 roadsters were produced in 1997. Of those, approximately 53 were painted blue and 64 were red. Black interiors were installed in 114 cars and three had a tan interior. There were also 114 cars with polished wheels and three with gold wheels.

1997 DODGE VIPER GTS COUPE

Chrysler said that the 1997 Dodge Viper GTS coupe was for the "discriminating sports car lover whose particular devotion is to the ultimate performance road car." The coupe was really much more than a Viper RT/10 roadster with a roof. Born of the same uncompromising passion and enthusiasm that created the raucous roadster, the closed car's design was a logical extension of the original Viper roadster form.

The GTS coupe stayed true to the front-engine, rear-drive layout that excited so many sports car lovers. It was strongly evocative of the greatest GT cars, particularly the 1965 World Championship-winning Daytona Cobra coupes. The GTS's functional, race-inspired details—the polished alloy quick-release fuel filler, twin helmet blisters in the roofline and NACA-ducted hood—tended to

draw the eyes of observers further into the car's athletic body work.

Inside, the cockpit was pure business. Ample comfort, accommodation and safety were provided by dual airbags, air conditioning, power windows and adjustable control pedals. Noise levels were pleasantly subdued, although one stab of the right foot could ignite the uneven-firing rasp of the 450-hp Viper V-10 engine.

The Viper's well-balanced chassis provided a feeling of stability and prodigious grip. During the 24 Hours of Daytona, one Viper GTS-R driver described his car as "built like a battleship." In their first season on the track, factory-backed GTS-Rs finished both the grueling 24 Hours of Daytona and 12 Hours of Sebring. They then qualified for the 24 Hours of LeMans, at speeds well above 200 mph.

New features for the 1997 GTS included a clutch disc with idle damper springs, a revised unibelt seat belt system, a new energy-absorbing tilt steering column, new seats and tracks, a new interior multi-function switch, a new instrument panel, an improved HVAC system with re-circulation mode and a new indicator lamp module. Standard equipment included the 8.0-liter V-10, six-speed manual transmission, polished five-spoke aluminum wheels, driver and passenger air bags, an alarm system with integrated remote keyless entry, power windows and locks, a one-piece glass hatch with defroster, GTS badging and GTS blue pearlcoat paint with dual stone white stripes.

The 1997 GTS coupe had a production run of 1,671 units. Of these, 965 cars were the standard Viper blue color and 706 were finished in Viper red. All of them had a black interior. Polished wheels were used on 1,657 coupes, 14 were Viper red cars with yellow wheels and seven were Viper red coupes with gold wheels and hood side emblems.

Most of the changes to the 1997 Viper GTS coupe were to the interior.

1998 DODGE VIPER RT/10 ROADSTER

Like the latest Dodge Viper GTS coupe, the 1998 Viper RT/10 roadster delivered the most exhilarating driving experience of any regular American production car. The open version of Dodge's powerful sports car also raced into the new model year with a list of similar product enhancements and refinements.

They included the use of new, weight-cutting tubular exhaust manifolds, the change to a low-overlap camshaft, a new electronic radiator fan control, next-generation air bags with a passenger air bag cut-off switch, revised key locks, a keyless entry system, a new instrument panel with full analog instrumentation, new Viper bright metallic silver and Viper red colors, a leak-resistant battery case, a "response-enhanced" evaporative emissions system, improved windshield washer nozzles, an automatic interior lamp shut off (to save battery power) and a quieter alternator.

Specifications for the two-passenger roadster were also very similar to those of previous models. Power from the 8.0-liter V-10 was now up to 450 hp at 5200 rpm and torque was 490 ft. lbs. at 3700 rpm. The 9.6:1 compression engine redlined at 6,000 rpm. It

again drove through a standard six-speed manual gearbox to a 3.07:1 ratio rear axle. A frame-mounted, bevel-gear-with-clutch type limited-slip differential was also standard equipment.

With a 96.2-inch wheelbase, 175.1-inch overall length, 75.7-inch overall width and 44-inch height, the roadster tipped the scales at 3,319 lbs. With only 7.37 lbs. per horsepower to move, it was one very fast machine. Dodge's 1998 press kit even pointed out that the Viper now held the United States Autoracing Club's (USAC) record for 0 to 100 mph in 14.78 seconds.

During 1998, Dodge issued demographic materials showing that current Viper buyers were 51-57 years old and 94 percent male with an average annual income of $225,000. The study also profiled the "target buyer" for 1998 models as a 52-58 year old in the 95 percent male category, also with an annual household income of $225,000.

The production total for the 1998 RT/10 roadster was 379 units. Of these, 252 cars were done in red and 127 were silver. Of those, 379 had polished wheels.

1998 DODGE VIPER GTS COUPE

The legend of the Dodge Viper—from the original RT/10 roadster to the 1996 Viper GTS coupe—had grown to near mythic proportions since the first concept car version was shown almost a decade earlier. So for 1998, the Viper GTS stayed true to the marque's heritage of delivering the most exhilarating driving experience of any regular American production car. The sleek Dodge coupe powered into 1998 with several product enhancements and refinements.

The curb weight had been further cut from the 1997 model through the use of new tubular exhaust manifolds. In addition, the use of a low-overlap camshaft helped to reduce emissions and improve fuel economy. A new electronic radiator fan control was adapted to help reduce cooling system noise.

In the safety area, the 1998 Viper GTS benefited from next-generation air bags and a passenger air bag cut-off switch. Security was

improved with revised key locks and a keyless entry system. The instrument panel featured full analog instrumentation with a 7,000-rpm tachometer, 200-mph speedometer, engine coolant gauge, oil pressure gauge, fuel gauge and a voltmeter.

Colors available for the 1998 GTS coupe included white, Viper bright metallic silver and Viper red. The year's production total included 102 white coupes, 436 monotone red coupes, 11 red coupes with silver stripes, 267 monotone silver coupes and 21 silver coupes with blue stripes. Of the 837 GTS coupes made for the model year, 735 had the standard black interior and 102 had blue interiors. Optional GT-2-style wheels were used on only 102 cars.

Other highlights included a leak-resistant battery case, "response-enhanced" evaporative emissions system, improved windshield washer nozzles, automatic interior lamp shut off (to save battery power) and a quieter alternator.

1999 DODGE VIPER GTS COUPE

Changes made to the 1999 Dodge Viper GTS coupe were mostly the same as those that the 1999 RT/10 roadster underwent. Larger wheels and tires (18-inch aluminum wheels with Michelin Pilot MXX3 speed-rated tires—P275/35ZR18 in front and P335/30ZR18 at the rear) enhanced the coupe's cornering ability without sacrificing other ride characteristics. Painted wheels were standard and polished wheels were optional.

Other 1999 changes included the reintroduction of a black factory color choice and release of the new cognac-colored Connolly leather option (that was ordered for 128 coupes.) Three GTS coupes had red interiors (a late-in-the-year option), 22 were trimmed in silver, 77 were done in solid black and 26 had a black interior with silver stripes.

A total of 699 GTS coupes were built in 1999, with 549 going into the U.S. market, 72 going to Canadian buyers and 78 shipped to other foreign countries. The first Viper GTS coupe retailed as a 1999 model was a Viper red car that was built on December 11, 1998. It had VIN (serial) number XV502442. The year's last GTS coupe built had VIN XV503946. It was also the last Viper sold in 1999. As in the case of RT/10s, the 1999 GTS models shared serial numbers with the Plymouth Prowler, which can cause some confusion.

The 1999 Dodge Viper GTS coupe received larger tires and wheels, but only 699 lucky buyers ever brought one home.

1999 DODGE VIPER GTS-R COUPE GT2 EDITION

Chrysler raced and won races with its factory-sourced, factory-sponsored Viper GTS-R competition coupe. The ultra-powerful muscle cars took the FIS's GT2 Manufacturer's Championship in 1997 and 1998 and had a hard-to-forget 1-2 victory in their class at the French Grand Prix at LeMans in 1998. Those wins inspired Dodge to produce an $82,500 GT2 Championship Edition Coupe for private buyers.

The GT2 version of the racing car came only in white with blue stripes. The aluminum-block-and-heads engine was a tweaked version of the standard GTS and RT/10 power plant with an additional 10 hp. The vital statistics showed a stock-looking 4.00 x 3.88-inch bore and stroke and 488-cid, but didn't tell the whole story. The Dodge boys revamped the intake system with K & N low-restriction air filters, new hoses and an air cleaner housing used on 1992 to 1996 Vipers, but sealed off the functional air scoop. The result was

460 hp at 5200 rpm and 500 ft. lbs. of torque at 3700 rpm.

The car got a couple of changes to its underpinnings, too. Great-looking BBS 18-inch alloy wheels were mounted and shod with Michelin Pilot MXX3 tires. Otherwise, the chassis had the stock layout using upper and lower A arms, coil springs all around and front and rear anti-roll bars. The 16.7:1 power rack-and-pinion steering was carried over from other Vipers along with the vented all-wheel (18 x 10 front and 18 x 13 rear) disc brakes.

Included as part of the GT2 Championship Edition coupe was a special front air splitter, ground effects, "dive bomber" spoilers and a carbon-fiber rear deck airfoil that resembled that used on the actual racing cars. The interior featured black leather seats with blue accents. In 0 to 60-mph acceleration testing, the GTS-R coupe pulled a 4.0-second time. It did the quarter mile in 12.1 seconds at 120.5 mph.

1999 DODGE VIPER RT/10 ROADSTER

On July 6, 2001, Dodge announced that with the beginning of 1999 model output in late 1998, the venomous Viper RT/10 roadster was about to receive a range of enhancements aimed at bringing its appearance and road-biting ability up to even higher levels than before.

One new feature on Viper roadsters was larger wheels and tires to enhance the car's cornering ability without sacrificing other ride characteristics. Replacing the 17-inch wheels were 18-inch aluminum wheels with Michelin Pilot MXX3 speed-rated tires mounted on them. The tires were P275/35ZR18 in front and P335/30ZR18 at the rear. Painted aluminum wheels were standard and polished wheels were considered optional equipment.

Another change for model year 1999 was reintroduction of black as an addition to the existing factory color choices of Viper red and silver. The RT/10 roadster was offered in all three colors without

The Dodge Viper RT/10 roadsters were as fast and flashy as ever in 1999.

racing stripes. A total of 549 were built, with 498 going into the U.S. market and 51 going to Canadian buyers.

Several interior enhancements were made, including a new Cognac-colored Connolly leather option that was ordered for 169 roadsters. Three RT/10s had red interiors, 50 were trimmed in silver and 116 were done in black. The Connolly package included leather seats, a leather steering wheel, a leather-wrapped shift knob, and

leather parking brake boot and grip. It was not offered for Red cars.

The first 1999 model was a Viper red car built in late 1998 and actually sold on January 4, 1999. It had VIN (serial) number XV502445. The year's last roadster built had VIN XV503935. An interesting thing about 1999 Vipers is that they shared serial numbers with the Plymouth Prowler. This can cause confusion when trying to research and authenticate a Viper, but it's true.

2000 VIPER GTS COUPE

The 2000 Dodge Viper GTS had a base price of $67,225.

(Jerry Heasley photo)

As the spiritual reincarnation of the Shelby Daytona coupe, the Dodge Viper GTS quickly developed a passionate following and changed very little from one season to the next because there was little motivation to mess with near perfection. A new steel gray color was the main update for 2000.

The coupe—which first appeared at Dodge dealerships in 1996—was based on the original RT/10 roadster and had virtually identical specifications, although there were minor differences between the two body styles. The RT/10 was 175.1 inches long, while the GTS was 176.7 in length. Overall height was 44 inches for the roadster and 47 inches for the coupe. The closed car was also a

little heavier, at 3,383 lbs., than the 3,319-lb. roadster.

Other minor dimensional differences were a 19.3-sq. ft. frontal area on the RT/10 compared to 20.5 on the GTS. The drag coefficient was 0.495 for the roadster without a top and 0.46 with one. The coupe's was 0.35. The 2000 Viper GTS coupe had a base price of $67,225. You could add the $10,000 American Racing Club (ACR) package that added 10 hp, stiffened the suspension and deleted items like air conditioning, a stereo and fog lights.

The base aluminum-block-and-heads V-10 engine was rated at the familiar 450 hp at 5200 rpm and 490 ft. lbs. of torque at 3700 rpm. With the ACR package it was 460 hp and 500 ft. lbs. of torque! The engine was linked to a six-speed manual transmission that had gear ratios of 2.66:1 in first, 1.78:1 in second, 1.30:1 in third, 1.00:1 in fourth, 0.74:1 in fifth and 0.50:1 in sixth. The 2000 Viper was easily capable of a 4.3-second 0-to-60 times and had a top speed of 185 mph.

Total production of 2000 GTS models was 949, with 804 marketed in the U.S., 92 sold in Canada and 53 going overseas. In addition, 218 ACR coupes were made. Monotone red finish was used on 111 cars of which 32 had cognac interiors and 79 had black interiors. An additional 55 red cars had stripes and black interiors. The new-for-the-year steel gray finish was used on 166 cars without stripes, of which 38 had cognac interiors and 128 had black interiors. Another 126 cars had steel gray bodies and stripes. The most popular 2000 Viper GTS color—solid black—was sprayed on 179 cars of which 66 had cognac interiors and 113 had black interiors. Finally, 94 cars were finished in black with stripes and 13 had cognac interiors and 81 had black interiors

2000 VIPER RT/10

The Dodge Viper didn't change very much since its inception in mid-1992. Steel gray exterior finish was probably the most obvious change in the 2000 model—if you ordered it, of course. You could, if you preferred, still get your car in red or black.

The RT/10 roadster continued with its longitudinal front engine and rear-wheel-drive power train layout. It again rode a 96.2-inch wheelbase and measured 176.7 inches front to rear. It was 75.7 inches wide with a track width of 59.6 inches front and rear. The roadster's height also remained at 44 inches.

The aluminum-block-and-heads V-10 engine was rated at the familiar 450 hp at 5200 rpm and 490 ft. lbs. of torque at 3700 rpm. As usual, the engine drove to a six-speed manual transmission that had gear ratios of 2.66:1 in first, 1.78:1 in second, 1.30:1 in third, 1.00:1 in fourth, 0.74:1 in fifth and 0.50:1 in sixth. The 2000 Viper was easily capable of 4.3-second 0 to 60-mph times and had a top speed of 185 mph.

Total production of 2000 RT/10 models was 840, with 757 marketed in the U.S. and 83 sold in Canada. The last car retailed by a Dodge dealer had the VIN ZV606129. Red finish was used on 255 cars, of which 76 had cognac interiors and 179 had black interiors. The new-for-the-year steel gray finish was the most popular 2000 color and was used on 296 cars—99 with cognac interiors and 197

with black. The second most popular 2000 Viper color—black—was sprayed on 289 cars of which 131 had cognac interiors and 158 had black interiors.

Other carryover technical features included rack-and-pinion steering with power assist and four-wheel disc brakes (18 x 10 inches in front and 18 x 13 inches in the rear). The tires used up front were P275/35ZR18s with P335/30ZR18s in the rear.

The 2000 Dodge Viper RT/10 was largely unchanged.

(Jerry Heasley photo)

2001 DODGE VIPER RT/10-GTS-ACR

(Jerry Heasley photo)

The 2001 Viper RT/10 featured a foldable and stowable top.

Thanks to the magic of the worldwide web, anyone with a computer and an interest in buying a Viper can get all the information they need by visiting www.4adodge.com/viper/models/index.html. But in case there are muscle car fans out there without a computer, here's the basics on the 2001 models.

2001 Viper RT/10 Roadster

Lightweight, all-aluminum 8.0-liter V10 engine with sequential bottom-fed multipoint electronic fuel injection. Foldable and stowable soft top. Remote keyless entry. Four-wheel high-performance power-assisted brakes with ABS. Seatbelt cluster lamp stays on after engine start until driver buckles up. Inside emergency trunk lid release. User-ready child seat top tether anchorage in the front passenger seat. Next-generation driver and front passenger air bags with front passenger air bag on/off switch. Fully independent suspension system. Rack-and-pinion steering.

2001 Viper GTS Coupe

Lightweight, all-aluminum 8.0-liter V10 engine with sequential bottom-fed multipoint electronic fuel injection. Foldable and stowable soft top. Remote keyless entry. Four-wheel high-performance power-assisted brakes with ABS. Seatbelt cluster lamp stays on after engine start until driver buckles up. Inside emergency trunk lid release. User-ready child seat top tether anchorage in the front passenger seat. Next-generation driver and front passenger air bags with front passenger air bag on/off switch.

Fully independent suspension system. Rack-and-pinion steering.

2001 Viper ARC Coupe

Lightweight, all-aluminum 8.0-liter V10 engine with sequential bottom-fed multipoint electronic fuel injection. Resin composite body with sheet-molded compound (SMC) hood. Special ACR Viper badging and graphics, including interior identification plaque. Unique 18-inch, one-piece BBS forged aluminum wheels.

Supplemental five-point restraint system. Four-wheel high-performance power-assisted brakes with ABS. Seatbelt cluster lamp stays on after engine start until driver buckles up. Inside emergency trunk lid release. User-ready child seat top tether anchorage in the front passenger seat. Next-generation driver and front passenger air bags with front passenger air bag on/off switch. Fully independent suspension system. Rack-and-pinion steering.

2001 DODGE VIPER GTS-R COUPE GT2 EDITION

Chrysler raced and won with its factory-sourced, factory-sponsored Viper GTS-R competition coupe. The ultra-powerful muscle cars took the FIS's GT2 Manufacturer's Championship in 1997 and 1998 and had a hard-to-forget 1-2 victory in their class at the French Grand Prix at LeMans in 1998. Those wins inspired Dodge to produce an $82,500 GT2 Championship Edition Coupe for private buyers.

The GT2 version of the racing car came only in white with blue stripes. The aluminum-block-and-heads engine was a tweaked version of the standard GTS and RT/10 power plant with 10 additional hp. The vital statistics showed a stock-looking 4.00 x 3.88-inch bore and stroke and 488-cid, but didn't tell the whole story. The Dodge boys revamped the intake system with K & N low-restriction air filters, new hoses and an air cleaner housing used on 1992 to 1996 Vipers, but sealed off the functional air scoop. The result was 460 hp at 5200 rpm and 500 ft. lbs. of torque at 3700 rpm.

The car got a couple of changes to its underpinnings, too. Great-looking BBS 18-inch alloy wheels were mounted and shod with Michelin Pilot MXX3 tires. Otherwise the chassis had the stock layout using upper and lower 'A' arms, coil springs all around and front and rear anti-roll bars. The 16.7:1 power rack-and-pinion steering was carried over from other Vipers along with the vented all-wheel (18 x 10 front and 18 x 13 rear) disc brakes.

Included as part of the GT2 Championship Edition coupe was a special front air splitter, ground effects, "dive bomber" spoilers and a carbon-fiber rear deck airfoil that resembled that used on the actual racing cars. The interior featured black leather seats with blue accents. In 0-to-60 acceleration testing, the GTS-R coupe pulled a 4.0-second time. It did the quarter mile in 12.1 seconds at 120.5 mph.

FORD

1960 FORD GALAXIE 352/360 SPECIAL

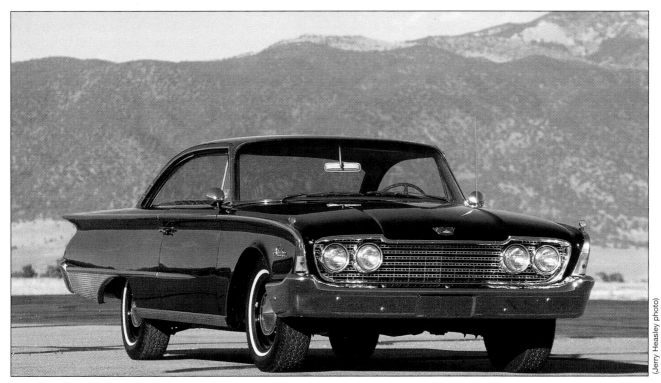

The 1960 Ford Galaxie Starliner hardtop was available with the 360-hp Thunderbird Super V-8.

As the 1960 full-sized domestic cars began appearing in the showrooms, it became quite apparent at the drag strips and on the racetracks that "performance options" was no longer the dirty term it had been for the past two or so years. Cubic inches, ram induction, multi-carburetor setups and different combinations of each were made widely available.

An exception at the start of the model year was the full-sized Ford. Its hottest option since 1958 was the 352-cid 300-hp V-8.

The big Fords were bigger than ever. Their wheelbase was up an inch to 119 inches. The overall length increased 5.7 inches to 213.7 inches. Overall width was the widest ever at 81.5 inches, an increase of 3.9 inches.

Styling departed radically from the popular and conservative 1959 Fords. Grille-mounted headlights and gull-wing fins gave deep meaning to the often-used term "all-new." At the top of the line was the sleek Starliner two-door hardtop and its convertible counterpart the Sunliner. Technically, they were in a Galaxie Special series. They came with six-cylinder engines or a variety of V-8s.

Ford got a late start in the new performance sweepstakes, but before the end of 1959 it had released its 360-hp Thunderbird Super V-8, which was based on the 352. It was also called the "Interceptor" or "Super Interceptor" and carried an "R" code. This engine was not initially available with Cruise-O-Matic, but only with a Borg-Warner T-85 three-speed manual gearbox, with or without overdrive. A Holley 540-cfm four-barrel carburetor, an aluminum intake manifold, new cast-iron exhaust headers, a cast nodular crank, solid valve lifters, a 10.6:1 compression ratio and a dual-point ignition system all helped.

The muscular combination was available on any full-sized 1960 model. *Motor Life* magazine got hold of a pre-production example and found it capable of going from 0 to 60 mph in 7.5 seconds with a top speed of 152 mph. Obviously, it had been modified a bit over the production version.

The most desirable combination for the 360-hp 352 is with a Starliner two-door hardtop or a Sunliner convertible.

1961 FORD GALAXIE STARLINER 390

A big year for Ford performance was 1961. Inspired by the "win-on-Sunday-sell-on-Monday" marketing mentality, the company released a 390-cid V-8 at the start of the year and a four-speed manual transmission near the end of the season. Both performance add-ons were hot options for the steamy Starliner hardtop.

In 1960, Ford had advised the Automobile Manufacturers Association (AMA) that it was suspending its support of the trade organization's 4-year-old ban on stock car racing. The company then showed up at the Daytona Motor Speedway with a 360-engined Starliner that ran 40 laps at an average of 142 mph.

By fall, similar cars had been put into the hands of racing car drivers and racked up 15 checkered flags in Grand National stock car competition. At the same time, a re-entry into factory-backed drag racing was made and a "three deuces" carburetor setup was legalized by the National Hot Rod Association.

The new-for-'61 Starliner was smaller, but had a bigger engine. Three versions of the 390-cid V-8 were offered. The standard rating was 300 hp. A police car variant was rated for 330 hp. Tops on the list was the 375-hp Thunderbird Super edition with a four-barrel carburetor. At midyear, when the triple two-barrel car-

(Jerry Heasley photo)

The 1961 Ford Galaxie Starliner was smaller than before, but it had a bigger engine in the 390-cid Thunderbird Super V-8 .

buretor system was released, it pushed the big engine up to 401 hp. After it was approved for NHRA racing, Fords dominated their classes.

Both engines featured a 4.05 x 3.78-inch bore and stroke and 10.6:1 compression ratio. The Thunderbird Special generated 375 hp at 6000 rpm. The Thunderbird Special 6V gave 401 hp at 6000 rpm.

The V-8 Starliner had a base price of $2,713 and tipped the scales at 3,615 lbs. Prices on the engine options were about $199 for the 300-hp V-8, $350 for the 375-hp job and $425 for the 401-hp edition.

Performance-wise, the 6V (six venturi) engine was capable of 7-second 0-60 mph runs and quarter miles with ETs just over 15 seconds. This definitely put it into the "muscle car" category. Starliner production—including sixes and smaller V-8s—was 29,669 units. However, the number of 390-cid 401-hp and 390-cid 375-hp cars built was smaller.

1962 FORD GALAXIE 500/500XL

The 1962 Galaxie 500XL hardtop could nudge 140 mph with a 390-cid triple-carburetor V-8 that produced 405 hp.

Certainly not the least significant attraction of the 1962 Fords was their appearance. They stand out as one of the best examples of Ford's competence level in car design.

With a 209-inch overall length they were large automobiles, but their clean lines—now totally free of fender fins and devoid of any overtones of General Motors influence—gave them a handsome appearance.

Ford got back into performance in 1960. It was more of the same in 1961. The results included the debut of the triple-carbureted 390-cid V-8 with 401 hp and a Borg-Warner four-speed gearbox for any 390 engines.

Shortly after New Year's celebrations ended in 1962, Ford piped on board a new 406-cid V-8 packing 405 hp at 5800 rpm. This "Thunderbird Special 406" carried over the triple carbs, special cam, valve gear, ignition, bearings and exhaust system of the 390-cid 401-hp engine. A 385-hp version with a single four-barrel carburetor was also available.

Despite the similarity to previous engines, there were some changes that reflected Ford's growing expertise in developing modern, high-performance automobiles. The 406-cid engine block, with its larger 3.78-inch bore, used a totally different casting that provided thicker cylinder walls.

To cope with the 406's added power, stronger pistons and connecting rods were installed and the oil relief valve was set at 60 psi instead of 45 psi. Dual valve springs with greater maximum load were also used on the 406.

Included in the $379.70 price tag of the 406 engine (one of which was Ford's 30,000,000th V-8) was a comprehensive performance package. Its most obvious feature was an excellent Borg-Warner four-speed transmission with ratios of 2.36:1, 1.78:1, 1.41:1 and 1.0:1. Less apparent—until the 406 Ford got into motion—were its stiffer (by 20 percent) springs and shocks.

Ford didn't offer sintered metallic brake linings, but 3-inch brake drums fitted with harder linings did a respectable job of hauling the 2 tons of Ford down from a maximum velocity approaching 140 mph.

Ford also added substantial strength to its high-performance driveline. For example, a 9-inch diameter ring gear was found at the rear, in place of the 8.75-inch unit used in 1961. A 3-inch diameter drive shaft was also fitted, along with a four-pinion differential.

With Ford's standard 3.56:1 ratio rear axle, the typical 405-hp Galaxie was capable of 0 to 60-mph runs in 7 seconds and of doing the quarter mile in 15.5 seconds at 92 mph.

1963 FORD GALAXIE 427

(Jerry Heasley photo)

In 1963, Ford offered two-door hardtop Galaxies and Galaxie 500XLs with a 427 V-8.

Ford Motor Company realized that it was going to be necessary to support a drag racing program if it expected to compete in the muscle car market of the 1960s. That thinking was behind the company's late 1962 release of two powerful new engine options based on a 406-cid V-8. Version one used a single four-barrel carburetor to generate 385 hp. The second carried three two-barrel carburetors and was advertised at 405 hp.

Ford really got its act into gear around the middle of 1963. Its first step was the release of the good-looking 1963 1/2 Galaxie fastback. Then came a new 427-cid V-8 with massive muscle for the street, the drag strip and the NASCAR superspeedways.

To promote the 427-powered 1963 Galaxie, Ford manufactured 50 special cars at its factory in Atlanta, Georgia. These cars were "factory lightweights" made exclusively for going down the quarter mile faster than the competition. They had fiberglass doors, hoods, trunks and front-end components. The bumpers and other parts were made of aluminum. Virtually everything that wasn't needed for rac-

ing was left off the cars.

For motivation, the Galaxie lightweights got a 427-cid V-8 with two Holley 600-cfm four-barrel carburetors advertised at 425 hp at 6000 rpm. The actual output was much higher. The engine was attached to a special version of Ford's "top-loader" four-speed manual gearbox that had an aluminum case to cut even more weight off. These cars tipped the scales at below 3,500 lbs. and ran the quarter mile in the low-12-second bracket at just under 120 mph!

In addition to the just-for-racing cars, FoMoCo produced 4,978 big Fords with one of two versions of the 427-cid V-8. One was the 425-hp engine tuned for the street. It had dual Holley 540-cfm carburetors on top of a cast-aluminum intake manifold and most owners who took these cars racing on weekends felt that the power rating was very conservative. The second street engine was a 427-cid V-8 with a single four-barrel carburetor. It produced 410 hp. Both of the big engines were available in Galaxie or Galaxie 500 XL two-door hardtops. The dual-quad engine was a $461.60 option.

1963 FORD GALAXIE LIGHTWEIGHT

(Jerry Heasley photo)

The 1963 Ford Galaxie factory lightweight with a 427-cid V-8 was ideal for the drag strip.

Although some people regarded 1963 Ford styling changes as "minor," it wasn't hard to identify the new models. For those interested in how the new Ford would "go," the car shined on race tracks early in the year, showing off both of Ford's new 427-cid V-8 and 1963 1/2 fastback body.

The 427-cid engine was based on the 406-cid V-8 with a 4.23-inch bore and 3.78-inch stroke. It encompassed design improvements outlined in Ford's "Total Performance" program.

Beginning with cross-bolted mains (numbers two, three and four), lighter-weight impact-extruding aluminum pistons and stronger connecting rods, the 427 had many advantages over the 406. With twin fours, the Thunderbird 427-cid high-performance V-8 produced 425 hp at 6000 rpm and 480 ft. lbs. of torque at 3700 rpm.

Since NASCAR did not allow multi-carb setups to run on its superspeedways, Ford also offered a single four-barrel 427-cid 410-hp (at 5600 rpm) job with 476 ft. lbs. of torque at 3400 rpm.

Although some questioned the use of the term "fastback" for Ford's 1963 1/2 model, there was good reason for its existence. By adopting the "sportsroof" for NASCAR competition, Ford had a car that could maintain 160 mph with 100 less hp.

The lightweight fastbacks were made to let it all hang out on the drag strip. Ford offered these hardtops only in a white-and-red exterior/interior color combination.

Although the drag model's steel body was identical to that of a stock Galaxie, all bolt-on items, such as the doors, trunk lid, hood and front fenders, were constructed of fiberglass. Aluminum was used for the bumpers. The interiors offered only the basics: skinny front buckets, cheap floor mats and absolutely no sound deadening.

With 425 hp, these Galaxies—which the NHRA declared eligible for both super stock and stock eliminator competitions—were capable of quarter-mile marks of 12 seconds and 118 mph.

Hot Rod (July 1963) asserted, "a tremendous improvement over 1962 … from the 352 high-performance of 1960 to this 427 engine, there has been a constant flow of improvement."

Before the competition season came to a close, Ford offered a "Mark II" version of the 427-cid V-8 with new cylinder heads. It had larger ports and valves, an aluminum high-rise manifold, stronger connecting rods, a forged-steel crankshaft and a 10-quart oil pan.

The tremendous performance of the 427-cid NASCAR Ford was demonstrated in a road test of a car that stock-car builders Holman & Moody had prepared. It was conducted by *Car Life* magazine. Although rated at 410 hp, the true output of the 427, after the Holman & Moody treatment, was closer to 500 hp. With a 3.50:1 rear axle, the Ford's top speed was approximately 155 mph. Even with this gearing, however, the Ford was a strong sprinter with *Car Life* (February 1964) reporting the following acceleration times: 0 to 30 mph in 2.3 seconds; 0 to 60 mph in 6.3 seconds and 0 to 100 mph in 13.2 seconds. The same car did the quarter mile in 14.2 seconds at 105 mph.

1964 FORD FAIRLANE HI-PO ("K" CODE)

Along with new styling, the 1964 Ford Fairlane offered some neat engine options based on he 289-cid small-block V-8. The original version of this engine was the 221-cid V-8, which grew to 260 cid and then to 289 cid. The 289 was originally designed for use in the mid-sized Fairlane and was an option for Falcons and Comets. However, it was most famous as a Mustang power plant and the Mustang was marketed with the support of a "Cobra" parts program that could take the hot "K" code 271-hp of the 289 and make it even hotter.

In 1964, the basic "C" code version of the Challenger 289 had a 9.0:1 compression ratio and a two-barrel carburetor. It generated 195 hp at 4400 rpm and there was nothing "muscular" about that. There was an "A" code edition with a four-barrel carburetor and a 9.8:1 compression ratio, which generated 225 hp—acceptable for keeping up with traffic on the freeway. But for muscle car fans, the only way to order it was as a "K" code or "Hi-Po" version. This meant that you got a 10.5:1 compression ratio and 271 horses at 6000 rpm with a single Holley four-barrel carb.

(Jerry Heasley photo)

The 1964 Fairlane could be ordered with a 289-cid 271-hp "Hi-Po" V-8.

Ford Motor Company realized that it was going to be necessary to support a drag racing program if it expected to compete in the muscle car market of the 1960s. That thinking was behind the company's late 1962 release of two powerful new engine options based on a 406-cid V-8. Version one used a single four-barrel carburetor to generate 385 hp. The second carried three two-barrel carburetors and was advertised at 405 hp.

Ford really got its act into gear around the middle of 1963. Its first step was the release of the good-looking 1963 1/2 Galaxie fastback. Then came a new 427-cid V-8 with massive muscle for the street, the drag strip and the NASCAR superspeedways.

To promote the 427-powered 1963 Galaxie, Ford manufactured 50 special cars at its factory in Atlanta, Georgia. These cars were "factory lightweights" made exclusively for going down the quarter mile faster than the competition. They had fiberglass doors, hoods, trunks and front-end components. The bumpers and other parts were made of aluminum. Virtually everything that wasn't needed for racing was left off the cars.

For motivation, the Galaxie lightweights got a 427-cid V-8 with two Holley 600-cfm four-barrel carburetors advertised at 425 hp at 6000 rpm. The actual output was much higher. The engine was attached to a special version of Ford's "top-loader" four-speed manual gearbox that had an aluminum case to cut even more weight off. These cars tipped the scales at below 3,500 lbs. and ran the quarter mile in the low-12-second bracket at just under 120 mph!

In addition to the just-for-racing cars, FoMoCo produced 4,978 big Fords with one of two versions of the 427-cid V-8. One was the 425-hp engine tuned for the street. It had dual Holley 540-cfm carburetors on top of a cast-aluminum intake manifold and most owners who took these cars racing on weekends felt that the power rating was very conservative. The second street engine was a 427-cid V-8 with a single four-barrel carburetor. It produced 410 hp. Both of the big engines were available in Galaxie or Galaxie 500 XL two-door hardtops. The dual-quad engine was a $461.60 option.

1964 FORD FAIRLANE "THUNDERBOLT"

The 1964 T-Bolt's engine bay held a 427-cid V-8 with up to 425 hp.

Along with new styling, the 1964 Ford Fairlane offered some neat engine options based on the 289-cid small-block V-8. The original version of this engine was the 221-cid V-8, which grew to 260 cid and then to 289 cid. The 289 was originally designed for use in the mid-sized Fairlane and was an option for Falcons and Comets. However, it was most famous as a Mustang power plant and the Mustang was marketed with the support of a "Cobra" parts program that could take the hot "K" code 271-hp of the 289 and make it even hotter.

In 1964, the basic "C" code version of the Challenger 289 had a 9.0:1 compression ratio and a two-barrel carburetor. It generated 195 hp at 4400 rpm and there was nothing "muscular" about that. There was an "A" code edition with a four-barrel carburetor and a 9.8:1 compression ratio, which generated 225 hp—acceptable for keeping up with traffic on the freeway. But for muscle car fans, the only way to order it was as a "K" code or "Hi-Po" version. This meant that you got a 10.5:1 compression ratio and 271 horses at 6000 rpm with a single Holley four-barrel carb.

(Jerry Heasley photo)

Just over 100 Fairlane Thunderbolts were produced in 1964 for drag racing.

These cars had fiberglass fenders, teardrop-shaped hood blisters, Plexiglas windows, lightweight bucket seats, a cold-air induction system, 8000 rpm Rotunda tachometers, modified front suspensions (to accommodate the 427), a long list of equipment deletions and many special competition equipment features. The 425-hp big-block V-8 actually cranked out more like 500 hp. It was linked to a beefed-up Lincoln automatic or a Borg-Warner T-10 four-speed manual transmission.

The 1964 Fairlane Special Performance drag vehicles soon adopted the Thunderbolt name and also became known as "T-Bolts." Demand was strong enough to prompt the ordering of a second batch of 54 all-white cars. Racing driver Gas Ronda dominated NHRA's 1964 World Championship with 190 points by running his T-Bolt through the quarter mile in 11.6 seconds at 124 mph.

Ford records show that the first 11 cars left the factory painted maroon and 10 of them had four-speed transmissions. The 100 additional cars produced were painted white when they were built and 89 of them had four-speed gearboxes. At least one 1965 Thunderbolt-style car was raced by Darrell Droke. However, the new Mustang soon took over as Ford's best offering for drag-car enthusiasts and the short life of T-Bolts halted at that point.

1964 FORD FALCON SPRINT

Had it not been for the introduction of the Ford Mustang in the spring of 1964, the 1964 Ford Falcon Sprint option for the Futura Sports two-door hardtop and convertible would likely have gone down as one of the year's sportiest and best high-performance offerings.

Released before the announcement of the Mustang (which was heavily based on the Falcon), the Falcon Sprint option incorporated a neat package. When the new 1964 American cars arrived in showrooms, Rambler's American, Plymouth's Valiant and Dodge's Dart didn't offer V-8 engines. The Chevy II line had lost its convertible and two-door hardtop models.

A V-8 was added to the Falcon lineup in midyear 1963. It was the mild 260-cid small-block V-8 with a Holley two-barrel carburetor and a 164-hp rating. Added to the Falcon options list at the same time was the Sprint option for the convertible and newly introduced two-door hardtop.

New, squared-off styling from the belt line down marked the Falcon's fifth model year. It used the same unitized chassis it had since its introduction as a 1960 model.

The Sports Futura hardtop listed for $2,314 and the Sprint package added $275 extra. The Sports Futura convertible started at $2,586 and $238 more bought the Sprint setup. Sports models started with front bucket-type seats and a center console, although not all Sprints had these items. The Sprint option also added the V-8 engine, complete with a chrome dress-up kit, wire wheel covers, a sports-type steering wheel, a tachometer and appropriate model badging. For $188 more, a four-speed manual floor shift was available.

Car Life tested a four-speed equipped Falcon Sprint convertible and found it did 0-60 mph in 12.1 seconds and had a top speed of 105 mph. By the time the road test appeared in print, in the magazine's June 1964 issue, the Mustang legend was already approaching full gallop.

With much other competition as well, the Falcon Sprint returned for model year 1965, but it was even more overshadowed by its Mustang stablemate. Today, the most collectable Falcon Sprints are into five-figure prices, which is getting respectable, but not as high as Mustang prices.

1964 FORD GALAXIE 427

(Jerry Heasley photo)

The 1964 Ford Galaxie was available with a 427-cid V-8.

Despite their best-ever-for-Ford performances on drag strips and racetracks, the 1963 Galaxie lightweights had not dominated quarter-mile competition the way Ford hoped they would. At first they competed with Pontiac's powerful 421 Super Duty V-8 and later the Chrysler Hemi came along. To keep up with the Joneses, Ford changed its focus to mid-size muscle by launching its fleet of Fairlane-based Thunderbolts that could run down a drag strip in less than 12 seconds at close to 125 mph.

However, the 427-powered full-sized Fords were still the hot ticket for stock car racing and to get them sanctioned for NASCAR competition the company kept producing big muscle cars and a big-car-based lightweight drag package as well. In 1964, a Galaxie A/Stock dragster package was offered for two-door models. Also available was a B/Stock Dragster package with added a low-riser manifold for the 427-cid V-8. These cars came in white with red interiors. Body sealer, sound deadening insulation and heaters were deleted. Added were lightweight seats and a fiberglass "power bubble" hood. The grilles were modified with fiberglass air induction vents.

The 427-cid V-8 was also offered in two versions for production-type full-sized 1964 Fords. The "Thunderbird High-Performance" option carried code "Q" and was the 410-hp (at 5600 rpm) version. The specifications for this power plant included a 4.23 x 3.78-inch bore and stroke, an 11.5:1 compression ratio and a single Holley four-barrel carburetor. The "Thunderbird Super High-Performance" engine carried code "R" and added two larger Holley carburetors to boost output to 425 hp at 6000 rpm. A 427-powered stock-bodied Ford was basically good for a 0-to-60 time of just over 6 seconds and a quarter-mile time of just under 15 seconds.

By 1964, the full-sized Fords had grown a little big for even NASCAR racing. Dodges and Plymouths were not only lighter, but had the Hemi engine to help them set the pace in stock car racing. Ford tried to get an overhead cam version of the 427-cid V-8 sanctioned, but NASCAR said that it didn't qualify as a production engine. Instead, a high-riser manifold and "high-rev" package were certified as production options and legalized for racing.

A 1964 Ford Galaxie with the dragster option.

(Jerry Heasley photo)

1965 SHELBY-AMERICAN AC/COBRA 289

(Jerry Heasley photo)

The 1965 AC Cobra 289 roadster was unique and very fast.

The Cobra is perhaps the ultimate American road warrior because it brought this country its first and only World Manufacturer's Championship in auto racing. The year was 1965 and the car was the 289 Cobra roadster. Despite the British origins of its AC Ace chassis, which was highly beefed-up and modified to accept American V-8 power, the Cobra was by rights its own unique marque. It was built by Shelby-American of Los Angeles, California. Carroll Shelby contracted with AC of England for the chassis and body and put the dream together using engines from Ford.

When the Cobra became a reality, AC had its name on the car. So did Ford, thanks to the use of "Powered By Ford" fender badges. However, the Cobra vision belonged to Carroll Shelby and Cobra was officially the name of the marque. A Cobra is not an AC and it is not a Ford. A Cobra is a Cobra. Shelby built small-block-powered versions from 1961 to 1965 and big-block versions from 1965-1967 (big-blocks).

The small-block Cobra, which weighed slightly over 2,000 lbs., was easily capable of speeds topping 150 mph, and was quicker than literally any other sports car sold to the public. That's why *Car Life* magazine, in its June 1962 drive report stated, "When the Cobra is certified for production sports racing, a fox will have been dropped among the chickens."

Shelby's original idea was to sell a street version of the race vehicle to finance the cars on the track, although any final accounting would certainly reveal that Ford Motor Company backed the Shelby-American racing program to benefit from the on-track publicity associated with its new small-block V-8.

Shelby accomplished the ultimate with his Cobra, beating arch rival Ferrari for the World Manufacturer's Championship.

At the end of the production run of the small-block roadster, Shelby-American built about 30 cars with automatic transmissions. Carroll Shelby drove one, and still owns it to this day. He favored the automatic for everyday use, but still also owns a big-block 427 Cobra roadster.

Sadly, most of the automatics were changed over to four-speeds, but a few do exist today, including CSH 2549. According to the salesman who sold this Cobra (originally silver, but now black) at Ron Tonkin Ford in Portland, Oregon, in 1967, Shelby himself drove this car its first two years. "We bought the car off Carroll. He was driving it as a demo then," Tonkin said.

1965 FORD GALAXIE 427

The 1965 full-sized Fords were billed as "the newest since 1949." Luxury and comfort were emphasized in the new Custom, Custom 500, Galaxie 500, Galaxie 500XL and Galaxie 500 LTD series. It was the first year for coil spring rear suspension and promotions were geared towards the new LTD being quieter than a Rolls-Royce.

Clean, sharp, square lines characterized the fresh new body styling that was set off by a radiator grille with thin, horizontal bars and dual headlights stacked on top of each other. There was a slight "Coke bottle" shape to the rear of the body.

With a move towards selling luxury and comfort, it might seem strange that Ford continued offering the 427-cid V-8 for the big cars, but remember that this engine was needed to help maintain Ford's "total performance" image and it didn't fit into other models like the Falcon, Mustang and Fairlane without extensive modifications. In fact, NASCAR had kicked the Chrysler Hemi V-8 out of stock car racing, so the 427-powered full-sized Fords took a record of 48 Grand National wins.

The 1965 Ford Galaxie was available with a 427-cid V-8.

(Jerry Heasley photo)

The Galaxie 500XL series was the sport trim version of the Galaxie 500 two-door hardtop ($3,167) and convertible ($3,426) and included all Galaxie 500 trim plus bucket seats, a floor-mounted shift lever, polished door-trim panels and carpeting on the lower portion of the doors. It's likely that the majority of full-sized Fords fitted with the 427 (except for all-out race cars) were Galaxie 500XL models.

A Galaxie 500XL two-door hardtop with the 427-cid 425-hp Thunderbird Super High-Performance V-8 could be purchased for as little as $3,233 in 1965. And even though it was a big car with a 119-inch wheelbase, a 210-inch overall length and a curb weight of 3,507 lbs., it still carried only 9.6 pounds per horsepower with the big-block V-8 installed. It could fly from 0 to 60 mph in 4.8 seconds and did the quarter mile in only 14.9 seconds.

1965 FORD MUSTANG GT

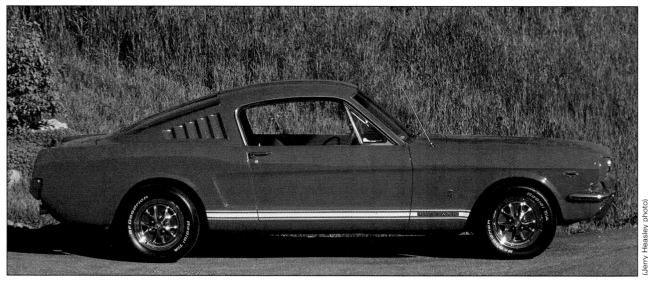

The 1965 Mustang GT 2+2 fastback was the beginning of a long line of successful Mustang muscle cars.

(Jerry Heasley photo)

It is not often that a car comes along and gets to create its own market segment, but that is what happened when Ford introduced the Mustang sporty compact on April 17, 1964. Mustang initiated the all-new "pony car" segment, and the market for the cars was large and long lasting.

There is argument among purists over whether the Mustangs produced prior to September 1964 are 1964 1/2 or 1965 models. However, when it comes to the interesting and collectible GT equipment group, there can be no question, as it was introduced for the first anniversary of the Mustang's introduction on April 17, 1965.

(Jerry Heasley photo)

The 1965 Mustang GT convertible had plenty of appeal.

The Mustang had already become a desirable commodity. Its standard equipment included bucket seats. It had the immediately popular long hood, short deck look. At first it came as a sport coupe (two-door hardtop) and a sporty-looking convertible. In the fall of 1964, a fastback model called the 2+2 was added to the lineup. From the outset, the options list was important in marketing the Mustang. Buyers could add lots of appearance and convenience extras, plus some bolt-on high-performance hardware. However, being based on the low-priced compact Falcon, there was some room for improvement in the go-fast department.

Combining available mechanical features with new visual pieces made the GT package a fairly thorough upgrade. First, the buyer had to order an optional V-8 engine, which at the time includ-ed the 225-hp Challenger Special 289 at $157, or the high-performance 271-hp 289-cid engine for $430.

The GT option included quick-ratio steering, disc front brakes, chromed dual exhaust tips that exited through the rear valance panel, a new grille bar with fog lights built in and GT instrumentation—which replaced the Falcon-based instrument panel with five round dials. Throw in GT badging and lower body striping and you had a bargain for around $150.

Although the exact number of Mustangs built with GT equipment is not available, they had a massive following and the installation rate for this option increased even more when Ford later released the appearance items separately for dealer installation.

1965 FORD SHELBY-MUSTANG GT 350 "R" CODE

(Jerry Heasley photo)

Shelby and Ford combined to build a race winner in the GT 350.

The "R" is for race, no joke. After serial number 34, Shelby-American began inserting an R as the second digit of the vehicle identification number (VIN). But in the early days, both Ford and Shelby-American were not entirely clear on the direction of this new high-performance Mustang.

Two things were certain. First, Ford wanted a higher-performance, specialty version of the Mustang. Second, it wanted a car that could compete with Chevy's Corvette. The latter suggested a two-seat car and this could be achieved by removing the back seat from a Mustang 2+2 fastback. Higher performance meant hopping up the 289-cid V-8, since Ford's big-block engines would not fit in the Mustang and because the small-block worked best for road racing.

Both jobs were turned over to Shelby-American of Los Angeles, which had taken the AC-based Cobra roadster and thrashed Corvettes in USRRC (United States Road Race of Champions) racing. At the same time, the Cobra completely overpowered the Corvette in SCCA A-production racing and beat out Ferrari for the World Manufacturer's Championship.

The GT 350 R Code was loaded with racing features, but only 36 were sold.

(Jerry Heasley photo)

Ford felt that it made a lot of sense to hire Shelby to turn the Mustang into a car that could beat the Corvette in SCCA B-production racing. The automaker knew this would further reinforce the muscular image of Ford's new pony car.

Shelby-American proceeded to build a street version of a new GT Mustang, which Carroll Shelby himself named the GT 350. It was a rather obvious reference to the 350-cid small-block engine from Chevrolet, although Shelby gave the press some story about walking off 350 steps.

With racing victories a major goal, Shelby-American also built a race-ready competition model that was not meant for street use. It was called the R-model.

To satisfy SCCA regulations at least 100 cars (race and street versions) had to be built. Therefore, 100 white fastbacks—each fitted with 289-cid high-performance K-code V-8s with solid valve lifters and 271 hp—were lifted off an assembly line at the Ford plant in San Jose, California.

The R-model came with the high-performance features of the street GT 350—the 289-cid 306-hp small-block with a hi-rise alu-minum intake manifold, four-speed transmission, No-Spin differential, lowered suspension and lots more—plus special R-model features. According to the *Shelby American Automobile Guide*, the latter included: "A fiberglass front lower apron panel, an engine oil cooler, a large-capacity radiator, front and rear brake cooling assemblies, a 34-gallon fuel tank, a 3.5-inch quick-fill gas cap, an electric fuel pump, an exhaust system with large-diameter pipes and no mufflers, five magnesium bolt-on 7.15-inch wheels, revised wheel openings, an interior safety group roll bar, a shoulder harness, a fire extinguisher, a flame-resistant interior, a plastic rear window, aluminum-framed sliding plastic side windows, complete instrumentation with a tachometer, speedometer and oil pressure, water temperature and fuel pressure gauges, a full Shelby-American competition-prepared and dyno-tuned engine and final track test and adjustments."

The GT 350 R code Mustang was so specialized that a mere 36 were sold. However, they were available to anyone willing to pay the base price of $5,950 to buy an out-of-the-box race winner. The 1965 GT 350 R was the SCCA B-production national champion in 1965, 1966 and 1967.

1966 FORD FAIRLANE 427

The 427 Fairlane was the product of corporate thinking; an attempt to salvage some commercial benefit from the 1963 Thunderbolt drag-racing program. While the T-Bolts had been built for racing only, the later big-block Fairlanes were meant to excite showroom shoppers seeking the ultimate in street performance machines.

Ford did a total redesign of the Fairlane for 1966. The engineers specifically left enough room in the engine compartment so the 427 could be shoehorned under the hood. Nothing was held back because of the sales theme Ford wanted to push at the time. When *Hot Rod's* Eric Dahlquist reviewed a 427-powered Fairlane in the magazine's July 1966 issue he pointed out that Charlie Gray of Ford's Performance Division and Bill Hollbrook of the company's Performance & Economy Section had helped to develop the car as part of the company's "Total Performance" program.

This program was aimed at taking the wind out of the sails of Mopar and General Motors. FoMoCo's 390 V-8 was eating the dust generated by Hemis, GTOs, 4-4-2s and SS-396 Chevelles. The fact that the 427 out-cubed Mopar's various 426s was no coincidence. It was an engine designed to turn on the hot rodders who wanted a Ford that could smoke the competition.

Identified by a big, long lift-off fiberglass hood with a huge scoop taking in air just above the grille, the Fairlane 500s and 500XLs equipped with the big-block came in 410 hp (single four-barrel) and 425 hp (with twin Holley four-barrel carburetors) configurations. The cars also featured NASCAR-style hood locking pins, chrome engine parts, 11.2-inch diameter disc brakes, a 2 1/4-inch diameter exhaust system, a heavy-duty suspension and a tachometer.

Hot Rod did not do a full road test of the 1966 Fairlane 427, but reported some figures quoted by "some of the mechanics on the project" which indicated quarter-mile runs in 14.5 to 14.6 seconds at 100 mph. Later, on drag strips with some tuning and racing slicks, the cars were found capable of doing the distance in just under 13 seconds at nearly 114 mph.

Only about 60 such cars were produced in 1966, but they gave the midsize Fords a muscle car image that boosted the entire line's market impact. In drag racing, the Fairlane 427s were so dominant that the rules were soon changed and they wound up in F/SX class, even though they were technically factory production models. In stock car racing, the medium-riser 427s were deemed legal and gave Ford a winning advantage over single four-barrel Mopars. (Dual quad Hemis were not sanctioned to compete.)

1966 FORD FAIRLANE GT/GTA

(Jerry Heasley photo)

The 1966 Fairlane GTA convertible was fast and plenty stylish.

(Jerry Heasley photo)

The 1966 GTA had plenty of exterior bells and whistles and a 335-hp V-8.

The first *production* Fairlanes able to carry a big-block V-8 were the totally redesigned 1966 models. The size of the Fairlane body didn't change much on the outside, but the increased dimensions under the hood became important in the muscle car era. These cars served as Ford's factory hot rods when they were equipped with the monster V-8s. They competed head to head with Pontiac's GTO and a Ford advertisement for the high-performance model was titled "How to cook a tiger!"

The Fairlane GT came with a 390-cid 315-hp V-8 as standard equipment. The Fairlane GTA included a 335-hp version of the 390-cid V-8, chrome-plated rocker covers, oil filter cap, radiator cap, air cleaner cover and dip stick, a high-lift cam, a bigger carburetor and the two-way three-speed Sport Shift automatic transmission that could be used like an automatic or like a manual gearbox.

A limited number of Fairlanes were sold with "side-oiler" 427-cid wedge engines. Some of these cars even hit the NASCAR ovals.

The 427-powered Fairlanes were characterized by a big air scoop that gulped cold air at the front of the hood. Only about 60 Fairlanes with 427s were produced.

Both Fairlane GT models were part of the fancy 500/XL line. The two-door hardtop sold for $2,843 and 33,015 were built. With the production of 4,327 units, the $3,068 based-price convertible was much rarer.

Included in the GT package were badges, a special hood, body striping, engine dress-up parts, a heavy-duty suspension, front disc brakes, bucket seats, a center console and a sport steering wheel. The base 315-hp V-8 featured a hot cam, special manifolds and a single four-barrel carb.

A 1966 Fairlane GTA two-door hardtop with the 390-cid 335-hp V-8 carried only about 10.5 lbs. per horsepower. It could move from 0 to 60 mph in a mere 6.8 seconds and did the quarter mile in 15.2 seconds.

1966 FORD GALAXIE "7-LITRE"

I chose a sporty new XL Hardtop by Ford like I make a business decision: with cold facts.
Cold fact 1—Ford has one of the world's quietest rides. That shows it's solidly built.
Cold fact 2—Ford has better ideas, like a SelectShift transmission that you can use as an automatic or a manual.
Cold fact 3—My wife likes Ford's looks.

And who'd argue with that? Certainly no one who's seen the new Ford XL. Bristling 289 cu. in. V-8 is standard. So are the foam-padded Thunderbird bucket seats and new SelectShift transmission that shifts automatically when you want it, and manually when you need it on ice or snow or on twisting mountain roads. And, of course, every '67 Ford is equipped with Ford Motor Company Lifeguard-Design Safety Features. Plus the rock-solid durability that is winning new Ford boosters in record-breaking numbers.

You're ahead in a FORD

Quieter because it's stronger...stronger because it's better built.

The 7-Litre series of the 1966 Ford Galaxie 500XL hardtop featured a high-performance 427-cid V-8.

While the 1965 and 1966 full-sized Fords shared a similar overall design character, the hood is the only body panel that can be interchanged between the two years. The 1966 feature lines were a bit more rounded and the Galaxie 500 two-door hardtop with its semi-fastback roofline had particular eye appeal.

In the muscle car marketplace, at this time, the demand for big cars was declining. The mid-sized models, sporty "senior" compacts and pony cars like the Mustang were offering go-fast options designed to steal high-performance buyers away from full-sized models. In reaction to this, Ford decided to package the big-engine Galaxie as a separate, sporty model aimed at mature muscle car mavens.

The Galaxie 500XL "7-Litre" series offered high-performance versions of the Galaxie 500XL two-door hardtop and convertible with a 428-cid 345-hp V-8 engine as standard equipment. Also included was a Cruise-O-Matic automatic transmission, but a four-speed manual gearbox was optional at no extra cost.

Along with the 428-cid power plant, the features of this model included a sport steering wheel with simulated English walnut finish, bucket seats, a floor-mounted gear shifter, a low-restriction dual exhaust system, power disc brakes and a non-silenced air cleaner.

The code "Q" 428-cid "Thunderbird Special" V-8 had a 4.13 x 3.98-inch bore and stroke. With a single Holley four-barrel carburetor and a 10.5:1 compression ratio, it developed 345 hp at 4600 rpm. A "Police Interceptor" version (Code "P") with 360 hp at 5400 rpm was optional. With its small-bore, long-stroke configuration, the 428-cid V-8 was designed for smoothness rather than competition. The 1966 Galaxie 500XL "7-Litre" hardtop could do 0 to 60 mph in about 8 seconds and the quarter mile in 16.4 seconds.

The 7-Litre fastback two-door hardtop had a suggested retail price of $3,596 and weighed 3,914 lbs. Ford records show that 8,705 were made. The convertible version had prices starting at $3,844 and weighed 4,059 lbs. Its production total was 2,368 units.

Ford did build 237 427-cid V-8s in 1966, but many of them were installed in Fairlanes, which had become wide enough to accept the big-block V-8 under the hood. Therefore, only a handful of 427-powered 1966 Galaxie 500XLs were produced.

1966 FORD MUSTANG GT

The 1966 Mustang GT was largely unchanged from the previous model year.

(Jerry Heasley photo)

For 1966, little change was made to the Mustang. A revised instrument panel, that looked less like the Falcon's, was used. The grille retained its now-familiar shape, but had the Mustang horse emblem "floating" in the "corral" in its center, with no horizontal or vertical dividing bars. A wind split ornament was added at the end of the "cove" on the body sides. Federally mandated safety features including seat belts, a padded instrument panel, emergency flashers, electric windshield wipers (with washers) and dual padded sun visors were made standard. Prices increased $44 for the hardtop, $18 for the 2+2 and $49 for the convertible.

(Jerry Heasley photo)

The cool convertible helped boost Mustang GT sales to about 30,000 in 1966.

The GT Equipment Group continued to be available in 1966 as a $152.50 package for Mustangs with high-performance V-8 power plants. It included a dual exhaust system, front fog lamps, special body ornamentation, front disc brakes, GT racing stripes (in place of rocker panel moldings), and handling package components. The handling package (normally $30.84 extra by itself) included increased-rate front and rear springs, larger-diameter front and rear shock absorbers, a steering system with a 22:1 overall ratio and a large-diameter stabilizer bar.

The base V-8 engine for 1966 was the Code "G" 4.00 x 2.87-inch bore and stroke 289-cid with a 9.3:1 compression ratio and an Autolite two-barrel carburetor. It generated 200 hp at 4400 rpm. The performance options included the Code "A" 289-cid Challenger V-8

with a 10.1:1 compression ratio and four-barrel Autolite carburetor, which produced 225 hp at 4800 and the Code "K" Challenger High-Performance V-8. This version of the "289" featured a 10.5:1 compression ratio, a four-barrel Autolite carburetor and solid valve lifters, which helped it to make 271 hp at 6000 rpm.

A Mustang 2+2 with the Challenger High-Performance V-8 could do 0 to 60 mph in 7.6 seconds and needed about 15.9 seconds to make it down the quarter mile. The GT package was twice as popular as it had been in 1965 and its sales increased from about 15,000 the earlier year to approximately 30,000. And that didn't include the toy Mustang GTs that Ford dealers sold for $4.95. Ford even took out a full-page ad showing a young boy pushing one of the miniature Mustangs along under his Christmas tree.

1966 SHELBY-MUSTANG GT 350H

(Steve Mason photo)

The 1966 Shelby-Mustang GT 350H fastback was quite a ride for a rental car.

"Rent-A-Race-Car" may seem like an oxymoron, but then, you might have forgotten about the Shelby GT 350H. The H stood for Hertz and it was a special version of Carroll Shelby's legendary conversion of the Mustang pony car into a true muscle car. The GT 350H was not Hertz's first venture involving rental cars that weren't totally ho-hum. Prior to 1965, Hertz had rented Corvettes.

In any case, during 1966 you could walk up to the Hertz counter in many major cities and ask for one of the hottest cars of the era. You *did* have to be a member of the Hertz Sports Car Club. You also

had to be at least 25 years old and able to demonstrate "driving skills." The latter often involved no more than a quick spin around the block.

When Hertz switched its allegiance to Ford products, renting 'Vettes didn't seem appropriate. Carroll Shelby's astute sales manager saw the promotional possibilities in having the Shelby-Mustang replace the Corvette. This would be great advertising, as well as a way to get potential buyers in the driver's seat.

While Shelby initially hoped to sell a couple dozen cars to

Hertz, the ultimate order was larger. The final tally came to 936 GT 350s out of a total run of 2,380 in 1966.

It came as no surprise—except possibly to Hertz—that these muscular rent-a-cars would create some maintenance headaches after being put into the hands of weekend racers. There are tales of "Rent-A-Racers" showing up at drag strips. When the remnants of a roll bar were found under the carpeting in one car, it was concluded that it had seen some track time in SCCA competition.

At a cost of only $17 dollars a day and 17 cents per mile (still about twice the rate of a regular Hertz rental at the time) the GT 350H offered a cheap car to use for a weekend of racing. After the race, Hertz could take care of any needed repairs.

The original Borg-Warner T-10 close-ratio four-speed manual transmissions were a real problem . . . especially when used by inexperienced drivers. Hertz later switched to Ford's C-4 automatic, which became an option on all Shelbys for 1966. Although lacking a stickshift, this was still a rental car with over 300 hp.

With the automatic, the "Cobraized" 289-cid High Performance small-block V-8 was fed by a 595-cfm Autolite carburetor that replaced the regular 715-cfm Holley. Another running change was to Mustang-type front disc brakes and a revised master cylinder. This lowered the pedal pressure a bit with sintered metallic brake pads and linings. A warning that read, "This vehicle is equipped with competition brakes. Heavier than normal pedal pressure required" was displayed on the instrument panel.

The GT 350H had some visual differences from normal '66 GT 350s. Most were finished in black with gold decals (a color scheme Hertz had used when it built its own taxicabs in the 1920s.) A few GT 350Hs were painted white, red, blue and green. Most of these also got gold striping.

After serving Hertz, the GT 350Hs were returned to Ford for minor refurbishing. Then, they were resold to the general public through selected dealers. Unfortunately, during refurbishing, the high-performance parts sometimes got "lost." While there were no special Hertz models in later years, the company did rent GT 350s through 1969.

Today, an excellent GT 350H will bring a couple of thousand dollars more than a "plain" GT 350.

1967 FORD FAIRLANE 427

A new taillight configuration was one of the changes on the Fairlane in 1967.

(Jerry Heasley photo)

The 1967 Ford Fairlane continued to use the body introduced in 1966 with minor trim changes. The 1967 grille was a single aluminum stamping in place of the two grilles used in the previous models. The 1967 taillights were divided horizontally by the back-up light, instead of vertically as in 1966.

The 427-cid "side-oiler" V-8 was again available on the Fairlane options list. The 1967 edition of *Car Fax* indicated that it came only on non-GT club coupes and sport coupes. Prices for the 410-hp engine in Galaxies without the 7-Litre package was $975.09, which is probably in the general ballpark for the Fairlane engine option.

The milder 410-hp single-four-barrel-carburetor version was not the only choice. There was the hairier 425-hp version that carried two four-barrel Holleys. Both of these options included a transistorized ignition, heavy-duty battery, heavy-duty suspension, extra cooling package and four-speed manual transmission. Also mandatory on Fairlane 427s at $46.53 extra were 8.15 x 15 four-ply-rated black nylon tires. Fairlane 427 buyers could opt for 8.15 x 15 four-ply-rated whitewall nylon tires for $82.83 extra or for blackwall ($62.22 extra) or whitewall ($98.52) models of larger 8.45 x 15 four-ply-rated nylon tires.

Racing versions of the 427-cid V-8 were offered with goodies like a new eight-barrel induction system that put about 30 extra horses on tap. A tunnel-port version of the 427 was available as an over-the-counter kit, with a tunnel-port intake on special cylinder heads and a special intake manifold.

In NASCAR competition, the 427-powered Fairlanes swept a bunch of early-in-the-year races before Chrysler complained. The sanctioning rules were then changed again to handicap the midsize Fords. Similarly, NHRA placed the Fairlane 427s in SS/B class to keep them from totally dominating the quarter-mile sport.

(Jerry Heasley photo)

The 1967 Ford Fairlane "427" sport coupe was a standout on the racetrack.

1967 FORD FAIRLANE GT/GTA

The 1967 Fairlane continued Ford's trend toward sporty, youthful styling and away from the dowdiness of the model's earlier years. GT models carried a narrow-wide-narrow side stripe motif just above the rocker panels. A new deeply recessed grille added to the midsize Fairlane's performance image and the vertically mounted dual headlamps created instant Ford identification.

For 1967, standard equipment for the Fairlane GT included all Fairlane, Fairlane 500 and Fairlane 500XL features plus power disc brakes; wide oval white tires, a special GT hood with simulated "power domes" with integral turn signals, GT body stripes, GT fender plaques, a GT black-out style grille, deluxe wheel covers, a 289-cid V-8, outside left-hand remote-control mirror and deluxe seat belts.

The 390-cid V-8 was optional. For $78.25 you could get it with a two-barrel carburetor and 270 hp. For $158.08 you could get a 320-hp version with a

four-barrel carburetor, but only if you also ordered an extra-cost transmission. The cheapest option was the heavy-duty three-speed manual gearbox for $79.20 extra. You could also get the 390 hooked to a four-speed manual for $184.02. The Sport Shift Cruise-O-Matic was $220.17 extra. When this transmission was ordered, the car became a GTA. A heavy-duty suspension was standard equipment on 1967 Fairlane GTs and GTAs with the big-block 390-cid V-8.

The Model 42 Fairlane GT sport coupe (two-door hardtop) sold for $2,838.88. The Model 43 convertible version had a $3,063.67 sticker price. Only 18,670 hardtops and 2,117 convertibles were made. The 390-cid engine added $184 to the prices ($264 when fitted with a four-barrel carburetor).

A 289-equipped Fairlane hardtop could go from 0 to 60 mph in 10.6 seconds and do the quarter mile in 18 seconds at 79 mph. The 390-cid 320-hp version required 8.4 seconds to reach 60 mph and did the quarter mile in 16.2 seconds at 89 mph.

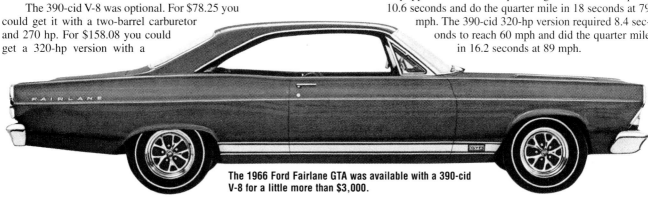

The 1966 Ford Fairlane GTA was available with a 390-cid V-8 for a little more than $3,000.

1967 FORD GALAXIE 500XL

Full-size Fords were completely restyled in 1967. They continued to ride on a 119-inch wheelbase and had an overall length of 213.9 inches, making them nearly 4 inches longer than in 1966.

The new models were even more rounded than the previous Fords, with rounder tops and fenders. On the front end, dual stacked headlights were seen once again, but the grille was all new. It was a double-stamped aluminum piece featuring horizontal bars divided by five vertical bars. The center portion of the grille projected forward and this pointed shape was carried over on the hood.

Stylists emphasized the "Coke-bottle" look even more in the body feature lines and the taillights were vertically positioned rectangles with chrome moldings and chrome crosshairs. Inside, Ford fans found a new energy-absorbing steering wheel with a thickly padded hub.

Offered again were Custom, Custom 500, Galaxie 500, Galaxie 500XL and LTD lines, but there was no Galaxie 500XL "7-Litre"

series. Instead, the 7-Litre goodies were offered as an option package for Galaxie 500XL two-door hardtops and ragtops.

The basic Galaxie 500XL featured bucket seats, a center console, special ornamentation, courtesy lights, foot pedal trim, a 289-cid 200-hp V-8 engine and SelectShift Cruise-O-Matic transmission. The 3,594-lb. fastback coupe sold for $3,243 and the 3,704-lb. convertible sold for $3,493. The 428-cid 345-hp "Thunderbird Special" V-8 was part of the 7-Litre option and you could order the 360-hp "Police Interceptor" version at additional extra cost.

Also continuing to be optional at extra cost was the hotter 427-cid V-8 in both the 410-hp "Thunderbird High-Performance" version and the 425-hp "Thunderbird Super High-Performance" version. There was even a tunnel port version of the 427 that was made available as an over-the-counter Ford dealer kit. It featured a tunnel port intake on special cylinder heads and special manifolds.

1967 FORD MUSTANG GT/GTA

For 1967, competition in the so-called sports-compact market was noticeably stiffer. Mercury introduced its fancy version of the Mustang—the Cougar—in 1967. Chevrolet, which had made little effort to respond to the Mustang with the dying Corvair, chose to develop its own, entirely new sports-compact model for 1967. It was called the Camaro. The Firebird was Pontiac's version of the Camaro. It bowed in mid-1967, six months after the Camaro.

Ford was hard pressed to improve on the "classic" Mustang it had introduced in 1964, but it had to. The competition was getting

very keen, indeed. Iacocca and company did a great job with a tough assignment. The 1967 Mustang got a jazzy new body, a wider tread for better road grip and a wider range of engines. Option choices were widened, too. They now included a tilt-away steering wheel, a built-in heater/air conditioner, an overhead console, a stereo-sonic tape system, a SelectShift automatic transmission that also worked manually, a bench seat, an AM/FM radio, fingertip speed control, custom exterior trim group, and front power disc brakes. Styling followed the same theme, but in a larger size.

The stylish 1967 Mustang GT convertible helped Ford hold its own in the battle with GM's new Camaro and Firebird.

The 1967 Mustang GT fastback featured all new lines and a distinctive rear shape.

On the exterior, the 1967 Mustang was heftier and more full-fendered. Especially low and sleek was the new 2+2 fastback, which featured all-new sheet metal. The roof line had a clean, unbroken sweep downward to a distinctive, concave rear panel. Functional air louvers in the roof rear quarters were made thinner than before. The wheelbase was unchanged, but overall length grew by nearly 2 inches. Front and rear tread widths went up by 2.1 inches and overall width was 2.7 inches wider at 58.1 inches.

All Mustangs had bigger engine bays. This was very necessary, because the first "big-block" option was among the many 1967 hardware upgrades. It was a 390-cid V-8 with 315 hp. This small bore-long stroke power plant was related to the Ford "FE" engine, introduced way back in 1958. It provided a good street-performance option with a low $264 price tag, lots of low-end performance and plenty of torque.

All of the 1966 engines were carried over, plus there was a new 200-hp version of the Challenger 289 V-8 with a two-barrel carburetor. This motor was standard in cars with the GT option. A new designation used on cars with automatic transmission and GT equipment was "GTA."

Other technical changes included front suspension improvements. A competition handling package was released, but it cost quite a bit extra and didn't go into too many cars. The 1967 Mustang GT 2+2 with the 390-cid 335-hp V-8 could do 0 to 60 mph in 7.4 seconds and the quarter mile in 15.6 seconds.

1968 FORD FAIRLANE COBRA 428-CJ

The 1968 Fairlane Cobra 428-CJ had a hot new body and a hot new engine.

(Jerry Heasley photo)

The Fairlane grew in 1968. It retained a 116-inch wheelbase, but overall length grew by 4 inches to 201. Some enthusiasts felt that it looked almost like a full-size car, although the big Fords of the day were still a whole foot longer. In addition to the Fairlane, Fairlane 500 and Fairlane GT series, there was a new Fairlane Torino top trim level.

In 1968, the fastback version that muscle car fans favored did not come as a Torino, only as a Fairlane 500 (six or V-8) or Fairlane GT (V-8). The GT was usually the version that showed up at drag strips and not with the base 302-cid V-8 or the optional 390-cid "big block." At the start of the year, racing buffs could order the 427-cid monster mill in a de-tuned 390-hp state, but this option was soon replaced with a new 428 Cobra-Jet engine that came in two versions.

The 428-CJ had a 4.13 x 3.98-inch bore and stroke, which made it a totally different engine than the 427. The base version, code "Q," came with 10.7:1 compression heads and a single Holley four-barrel carburetor. It was advertised at 335 hp at 5600 rpm. The Super Cobra-Jet (SCJ) version, code "R," had a 10.5:1 compression ratio, a four-barrel with ram-air induction and advertised 360 hp at 5400 rpm.

The Cobra-Jet V-8 was basically the 1966 Ford "FE" big block fitted with 427-type cylinder heads. The factory grossly underrated the power of the Cobra-Jet V-8 in the mid-sized cars to give them an advantage in drag racing classifications. Later, it was revealed that the CJ-428 produced something like 410 hp in the 1968 Fairlanes and Torinos. No wonder they could run from 0 to 60 mph in just over 6 seconds and do the quarter mile in 14.5 seconds.

1968 FORD 427

For 1968, the full-sized Fords continued with the same basic body introduced in 1967, but there were some significant revisions to the front-end sheet metal that make the two designs look more different than they really are. The new grille work was less protruding and hidden headlights were used on the upper series. The new grille had a honeycomb texture with a single vertical division bar in its center. The Ford name in block letters and a Ford crest appeared. Rooflines were generally more formal looking and the taillights were divided horizontally (instead of vertically, as in 1967) by the back-up light lenses.

The legendary "side-oiler" 427-cid V-8 made its last appearance in big Fords in 1968. It was slightly de-tuned to 390 hp at 5600 rpm and 460 ft. lbs. of torque at 3200 rpm.

This year's big Fords came in Custom, Custom 500, Galaxie 500, Ford XL and Ford LTD series. If you wanted a hardtop or a convertible (like many buyers interested in big-block engines did) you had to shop the upper three series. In the Galaxie 500 line the prices were $2,964.55 for the sportier fastback hardtop, $2,999.28 for the formal roof hardtop and $3,215.20 for the ragtop. The Ford XL line offered just the fastback hardtop at $3,068.94 and the ragtop at $3,320.65. The LTD came only as the formal roof hardtop at $3,129.87. There was no LTD convertible. Of course, those with serious racing in mind could get the 427 in a $2,667.49 Custom two-door sedan and go lots faster without the eye appeal.

The 427-cid engine had a dealer wholesale price of $449.53. Once the Ford dealer tacked on federal excise tax and his normal profit, the price tag for the monster motor was up to $622.97.

At midyear 1968, Ford Motor Company discontinued making the 427-cid V-8. In the Fairlane and Mustang series, the 427 was replaced by the equally famous and powerful Cobra Jet 428 and Super Cobra Jet 428 engines. The big cars got a new Thunder-Jet 429-cid V-8 that sounded formidable but produced only 340 and 360 hp—not quite enough to turn the later big Fords into muscle cars.

QUIET. STRONG. BEAUTIFUL.

A GREAT ROAD CAR.

'68 FORD

1968 Ford XL. Latest version of the Fords shown quieter than Europe's finest luxury cars, strong enough to leap off an Olympic ski jump. This year, Ford XL leaves its rivals farther behind than ever. No other car in its field offers disappearing headlamps as standard equipment. Or front power disc brakes at the XL price. Or a transmission like SelectShift on any model, with any engine. Or a 5-passenger fastback with XL's unique styling. Or the stripes that specially modified Ford cars won at LeMans, Sebring, Daytona. Ride this great road car.

See the light!

FORD has a better idea.

The 427-cid 390-hp V-8 was offered for any full-size 1968 Ford, including the Galaxie LX fastback.

1968 FORD MUSTANG CJ 428/SCJ 428

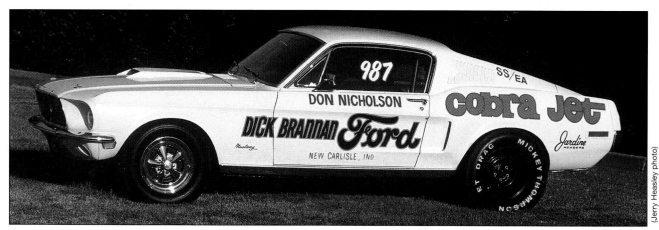

The 1968 Ford Mustang CJ fastback was right at home on the drag strip, thanks to an imposing Cobra Jet 428 V-8 capable of producing up to 400 hp.

Ford introduced the 428 Cobra Jet engine option on April 1, 1968 as its big-block performance leader. Production of the engine continued through 1970. Rated conservatively for 335 hp at 5200 rpm, the 1968 Mustang CJ 428 put out more like 375 to 400 ghp. It was hot competition for the SS 396 from Chevrolet, the 400 HO from Pontiac, the 440 Magnum from Mopar and literally any other muscle car on the street in 1968. After a drag-strip test, *Hot Rod* magazine declared the Mustang's 428 CJ to be "the fastest running pure stock in the history of man."

A high-performance variant of the basic 428-cid V-8, the main features of the CJ were revised heads—similar to the Ford 427 "low-riser" type—with bigger ports, a camshaft from the 390-cid GT engine, a cast-iron copy of the 428-cid Police Interceptor intake manifold and a 735-cfm Holley four-barrel carburetor.

For 1968 1/2, all Cobra Jets were coded "R" in the fifth digit of the vehicle identification number (VIN) and all were Ram-Air cars (featuring an air cleaner and flapper assembly mounted underneath the hood). A small scoop sat atop the hood to admit cold air to the Holley four-barrel.

The 428 SCJs were built with drag-strip duty in mind, which is why Ford beefed up the bottom end and added an oil cooler, but left the top end alone. SCJs came with hardened cast-steel crankshafts (regular CJs had nodular iron cast cranks) and LeMans rods that were externally balanced with a large vibration damper. Of course, the CJ was already stock with a nodular-cased 9-inch differential and 31-spline axles.

SCJs did not have a unique engine code, but they were mandatory with either a 3.9:1 Traction-Lok (code V) or a 4.30:1 Detroit Locker (code W) axle.

1968 FORD MUSTANG GT/GTA
AND CALIFORNIA SPECIAL

The 1968 Mustang GT 390 fastback cranked out about 325 hp to go along with its good looks.

Ford invited 1968 car shoppers to "Turn yourself on, switch your style and show a new face in the most exciting car on the American road," in its advertising for the 1968 Mustang.

Only subtle changes were actually made to the new-in-1967 design. Bucket seats, a floor-mounted stick, a sports steering wheel and rich, loop-pile carpeting remained standard. Minor trim updates included a front end with the Mustang emblem "floating" in the grille, script-style (instead of block letter) Mustang body side nameplates and cleaner-looking bright metal trim on the cove. There was a new two-tone hood. Still, prices rose substantially, averaging about

The "California Special" 1968 Mustang GT had some special exterior goodies, including a spoiler.

(Jerry Heasley photo)

$140 more per model.

The $147 GT option included a choice of stripes. Either the rocker panel type or a reflecting "C" stripe could be specified. The latter widened along the ridge of the front fender and ran across the door, to the upper rear body quarter. From there, it wrapped down, around the sculptured depression ahead of the rear wheel, and tapered forward, along the lower body, to about the midpoint of the door. Other GT goodies included fog lights in the grille, a GT gas cap and GT wheel covers. The fog lights no longer had a bar between them and the "corral" in the grille. Disc brakes were usually extra, but made the standard equipment list when big-block V-8s were ordered. A total of 17,458 GT's were made in 1968. A GT equipped with the 390-cid V-8 is considered a very desirable collector's car.

Many new engine options were offered in 1968. Some reflected midyear changes. There were no options with the base 289-cid 195-hp V-8. Instead, a 302-cid V-8 was added. This was initially seen with a four-barrel carburetor and 230-hp output rating. Later, a 220-hp version with a two-barrel carburetor came out. Big-block options included two "FE" series engines, the 390-cid V-8 (with 320/325 hp) and the 390-hp 427-cid V-8. This engine was used in only a handful of cars before it was phased out in December 1967. Starting in April 1968, a new 428-cid Cobra-Jet V-8 with 335 hp was put into about 2,817 Mustangs. Cars with four-speed transmissions included strengthened front shock absorber towers and revised rear shock absorber mountings. Ram Air induction was available.

About 5,000 GT/CS "California Special" Mustangs were produced in 1968. Their features included a Shelby-style deck lid with a spoiler, sequential taillights and a blacked-out grille. They had no Mustang grille emblem. The wheel covers were the same ones used on 1968 GTs, but without GT identification.

1968 SHELBY-MUSTANG GT 500KR

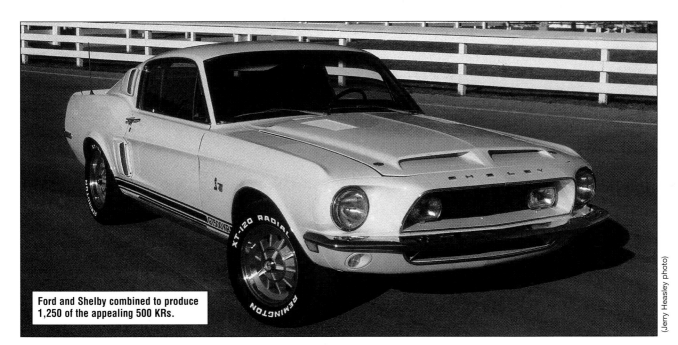

Ford and Shelby combined to produce 1,250 of the appealing 500 KRs.

(Jerry Heasley photo)

Somebody stole the Shelby GT 500KR that *Car Life* magazine was going to test drive. You couldn't blame them — the under-$5,000 fastback had a lot of appeal. With its 428-cid Cobra Jet engine, it was a big temptation to any car-loving cat burglar. After a rough three-day break-in, the LAPD recovered the car, but a Ford public relations guy had to call *Car Life* and admit it was in no shape for a national article. The magazine wound up with a replacement car and a good lead-in to introduce it.

Actually, the hot Mustang didn't need too much of an introduction. Everyone knew what Cobra meant and the GT 500 designation was well understood by 1968. As for "KR," the folks at Ford and Shelby said it stood for "King of the Road." With a 6.9 second 0-to-60 mph speed and 14.57 second quarter-mile ET, the GT 500KR wasn't the undisputed king of drag racing. "But, there's more to life than the quarter-mile," *Car Life's* editors maintained.

Tucked below the hood was a 428-cid Cobra Jet V-8 with 4.13 x 3.98-inch bore and stroke, 10.6:1 compression, special hydraulic lifters, dual branched headers and one extra-big Holley four-barrel. It was rated for 335 hp at 5200 rpm and 440 ft. lbs. of torque at 3400 rpm. True horsepower, however, was 435-500.

The Shelby KR package, for a coupe or convertible, also included a fiberglass hood and front panels, functional air scoops and hot-air extractors. A big speedometer and tachometer were added to the instrument panel and other gauges were moved to the console. Vinyl buckets and thick carpeting were standard. There was wood-look dash trim, suspension upgrades (including staggered shocks), E70-15 Goodyear Polyglas tires, a limited-slip differential, engine dress-up items and special stripes and badges.

Large, but ineffective air scoops were attached to the body sides to cool the disc/drum power brakes. During a test drive, the binders got so hot that they started pouring smoke out of the scoops. No wonder *Car Life* rated overall braking performance poor.

Although it was not the fastest car ever made, the GT 500KR was the fastest Shelby-Mustang made up to its time. Some racers registered ETs below 13 seconds and top speed was around 130 mph. The fastback model was base-priced at $4,473 and ran about $4,900 with a nice selection of options. Production counts were 933 units for the fastback and 318 for the convertible.

1968 FORD TORINO GT

The 1968 Ford Torino Cobra Convertible is relatively rare, and worth far more than its original $3,020 sticker price.

The 1968 Ford Torino GT was the sporty version of the Fairlane 500 and was based on that model. The Torino GT actually came in three versions. Model 65D was the two-door hardtop, which sold for $2,768.17, weighed 3,194 lbs. and had a production run of 23,939 units. The convertible—Model 76D—was much rarer and only 5,310 were made. Prices for the ragtop began at $3,020.40 and it tipped the scales at 3,352 lbs. in showroom stock condition. The real image car was the Model 63D two-door fastback, with its $2,742.84 window sticker, 3,208-lb. curb weight and 74,135 units produced. Dubbed the "SportsRoof" by Ford, this car had lots of buyer appeal in its era.

Fairlane standard equipment included government-mandated safety equipment, a 200-cid six or a 302-cid V-8 and 7.35-14 tires. The standard Torino models (sports coupe, sedan or wagon) added wheel covers and an electric clock. The sporty Fairlane GT included all this plus a vinyl bench seat, a GT handling suspension, argent silver styled wheels with chrome trim rings, F70 x 14 wide oval tires, GT body stripes, a gray GT grille, GT nameplates and a 302-cid 210-hp V-8. Power brakes were required if the optional 390-cid big-block V-8 was ordered.

The 390-cid engine came in two versions. The 265-hp edition with a single two-barrel carburetor added just $78.25 to the price of a Torino V-8. The 325-hp four-barrel version was $158.08 extra and also required an extra-cost transmission (either the heavy-duty three-speed at $79.20, a four-speed manual at $184.02 or Ford's Select Shift Cruise-O-Matic at $233.17).

Real muscle car lovers were probably more interested in getting a Torino GT with a 427-cid 390-hp V-8. It was a $622.97 option for all Fairlane two-door hardtops and you could not get it with Select Aire air conditioning, power steering, a 55-amp generator, a heavy-duty suspension or optional tires as extras either because it didn't make sense or these options were already required.

Motor Trend (December 1967) tested a 1968 Torino GT SportsRoof and liked most things about it, except the vision to the rear with the radical fastback styling. Other minor criticisms were made, but the overall impression was positive. "The new breed of super car from Ford is a full step ahead of its '67 counterpart," the magazine concluded.

The test car had the 390-cid four-barrel engine, which developed 335 hp at 4800 rpm and 427 ft. lbs. of torque at 3200 rpm. It had a 10.5:1 compression ratio, three-speed manual attachment and 3.25:1 rear axle. *Motor Trend* reported 7.2 seconds for 0 to 60 mph and 15.1 seconds at 91 mph for the quarter mile.

1969 FORD FAIRLANE "COBRA" 428-CJ

The hit of the season in Ford's mid-sized line for 1969 was a low-buck muscle car called the Torino Cobra. Designed to steal sales away from the surprisingly popular Plymouth Road Runner, the Torino Cobra was offered in both notchback and fastback models with the 428-CJ engine as standard equipment. Also standard was a four-speed manual gearbox, a heavy-duty suspension and cartoon decals of the coiled-snake Cobra emblem.

At the time, the idea of a "stripper" performance car at a budget price had great appeal to many people, but there were those who liked their muscle cars with a bit more spit and polish, so Ford also offered the same goodies, as optional equipment, in all 1969 Fairlanes—not just the Fairlane Torino models.

In all likelihood, few if any such engines made their way into base Fairlane models, since this series did not offer the fastback

body style. This model was merchandised in the Fairlane 500 line with a base price of $2,674 for a V-8 version. Of course, you could also get a 428 CJ in the regular hardtop—which listed for $2,699—if you wanted a "sleeper" type muscle car.

As in 1968, the 428-CJ had a 4.13 x 3.98-inch bore and stroke. The base version came with 10.6:1 compression heads, a single Holley four-barrel carburetor and 335 hp at 5600 rpm. The Super Cobra-Jet (SCJ) version had a 10.5:1 compression ratio, a four-barrel with ram-air induction and 360 advertised horsepower.

One of the buff books tested a 1969 Fairlane Cobra two-door hardtop with the 428-cid 335-hp engine option. It gave the price of the car as $3,139. The hot Fairlane moved from 0 to 60 in 6.3 seconds and did the quarter mile in 14.5 seconds.

1969 FORD MUSTANG BOSS 302

(Jerry Heasley photo)

The flat black paint on the hood and trunk was a trademark of the 1969 Ford Mustang Boss 302.

In the slang of the '60s the word "boss" had a bundle of connotations. It meant "tough" or "awesome" (in the sense kids use the word today) and something that was "boss" was something every right-minded person aspired to. So, Ford picked it as a good name for its hot Mustang with the new 302-cid V-8.

Actually there were two Bosses. The first was a race-ready Boss 429 with Ford's NASCAR racing engine and completely redesigned front suspension. Then came the Boss 302, which was intended for high-performance street use.

The Boss 302 was Ford's answer to the Camaro Z/28 and was as likely to wind up in the hands of a hard-working kid as a middle-to-upper income youth who wanted to put a little excitement into his life.

What made the Boss special was a beefed-up 302-cid V-8 with four-bolt main bearing caps, a stronger crankshaft and—most important of all—redesigned cylinder heads that allowed dramatically better breathing. These "Cleveland" heads (as they are called) were also designed to sit atop Ford's 351 Cleveland V-8. In stock tune, a Boss 302 could turn in 0 to 60-mph times of under 7 seconds and nudge the century mark in a standing-start quarter mile.

While a Boss 302 in the hands of a collector is likely to be driv-

en a little more gingerly than the paces original owners put these cars through, Ford built an rpm limiter to keep lead-footed types from blowing up the engine. Basically, the limiter worked by counting ignition impulses and not allowing the engine to exceed 6,000 rpm.

Besides the special 302 engine, a Boss can be recognized by the matte black paint on its hood and trunk, Boss 302 name swatches on its sides, a front spoiler and styled steel wheels. Its performance equipment includes front disc brakes and a four-speed manual transmission. The optional rear spoiler was obviously decorative. (If this feature had been functional it would have been standard, right?)

Unlike other performance cars of the period, the Boss 302 had exceptionally good street manners—although the firm suspension did broadcast tar strips and other pavement irregularities.

Open the door and the Boss became just another Mustang. The interior is attractive, but it also features the infamous Mustang "park bench" rear seat. That's okay, though; the Mustang fastback wasn't really designed to be a four-seater.

If you've had a chance to own or drive one of these cars you'd probably agree with its original admirers: "Hey, man, this car is Boss!"

1969 FORD MUSTANG CJ 428/SCJ 428

The 1969 Mustang SCJ 428 convertible featured the same Super Cobra Jet engine as the CJ, but also had a few extra high-performance options.

(Jerry Heasley photo)

A 1969 Mustang GT sport coupe with the CJ 428 option generated about 335 hp.

(Jerry Heasley photo)

For model year 1969, the Mustang got its third major restyling. Its new body wasn't drastically changed, but it grew 3.8 inches. There was no change in wheelbase, which was still the same 108 inches as in 1965. The windshield was more sharply raked and quad headlamps were used. The outer lenses were deeply recessed into the fenders and the inboard lenses were set into the grille.

Missing for the first time was a side scoop (or cove) on the body. This styling gimmick was replaced with a feature line that ran from the tip of the front fender to just behind the rear-most door seam, at a level just above the front wheel opening. On convertibles and hardtops there was a rear-facing, simulated air vent in front of the rear wheel opening on both sides. On fastbacks, this feature line lead to a backwards C-shaped air scoop *above* the main feature line.

The fastback was now referred to as the SportsRoof or Sports Roof (various Ford ads spelled the term differently). It had a 0.9-inch lower roofline than earlier fastbacks. Also, Mustang fastbacks were now true hardtops. The rear quarter louvers were gone. Instead, a small window abutted the door glass.

Though the styling theme remained Ford-like, the Mustang adopted GM-like models to suit the tastes of different buyers. Mustangs now came in basic, luxury, sporty and high-performance formats like a Camaro or Firebird. This may have reflected the influence of Semon "Bunkie" Knudsen, a longtime GM executive who became president of Ford on February 6, 1968. While he didn't have time to change the cars, it's just about certain he changed marketing ideas.

Knudsen's background included a heavy emphasis on high-performance cars. He liked the look of the SportsRoof and this body style became the basis for a series of hot-forming "buzz bombs" like the Mach 1 and the soon-to-be-released Boss 302 and Boss 429.

One nice performance option available to enthusiast buyers in 1969 was a Mustang GT or Mach 1 with the Cobra Jet 428 engine. This motor was Ford's big-block performance leader. It came in Cobra Jet (CJ 428) or Super Cobra Jet 428 (SCJ 428) versions. The former was called the "standard Cobra engine" in the 1969 *Performance Buyer's Guide*. It generated 335 hp at 5200 rpm and 440 ft. lbs. of torque at 3400 rpm. The latter was the same engine with Ram Air induction, a hardened steel cast crankshaft, special "LeMans" connecting rods and improved balancing for drag racing. It had the same advertised horsepower.

A 1969 Mach 1 two-door hardtop with the 428-cid 335-hp engine carried just 9.6 lbs. per hp. It could do 0 to 60 mph in 5.5 seconds and cover the quarter mile in 13.9 seconds according to one road test. *Car and Driver* tested a Mach 1 fastback with the regular Cobra Jet V-8, automatic transmission and a 3.91:1 limited slip axle. This combination produced 5.7-second 0-to-60-mph performance and a 14.3-second quarter mile at 100 mph. The car had an estimated top speed of 115 mph.

1969 FORD MUSTANG MACH 1

The 1969 Mustang Mach 1 SportsRoof showed off the Mustang's new styling.

(Jerry Heasley photo)

For model year 1969, the Ford Mustang got its third major restyling. A new body introduced for 1969 kept the Mustang image. The fastback, formerly known as the 2+2, was now referred to as the SportsRoof.

The Mach 1 was based on the SportsRoof. "Mustang Mach 1— holder of 295 land speed records," said Ford's *1969 Performance Buyer's Digest*. "This is the one that Mickey Thompson started with. From its wide oval, belted tires to its wind tunnel designed SportsRoof, the word is 'go.'" The company pointed out that the production car had "the same wind-splitting sheet metal as the specially modified Mach 1 that screamed around Bonneville clocking over 155, hour after hour, to break some 295 USAC speed and endurance records."

Standard on all Mach 1s was a spoiler, matte black hood, simulated hood scoop and exposed NASCAR-style hood lock pins, which could be deleted. A reflective side stripe and rear stripes carried the model designation just behind the front wheel arches and above the chrome pop-up gas cap. Chrome-styled steel wheels and chrome exhausts tips (with optional four-barrel carburetors) were other bright touches. Also featured were dual color-keyed racing mirrors, and a handling suspension.

Mach 1s had the Mustang's fanciest interior with high-back bucket seats, black carpets, a rim-blow steering wheel, a center console, a clock, sound-deadening insulation and teakwood-grained trim on the doors, dash and console.

The Mach 1's base engine was a 351-cid two-barrel Windsor V-8. This was essentially a stroked 302-cid Ford V-8 with raised deck height, which created a great street performance engine. Options included the 351-cid 290-hp four-barrel V-8 and a 390-cid 320-hp V-8. Another option available to enthusiast buyers was a Mustang GT or Mach 1 with a Cobra Jet 428 or Super Cobra Jet 428 engine.

Exterior features such as a spoiler only enhanced the Mach 1's formidable go-fast potential.

(Jerry Heasley photo)

1969 FORD TORINO GT

The 1969 Ford Torino GT lineup again came in three versions. Model 65D was the two-door hardtop, which sold for $2,848, weighed 3,173 lbs. and had a production run of 17,951 units. The convertible—Model 76D—was much rarer than even the 1968 version and only 2,552 were made. Prices for the ragtop began at $3,073 and it tipped the scales at 3,356 lbs. in showroom stock condition. Still the most popular body style was the Model 63D two-door fastback, with its $2,823 window sticker, 3,220-lb. curb weight

and 61,319 units produced.

The 1969 Torino GT included all Fairlane 500 features plus the 302-cid 220-hp V-8 engine, bucket seats, a center console, special GT nameplates, GT exterior trim, argent silver finished styled steel wheels, a heavy-duty suspension, wide oval fiberglass-belted white-sidewall tires, hood scoop turn signals, lower body side stripes on sport coupes and convertibles and a C-style body side stripe on fastbacks. A power top was included on convertibles.

For $420.96 extra, buyers could get a 428 Cobra Jet Ram Air engine under the hood of their 1969 Torino.

This year a 351-cid 250-hp two-barrel V-8 was the first option for Torino GTs (at $58.34 over the 302) and actually replaced the two-barrel version of the 390-cid Ford big-block V-8. The four-barrel version of the 390, now rated for 320 hp, was $163.24 extra and also required an extra-cost transmission (either the heavy-duty three-speed at $79.20, a four-speed manual at $194.31 or Ford's Select Shift Cruise-O-Matic at $222.08).

The 427-cid 390-hp V-8 was no longer available. Its replacement in the "Fairlane" models (including Torino GTs) was a new 428-cid 335-hp V-8 for only $287.53 extra. This option also required an extra-cost transmission and included a heavy-duty battery, a 55-amp alternator, dual exhausts, the extra-cooling package, bright engine dress-up parts, cast aluminum rocker covers and a 3.25:1 non-locking rear axle. This was the non-Ram Air version.

The 428 Cobra Jet Ram Air V-8 was an additional $420.96 for Fairlanes that were not already Cobra models. This included all of the same goodies as the "regular" 428 Cobra Jet option, plus a 3.50:1 non-locking rear axle and a functional hood scoop.

In one magazine test, the 1969 Torino GT with the 428-cid big-block V-8 turned in a 14.5-second quarter-mile run. It could also scat from 0 to 60 mph in just 6.3 seconds.

1969 FORD TORINO COBRA

A new sub-series showed up in the 1969 Ford Torino GT line-up. This Cobra line included just two body types, the Model 65A formal hardtop base priced at $3,208 and the Model 6B sports roof base priced at $3,183. The emphasis was on performance when you went Cobra shopping and the standard equipment included a 428-cid 335-hp Cobra Jet V-8, a four-speed manual transmission, competition suspension, wide oval belted black sidewall tires and 6-inch wide wheels with hub caps.

The base Cobra engine featured a 4.13 x 3.98-inch bore and stroke, a 10.6:1 compression ratio, 335 hp at 5200 rpm and 440 ft. lbs. of torque at 2600 rpm. You could get it with an optional 351-cid 290-hp V-8 if you wanted to save on gas, but few muscle car buffs did. Also optional on the Torino Cobra was the 428 Cobra Jet "Ram Air" V-8, which also carried a 335-hp rating but achieved it at a higher 5600 rpm peak. Its torque output was 445 ft. lbs. at 3400 rpm and it had a 10.7:1 compression ratio.

The Ram Air engine featured a functional hood scoop to "ram" cold air into its single Holley four-barrel carburetor. This setup was only $133.44 extra on the Cobra, compared to $420.96 when ordered for other "Fairlane" models, including Torino GTs.

If you did not want to shift for yourself, a Select Shift automatic transmission was optional for $37.06 and it came with a floor shift and optional center console. The 3.25:1 rear axle was standard and optional axle ratios included 3.45:1, 3.91:1 and 4.30:1. Power disc brakes were also available for $64.77. A Traction-Lock differential was $63.51 extra and getting a factory tachometer added $47.92 to the price tag.

Motor Trend road tested a Cobra with the Ram Air engine and liked the car. The magazine charted 0-to-60 performance at 6.3 seconds and the quarter mile at 14.5 seconds and 100 mph. "Torque gives rubber big bite for fast acceleration," the buff book summarized. "Four-speed helps. Ford has many hop-up parts for 428." They included special camshafts, special cylinder heads, an aluminum intake, "eight-barrel" induction, flat-top pistons, a cast crankshaft, a dual-point distributor and a heavy-duty oil pump.

(Jerry Heasley photo)

The 1969 Ford Torino could hit 100 mph in the quarter mile with the Cobra Jet Ram Air 428 engine.

1969 FORD TORINO TALLADEGA

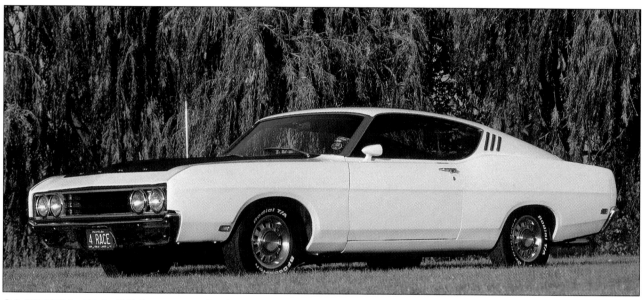

(Jerry Heasley photo)

Only 754 1969 Ford Torino Talladegas were produced.

At the time they were built, the fastback cars that became combatants in the "aerodynamic wars" on the 1969-1970 NASCAR Grand National superspeedways were more of a headache to their manufacturers than the worshipped treasures they are today. Requirements to "legalize" them for racing meant at least 500 examples had to be produced during the 1969 model year. That minimum production level was raised to one car per dealer for 1970.

Ford's hopes rode on the sloped-nosed 1969 Torino Talladega, which was part of the midsized Fairlane model lineup. A similar, but not identical, Mercury Montego counterpart was produced and called the Cyclone Spoiler II.

Ford called its fastback-styled two-door hardtops "SportsRoof" models at this point and the Talladega model was one of them. It was named after a town in Alabama where a new 2.66-mile NASCAR superspeedway was opening. The Talladega had an extended, sloped nose and a flush radiator grille. A revised Torino rear bumper was used in front of this model and the rocker panels were reworked a bit. The result was a car that was nearly 6 inches longer and 1 inch lower than a stock Torino SportsRoof. Of course, NASCAR racing teams started from there and continued to enhance their Talladegas.

In the stock version, power came from a 335-hp Cobra Jet 428-

cid "FE" block V-8, which was pretty potent, but came only with a C-6 Cruise-0-Matic automatic transmission. The racing cars ran the 427-cid big-block at the beginning of the season. Beginning in March, they were allowed to use the new 429-cid "semi-hemi" V-8. These engines were *not* installed in showroom Talladegas however, since the Mustang Boss 429 was utilized to meet the requirements of the race-sanctioning groups.

Counting prototypes, Talladega production easily passed the required 500 units and wound up at 754. The cars came in Wimbleton white, royal maroon or presidential blue. They had black interiors and came only with bench seats.

The idea behind the Talladega was to get the production work over with as quickly as possible and let the racers create a performance image for the Torino series. They did this, too. David Pearson won his second straight NASCAR Grand National championship driving for race team owners Holman and Moody.

The 1969 Talladegas proved very adept at racing. In fact, test drivers found that their 1970 replacements were some 5 mph slower on the big tracks. As a result, Ford's factory-backed teams ran year-old models at many tracks during the 1970 racing season.

1970 FORD MUSTANG CJ 428/SCJ 428

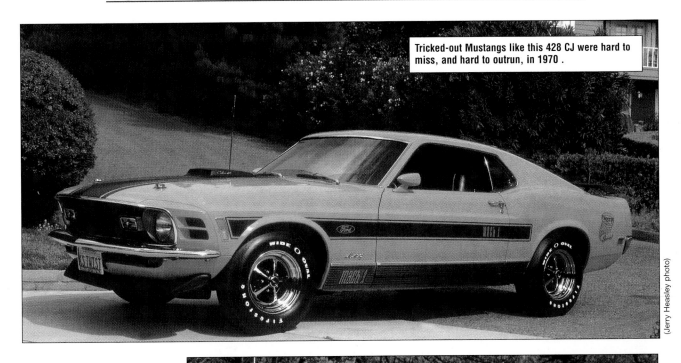

Tricked-out Mustangs like this 428 CJ were hard to miss, and hard to outrun, in 1970 .

(Jerry Heasley photo)

The new headlight setup was one obvious difference in the 1970 Mustangs. This 428 CJ coupe could be had with nine different engine packages.

(Jerry Heasley photo)

The 1970 Mustang had some distinctions to set it apart from the 1969 edition. The biggest change was a return to single headlamps. They were located inside a larger new grille opening. Simulated air intakes were seen where the outboard headlights were on the 1969 models. The rear end was also slightly restyled.

Mustang standard equipment included wall-to-wall carpeting, bucket seats, belted bias-ply tires, a locking steering column, a full synchronized manual transmission, a sporty floor-mounted shift lever and a rear deck lid spoiler on SportsRoof models. Among the many muscle car options were power front disc brakes, a functional hood scoop, rear window louvered sport slats, a Hurst shifter, a tachometer and a Drag Pack package.

In addition to the base hardtop and convertible, Mustangs came as the hot Mach 1 fastback, the luxurious Grande hardtop and the race-bred Boss 302 fastback. With engine option selections, you could change the Boss 302 into a Boss 351 or a Boss 429. In total, Ford offered nine Mustang engines to pick from and the lineup was the same as 1969, except that the 390-cid V-8 was discontinued.

While the pre-package Boss models were the hit of the enthusiast magazines this season, the CJ 428 and SCJ 428 engines were both back. The former listed for $356 in all Mustang models except the Mach 1, which offered it for $311 over the price of its standard 351-cid V-8. The Ram-Air version was $376 extra in the Mach 1 and $421 extra in other models. A 2.32:1 close-ratio four-speed manual gearbox ($205) or a Cruise-O-Matic automatic transmission ($222) was required with both of the Cobra Jet engines. In addition, on base Mustangs F70-14 whitewall tires were required over E78-14 black sidewall tires when either of these engines was ordered. On Mach 1s, Boss models and convertibles, E70-14 whitewalls were required.

1970 FORD MUSTANG MACH 1

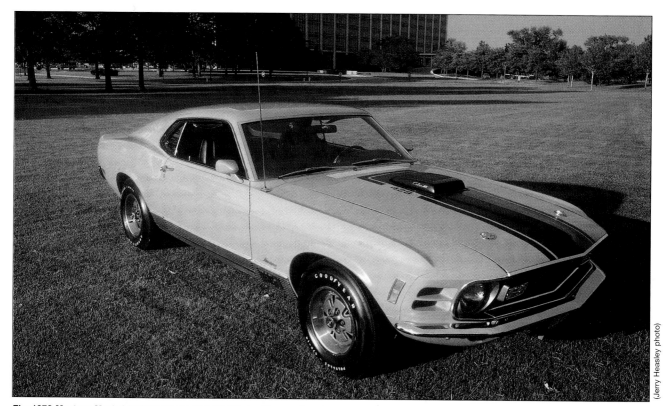

(Jerry Heasley photo)

The 1970 Mustang Mach 1 had all the exterior trimmings of a muscle car.

"Five years ago, Mustang started a whole new idea in sporty cars," said one 1970 Ford advertisement. "And Mustang's been first ever since." The ad listed "sporty facts" that made the Mustang favored in its market segment:

"**Fact.** Six great Mustangs models. They include the hot Mach 1, luxurious Grande, and the race-bred Boss 302. (Three roof lines, too. Hardtop, Convertible and a SportsRoof, a choice no one else can give you.)

"**Fact.** Power your Mustang your way. With nine Mustang engines to pick from (the lineup was the same as 1969, except that the 390-cubic-inch V-8 was discontinued). Economical 200-cid six all the way up to the 429 cube V-8.

"**Fact.** Loaded with sporty features. Mustang standards: Wall-to-wall carpeting. Bucket seats. Belted bias-ply tires. Locking steering column. Full synchronized manual transmission. Sporty floor-mounted shift. Rear deck spoiler on SportsRoof models.

"**Fact.** You can design it yourself. With more options than ever. Power front disc brakes. Functional hood scoop. Rear window louvered Sport Slats. Vinyl roof. Hurst Shifter. SelectAire Conditioning. Stereo system. Tachometer. Drag Pack. "Grabber"

exterior paint colors."

The 1970 Mach 1 featured the new year's front end styling and had its taillights recessed in a flat panel with honeycomb trim between them. Ribbed aluminum rocker panel moldings with big Mach 1 call-outs and a cleaner upper rear quarter treatment without simulated air scoops at the end of the main feature line were seen. A black-striped hood with a standard fake scoop replaced the completely matte-black hood. New twist-in hood pins held the hood down.

You could also get a shaker hood scoop on Mach 1s with the standard 351-cid V-8. A redesigned steering wheel was the big interior change. A larger rear stripe, larger rear call-out, mag-type hubcaps, wide 14 x 7-inch wheels and bright oval exhaust tips were also new. Black-painted styled wheels were a no-cost *option*.

Motor Trend tested a 1970 Mustang Mach 1 with the 351-cid four-barrel V-8. It had a 4.002 x 3.50-inch bore and stroke. With an 11.0:1 compression ratio it developed 300 hp at 5400 rpm and 380 ft. lbs. of torque at 3400 rpm. With automatic transmission and a 3.00:1 axle the car turned 0 to 60 mph in 8.2 seconds and did the quarter mile in 16 seconds at 86.2 mph.

1970 FORD TORINO COBRA

Ford had its intermediate cars on a two-year styling cycle at the time, so no matter how good the 1968 and 1969 Fairlane fastbacks looked or how fast they were in stock car racing competition, by the time the 1970 model year rolled around, it was time for a new batch of sheet metal.

Ford also had its intermediates (and most other lines) on a growth binge and the new 1970 Torino wheelbase increased from

116 to 117 inches. Length was up half a foot and width increased about 2 inches.

A full line of models was again available, being topped by the Torino Cobra. At $3,270 it had the most expensive base price in the line, even more than the sole remaining convertible—the GT at $3,212.

Part of the cost could be attributed to its new standard power

The 1970 Ford Torino Cobra packed 370 hp, but it wasn't as fast as the '69 model .

plant, the 385 series big-block 429. The 428 was gone from the intermediates for the new year. Torinos got the milder 360-hp engine with a single four-barrel carburetor. Cobras came with Ford's top-loader four-speed manual transmission (capped by a Hurst shifter), a competition suspension with staggered rear shocks, 7-inch wide steel wheels, F70-14 wide oval tires, a black hood with locking devices, black-out trim and Cobra badging. Bench seats were standard. Engine options included the 370-hp Cobra 429 or Cobra Jet Ram Air 429 with the same rating. For $155 you could get the Traction-Lok differential and for $207 the 4.30:1 Detroit Locker rear axle was available.

Production was 7,675, which was overshadowed by the 56,819 Torino GTs produced, which were flashier and cheaper at $3,105, thanks to a standard 302 cid V-8.

Torino Cobra was supposed to be the car of record for NASCAR Grand National racers, but it was slower than the 1969 Talladegas, forcing teams to run year-old cars. An answer to the winged Dodge Charger Daytona and Plymouth Superbird, the King Cobra was stillborn.

1971 FORD MUSTANG BOSS 351

The Mustang Boss 351 was rare in 1971, and a definite collector car today.

Ford Mustangs grew to their all-time largest for the 1971 model year. Wheelbase was up an inch to 109 inches, length increased 2.1 inches to 189.5 inches and width grew 2.4 inches to 74.1 inches. The latter was accompanied by a tread increase that permitted the 429-cid big-block V-8 to fit in the engine compartment with ease. Although the 429-powered cars were the most muscular, the Boss 351 was perhaps the most interesting.

The Boss 429 was curtailed early in the 1970 model run and the Boss 302 was of no more use after it was gone. Racing rules had changed and engine size was no longer critical to racing legalization. As a result, the Boss 351's purpose was just to tap what was left of the declining high-performance market.

Like its predecessors, the Boss 351 was based on the SportsRoof or fastback model. It was considered an option package and brought the base Mustang price of $2,973 up to $4,124. The heart of the new Boss 351 package was a 351-hp Cleveland V-8 with four-bolt main bearings, solid valve lifters and a four-barrel carburetor. The 1971 models were the last for Ford high-compression engines and the last for gross advertised horsepower numbers, which were 330 hp for the Boss 351.

Other mechanical features included a four-speed "top-loader" manual transmission with a Hurst gear shifter, a competition-type suspension, power front disc brakes, 3.91:1 Traction-Lok gearing, dual exhausts with non-exposed tips and the infamous rev limiter. Visuals were plentiful with side and rear identification decals, a matte black hood with functional scoops and locks and side stripes.

Only about 1,800 Boss 351s were made, which adds up to rarity today. There was no 1972 Boss Mustang of any kind, but by playing with the options list, you could come close to "building" one. The last year for the "big" Mustang was 1973.

1971 FORD MUSTANG MACH 1

The '71 Mach 1 featured a new paint scheme in addition to traditional muscle car features, including a rear deck spoiler.

The 1971 Mustang Mach 1 was redesigned and bigger all over, but still sported the Super Cobra Jet 429 power plant.

For 1971, Ford completed its fourth redesign of the Mustang. This created a bigger car. It had the basic Mustang look, with a longer wheelbase, a stretched length, more width, wider front and rear tracks and a heavier curb weight. A raked windshield, bulging front fenders and aerodynamic enhancements were evident.

The Mach 1 package returned. It included color-keyed mirrors, a honeycomb grille, color-keyed bumpers, sport lamps, a new gas cap, special decals and tape stripes and black or argent silver finish on the lower body perimeter. A special hood with NASA-style air scoops was a no-cost option with the base 302-cid V-8 and standard otherwise.

Available for the last time was a 429-cid big-block engine, which came in Cobra-Jet Ram Air and Super-Cobra-Jet Ram Air versions. Ford put together 1,255 of the CJ-R equipped Mach 1s and 610 of the SCJ-Rs.

Basically a de-stroked Thunderbird/Lincoln 460-cid V-8, the 429 had a wedge-head-shaped combustion chamber derived from up-to-date performance technology. The CJ-R version utilized large

valves, a hydraulic camshaft, four-bolt main bearing caps, re-worked porting and a 700-cfm Quadrajet carburetor (sourced from General Motors). A Ram Air induction system was included. Advertised horsepower for the 429 CJ-R was 370 at 5400 rpm.

The 429 SCJ-R put out 375 hp at 5600 rpm. A Drag Pack option with either a 3.91:1 Traction-Lok differential or a 4.11:1 Detroit Locker axle was mandatory. The option also included an oil cooler for when things really got hot at the drag strip. Other 429 SCJ-R performance features included solid valve lifters, adjustable rocker arms, drop-forged pistons and a 780-cfm Holley carburetor.

Both Cobra Jet engines had 11.3:1 compression and produced 450 ft. lbs. of torque at 3400 rpm. The SCJ-R had a bit more camshaft duration (200/300 degree versus 282/296 degrees).

Car Life (July 1969) tested a 375-hp Boss 429 with a four-speed manual transmission and 3.91:1 axle. It did 0 to 60 mph in 7.1 seconds. The quarter mile took 14.09 seconds with a terminal speed of 102.85 mph. Top speed on the car was about 116 mph.

1971 FORD TORINO COBRA

Updated trim and a slightly revised grille made the 1971 Ford Torino Cobra look slightly different than the 1970 version. This year's Cobra was technically a high-performance version of the Torino Brougham series and included all of the Brougham's standard features plus a base V-8 (the 351-cid 285-hp "Cleveland" engine), a four-speed manual gearbox with a Hurst shifter, special Cobra identification, a heavy-duty suspension, 7-inch-wide argent silver painted wheels with chrome hub caps, a blacked-out grille and lower escutcheon panel, a black-finished hood with non-reflective paint, polished aluminum wheel well moldings, F70-14 white sidewall wide oval tires, a 55-amp heavy-duty battery, a dual exhaust system and pleated vinyl seat trim.

For 1971, the Model 63H Cobra came only in the SportsRoof format and had a dealer cost of $2,504.84. After mark-up and federal excise tax, the suggested retail price was $3,295. It weighed 3,594 lbs. and only 3,054 were manufactured.

In addition to the standard 351-cid V-8, Cobras could be ordered with two versions of Ford's 429-cid V-8. The 370-hp Cobra Jet version without ram-air induction was a $372 option and, in addition to the big engine, it included a competition suspension, a "sporty" exhaust noise feature, an 80-amp battery, a 55-amp alternator, dual exhausts, an extra-cooling package, bright engine dress-up parts, cast aluminum rocker covers and a non-locking rear axle with a 3.25:1 ratio. The 429-cid 370-hp Cobra Jet Ram-Air V-8 was a $343 extra. It included all the extras that came with the base Cobra Jet V-8 plus a "shaker" hood scoop.

Muscle options available for the Cobra included high-back bucket seats and a console for $150, power front disc brakes for $70, a "shaker" hood scoop (with the 351-cid engine only) for $65, "laser" body side stripes for $39 and Select Shift automatic transmission ($22 with the 351 or $43 with the 429).

The 370-hp version of the Cobra formal hardtop carried about 10.5 lbs per horsepower and could run from 0 to 60 mph in 6 seconds flat. It did the quarter mile in 14.5 seconds.

1978 FORD MUSTANG II "KING COBRA"

The 1978 Mustang II King Cobra won't win many races, but it was fast for its day.

(Jerry Heasley photo)

During the mid- to late-1970s, a number of "visual" muscle cars were offered by domestic automakers. Their mission was to drum up enthusiasm in the youth market and to snare what was left of the old high-performance car buyers. Exemplifying this was the 1978 King Cobra. It dressed the not-universally-loved lines of the Mustang II hatchback in the most garish (or garnished, depending on your point of view) format it had ever come in.

The King Cobra followed the Cobra II option that came out in mid 1977. The Cobra II's huge side stripes, lettering and front and rear spoilers probably did more to anger purists than to attract serious performance fans. It returned for 1978, but at the start of the model year the King Cobra was added. It featured a more complete front air dam, a similar rear spoiler, a wheel flair treatment, the same fake hood scoop and graphics that differed from those of the Cobra II. The subdued lettering on its body sides and rear spoiler were a big contrast with the giant Cobra hood decal that the King carried. Its $1,293 premium on the hatchback's $4,011 base price also bought

color-keyed dual sport mirrors plus blackout-style grille and headlight door trim. Thankfully, it didn't include the window slats the Cobra II often got.

Power front disc brakes, power steering and heavy-duty suspension were part of the package along with a standard four-speed manual gear shift. Its clutch was attached to a 302-cid V-8, also standard. Before visions of Boss 302s and High Output 302s dance through your head, please note that the King Cobra's 302 was the "F" Code version, which breathed through a Motorcraft 2150 two-barrel carb and churned out a lazy 139 hp at 3600 rpm.

While scorned by today's collectors, the King Cobra wasn't all that inferior to the rest of the visual muscle cars of its time. With around 500 made, the King Cobras are getting rare. They also offer somewhat unique styling touches and salvage yards full of replacement parts and bring a 50 percent premium over today's regular Mustang II prices.

1979 FORD MUSTANG INDY PACE CAR

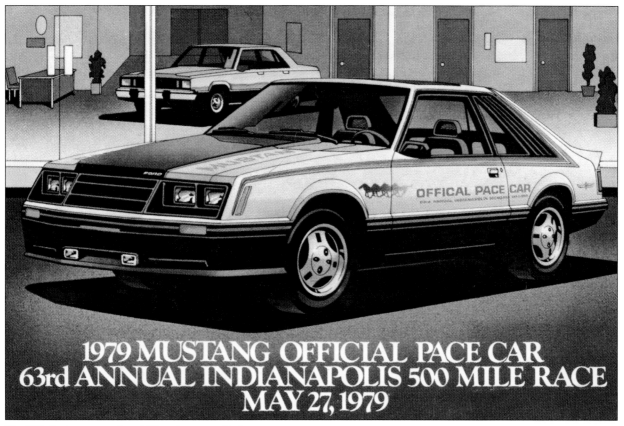

The 1979 Mustang was a sign of things to come at Ford.

In his book *Fast Mustangs*, high-performance Ford enthusiast Alex Gabbard states, "The appearance of the 5-litre Mustang in 1979 caused many enthusiasts to applaud. As usual, the segment of the market that likes the feel of brawn found in the torque of a V-8 was somewhat impressed. As the engine increased in power, impression grew increasingly until the modern version of the HO 5-litre had become a real muscle car by any definition."

A whole new breed of Mustang was presented for 1979. It was derived from the Ford Fairmont platform and featured unit-body construction. With dramatic new sports car styling, it had one of the most efficient, aerodynamic body designs of its era and also had 20 percent more interior space than the previous model.

The Mustang now had a 100.4-inch wheelbase, a 179.1-inch overall length and weighed around 2,600 lbs. Precise handling was delivered by a variety of suspension improvements. The two-door notchback model was priced at $4,858 with V-8 power and the three-door hatchback ran about $5,223 with the big engine.

The 1979 V-8 had a 4.00 x 3.00-inch bore and stroke for a familiar-sounding 302 cubic inches. With a single Motorcraft two-barrel carburetor and an 8.4:1 compression ratio, it was no muscle car compared to those of the '60s or those available today, but it was pretty snappy for 1979. The 5.0-liter V-8 generated 140 hp at 3600 rpm and 250 ft. lbs. of torque at 1800 rpm. While this was obviously not a real drag racer, the Indy Pace Car model had the "look" of a genuine performance car and more or less honored the return of the V-8 which started the ball rolling to a lot better things in the years to come.

The V-8-powered Mustang three-door hatchback that paced the 63rd running of The Indianapolis 500-Mile Race on May 27, 1979, had a T-top and special silver and black finish with red-orange striping and Official Pace Car graphics. It wore stock, forged-metric aluminum wheels. A limited edition of Indy Pace Car replicas was marketed to the public.

1980 FORD SVO-MCLAREN TURBO MUSTANG

The McLaren Mustang was created by Ford Motor Co.'s newly formed Special Vehicle Operations (SVO) group. The "semi-aftermarket" modern muscle car hit the market in late 1980. It represented the ultimate-for-the-era, small-displacement street performance car. Unfortunately, its price tag of $25,000 was anything but small.

Under the car's hood was a high-tech 2.3-liter turbocharged four-cylinder engine. It had a special variable-boost turbocharger that provided from 5 to 11 psi. This provided optimum road and track driving performance.

Compared to the stock Ford turbo four, with its set pressure of

5 psi (and an estimated 131 hp), the McLaren Mustang was a screamer. It was rated for 175 hp at 2500 rpm with the turbocharger boost running 10 psi.

Flared fenders and a functional air dam were among body changes that set the McLaren apart. Designers Todd Gerstenberger and Harry Wykes went after an International Motor Sports Association (IMSA) racing car image. They did a great job of achieving just the look they wanted. The air dam directed cold air to the front disc brakes through the hairy-looking wastegate hood.

Other features of the McLaren Mustang included BBS Euro-

The 1980 Ford SVO-McLaren Mustang Turbo was a much different animal than its muscle car ancestors, but it was fast for its generation and scarce today.

-styled laced wheels shod with Firestone 225/55R-15 HPR tires, Koni shocks, Stewart-Warner gauges and Recaro seats. To complement the McLaren's competition look, there was a competition-type roll bar in the car's interior. A dress-up kit made the mighty little engine shine like a jewel.

Part of the SVO concept was to showcase high-performance components in cars such as the McLaren—which was virtually hand-built—and determine the most popular equipment. The favorites could then be made available through the performance parts aftermarket at a later date.

No one expected to see the production of thousands of McLaren-Mustangs. Instead, the idea was to get lots of enthusiasts interested in bolt-on hardware for thousands of late-model

Mustangs. Consequently, production of the cars was extremely limited. No more than 250 examples—including the prototype—were believed put together. Some experts think that the real number was substantially lower than that.

Loaded with good looks and outstanding performance capabilities, the McLaren exudes collector appeal as well. It has always been a special and rare machine that few people have owned.

Of course, the package isn't really that well known. This might translate into a bargain, should a second or third owner obtain such a car and confuse it with a dressed-up stock Mustang. Therefore, the McLaren is something to keep your eyes open for. Our guess is anything just under the original price would be about right, today, at least for examples in top condition.

1984 FORD MUSTANG SVO

The 1984 Mustang SVO could crack the 130-mph mark with its turbocharged 2.3-liter, four-cylinder engine.

The release of the 5.0-liter V-8 in 1979 Mustangs was the beginning of the marque's high-performance revival, but getting back to a traditional, high-torquing V-8-powered muscle Mustang didn't happen overnight. Ford reverted to a smaller 4.2-liter (255-cid) V-8 in 1980, but gas shortages during the 1970s had put the focus on finding ways to make smaller, more efficient cars go faster. Ford tried four-cylinder turbo power in its Cobra model and the limited edition 1980 McLaren Mustang and the company had no intentions of stopping there.

On April 17, 1984, Ford distributed a letter noting the Mustang's 20th birthday and mentioning two hot cars the company was offering that year. One was a more powerful midyear GT with a 5.0-liter V-8 that wound up being delayed. The other was the Mustang SVO, which was named after the automaker's Special Vehicle Operations team.

Featuring a touch of European-inspired technology, the

$15,596 SVO model (about $6,000 more than a regular Mustang Turbo GT) was promoted as a "machine that speaks for itself." Special features included multi-adjustable articulated bucket seats, a performance suspension with adjustable Koni gas shocks and a 2.3-liter port-fuel-injected turbocharged four-cylinder engine with an air-to-air intercooler. The engine had an 8.0:1 compression ratio and produced 175 hp at 4400 rpm and 210 ft. lbs. of torque at 3000 rpm. A functional hood scoop designed to "ram" cold air into the engine was also part of the package.

The SVO engine was linked to a five-speed manual transmission with overdrive fifth gear and a Hurst shift linkage. It had a Traction-Lok rear axle with a 3.45:1 final drive ratio. Disc brakes were fitted on all four corners, as were Goodyear NCT steel-belted radial tires on 16 x 7-inch cast-aluminum wheels.

Only the three-door Hatchback body was delivered as an SVO.

Identification features included unique single rectangular headlamps, a front air dam with integral spoiler, a functional hood scoop, rear wheel opening "spats," a dual-wing rear spoiler, a full wrap-around body-side protection molding system and dual remote rearview mirrors. The SVO's leather bucket seats were trimmed with unique all-cloth seat material and the steering wheel, emergency brake handle, shift boot and shift knob were leather wrapped. A console with an integral armrest and glove box and a premium AM/FM sound system were other attractions.

According to Ford, the SVO could do 0 to 60 mph in 7.5 seconds and had a top speed of 134 mph. *Motor Trend* called the SVO "the best driving street Mustang the factory has ever offered." *Road & Track* said "the SVO outruns the Datsun 280ZX, outhandles the Ferrari 308 and Porsche 944 and it's affordable."

1985 FORD MUSTANG GT 5.0-LITER HO

(Jerry Heasley photo)

The 1985 Mustang GT 5.0-Liter was rated at 210 hp and brought Ford closer to its muscle car roots.

The 1985 5.0-Liter Mustang GT proved that powerful V-8s had a future under the Mustang's hood, even if Ford Motor Company wanted enthusiasts to think that cars with turbocharged four-cylinder engines were poised to take over in the enthusiasts' market niche. One reason for the popularity of the V-8 was price. You could purchase a Mustang GT three-door hatchback with a 302-cid engine for $9,885 as compared to the Mustang SVO's base window sticker of $14,521.

Ford had upgraded the 5.0-liter V-8 to a Holley four-barrel carburetor in 1984, a year in which the motor cranked out 175 hp at 4000 rpm and 210 ft. lbs. of torque at 3000 rpm. In 1985, the news was a new HO (high-output) version of the 5.0-liter engine with 210 hp at 4400 rpm and 270 ft. lbs. of torque at 3200 rpm. *Motor Trend*

said it had "lovely axle-creaking torque of another time."

In addition to having a Holley four-barrel carburetor like the previous year's model, the 1985 version of the Mustang GT 5.0-liter HO featured a high-performance camshaft, roller tappets and a two-speed accessory drive system. The small-block V-8 was connected to a floor-mounted gear shifter with a tighter shift pattern and new gear ratios. This engine was hot and as the word about it got out, the production of V-8 Mustangs leaped from 36,038 in 1984 to 45,463 for 1985.

All Mustang GTs had the V-8 engine as standard equipment. The three-door hatchback model sold for $9,885 and weighed 2,899 lbs. while the ragtop listed for $13,585 and weighed 3,043 lbs.

1985 FORD MUSTANG SVO

The 1985 Mustang SVO three-door hatchback wasn't a huge hit with buyers, despite its 205 hp and appealing looks.

The Mustang was again available in base LX and GT car lines in 1985. Base models included the two-door sedan and the three-door hatchback. The LX and GT series both also offered convertibles. The SVO specialty hatchback was also back again. It had a few changes, such as a switch to Eagle 50-series tires on 16-inch wheels.

The SVO again featured a 2.3-liter port-fuel-injected turbocharged four-cylinder engine with an air-to-air intercooler. Early in the year the 175-hp 1984 type engine was used. Then, in the middle of the 1985 model year, the SVO got flush-mounted aerodynamic headlamps and turbo improvements that boosted its output to 205 hp.

Racing driver Jackie Stewart, who was working as a consultant to Ford Motor Company, promoted the SVO Mustang in an advertisement headlined: "The New Turbo Math. Ford's turbo gives four cylinders the power of eight." It pointed out that cooling the air that came out of a turbo resulted in a cooler, denser "air charge" and a 30 percent increase in power over an ordinary turbo.

"When the four-cylinder car was thrust upon America by the energy crisis, it looked for awhile as though the American driver was going to have to put up with weak-kneed performance to get gasoline economy," the ad stated. "But technical finesse triumphed. The turbocharger was tamed for the street legal car and the four-cylinder car got the power of an eight."

Stewart also pointed out that the high-tech four-cylinder turbo engine had the advantage of a computer command control system with a "computer capable of taking 250,000 commands a second, so there is absolute split-second monitoring of your exact fuel and spark needs."

Despite the backing of Stewart, sales of the 2,881-lb. SVO Mustang dropped slightly to 1,954 units, even though the price was decreased to $14,521.

1986 FORD MUSTANG GT/SVO

The 1986 Mustang SVO was largely unchanged from the previous years, and was available in a three-door hatchback or convertible.

(Jerry Heasley photo)

There were not many changes made to the 1986 Mustangs. Ford increased its anti-corrosion warranty, added sound-deadening material and adopted a single-key locking system. A revised port-type fuel-injection system and a 200-hp V-8 for GT models were other changes.

Ford continued to offer an 88-hp four-cylinder engine and a 120-hp throttle body-injected V-6 in Mustangs, but the updated 5.0-liter HO V-8 was standard in GTs. It was revised from 1985's four-barrel carburetor induction system to a multi-port fuel injection system and lost 10 hp in the process, although performance was still quite impressive. The 302-cid cast-iron V-8 had a 9.2:1 compression ratio and produced 200 hp at 4000 rpm and 285 ft. lbs. of torque at 3000 rpm.

Other standard equipment on GTs was oriented towards performance car buyers and included a five-speed manual overdrive transmission, Goodyear Eagle VR tires, quick-ratio power steering, a special heavy-duty suspension and articulated front sports seats. An automatic overdrive transmission was optional for $622.

The Mustang GT was available in two models. One was a three-door hatchback with a $10,691 price tag and curb weight of 2,976 lbs. The other was the convertible, which listed for $14,523 and weighed in at 3,103 lbs.

The computer-controlled 2.3-liter turbocharged and intercooled four-cylinder engine with a 205-hp rating was standard in SVOs. The SVO included a five-speed transmission with Hurst shifter with short, quick throws, four-wheel disc brakes and all of the other special goodies that the previous SVO models came with. In 1985, the SVO Mustang carried a higher $15,272 price tag. It sold a slightly higher total of 3,382 units before it was dropped.

1987 FORD MUSTANG GT

An attractive styling revamp made the 1987 Mustang look more changed than it really was. Although it was not an all-new car, a package of new front and rear body fasciae, aero headlamps and a prominent lower feature line with heavy moldings made it seem like a different car. It also sported a redesigned instrument panel, pod-mounted headlamp switches and a center console.

With the SVO model and its sizzling turbocharged four gone, the 5.0-liter HO V-8 took over as the top performance option and the ante was upped with a pair of new cylinder heads that added 25 hp. The engine's compression ratio remained at 9.2:1, but the revised heads and sequential fuel-injection system boosted output to 225 hp

at 4000 rpm and 300 ft. lbs. of torque at 3200 rpm.

The Mustang GT was again offered in two models. One was a three-door hatchback with a $11,835 price tag and curb weight of 3,080 lbs. The other was the convertible, which listed for $15,724 and weighed in at 3,214 lbs. GT models had a lower front air dam with integrated fog lamps and air scoops and "Mustang GT" lettering formed into the flared rocker panel moldings and rear fascia. The GT hatchback also had a large spoiler with a high-mounted stop-light. The wide taillights on the GT models were covered by a lou-ver-like appliqué. Inside was the new "Euro" dash and a two-spoke steering wheel.

1988 FORD MUSTANG GT

After the extensive changes that it underwent in its 1987 makeover, the Mustang was little changed for 1988. The base-level LX models got a battery with more juice and it was about the extent of all revisions. Three basic body styles were offered in LX trim and a pair of Mustang GTS continued to be offered in hatchback and convertible styles. Prices jumped about $700 for the closed cars and $1,100 for ragtops.

The Mustang GT came once again in two body styles. One was a three-door hatchback, now with a $12,745 price tag and curb weight of 3,193 lbs. The other was the convertible, which listed for $16,610 and weighed in at 3,341 lbs. GT models had a lower front air dam with integrated fog lamps and air scoops, "Mustang GT" let-tering formed into the flared rocker panel moldings and rear fascia,

a large rear spoiler with a high-mounted stop light on hatchbacks, wide tail lamps covered by a louver-like appliqué, and P225/60VR16 Goodyear Eagle GT Gatorback tires.

Back again was the 5.0-liter V-8 with its 4.00 x 3.00-inch bore and stroke, five main bearings, hydraulic valve lifters and sequential fuel injection system. Its compression ratio rose to 9.5:1 so that the peak of 225 hp came at a slightly higher 4200 rpm. Advertised torque remained at 300 ft. lbs. at 3200 rpm. In *Motor Trend* maga-zine editor Tony Swan noted, "Ironically, the best all-out performer in the Ford power ladder is another yestertech 5.0-liter pushrod V-8, the one that's almost as venerable as those employed by General Motors."

1989 FORD MUSTANG 5.0-LITER HO

The 1989 Mustang GT 5.0-Liter HO convertible was a hot ride with a price tag of about $17,500.

(Jerry Heasley photo)

For the 25th anniversary of the nameplate in 1989, the 5-liter Mustang was back offering go-fast enthusiasts as much performance at the 5.7-liter Camaro IROC Z with less bulkiness and a lower price tag. The Mustang continued on its trim 100.5-inch wheelbase with an overall length of 179.6 inches. It was 69.1 inches wide and 52.1 inches high. Ford now offered the 302-cid V-8 in a new LX series and well as in the GT line.

All three LX body styles could be ordered with the V-8. The coupe listed for $11,410 and weighed 3,045 lbs., the hatchback list-ed for $12,265 and weighed 3,110 lbs. and the convertible carried a $17,001 price tag and weighed in at 3,257 lbs. The V-8 package for LX models included articulated sport seats, as used in the Mustang GT.

The Mustang GT came once again in two body styles. One was a three-door hatchback, now with a $13,272 price tag and curb

weight of 3,194 lbs. The other was the convertible, which listed for $17,512 and weighed in at 3,333 lbs. GT models continued to fea-ture a lower front air dam with integrated fog lamps and air scoops, "Mustang GT" lettering formed into the flared rocker panel mold-ings and rear fascia, a large rear spoiler with a high-mounted stop light on hatchbacks, wide tail lamps covered by a louver-like appliqué; and P225/60VR16 Goodyear Eagle GT Gatorback tires.

This year's version of the 5.0-liter V-8 had a 9.2:1 compression ratio. It produced 225 hp at 4200 rpm and 300 ft. lbs. of torque at 3200 rpm. Said *Motor Trend's Automotive Yearbook* for 1989, "It's a very hot package with a '60s ring and a torque curve that'll tight-en your skin, all for the price of a Honda Accord. Ford has vowed to keep the V-8 Mustang as you see it here through the early '90s. And you thought Santa had forgotten."

1990 FORD MUSTANG 5.0-LITER HO

(Jerry Heasley photo)

The 1990 Mustang GT 5.0-Liter HO had a small-block V-8 that produced 225 hp.

For 1990, Ford Motor Company gave the Mustang a driver's side air bag and standard rear shoulder belts. Map pockets were added to the door panels, while tilt steering and an armrest on the console disappeared. Since there had been no anniversary model in 1989, the nameplate's quarter century of tradition was recognized in sales literature that emphasized that the first Mustang, although released in April 1964, was technically a 1965 model. (So why did Ford make anniversary editions in 1984 and 1994?)

Sedans, hatchbacks and ragtops again came in the LX 5.0-Liter series and these actually had the beefiest suspension. The hatchback and convertible came in GT trim, which primarily added spoilers and air dams. The small-block V-8 had a 9.0:1 compression ratio and again made 225 hp at 4200 rpm and 300 ft. lbs. of torque at 3000 rpm. "225 horses are bound to kick something" said an advertisement for the Mustang GT. Once again, the Borg-Warner five-speed

manual gearbox was linked to it as standard equipment.

Cars with the 5.0-liter EFI HO V-8 and the five-speed manual gearbox came standard with a 2.73:1 axle and a 3.08:1 Traction-Lok rear end was optional. With automatic overdrive transmission, the 2.73:1 axle was standard and a 3.27:1 Traction-Lok unit was optional. The wheels used on the Mustang GT and 5.0-Liter LX models were 15 x 7.0-inch aluminum rims compared to 14 x 5.0-inch standard steel wheels on the Mustang LX. They carried P225/60VR15 Goodyear unidirectional "gatorback" tires.

A limited-edition metallic emerald green convertible with a white interior was announced, in the spring of 1990, as a "25th anniversary" model. There were rumors of a Mustang "street racer" with a 351-cid V-8 being built, but Ford eventually dropped this idea because such a model would have been too costly to produce.

1993 FORD MUSTANG COBRA

Model year 1993 could easily have been one in the "live bait" category for the Ford Mustang. It was in the last year of a long run (since 1979) before the all-new 1994 models bowed. Chevrolet's Camaro and Pontiac's Firebird were also redesigned and available in performance trim. Both shared a 350-cid 275-hp V-8 that could beat

the Mustang's 302-cid 205-hp H.O. V-8.

Ford was well aware of Steve Saleen's hot Mustangs and other "tuner" versions of the Mustang that were much more powerful than production cars. However, the need to meet CAFE standards and warranty claims precluded production-line attempts to match such

The 1993 Mustang Cobra was the first offering from Ford's SVT team.

aftermarket creations. Still, the Cobra and Cobra R—introduced in mid-1993—turned out to be a great warm-up act for future performance Mustangs from Ford. In the end, the Camaro Z/28, Firebird Formula and Firebird Trans Am wound up leading the pony car class in ultimate performance numbers, but not by very much.

Ford had called on its legendary snake nameplate in the past when it needed image to spice up its vehicles, but some summons were more for show than go, such as the Mustang II derivatives called the Cobra II and the King Cobra. This time it was a different story, as the show items were few and the go items were abundant, thanks to the effort of the new Special Vehicle Team. The "SVT" group was a sort of "skunkworks" that fit in somewhere between racing and production cars—and even trucks, a few years later on. The SVT method was to take a production car, go over it top to bottom and make it a better performing and handling vehicle, *then* add a few dress-up items to set it apart from the common models.

For the 1993 Cobra, they took the 302-cid V-8 and added GT-40 cast-iron cylinder heads with larger valves, stronger valve springs, a two-piece intake plenum and manifold, a hotter cam, higher-ratio rocker arms, higher-flow fuel injectors and air management and a less-restrictive exhaust system. The result was a conservative 235 hp at 5000 rpm.

Other mechanical improvements included stronger insides for the Borg-Warner T-50D transmission, much-needed four-wheel disc brakes, cast-aluminum 17 x 7.5-inch wheels (wrapped in 245/45ZR-17 Goodyear tires) and suspensions softened up a bit for more travel and better road contact.

Changes made to the inside of the Cobra were more minimal, with a Mustang horse badge on the dash and Cobra floor mats. The badge was also in the reworked front grille and air dam, which included fog lights. Cobra badges were affixed to the front fenders and deck lid. "It is the hardest accelerating, quickest stopping, best handling pony car from Ford yet," said *Road and Track* of the Cobra.

Naturally, the Cobra had to go door to door with its GM counterparts. *Motor Trend* put one up against a six-speed Camaro Z/28 and wound up with a 0-to-60 time of 6.2 seconds for the Ford versus 5.6 seconds for the Chevrolet. The Camaro covered the quarter mile in 14.0 seconds and 98.8 mph compared to 14.4 seconds and 97.4 mph for the Cobra. Considering Chevy's cubic inch and horsepower advantages, it was really a very close contest. As a comparison, *Motor Trend* tested a 1993 Mustang GT convertible that did 0 to 60 in 8 seconds flat and the quarter in 16.1 seconds at 85 mph.

Stretching things a bit, *Car Craft* took a heavily modified Mustang Cobra and ran it at over 200 mph at an 7.5-mile test track in Ohio. Its engine was said to produce 750 hp.

The Cobra was not the final performance chapter in the 1993 Mustang story. Under the guidance of SVT—with help from road racer Paul Rossi—about 100 Cobra R versions were made for racing-only purposes, even though they met showroom emission and safety requirements. While the driveline retained its stock Cobra goodies, changes included bigger brakes, five-lug hubs, 17 x 8-inch alloy wheels, Koni double-adjustable shocks, a bigger aluminum radiator, oil coolers and even power steering coolers.

Body modifications included a stiffer convertible floor pan, reinforced front strut towers, basic bucket seats up front and no further seating behind them. There were wind-up windows, no radio and no option for air or other power goodies, just like the lightweight drag cars of the 1960s. The price for the Cobra R was $25,692 compared to the base Cobra's sticker price of $18,555 plus $475 shipping.

1994 FORD MUSTANG COBRA

Ford bragged that 85 percent of the 1994 Mustang body and chassis was all-new or modified over the 1993 model. The bodies were completely redone and the Fox-4 chassis was beefed up considerably over the earlier design, which traced its roots directly to the non-performance Fairmont of 1978.

Unfortunately for the Ford-eats-Chevy gang, under the hood it was pretty much the same story as 1993 and years before with the 302-cid V-8 motivating the GT and midyear Cobra models.

Simplification hit the model lineup with only a fastback-like coupe and a convertible being offered in the base and GT series. The former got new 3.8-liter V-6 power and the latter had a 215-hp rendition of the 302. The 215 was 10 horses to the plus side of 1993, thanks to revised intake plumbing from the Thunderbird. All models also got four-wheel disc brakes.

While the Mustang GT was quite a performance ticket in the 1980s, competition from Chevrolet's Camaro Z/28 and Pontiac's Firebird Formula and Trans Am raised the bar. A superior defense of Ford's honor was offered, for the second straight year, by the Cobra. This model was again released as a midyear offering through Ford's Special Vehicles Team (SVT).

Following the 1993 game plan, the Cobra's use of cast iron GT-40 heads, a revised intake setup, a special camshaft and rockers, fuel injection, valves and low-restriction exhausts resulted in a gain of 25 hp to 240. Underneath there were now 13-inch Kelsey-Hayes discs up front and 11.65-inch discs in the rear, with Bosch anti-lock hardware worked in. Polished 17 x 8-inch five-spoke alloy wheels sported 255/45ZRx17 Goodyear GS-C tires. The suspension was revised from the GT with a bit softer springs for more suspension travel and improved road holding.

A new front treatment with crystal headlight lenses, a different grille and fog lamps was balanced by a new curved rear soiler. Badging was conservative with snakes on the fenders and a Cobra plate on the deck lid. A peak inside revealed white-faced instruments and a 160-mph speedometer. Cobra floor mats and an airbag cover were subtle touches.

Coming only in Rio red was a Cobra convertible, intended to commemorate Mustang pacing the Indianapolis 500 for the third time (1964 and 1979 came first). Plans called for making just 1,000 of them, compared to 5,000 coupes. Small badges were the main difference. A set of pace car decals came with each car, packaged in the trunk. The price was $23,535 compared to the coupe's $20,765.

Testers found the new Cobra was a fine performer for a Mustang, but also discovered that the GM bullies still ruled the pony car farm. They also noted the Cobra's "power band" falling off at 5500 rpm compared to the 1993's pulling strong in the upper 5000s range. In a Cobra vs. Firebird Formula convertible showdown, *Road and Track* gave the Firebird (6.7 seconds) the edge in the 0 to 60-mph category against the Cobra, which took 6.9 seconds. The quarter mile didn't change things with the GM pony's 15.1 seconds and 95 mph shutting down the Ford snake's 15.3 seconds and 93 mph performance.

1995 FORD MUSTANG COBRA/COBRA R

The 1995 SVT Ford Mustang Cobra had a base 302 V-8, but the R version's 351 could bring the horsepower output up to 300.

(Jerry Heasley photo)

The Mustang Cobra returned for 1995, again in two forms. As in 1994, it relied on the 302-cid V-8 for power. By then, a base coupe listed for $21,300 to $18,105 for a GT. For the ragtops the margin was $25,605 to $22,795. Destination charges for all ran $500.

No longer relying on 302 power was the racing version of the Cobra, the Cobra R, which returned after having a limited run in 1993. After that, SVT rationed about 250 additional cars to licensed racers. This car used Ford's 351 "Windsor" V-8, which was rated for 300 hp. The Cobra R came finished only in white. It featured all legal emissions and safety equipment, minimal bucket seats, a shelf in place of the back seats, no power accessories, no air conditioning, no radio and a raised fiberglass hood with appropriate bracing.

A Tremec 3550 five-speed transmission sent the horsepower to Traction-Loc 3.27:1 gears and out to 17 x 9-inch alloy wheels with Comp T/A P255/45ZR17 tires. Koni adjustable shocks, revised springs and anti-roll bars and standard Cobra discs all contributed to its race-car-like handling. A 20-gallon fuel cell, a larger radiator and assorted auxiliary coolers were among the few items that didn't come from the assembly line.

Just about every Cobra R was quickly grabbed by serious racers, but *Motor Trend* got its hands on a 1995 Cobra R to test. The magazine reported that it was good for 151 mph, 0 to 60 mph in 5.4 seconds and a 14.0-second quarter mile at 99 mph.

1999 FORD SVT MUSTANG COBRA

The new-for-1999 SVT Cobra Mustang was a modern pony-car class muscle car. Taken in that context, it has direct links to the hot Mustangs of the '60s.

The SVT Cobra sits on a 101.3-inch wheelbase and stretches 183.5 inches bumper to bumper. It stands 53.5 inches high and weighs in at 3,588 lbs. While the regular version of the ragtop priced out at $31,995 in 1999, the SVT Cobra Mustang convertible went for $32,190.

Basic features of the car included an independent-struts type front suspension with coil springs and an anti-roll bar. The rear independent suspension used unequal-length control arms with a toe control link, coil springs and an anti-roll bar. The ABS brakes used vented discs at all four corners. Attaching the car to the ground were 245/45ZR-17 B.F. Goodrich Comp T/A tires.

Below the hood was where the Ford SVT (Special Vehicles Team) group really worked some muscle magic. Tucked there was a 281-cid 32-valve V-8 with an aluminum engine block, aluminum cylinder heads and port fuel injection. It served up 320 hp at 6000 rpm and 317 ft. lbs. of torque at 4750 rpm. An SVT Cobra Mustang with five-speed manual gearbox and 3.27:1 rear axle ran from 0 to 60 mph in 6 seconds flat, from 0 to 100 mph in 15.3 seconds and from 0 to 130 mph in 31.8 seconds. The same car covered the quarter mile in 14.6 seconds at 98 mph and had a top speed of 149 mph.

Car and Driver magazine (August 1999) reported that the SVT Mustang Cobra had fresh-looking styling, a high-tech power plant, a top-notch independent rear suspension and outstanding brakes, as well as a very affordable price for this type of car. It rated the SVT "competent, quick and exclusive," but said the transmission could use an additional gear to win more races in the "Stoplight Grand Prix."

2000 FORD SVT MUSTANG COBRA R

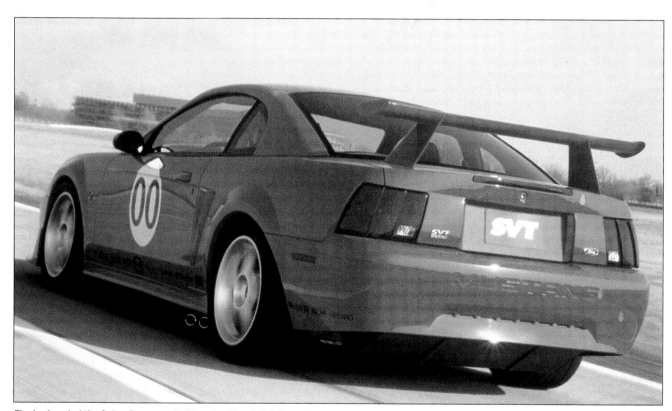

The back end of the Cobra R was marked by a functional airfoil—a nice feature on a car with 385 hp.

Ford's Special Vehicles Team built the 2000 Mustang Cobra R to go, turn and stop very quickly. With performance figures that showed the car could do 0 to 60 mph in 4.7 seconds and cover the quarter mile in 13.2 seconds at 110 mph, *Car and Driver* (April 2000) described it as "The fastest Mustang ever."

With a $55,845 price tag, the Cobra R drew a limited amount of buyer interest and that was also partly due to production limitations. Only 300 of the cars were scheduled to be built in the model year. However, that was considered a lot, since the 1993 Cobra R had a 109-unit production run and the 1995 model climbed to a total of 250 copies.

Like any real muscle car, the 2000 Cobra R had a lot of goodies to make it look fast and handle well. The list included a massive spoiler on the front end and a functional stationary rear airfoil. Each car came from SVT with a front air splitter that could be attached to the nose. Buyers were warned to use it only for show or racing purposes as street use might damage it. The R continued a tradition of some top muscle cars by being offered only in a single color called "performance red." The interior was dark charcoal.

Under the Cobra R's louvered hood scoop sat a 5.4-liter V-8 with a 9.6:1 compression ratio and port-fuel injection system. The engine was fitted with a number of hardware items from the Ford

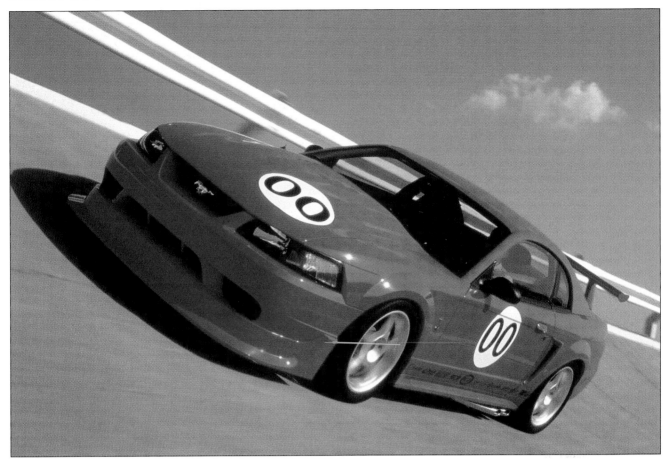

The 1995 SVT Ford Mustang Cobra R was pricey at almost $56,000, but it was attractive and had a top speed of about 175 mph.

parts bin, such as a special cylindrical K & N air filter, a larger single-bore throttle body, high-performance heads from Ford's off-road truck racing program, higher-lift camshafts, flat-top aluminum pistons, Carrillo billet steel connecting rods and tubular steel exhaust manifolds connected to Borla mufflers with a beautiful rumble. It generated 385 hp at 5700 rpm and 385 ft. lbs. of torque at 4500 rpm. The redline was 6,500 rpm and the top speed was 175 mph.

The Cobra R's suspension was suitably beefed up front and rear with Bilstein gas shocks up front, twin-tube gas shocks in the rear, heavy-duty Eibach springs and fat anti-roll bars at each end. The 9.5-18 five-spoke aluminum alloy rims were mounted with 265/40ZR-18 B.F. Goodrich G-force KD radial tires.

Best of all, you no longer had to have SCCA or NHRA credentials or some other type of competition license to buy a Cobra R, as had been the case in the past.

2001 FORD BULLITT MUSTANG

Ford's youthful styling chief J Mays, who created the retro two-seat Thunderbird, was also responsible for the "Bullitt" concept car. Named for the 1968 Mustang GT that actor Steve McQueen drove when he played detective Frank Bullitt in the cult-classic motion picture of the same name, this hot 2001 model is based on a Mustang GT with $3,695 worth of upgrades.

The car's body is modified to reduce the size of the rear quarter windows and lowered 3/4 inch all around. The traditional Mustang side scoops are covered, a crushed-aluminum flip-up gas filler added and the Bullitt Mustang rides on Torq Thrust D-style wheels sourced from American Racing Wheels.

Under the hood, the 4.6-liter (281-cid) single overhead cam V-8 features the SVT Cobra model's cast-aluminum intake manifold, a twin-bore 57-mm throttle body, cylinder heads and a high-

flow exhaust system. The changes produce 265 hp at 5000 rpm and 305 ft. lbs. of torque at 4000 rpm, which can move the car from 0 to 60 mph in 5.7 seconds. The quarter mile takes 14.1 seconds at 98 mph.

The engine is attached to a five-speed manual gearbox. It has heavy-duty shocks, special anti-roll bars and 17-inch diameter Goodyear Eagle tires. Its curb weight is 3,273 lbs.

The $27,000 Bullitt Mustang had perforated black leather upholstery and interior trim, a black leather steering wheel, white-faced gauges and an aluminum gearshift knob. The car came in dark highland green—just like the famous movie car—as well as optional true blue or black. Ford projected that it would build 6,500 of them in 2001.

MERCURY

1964 MERCURY COMET CYCLONE

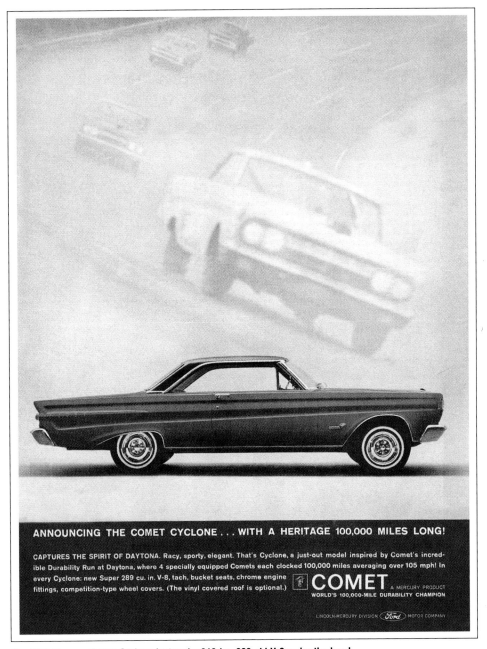

The 1964 Mercury Comet Cyclone featured a 210-hp, 289-cid V-8 under the hood.

In the middle of model-year 1964, Lincoln Mercury Division's new Comet Cyclone high-performance model arrived in showrooms. It featured less chrome than other Comets. There were thin moldings over the wheel wells and under the doors and "C-O-M-E-T" lettering only on the rear fins. Marauder-like "Cyclone" front fender badges sat low on the fenders.

The standard engine provided in the Cyclone was the four-barrel, 210-hp version of the "289" with 9.0:1 compression. It also featured 14-inch chrome wheels. Camera-case-grained black vinyl replaced wood trim on the instrument panel. It came with new, pleated black bucket seats and a console with color-keyed vinyl in special colors. A special option was a "convertible" style vinyl roof. Cyclones offered a three- or four-speed manual transmission, plus Merc-O-Matic. Promotions for the car were tied into the 100,000-mile endurance run at Daytona.

As tested in *Car Life* (April 1964), the Cyclone priced-out at $3,027 with options. The magazine listed 0 to 60-mph times of 11.8 seconds with automatic transmission and 10.2 seconds with a four-speed. The quarter mile was covered in 16.5 seconds at 73.8 mph by the Merc-O-Matic-equipped Cyclone and 16.4 seconds at 77 mph by the four-speed Cyclone. The car with automatic averaged 12 to 15 mpg in normal driving, while the stick-shift car did a bit better at 13 to 16 mpg. Top speed was listed as 109 mph.

There was also a fastback Comet "Super Cyclone" concept car that debuted at the New York Automobile Show. It had a special body with a Plymouth Barracuda-like glass back window. Also featured were chrome racing wheels, Cibie rectangular headlamps, through-the-rear-fender exhausts; "Rally-Pak" instrumentation with a vacuum gauge, a tachometer and an elapsed time clock, a walnut steering wheel with flat aluminum spokes, a "radar" warning device (for driving in fog) and a vertical bar grille with a horizontal center molding.

1965 MERCURY COMET CYCLONE

The 1965 Mercury Comet Cyclone came only as a two-door hardtop.

Mercury's 1965 Comet Cyclone series consisted of a single two-door hardtop priced at $2,683. That made it the second-most expensive Comet (the Villager station wagon was the priciest model).

The 1965 Cyclone had a special grille with only two groups of horizontal blades and blacked-out finish around its perimeter. Cyclones had all the equipment that came on Calientes, plus bucket seats in front, a center console, a tachometer, unique deluxe wheel covers, curb moldings and a 289-cid "Cyclone" V-8 engine with a two-barrel carburetor. A distinctive twin-air-scoop fiberglass hood was optional.

In May 1965, *Motor Trend* printed a road test titled "2 Comets: Hot & Cool" that compared the Caliente and Cyclone two-door hardtops. The Caliente had the 289-cid, 200-hp engine and Merc-O-Matic transmission. It did 0 to 60 mph in 11 seconds and ran down the drag strip in 18.1 seconds with a 76-mph terminal speed. Its top speed was 96 mph. The Cyclone had the 225-hp version of the "289" and a four-speed gearbox. It trimmed 2.2 seconds off the other car's 0 to 60-mph time and the quarter-mile took 17.1 seconds at 82 mph.

Its top speed was 108 mph.

The magazine liked the restyled Comet front end, the higher horsepower, its handling and its large trunk. The brakes (the Caliente's brakes had power assist and the Cyclone's did not) were both good. Stopping distance from 60 mph was 158 feet with assist and 161 feet without assist. Technical editor John Ethridge's major criticisms concerned the Cyclone's wheel-spinning ability and its rear axle hop (which hurt acceleration times). He also said that the Caliente's "hang-under-dash" air conditioner interfered with the driver's right leg.

The 195-hp "Cyclone V-8" engine was a $108 option for non-Cyclone models. It had a 9.3:1 compression ratio. In addition, there was a 220-hp "Super Cyclone 289" with a 10.0:1 compression ratio and a four-barrel carburetor. This engine cost $45.20 extra in Cyclones and $153.20 additional in other models.

A three-speed manual gearbox was standard with all engines. A four-speed manual transmission was $188 extra, and Multi-Drive Merc-O-Matic ran $189.60 additional. This was, again, a three-speed automatic, comparable to the Ford Cruise-O-Matic.

1966 MERCURY COMET CYCLONE GT

It was a mod world in 1966. Women's skirts were shorter. Men wore their hair long. Notre Dame went for a tie instead of a win in its dream football game against Michigan State. It appeared America was doing the same in Vietnam.

In Detroit, the muscle-car craze that had been triggered by Pontiac's GTO was in high gear. Mercury stole some of the thunder with its own Cyclone GT in 1966. To remind us of Mercury's serious performance intentions, the Cyclone GT was selected to be the Indianapolis 500 pace car.

After bidding itself into providing the mandatory matched set of Cyclone GT convertibles for the revered Memorial Day race, Mercury built some 100 pace car replicas that found their way to Indiana. There they were used to transport parade queens and

celebrities in conjunction with the pre-race festivities. Unlike other automakers, Mercury made no attempt to market the replica pace cars through its dealers.

The base Cyclone version of the mid-sized Comet had premiered in midyear 1965. The high-performance 1966 Cyclone GT came out in the fall of 1965, along with the rest of the new Comet line.

From its inception, the Comet and Cyclone body had grown almost every year. The 1966 version was based on Ford's Fairlane body shell. It rode on a 116-inch wheelbase. This moved it out of the *compact* category and into the *intermediate* size class. For performance buffs, this change made the Cyclone a viable contender against the small-bodied, big-engined muscle cars of the period.

For 1966, Mercury went full blast and brought out the Cyclone GT. Powered by Ford's popular 390-cid 335-hp V-8, the Cyclone GT had an optional handling package, front disc brakes and optional four-speed manual or automatic transmission. (A three-speed manual was standard.) Also standard were dual exhausts, a fiberglass hood with twin non-functional scoops and GT identification and stripes.

The 390-cid V-8 used a four-barrel carburetor and had a 10.5:1 compression ratio. The optional Merc-O-Matic transmission only came with a GT Sport Shift enabling manual inter-range control via a floor-mounted lever. When so equipped, the Cyclone GT was capable of 0 to 60 mph in 7 seconds and quarter-mile runs in the high 14s. And this was in spite of the fact that the 390-cid engine added some 430 lbs. to the standard six-cylinder Comet.

Mercury's director of high-performance projects, Fran Hernandez, and his assistant, Paul Preuss, oversaw the 1966 pace car effort. The two actual pace cars that emerged were candy apple red Cyclone GT convertibles capable of 115-mph cruising speeds. Modifications and engine blueprinting were done at Bud Moore Engineering in Spartanburg, South Carolina. The pace car rode on 7.75 x 14 Firestone wide oval Super Sport tires mounted on optional styled steel wheels. Benson Ford was behind the wheel for the Cyclone GT's parade lap.

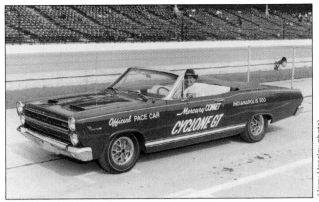

(Jerry Heasley photo)

The 1966 Mercury Comet Cyclone GT convertible was chosen to pace the Indianapolis 500.

Graham Hill won the 500-miler that day, but the Cyclone GT subsequently proved to be a loser in Lincoln-Mercury showrooms. Only 13,812 hardtops and 2,158 convertibles were built.

1967 MERCURY COMET CYCLONE GT

(David Hooten photo)

The 1967 Mercury Comet Cyclone GT hardtop got plenty of muscle from its optional 390-cid big-block V-8.

Mercury had a hard time attaining a presence in the booming intermediate market in the 1960s. Its cars were always in the shadows of other Ford products. The Mercury Meteor and the Ford Fairlane were both introduced as intermediates for 1962. The Meteor died of lack of interest after the 1963 models were done, but the Fairlane continued on.

For 1966, the formerly compact Comet was upgraded to the same 116-inch wheelbase the midsized Fairlane. Just when people were starting to get used to that, the mildly face-lifted 1967 models came along and the Comet name was only applied to the lowest-priced series, leaving Mercury awkwardly calling its offerings the Mercury intermediates. This changed for the better in 1968, when the Montego name was introduced. However, for 1967, not only were the intermediates lacking a name, but promotional backing as well, since the new Cougar—a luxury sports compact—was getting all the hype.

For the performance buyer, Mercury continued its Cyclone series. It again offered two-door hardtop and convertible models. While a rather meek 200-hp version of the 289-cid V-8 was standard, knowledgeable buyers selected the GT Performance Group from the Cyclone options list. Doing so substituted the 390-cid "FE" big-block V-8 with a rating of 320 hp. That was down 15 hp from the 1966 version, but still fairly hot.

The Cyclone with the GT Performance Group also included a four-barrel carburetor, a dual exhaust system, an engine dress-up kit, a hood with two non-functional air scoops, 5 1/2 x 14-inch wheels, wide oval tires, heavy-duty shocks and springs, a thicker front sway bar, 3.25:1 gearing, body side stripes with GT badges and interior GT badging. Cyclones also came standard with front bucket seats. Options included a four-speed manual gearbox.

The recession of 1967 was not kind to car sales and the Mercury intermediates took a beating. A total of 6,910 were made compared to 24,164 for 1966. The 1967 models with the GT option included 3,419 hardtops and 378 convertibles, meaning the GT-embellished cars outnumbered the regular Cyclones. The 1967 Cyclone GTs, and all Cyclones for that matter, are rather rare today.

Racing promotion for the 1967 Cyclone was limited to its body lines being used atop funny cars for drag racing, but better things were ahead for Cyclones. They would become the NASCAR superspeedway stars of 1968 and beyond, finally helping Mercury's intermediate-sized models to establish a name for themselves.

1967 MERCURY COUGAR GT 390

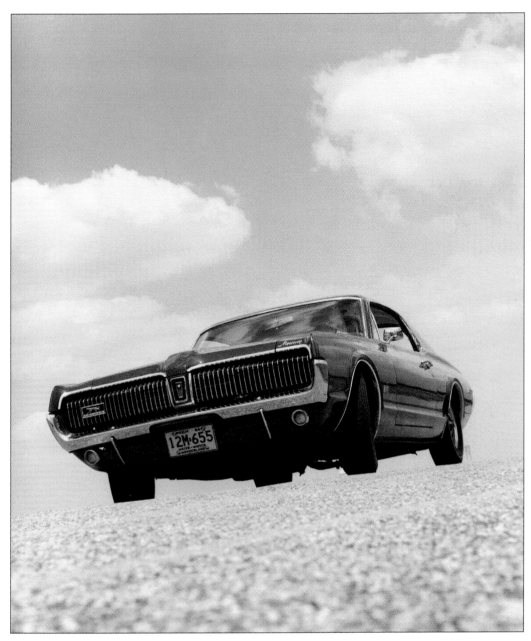

The 1967 Mercury Cougar hardtop was designed to be a more refined, shapely muscle car.

The 1967 Mercury Cougar GT with the optional 390-cid 335-hp engine was a muscle car for the man on his way to a Thunderbird. Although this power plant was equipped with hydraulic lifters, a fairly mild cam and street-type valve timing, it produced a 1:10 power-to-weight ratio that was good for some driving excitement.

The Cougar, said *Car Life,* was best described as a "Mustang with class." It had a shapely, graceful appearance and jewel-like trimmings. Only the two-door hardtop was available at first. A convertible would come along later.

While based on the Mustang platform, the Cougar received some upgrades to its suspension componentry. They included a hook-and-eye joint in the lower front A-frames to dampen ride harshness, 6-inch-longer rear leaf springs and better-rated rear spring and axle attachments.

The GT, however, came more firmly sprung with solid rear bushings, stiffer springs all around, bigger 1.1875-inch shocks and a fatter .84-inch anti-roll bar. Power front disc brakes, 8.95 x 14 wide oval tires and a 390-cid 335-hp V-8 were included, as well as a low-restriction exhaust system and special identification features.

A Holley C70F carburetor with four 1.562-inch venturis and vacuum-operated secondaries sat on the 390-cid engine. With a 10.5:1 compression ratio, it required premium fuel. The horsepower peak came at just 4800 rpm. A husky 427 ft. lbs. of torque was produced at 3200 rpm. Transmission choices included three- or four-speed synchromesh gearboxes or a three-speed Merc-O-Matic with manual shift capabilities for downshifting to second below 71 mph or to first below 20 mph.

The manual gearboxes used with the 390 were different from those used with the 289. The three-speed with the big-block had ratios of 2.42:1 and 1.61:1. For the four-speed attachment, 2.32:1, 1.69:1 and 1.29:1 ratios were provided. Smaller-engined "stick" cars used numerically higher gear ratios. In the rear axle department, the 390 came standard with a 3.00 axle. A 3.25 unit was optional. They called this the "power transfer" axle.

The Cougar GT 390 was good for 0 to 60 mph in 8.1 seconds and 16 second quarter miles. Only 53 percent of all Cougars had four-speed manual gearboxes in 1967.

1968 MERCURY COUGAR GT-E

The Mercury Cougar followed the pioneering Ford Mustang into the "pony car" marketplace. It came along three-and-one-half model years later than the Mustang and had a fancier image. When it bowed in model-year 1967, the Cougar (as well as its restyled Mustang cousin) could accept Ford big-block V-8s between its front wheels, which is something the 1964 1/2 to 1966 Mustangs could not do.

The hottest engine showing up on the 1967 Cougar options list was the 390-cid 320-hp fat block. Then, as model year 1968 bowed, the Cougar got its first real high-performance package with the 7.0-liter GT-E, which was an option for both the base Cougar and the even fancier XR-7. The option included the mild 390-hp "E" version of Ford's 427-cid engine, plus a SelectShift Merc-O-Matic transmission, a performance handling package, styled steel wheels, power disc brakes and a non-functional "power dome" hood air scoop.

When the nose-heavy 427-cid V-8 was installed in the Cougar, which had a 111-inch wheelbase (3 inches longer than the Mustang), it produced average performance for the muscle cars of that era. A 7.1 second 0-to-60 time was published in the enthusiast magazines.

The mating of the 427 to the Cougar was a short-term offering because the 427-cid option was discontinued late in 1967. Later in the model year the Cougar—like Ford's other sporty and mid-sized cars—received an injection of Cobra Jet 428 power. To keep insurance agents and bean counters happy, the 428-cid big block carried a rating of 335 advertised hp. Because it had a longer stroke, the 428-cid engine had an easier time with emission requirements. However, its actual power output was estimated to be closer to the choked-down 427E it replaced.

Although the Cougar concept was aimed at sporty luxury instead of high performance, the 1968 GT-E was the nameplate's first step into the muscle-car sweepstakes and would not be its last.

1968 MERCURY COUGAR XR-7G "DAN GURNEY"

The flashy 1968 Mercury Cougar XR-7G hardtop is a collector gem today.

Signature models of high-performance cars were "in" during the late 1960s and early 1970s. AMC had its "Mark Donohue" editions and Mercury offered a limited-edition Cougar now called the "Dan Gurney" edition. Today, models like these are usually popular with car collectors even though they were not all that popular with the buying public when they were originally introduced years ago.

Such is the case with the 1968 1/2 Mercury Cougar XR-7G. This was actually an upscale Cougar XR-7 with a personalized option. The "G" stood for "Gurney," an American racing hero of the day who was under contract to Lincoln-Mercury Division. Gurney was a member of the driving team that piloted the Bill Stroppe-prepared 1967 Cougars that raced in the Sports Car Club of America (SCCA) Trans-American sedan series competition.

The Cougar would be the first of two Mercury specials named for Gurney. The second was a version of the 1969 1/2 Cyclone

Spoiler. After 1969, Gurney's racing and car-building services were contracted by Plymouth and the string of Gurney editions ended.

The Cougar's rather rare XR-7G option package was mainly an assortment of "gingerbread" and any available power plant from the base 302-cid V-8 on up could be used to power cars with the package. The features of the G option included a fiberglass hood scoop, road lamps, a racing mirror, hood pins and a new power sunroof (which could also be ordered for other 1968 Cougars).

At the rear of the car, four exhaust tips exited through the valance panel. New styled wheels held radial FR70-14 tires. Badges showing a special emblem decorated the instrument panel, roof pillar, deck lid and grille. The XR-7G Cougars were not widely promoted back in 1968 and very few were made, making the survivors highly prized by collectors today.

1968 MERCURY CYCLONE GT

The Comet was restyled for 1968 and looked like a full-size Mercury that went on a diet. There was a new horizontal grille, bright rocker-panel moldings, side marker lights and chrome-encased, vertical taillights. Among the standard features were an energy-absorbing steering column and steering wheel, front and rear seatbelts, shoulderbelts, padded dash, padded sun visors, dual brakes with warning light and two-speed windshield wipers and washers.

Only one model was left in the base series. It was the two-door hardtop with a base price of $2,477. The new Mercury Montego looked about the same as the Comet. It had all the same standard features, plus curb moldings, a cigar lighter and a glove box lock. There were two variations: The four-door sedan prices started at $2,504 and the two-door hardtop sold for $2,552.

The Montego MX had full-length upper and lower body trim, chrome wheel well trim, and a vinyl. It also had bright metal upper door frames, simulated wood-grain inserts in the lower body molding, wood-grain door trim panels inserts and carpeting. The Montego MX line offered a four-door sedan, two-door hardtop, convertible and station wagon from $2,657 to $2,935.

Cyclones had a mid-tire level tape stripe. The GT option was still around and added only $168 to the $2,768 base price, but no longer included the 390 four-barrel engine. A two-barrel 302 cid V-8 rated at 210 horses was standard for all Cyclones. The GT option now brought you bucket seats and trim changes.

Residing on the option list was a four-barrel, 230-hp 302-cid engine, a mild 265-hp version of the 390-cid V-8 and a stronger 325-hp version, plus the 390-hp edition of the 427-cid V-8. It would be the only official time that the 427 was offered and it was a short one. This engine was axed a couple of months into production and replaced in sparse numbers by the 428 Cobra Jet V-8, rated at 335 insurance-pleasing horses. The real power was indicated by a 0-to-60 magazine road-test time of 6.2 seconds.

Cars with the GT option had an upper-body racing stripe, bucket seats, wide tread whitewalls, special wheel covers, an all-vinyl interior and a special handling package. Cyclones were offered in two-door hardtop and two-door fastback models and both had a base price of $2,768. The public voted overwhelmingly for the fastback, of which 6,105 GT-optioned Cyclones were made compared to 334 for the notchback.

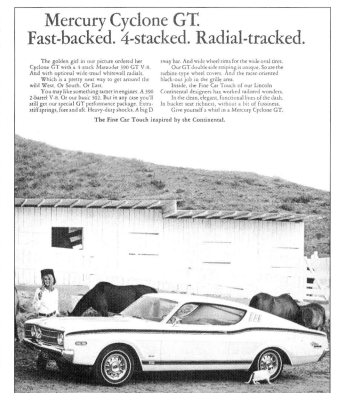

1968 Mercury Comet Cyclone GT came out with an optional 390-hp 427-cid engine, but that was soon replaced by a 428 Cobra Jet.

1969 MERCURY COUGAR ELIMINATOR

(Jerry Heasley photo)

The Eliminator could be had with several different engines, including a CJ 428.

The 1969 Mercury Cougar was wider, longer and heavier. Attractions for model year included the nameplate's first convertible. A midyear muscle car offering—the Eliminator—came only in two-door hardtop form.

The 1969 Cougar's grille had horizontal pieces that protruded slightly at the center. Bucket seats and retractable headlights were standard. Rocker panel strips, wheel opening moldings and two parallel full-length, upper-level pinstripes decorated the body sides. The back-up lights wrapped around the rear fenders and the taillights were trimmed with concave vertical chrome pieces. A vinyl interior with foam-padded bucket seats and carpeting was standard.

The Cougar two-door hardtop ($2,999) and convertible ($3,365) were the base models. A GT appearance group option included: Comfortweave vinyl bucket seats, a rim-blow steering wheel, a remote-control left-hand racing mirror, turbine wheel covers, GT decals, a GT dash nameplate and F70 x 14 fiberglass belted tires for $168.40. The XR-7 looked like the basic Cougar outside. Its extras included a rim-blow steering wheel, a courtesy light group, a visual check panel, a left-hand remote-control racing mirror, an electric clock, deluxe armrests, a walnut-toned instrument panel with tachometer and trip odometer, leather-and-vinyl upholstery, vinyl door panels and special wheel covers.

Standard in the Eliminator was a four-barrel version of the Windsor 351 cid V-8, rated at 290 hp. Other Cougar options were available, including the last of the 390-cid V-8s and the 428 CJ with and without Ram Air. Both of these were rated at 335 hp, far under

their true output on a dyno. Another notable engine option—the Boss 302—was new and came in "street" and "racing" versions. The former had a single four-barrel carburetor and was advertised at 290 hp, a fraction of its actual output. The latter had two four-barrel carburetors, but its horsepower rating was never advertised.

The Eliminator and Boss 302 were a curious combination. The term "eliminator" comes from drag racing and the Boss 302's forte was sports sedan racing. The wisdom of sticking it in the 3,500-lb. Cougar was questionable. Factory-backed Mustang Boss 302s were raced in SCCA Trans-American sedan events, but Cougar Eliminators were not.

Visuals with the Eliminator package included front and rear spoilers, a blacked-out grille, a hood scoop, argent styled steel wheels similar to the Torino GT type, appropriate side striping and a rally clock and tachometer. With the CJ 428-cid engine option you got a hood scoop, hood hold-down pins, a competition handling package and hood striping.

1969 MERCURY CYCLONE GT

The Mercury Cyclone fastback body style had outsold the two-door hardtop model by a wide margin in 1968, so Lincoln Mercury brass took the hint and dropped the notchback version for 1969. A slightly re-trimmed fastback returned for the new model year, while the Cyclone GT was reduced to an appearance group option. There was also a very hot, all-new Cyclone CJ model.

The 1969 Cyclone CJ included a blacked-out grille that was framed in chrome. There was a single chrome piece in the middle, running from each end of the grille. A Cyclone emblem in the center of the grille highlighted the CJ model's front end. Additional features included wheel opening moldings, a dual exhaust system, a 3.50:1 ratio rear axle, an engine dress-up kit, a hood tape stripe and a competition-type handling package. A sports appearance group with bucket seats, remote-control left-hand racing mirror, turbine-style full wheel covers and a rim-blow steering wheel was optional

for the Cyclone CJ at $149 extra.

The Cyclone CJ came with Ford's big-block 428-cid 335-hp Cobra Jet V-8 as *standard* equipment. Also included were a four-speed manual gearbox, a competition handling package and a plain bench seat interior. The CG sold for $3,224. That was just a tad more than a regular Mercury Cyclone V-8 with the 302-cid base engine (which had a base retail price of $2,771).

The Cyclone CG was aimed at the budget-priced super car niche that Plymouth's Road Runner had carved out of the muscle car marketplace. It had a list price of $3,207 and only 3,261 copies were assembled. A Cyclone CJ with a 435-hp version of the 428-cid V-6 carried only 11.6 lbs. per horsepower. It could do 0 to 60 mph in 6.1 seconds and fly down the quarter mile in 13.9 seconds.

The CJ might easily have been the most desirable Cyclone for 1969, but at midyear the Cyclone Spoiler II came along

1969 MERCURY CYCLONE SPOILER II

When NASCAR Grand National stock car racing teams tested the new 1968 body styles, they found the Mercury Cyclone fastback to be a bit faster than its Ford Fairlane fastback counterpart. A more aerodynamic nose design was said to be the reason.

When Cale Yarborough drove the Wood Brothers Cyclone to victory in the Daytona 500 in February 1968, the battle of the NASCAR noses was on. Dodge countered with the Charger 500 for 1969. Ford forces fought back with the Torino Talladega and Mercury Cyclone Spoiler II. Both featured flush grilles and extended noses.

The Talladega was fairly simple, but the Cyclone Spoiler was not. Mercury announced the Spoiler as a midyear model to go on sale in January 1969. The main feature in early information was a spoiler bolted on the trunk deck. It was nice, but the device was not legal in NASCAR at the time. Originally, an extended nose similar to the Talladega was to be an option.

After considerable confusion, the long-nosed Spoiler came to be known as the Cyclone Spoiler II. A total of 519 were made, all with the 351-cid four-barrel V-8 despite an announcement that there also would be a 428-cid Cobra-Jet Ram-Air option. At least 500 needed to be produced to qualify the car as a production model so it could be raced.

Cyclone Spoilers came in two trim versions. A "Dan Gurney" Spoiler had a dark-blue roof, dark-blue striping and a signature decal on the white lower portion. A "Cale Yarborough" edition featured red trim similar to his Wood Brothers stock car. It, too, had a signature decal.

(David Hooten photo)

The 1969 "Cale Yarborough" Cyclone Spoiler II had special striping and a rear spoiler.

As it turned out, the Spoiler wasn't declared legal in NASCAR until the Atlanta 500 on March 30. This put Cyclone pilots in Talladegas for the Daytona 500 race, which was won by Lee Roy Yarbrough in Junior Johnson's Talladega.

Yarbrough turned out to be the year's hottest driver, but his Spoiler season was short since Ford was worried that it wouldn't win the manufacturer's title. As a result, the company put him back in a Talladega at mid-season. The aerodynamic wars got hotter late in the season when Dodge announced the Charger Daytona and later the cartoon-inspired 1970 Plymouth Road Runner SuperBird. The latter helped Plymouth snag Gurney to drive its racing cars.

1970 MERCURY COUGAR ELIMINATOR

(Jerry Heasley photo)

A 1970 Mercury Cougar Eliminator hardtop with a Boss 302 like this one could pull a 15.8-second quarter mile.

Evolutionary design changes characterized the 1970 Mercury Cougars. They included a new vertical grille and a forward-thrusting front end. Promoted as "America's most completely equipped sports car," the new Cougar grille had a center hood extension and an "electric shaver" style insert. Its design was reminiscent of the 1967 and 1968 models' grilles.

Features for the basic Cougar models included upper body pin stripes, wheel opening moldings, roof moldings and windshield and rear window chrome accents. The sporty interior featured high-back bucket seats, courtesy lights, carpeted door trim panels, a vinyl headliner and a rosewood-toned dash panel. The Cougar convertible had a Comfortweave vinyl interior, door-mounted courtesy lights, a three-spoke steering wheel and a power top with a folding rear glass window. There was a two-door hardtop with a base retail price of $2,917. Prices for the convertible started at $3,264. Only 2,322 ragtops were made.

The Cougar XR-7 had distinct wheel covers, rocker panel moldings, a remote-control racing mirror and an emblem on the rear roof pillar. Interior features included vinyl high-back bucket seats

with leather accents, map pockets on the seat backs, a tachometer, a trip odometer, a rocker-switch display, a burled walnut vinyl applique on the instrument panel, rear seat armrests, map and courtesy lights, a visual check panel, loop yarn nylon carpeting and an electric clock with elapsed-time indicator. The XR-7s came in the same body styles as the base Cougar, at $3,201, and $3,465, respectively. The XR-7 ragtop had a run of just 1,977 units.

The Eliminator returned for one final time. Now standard was the new 351 Cleveland four-barrel V-8 that was rated at 300 hp. There were options galore for the muscle car's engine compartment including the Boss 302, the 428 CJ and a new version of the 385 series big-block 429. This "Boss 429" package included Ram-Air induction and a 375-hp rating. "Call it the road animal," said Cougar literature. A rear deck lid spoiler, body graphics and a restyled scooped hood returned as part of the Eliminator's image.

One car enthusiast magazine of the era tested a 1970 Cougar Eliminator with the 290-hp version of the "Boss 302" V-8. It carried 12.4 lbs. per hp and did 0 to 60 mph in 7.6 seconds. The quarter mile took 15.8 seconds.

1970 MERCURY CYCLONE SPOILER AND GT

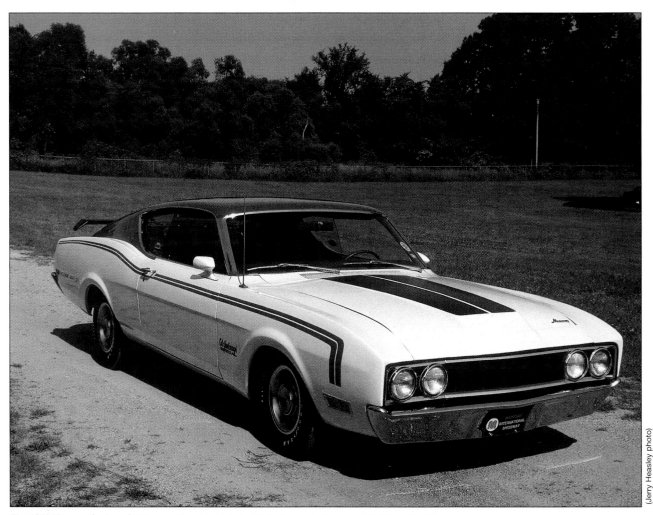

The 1970 Mercury Cyclone Spoiler was the fastest of the 1970 Mercurys, thanks to a 370-hp 429 V-8.

Mercury Cyclones got all kinds of things when they were restyled for 1970 after a two-season stint with a more radical fastback roofline. Some of the changes made for 1970 were good for muscle car fans and some were not.

Though the same unitized chassis was used, the Cyclone wheelbase grew by 1 inch to 117 inches and the overall length of the cars was extended by a hefty 6.7 inches. The latter alteration was due primarily to a protruding nose and fender design that produced somewhat questionable styling. Cyclones also got a gun sight-type design in the center of their grilles.

While their Ford Torino cousins got new fastback designs, Mercury intermediates did not. The Cyclone hardtops had trunk lines about halfway between the old notchback hardtop and a true fastback. There were three Cyclones for 1970: The base model that retailed for prices starting at $3,238, the Cyclone GT base priced at $3,226 and the Spoiler, which listed for $3,759 and up.

The base Cyclone came with the 429-cid 360-hp version of the Ford 385 Series big-block V-8. Standard equipment included a four-speed manual transmission with a floor-mounted Hurst shifter, a competition handling package, a 3.25:1 ratio rear axle, a blacked-out performance styled grille with vertical running lights, exposed headlights, a silver- or black-finished lower back panel, loop carpeting, G70-14 fiberglass-belted tires and a bench seat. Options included the 370-hp CJ 429 engine, the 375-hp Super CJ 429 V-8 and—in extremely limited production numbers— the Boss 429.

The Cougar GT, which had once been the hottest Cyclone model, was now the mildest. It came with a 351-cid 250-hp V-8 with a two-barrel carburetor. Other standard features included a choice of seven unique exterior tone-on-tone color combinations, a three-pod taillight treatment, lower body side moldings, a non-functional performance hood with integral air scoop, a left-hand remote-control racing mirror, a right-hand manual racing-style mirror, concealed headlights, bright belt and trunk lid moldings, high-back bucket seats, Comfortweave vinyl upholstery, a three-spoke sports steering wheel with rim blow and unique door and quarter trim panels. The new 351-cid "Cleveland" V-8 was among the available engine options.

A Ram-Air equipped 370-hp 429 was standard motivation for the Spoiler. High-back buckets were also a part of the package.

1971 MERCURY COUGAR GT CJ 429

(Jerry Heasley photo)

The Mercury CJ 429s of 1971 were about as big as muscle cars get.

The 1971 Mercury Cougar GT CJ 429s were bigger, longer and heftier looking from in front and behind.

(Jerry Heasley photo)

The 1971 Cougars had the most dramatic changes seen since the marque's 1967 introduction. There was a longer wheelbase, a lower silhouette, interior refinements and a muscular new GT option to fill up the gap left by the discontinued Eliminator. The styling inspiration for the Cougar's thinner roof and windshield pillars was said to have come from Europe.

The 1971 models were "horse-sized" ponies, based on the big, new Mustangs. They were 4 inches longer (113 inches) in wheelbase and 7 inches longer (197 inches) in overall length. With a radiator-style grille, they looked even heftier than that.

The Cougars had better manners than the Mustang, with more sound-deadening materials and nicer trim and interior appointments. Only big V-8s went under the hood. They included a 351-cid engine with a two-barrel carburetor and 240 hp, a 351-cid V-8 with a four-barrel carburetor and 285 hp and a 429-cid four-barrel job with 370 hp.

There were two Cougar series, each with a hardtop and a con-vertible. The XR-7 was the sporty version with bucket seats, full instrumentation and a vinyl half-roof. Cougar list prices started at $3,289 and went to $3,877.

The $129.60 GT package was available only for the base Cougar hardtop. It included a high-ratio rear axle, a competition sus-pension, dual racing mirrors, a hood scoop, a performance cooling package, a tachometer, a rim-blow steering wheel, F78 x 14 white sidewall tires, hub caps with bright trim rings, GT fender identifica-tion and a black instrument panel. The hood scoop was non-func-tional, except when the 429 CJ engine option was installed.

The 429 CJ engine listed for $310.90 in all Cougars with the Select-Shifter four-speed manual transmission (which cost $215.10 extra). This engine also included cast-aluminum rocker-arm covers, a bright dipstick handle, oil filler cap, radiator cap and air cleaner (on cars without Ram Air) and a heavy-duty battery. Other options required with the 429 CJ package were power disc brakes and F70 x 14 or larger tires.

1971 MERCURY CYCLONE SPOILER AND GT

The intermediate-size Montego continued to be the basis for the performance models remaining available from Lincoln Mercury Division in 1971. The new models were again actually based on the mid-sized Ford Falcon-Torino series first launched in 1968.

Montego, Montego MX, Montego MX Brougham, Montego Cyclone, Montego Cyclone GT and Montego Cyclone Spoiler series were offered. All Cyclones were two-door hardtops. Base retail prices were $3,369 for the Montego Cyclone, $3,680 for the Montego Cyclone GT and $3,801 for the Montego Cyclone Spoiler.

The Montego Cyclone's standard equipment included color-keyed deep-loop carpeting; concealed windshield wipers, a "cross country ride" package, dual racing mirrors, flow-thru ventilation, a non-functional hood scoop, Cyclone running lights, dual pod tail-lights, F70-14 traction-type tires, a 351-cid 285-hp four-barel V-8 and a four-speed manual transmission with Hurst shifter.

The Cyclone GT included the cross country ride package, a performance hood with integral scoop, concealed headlights, Cyclone running lights, deluxe wheel covers, dual racing mirrors (left-hand remote controlled), full instrumentation, high-back bucket seats, a deluxe three-spoke steering wheel, F70-14 white sidewall tires, a 351-cid 240-hp V-8 with a two-barrel carburetor and Select-Shift automatic transmission.

The Montego Cyclone Spoiler included the same ride package; a Traction-Lok differential, a 3.25:1 rear axle, a front spoiler under the bumper, a rear deck lid spoiler, a performance hood with an integral air scoop, dual racing mirrors (left-hand remote-controlled), Cyclone running lights, hub caps with bright trim rings, Spoiler tape stripes, full instrumentation, high-back bucket seats, a deluxe rim-blow steering wheel, G70-14 fiberglass-belted raised-white-letter tires, a 351-cid 285-hp V-8 with a four-barrel carburetor and a four-speed manual gearbox with a Hurst floor-mounted shifter.

With these cars, the longer their model names, the better their collector-car potential is. The Cyclones were tough cars with good reliability, but 1971 was the final year for the Cyclone name.

A 429-cid "Super Cobra Jet" V-8, with 370 hp, was optional in 1971 Cyclones and Cyclone Spoilers at $257.80 extra. The "427" got less than 10 mpg, but it had some real muscle. The 429 CJ package included cast-aluminum rocker arm covers and a bright dipstick handle, oil filler cap, radiator cap and air cleaner (on non-Ram-Air cars). Power disc brakes were mandatory and, if you wanted air conditioning, you also had to add power steering

OLDSMOBILE

1964 OLDSMOBILE 4-4-2

The first Oldsmobile 4-4-2 was a 1964 3/4 offering for drivers who wanted just a bit more performance and handling. On the official price sticker, this $285.14 package was described as "Option number B-09 Police Apprehender Pursuit." One piece of Oldsmobile literature called *Product Selling Information for Oldsmobile Salesmen* explained the 4-4-2 like this, "police needed it—Olds built it—pursuit proved it." This literature clearly pointed out the *original* meaning of the 4-4-2 designation as follows:

"4-BARREL CARBURETION—plus high-lift cams boost the power of the "4-4-2" Ultra High-Compression V-8 to 310 hp—up 20 hp over Cutlass V-8.

4-ON-THE-FLOOR—stick shift synchromesh transmission captures every power advantage both up and down the entire gear range.

2 DUAL EXHAUSTS—complete dual exhaust system features less back pressure for better performance … aluminized for longer life."

Other 4-4-2 features included heavy-duty shocks and springs, a rear stabilizer bar, dual-snorkel air cleaner, higher-lift camshaft and extra-high-quality rod and main bearings.

Motor Trend tested an Oldsmobile F-85 Cutlass 4-4-2 two-door hardtop in September 1964. The car had a base price of $2,784 and an as-tested price of $3,658.74. Options on the test vehicle included power steering two-speed windshield wipers an electric deck-lid release back-up lights a crankcase vent an outside rear view mirror a power seat simulated wire wheel covers and the Police Apprehender Pursuit package. The car had a 3.55:1 non-Positraction rear axle.

The car accelerated from 0 to 30 mph in 3.1 seconds and from 0 to 60 mph in 7.5 seconds. It could do the standing-start quarter mile in 15.5 seconds at 90 mph. *Car Life* (August 1964) reported a 7.4-second 0 to 60-mph time and a 15.6-second quarter mile.

"What Olds engineers have done, in the final analysis, is produce a car which at long last lives up to the claims of the company's advertising copywriters and top-level spokesmen," said *Car Life*. "The 4-4-2 is indeed 'where the action is.' No better Oldsmobile has rolled off the Lansing assembly line in many a year and though it isn't quite the sports car that corporate brass likes to think, it doesn't miss by much."

1965 OLDSMOBILE 4-4-2

The new 400-cid engine in the 1965 Oldsmobile F-85 4-4-2 cranked out 345 hp.

The F-85 Cutlass line was mildly face lifted for 1965 and the 4-4-2 performance and handling package gained in popularity. Noting the runaway success of the Pontiac GTO with its 389-cid engine, Oldsmobile engineers saw the need to cram more cubes into their creation. Reducing the bore of the new Olds 425-cid engine from 4.125 inches to an even 4.0 produced an engine ideally sized for the 4-4-2 at 400 cid.

This year the 4-4-2 package was offered with an optional Hydra-Matic transmission. Since the second "4" in the 1964 model designation had stood for "four-speed manual transmission," Oldsmobile had to explain the 4-4-2 name a different way. The company now said that the first four (4) stood for the new 400-cid V-8, the second four (4) meant four-barrel carburetor and the two (2) meant dual exhaust. This sounded a little awkward, since "4" and "400" aren't the same, but who cared?

With the 400-cid engine, power rose by 35 horses to a

total of 345 hp at 4800 rpm and torque increased by 85 ft. lbs. to 440 at 3200 rpm. The new engine had a 10.25:1 compression ratio and a single Rochester four-barrel carburetor. *Car and Driver* magazine test drove a 1965 Olds 4-4-2 convertible with a four-speed manual gearbox and a 3.55:1 axle in May 1965. Its 0 to 60-mph time was recorded as 5.5 seconds and the quarter-mile run took 15.0 seconds at 98 mph.

Said *Car and Driver*, "Summed up, the Oldsmobile 4-4-2 is another one of those 'special purpose' American cars that should really be sold as the *all*-purpose car. It really isn't a sports car, and it isn't exactly like the imported sports sedans—even though that seems to have been the aim of its manufacturer—but it *does* approach a very worthwhile balance of all the qualities we'd like to see incorporated in every American car."

A standard 1965 Olds F-85 coupe with the 4-4-2 option sold for $2,605. The Cutlass version came in coupe ($2,799), hardtop ($2,940) and convertible ($3,139) versions. A total of 25,003 cars had the 4-4-2 package installed this year.

1966 OLDSMOBILE 4-4-2

(Jerry Heasley photo)

The Oldsmobile F-85 4-4-2 hardtop got some styling revisions for 1966, and featured a 400-cid engine that could take the car a quarter mile in 14.8 seconds.

When it was restyled for 1966, the Oldsmobile Cutlass F-85 took on a more massive, creased-edge look. The 4-4-2 high-performance package now included seat belts, an instrument panel with a padded dashboard, a windshield washer system, two-speed windshield wipers, a left-hand manual outside rear view mirror, foam padded seat cushions, carpeting on the floor front and rear, chrome roof moldings, a deluxe steering wheel, bucket or custom seats, deluxe armrests, a courtesy lamp package, 7.35 x 14 tires and seat upholstery in either vinyl or cloth.

Under the hood of the 4-4-2 model, the 400-cid V-8 had been tweaked by another 5 horsepower (to 350 hp) thanks to a slight increase in compression ratio. Late in the model year, the 4-4-2 received another adrenalin injection (to 360 hp) with the one-year-only triple two-barrel carburetor setup. *Car Life* magazine took one of these screamers from 0 to 60 mph in a mere 6.3 seconds and called it the "civilized supercar." Quarter-mile runs were made in as little as 14.8 seconds.

From the standpoints of both performance and rarity, the 1966 Olds Cutlass 4-4-2 equipped with the 360-hp factory Tri-Power installation is the most desirable example of these production years to a real muscle-car enthusiast.

1967 OLDSMOBILE CUTLASS SUPREME 4-4-2

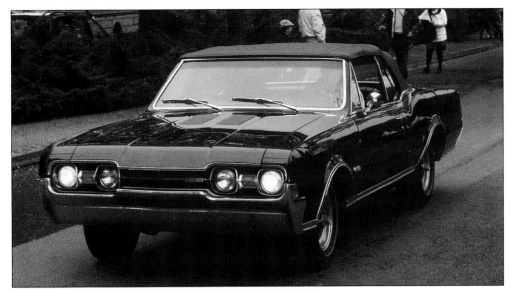

The 1967 Oldsmobile Cutlass Supreme 4-4-2 convertible was a slick, attractive muscle car for less than $3,200.

Today it matters little that the 1967 Oldsmobile 4-4-2 was only an option for the intermediate Cutlass Supreme series. It wouldn't be until the 1968 models bowed that the performance edition would get full model status.

If you've got a 1967 4-4-2, be it a two-door sedan, two-door hardtop or convertible, you've got a full-fledged muscle car that makes no excuses, unlike some of the later 4-4-2-badged cars that Oldsmobile turned out.

The original 1964 Cutlass 4-4-2 option was a quick, midyear answer to the GTO option for the Pontiac Tempest. It utilized parts and pieces from the police package available at the time. By 1967, Olds and its competitors were turning out nicely packaged hot intermediates with visual and mechanical performance galore.

The 1967 Cutlass 4-4-2 option was available for the top-of-the-line Cutlass Supreme series, which grew from a single four-door hardtop in 1966 to a full model range for 1967. You could add the 4-4-2 package to all of the series' two-door models. Base prices were $2,694 for the sedan, $2,831 for the hardtop and $3,145 for the convertible. They came with a standard 330-cid 320-hp V-8.

Checking option box L78 brought the 4-4-2 option and added only $184 to your bill. For that small sum came the 440-cid 350-hp V-8, heavy-duty suspension, wheels and engine mounts, F70 x 14 Red Line tires, bucket seats and 4-4-2 badging front, rear, sides and inside. Another $184 could be spent on the four-speed floor-shifted

manual gearbox and the whole package could be delivered to the pavement via a limited-slip differential for $42. Axle ratios ranged to 4.33:1.

For those who preferred something simpler to drive, 4-4-2s could be had with the Turbo Hydra-Matic three-speed automatic that was available for $236. For the less sporty, bucket front seats could be deleted in favor of a bench seat. On the other hand, those interested in a sportier car could opt for a console between the bucket seats.

While a standard rating of 350 hp was good for openers in 1967, it was necessary to have a trick setup a step beyond that. General Motors bureaucracy had undergone another of its periodic soul cleansings and banned Tri-Power in all cars except the Corvette. Oldsmobile's reaction was the W-30 option.

The flush hood louvers over the air cleaner were functional on the 4-4-2, but they did not have any ram-effect needed for added horses. Using factory ducting from the front of the car, the 1967 W-30-optioned version was advertised at 360 hp, the same as the 1966 Tri-Power Cutlass 4-4-2. Performance tests of the 1966 and 1967 Cutlass 4-4-2s, however, revealed nearly a second lost in the 0-to-60 runs and quarter-mile sprints were down about the same for the 1967s. However, that doesn't prevent a 30-percent price premium today for W-30-equipped 1967 4-4-2 examples.

1968 OLDSMOBILE 4-4-2

In June 1968, *Car Life* nicknamed the Olds 4-4-2 "The Handler" and called it one of the best high-performance packages built in America. The magazine also noted the car's lack of recognition due to the high-priced and luxurious Oldsmobile image that made a muscle car an odd fit in the product mix.

But Olds was trying. Along with the car's all-new General Motors A-car body, the 4-4-2 also had separate model status for the first time in 1968—it was no longer a Cutlass add-on. There were three models: Holiday hardtop, sports coupe (post sedan) and convertible in this first 4-4-2 series.

The new 4-4-2 had more curves than ever on its long hood and short deck body with razor edge fenders and a swoopy rear. Big 4-4-2 emblems and dual through-the-bumper exhaust made it easy to

spot. On a 112-inch stance, the 4-4-2 was 201.6 inches long, 76.6 inches wide and 52.8 inches tall. Front and rear tracks were both 59 inches.

A coil spring front suspension with anti-roll bar was mated with a coil spring link-coil live axle rear suspension. The recirculating ball gear steering (with integral assist) had a 20.7:1 overall ratio and 4.3 turns lock-to-lock. Brakes were discs up front and drums rear. Tires were F70-14s.

As in 1967, a 400-cid V-8 was standard, but it was a totally new one with 3.87 x 4.25-inch bore and stroke (4 x 3.975-inch bore and stroke in 1967). There were three basic four-barrel versions of this 10.5:1 compression engine, the hottest with the W-30 Force Air package added. They gave 325 hp (automatic), 350 hp (stick) and

360 hp, respectively. However, a milder two-barrel "turnpike cruiser" economy engine with 9.0:1 compression and 290 hp (including Turbo Hydra-Matic) could be had, too.

Shift-for-yourself choices included a three-speed gearbox and wide- and close-ratio four-speed manual transmissions. A slew of rear axle options were available. Other popular extras included power steering, a high-voltage ignition system, a tilt-away woodgrain steering wheel, a so-called "Rocket Rally Pac," an AM radio, a center console and a remote-control outside rearview mirror. Bucket seats were standard.

Buyers who ordered the Force Air induction system got large 15 x 2-inch air scoops below the front bumper, a special camshaft for a higher torque peak, modified intake and exhaust ports, a free-flowing exhaust system and low-friction componentry.

Car Life's 4-4-2 Holiday listed for $3,127 f.o.b. in Lansing, Michigan, but went out the showroom door at $4,059. It had the 350-hp engine and took 15.13 seconds to do the quarter mile at 92.2 mph. According to the magazine, overall braking was poor and fuel consumption was in the 11 to 16 mpg range for normal driving (12.2 mpg for the test). "A true high-performance car and the best handling of today's supercars," the editors wrote.

Production of the 1968 Olds 4-4-2 totaled 4,282 sports coupes, 5,142 convertibles and 24,183 Holiday hardtops for a total of 33,607 units compared to 24,829 the previous year.

1968 HURST/OLDS

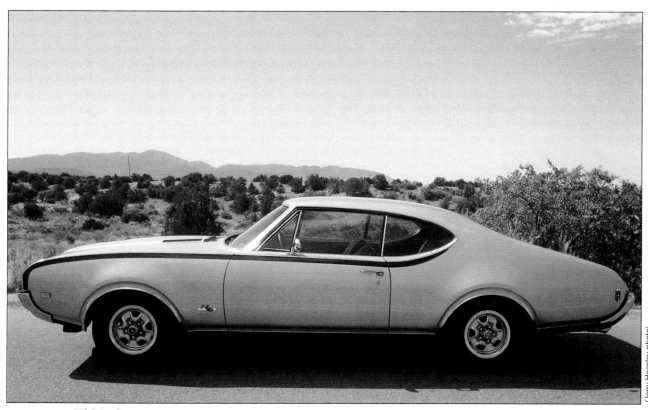

(Jerry Heasley photo)

A total of 515 1968 Hurst/Olds were built in 1968.

For 1968, what had formerly been the largest Olds engine offering, at 425 cid, was punched out to a full 455 cid. GM brass would not permit the cramming of the new 455 into the 4-4-2 platform, but this didn't stop George Hurst, of Hurst Performance Products, from trying it on his own. So successful was his effort that he—along with Olds officials—got entrepreneur and Oldsmobile supplier John Demmer, of Lansing, Michigan, to assemble clones of Hurst's car in his own facility on a limited basis. This is how the first Hurst/Olds was born!

To power the Hurst/Olds, the 4-4-2's standard 400-cid engine was replaced with a Force Air 455 with a 10.5:1 compression ratio that was beefed-up internally to develop 390 hp at 5000 rpm and 500 ft. lbs. of torque at 3600 rpm. The big W45 motor was based on the Toronado engine, but built with a special crankshaft, a custom-curved distributor, special carburetor jets, a 308-degree camshaft with a .474-inch lift and hand-assembled Ram-Air cylinder heads. The power plant was hooked to a modified Turbo Hydra-Matic with a Hurst Dual-Gate shifter that could be shifted like a manual transmission or used like an automatic.

A heavy-duty rear end incorporated a standard 3.91:1 rear axle. Also included as part of the package were specially calibrated power disc-drum brakes, a heavy-duty suspension, a heavy-duty cooling system with a high-capacity radiator and viscous-drive fan and G70-14 Goodyear polyglas tires. The entire car was dressed up in a special silver and black trim package that looked very distinctive.

A total of 515 Hurst/Olds were built for 1968. Of these, 451 were based on the 4-4-2 Holiday two-door hardtop while the remaining 64 were originally 4-4-2 coupes. No Hurst/Olds were produced in convertible form. In August 1968, *Super Stock* magazine road tested the 4-4-2 and reported a top run of 12.90 seconds for the quarter mile at 109 mph.

The Hurst/Olds partnership proved to be quite an image-boosting program for the GM division and the two companies went on to team up on other Hurst/Olds models for many years.

1969 OLDSMOBILE 4-4-2

A 1969 Oldsmobile 4-4-2 sports coupe with a 400-cid V-8 could reach 123 mph on the speedometer.

A new pitchman named Dr. Oldsmobile prescribed image enhancements for the 4-4-2 in 1969. They included a bolder split grille, fat hood stripes and bright, new name badges. Also, the two-barrel "turnpike cruiser" option was eliminated to purify Oldsmobile's muscle car reputation.

Hotter than all but the Hurst model was the heavy-breathing W-30 option. Its specifications were about the same as in 1968, except for the torque rating, which went to 400 ft. lbs. at 3600 rpm compared to 440 ft. lbs. a year earlier. The same 400-cid 360-hp at 5400 rpm V-8 could push the W-30 to 123 mph tops.

Transmission options were also unchanged. Hurst shifters again came with stick-shift cars. Turbo Hydra-Matic buyers got a column shift, although a console mount was optional.

Axle ratios were expanded, with some applications changed, too. The 4.33:1 rear, formerly standard with stick shift cars, was now standard only with the optional close-ratio four-speed manual transmission. A 3.42:1 axle was attached to wide-ratio four-speeds, as well as to Turbo Hydra-Matics. The 3.08:1, 3.23:1 and 3.91:1 axles were back from the 1968 options list and a 4.66:1 option was new.

A divider between the halves of the grille, finished in body color, carried big 4-4-2 identifiers. W-30s had special hood stripes and front fender decal cutouts. Front parking lights were moved from between the headlamps to the front bumper. Strato bucket seats, red-stripe wide-oval tires, a juicy battery, dual exhausts and beefy suspension goodies were included. An anti-spin rear axle was mandatory.

The coupe ($3,404), hardtop ($3,467) and convertible ($3,658) with W-30 Force Air induction accounted for 5 percent of production, or 1,389 cars. Total 4-4-2 output, by body style, included 2,475 coupes, 19,587 hardtops and 4,295 ragtops.

New for the year was a calmer W-31 Force-Air setup for the F-85 with Turbo Hydra-Matic transmission. This was a "for-the-street" extra for those with milder street use in mind and was aimed at the younger set where heavy breathing and heavy spending didn't co-mingle. At $310, the package was actually higher than the W-30 at $264. However, the car-and-equipment tab was lower. So was production. Only 1 percent of all Oldsmobiles were W-31s in 1969.

1969 HURST/OLDS

The 1969 Hurst/Olds hardtop featured a distinctive gold-and-white paint job.

Olds 4-4-2 styling was altered only slightly for 1969. Essentially, each pair of lamps in the quad headlight system was brought closer together. This, along with some modification of the central grille and bumper area made for a smoother, less-cluttered frontal appearance. Taillights were recessed and took on a vertical theme, as opposed to the horizontal orientation of the year before.

Production of the Hurst/Olds nearly doubled for 1969 with a total of 906 making it to the pavement. For this year, all Hurst/Olds were based on the 4-4-2 Holiday two-door hardtop body style.

(Jerry Heasley photo)

Stimulated by a special 455-cid 380-hp "Rocket" V-8, this year's Hurst Olds—while slightly heavier (3,885 lbs.) than its '68 counterpart (3,870 lbs.)—bettered the original version's 0 to 60-mph acceleration times (5.9 seconds versus 6.7 seconds), but took slightly longer to cover the quarter mile (14.0 seconds versus 13.9 seconds).

At a price that ranged from $4,500 to $4,900, the Hurst/Olds buyer had to part with a few more pennies than it took to buy Oldsmobile's factory hot rod, the 4-4-2 model. But in return for paying that premium, the Hurst/Olds buyer got the optimum balance of luxury and performance available in an Oldsmobile muscle car.

Power was transmitted from the engine through a heavy-duty Turbo Hydra-Matic or the buyer's choice of a close- or wide-ratio four-speed manual transmission, all Hurst-shifted, of course. The package was finished off with an eye-popping gold-and-white color scheme complete with strut-mounted rear deck spoiler.

1970 OLDSMOBILE 4-4-2 (W-30)

(Jerry Heasley photo)

The 1970 Oldsmobile 4-4-2 W-30 Holiday hardtop got high marks for its 455-cid engine and handling capabilities.

The W-30-equipped 4-4-2 was Oldsmobile's response to the lifting of General Motors' ill-conceived mandate prohibiting the use of engines exceeding 400-cid in its A-bodied automobiles.

On a limited scale—and well beyond the reach of GM's authority—this wall of separation had already been breached by the Hurst Corp.'s 1969 Hurst/Olds. Either in a "bandit" Hurst or a W-30-optioned Olds 4-4-2, the division's 455-cid V-8 represented a major advance in straight-line performance. And it did not adversely affect the 4-4-2's handling, since it weighed about the same as the smaller and less-powerful 400-cid V-8 used in 1969 Olds 4-4-2s.

The 4-4-2 had, since its introduction in 1964, enjoyed a deserved reputation for handling far above the existing norm for American supercars. The W-30 version, along with its stature as a powerful 370-hp automobile, maintained the tradition of being a handler. There was nothing magical or exotic about the W-30 Olds 4-4-2 suspension, which consisted of front coil and rear leaf springs. Like all 4-4-2 Oldsmobiles, the W-30 was equipped with a rear stabilizer bar. *Car Life* magazine, in its March 1970 issue said, "At last people who want more power, but still want their car to handle, have a car that does both."

Also adding to the W-30 Olds 4-4-2's performance profile were standard 10.88-inch front power disc brakes that were optional for standard 4-4-2s. At the rear, 9.5 x 2.0-inch drum brakes were utilized. This setup wasn't flawless, but *Car Life* noted that on its W-30 test car, "The front disc brakes came through the brake fade test smoking, but working well."

The source of all the kinetic energy in the W-30 was, at least officially, only slightly different from the standard 4-4-2 engine. Both engines displaced 455 cubic inches and had 10.5:1 compression ratios, but the standard 4-4-2 engine developed 365 hp at 5000 rpm and the W-30 was said to put out 370 hp at 5400 rpm.

Virtually identical to the one used on the 1969 Hurst/Olds was the 1970 W-30 model's fiberglass hood. Unlike the air ducts installed on the W-31, which were mounted under the front bumper, those for the W-30 were mounted on the hood. The twin intakes rammed a flow of cool air through a mesh filter and were linked to a low-restriction air intake by a sponge-like material that acted as a gasket seal with the hood.

The W-30's standard transmission was identified by Oldsmobile as the "Muncie Close Ratio." *Car Life* described it as "Oldsmobile's version of Chevy's M22 'Rock Crusher.'" For an additional $227, the M40 version of the Turbo Hydra-Matic 400 was available. Compared to a normal Turbo Hydra-Matic transmission, the M40 had higher rpm shift positions and sharper shifts.

Hurst made all floor shifts for the W-30. Oldsmobile reported: "They are the same basic construction as the aftermarket Hurst competition shifter, except there are not stops and there is sound insulation on the production shifter."

The W-30 was capable of 0-to-60 times of under 6 seconds and quarter-mile runs of 14.36 seconds at 100.22 mph.

1970 OLDSMOBILE RALLYE 350

(Jerry Heasley photo)

The 1970 Rallye 350 is nicknamed the "yellow peril."

While not the brawniest muscle car ever built, the Oldsmobile Rallye 350 was surely one of the brightest. Its smart Sebring yellow paint makes it stand out wherever it's seen. So does the fact that its urethane-clad bumpers and Rallye spoke wheels are done in the same color. In addition, it's trimmed with bold orange and black stripes along the tops of rear fenders and over the backlight.

Introduced in February 1970, the car was initially planned as a Hurst/Olds, but Lansing wound up marketing it as a new option that combined the looks of a limited-edition muscle car with a more "streetable" power-train package. It could be added to either the F-85 coupe or the Cutlass 'S' coupe or hardtop.

The base engine, of course, was the 350-cid V-8 with a 4.057 x 3.385-inch bore and stroke. This version developed 310 hp at 4200 rpm. A W-31 Force Air package was available for cars with the Rallye 350 option. It boosted compression from 10.25:1 to 10.5:1 and gave 325 hp at 5400 rpm. Also included on W-31s were aluminum intake manifolds, a heavy-duty clutch, front disc brakes, a special hood and decorative touches such as decals, paint stripes and specific emblems.

When the Rallye 350 equipment was added to an F-85 or Cutlass 'S,' the following extras were mandatory: Rallye sport suspension, Force Air fiberglass hood, dual sport mirrors and a sport steering wheel. Retail price for the F-85 option package was $3,163. The Cutlass 'S' based editions were $3,283 (coupe) and $3,346 (hardtop).

Transmission attachments included three-on-the-floor or four-on-the-floor, the latter available with wide- or close-ratio choices (all with Hurst shifters). Three-speed Turbo Hydra-Matic could be had with regular column shift or optional console shift. Axle ratios were 3.23:1 (manual) or 3.42:1 (automatic), with 3.42:1 and 3.91:1 options.

Like the GTO "Judge," this trendy-looking Olds was aimed at a market niche that proved to be smaller than sales projections forecasted. Only 3,547 of these "yellow perils" were assembled: 2,527 were Cutlass S-based and 1,020 were F-85s. Many of the cars came with a rear deck lid spoiler, which cost $74 extra.

In February 1970, *Motor Trend* tested a Rallye 350 with the 310-hp engine, three-speed manual transmission and 3.23:1 rear axle. It did 0 to 60 mph in 7.7 seconds and covered the quarter mile in 15.4 seconds at 89 mph.

1971 OLDSMOBILE 4-4-2

This was the last year that Oldsmobile would have the 4-4-2 as a separate model. In 1972, the 4-4-2 would become an appearance and handling option for the Cutlass 'S.'

For its last year as a separate series, the 4-4-2's standard equipment included a special 455-cid engine, a dual exhaust system, carpeting, special springs, stabilizer bars, special engine mounts, Strato bucket seats, heavy-duty wheels, special emblems and a deluxe steering wheel. Oldsmobile offered a choice of vinyl or cloth upholstery. The standard tires were G70-14s.

The W-31 version of the 350-cid 1970 Cutlass V-8 had to be discontinued in 1971 since it couldn't pass emission control tests that were coming online at the time, but W-30-optioned 4-4-2 models were continued in 1971. The W-30s had an 8.5:1 compression ratio, accomplished by using a piston with a dished-out top.

The 455-cid engine used in the 4-4-2 had a net horsepower rating of 260. The gross horsepower rating shown in the *Standard Catalog of American Cars 1946-1975* is 340 at 4600 rpm. While Oldsmobile was reluctant to give out the W-30's ratings for 1971, the 1970 rating was 470 gross hp.

A unique 1971 feature was the use of valve rotators on the exhaust valves of 4-4-2 and W-30 engines. In addition, valve rotators were fitted on the intake valves. Special alloy exhaust valve seats were installed in the cylinder heads and the valves themselves had aluminum seats and hardened tips. To ensure that the calibrated settings on the Rochester 4MC four-barrel carburetor stayed constant, plastic caps were snapped over the idle mixture screws.

Because the lowered compression ratio used in 1971 generated more heat than previous 4-4-2 high-compression engines, the fan speed was increased. To counter the resultant increase in fan noise, Oldsmobile used a new clutch designed to release the fan before an objectionable noise level was reached. It was used with fans set up to increase speed faster from idle.

The Olds 4-4-2 was a separate model for the last time in 1971.

The rear ends on all Cutlass-based cars were given larger pinion bearings and stronger pinion shafts while the clutches in limited-slip differentials were such that they developed higher maximum friction torque. Optional on the W-30 cars was a dual-disc, dual-plate clutch that offered 10 percent greater torque capacity, 40 percent less pedal effort and a 100 percent increase in clutch life.

Hot Rod magazine drove a dual-disc equipped W-30 Olds 4-4-2 with a 455-cid engine and four-speed gearbox and found the shifts "startlingly quick and effortless." The writers said, "You really have to get used to using a light foot." A heavy-duty close-ratio four-speed gearbox could be ordered on the W-30 machines. *Hot Rod* magazine, went on record saying, "It isn't recommended for sus-

tained street driving." W-30 machines also got a full complement of suspension pieces for taking on all kinds of highway outings. Disc front brakes were also available.

On balance, *Hot Rod* concluded that the 1971 version of the 4-4-2 and its W-30 variant represented no appreciable performance sacrifice. As the last of the special series, the '71 4-4-2 is worth collecting. *Car & Driver* once characterized it as, "strictly speaking, a muscle car, but one … too gentlemanly to display the gutter habits of its competitors." Among the '71s, the 4-4-2 convertible is definitely the rarer piece with 1,304 produced. Oldsmobile also made 6,285 two-door hardtops.

1979 HURST/OLDS W-30

The 1979 Hurst/Olds had a long list of muscle car extras to make the pedestrian 350-cid engine more attractive.

(Oldsmobile Division photo)

As the 1970s waned, domestic automakers gradually were growing bolder and openly offering specialty performance cars again. Oldsmobile made such a step early in calendar year 1979 when it introduced the Hurst/Olds option for its Cutlass Calais coupe.

The first Hurst/Olds model was built in 1968 when Oldsmobile used the back-door approach and hired Hurst to stuff the big 455-cid engine into the intermediate Cutlass model. Later versions ended up being more for dress than speed with the last offering prior to 1979 being the 1975 model.

For 1979, the downsized Cutlass Calais needed some dressing up and got it with a Hurst/Olds package. For $2,054 tacked on to the $5,631 base price you got option W-30 (a decal stating such was on each front fender). This extra-cost package included gold paint trim, gold aluminum wheels, gold sport mirrors, Hurst/Olds emblems on the sail panels, a Hurst Dual-Gate shifter on the mandatory Turbo Hydra-Matic 350 and the Oldsmobile 350-cid V-8 (which was not available on some other models at the time). The output of 170 net hp was nothing to brag about, but it bested the 130 being put out by the 305-cid V-8 used in most other GM vehicles at the time.

In the past, Hurst/Olds cars had been shipped to a separate factory for the Hurst conversion, but the 1979 examples were set up for conversion right at the Oldsmobile factory. That didn't seem to bother the buyers in 1979 as 2,499 were made, just short of the 2,535 record set by the 1975 model. Of the 1979 total, 1,334 were finished in black and 1,165 were done in white. Optional T-top roofs ended up on 537 Hurst/Oldsmobiles.

Despite little promotion, the sales tally wasn't enough for the Hurst/Olds to return until the 1983 model year. A second so-called energy crisis in the 1979-'80 period also was a factor.

1984 HURST/OLDS

A 1984 Hurst/Olds coupe could be purchased new for about $12,700.

The ninth edition of the Hurst/Olds came in model year 1984 and for the first time, the Hurst/Olds was not a midyear model. It was announced with the rest of the line on September 14, 1983. Hurst's parent company—Cars & Concepts—started production in December in the company's Brighton, Michigan, facility.

Black and silver exterior colors were reversed from the 1983 model with red trim continuing. The hood bulge and the front and rear spoilers from the previous year were also carried over. Returning, too, was the next best thing to a video arcade in the front seat, the Lightning Rod Automatic Shifter. Instead of the usual single lever popping up from the console, there were three. They controlled the overdrive automatic transmission. The extra levers gave you manual control of first and second gear selections.

Power continued from the Olds-built 307-cid V-8, which was rated at 180 hp, the same as the Chevrolet Monte Carlo SS. A Rochester 4MV Quadrajet carb and aluminum intake manifold did the best job it could offer under the stringent emission and CAFE requirements of the time. A heavy-duty suspension, front and rear sway bars, chrome-plated super stock wheels and Goodyear Eagle GT P215/65R15 rubber got the power to the ground.

The price of the package on the Cutlass Supreme Calais coupe was $1,997 above the base price of $10,649. About 3,500 of the 1984 model were produced, making it the most popular car in the Hurst/Olds series.

PLYMOUTH

1962 PLYMOUTH MAX WEDGE 413

During early 1962, Plymouth sales were hurting. Then an announcement in *Motor Trend's* "Spotlight on Detroit" column in May 1962 publicized a new engine option that would help turn things around. "A new 410-hp, 413 cubic inch V-8 engine with ram-tube manifolding will be available as a factory-installed option on many Plymouths and Dodge Darts beginning this month," said the brief photo caption. "The big power plant will have an 11-to-1 compression ratio, a newly designed short ram-tube intake manifold, two four-barrel carburetors and high-velocity exhausts."

A closer look at the 413-cid engine written up in *Motor Trend's* August 1962 issue was described as "the first report on the Plymouth-Dodge Super Stock engine." Technical editor Roger Huntington got his hands on a Super Stock Dodge Dart two-door sedan with the Ramcharger V-8. In his story, he explained that this engine was the same as the Plymouth version.

Amazingly, the big monster motor cost only $374.40 more than a base 230-hp V-8. With that option you got a big-block V-8 with a 4.19 x 3.75-inch bore and stroke, an 11.0:1 compression ratio and two 650-cfm Carter AFB four-barrel carburetors mounted on a newly designed cross-ram intake manifold. The Max Wedge V-8 was linked to a three-speed TorqueFlite automatic transmission. In the 3,440-lb. car, this combination was good for 5.8-second 0-to-60 times and a standing-start quarter mile in 14.4 seconds at 101 mph.

Max Wedge racing cars with some aftermarket enhancements and other tweaking could do even better than that, and did. On July 15, at a drag strip in Fremont, California, Tom Grove became the first Super Stock driver to run the quarter mile in under 12 seconds. His 413-powered 500-hp "Melrose Missile" ran down the drag strip in 11.93 seconds with a trap speed of 118.57 mph.

1963 PLYMOUTH MAX WEDGE 426

(Jerry Heasley photo)

The 1964 Max Wedge 426s were designed with racing in mind, and they proved successful on both drag strips and stock car tracks.

In 1963, the National Hot Rod Association (NHRA) and the National Association for Stock Car Auto Racing (NASCAR) and several other groups that sanctioned automobile racing established an engine displacement limit of 7 liters or 427 cubic inches. As a reaction to this, in June of 1963, Plymouth announced its development of a 426-cid "Max Wedge" V-8 for Super Stock class drag racing. The 426-cid engine block had been introduced only in upper-

level Chryslers in 1962 and had not been tuned for drag racing.

The so-called Stage II version of the motor brought out in 1963 was intended for sale only to those competing in supervised drag racing and stock car racing. At 1 cubic inch under the new limit, this engine increased Chrysler's ability to win in both drag and oval-track racing. By the end of the year, a total of 2,130 Plymouths and Dodges with this motor would be built.

The three Max Wedge 426 engine options all produced more than 400 hp.

(Jerry Heasley photo)

The new Max Wedge 426 engine looked identical to the Max Wedge 413 V-8, but had a larger bore size of 4.25 inches. It came in three different versions. The first version, with a single four-barrel carburetor, was designed for stock-car racing rules. It put out 400 hp. The second version, with an 11.0:1 compression ratio and dual four-barrel carburetors on a cross-ram manifold, produced 415 hp at 5600 rpm and 470 ft. lbs. of torque at 4400 rpm. The third version had a 13.5:1 compression ratio and dual four-barrel carburetors, also on the cross-ram intake. It produced 425 hp at 5600 rpm and 480 ft. lbs. of torque at 4400 rpm.

Many of the Max Wedge 426s also carried a new Super/Stock package designed for drag racing. It included lightweight aluminum front-end sheet metal, a large air scoop for the hood and some trim deletions designed to shave off pounds.

1964 PLYMOUTH BARRACUDA

The 1964 Plymouth Barracuda came with an optional 273-cid small-block V-8 and a few other add-ons that inflated its $2,365 base price.

"We are sure the Plymouth Barracuda is just right for young, sports-minded Americans who want to enjoy the fun of driving a car that also fills their general transportation needs," said Plymouth's general manager P.N. Buckminster, when the Barracuda arrived in April 1, 1964.

The Barracuda was a reaction to the Ford Mustang and the Corvair Monza. It was based on the Valiant's 106-inch stance and shared most of its front sheet metal with that compact-size Plymouth. The rear of the body was turned into a dramatic fastback roofline that was created primarily through the use of a very large, lift-up rear window.

Like the Valiant, the Barracuda featured front torsion bars and leaf springs at the rear. Power brakes were standard equipment. Tires were size 6.50 x 13. Chrome-plated lugs for the 13 x 4 1/2-inch safety-rim wheels were optional, as were finned wheel covers with simulated knock-off hubs.

Barracuda buyers had a choice of three engines, and two of them were in-line version of the Chrysler "slant six." The third was a 273-cid V-8 that produced 180 hp at 4200. This small-block engine had solid valve lifters, a 3.62 x 3.312-inch bore and stroke, an 8.8:1 compression ratio and a Carter Type BBS two-barrel carburetor. You could settle for the standard three-speed manual transmission, but muscle-car fans usually opted for a new four-speed manual gearbox with a Hurst shift linkage. You could also order a three-speed TorqueFlite automatic at extra cost.

The Barracuda had a base price of $2,365 and weighed 2,740 lbs. Some popular options included racing stripes for $31, a Transaudio radio for $59, and performance group equipment fort $156. The latter included a four-barrel carburetor for the 273-cid V-8 plus a heavy-duty suspension package. While it was a neat package, the 1964 Barracuda did not strike a hit with buyers like Ford's Mustang did. In the eight months that it was on the market, only 23,443 copies were built.

1964 PLYMOUTH 426-R/426-S

(Jerry Heasley photo)

The 1964 Plymouth 426 Fury came in both racing and street versions.

In 1964, Plymouth continued to offer the "Super Stock" Max Wedge Stage III 426-cid engine. Dodge offered the same motor of course, the only difference being the Plymouth version had a black cooling fan and the Dodge engine had a chrome-plated fan blade. It was a competition-only option and carried the code 426-R, with the "R" indicating "racing." It had an option price in the $500 range.

The 426-R engine was again available in 415- and 425-hp versions. The former had the 11.0:1 compression ratio and the latter had the 13.5:1 ratio. The more powerful version also had nifty "Tri-Y" exhaust headers.

New this year was a 426-S "street" version of the 426-cid V-8 that was rated for 365 *advertised* horsepower, but actually produced around 410 hp. This engine did not include most of the Max Wedge hardware, but because of the similar displacement numbers, many buyers thought it was nearly the same engine. It ran a single four-barrel carburetor on a cast-iron intake and a 10.3:1 compression ratio. It used a standard type exhaust system. With 470 ft. lbs. of torque at 3200 rpm, it was no slouch and it was far more "streetable" than the race versions of the 426.

Most of 426-R engines went into cheap Savoy two-door sedans because they were the lightest-weight full-size models made by Plymouth and thus went the fastest with the big engine. The NASCAR racing cars carried four-barrel carburetors. The drag racers went for the dual-quad setups and many had the lightweight aluminum front-end sheet metal, large hood scoops, etc. They were plain-Jane machines, but amazingly fast with performance in the same range as 1963.

The street version of the 426 could be had in any model from the Savoy to the Sport Fury hardtop or convertible. A 1964 Sport Fury two-door hardtop with the 426-cid 365-hp V-8 carried about 9.5 lbs. per horsepower and could turn in 6.8-second 0 to 60-mph runs. The same combination was good for a 15.2-second quarter-mile run.

1964 PLYMOUTH 426 RACE HEMI

Plymouth's "Super Commando" 426-cid Hemi V-8 was released around February 9, 1964, for competition use. Its purpose was to help Mopar drivers take checkered flags at NASCAR superspeedways and to allow them to dominate Super Stock drag racing classes.

It didn't take Plymouth very long to achieve one of these goals. On February 23, 1964, three Hemi-powered Belvederes and one of their Dodge cousins swept the field at the Daytona 500, taking the first four places in order. The race winner was Richard Hemi in his electric blue No. 43. Running behind him, in order, were Plymouth drivers Jimmy Pardue and Paul Goldsmith.

In order to "legalize" the Hemi engine for NASCAR racing, Chrysler had to build several thousand of them and offer them in production cars. In 1964, the corporation made 6,359 (Hemi and Wedge) 426-cid engines and put them in both Plymouths and Dodges. On an in-the-crate basis, the Super Commando 426-cid

415-hp version of the Hemi added $1,800 to the price of a 1964 Plymouth V-8. The Super Commando 426-cid 425-hp Hemi engine was a $2,000 in-the-crate option.

The 1964 Hemi had a cylinder head design similar to that used on the "Firepower" Hemi of the 1950s. However, in this case the cylinder heads were made of aluminum, rather than cast iron. The official horsepower ratings, advertised as being the same as those for the 426 Wedge V-8, were a figment of someone's vivid imagination. There are rumors that dynometer tests registered Hemi output at over 600 hp.

Plymouth dealers sold the Hemi engines over the counter, but they also came in factory-built super stock drag-racing cars. On the NASCAR circuits, the Hemi ran nearly 175 mph at Daytona. Richard Petty's Hemi-powered Belvedere brought Plymouth its first ever Grand National championship.

1965 PLYMOUTH BARRACUDA

Although the 1964 1/2 Barracuda had represented a departure in the right direction for Plymouth, it wasn't all that it could have been. *Car and Driver* (May 1964) concluded, "We'd be the first to applaud a product from Chrysler that really puts them into the sports car business, but this car, with nothing but a slick-looking body, seems superfluous."

This may explain the Barracuda's return, in 1965, with a hotter engine and a rally-bred suspension package. While the standard Barracuda had no real changes other than the elimination of "Valiant" nameplates on the exterior, the more muscular version inspired *Car and Driver* (October 1964) to change its tune a bit about the car's performance. "Our test Barracuda, with its warmed-up 273 engine, is everything you'd like it to be," wrote the magazine. "In fact, it may well be the most satisfactory enthusiast's car of all three of the sporty compacts."

The new "Golden Commando" version of the 273-cid V-8 was definitely a step towards improving the breed. It upped the compression ratio to 10.5:1 and added a single four-barrel Ball & Ball carburetor. This was enough to produce 235 hp at 5200 rpm and 280

ft. lbs. of torque at 4000 rpm. In terms of performance, a Barracuda with a 3.23:1 rear axle and four-speed all-synchro manual transmission tested by *Car and Driver* was able to run from 0 to 60 mph in 9.1 seconds and do the quarter mile in 17.5 seconds at 88.5 mph. *Road & Track* (April 1965) got a like-equipped Barracuda to do 0 to 60 mph in 8.2 seconds and cover the quarter mile in 15.9 seconds at 85 mph.

The list price of the 1965 Barracuda V-8 was $2,535, but the hot engine was merchandised as part of the Formula S package, which also included heavy-duty front torsion bars, heavy-duty rear springs, firm-ride shock absorbers, a sway bar, rally stripes, extra-wide wheel rims, Goodyear Blue Streak wide oval tires and "Formula S" medallions ahead of the front wheel openings. With this option the base price was $3,169.

Along with better performance came better sales, and by the time the model year ended, a total of 64,596 Barracudas left Plymouth assembly lines. Of these, 19.4 percent had four-speed manual transmissions and 100 percent had front bucket seats.

1965 PLYMOUTH BELVEDERE SATELLITE MAX WEDGE STAGE III/RACE HEMI

Promoted as "the roaring '65s," mid-sized Plymouths boasted new lower body styling, carryover roof lines, a return to single headlamps and a new high-performance line called Satellite. Starting at $3,045, this 116-inch wheelbase, Belvedere-based intermediate assumed the muscle car role heretofore filled by Sport Furys (which had become sports/luxury cars). A four-section aluminum grille and a crisp, tapering body-side feature line dominated the round-cornered, but mostly square styling. Rear fenders had a set of dummy louvers for image.

Bucket seats, a center console and all-vinyl upholstery were standard in two-door hardtops and ragtops. Chrysler's top trim levels had a glittery, rich look and the Satellite filled the bill. Sales literature showed the 426-cid 425-hp "Max Wedge" on the options list, as well as the 426-cid 365-hp "Street Wedge," the 383-cid 360-hp big-block V-8, the 361-cid 265-hp V-8 and the 318-cid 230-hp V-8.

Often confused with the Hemi due to similar displacement and horsepower numbers, the 426 Max Wedge Stage III was a race-bred engine with a different combustion chamber configuration. It had 12.5:1 compression, a NASCAR "Tri-Y" exhaust system, a cam with 320 degrees of overlap, reworked combustion chambers, notched valves and big, twin Carter four-barrels with giant air cleaners. Chrysler did not warranty this engine as it was "not recommended for general driving." The tamer, 426-cid 365-hp Street Wedge, with 10.3:1 compression and a single four-barrel on a cast-iron intake had better street driveability, due to its lower state of tune.

A rare Plymouth engine was the 426-cid "Race Hemi." Introduced in 1964, it was intended for off-road (race) use only. It used a cast-iron block with 4.25 x 3.75-inch bore and stroke, a forged and shotpeened crankshaft, impact extruded pistons, cross-

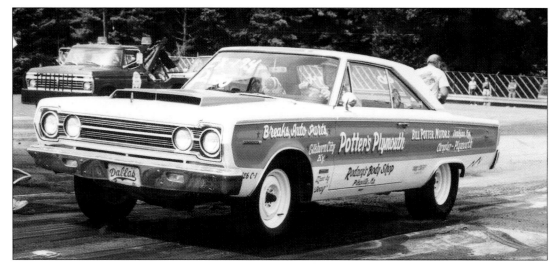

The 1965 Plymouth Belvedere Satellite Stage III Race Hemi engine was not covered by warrantee and not recommended for street use.

bolted main bearing caps, forged rods and solid lifters, all of which would be carried over for "Street Hemis." But, the Race Hemi also had a magnesium dual-four-barrel intake manifold, aluminum cylinder heads, a header-type exhaust system, a 328-degree cam (with 112 degree overlap), bigger valves with stiffer springs and 12.5:1 compression. Chrysler built 360 Race Hemi engines in 1965. Typically, 60 percent went into Plymouths. Most likely, the majority of Hemis went into base Belvedere coupes—the lightest model in

the lineup. A '65 Hemi Satellite would, however, be a rare possibility. Chrysler was known to do just about anything to sell a car.

A Hemi-powered '65 Plymouth racing car, competing in S/SA drag classes with "Drag-On-Lady" Shirley Shahan behind the wheel, went 129.30 mph in the quarter mile. While NASCAR issued a temporary ban on the $1,800 engine, Hemi Belvederes won many events in USAC, NHRA and AHRA competition during 1965.

1966 PLYMOUTH BARRACUDA 'S'

The 1966 Plymouth Barracuda 'S' had a little more muscle than the previous year's model.

By 1966, the Barracuda 'S' had clawed its way to the championship in the Sports Car Club of America's (SCCA) national rallying class. That was not bad for a car that had suffered through its first year, in 1965, as a "pretty face" without much real performance behind it. The "Golden Commando" version of the 273-cid V-8 was the "hot-ticket" engine option again. It had a new unsilenced air cleaner, but no real specifications changes.

Prices for the 1966 Barracuda V-8 started at $2,655. There was not a whole lot that was really new about the car's appearance, although it did get the year's new split grille with criss-cross inserts (as used on the 1966 Valiant) and a large, circular center medallion with an image of a fish (repeated on the rear of the car). A Barracuda script appeared on the front fenders. When the Barracuda 'S' package was added, this was noted with small, circular badges below the Barracuda name on the front fenders. New pinstriping decorated the body and a vinyl top was a new option. Six types of optional racing

stripes were available.

Standard equipment included new thin-shell bucket seats, front fender turn indicators, rocker panel moldings, special full wheel covers and floor carpeting. *Motor Trend* decided to test a Barracuda 'S' with $400 worth of options to prove that "Barracudas can bite." The car had the following extras: 235-hp V-8 (97.30), automatic transmission ($177.30), heavy-duty suspension ($13.60), disc brakes ($81.95), power brakes ($41.75), power steering ($80.35), AM radio ($57.35), tinted glass ($27.90), tachometer ($48.70), some of which were included in the Barracuda 'S' model's price.

The resulting car was featured in the February 1966 edition of *Motor Trend*. It had an as-tested price of $3,616.50. In the test, it achieved 0 to 60 in 8.9 seconds and did the quarter mile in 16.5 seconds at 84 mph. In production terms, the 1966 Barracuda's popularity leveled off at 38,029 units.

1966 PLYMOUTH SATELLITE "STREET HEMI"

According to Chrysler's historical archives, 844 Hemi-powered Plymouth Satellites were built in 1966. Hardtops accounted for 817 of these, including 503 with four-speeds and 314 with TorqueFlite. Ragtops with Hemis installed totaled 27 units. All had the "Street Hemi" engine. Although similar to a race Hemi, this 426-cid engine used a dual four-barrel aluminum intake, milder valve-train specs, different 10.25:1 pistons and a big single air cleaner. A pair of tubes were added to the right-hand exhaust manifold to handle heat riser functions. Chrysler rated the engine for 425 hp at 5,000 rpm and 490 ft. lbs. of torque at 4,000 rpm.

Like other Plymouth Belvederes, the Satellite featured a major restyling for 1966, highlighted by a slab-sided body with crisper fenders and mild body side sculpturing. Cantilevered rooflines continued on hardtops, with the pillars slightly widened. The windshield was larger and flatter. Up front, parking lamps changed from rectangles in the bumper to circles in the grille. Satellites had bucket seats, consoles, full wheel covers and vinyl trim. Prices began at $2,695 for the hardtop with a 273-cid V-8 and $2,910 for the similarly powered ragtop. The Hemi package was about $1,105 extra.

Early in the season, the biggest engine for Satellites was the 383-cid big-block V-8 with 325 hp. Use of a new 440-cid 365-hp V-8 was limited to Plymouth Furys. Dodges got the Hemi first, a few months into the season. Then, Plymouth released it.

Included in the engine package were heavy-duty suspension, larger drum brakes, wide wheels and 7.75 x 14 Goodyear high-speed tires. Three-on-the-tree couldn't handle the Hemi's torque, so a four-speed or TorqueFlite transmission had to be added, the latter including a transmission fluid cooler. The standard 3.23:1 axle was suitable for the TorqueFlite Hemis, while those with stick shift needed a Dana 60 truck-type axle with identical gear ratio. A Sure-Grip differential was extra. To announce the Hemi, HP2 badges were placed on the front fenders.

Hemi Satellites were good for 7.4-second 0-to-60 runs and 14.5 second ETs. Eight wins by Richard Petty announced the engine's induction into NASCAR circles. USAC saw the Hemi-powered cars take its annual championship. In professional drag racing, A/Stock class Belvederes were going 122 mph in 11.6-second quarter-miles, so the Satellites should be in the same bracket. Production of Hemi Belvederes was a bit lower with 136 coupes, 531 hardtops and 10 convertibles recoded.

1967 PLYMOUTH BARRACUDA

Barracuda's sporty split grille was all new for 1967.

Plymouth's sports compact, the Barracuda, came of age for 1967. It was no longer just a fastback version of the Valiant, but was now its own separate sub-make. It grew to three distinct models including a much smoother looking fastback two-door hardtop, a uniquely styled notchback two-door hardtop and a convertible.

It officially bowed on November 26, 1966, about two months after the rest of the 1967 Plymouth lineup. In so doing it avoided being buried by the hoopla surrounding two other new sports compacts introduced in early fall, the Chevrolet Camaro and Mercury Cougar.

Barracuda basics were still Valiant-related, like a longer 108-inch wheelbase, but the relationship was far less apparent from the outside package. Curved side glass, mostly its own body panels and unique rooflines, plus a 4.4-inch greater overall length (192.8 inches) all added to the impression of the Barracuda as its own car line.

The fastback (sports) hardtop continued the interior with fold-down rear seats and access to the trunk area. The new notchback hardtop featured a small greenhouse area with a concave rear window. It looked a little like the 1960-'64 Corvair coupes. The notchback did serve as a basis for the convertible, which came out a few weeks later than the hardtops. It featured a glass rear window and power top. A split grille with directional and parking lights inside added to the Barracuda's sporty flair.

Power plants were the same used in the earlier models, with one big exception—for the first time you could get a production B-block V-8 in a Barracuda. This was the 383-cid engine, which came with a Carter four-barrel carburetor and a 10:1 compression ratio. It was advertised at 280 hp.

One way to assure that all the right stuff showed up when you ordered your Barracuda was to order the Formula S package. Just as on the earlier Barracudas, it included the Commando 273 engine, wide oval 14-inch tires, heavy-duty suspension, anti-sway bar and appropriate S badges. Actually, there were two Formula S options for 1967, the second coming on stream a bit later and including the 383—the only way you were supposed to be able to get it.

Option lists were up to speed with the competition and included a four-speed manual ($179), TorqueFlite automatic ($181-$206) and Sure-Grip differential ($39). You could also get disc front brakes, bucket front seats, console and even stripes. Base prices for V-8-powered Barracudas were competitive with the fastback at $2,270, notchback at $2,530 and convertible at $2,860.

The buying public responded, calling for a production run of 62,534 (30,110 fastbacks, 28,196 notchbacks and 4,228 convertibles). It was the most popular Barracuda model year ever. Only the restyled 1970 models would come close (55,499).

Today, 1967 Barracuda prices reach into five figures in No. 1 condition, with Formula S models commanding a 10 percent premium and 383s a whopping 40 percent.

1967 PLYMOUTH BELVEDERE GTX

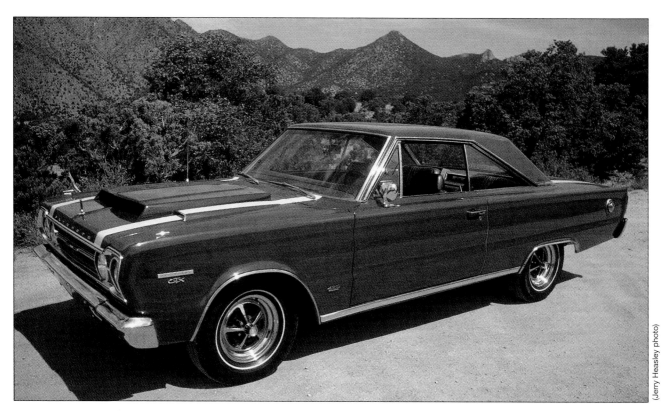

(Jerry Heasley photo)

Plymouth put out about 12,500 Belvedere GTXs in 1967, and only 720 had the Hemi options.

Having a big-inch performance model in your lineup was mandatory if you wanted to market your muscle in the mid-1960s. Pontiac started it with its GTO option for the intermediate Tempest in 1964. One by one the competition followed. One of the last to arrive was the 1967 Plymouth Belvedere GTX.

With its lightweight Super Stocks and its big Wedge and Hemi V-8s, Plymouth built, in limited numbers, cars that were far faster than the GTO, but it was reluctant to do up a package that put all the parts together.

Two vital elements of the Plymouth GTX were the model year 1966 introduction of the Street Hemi and the 440-cid Wedge V-8 in Super Commando form for 1967. Combine them with the Belvedere's 116-inch wheelbase, throw in top-of-the-line bucket seats, fake hood scoops and stripes and the GTX was ready.

Standard for $3,178 in two-door hardtop form and $3,418 for a convertible, you got the 375-hp 440-cid V-8, TorqueFlite automatic, heavy-duty suspension and even a pit-stop gas filler. Spend an extra $564 and you got the Street Hemi fed by a pair of Carter AFB four-barrels and rated at a conservative 425 hp. Magazine tests rated the Super Commando GTX as capable of 0 to 60 mph in 7 seconds or less.

The exact number of GTXs sold during the model year is not known, as their total was included with Satellite models. What is known is that the Hemi-optioned GTXs are rare with only 720 of the approximately 12,500 GTXs built equipped with them. Of those, 312 had four-speed transmissions and 408 were attached to TorqueFlite automatics. Estimates put the number of Hemi convertibles built at only 17.

1968 BARRACUDA "HURST HEMI"

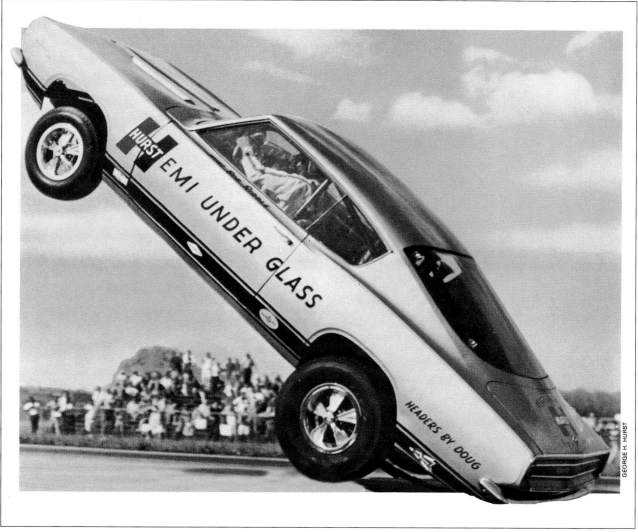

GEORGE H. HURST

Hurst used its 1965 "Hemi Under Glass" Barracuda exhibition drag car to draw attention to the company's racing acumen.

The original 1964 Plymouth Barracuda was one of the first muscle cars to utilize a Hurst shifter as standard equipment on cars with four-speed transmission options. To help promote this product association, in 1965, Hurst Performance Research Co. built the famous "Hemi Under Glass" exhibition drag racer.

Using a modified Chrysler Hemi mounted amidships below the large Barracuda back window, this gold-colored "funny car" could stand on its bumper to reveal the words "Bear of a 'Cuda" written on its modified belly pan. In 1967, the racing car was updated to second-generation Barracuda styling.

Then, for 1968, Chrysler came up with the idea of stuffing the 426-cid 425-hp Street Hemi into Plymouth Barracudas and Dodge Darts. The purpose was to build the ultimate, big-engined, lightweight, production-based muscle car. These cars were made with the help of George Hurst and his company.

Hemi production totals at the Chrysler Historical Archives do not include the 1968 Hemi Barracudas and Hemi Darts, since they were not considered factory-built vehicles. However, in this case, the Hurst association with the cars *increases* their collectibility. Former

employees of Hurst Performance Products estimate that 70 Hemi Barracudas and 80 Hemi Darts were made.

The cars were built by Hurst mainly for professional drag racers, so they did not get a standardized cosmetics package. After all, the pros were only going to decorate them in their own colors and graphics. Hurst did replace some stock steel body panels with fiberglass replicas. The interiors were gutted and fitted with lightweight truck bucket seats.

Hurst added headers to the cars. Of course, the company's own shifter kits went in, too. Hefty S/S axles were used, with various gear ratios available. All of the cars had either modified TorqueFlite transmissions or four-speed manual gearboxes.

When delivered, the cars were finished in primer and wore standard E70-14 street tires. It was up to the individual buyers to paint and decorate the cars and bolt on racing slicks.

With about 500 actual hp and low 3,400-lb. weights, the cars could fly down a drag strip. One, piloted by Judy Lilly, was christened "Miss Mighty MoPar" and campaigned in NHRA and SS/AA class racing.

1968 PLYMOUTH BELVEDERE GTX

(Jerry Heasley photo)

The 1968 Plymouth Belvedere GTX proved to be an under-appreciated muscle car.

Plymouth's intermediate-size performance model — the Belvedere GTX — should have been one of the more popular muscle machines in its market segment as the 1960s waned, but that just didn't turn out to be the case. Instead, the potent high-performance model was forced to play second fiddle in the Plymouth lineup to the Spartan-looking, lower-priced and more imaginative Road Runner.

The Belvedere GTX never wavered from its mission of being a high-content muscle car with a nice assortment of big-block power plant offerings. However, since it was only a year old when the redesigned 1968 Plymouth models were introduced, it didn't have a loyal following to see it through. It shared the new Belvedere body—including the special high-performance hood—with the Road Runner.

For 1968, the Super Commando 440-cid V-8 again came as standard equipment in the GTX. It had a 4.32 x 3.75-inch bore and stroke, hydraulic valve lifters, a 10.1:1 compression ratio and a single Carter AFB four-barrel carburetor (model No. 4326S). This engine developed 375 hp at 4600 rpm. *Car Life* road tested a 440-powered GTX with automatic transmission and reported a 0-to-60 time of 6.8 seconds. It did the quarter mile in 14.6 seconds with a 96-mph terminal speed. Top speed was about 121 mph.

Base prices were $3,329 for the hardtop and $3,590 for the soft top. Production figures were kept and with 17,914 hardtops and 2,026 ragtops built, the numbers were surely higher than those for the 1967 models. However, these figures paled by comparison to the 44,599 Road Runners that came off the assembly line.

For $605 extra, you could get the 426-cid Street Hemi stuffed into your GTX. Hemi-equipped GTXs continued to be rare, with only 410 hardtops and about 36 convertibles believed to have been made.

1968 PLYMOUTH ROAD RUNNER

Plymouth may have been about the last nameplate to bring out an intermediate muscle car model when it introduced the 1967 Belvedere GTX. However, it was the first automaker to exploit the potential market for a low-buck performance car when it introduced the 1968 Road Runner.

The idea of putting a powerful engine in the cheapest, lightest model available was not a new one and wise users of the option list had been ordering "Q-Ships" for years. What Plymouth did with the Road Runner was to do all the work for the customer. The company gave the car a low price that youthful buyers could more easily afford and wrapped it all up in a gimmicky fashion—using a popular Warner Bros. cartoon character as the car's namesake.

Using Road Runner identification and a cheap horn that emulated the cartoon bird's well-known "beep-beep" got attention in the marketplace. The lowest-priced Belvedere two-door sedan was the basis for the Road Runner and came "complete" with such standard fleet items as plain bench seat and rubber floor mats.

The first Road Runner's standard engine was a 335-hp version of the 383-cid Chrysler B-block. It was rated at only 5 hp more than the regular 383, but it probably had more power than that due to the use of cylinder heads, intake and exhaust manifolds and a camshaft from the Chrysler 440-cid V-8. Added to the mechanical goodies were a standard four-speed manual transmission, a heavy-duty suspension, 11-inch drum brakes and Red Stripe tires.

(Jerry Heasley photo)

The Road Runner was the quintessential muscle car for the masses when it came out in 1968, thanks to its affordable price.

The kicker for the Road Runner was its low $2,870 price. If you wanted some interior niceties such as carpeting and bright trim, you had to invest $79.20 for the Road Runner Decor Group. If you wanted to kick the toy image, you had to ante up $714.30 extra for the 426-cid 425-hp Street Hemi.

A two-door hardtop was added midyear and its 15,359 production run was added to the coupe's 29,240 tally to make the Road Runner a winner. Of those, 1,019 were Hemi-powered.

1969 PLYMOUTH BELVEDERE GTX

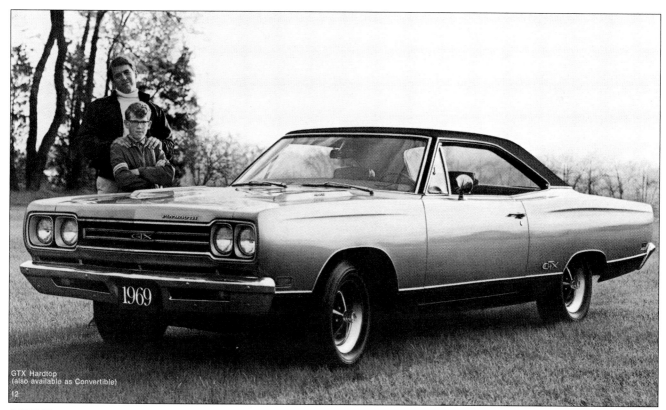

GTX Hardtop
(also available as Convertible)

12

A 1969 Plymouth Belvedere GTX with a 375-hp 440 could clock a 13.7-second quarter mile.

"No matter how you may try to camouflage it by loading a car with power and comfort options, when you get down to the nitty gritty of supercar existence, an inescapable, basic fact always remains on the surface," said *Motor Trend's* Bill Sanders in January 1969. "One primary purpose of a super car is to get from here to there, from this light to the next, in the shortest elapsed time. To this end, the Plymouth GTX is the flat out, best qualifier of all."

Sander's magazine test car had the 440-cid base engine, rather than the Street Hemi. It produced the same 375 hp at 4600 rpm and 480 ft. lbs. of torque at 3200 rpm that it had in 1968. The test car was also equipped with automatic transmission and a 4.10:1 rear axle. Sanders managed to achieve 0 to 60 mph in 5.8 seconds. The car did the quarter mile in a mere 13.7 seconds at 102.8 mph.

The GTX two-door hardtop Model RS23 had a dealer cost of $2,710.82 and retailed for $3,329. The convertible, Model RS27, cost dealers $2,924.89 and sold for $3,590. Sanders listed the base price of his test car as $3,433, which included federal excise tax.

Standard GTX equipment included a heavy-duty rear suspension, heavy-duty front torsion bars, anti-sway bars, the 440-cid Super Commando V-8, foam padded bucket seats, simulated woodgrain trim on the doors and the instrument panel, carpeting, F70 x 14 red streak or white streak tires, body accent stripes, heavy-duty

brakes, a 70-amp battery, roof drip-rail moldings, firm-ride shocks, custom sill moldings, front foam cushions, arm rests with ash trays and dual horns.

Sander's test car also included a Super Performance axle ($271.50), a center console ($54.45), TorqueFlite transmission ($40.40 on the GT), three-speed windshield wipers ($5.40), undercoating ($16.60), front and rear bumper guards ($32), a tachometer ($50.19), the famous "Air Grabber" hood scoop ($55.30), an AM solid-state radio ($63.35), a rear seat speaker ($14.45), power steering ($97.69), performance hood paint ($18.05), red streak fiberglass-belted tires ($34.10) and a destination charge of $149. If he had ordered the Street Hemi it would have cost $604.75 extra.

For 1969, Plymouth made only 17,914 GTX hardtops and just 1,026 GTX convertibles.

1969 PLYMOUTH ROAD RUNNER

(Jerry Heasley photo)

The Road Runner maintained a no-nonsense look in 1969, but it did receive a few minor cosmetic changes.

New grilles and new rear-end styling characterized the 1969 Plymouth Road Runner models, which were now available in three different body styles. The original coupe version Model RM21 carried at $2,945 window sticker and weighed the least at 3,435 lbs. It attracted 33,743 buyers. The hardtop Model RM23 raced to the head of the pack with 48,549 assemblies. It cost a bit more at $3,083 and weighed 15 additional lbs., but customers liked its styling. The $3,313 convertible, Model RM27, was a rarity with only 2,128 of the 3,790-lbs. ragtops being turned out.

Standard features of the 1969 Road Runner included a heavy-duty suspension, heavy-duty brakes, heavy-duty shocks, a dash nameplate, a deck lid nameplate, door nameplates, top-opening hood scoops, chrome engine parts, an un-silenced air cleaner, Hemi orange paint treatment, red- or white-streak tires, a four-speed manual transmission with a Hurst gear shifter, a fake walnut shift knob, back-up lights and a deluxe steering wheel.

The standard engine for the Road Runner was the 383-cid V-8, which had a 4.250 x 3.375-inch bore and stroke. With a Carter AVS four-barrel carburetor and 10.0:1 compression ratio, the Road Runner engine produced 335 hp at 4600 rpm. Engine options included the 440-cid V-8 or the 426-cid Street Hemi.

Car and Driver magazine included a Hemi Road Runner coupe in its comparison test of six "econo-racers" in January 1969. It showed the list price of the car to be $4,362.05 as tested. That included the Hemi for $813.45, an automatic transmission for $39.50 over the base four-speed, a performance axle package ($64.40 with automatic), the décor package for $81.50, a remote-control mirror for $10.45, power steering for $100, power disc brakes for $91.65, an AM radio for $61.55, a rear speaker for $14/05, a tachometer for $50.15, undercoating for $16.60 and F70 x 15 belted tires for $90.95.

The Street Hemi also had a 4.25 x 3.75-inch bore and stroke,

but the Hemi heads, a 10.25:1 compression ratio and dual four-barrel Carter carburetors helped boost its output up to 425 hp at 5000 rpm and 490 ft. lbs. at 4000 rpm.

The Hemi Road Runner coupe was on a 116-inch wheelbase and had a curb weight of 3,938 lbs. It had a 3.54:1 rear axle. *Car and Driver* recorded 0 to 60 mph in 5.1 seconds. The quarter mile was covered in 13.54 seconds with a trap speed of 105.14 mph. It had an estimated top speed of 142 mph.

"To say that the Road Runner scored heavily in the performance part of the test is Anglo Saxon understatement in the best tradition," said the writer. "It was the quickest in acceleration, stopped in the shortest distance and ranked second in handling. That's a pretty tough record."

The 1969 Plymouth Road Runner came with a standard 383-cid V-8.

1970 PLYMOUTH AAR 'CUDA

(Jerry Heasley photo)

Bold graphics gave the 1970 Plymouth AAR 'Cuda a distinctive look.

Having a player in the Sports Car Club of America (SCCA) Trans-American sedan racing series was a must for the Detroit purveyors of pony cars in 1970. There were factory-backed efforts from American Motors, Ford, Dodge and Plymouth. Chevrolet and Pontiac had back-door programs.

Open Plymouth and Dodge participation was new. It came together because there were new Plymouth Barracuda and Dodge Challenger designs and because rules changed so that the 5.0-liter engines used in the racing cars didn't have to be exactly the same size as the production engines they were derived from.

This meant that Chrysler's potent 340-cid small-block could be de-stroked to 303.8 inches to meet the limit. Plymouth could legalize its Trans-Am racing equipment by building 1,900 or more special models. The result was the 1970 AAR 'Cuda.

The new option package for the Barracuda two-door hardtop was named after Dan Gurney's All-American Racers (AAR) team. Gurney was signed for 1970 after driving the previous few seasons for Mercury. He would enter a 'Cuda in the Trans-Am series with Swede Savage as the driver.

Powering the AAR 'Cuda was a 340-cid small-block V-8 with high-performance heads and thicker webbing in the block to allow the racing team to use four-bolt mains. Even though only a single four-barrel carb was allowed in racing, that didn't prevent triple two-barrel Holleys from being used in the production model. A fiberglass, cold-air-induction hood let the carburetors breathe fresh air.

Other parts of the package for Plymouth's E-body model were a rear spoiler, front and rear sway bars, exhaust that exited in front of the rear tires, rally wheels with E40 x 15 tires up front and large G60 tires in the back. Transmission choices included the A-833 four-speed manual gearbox with a Hurst gear shifter or the Chrysler 727 TorqueFlite automatic. AAR decals and striping identified the package.

Compared to other specialized offerings of the time, the AAR 'Cuda was plentiful, with 2,724 being built.

Despite Gurney's efforts, Barracuda did not win a Trans-Am race in 1970. Factory support for racing was quickly eroding at the time and there was no 1971 AAR 'Cuda or racing team.

1970 PLYMOUTH BELVEDERE GTX

A redesigned grille, a new hood and restyled front fenders characterized Plymouth's intermediate models in 1970. The Belvedere GTX featured much of the same standard equipment as the Road Runner, including heavy-duty suspension, heavy-duty brakes, a dual exhaust system, a high-performance hood with the "air grabber" hood scoop, front and rear bumper guards, a 150-mph speedometer, F70-14 red or white stripe tires, three-speed wipers, heavy-duty

shock absorbers and roof and door moldings. In addition, it also had the 440-cid Super Commando V-8, a deluxe vinyl interior, foam seat padding on its new-for-1970 high-back front bucket seats and rear bench seat, body-side reflective tape stripes, side markers, dual (non-beep-beep) horns, a 70-amp battery and bright exhaust trumpets.

The Belvedere GTX lineup lost its convertible for 1970.

(Jerry Heasley photo)

The hardtop was the only 1970 Plymouth Belvedere GTX model available.

The only body style left was the hardtop, which Chrysler sold to Plymouth dealers for $2,703.36. They then retailed the car to the public at around $3,535. The 1970 model wound up drawing only 7,748 orders, with a mere 72 of the cars getting Street Hemi V-8s installed at a cost of $710.60. In addition, Belvedere GTX buyers could also get the 440-cid six-pack option (with three two-barrel carburetors) for just $119.05 above the price of the base 440. "A GTX six-barrel is no slouch in the performance department either," said *Motor Trend* in its fall 1969 review of the hot '70s models.

The TorqueFlite automatic transmission was standard in the 1970 Belvedere GTX. A four-speed manual transmission was also available at no extra cost. The Trak Pak option was $142.85 extra and the Super Trak Pak was $235.65 extra. The ingredients of these packages are described in the 1970 Road Runner section of this book. Also available was a "super performance axle package" with a 9 3/4-inch Dana rear axle, a 4.10:1 axle ratio and power front disc brakes.

1970 PLYMOUTH 'CUDA 340

Barracuda entered its third and final generation for the 1970 model year, when the distance between the front wheels was upped to comfortably swallow everything from a slant-six to the Hemi. The fastback coupe was axed, but attractive two-door hardtop and convertible versions were left.

All 'Cudas sat on a 108-inch wheelbase and had an overall length of 186.7 inches. The width was 74.9 inches and height was 5.9 inches. At 59.7 inches the front track was a bit narrower than the 60.7-inch rear track.

Attracting less media attention than the big-block 'Cudas was the 'Cuda 340, which continued as an option for the 'Cuda (on which a 383-cid V-8 was standard). The 340-cid V-8, with its 4.04 x 3.31-inch bore and stroke, was a nice alternative, especially for youthful muscle car buyers who couldn't quite hack the price of a 440 or a Hemi. It ran with a 10.5:1 compression ratio and a single

four-barrel carburetor and that was enough to generate 275 hp at 5000 rpm and 340 ft. lbs. of torque at 3200 rpm.

Motor Trend ran a comparison test between 'Cudas with all three engines. In the 0 to 60-mph category, the 340-powered version needed 6.4 seconds compared to the 440's 5.9 seconds and the Hemis 5.8 seconds. Its quarter-mile performance was 14.5 seconds (96 mph) compared to 14.4 seconds and 100 mph for the 440 version and 14 seconds and 102 mph for the Hemi 'Cuda. The 440-powered test car had a four-speed manual transmission, while the 'Cuda 340 and the Hemi 'Cuda had automatics.

For all-around use, the 'Cuda 340 was really a nicely balanced package. After driving all three cars, *Motor Trend's* A.B. Shuman admitted to his readers, "From the foregoing you may have detected a 'slight' preference for the 340 'Cuda. This was intentional. It was the best of the lot!"

1970 PLYMOUTH DUSTER 340

Plymouth certainly didn't anticipate the public's response to Plymouth's compact Valiant lineup for 1970. Led by the redesigned Duster coupe, Valiant production increased from 107,218 in 1969 to 268,002 in 1970. Of that number, 192,375 were regular Duster coupes and 24,817 were examples of an entry-level car for Plymouth's "Rapid Transit System"—the Duster 340.

The Duster replaced the rather staid two-door sedan in the Valiant lineup. Styling was characterized by a contemporary look, with bulging lines from the firewall back. The same 108-inch wheelbase unitized chassis was used for both models.

Doing for compact cars what the Road Runner did for mid-sized cars, the Duster 340 was the low-priced performance machine.

It came standard with a 340-cid 275-hp V-8 that had been used in Plymouths since 1968. More goodies included a floor-mounted three-speed manual shift, heavy-duty suspension, E70 x 14 belted tires, styled steel wheels, striping and the obligatory cartoon character—in this case a friendly dust devil.

The Duster 340's bottom-line base price was only $2,547. Bucket seats and other dress-up items were optional, ala Road Runner. *Car Life* tested an automatic-equipped Duster 340 and found that it could go from 0 to 60 mph in only 6.2 seconds and that it was a great buy. The buying public felt the same, which made the Duster a success in general and the 340 version a particular hit.

1970 PLYMOUTH HEMI 'CUDA

(Jerry Heasley photo)

It was easy to go fast in a 1970 Plymouth Hemi 'Cuda, but it wasn't easy to insure them.

When the redesigned 1970 Plymouth Barracuda came to the muscle-car market, there would be no excuses for not putting a big engine under its wide hood. Design engineers had widened the car by more than 5 inches and increased both the front and rear tracks by 3 inches. As a result, any Chrysler Corporation engine would fit in the engine bay, right up to the street version of the "King Kong" racing power plant—the 426-cid Hemi.

The Hemi was an $871.45 option for the muscular 'Cuda hardtop (which was base priced at $3,164) and the convertible (which carried a $3,433 window sticker). The 'Cuda came standard with another big-block mill—the 383-cid 355-hp V-8. No wonder Chrysler listed the 'Cuda as a member of its "Rapid Transit System."

Street Hemis got new hydraulic lifters for 1970, but a new cam profile gave the Mopar engineers no reason to alter the 425 advertised hp rating. The Hemi's two Carter AFB four-barrel carburetors breathed through the Air Grabber "shaker" hood scoop.

In order to get the horses to the pavement, Hemi-powered 'Cudas and other big-engined Barracudas relied on heavy-duty drive-line parts. There was a choice of the New Process A-833 four-speed manual gearbox or the 727 TorqueFlite automatic. A Dana 9-3/4-inch differential was kept in place by a leaf-spring rear suspension with six leafs on the right and five leafs plus two half-leafs on the left. Fifteen-inch-diameter, 7-inch-wide wheels held F60 x 15 tires

In short, power was the Hemi 'Cuda's long suit. Not long was the list of buyers. Insurance companies did not look kindly on Hemi 'Cudas and did not care if they could do 0 to 60 mph in 5.8 seconds and run down the quarter mile in 14.1 seconds at 103.2 mph. By the time the 1970 run came to an end, only 652 hardtops had left the factory with Hemi power and 284 of them had four-speed transmissions. Far more spectacular in terms of rarity was the convertible with only 14 being made, five with a manual gearbox.

1970 PLYMOUTH ROAD RUNNER

The 1970 Plymouth Road Runner two-door hardtop with a 383-cid V-8 sold new for just over $3,000.

For 1970, the third year Plymouth's Spartan muscle car utilized the same basic Belvedere body. Standard Road Runner equipment was listed in *Car Fax* as follows: Three-speed manual transmission with floor shift; front armrests, rear armrests, cigar lighter, glove box light, "beep-beep" horn, high-performance hood, front bumper guards, 150-mph speedometer, Road Runner emblems, 383-cid Road Runner V-8, F70-14 white-line tires on wide safety rim wheels, three-speed windshield wipers, roof-drip rail and upper door-frame moldings and heavy-duty shock absorbers.

There were again three Road Runner models. The dealer price

on the coupe was only $2,210.28 and it carried a $2,896 suggested retail price. The two-door hardtop was dealer priced at $2,316.23 and sold for $3,034. The convertible cost the dealer $2,513 and retailed for $3,298 including federal excise tax.

To a degree, it seemed as if Plymouth was gradually losing sight of the Road Runner's original concept of being a "real" muscle car with a low price tag. Replacing the four-speed manual transmission with a three-speed gearbox was one sign of this. Another was the use of hydraulic valve lifters on the Hemi, which cost $841.05 extra. You could also get the 440-cid six-pack engine for $249.55 extra, as long as you could live without air conditioning and

were willing to add either the four-speed or an automatic transmission.

Another option for Road Runner owners with drag racing in mind was the A33 Super Trak Pak package, which included a heavy-duty 9 3/4-inch Dana Sure-Grip 3.55:1 rear axle, a dual breaker-point distributor, a woodgrained gear shift knob and recess warning light and the heavy-duty four-speed manual gearbox with Hurst shifter. It cost $142.85 extra. Or they could order the Super Trak Pak version, which included all of the same extras with a 4.10:1 ratio Dana rear axle and power front disc brakes for $235.65.

1970 PLYMOUTH ROAD RUNNER SUPERBIRD

The Superbird was a potent force on the racetrack in the early 1970s and had a rolling billboard for a spoiler.

The final volley in the battle of muscle-car aerodynamics was the 1970 Plymouth Road Runner Superbird. With a 7.0-liter engine-displacement limit, competing auto makers armed themselves with more wind-cheating body designs, culminating with the "winged warriors" from Chrysler—the 1969 Dodge Charger Daytona and 1970 Plymouth Road Runner Superbird. Designed for use on the NASCAR Grand National superspeedway oval tracks, these Mopars featured a long, peaked nose and a high airfoil on struts above the rear deck.

Though similar in concept, the 1970 Plymouth Superbird and 1969 Dodge Daytona shared little in the way of specialized parts. The noses, airfoil and the basic sheet metal of the Charger and Road Runner two-door hardtops differed. The nose added 19 inches of length.

Rules in 1969 called for only 500 copies of each model to be made to make it "legal" for racing. For 1970, manufacturers had to build one for each dealer. Experts believe that, when it was all over, a total of 1,971 Superbirds were built.

The most popular engine was the 440-cid Super Commando V-

8 with a single four-barrel carburetor. It was rated at 375 hp and priced at $4,298. A total of 1,120 Superbirds came this way. Another 716 cars were equipped with the 440-cid 390-hp V-8 with three two-barrel carburetors. That leaves just 135 cars that were equipped with the 426-cid, 425-hp, twin four-barrel Street Hemi (77 with automatic transmission and 58 with four-speed manual transmission). The racing cars used the Hemi racing engine.

Speaking of racing, the Superbird was big enough bait to lure Richard Petty back to racing Plymouths after his one-year hiatus with Ford. Petty Engineering hired Pete Hamilton to run a second Superbird at selected events in 1970 and he promptly won the big one—the Daytona 500.

Plymouth intermediates were redesigned for 1971 and, with the performance market shrinking and budgets for racing being shifted to meeting Federal safety and emission standards, there was no follow-up to the Superbird. That made the limited-edition Mopar winged machines among the first muscle cars to start climbing in collector value.

1971 PLYMOUTH BELVEDERE GTX

The 1971 Plymouth Belvedere 440-cid V-8 produced 375 hp.

(Jerry Heasley photo)

The 1971 Plymouth Hemi Belvedere had plenty of muscle-car features inside and out, but only 30 were built.

(Jerry Heasley photo)

With annual sales of the upscale high-performance model running much below expectations for several years, many people were surprised when the Belvedere-based, mid-sized GTX showed up for one more appearance in the 1971 Plymouth lineup. This year it once again came only as the Model RS23 two-door hardtop. At the beginning of the model year it had a $3,707 window sticker and weighed 3,675 lbs. By May, the price was increased to $3,733.

As usual, the GTX's standard equipment assortment picked up where the Road Runner's list left off. Additional items included with the 1971 GTX were the 440-cid 375-hp Super Commando V-8, the TorqueFlite automatic transmission, high-back front bucket seats, a low-restriction dual exhaust system with chrome exhaust trumpets, dual horns; vinyl interior trims (cloth-and-vinyl interiors were a no-cost option), a 70-amp 12-volt battery, custom body sill moldings, wheel opening moldings, drip rail moldings, an extra-heavy-duty

suspension (front and rear) and G70 x 14 black sidewall tires with raised white letters.

A bench seat with cloth-and-vinyl trim and a center armrest was a no-charge option and white sidewall tires could be substituted in place of the white-lettered style at no extra cost. GTX buyers could also opt for a floor-mounted three-speed manual gearbox in place of the TorqueFlite automatic. The Hemi engine was still available for $746.50.

The Air Grabber hood was standard with the Hemi and the four-speed manual gearbox was a no-charge item on Hemi GTXs. This was the last year for the Street Hemi and Chrysler built only 356 of the engines for *all* of its lines. In the GTX series, only 30 cars were Hemis and of those, a mere 11 units had the four-speed manual transmission.

227

1971 'CUDA 340

"The 'Cuda 340 is the kind of car a person could like," said Steve Kelly in the January 1971 issue of *Hot Rod* magazine. "It runs low-14 without breathing hard, takes corners without yelling and is big enough to be seen." Kelly admitted that the 'Cuda 340 was not the ultimate Trans-Am racer, but he also pointed out that it could beat a stock Camaro Z/28 or Mustang Boss 302 through the quarter mile.

Early in model year 1971, the 'Cuda sport coupe cost Plymouth dealers $2,508.57 and retailed for $3,134. The ragtop had a $2,716.34 dealer cost and a $3,391 window sticker. In May, the dealer costs were increased to $2,525.67 and $2,733.44 respectively, and the window stickers rose to $3,155 for the hardtop and $3,412 for the ragtop. That compared to $253.20 extra for a 440 engine or $883.90 for the Hemi.

Standard equipment on the 'Cuda included all Barracuda features plus a performance hood, chrome wheel lip and body-sill moldings, a color-keyed grille, a black-out-style rear deck panel, a heavy-duty suspension front and rear, heavy-duty brakes, 'Cuda ornamentation and whitewall tires as a no-cost option. The 383-cid V-8 was again standard and the 340-cid four-barrel V-8 was a $44.35 option.

Production of 'Cudas in general was very low this year. Plymouth made only 6,228 hardtops and 374 convertibles. It is known that a total of 153 cars had Hemis. Although we have never seen production breakouts for 340s, 383s and 440s, with so many options available, the number made of each is probably fairly low and since the 383-cid V-8 was bigger and less expensive, it's likely that it drew the bulk of orders.

Hot Rod managed to turn in a best run of 14.18 seconds for the quarter mile (100.33 mph) with its 1971 'Cuda 340 after emptying the trunk and removing the air cleaner element. In addition, it also proved to be a superior road car.

1971 PLYMOUTH HEMI 'CUDA

(Jerry Heasley photo)

This 1971 Plymouth Hemi 'Cuda convertible was one of only seven built.

Sox & Martin and PeeWee Wallace were burning up the drag strips in Barracudas back in 1971 and also helping to generate interest in Plymouth's "fish car." A lot of that interest went to non-Hemi-powered cars, however, as the $884 Hemi option was ordered for just 108 hardtops (60 with four-speed manual transmissions) and a mere seven convertibles. Two of the ragtops had four-speeds.

Seven other engines were offered for 1971 Barracudas and a number of them fit into the muscle car category. The three smallest engines did not fill the bill. They included the 198-cid 125-hp slant six, the 225-cid 145-hp slant six and the 318-cid 230-hp V-8.

The 340-cid V-8 with a four-barrel carburetor was a little hotter, generating 275 hp and 340 ft. lbs. of torque at 3200 rpm. Then came the 383-cid big-block V-8, which was offered in two-barrel and four-barrel versions. The former was good for 275 hp and 375 ft. lbs. of torque at 2800 rpm and the latter just hit the 300-hp bracket and pumped up 410 ft. lbs. of power at 3400 rpm.

That left two V-8s for the true muscle-car crowd. The 440-cid "six pack" version climbed up to 385 hp and 490 ft. lbs. at 3200 rpm. Then came the top-of-the-hill Hemi, which had 426 cubic inches, 425 hp and 490 ft. lbs. of twisting power at 4000 rpm.

(Jerry Heasley photo)

The 1971 Plymouth Hemi 'Cuda came with a heavy-duty suspension, single four-barrel carburetor and either a four-speed manual or automatic transmission.

The 1971 Hemi engine featured a 10.2:1 compression ratio and a single four-barrel carburetor. It came attached to either a four-speed manual or an automatic transmission. The standard rear axle had a 3.23:1 ratio. Sure-Grip-only options included 3.55:1, 3.54:1 and 4.10:1. Plymouth's nifty S15 heavy-duty suspension package was standard with Hemi 'Cudas.

After model year 1971, Plymouth continued to offer Barracudas, but Hemi versions and convertibles didn't make the cut after the season came to its end.

1971 PLYMOUTH ROAD RUNNER

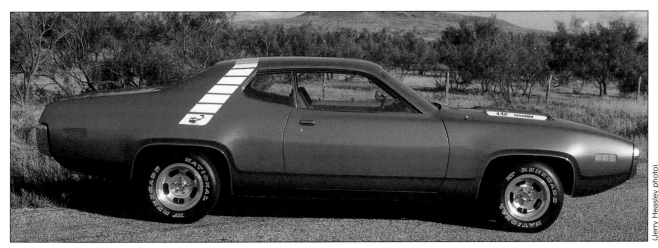

(Jerry Heasley photo)

The 1971 Plymouth Road Runner hardtop had several engine options, including a 425-hp Hemi, or a 385-hp 440-cid V-8.

Performance cars of all sizes continued to be available in large numbers of models and options during the 1971 model year, but low sales numbers put them on the endangered species list.

Returning for 1971 was just the two-door hardtop version of the Plymouth Road Runner. The new grille looked like a big loop around the front of the car. The totally revised sheet metal was shared with the Sebring and Sebring Plus coupes. The sedan and convertible versions did not get translated onto the newly designed Mopar mid-size body shell.

With the more expensive GTX still around, the Road Runner again filled its low-priced muscle car niche with its trick "beep-beep" horn, hot graphics and other solid performance. Standard in the Road Runner model was a 300-hp version of the trusty 383-cid V-8. It had a 4.25 x 3.38-inch bore and stroke and a single four-barrel carburetor and developed 400 foot-pounds of torque at 2400 rpm. Also standard were a floor-mounted three-speed manual transmis-

sion, heavy-duty underpinnings, deep-pile carpeting, rallye cluster instrumentation, a performance hood, a low-restriction dual exhaust system, heavy-duty brakes, F70-14 whitewall tires and all-vinyl bench seats with foam rubber front cushions. The Road Runner listed for $3,120 early in the year. Around May 31, the price increased to $3,147.

For $242 you could add the 440-cid V-8, which had a 4.32 x 3.75-inch bore and stroke. It developed 385 hp at 4700 rpm and 490 ft. lbs. of torque 3200 rpm thanks to its three two-barrel carburetors. The Hemi was an $884 option and still came with an advertised 425 hp. Other interesting options included the Air Grabber pop-up hood scoop for $67 and even a bolt-on rear deck spoiler.

In all, the production of 14,218 was not that bad. As for the rare variety, that was the Hemi option, which went into only 55 Road Runners this year.

1972 PLYMOUTH 'CUDA 340

The popularity of the Plymouth Barracuda was declining in 1972, as insurance companies and government watchdogs ganged up on the muscle car makers. The Barracuda convertible disappeared, as did 383-, 440- and 426 Hemi engine options for 'Cudas. Luckily, the 340-cid V-8 managed to slip by the gatekeepers.

Plymouth dealers had to part with $2,371.77 to floor plan a Model BH23 Barracuda hardtop with the base 318-cid V-8, which had a suggested retail price of $2,808. Its standard equipment included dual head lamps, dual horns, hub caps, an inside day-night mirror, a brake warning light, an outside rear view mirror, bucket seats, a cigar lighter, fuel, temperature and ammeter gauges and 7.35 x 14 black sidewall tires. A dealer cost of $2,495 applied to the year's only other Barracuda, which was the Model BS23 'Cuda hardtop. It retailed at $2,953.

In addition to Barracuda equipment, the 'Cuda included a 340-cid V-8 with a two-barrel carburetor; chrome wheel lip and body sill moldings, a performance hood, a color-keyed grille, a black rear deck panel, heavy-duty suspension and brakes, an electronic ignition system and F70 x 14 white sidewall tires.

A four-barrel version of the 340 was the only engine option. It was available for the special price of $209.70 in the 'Cuda. It cost $276.60 for other Barracudas. The A36 performance axle package could be ordered for all cars with 340-cid four-barrel engines. A four-speed manual gearbox was available only for 340-cid four-barrel cars for $192.85. TorqueFlite was $223.30 extra for cars with that same engine. Other than stripes, styled chrome rims or rallye road wheels and front disc brakes ($68.05), there was little left in the way of high-performance options.

Plymouth records show that 7,858 'Cudas were produced in 1972. All of them were 'Cuda 340s, but the numbers do not indicate how many were 340s with four-barrel carburetors. The 1970 340 with the four-barrel carburetor was rated for 240 net SAE hp. Weighing in at around 3,625 lbs., it carried about 15.1 lbs. per horsepower and could do 0 to 60 mph in 8.5 seconds. The quarter mile took 16.3 seconds. Hey, it was 1972!

1972 PLYMOUTH ROAD RUNNER

(Jerry Heasley photo)

The Plymouth Road Runner still had 400- and 440-cid engine options in 1972.

The 1972 Plymouth Road Runner received minor cosmetic changes. A new radiator grille design made it look a little different than it had in 1971. Although Plymouth offered buyers a choice of 16 hues, the psychedelic colors of the past few years were gone. The standard bench seat came trimmed in blue, green or black vinyl.

As in 1971, the model RM23 Road Runner was offered in only a single body style. The two-door hardtop had a $3,080 list price and a 3,495-lb. curb weight. Production dropped nearly 50 percent to 7,628 cars.

The Road Runner equipment list started with all features that were considered standard on the Plymouth satellite, plus the following additions or substitutions: three-speed manual transmission with floor-mounted gear shifter, heavy-duty suspension, heavy-duty brakes, front and rear sway bars, pile carpets, a performance hood, a low-restriction dual exhaust system, a beep-beep horn, a rallye instrument cluster with a 150-mph speedometer, Road Runner trim and ornamentation, F70-14 white sidewall tires and a 400-cid four-barrel V-8.

The Code E86 440-cid V-8 with a single four-barrel carburetor was optional in the Road Runner for $152.70, but could not be ordered in combination with the three-speed manual transmission. You had to add either a four-speed manual gearbox for $201.85 extra or TorqueFlite automatic for $231.65. Plymouth sales literature did not list the output for this engine, but other sources put it at 280 net hp at 4800 rpm and 375 net foot-pounds of torque at 3200 rpm.

An "Air-Grabber" hood scoop could be substituted for the regular style when buyers were willing to pay $67.40 extra. In this case, a different tape stripe treatment (a $22 option) was used. A 3.23:1 axle was standard and options in that department included a 2.76:1 that was available with the 340- and 400-cid four-barrel V-8s only. Hood locking pins were $16.20 extra and a tachometer cost $51.55. A performance axle package retailed for $93.65 and included a Sure Grip differential, heavy-duty 3.55:1 rear axle, seven-blade torque fan, 26-inch high performance radiator and a fan shroud. It was not available for cars with the 440-cid four-barrel V-8 and four-speed manual transmission. A Track Pack option for $160 extra included all of the same items, but the axle was a Dana model with a 3.54:1 ratio. You could not mix the Track Pack option with air conditioning.

PONTIAC

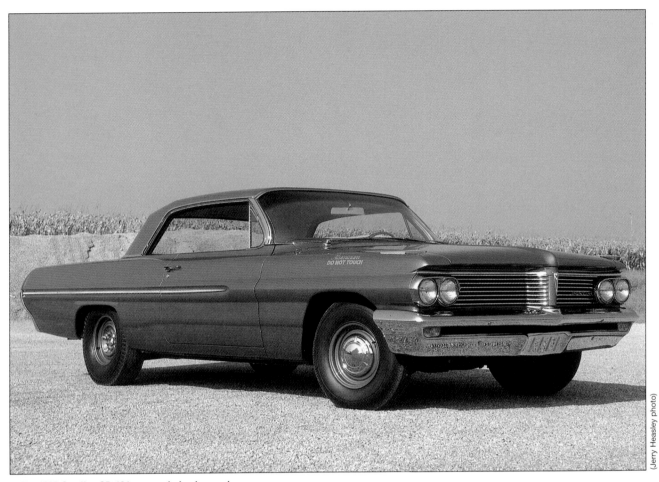

(Jerry Heasley photo)

The 1962 Catalina SD-421 was made for drag racing.

Pontiac was the first automaker to build factory lightweight drag racing cars. Ever since its NASCAR engine options were issued in mid-1957, the company found that racing sold cars. By 1960, the "Poncho" performance image had made Pontiacs the third-most popular American cars for the first time. Chevy's new-for 1962 409-cid engine was a threat, though. Pontiac's best match for a 409-powered Chevy was the 1961 Super-Duty 389 Catalina, which had 368 hp with Tri-Power. Perhaps 25 of these cars were built.

More power and less weight was needed to keep the Pontiacs competitive, so Pontiac Motor Division put its lightest, most powerful car on a diet with a horsepower supplement. Extensive use of aluminum body parts and a special 421-cid 405-hp V-8 created the 3,600-lb. 1962 Super-Duty Catalina.

The new 421-cid V-8 featured four-bolt main bearing caps, forged pistons and twin Carter four-barrel carburetors on a special manifold linked to either a Borg-Warner T-85 three-speed manual transmission or a T-10 four-speed manual gearbox. Actual output from this massive motor was over 500 hp.

Lightweight parts, in addition to the front-end sheet metal like the fenders, hood and grille sections, included an aluminum back bumper and dealer-optional Plexiglas windows. Many of the Super-Duty Catalinas used a functional hood scoop that was actually a Ford truck part that Pontiac purchased in quantity and issued a GM parts number for. An unusual Super-Duty option was a set of cast aluminum Tri-Y exhaust headers.

Pontiac promotional expert and racing personality Jim Wangers found the 1962 Super-Duty Catalina to his liking and turned in performances like a 12.38-second quarter mile at 116.23 mph at Detroit Dragway. In all, 225 of the 421-cid motors were built in 1962. They went into 162 cars and 63 engines were made as replacement motors. Not all cars that got the 421-cid Super-Duty engines had factory lightweight body parts.

1963 PONTIAC SUPER-DUTY CATALINA

For 1963, Pontiac Motor Division took the Super-Duty Catalina 421 program a few steps further. The cylinder heads got higher intake ports and oval-shaped exhaust ports, plus larger valves and higher-compression (12.5:1) cylinder heads. A new McKellar No. 10 solid lifter camshaft was released for use in engines with dual valve springs. A transistorized ignition system was added. A few cars even had 13.0:1 compression ratios. Official ratings for the hottest setup went to 410 hp, but the actual output of the 421-cid Super-Duty engine was somewhere between 540 hp and 550 hp.

The 1963 factory lightweight cars lost about another 100 lbs.

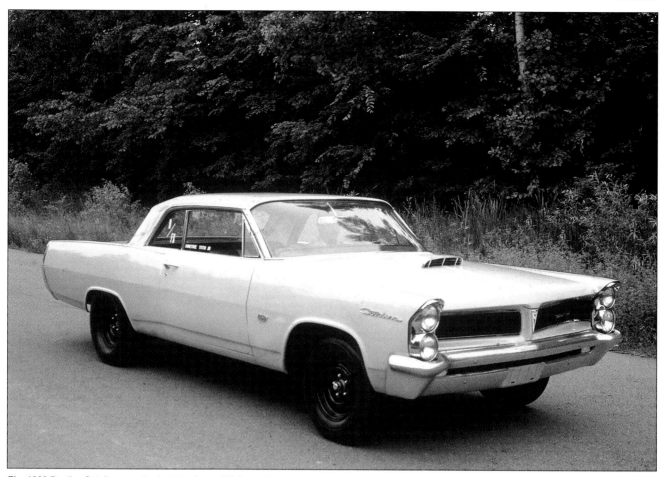

The 1963 Pontiac Catalina was the last to offer a 421 Super-Duty option.

through the use of Plexiglas windows and aluminum trunk lids. Also available were aluminum splash pans, radiator core supports and bumper-attaching parts. In addition, some Catalina frames were "Swiss cheesed" by drilling large holes through them. They weighed in at about 3,325 lbs. in ultimate lightweight form.

Drag racer Arnie "Farmer" Beswick campaigned one of the 15 "Swiss cheese" Catalinas that was built before General Motors management issued an all-out ban on factory racing efforts in January 1963. His "passionate Poncho" racked up a low elapsed time of 11.91 seconds in the quarter mile. With their low production numbers, the "Swiss cheese" cars did not qualify for S/S "super stock" drag racing classes. Instead, they competed in the F/SX "factory experimental" class.

In addition to 77 Super-Duty Catalinas and Grand Prixs (including the "Swiss cheese" units) 11 Super-Duty Tempests were also constructed. The late Mickey Thompson dreamed up this com-

bination for A/FX competition. Another pair of A/FX-class 421-powered Tempests—a coupe and a station wagon—were campaigned by Beswick.

After General Motors issued its anti-racing edict, Jim Wangers and a group of Pontiac Motor Division engineers known as the "Young Turks" turned their energies in a new and very successful direction. Wrapping up a package of performance extras as a LeMans option package, they snuck the first GTO onto the streets in 1964 and the rest is history.

The Super-Duty Catalinas helped Pontiac spin its racing reputation into a winning production vehicle that became a champion in the sales race and lasted for 10 glorious years. Today, a Super-Duty 421 Catalina factory lightweight car should fetch at least $65,000 in the collector's market and a car with a famous racing history that's fully documented could bring $100,000. A Swiss cheese car will go even higher.

1964 PONTIAC CATALINA 2+2

The 1964 Pontiac lineup included seven Catalinas, two Star Chiefs and four Bonnevilles. However, this did not count the various model-options, which were base cars with specific extra-equipment packages. Important new full-size option-created-models introduced that year included the Catalina Ventura and the Catalina 2+2.

A more-rounded Pontiac front end kept the split grille and vertical headlamps of previous years. The new front fender line was squared off flush with the headlamps instead of being cut back. The

tail lamps were boomerang-shaped and vertical.

Catalinas were Pontiac's "small" full-sized cars. The sport coupe and convertible body styles could be ordered with the 2+2 sports option package for the first time. Catalina 2+2s had identification badges below the Catalina name on the front fenders. The option included a 389-cid V-8 that generated 267-hp with Hydra-Matic transmission or 283-hp with a four-speed manual gearbox plus bucket seats, a center console with a vacuum gauge, a special

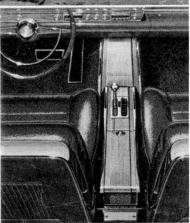

The 1964 Pontiac Catalina 2+2 boasted plenty of luxury, but it was also plenty fast for a full-sized car.

Morrokide interior and fender and rear deck identification badges for $291 extra. Only 7,998 Catalinas were built with the 2+2 option in 1964.

Picture a big GTO and you've got the 1964 Catalina 2+2. This was a model option designed to give the family a real sports car that was big enough for five passengers. Convertibles with the option will go for more than hardtops, but as automotive investments, both body styles will appreciate in price at about the same strong rate.

The 421 HO—a hot street version of the big-block Pontiac V-8—was also available in Catalina 2+2s. It came in three versions with 320-, 350- and 370-hp. The most powerful was equipped with Tri-Power and generated 460 ft. lbs. of torque at 3800 rpm. This was the real muscle-car edition and even though it had a curb weight of 4000 lbs., it carried just 10.8 lbs. per horsepower. It did 0 to 60 mph in only 7.2 seconds and covered the quarter mile in 16.1 seconds.

1964 PONTIAC GTO

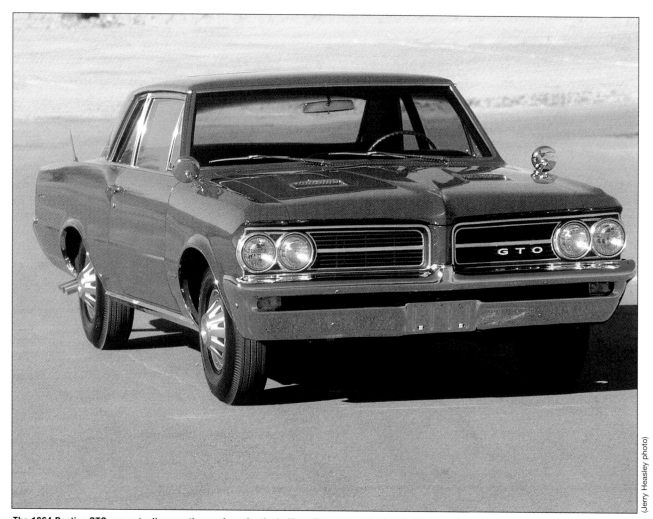

(Jerry Heasley photo)

The 1964 Pontiac GTO was actually an option package for the LeMans Tempest and included a 325-hp, 383-cid engine.

Often regarded by automotive enthusiasts as the first true muscle car, in the sense of being a mid-size car with a big-block V-8 engine, the original GTO was not really a model at all. Due to General Motor's fall 1963 ban on divisional participation in high-performance marketing, Pontiac was prevented from putting an engine with more than 300 cubic inches into an intermediate-size model. That's why Pontiac's "Young Turk" executives and an ad man named Jim Wangers snuck the GTO into existence as an extra-cost package for the Tempest LeMans.

Late in October of 1963 the Grand Turismo Omologato package was announced for the LeMans coupe, hardtop and convertible as a $295 option. GTO equipment included a 325-hp 389-cid V-8 with a special camshaft, special hydraulic lifters and 421-style cylinder heads. It had a single Carter four-barrel carburetor. Also included in the option were specially valved shock absorbers; a seven-blade, 18-inch cooling fan with a cut-off clutch; a dual exhaust system; special 6-inch-wide wheel rims; red-stripe nylon low-profile tires; GTO identification medallions; twin-simulated hood scoops; six GTO emblems; an engine-turned dash insert; bucket seats; special high-rate springs and longer rear stabilizers.

Desirable GTO options included a center console, Hurst-Campbell four-speed manual shift linkage, custom exhaust splitters, no-cost whitewall tires, special wheel covers and a Tri-Power engine option with three two-barrel carburetors. The Tri-Power version of the 389-cid V-8 produced 348 hp at 4900 rpm.

In January 1964, *Motor Trend* magazine found a four-speed GTO convertible capable of doing the quarter mile in 15.8 seconds at 93 mph. The same car's 0-to-60 performance was 7.7 seconds and it had a 115-mph top speed.

By the year's end, the GTO was considered a huge sales success. Pontiac records showed production of 7,384 GTO coupes, 18,422 two-door hardtops and 6,644 convertibles.

1965 PONTIAC CATALINA 2+2

At a bargain base price of around $3,300, the Catalina 2+2 was tough to beat as an all-around driving machine in 1965.

Pontiac originally offered a 2+2 option for its 1964 Catalina sport coupe and convertible. Modest sales of the original bucket-seats-and-badges package were taken in stride by Pontiac Motor Division, which made the 2+2 a "sports option" for 1965. This blossoming of the 2+2 coincided with new styling and a chassis redesign for all full-sized Pontiacs. The result was an extremely attractive automobile with outstanding performance.

The second 2+2 was available again in either two-door hardtop or convertible body form. The 2+2's performance was given a strong starting point thanks to the 1965 Pontiac's bold "ship's prow" front end with its stacked headlights and a fresh variation on the neo-classic divided grille. Providing sufficient identification were front fender louvers and 2+2 emblems on the hood, rear fenders and rear deck.

The Catalina 2+2 base engine was now Pontiac's 421-cid V-8 with a 10.5:1 compression ratio and four-barrel carburetor. Its ratings were 338 hp at 4600 rpm and 459 ft. lbs. of torque at 2800 rpm. The standard transmission was an all-Synchromesh close-ratio four-speed. Pontiac specified a 3.42:1 standard axle ratio for the 2+2. It provided excellent all-around performance as reflected in the car's 0-to-60 time of 7.2 seconds, its 0-to-100 time of 20.5 seconds and a standing-start quarter-mile completed in 15.8 seconds at 88 mph.

If a Catalina 2+2 of this caliber didn't satisfy a buyer's performance desires, Pontiac offered a 421 HO version. *Car Life*, April 1965, quoted one happy 421 HO owner as saying "I will say this is the finest road machine I have ever driven—foreign cars included. It has comfort, performance and, in my opinion, handling that should satisfy anyone but a road course driver." The 421 HO had ratings of 376 hp at 5000 rpm and 461 ft. lbs. of torque at 3600 rpm. Replacing the standard Carter AFB four-barrel carburetor was Pontiac's Tri-Power setup featuring three two-barrel carburetors. The 421 HO also benefited from its quick-bleed hydraulic valve lifters, which made

5400 rpm a realistic rev limit.

It was possible to equip the Catalina 2+2 with a "ride and handling package" consisting of extra-stiff front and rear springs, heavier-duty shock absorbers, a front sway bar, aluminum wheel hubs, quicker-ratio power steering, a tachometer, a gauge package and a close-ratio four-speed manual transmission.

A Catalina 2+2 so equipped (and running a 4.11:1 "Saf-T-Track" limited-slip differential) was tested by *Car Life* in April 1965. Although its 0-to-60 performance of 7.2 seconds and its quarter-mile time of 15.5 seconds (at 95 mph) were impressive, *Car Life* said the car fell short of true 2+2 potential. "Optimum time for the quarter-mile," said *Car Life*, "should fall into the low 14-second category when the car is more suitably tuned and equipped."

At the opposite end of the 2+2 performance spectrum was a Catalina 2+2 prepared by Royal Pontiac of Royal Oak, Michigan. This aftermarket-modified example was tested by *Car and Driver* against a Ferrari 2+2. Equipped with the 421 HO engine, a close-ratio four-speed manual transmission and virtually every performance and handling item in Pontiac's inventory, this superb machine had a top speed of 132 mph. It accelerated from 0 to 60 in 4 seconds and had handling that prompted Walt Hansgen to comment, "the Pontiac 2+2 is no sports car or GT car, but it really is an excellent automobile."

With a list price of $3,287, the Catalina 2+2 was a tremendous performance bargain. Even when equipped in its Royal Oak form, it listed for just over $4,200.

Along with the GTO, the 2+2 further contributed to Pontiac's mid-1960s performance image that has become a modern day legend. Exciting to look at, exciting to drive and, most of all, exciting to own, the Catalina 2+2 was in a class by itself among American automobiles.

1965 PONTIAC GTO

(Jerry Heasley photo)

The 1965 Pontiac GTO convertible had a 389-cid V-8 with a four-barrel carburetor and 335 hp.

For the 1965 model year, the Pontiac GTO was continued as an option package on Tempest LeMans coupes, two-door hardtops and convertibles. This year the car had twin staked headlights and the front fenders had small hoods. While sales of the original 1964 model had been held down by autoworker strikes and an abbreviated model year (after the option's midyear introduction), this year Pontiac was ready to open the flood gates.

Advertising promotions included five huge 26 x 11 1/2-inch full-color photos of the so-called "GeeTO Tiger" in action for only 25 cents and a GeeTO Tiger record for 50 cents. The latter captured the sounds made as a company test driver put a 1965 GTO through its paces at the GM Proving Ground in Milford, Michigan. At the same time, Hurst Performance Products Co., of Glenside, Pennsylvania, sponsored a GTO pace car for *Motor Trend* magazine's Riverside 500 race.

Pontiac held the price of the GTO option at $295.90 for 1965. It included most of the same items it did in 1964, except that a single dummy hood scoop was used in place of two. The 421-style cylinder heads were re-cored to improve the flow of gases.

The standard 389-cid GTO V-8 was a four-barrel-carburetor job with 10.75:1 compression and 335 hp. It was good for 16.1-second quarter mile acceleration runs at 89 mph. Its 0 to 60-mph time was 7.2 seconds. For only $115.78 extra buyers could add Tri-Power carburetion with a special 288-degree camshaft that provided 360 hp from the same block.

The GTO convertible was available for as little as $3,092.90 and 11,311 were made. The coupe had a base price of $2,786.90 and 8,319 assemblies. The sales leader was the two-door hardtop, which could be had for as little as $2,854.90. It was the choice of 55,722 buyers.

1966 PONTIAC CATALINA 2+2

Throughout the late 1960s, Pontiac Motor Division remained America's No. 3 automaker. The company had built its post-1957 image on the youth-market appeal of full-sized performance cars. Under-the-table factory support of drag and stock car racing helped move the big, "brutaful" Pontiacs out of showrooms across the United States. In the mid-1960s, big-car sales started gradually declining and the performance emphasis switched to the midsize cars where the Pontiac GTO ruled the roost.

Pontiac big cars continued to come on two wheelbases (as they had since 1958). From 1965-1969, the smaller stance—which measured 121 inches—was used for Catalinas and all Safari station wagons (regardless of trim line). The larger 124-inch stance was reserved for Star Chiefs, Executives and Bonnevilles.

Sporty luxury, smooth performance and high style were the keynotes of Pontiac's larger cars during this six-year period. Playing off the glory of the Super-Duty high-performance engine series, big-cube, multi-carbureted engines and 300-plus-hp ratings continued to be offered. However, 0-to-60 acceleration suffered due to added weight. The big-boat Bonnevilles were super cars to drive on super-highways, but rarely did much at a drag strip. The opposite was true of the Catalina 2+2, which became Pontiac's full-sized performance car.

One of Pontiac's top full-size collector cars of the era, the Catalina 2+2 has a mystique of its own. It came—on either hardtop coupes or convertibles—as a pre-packaged group of equipment. Individual options could also be added. For 1966, small changes were the rule. An industry-first plastic grille was among them. A two-stage exhaust system with resonators was new. Added options included manually inflatable Super-Lift air shocks, Strato bucket or Strato bench seats and headrests.

The package included all-vinyl bucket seats, louvered fender trim, 2+2 badges, a 421-cid V-8, a three-speed transmission with a Hurst floor shifter, heavy-duty shocks and springs, chrome engine parts, full wheel discs and special fender pin striping.

With a weight in the over-2-ton range, the 2+2 with the Tri-Power 421 HO engine and four-speed gearbox could hit an incredible 95 mph in the quarter mile. Pontiac installed the 2+2 option on 6,383 Catalinas in 1966, but Pontiac's records do not indicate how many cars with the option were sport coupes or convertibles. Of the total, 2,208 cars had manual transmissions and 4,175 had Hydra-Matic drive.

1966 PONTIAC GTO

The 1966 GTO with its standard 389-cid engine could clock a more-than-respectable 15.4 seconds in the quarter mile.

Pontiac's mid-size A-body cars had a new, smoother and rounder appearance for 1966 with wide wheel openings and a recessed split grille. GTOs were in their own series. It was the last year for the Tri-Power three two-barrel-carb option.

A distinctive mesh grille incorporating rectangular parking lamps characterized 1966 GTOs. Features included bucket seats, a single hood scoop, walnut grain dash inserts, specific ornamentation, dual exhausts, heavy-duty suspension and 7.75 x 14 red-line or white-stripe tires.

Coupe prices started at $2,783 and 10,363 were built. Hardtops prices started at $2,847 and 73,798 were built. The $3,082 convertible found 12,798 buyers. Sales included 77,901 cars with the base 335-hp V-8, 18,745 with Tri-Power 360-hp engines and about 30 with 360-hp Ram Air Tri-Power engines. Most GTOs (61,279) had manual gearboxes.

Car Life magazine (May 1966) asked for and almost got a "standard" GTO to test drive. Pontiac supplied a sport coupe with the 389-cid 335-hp four-barrel engine, four-speed manual gearbox, a console, tinted glass, rally gauges, a tachometer, rally wheels, a radio, a remote rearview mirror and air conditioning. It booked out at $3,589, a bit more than the sport coupe's base price of $2,763. The car had a 3.08:1 rear axle and a dual reverse-flow exhaust system with mufflers and resonators.

The 389-cid V-8 had a 4.064 x 3.75-inch bore and stroke. It featured a single Carter four-barrel carburetor, a 10.75:1 compression ratio and hydraulic lifters. Output was rated at 335 hp at 5000 rpm and 431 ft. lbs. of torque at 3200 rpm. *Car Life's* 3,950-lb. GTO carried 11.6 lbs. per horsepower and delivered outstanding performance. It went from 0 to 60 mph in 6.8 seconds and did the quarter mile in 15.4 seconds at 92 mph. Another publication test drove a heavier '66 GTO convertible with the 360-hp Tri-Power V-8 and did not do any better, running 0 to 60 in the same 6.8 seconds and using 15.5 seconds to cover the quarter mile.

1967 PONTIAC CATALINA 2+2

The market for full-sized (read *huge*) performance cars was a small one by the time the 1967 model year rolled around. One by one the full-sized models dropped their specially trimmed, big-engine variants in favor of the plush, quiet motoring experience sought by luxury-oriented buyers. As a result, the Pontiac Catalina 2+2 reverted to option-package status in 1967, the last year it was offered as a U.S. model (a Canadian version was seen as late as 1970 and a different type of 2+2 would surface in the mid- to late-1980s).

Only technically minded people noticed this 1967 change, however, as the 2+2-optioned Catalina gave all the appearance of an integrated package. A 428-cid 360-hp V-8 came as standard equipment, as did a heavy-duty suspension, a floor-mounted three-speed manual transmission and front bucket-type seats. Exterior trim boasted front, side and rear 2+2 badges, plus a row of imitation vents on the front fenders.

A General Motors edict of the 1967 model year dropped all multiple-carburetor setups at Pontiac, but there were some high-performance options. A 428-cid 376-hp V-8 with a four-barrel carburetor cost $119 extra. An additional $226 bought a four-speed manual transmission. You could also add the usual Pontiac goodies like eight-lug wheels for $135 and Rally II steel wheels for $56. Of course, you had to start by checking the 2+2 option box on the order form. That added $410 to the $2,951 two-door hardtop and $389 to the $3,276 convertible.

When the model year was over, only 1,768 2+2-equipped Catalinas were built. No hardtop and convertible production breakout is available. Low sales sealed the fate of the option, ending its four-year run.

Pontiac still offered the Catalina 2+2 as both a convertible and sport coupe in 1967, but low sales figures eventually ended its four-year run.

TWO PLUS TWO

What happens when you take a lean, lithe road machine, stuff in a big, capable 428 cubic inch V-8 that produces 360 horsepower from four barrels, tie it to an all-synchro floor-mounted heavy-duty 3-speed, and add bucket seats, carpeting and special suspension? You'll find out when you drive one—if you stop staring lovingly at it long enough to climb behind the wheel. But beware—once inside you may never want to get out. Options? How about a 376-hp Quadra-Power 428? Or a hood-mounted tach? Or special wheels? The list goes on and on.

1967 PONTIAC FIREBIRD 400

Pontiac's general manager, John DeLorean, gave the Firebird a strong send off. On January 27, 1967 he noted, "The personal sports car field is probably the most rapidly growing in the industry. With the introduction of the Firebird we hope to attract new buyers who want to step up to something extra in styling as well as performance in this segment of the market."

The most potent of the five new Pontiacs, the Firebird 400, boasted a 400-cid engine with a single four-barrel carburetor and 10.75:1 compression ratio. It developed 325 hp at 4800 rpm and 410 ft. lbs. of torque at 3400 rpm. A heavy-duty three-speed transmission was standard with a four-speed or automatic transmission optional. The Firebird 400 model had twin traction bars that helped minimize the negative impact of the single leaf spring rear suspension.

Since the Firebird 400 and GTO engines had identical specs, enthusiasts wondered why the Firebird developed 325 hp compared to the GTO's 350. The answer was a small steel tab positioned on the linkage between the Rochester carburetor's primary and secondary barrels. It limited the second venturi's opening to 90 percent of capacity. This restrictive act, performed in the name of corporate policy prohibiting any GM product to leave the factory with less than 10 lbs. per horsepower, was easily circumvented by removing or bending this innocent-looking, but power-robbing tab.

The Firebird 400's styling left no doubt that it was pure Pontiac. Most apparent was its divided front grille, which successfully continued a Pontiac styling theme dating back to the original Wide-Tracks of 1959. At the rear, horizontally divided tail lamps linked the Firebird to the GTO. The most audacious of the several instrument packages offered for the Firebird was the hood-mounted tachometer. This had been introduced on the GTO and it further reinforced the Firebird's performance image.

Car Life dubbed the Firebird 400 "the enthusiast's choice" and discovered that it could deliver a 0 to 60-mph time of 6.5 seconds with the four-speed all-synchromesh transmission and a 3.36:1 axle. Aside from its engine, the 400 option included (as standard equip-

The 1967 Pontiac Firebird 400 was a new muscle creature with some definite similarities to the GTO.

ment) a chrome air cleaner, chrome rocker covers, a chrome oil cap, a dual exhaust system, red or white E70 x 14 wide-oval tires, a heavy-duty battery, a heavy-duty starter, a de-clutching engine fan and dual hood scoops.

When the Ram Air option was ordered it added direct-air induction, a longer-duration cam with more overlap, a more efficient cast-iron exhaust manifold and different valve springs with flat metal dampers. The carburetor was also recalibrated. Power ratings with the Ram Air option were deliberately understated at 325 hp at 5200 rpm and 410 ft. lbs. of torque at 3600 rpm. Firebirds with this option were truly rare birds, as only 65 400s were so equipped.

The 400 convertible listed for $3,346.53 and the coupe for $3,109.53. With the rare Ram Air option the prices were $3,609.39 and $3,372.36, respectively. Prices for the Firebird 400 included installation of either a four-speed manual or Turbo Hydra-Matic transmission. If a heavy-duty three-speed manual gearbox was selected, the Firebird 400 price differential was $358.09.

1967 PONTIAC GTO

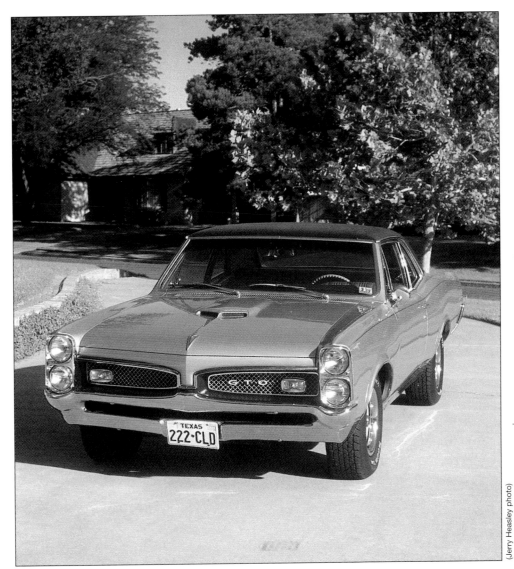

The 1967 Pontiac GTO came with a 400-cid V-8, but plenty of buyers opted for the 400 HO engine that generated 360 hp.

(Jerry Heasley photo)

Minor trim revisions and wide, bright body underscores identified 1967 GTOs. The Model 24207 coupe was the lowest-priced body style, costing dealers $2,174.04 and having a suggested retail price of $2,871. It saw 7,029 assemblies. The Model 24217 hardtop's dealer price was $2,222.64 and it retailed for $2,935. Its production was 65,176 units. A total of 9,517 customers bought the Model 24267 convertible, which wholesaled for $2,399.22 and sold for $3,165 at showroom level. This year, stick-shift cars totaled 39,128 versus 42,594 with Pontiac's new three-speed Turbo Hydra-Matic transmission.

GTOs included all LeMans equipment plus a specific base engine, bucket seats, body paint striping, a walnut-grain-style dash panel, dual exhausts, heavy-duty shocks, heavy-duty springs, heavy-duty stabilizer bars and red line or whitewall tires.

A new 400 cid V-8 replaced the 389-cid. It had a 4.12 x 3.75-inch bore and stroke. A two-barrel "economy" version with an 8.6:1 compression ratio and a Carter AFB carburetor went into 2,967 GTOs. This motor was available at no extra cost only in cars with automatic transmission. It produced 255 hp at 4400 rpm and 397 ft. lbs. of torque at 4400 rpm.

The base GTO engine was put under 64,177 hoods. This version of the 400-cid V-8 had a 10.75:1 compression ratio and a Rochester four-barrel carburetor. It generated 335 hp at 5000 rpm and 441 ft. lbs. of torque at 3400 rpm.

Another option was the 400 HO engine, which was factory installed in 13,827 cars. With manual transmission attachment this engine was $76.89 extra whether or not the car had the RPO 612 air injection exhaust control system. The price was the same for cars with automatic transmission. The HO engine had a 10.75:1 compression ratio. It developed 360 hp at 5100 rpm and 438 ft. lbs. of torque at 3600 rpm.

The Ram Air I engine was installed in 751 cars (only 138 with automatics). This version of the 400-cid V-8 was $263.30 extra with both manual or automatic transmissions and with or without RPO 612. It had the same basic specs as the HO engine, except that the horsepower curve peaked at 5400 rpm and the torque curve peaked at 3800 rpm.

Motor Trend did a comparison test of two Ram Air 400 GTOs. One car had a four-speed manual gearbox and the other had Turbo Hydra-Matic. The manually shifted car was faster from 0 to 60 mph, doing the run in 4.9 seconds versus 5.2 seconds for the car with automatic. With standard tires, the stick-shift GTO did the quarter mile in 14.21 seconds at 102.97 mph, while the second one took 14.09 seconds at 101 mph. Both cars were then fitted with M & H drag tires and tested again. The stick version took 13.09 seconds at 106.5 mph and the THM version took 13.36 seconds at 105 mph.

1968 PONTIAC GTO

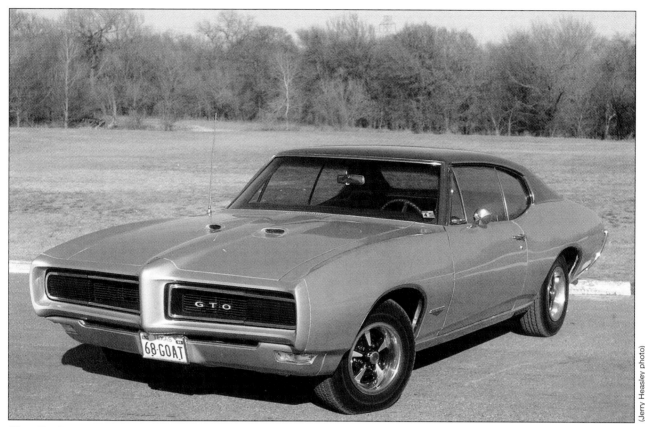

(Jerry Heasley photo)

Motor Trend named the 1968 Pontiac GTO its "Car of the Year."

A long hood and short deck highlighted a more streamlined-looking Tempest line. Two-door models, including all GTOs, were on a shorter 112-inch wheelbase. GTOs added dual exhaust, a three-speed transmission with a Hurst shifter, heavy-duty underpinnings, red line tires, bucket or notchback bench seats, a cigar lighter, carpeting, disappearing windshield wipers and a 400-cid 350-hp V-8. New and highly touted was the unique Endura rubber-clad front bumper (a GTO exclusive). GTO emblems, distinctive taillights and hood scoops rounded out the GTO goodies.

Base prices for the two 1968 models (there was no more "post" coupe) were $3,101 for the two-door hardtop and $3,996 for the convertible. Production of these body styles was 77,704 and 9,980, respectively. Although the Endura bumper was a hit of the year, those who didn't like it could get the standard 1968 Tempest chrome bumper as a delete option on GTOs. Engine options for 1968 were the same as in 1967.

The 1967 GTO production figures included 2,841 hardtops and 432 ragtops with the 400-cid 255-hp two-barrel V-8 and automatic; 39,215 hardtops and 5,091 convertibles with the 400-cid 335-hp four-barrel V-8 and automatic; 25,371 hardtops and 3,116 ragtops with the 400-cid 335-hp four-barrel V-8 and manual transmission; 3,140 hardtops and 461 ragtops with the 360-hp 400 HO V-8 and automatic; 6,197 hardtops and 766 ragtops with the 360-hp 400 HO V-8 and stick shift; 183 hardtops and 22 convertibles with the Ram Air 400 V-8 and automatic; and 757 hardtops and 92 ragtops with the Ram Air 400 V-8 and a stick shift.

Motor Trend named the 1968 GTO as its "Car of the Year" and tested two different versions. The first car had the 400-cid 350-hp V-8, a 3.23:1 rear axle and Turbo Hydra-Matic transmission. It did 0 to 60 mph in 7.3 seconds and the quarter mile in 15.93 seconds at 88.32 mph. The second car was a 360-hp Ram Air model with a four-speed manual gearbox and a 4.33:1 rear axle. It went from 0 to 60 mph in 6.5 seconds and covered the quarter mile in 14.45 seconds at 98.20 mph.

1969 1/2 PONTIAC FIREBIRD TRANS AM

This muscle machine started out as a sports-racing car. It was planned as a sedan racer that could compete in the Sports Car Club of America (SCCA) Trans-American Cup series. The racing version was supposed to be powered by an ultra-high-performance, low-compression 303-cid small-block V-8. The engine was designed specifically to "fit" the displacement limits of the racing class. Only 25 of these engines were ever made. They were sold to competitors

to replace the 400-cid big-block V-8s their cars left the factory with.

The base 400 HO engine (which Pontiac engineers called the Ram Air III V-8) was used in 634 cars (including all eight convertibles). Of these, 114 cars (including four of the convertibles) had a manual gearbox. Fifty-five other cars (all coupes) came with a Ram Air IV engine, which cost $390 extra. Of these, nine cars had Turbo Hydra-Matic transmissions and the other had stick shift.

(Jerry Heasley photo)

All 1969 1/2 Trans Ams were white with blue stripes.

The WS4 Trans Am package for base Firebirds included the Ram Air III engine, a three-speed heavy-duty floor shifter, functional hood scoops, heavy-duty running gear, special interior and exterior trim, a rear deck lid airfoil, full-length body stripes and front fender air extractors. All Trans Ams—except one all-silver prototype fitted with a 303-cid V-8 that underwent extensive testing by *Motor Trend*—were cameo white with blue stripes. Ram Air III cars had 335 hp at 5000 rpm and 430 ft. lbs. of torque at 3400 rpm. Ram Air IVs had 345 hp at 5400 rpm and 430 ft. lbs. at 3700 rpm.

Big-block-powered Trans Ams were found to be better suited for drag racing than road racing. They could do the quarter mile in 14.1 seconds at 101 mph.

Prices for the WS4 option varied by body style and transmission, but were around $725. That put the Trans Am sport coupe's window sticker at around $3,556. Only eight convertibles (base priced around $3,770) were built.

Base Trans Ams came with standard steel disc wheels. Some had their stripes running over the rear spoiler, some below it. A rare option is the Code 293 special custom interior with gold genuine leather seat bolsters.

1969 PONTIAC GTO

For 1969, the GTO received a mild facelift wearing a new grille with a honeycomb texture. At the rear of the car, the taillights moved from in the bumper to just above it. There were two "regular" GTO models. The two-door hardtop listed for $3,080 and 58,126 were made. Convertibles—base priced at $3,553—found 7,328 buyers.

Standard features for 1969 GTOs included a 400-cid 350-hp V-8, dual exhausts, a 3.55:1 ratio rear axle, a heavy-duty clutch, a Power-Flex fan, a "pulse" windshield wiper system, three-speed manual transmission with a floor shifter, sports type springs and shock absorbers, red line wide oval tires, bucket seats or a notchback bench seat with a center arm rest,

carpeting, concealed windshield wipers, panel, courtesy and glove box lamps and a deluxe steering wheel. Buyers who opted for economy could substitute the 400-cid 265-hp regular-fuel V-8, with a two-barrel Rochester carburetor, at no extra cost, but only with Turbo Hydra-Matic transmission (which was $227.04 extra).

GTO production totals for 1969 included 1,246 hardtops and 215 ragtops with the "economy" 400-cid 265-hp two-barrel V-8 and automatic transmission. In addition, 32,744 hardtops and 4,385 convertibles came with the base engine and Turbo-Hydra-Matic transmission, while 22,032 hardtops and

The 1969 Pontiac GTO didn't lack speed, styling or creature comforts.

2,415 ragtops had this engine linked to a stick shift.

There were two Ram Air engine options this year. The first was identified as the HO option in several period sources, but is better known as the Ram Air III engine to car collectors today. It was a 400-cid V-8 with a 10.75:1 compression ratio, a single Rochester MV four-barrel carburetor and a functional hood scoop. It was rated for 366 hp at 5100 rpm and 445 ft. lbs. of torque at 3600 rpm. The second option was the so-called Ram Air IV version, which was another 400-cid V-8 with 10.75:1 compression and a Rochester 4M four-barrel carburetor. It generated 370 hp at 5500 rpm and 445 ft. lbs. of torque at 3900 rpm.

PMD records show that 2,417 "regular" GTOs had Ram Air engines, but these cars cannot be separated from GTOs having a new "The Judge" option, which is discussed separately in this book. According to contemporary sources, the 370-hp 1969 GTO coupe was good for 6.5-second 0-to-60 times and 14.6-second quarter-mile runs.

1969 PONTIAC GTO "THE JUDGE"

"Born Great" was the company slogan used for the 1969 GTO "The Judge." It was designed to be what *Car and Driver* called an "econo racer." In other words, it was a well-loaded muscle car with a price that gave you a lot for your money! It was a machine that you could take racing, pretty much "as is," for a lot less money than a purpose-built race car cost.

Pontiac Motor Division's release of the "The Judge" option came on December 19, 1968. At first, "The Judge" came only in bright orange with tri-color striping, but it was later made available in the full range of GTO colors. Special standard features of the package included a blacked-out grille, Rally II wheels (minus trim rings), functional hood scoops, "The Judge" decals on the sides of

"The Judge" 1969 Pontiac GTO originally came only in orange with tri-colored striping.

the front fenders and "Ram Air" decals on the hood scoops. At the rear there was a 60-inch wide "floating" deck lid airfoil with a "The Judge" decal emblem on the upper right-hand surface.

The standard "The Judge" engine was the 400-cid 366-hp Ram Air III V-8 linked to a three-speed manual transmission with a Hurst T-handle shifter and a 3.55:1 rear axle. A total of 8,491 GTOs and Judges were sold with this motor and only 362 of them were convertibles. The 400-cid 370-hp Ram Air IV engine was installed in

759 cars in the same two lines and 59 of these were convertibles.

"The Judge" option was added to 6,725 GTO hardtops and only 108 GTO ragtops. The editors of *Car Life* magazine whipped a Judge through the quarter mile at 14.45 seconds and 97.8 mph. *Supercars Annual* covered the same distance in a Judge with Turbo Hydra-Matic transmission and racked up a run of 13.99 seconds at 107 mph!

1970 1/2 PONTIAC FIREBIRD FORMULA 400

While the 1970 Trans Am was probably the hottest of the second-generation Firebirds introduced during the last week in February, the Formula 400 was right up there in terms of performance and had more of the street-racer look that said "muscle car" from the word go.

In addition to all the federally mandated GM safety features, the Formula models included a 330-hp 400-cid V-8 with a single four-barrel carburetor, a three-speed manual gearbox with a heavy-duty Hurst shifter, a 1 1/8-inch front and 5/8-inch rear stabilizer bar, high-rate springs, special wind-up rear axle controls, F70 x 14 bias-belted tires, 7-inch-wide wheel rims, Formula 400 trim, a deluxe steering wheel, carpets, a vinyl bucket seat interior, dual sport mirrors, concealed windshield wipers and manual front disc and rear drum brakes.

All Formulas had a special, tough-looking hood with long twin air scoops that opened at the front end, just above the grille. These scoops became functional when the L74 Ram Air V-8 was ordered for $168.51 extra. This was called the 400 Ram Air option and it put out 335 hp at 5000 rpm.

Car and Driver (June 1970) said the Formula provided "fast acting relief from everything but the highway patrol." The magazine's test car had an as-tested price of $5,058.38. That included

$227.04 for the 330-hp V-8 (there was no explanation of why they paid extra for the base engine), $42.14 for a 3.07:1 Safe-T-Track rear axle, $28.44 for F70-14 white-lettered tires, $239.08 for a AM/FM stereo radio, $47.49 for décor moldings, $18.96 for concealed windshield wipers, $12.64 for custom seat belts, $42.13 for a Formula steering wheel, $84.26 for Rally II wheels, $94.79 for a rally clock and tachometer, $58.98 for a center console, $105.32 for variable-ratio power steering, $42.13 for power disc brakes, $45.29 for a tilt steering wheel, $6.85 for floor mats, $32.65 for tinted glass, $105.32 for power windows, $375.99 for custom air conditioning, $78.99 for custom interior trim and $227.04 for Turbo Hydra-Matic transmission.

Pontiac's 400-cid V-8 had a 4.122 x 3.75-inch bore and stroke, a 10.25:1 compression ratio and a single four-barrel Rochester carburetor. It generated 330-hp at 4800 rpm and 430 ft. lbs. of torque at 3000 rpm. *Car and Driver* charted a 6.4-second 0-to-60 run and a 14.7-second quarter mile at 98.9 mph. That wasn't as fast as the Trans Am the magazine also tested, which also cost less ($4,663.63).

But the Formula's appeal was image. While the Trans Am looked like an exotic European road-racing car, the Formula had the look of a winner in the "Stoplight Grand Prix."

1970 PONTIAC-HURST GRAND PRIX SSJ

Car Life referred to the 1969 Grand Prix as "a stretched GTO" and named it the best-engineered car of the year. For muscle-car enthusiasts, the big news for 1970 was the SSJ Grand Prix with Hurst modifications. It could be ordered through Pontiac dealers. Pontiac built and painted 272 of the cars. They were then shipped to Hurst for the conversion work.

The SSJ was based on the 'J' model (the vinyl accent stripes used on factory-issued SJs were incompatible with Hurst SSJ features). The SSJs were painted either cameo white (code CC) or starlight black (code AA). Interiors were ivory, black or sandalwood in cloth or all-Morrokide. Mandatory options included body-color sport mirrors, G78 x 14 whitewalls and Rally II wheels. The space-saver spare and ride and handling package were recommended.

After assembly, these cars were shipped to a Hurst plant in Southfield, Michigan, where frost gold accents were applied to the hood, side window frames, front of the roof and Rally II wheels. A landau-style half-top (antique white, white or black) was installed,

as was a steel, electrically operated sunroof like those used in Cadillac Eldorados.

Engines for 1970 included the same base power plant as in 1969 or a 265-hp regular-fuel economy version of the 400-cid V-8 at no extra charge. However, the 428-cid V-8 was replaced with a 455-cid 370-hp big block.

In *Popular Science,* a road-tested Grand Prix proved faster than a Dodge Hemi Charger and Ford Fairlane GT around the road racing circuit at Bridgehampton. The car used for the test had a Turbo Hydra-Matic transmission, as did most Grand Prixs. Only 500 stick-shift models were built and just 329 of them had the four-speed manual gearbox.

Instead of the 370-hp engine, a code LS5 455 HO V-8 could be had as an option. The conversion took about 10 days. Special die-cast model SSJ emblems were featured for identification. Hurst and Pontiac also provided a special SSJ sales catalog.

1970 PONTIAC TEMPEST GT-37

An economy wave swept the American auto industry in 1970, with cheap, six-cylinder cars seeing renewed popularity. Pontiac Motor Division—with its 1960s performance image—was a little out of step with the new trend that inspired cars like Chevrolet's Vega, Ford's Maverick and Plymouth's Duster. In fact, Plymouth was able to knock PMD out of third place in sales.

By midyear, Pontiac simplified its Tempest hardtop to give it a more competitive price. It was released as the T-37, which was aimed at entry-level buyers. Although the "37" part of the designation was based on General Motors' code for a two-door hardtop model, Pontiac soon bent the rules a bit and released a T-37 coupe (two-door sedan) as well as the hardtop. With a $2,683 price tag, the cheap T-37 generated 20,883 sales in half a year.

It wasn't long after the T-37 appeared that somebody decided to issue a sporty variation. To create such a budget-priced muscle car,

it was decided to dress up the plain-looking coupe with GTO-like extras and call it the GT-37. The new model was a stripped-down muscle car with a V-8 engine. The fastest production car that Pontiac built in 1970 turned out to be the Tempest GT-37 two-door sedan with the Ram Air III engine.

Standard equipment for the GT-37 included any Tempest V-8 with low-restriction dual exhaust, a three-speed heavy-duty manual transmission with floor shift, G70-14 raised-white-letter tires, Rally II wheel rims, 1969 Judge-style stripes and a hood pin kit. A rear deck airfoil was optional, but bucket seats were not available.

The hot GT-37 engine was the 400 cid V-8 that came in 1970 1/2 models with stick shift. This was actually the Ram Air III V-8, without a Ram Air hood and dual-snorkel air cleaner. It did have the bigger Ram Air III valves.

Pontiac built 1,419 of the 1970 1/2 GT-37 coupes.

1970 PONTIAC GTO

Prominent styling changes on the 1970 GTO included smaller, split oval grilles, dual rectangular headlamp housings (with round lenses) and creased body sides. The hood had twin air scoops and a GTO nameplate was seen on the left-hand grille. The rear end also sported flared fenders and the exhaust pipes exited through a valance panel below the rear bumper.

Standard hardware for the two GTOs included: front bucket seats, a padded dashboard, a functional air-scoop with a handle under the dash for manual control, a heavy-duty clutch, sports-type springs and shock absorbers, courtesy lights, a dual exhaust system, a 350-hp V-8, a heavy-duty three-speed transmission with floor-mounted gear shifter and G78-14 fiberglass-belted tires. The "Goat" featured a total Endura nosepiece without a metal bumper and had cleaner styling than other Tempests.

It was $3,267 for the base hardtop and 32,737 were built. The

base 400-cid 350-hp V-8 was put in 27,496 of these cars, including 9,348 with stick shifts. Priced at $3,492, the convertible saw only 3,615 assemblies. The base engine went into 3,058 of the ragtops, including 887 with stick shifts.

The 1970 GTO engines had several innovations, including special spherical-wedge cylinder heads and a computer-perfected camshaft design. Ram Air III engines with 366 hp were used in 1,302 hardtops and 114 convertibles with stick shifts and 3,054 hardtops and 174 convertibles with Turbo Hydra-Matics. Ram Air IV engines with 370 hp were used in 140 hardtops and 13 convertibles with stick shifts and 627 hardtops and 24 convertibles with Turbo Hydra-Matic. Also available in non-Judges was a 455-cid 360-hp V-8. This engine was installed in 2,227 stick-shift cars (241 ragtops) and 1,919 cars with Turbo Hydra-Matics (including 158 ragtops).

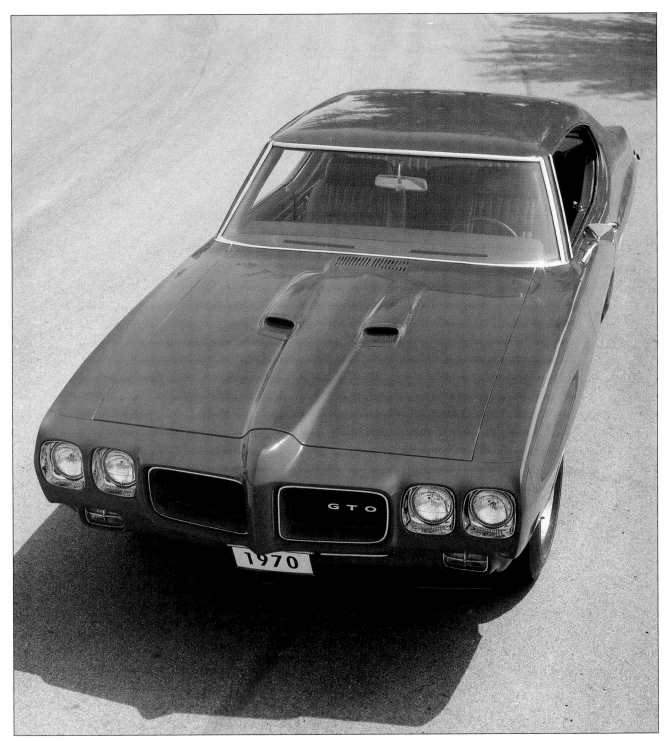

At a bargain base price of around $3,300, the GTO was tough to beat as an all-around driving machine in 1965.

A 1970 GTO hardtop with the 400-cid 366-hp V-8 did 0 to 60 mph in 6 seconds flat and covered the quarter mile in 14.6 seconds. With a 455-cid 360-hp V-8 the same model was actually slower, requiring 6.6 seconds for the 0-to-60 run and 14.8 seconds to cover the quarter mile. *Car and Driver* tested a 455-cid GTO coupe in its January 1970 issue. The car had a four-speed manual gearbox and 3.31:1 rear axle. The chart accompanying the article showed a 6.6-second 0 to 60-mph time and a quarter-mile run in 15 seconds at 96.5 mph.

1970 PONTIAC GTO JUDGE

"The Judge" came with a 455-cid, 360-hp base engine in 1970, but the 366-hp Ram Air V-8 was an even faster option.

The flashy "Judge" was hard to miss, from any angle.

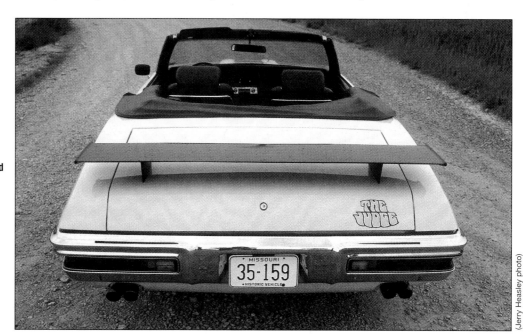

(Jerry Heasley photo)

(Jerry Heasley photo)

"The Judge" option package was again available for GTO hardtops and convertibles in model year 1970. It was coded as the 332-WT1 accessory group and included the 366-hp Ram Air V-8, Rally II wheels less trim rings, G70-14 black sidewall fiberglass-belted tires, a T-handle-shifted manual transmission, a rear deck lid airfoil, specific side stripes, "The Judge" decals and stripes and a black-textured grille.

Contrary to some reports, "The Judge" GTOs were not cheaper than base models, unless the base models had all of the same accessories installed individually. The 366-hp package added $337.02 to the price of the cars that it was ordered for, regardless of whether the car was a hardtop or a ragtop. That put the base price of a hardtop with "The Judge" equipment at about $3,604.02, although there may have been some mandatory options that added a little

more to that. Prices on the convertible version started at about $3,829.02.

Those who wanted to get their "Judge" with a more powerful Ram Air IV engine had to shell out $558.20 more. In addition, Ram Air IV cars could only be built with either a three-speed Turbo Hydra-Matic transmission or a four-speed manual gearbox. Pontiac Motor Division engine production records show that 42 GTO hardtops and 288 ragtops were built with Ram Air V-8s. As for the Ram Air IV V-8, it was used in 767 hardtops and just 37 convertibles. (These combined production figures are for plain GTOs and cars with "The Judge" option lumped together.)

Pontiac's base 455-cid 360-hp 1970 GTO "The Judge" two-door hardtop was good for 0 to 60 mph in 6.6 seconds. It did the quarter mile in 14.6 seconds.

1970 1/2 PONTIAC FIREBIRD TRANS AM

The Pontiac Firebird Trans Am coupe was a cutting-edge performance car in 1970.

The introduction of 1970 Firebirds was delayed until the winter of 1970. When they appeared they had a sleek new, half-inch-longer body shell on the same 108-inch wheelbase. There were now four separate Firebird series called Firebird, Espirit, Formula 400 and Trans Am. A Maserati-like, semi-fastback body made the second-generation Trans Am a sophisticated muscle car.

The No. 22887 Trans Am hardtop coupe had a base sticker price of $4,305 lbs. It weighed 3,550 lbs. and 3,196 were made. The Trans Am suspension was upgraded and big-block engines were carried over with Ram Air induction. The least-powerful engine option was the Ram Air 400-cid four-barrel V-8 connected to a four-speed, wide-ratio gearbox with a floor-mounted Hurst shifter.

Convertibles were no longer available. In addition to white paint with blue stripes, Pontiac offered blue cars with white stripes. Standard equipment included all mandatory safety features, a front air dam, front and rear spoilers, a shaker hood, side air extractors, a rear spoiler, aerodynamic mirrors (left-hand remote controlled),

1 1/4-inch front and 7/8-inch rear stabilizer bars, heavy-duty shocks and springs; an engine-turned aluminum instrument panel with a rally gauge cluster; concealed windshield wipers, bucket seats, carpets, all-vinyl upholstery, power brakes and steering and 15-inch Rally II wheels.

A higher 10.5:1 compression ratio gave the base 400-cid Ram Air III V-8 in 1970 1/2 models 345 hp. This engine went into 1,339 cars with automatic and 1,769 with stick. In addition to the standard four-speed manual transmission, Turbo Hydra-Matic, also with a floor shift, was a no-cost extra. Fifty-nine automatics and 29 sticks were built with the 370-hp Ram Air IV option. A Ram Air III-equipped Trans Am could do the quarter-mile in 14.5 seconds at 99 mph. *Car and Driver* (June 1970) road tested an Espirit, a Formula 400 and a Trans Am. The latter was the hottest of the three and moved from 0 to 60 mph in just 5.7 seconds. The standing-start quarter mile took only 14.1 seconds at 103.2 mph.

1971 PONTIAC FORMULA FIREBIRD

In 1971, GM made few alterations to the outside of its F-cars, but installed new high-back bucket seats and adopted some underhood changes dictated by forthcoming anti-pollution rules. A 350-cid small-block V-8 was made standard equipment and a 455-cid V-8 replaced the venerable 400-cid V-8 as the largest Pontiac engine. As a result of all these "engine swaps," the third-rung model in the Firebird line could be had as a Formula 350, a Formula 400 or a Formula 455. However, most people started to call it simply the "Formula Firebird."

Standard equipment on this model included vinyl bucket seats, a custom cushion steering wheel, a flame chestnut wood-grain-appearance dash panel, right- and left-hand body-color outside rearview mirrors (with a remote-control mechanism for the left mirror), an Endura rubber front bumper, a fiberglass hood with simulated dual air scoops, a black-textured grille with bright moldings, standard hubcaps, narrow rocker panel moldings, Formula 350/400/455

identification, a heavy-duty three-speed transmission with floor shifter, a high-performance dual exhaust system with chrome exhaust pipe extensions and a Power Flex cooling fan (with 400- and 455-cid engines).

Muscle car lovers were most interested in the Formula 455 version in 1971, although not all buyers understood that there were two 455-cid engine options. Both had the same 4.15 x 4.21-inch bore and stroke, but the least-powerful version used an 8.2:1 compression ratio. This engine, which cost $157.98 extra, produced 325 hp at 4400 rpm and 455 ft. lbs. of torque at 3200 rpm. The option was the same 455 HO version that Trans Ams got as standard equipment. It was good for 335 hp at 4800 rpm and 480 ft. lbs. of torque at 3600 rpm. This motor cost $236.97 extra in Formulas.

The Formula 455 with a four-speed manual gearbox and a 3.42:1 rear axle could go from 0 to 60 mph in 7.6 seconds and did the quarter mile in 15.5 seconds at 89.5 mph.

1971 PONTIAC GRAND PRIX SSJ

For 1971, the regular Grand Prix received a front and rear beauty treatment. There were single headlamps, a separate bumper (running across the grille) and a semi-boattail rear end that gave a dramatic new appearance to the back of the car. Two inches was added to the overall length.

Hurst again offered the semi-custom SSJ option package through Pontiac dealers. The basic package was about the same as it had been in 1970, although gold honeycomb wheels or American mag wheels could now be substituted for the factory-type Rally II rims. The Hurst sunroof was now described as "the same German type used in Mercedes-Benz." SSJ nameplates were located on the car's front fender tips. Hurst Fire Frost Gold accents highlighted the body.

A number of new Hurst accessories were made available for the 1971 model. They included an Auto-Stick gear shifter (for cars with bench seats only), a roll control device and a digital computer to calculate speed and elapsed times in the quarter mile. Also available were B.F. Goodrich radial T/A GR60-15 tires that could be installed in place of the standard G78-14 white-stripe tires.

Engines were the base 400-cid 300-hp L78 V-8 (that was standard in Grand Prix Js) and the 455-cid 325-hp LS5 V-8 (which was standard in SJ models and optional in Js). Only 116 stick-shift cars were made and half of them had four-speed manual transmissions. The available rear axles were reduced to three choices. A 3.23:1 ratio was used in conjunction with manual transmissions; a 3.08:1 ratio came with the 400-cid V-8 and Turbo Hydra-Matic and a 3.07:1 axle was used with the 455-cid engine and automatic.

Sales of Hurst SSJs dwindled to about 157 units. Apparently, the base price of the conversion ($1,147.25) remained the same as in 1970. It didn't include destination charges.

1971 PONTIAC TEMPEST GT-37

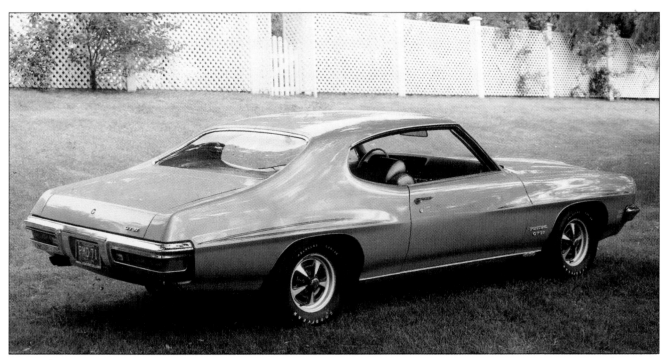

At about $2,800, Tempest GT-37s were Pontiac's lowest-priced cars in 1971.

Styling revisions to Pontiac Motor Division's 1971 Tempest intermediate-size models included redesigned grilles and a reworked nose and hood for GTOs. The year's lowest-priced Pontiacs were the Tempest T-37 models, which now included a four-door sedan that retailed for $2,795, a two-door coupe that sold for $2,747 and a two-door hardtop priced at $2,807.

In 1971, the GT-37 option was supposed to be made available for T-37 hardtops and coupes with a V-8 engine. However, no 1971 Tempest GT-37 coupes were ever made because the sport mirrors that were added to the package would have prevented the opening of vent windows on that particular body style.

The GT package cost dealers $187.47 and retailed for $236.97. It included vinyl accent stripes, Rally II wheels less trim rings, G70-14 white-letter tires, a dual exhaust system with chrome exhaust pipe extensions, a heavy-duty three-speed manual transmission with a floor-mounted gear shifter, body color outside rearview mirrors (with remote-control left-hand mirror), hood locking pins, GT decals and a GT-37 nameplate.

Changes for 1971 included the use of 1971 GTO "The Judge" stripes and a minor redesign of the hood locking pins. A third type of GT-37—with sword-shaped body stripes made of reflective foil—was seen in mid-1971.

For 1971, engines available in GT-37s started with a 350-cid two-barrel with 250 hp. Options included a two-barrel 400-cid 265-hp V-8 for $52.66 extra, a four-barrel 400-cid 300-hp V-8 for $221.17 additional, a four-barrel 455-cid 335-hp V-8 for $279.10 more and the four-barrel 455 HO with 335 hp, which added $358.09 to the price of the GT-37 with a standard V-8.

The 1971 GT-37s had a 5,802-unit production run, of which about 50 were 1971 1/2 models with foil stripes. About seven of these cars had a distinctive black-and-gold paint and interior trim combination.

1971 PONTIAC GTO

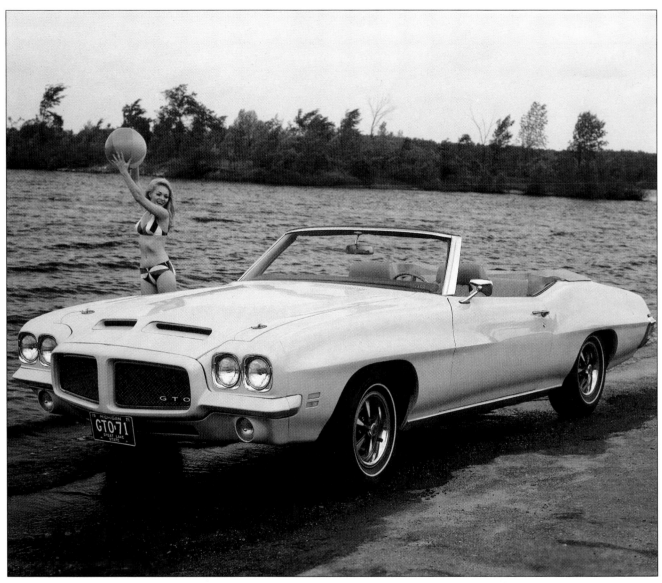

The 1971 GTO came with 455-cid and 455 HO engines, but the base 400 was the most common.

For 1971, Pontiac's legendary GTO—a part of the Series 42 Tempest line—still came in hardtop and soft-top models. Factory dealers paid $2,612.25 to get a Model 24237 hardtop with a suggested retail price of $3,446. The Model 24267 convertible wholesaled to dealers for $2,788.83 and went on the lots for as little as $3,676.

Larger grille cavities and round front parking lamps were 1971 GTO changes. The hood now had twin air slots at the front. GTOs came with all features of the LeMans Sport model plus an engine-turned aluminum instrument panel, special front-end styling with an Endura front bumper, a special hood with forward-mounted simulated air-intake scoops, a 400-cid four-barrel V-8, a heavy-duty three-speed manual transmission with floor-mounted shifter, dual exhausts with extensions exiting through the rear valance panel, a Power-Flex cooling fan, a 1 1/8-inch diameter stabilizer bar, a rear stabilizer bar, high-rate shock absorbers and springs, G70-14 black sidewall tires and GTO identification.

Engine and transmission combinations were cut from 17 to 10.

The base 400-cid V-8 was used in 6,421 hardtops and 508 convertibles with stick shift and 2,011 hardtops and 79 convertibles with automatic. It had an 8.2:1 compression ratio and a single four-barrel carburetor and was good for 300 hp at 4800 rpm and 400 ft. lbs. of torque at 3600 rpm.

The 455-cid V-8 went into 534 hardtops and 43 convertibles, all with stick shift. This engine also had an 8.2:1 compression ratio and a Rochester 4MV four-barrel carburetor. It developed 325 hp at 4400 rpm and 455 ft. lbs. of torque at 3200 rpm.

A 455-cid HO engine was used in some non-Judge-optioned GTOs. This engine had an 8.4:1 compression ratio and a four-barrel carburetor. It produced 335 nhp at 4800 rpm and 480 ft. lbs. of torque at 3600 rpm. It was used in 412 hardtops and 23 convertibles with stick shift and 476 hardtops and 21 convertibles with Turbo Hydra-Matic.

The regular GTO hardtop had a 9,497-unit production run. Only 661 GTO convertibles were made this year.

1971 PONTIAC GTO JUDGE

(Jerry Heasley photo)

The GTO "The Judge" hardtop was still a tough package to beat for the money in 1971.

Pontiac dealers didn't earn much of a mark-up on the 1971 GTO "The Judge" option. The package, which had the code No. 332, carried a dealer cost of $312.45 and a suggested retail price of $394.95. That certainly wasn't a bad deal for the buyer, considering all he or she got for the money.

The GTO was based on the LeMans Sport, which included all LeMans equipment plus dual horns, pedal trim plates, a lamp package; carpeted lower door panels; a custom cushion steering wheel and wheel opening moldings. Moving up to the GTO series got buyers an engine-turned aluminum instrument panel; an exclusive Endura front end treatment, a special scooped hood, a 400-cid 300-hp four-barrel V-8, a heavy-duty three-speed transmission with a floor shifter, a dual exhaust system, a power-flex fan, a 1 1/8-inch-thick front stabilizer bar, a beefed-up rear stabilizer, high-rate shock absorbers and springs, G70-14 black sidewall tires and GTO badges.

The "The Judge" option—available for the two-door hardtop and the convertible only—added a bigger engine (the 455-cid HO four-barrel V-8); Rally II wheels less trim rings; a hood air inlet, a T-handle shifter (with manual transmission), a rear deck lid airfoil, specific body side stripes, "The Judge" decals, Ram Air decals and a black texture in the grille.

Adding the option price to the base price of the hardtop gives you a total of $3,840 for "The Judge" of that body style. The very rare ragtop version (only 17 1971 GTO "The Judge" convertibles were actually built) went out the door for as little as $4,070 when no extras were added on. Actually, the price was about $10 higher for both body styles because the RPO 621 "ride & handling" shock absorber and spring package, which had a suggested retail price of $9.48, was a mandatory option.

1971 PONTIAC FIREBIRD TRANS AM

The muscular Pontiac Firebird Trans Am got new seats in 1971, but not much else.

(Jerry Heasley photo)

The 1971 Pontiac Firebirds were very close to a direct carry-over of the late-arriving 1970 1/2 models. The most obvious change between cars of the two years was the new high-back bucket seats used on the 1971 models. The lower-level models like the Firebird, Espirit and Formula also had new front fender air extractors and a

few other detail changes, but the 1970 and 1971 Trans Ams looked virtually identical, except for the new bucket seat design.

The style No. 22887 Trans Am hardtop coupe had a base sticker price of $4,590. It weighed 3,578 lbs. and only 2,116 were made. Standard equipment in Trans Ams included: all mandatory safety features; vinyl bucket seats; rally gauges; a clock; a tachometer; a Formula steering wheel; an Endura front bumper; body-colored mirrors; honeycomb wheels; functional front fender air extractors; a rear deck lid spoiler; a black textured grille with bright moldings; front and rear wheel opening flares; concealed wipers; identification badges; a performance dual exhaust system; a special air cleaner; a rear-facing cold-air hood intake with throttle control; a Power Flex fan; dual horns; front power disc brakes and rear drum brakes; F60-15 white-lettered tires; a close-ratio four-speed manual transmission with floor shift and—most important of all—a big 455 HO

four-barrel V-8.

With a change to lower compression ratios in 1971 (thanks to future leaded gas requirements), Pontiac found it prudent to substitute the 455-cid V-8 for the 400-cid engine. The 455 HO version had a 4.15 x 4.21-inch bore and stroke and used a single four-barrel Rochester carburetor. With 8.4:1 compression, it developed 335 hp at 4800 rpm and 480 ft. lbs. of torque at 3600 rpm. Trans Am buyers who preferred an automatic transmission could substitute a three-speed Turbo Hydra-Matic for the Hurst-shifted close-ratio four-speed manual gearbox at no charge.

1972 PONTIAC FORMULA FIREBIRD

The one-two punch of government regulation and restrictive liability insurance rates pounded the pony car market niche that Pontiac built the Firebird for. As a result, sales got very slow by 1972 and PMD cut the prices on all Firebird models to try to lure customers into the showrooms. Dealers were hoping to increase sales, but a crippling United Auto Workers Union strike at GM's Norwood, Ohio, assembly plant (where F-cars were made) caused production lines to grind to a premature halt. As a result, only 5,249 Formula Firebirds were built for the year.

Standard equipment on this model included: vinyl bucket seats; a custom cushion steering wheel; right- and left-hand body-color outside rear view mirrors (with a remote-control mechanism for the left mirror); an Endura rubber front bumper; a fiberglass hood with

dual air scoops (functional on Formula 455 models only); a black-textured grille with bright moldings; standard hubcaps; narrow rocker panel moldings; firm-control shock absorbers front and rear; Formula 350/400/455 identification; a heavy-duty three-speed transmission with floor shifter; a high-performance dual exhaust system with chrome exhaust pipe extensions and a Power Flex cooling fan (with 400- and 455-cid engines).

There was only one 455-cid engine option in 1972. It used an 8.4:1 compression ratio and produced 300 hp at 4000 rpm and 415 ft. lbs. of torque at 3200 rpm. It sold for $231 over the price of the base 400-cid 250-hp engine. The Formula 455 with a four-speed manual gearbox and a 3.42:1 rear axle could go from 0 to 60 mph in 7.6 seconds and did the quarter mile in 15.5 seconds at 89.5 mph.

1972 PONTIAC GRAND PRIX SSJ

Pontiac ads said, "the 1972 Grand Prix lacks the 1909 Tudhope-McIntyre's runningboards, but has the same enduring styling, innovations, exceptional engineering and construction." The ads also said that these cars were built only in Pontiac, Michigan, and Lakewood, Georgia, "By a select group of dedicated men."

New styling elements included an egg-crate grille with multiple fins between its main bars at the front of the car and triple-segment tail lamps at the rear. Finned wheel covers also appeared this year.

Also back was the SJ with body-color sport mirrors, vinyl pin stripes, luggage and door courtesy lamps, a rally gauge cluster and the 455-cid 300-hp V-8 with a single four-barrel carburetor. All Grand Prixs had Turbo Hydra-Matic transmissions and more than 90 percent of them had front bucket seats.

A very-hard-to-find (and perhaps impossible) Grand Prix is a 1972 Hurst SSJ. Hurst Performance Products Company had no record of producing any such cars, but some are claimed to exist. In their book *The Hurst Heritage,* Bob Lichty and Terry Boyce estimated that 60 examples of the 1972 Hurst SSJ were built. This estimate was based on an interview with a former company employee who recalled delivering about that many cars to Pontiac Motor Division for shipping.

According to the research conducted by Lichty and Boyce, Hurst SSJs were priced at about $5,132 in 1970, about $5,461 in 1971 and around $5,617 in 1972. During the last year of production they apparently came only with a dual-gate automatic transmission.

1972 PONTIAC LEMANS SPORTS GTO

The smog police and the insurance industry ganged up to bring an end to the muscle-car market niche that the GTO option for the LeMans had started in 1964. So as the muscle-car era drew near its close in 1972, it was perhaps somewhat fitting that the GTO returned to being an option for the LeMans.

This change was part of a general de-emphasis of the GTO, which actually helped it survive a few more years. In addition, Pontiac dropped the eye-catching "The Judge" option package along with the GTO convertible.

In terms of appearance, the 1972 GTO was very 1971-like. It had a revised grille mesh and new front-fender air extractors. It was still characterized by an Endura front end and a special hood with dual air scoops opening at the front. However, this treatment was no longer exclusive to the "Goat." You could order it as an option for any LeMans or LeMans sport model with a V-8.

The base engine for the new GTO was the 400-cid with a 4.12

x 3.75-inch bore and stroke. It had an 8.2:1 compression ratio and a single four-barrel carburetor. This motor generated 250 hp at 4400 rpm and 325 ft. lbs. of torque at 3200 rpm.

There were two 455-cid engine options, both with a 4.15 x 4.21-inch bore and stroke. The first had a single four-barrel carburetor and an 8.2:1 compression ration and cranked out 250 hp at 3700 rpm and 325 ft. lbs. of torque at 2400 rpm. The most powerful option was the 455 HO, which had an 8.4:1 compression ratio and a four-barrel. It was good for 300 hp at 4000 rpm and 415 ft. lbs. of torque at 3200 rpm.

A 1972 GTO hardtop with the 455 HP V-8 was base priced at about $2,968 and weighed 3,885 lbs. It carried 13 lbs. per horsepower and its performance really suffered for it. It required 7.1 seconds to scoot from 0 to 60 mph and the quarter mile took 15.4 seconds. No wonder GTO orders dropped to only 5,807.

1972 PONTIAC FIREBIRD TRANS AM

The Pontiac Firebird Trans Am was still in production in 1972, but it was almost identical to the previous year's model.

The Trans Am sported the familiar logo and blue-and-white paint scheme in 1972.

Late in 1971, rumors began to circulate around the auto industry that the Pontiac Firebird and Chevrolet Camaro were going to disappear from the GM family of cars. Ultimately, this did not happen because a number of enthusiasts who worked for Pontiac Motor Division fought very hard to keep the models alive. Still, PMD came very close to dropping the Firebird and as a result, very few styling changes were made for the model year. The 1972 Trans Am looked virtually identical to the 1971 model—which certainly wasn't a "bad" thing.

The No. 22887 Trans Am hardtop coupe had a lower base sticker price of $4,255. It weighed a lttle less, too—3,564 lbs. Production was extremely low, with only 1,286 cars leaving the factory.

Standard equipment in Trans Ams included: all mandatory safety features; vinyl bucket seats; rally gauges; a clock; a tachometer; a Formula steering wheel; an Endura front bumper; body-colored mirrors; honeycomb wheels; functional front-fender air extractors; a rear deck lid spoiler; a black textured grille with bright moldings; front and rear wheel opening flares; concealed wipers; identification badges; a performance dual-exhaust system; a special air cleaner; a rear-facing cold-air hood intake with throttle control; a Power Flex fan; dual horns; front power disc brakes and rear drum brakes; F60-15 white-lettered tires and a close-ratio four-speed manual transmission with floor shift.

Only one V-8 engine was used in 1972 Trans Ams. It was the 455-cid HO version with the 4.15 x 4.21-inch bore and stroke. It wore a single four-barrel Rochester carburetor and had an 8.4:1 compression ratio. The engine developed 300 hp at 4000 rpm and 415 ft. lbs. of torque at 3200 rpm. Trans Am buyers who preferred an automatic transmission could again substitute a three-speed Turbo Hydra-Matic for the Hurst-shifted close-ratio four-speed manual gearbox at no charge.

1973 PONTIAC FORMULA SD 455

In the early 1970s, the Formula Firebird had the image of being a street racer. As such, it was a great platform for the hottest Pontiac options and that's what it got when Pontiac Motor Division (PMD) decided to drop the optional SD 455 V-8 under the Formula model's hood.

The SD 455 mill was a very special big-block engine that had actually been derived from Pontiac's *small-block* racing program of 1970. PMD had worked up a powerful small-displacement motor to make it legal for Sports Car Club of America sedan racing. Only a few of these were sold in the crate, but much of the racing technology was then transferred to the RPO LS2 455-cid V-8.

The optional super-duty engine was the same one used in Trans Ams. All SD 455 V-8s featured a special block with reinforced webbing, large forged-steel connecting rods, special aluminum pistons, a heavy-duty oiling system, a high-lift camshaft, four-bolt main bearing caps, a special intake manifold, a dual exhaust system and upgraded valve train components. It had an 8.4:1 compression ratio and 310-hp rating.

A dual-scoop fiberglass hood characterized the third-step-up Formula Firebird, which came in Formula 350 (150 hp), Formula 400 (230 hp) and Formula 455 (250 hp) editions. The front fenders carried Formula lettering behind a Firebird emblem and engine call-out badge. Formulas also sported a new black-textured grille, high-rate rear springs and other high-performance equipment. A dual exhaust system was standard on all Formula models. Radial tires were a new option.

The Formula 350 hardtop coupe had a base price of $3,276. Late in the 1973 model year, the SD 455 was offered as a $675 option for the Formula. A total of 10,166 Formulas were made in 1973, but only 43 of those cars were actually sold with the ultra-high-performance engine.

1973 PONTIAC GRAND AM

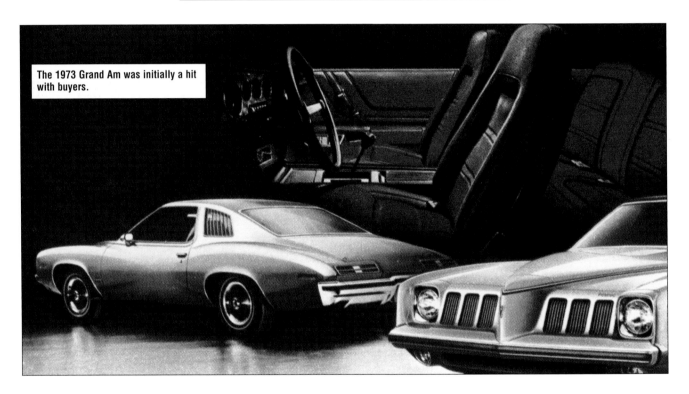

The 1973 Grand Am was initially a hit with buyers.

The Grand Am two- and four-door Colonnade hardtops bowed in the 1973 model year. Standard features included concealed windshield wipers, custom finned wheel covers, special taillights, dual horns, an in-the-windshield radio antenna, improved front and rear bumpers, a pliable plastic nose and fender caps, bumper impact strips, louvered quarter windows, bright metal moldings, black-accented rocker panels and body-colored door-handle inserts.

The interiors of both models featured reclining bucket seats in wide-wale corduroy or all-vinyl and Morrokide, a three-spoke custom steering wheel, African Crossfire mahogany dash trim, an electric clock, a Grand Prix-style dash with full instrumentation, a high-low ventilation system, a center console with a floor shift, a turn-signal dimmer switch, nylon-blend loop-pile carpeting, pedal trim and door-pull straps.

Grand Ams had 1.12-inch front and 0.94-inch rear stabilizer bars, variable-ratio power steering, power front disc brakes, four-wheel coil springs, a heavy-gauge perimeter frame, a Power-Flex cooling fan, 7-inch-wide wheels and GR70-15 steel-belted radials.

Standard power came from a 400-cid two-barrel V-8 with a Turbo Hydra-Matic transmission and a 3.08:1 rear axle. Options included a 400-cid four-barrel V-8 or a 455-cid four-barrel V-8. A four-speed manual transmission was optional with the "middle" engine, and 2.93:1, 3.23:1 and 3.42:1 axles were available. The new-for-1973 Super-Duty 455 V-8 was listed in the Grand Am sales catalog, but was never released in this model.

What really set the Grand Am apart was its front-end styling with a slim, ship's-prow nose that jutted out prominently. The grille slanted rearward at its top and had three vertical rectangular segments on either side of center. Each segment was filled with six vertical fins. Everything around the shelf-like bumper that looked like painted steel was actually made of a durable, squeezable rubber that gave upon impact, then sprung back to shape.

The Grand Am came in two- and four-door models in 1973.

The Grand Am was similar in dimension to a LeMans. Base retail prices were $4,264 for the two-door hardtop and $4,353 for the four-door hardtop. Shipping weights were 3,992 and 4,018 lbs., respectively.

A test of the two-door hardtop with a 455-cid 250-nhp V-8 gave performance figures of 7.9 seconds for 0 to 60 mph and 15.7 seconds in the quarter mile.

Sixteen colors were available for 1973 Grand Ams. The corduroy upholstery trim came in burgundy red or beige.

During its first season, the Grand Am did almost as well as the first GTO. Production of 43,136 units was realized. There seemed to be a substantial number of buyers interested in European-style high performance with good roadability, handling and driveability. However, the demand was either satisfied very rapidly or the buyers felt the Pontiac fell short on its promises. In 1974, production fell to 17,083. By 1975, the total had dropped to 10,679. The Grand Am left the lineup (temporarily) for 1976.

1973 PONTIAC LEMANS GTO

The 1973 GTO option is of great interest to collectors. Only 4,806 LeMans or LeMans Sport Colonnade coupes left the factory with this package, which cost approximately $368 over base price. For years, these cars were virtually ignored by GTO purists. Now, their rarity and high-performance characteristics, coupled with a dwindling supply of early GTOs, is beginning to change the picture.

The code 341 GTO option included a standard 400-cid engine with four-barrel carburetor, a blacked-out grille, dual NASA-type air scoops in a special hood, fat tires, a dual exhaust system, a floor-mounted three-speed manual transmission, super-firm shock absorbers, a rear sway bar, "baby moon" hubcaps, 15 x 7-inch wheels and specific body striping.

The base 400-cid engine had an 8.0:1 compression ratio. It developed 230 nhp at 4400 rpm and 325 ft. lbs. of torque at 3200 rpm. Also available was an optional 455-cid four-barrel V-8 with an 8.0:1 compression ratio. This engine developed 250 nhp at 4000 rpm and torque was listed as 370 ft. lbs. at 2800 rpm.

Sales catalogs also listed the 455 Super-Duty V-8, which was installed only in a handful of pre-production units and not in assembly line cars. At least one of these cars showed up at Pontiac's long-lead press conference in the summer of 1972. It was powerful and fast, but the Super-Duty option was later canceled.

A total of 544 cars with the GTO option were built with the regular 455 V-8. They included 25 LeMans two-door Colonnade coupes and 519 LeMans Colonnade two-door hardtops. All had Turbo Hydra-Matic attachments. According to experts, with all things considered, the 400-cid 230-nhp GTO engine was the best performance compromise.

GTOs with the 400-cid V-8 came standard with a 3.42:1 rear axle. Optional axle ratios were 3.08:1 and 3.23:1. When the 455-cid V-8 was added, the standard ratio was 3.08:1 with air conditioning and 3.23:1 without it. The 3.08:1 axle was also optional in 455-powered cars without air.

1973 PONTIAC TRANS AM SD 455

(Jerry Heasley photo)

The 1973 Pontiac Firebird Trans Am SD 455 coupe clocked a 13.54-second quarter mile in one magazine test.

Firebirds for 1973 had new colors, redesigned interiors, new hubcaps and a longer options list. The bumpers on the F-cars were redesigned to meet new federal standards. This made the cars slightly longer, which resulted in the new grille being slightly less recessed. The grille had an "egg-crate" pattern.

Like other Trans Ams that came before it, the 1973 model had special air dams, spoilers, flares and scoops. The hood scoops were now sealed and nonfunctional. A new feature was a large hood decal showing the American Indian Firebird icon that the basic car was named for. Enthusiasts soon dubbed this graphic the "screaming chicken." On 1973 models, the bird was always black, but the background color varied. It was orange on red cars, black on white cars and light green on Brewster Green Trans Ams.

The base engine used in the Trans Am was a 455-cid V-8 with a single four-barrel carburetor and 8.0:1 compression ratio that produced 250 hp. Pontiac built 4,550 cars with this engine and 1,420 of them had a stick shift. For real muscle, buyers could add a super-duty engine derived from Pontiac's experience in racing. The SD 455 featured a special block with reinforced webbing; large forged-steel connecting rods, special aluminum pistons, a heavy-duty oiling system, a high-lift camshaft, four-bolt main bearing caps, a special intake manifold, a dual exhaust system and upgraded valve train components. It had an 8.4:1 compression ratio and cranked out 310 hp.

The SD 455 Trans tested by *Hot Rod* magazine turned the quarter mile in 13.54 seconds at 104.29 mph. Going from 0 to 60 mph took all of 7.3 seconds. *Car and Driver* also tested an SD 455 and registered a 13.75-second quarter mile at 103.56 mph. The SD 455 engine designation appeared on the side of the hood scoop on these cars. Only 252 SD 455 Trans Ams were built and 72 had stick shift.

1974 PONTIAC FORMULA SD 455

For 1974, the model U 87 Formula Firebird was back with a new front-end treatment. A new, slanting "shovel nose" grille cap with an "electric shaver" insert was easy to spot. Rear styling was also revised.

Pontiac dealers had to send the factory $3,092.75 to get a Formula in their showroom. They could then hope to sell the car for its suggested retail price of $3,614.20.

Basic Firebird equipment included bucket seats, narrow rocker panel moldings, a deluxe two-spoke steering wheel, E78-14 black sidewall tires and a 250-cid in-line six-cylinder engine. The Formula model option also included a custom cushion steering wheel, hubcaps, a fiberglass hood with dual air scoops, dual outside rearview mirrors, a special heavy-duty suspension, a black textured grille,

F70-14 tires, dual exhausts and a 350-cid V-8 with a two-barrel carburetor. Automatic transmission was required on cars sold in California.

There were two 455-cid V-8s available in 1974 Formula Firebirds. The L75 version had a four-barrel carburetor with dual exhausts. It produced 250 nhp at 4000 rpm and 330 ft. lbs. of torque at 2400 rpm. Its price was $154 and the M40 Turbo Hydra-Matic transmission was mandatory. The 455-cid super-duty V-8 was a bit more expensive in Formulas than in Trans Ams. It cost $675 extra. The 1974 version was rated for 290 nhp at 4000 rpm and 395 ft. lbs. of toque at 3200 rpm. Only 58 Formulas were built with this engine during the 1974 model run.

1974 PONTIAC VENTURA GTO

Often cited as one of the major players in the 1960s muscle car era, the GTO, which bowed as a high-powered option for the intermediate Pontiac Tempest in late 1963, waxed and waned with most of the other muscle machinery. By the early 1970s, it was a different car. Its last appearance as an intermediate came as an option for the restyled 1973 LeMans. Generating only 4,806 orders, it was changed to a $195 option for the compact Ventura two-door sedan for the 1974 model run.

As a sports package for the 111-inch wheelbase car—which was one of seven Chevy Nova clones—it wasn't bad. Pontiac's 350-cid 165-nhp V-8 came as standard equipment. This engine breathed through an open-at-the-rear "shaker" hood scoop. A three-speed manual transmission with a floor-mounted gear shifter was standard. Buyers could add a four-speed manual transmission for $207 over the GTO's base price of $3,212.

The little GTO's other mechanical systems were also fairly adept. The beefy suspension featured front and rear stabilizer bars,

heavy-duty shock absorbers, heavy-duty springs, 6-inch-wide Rally II wheels with no extraneous trim, a 3.08:1 rear axle and E70-14 tires, all as standard equipment. A radial-tuned suspension cost extra.

For the first time, the standard GTO interior included a bench seat. Options ranged all the way up to all-Morrokide front bucket seats and a center console.

While it was different, the 1974 GTO was not a bad car and customers seemed to agree somewhat. A total of 7,058 were built. While that doesn't sound like the "good old days" it was an approximate 75 percent increase in production over the Lemans-based 1973 GTO. However, it was not enough to warrant another try in 1975.

Today the 1974 GTO is easily the most valuable of the Ventura compacts from Pontiac, but its value is a far cry from the five-digit prices that the early GTOs generate in the collectors' marketplace.

1974 PONTIAC TRANS AM SD 455

The 1974 Trans Am SD 455 was faster than the 1974 Corvette.

Extensive front-end styling revisions and an improvement in sales made headlines in the Firebird niche of the American muscle car marketplace in 1974. The Firebird ($2,895), the Espirit ($3,295), the Formula ($3,276) and the Trans Am ($4,204) models were carried over from 1973. The SD 455 engine option also remained in limited availability for the Formula Firebird and Trans Am models.

The new front end created by well-known designer John Schinella introduced an integrated "soft" bumper treatment, which was repeated at the rear of the F-cars. The front of all Firebirds carried a new, slant "shovel-nose" grille cap with an "electric shaver" grille insert made up of slanting, vertical blades. Black rubber bumper-face bars were featured. An air-scoop-like front valance panel contributed to a more massive overall look. Slimmer, wider front parking lamps without chrome protective grids were used. They carried textured, amber-colored lenses.

The Trans Am model option included a Formula steering wheel, rally gauges with a clock and a dash panel tachometer, a swirl-finish dash panel trim plate, a full-width rear deck lid spoiler, power steering, power front disc/rear drum brakes, a limited-slip differential, wheel opening air deflectors, front-fender air extractors, a dual exhaust system with chrome extensions; Rally II wheels with trim rings, a special heavy-duty suspension, dual outside rear view sports mirrors, F60-15 white-letter tires, a four-speed manual gearbox and a 400-cid 225-hp V-8.

The regular 455-cid 215-hp V-8 was $55 above the price of the 400-cid engine and the SD 455 V-8 was $578 extra. The SD 455 was installed in 212 Trans Ams with four-speed manual gearboxes and 731 with automatic transmission. Although it was relatively rare, the engine was popular with the editors of enthusiast magazines, who said it made the Firebird the hottest car of the year and slightly faster than the Corvette!

1977 PONTIAC CAN AM

The 1977 Pontiac Can Am Colonnade coupe was short-lived, but had plenty of personality.

Can Ams were constructed on an off-line basis by a specialty car company named Motortown Corp. The overall design was taken from a Pontiac factory concept car, exhibited in 1975. The show car was called the All-American Grand Am. Motortown started with a specifically equipped Lemans sport coupe and handled the conversion process.

The Can Ams had a flamboyant and competition-like appearance. Just one body style—the Colonnade coupe—was available with Can Am features. The package constituted a model option, rather than a separate series. It was introduced as a midyear addition to the line and was available for only a few months. This makes the Can Am a rare find.

Some ingredients of the Can Am option package were the same as Grand Am equipment, such as: a Grand Prix instrument cluster and clock, power front disc brakes, variable-ratio power steering, front and rear stabilizer bars, twin body-color sport mirrors, the RTS handling package, GR70-15 steel-belted radial tires, rubber bumper strips and a 400-cid V-8.

The 400-cid V-8 engine was not the two-barrel version used for base Grand Ams. Instead, the Trans Am's "T/A 6.6-liter" four-barrel V-8 was used. It was rated at 200 nhp. The Can Am had about the same 10-second 0-to-60 time as a 1975 midsized Pontiac with the 455-cid V-8.

Can Ams that were sold in California and in high-altitude counties used a different 403-cid 6.6-liter V-8 built by Oldsmobile.

Other elements of the $1,589 Can Am model-option included: cameo white body paint, a blacked-out grille assembly, black-fin-ished rocker panel moldings and window moldings, special identification badges and a "shaker" style hood scoop. Also included were a space-saver spare, body-color Rally II wheels, a black lower-body side with accent striping and Turbo Hydra-Matic transmission (a manual gearbox was not available).

The Can Am option was listed for the LeMans sport coupe (which included bucket seats) with louvered rear quarter windows. Can Am add-ons included a Safe-T-Track rear axle, white-letter tires, a custom sport steering wheel, Soft-Ray tinted glass, custom color-keyed seat belts, dual horns, front and rear floor mats, air conditioning, an AM/FM stereo with eight-track tape player, a CB radio, a tachometer, a front-seat console and an interior hood latch.

The graphics package for the Can Am was really an eye catcher. It used fade-away lettering and stripes with an orange base, red lower accents and yellow upper accents. The model name appeared in these colors on the front fenders behind the wheel openings and on the right-hand side of the deck lid. Similar stripes were used along the upper belt line's forward section, on the rear spoiler, on the mirrors, on the hood scoop and front spoiler and around the rear license recess. Engine call-outs in the same colors decorated the shaker hood scoop.

As the story goes, just when the production process was getting smoothed out, a machine that stamped out the special rear spoiler broke down. Motortown was unable to solve the problem cost effectively and, therefore, decided to cancel the model option after 1,130 cars had been assembled.

1986 1/2 PONTIAC GRAND PRIX 2+2 AEROCOUPE

(Jerry Heasley photo)

The 1986 1/2 2+2 Aerocoupe was the result of Pontiac's search for a slipperier race car.

Pontiac, like Chevrolet, had a tough time beating Ford Thunderbirds in general and Bill Elliott in particular in NASCAR Winston Cup stock car racing during 1985. In fact, Pontiac didn't win a single Winston Cup event that year. One of the reasons for this was unfavorable aerodynamics caused by the brick-like frontal design and nearly vertical rear window of the Pontiac Grand Prix, which was the model raced.

While the Chevrolet Monte Carlo SS had a sleek nose and only needed a rear window design modification, Pontiac had to make changes front and rear in order to make its package "slipperier." The resulting high-performance model arrived on January 3, 1986, when the Pontiac 2+2 was announced. Even though the Grand Prix name was absent from early publicity, the 2+2 equipment was an option package (RPO Y97) for the Grand Prix.

The 2+2 option included a rounded front fascia that was similar to that of the Monte Carlo SS, but not quite as sleek, a bubble-back rear window, a smaller-than-stock fiberglass deck lid with a spoiler, styled steel wheels, silver paint with medium gray lower trim and two-tone red accent striping around the perimeter. A gray interior was featured.

Mechanically, the LG4 305-cid Chevy small-block V-8 was rated at 165 hp, up 15 from the regular 305 in the Grand Prix. A four-speed automatic overdrive transmission and 3.08:1 rear end gearing kept things on the calm side. Front and rear stabilizer bars, stronger shocks and 215/65R15 Goodyear Eagle GT tires firmed up the ride and handling.

Not cheap, the $17,800 2+2 came loaded with air conditioning, AM/FM/cassette radio, cruise control, power locks and windows and full tinted glass. Sales to the public started in early March and except in the Southeast, the 2+2 was a slow mover. Only 200 are believed to have been built. A 1987 2+2 was announced at the start of the model year, but was never put into production, making the 1986-1/2 models rare indeed.

Pontiac racers didn't have to worry about production schedules as for $1,512.50, Pontiac Motorsports offered the 2+2 Race Body Pac (PN 100449830), which contained all the 2+2 pieces. The parts were also available to racers individually. Unfortunately, the 2+2 didn't prove all that successful on the track with only two wins in 1986-1987. Most NASCAR Winston Cup Pontiac competitors switched to the 1988 Grand Prix front-wheel-drive body for 1988.

1987 PONTIAC FORMULA

When Pontiac decided to use the Corvette-derived 5.7-liter (350-cid) V-8 in Firebirds in 1987, it returned the option of true "muscle-car-like" performance to fans of the Formula Firebird for the first time in a good many years.

The 1987 Formula Firebird wasn't actually a model at all—it was an option for the base Firebird. The Formula package came in two content levels, W61 for $1,273 and W63 (with lots more power goodies) for $1,842.

Cars with the Formula option had a real "street-machine" image with a sculptured "power dome" hood, a body-colored aero-wing spoiler and Formula graphics that spelled out the option name in big letters along the bottom of the doors. A 5.0-liter four-barrel V-8 was standard, but the choice of most muscle car nuts was the 5.7-liter "Corvette" engine. However, one road test showed that a cheaper option—a 5.0 liter TPI V-8—could perform a bit, too.

In September 1987, *Road & Track* did a unique four-car test comparing the Formula 5.0 TPI, a 1969 Trans Am, a 1987 Mustang LX and a 1970 Mustang Boss 302. The older cars were quickest, but the Formula did 0 to 60 in 6.3 seconds and the quarter mile in 14.9

seconds at 92.5 mph. That was just a tad slower than the numbers that the heavier 1987 Trans Am GTA with the 5.7-liter TPI V-8 registered!

Road & Track noted that while both of the older muscle cars accelerated faster, the performances of the 1987 muscle cars was better overall. Their aerodynamic enhancements and higher axle gearing gave them both higher top speeds and they also handled and braked better and had superior ride quality, plus much better fuel economy. And of course, if you wanted to go even faster, you could add the 5.7-liter TPI V-8 to your Formula Firebird at extra cost.

In addition, the 1987 Formula Firebird goodies included a WS6 performance suspension package, P245/50VR16 tires on 16 x 8-inch cast-aluminum wheels and backlit rally gauge instrumentation.

On the bottom line, the Formula could be turned into a real performer that could probably slightly outrun a Trans Am or GTA. In addition, it's a rarer car. Pontiac built 88,623 Firebirds in 1987 and approximately half were Trans Ams or GTAs. That means that less than half had the Formula option.

1987 PONTIAC TRANS AM/GTA

Starting with cars built to 1987 specifications, Firebird buyers were offered more models, more aerodynamic styling and more performance. The release of a powerful new 5.7-liter (350-hp) V-8 with Tuned Port Injection (TPI) brought the Trans Am and other Firebird models back into the "muscle car" category.

The Trans Am represented Pontiac's "driving excitement" car. It included a body aero package, an aero rear deck spoiler, bird decals, fog lamps, hood air extractors and louvers, neutral-density smooth contour taillights, deep-dish 15 x 7-inch gold or silver Hi-Tech Turbo Cast wheels and added gauges.

The Trans Am power train offering started with a base 165-hp V-8 and included a 5.0-liter TPI V-8 featuring a high-output cam good for 206 hp and 285 ft. lbs. of torque. Of course, if you wanted a muscle machine, the 5.7-liter engine was a must. It featured roller valve lifters, a hardened steel camshaft, fast-burn combustion chambers, a remote mounted coil and dual cooling fans. Essentially a slightly modified Corvette engine, the 5.7-liter V-8 produced 210 hp and 315 ft. lbs. of torque.

Third-generation Firebirds had not had this kind of power in

years. The 1982 model with the 5.0-liter V-8 had been tested for 9.2-second 0 to 60-mph runs and 17-second quarter miles at 80.5 mph. This was great performance in context of the time, but not really "muscular." By 1986, this had been slightly improved to an 8.4-second 0-to-60 time and a 15.2-second quarter mile. However, with the 5.7-liter TPI motor, *High Performance Pontiac* magazine reported a 0-to-60 time of 6.2 seconds and a 14.2-second quarter mile at 94 mph.

The GTA package was an option for the Trans Am and came in a choice of two content levels: W61 at $1,701 and W63 at $1,958. It was primarily a luxury performance option including a monochromatic exterior, a dressed-up interior, fancier wheels, a WS6 suspension upgrade, a 3.27:1 limited-slip rear axle and the 5.7-liter V-8 as standard equipment. So it gave you a pre-packaged muscle Trans Am, but you could make the regular TA just as fast with the right picks from the options list.

Pontiac Motor Division built a grand total of 88,623 Firebirds in the 1987 model year. About half of them were Trans Ams or GTAs.

1988 PONTIAC FORMULA 5.7-LITER TPI

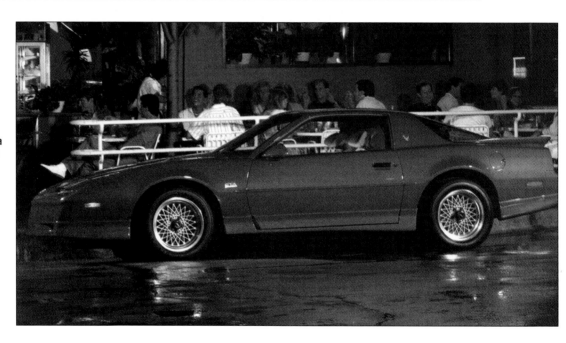

The Pontiac Formula Firebird got a bunch of refinements for 1988, including a new fuel-injection system.

For 1988, Pontiac enhanced the performance strengths that had been given to the 1987 Firebirds. The basic offerings remained the same, but each model or model-option gained some power train, trim and equipment features that underlined its role in the product mix.

After its well-received revival as an option package in 1987, the Formula package returned. It had the same status in 1988, although it was promoted more like a separate model. The base 5.0-liter V-8 was switched from a four-barrel carburetor to a throttle-body injection (TBI) induction system. This added 5 additional hp. The 5.0-liter TPI V-8 was available again, too. With air-induction improvements, the motor delivered 190 hp with a four-speed automatic transmission and 215 hp with a five-speed manual transmission. Once again, the 225-hp 5.7-liter automatic-only V-8 was a must for muscle-car mavens.

Formula Firebirds got new colors, revised interior trim and a different speedometer. Formula lettering on the doors was standard

along with 16 x 8-inch deep-dish Hi-Tech Turbo Cast wheels. The Formula's role in the product mix was to offer the acceleration and handling characteristics of the Trans Am and the GTA at a more attractive base price of $11,999, which represented a substantial savings to the buyer.

In 1987, Carroll Supercharging Co., of Wyckoff, New Jersey, advertised an aftermarket conversion called the VHO Formula in 1987. It added a belt-driven Paxton supercharger to the Formula 350. The blower provided a 5-psi pressure-boost raising output to 400 hp at 2500 rpm and torque to 475 ft. lbs. at 4000 rpm. *High Performance Pontiac* magazine tested the VHO Formula 350 and found that it did 0 to 60 mph in 6 seconds and the quarter mile in 13 seconds. The Carroll supercharging package retailed for $8,500. The conversion voided the Pontiac factory warranty, but engineer Greg Carroll said he would guarantee the VHO Formula 350 for 12 months or 12,000 miles. Very few of these cars were built.

1989 PONTIAC FORMULA FIREBIRD 5.7-LITER TPI

Every 1989 Firebird model had more reliable, foul-resistant Multec fuel injectors, improved rear disc brakes and Pass-Key anti-theft protection. The entire line now featured base coat/clear coat paint with a new bright blue metallic color offered. Door glass rubber was improved to cut wind noise and seal better. Three-point rear lap and shoulder belts were standard. The options list was expanded and all models could have T-tops, the full range of sound equipment and a digital CD player with a Delco II anti-theft system.

Base Firebirds continued to offer affordable performance. Prices started at $11,999 for the standard 135-hp MFI V-6. The 170-hp TBI V-8 was optional. Both of these came standard with a five-speed manual transmission, while a four-speed automatic was an extra-cost item. Firebird V-6s used a new FE1 suspension with 30-mm front and 18-mm rear anti-roll bars. With V-8s, the F41 Trans Am suspension was used and air conditioning was standard. Exterior graphics featured a narrower side stripe.

Street performance at a budget price was again the forte of the Formula Firebird or Model S87 with the W66 package. It had a dealer wholesale price of $12,456 and a suggested retail price of $13,939. The standard engine in this model was the 50-liter TBI V-8, but options included both the 5.0-liter 225-hp and 5.7-liter 235-hp TPI V-8s. Air conditioning was standard equipment, as was the WS6 suspension system. Body side striping was of the same style used on base Firebirds.

The 5.7-liter TPI V-8 (350 cid) had a 4.00 x 3.48-inch bore and stroke and a 9.3:1 compression ratio. It was rated for 235 hp at 4,400 rpm and 330 ft. lbs. of torque at 3200 rpm.

1989 PONTIAC TRANS AM/GTA 5.7-LITER TPI

The 1989 Pontiac Firebird GTA was high on the looks and performance charts, with a price tag just over $20,000.

The 1989 Pontiac Trans Am cost about $2,500 more than a Formula Firebird and even the base Trans Am had a few GTA-like extras, although engine choices were the same for both the Formula and the Trans Am. A limited-slip differential was standard with the 5.7-liter V-8 and this Corvette engine also came only with automatic transmission.

Added equipment on all Trans Ams included body skirting, an aero fascia, hood air extractors, front fender air extractors, hood louvers, fog lamps and Soft-Ray tinted glass. Also standard was the F41 suspension with 34-mm front and 23-mm rear anti-roll bars and recalibrated spring and shock absorber rates. Firestone Firehawk GTX tires were mounted on 15 x 7-inch cast-aluminum wheels.

At the top of the Firebird model line up, with a $20,339 price tag, was the 5.7-liter GTA. Finally released on the GTA was an optional new notchback hatch rear window designed to provide a more individual profile and a cooler interior. With 330 ft. lbs. of torque, the big-engined 1989 GTA was 0.2 to 0.3 seconds faster in the 0 to 60-mph sprint than ever before.

New deflected-disc valving for the gas shocks and struts gave the GTA's WS6 performance suspension a more comfortable ride. It had 36-mm front and 24-mm rear anti-roll bars, P245/50ZR16 Goodyear tires and lightweight 16 x 8-inch cross-lace aluminum wheels.

Cloth articulating seats were standard in the GTA and leather-covered bucket seats with increased thigh support—plus inflatable lumbar and side bolsters—were optional. Also available at extra cost was a full complement of power convenience accessories down to a high-tech radio with redundant controls on the wheel hub.

The 5.7-liter TPI V-8 (350 cid) had a 4.00 x 3.48-inch bore and stroke and a 9.3:1 compression ratio. It was rated for 235 hp at 4,400 rpm and 330 ft. lbs. of torque at 3200 rpm.

1989 1/2 PONTIAC TRANS AM INDY 500 PACE CAR

The 20th Anniversary Trans Am featured a hot turbo V-6 in addition to some very cool styling.

Sometimes a new car is an instant collectible. No experts are needed to debate its pros and cons or its future value. Such was the case with the 1989 1/2 20th Anniversary Firebird Trans Am. It had all the bases covered. Trans Ams have general collector value and the limited-production 20th Anniversary Edition was a plus, but topping this off was its Indy 500 Official Pace Car status.

For these reasons alone, the 20th Anniversary Trans Am is worthy of admiration, but the icing on the cake is its standard 231-cid 250-nhp Buick turbo V-6—the same V-6 used in the very hot 1987 Buick Regal Grand National.

Technically, the 20th Anniversary model was an option on the Trans Am GTA, which itself was a $4,340 option on the $15,999 Trans Am. Prices on the 20th Anniversary Indy 500 edition often passed $30,000. Pontiac said it would build only 1,500 copies.

Visuals included monotone white paint with a camel interior. There was a 20th Anniversary emblem on the nose, a similar emblem on each sail panel plus Turbo Trans Am and Indianapolis Motor Speedway emblems on the front fenders. Cars used at the speedway had hatch roofs, but this extra was optional on production models.

Road and Track tested a 20th Anniversary Trans Am Indy 500 Pace Car and found it could do 0 to 60 mph in 5.3 seconds and 0 to 100 in 13.9 seconds. "It might be a good idea to get in the Turbo Trans Am line now," *Road and Track* recommended in its January 1989 issue.

Three actual Pace Cars were outfitted with strobe lights and other special equipment by Dave Doern of Chicago, Illinois. They had been driven to his shop from different points and one car was actually wrecked by a PR man, who had it fixed on the hush-hush. After the strobes were added, the cars went to Indy. Bobby Unser drove one of them on the Indy 500 pace laps. The others were back-ups. Emerson Fittipaldi took one home after his win.

1990 PONTIAC TRANS AM/GTA/ FORMULA 5.7-LITER TPI

As the years went by, Pontiac continued to upgrade each model in the Firebird line. The base Firebird got more Formula-like, the Formula got more Trans Am-like and the Trans Am got more like the GTA. All three of these models could be had with the muscular 5.7-liter TPI V-8, which was standard in the GTA and optional in the Formula and the Trans Am.

This engine was the Chevrolet-made 350-cid with tuned-port injection and a 9.3:1 compression ratio. The 1990 hp rating was 235 at 4400 rpm and torque output was 340 ft. lbs. at 3200 rpm.

The 1990 Formula Firebird had a base retail price of $14,610. It had most of the features of the base Firebird plus standard air conditioning, an aero wing spoiler, tinted glass, a domed hood and Formula door graphics. The 5.7-liter engine (RPO BL2) was a $1,045 option. It required automatic transmission, an engine oil cooler, four-wheel disc brakes, a limited-slip differential and the RPO QLC high-performance tire package, which incorporated the WS6 performance suspension with P245/50ZR16 steel-belted radials and deep-dish high-tech wheels.

The Trans Am retailed for $16,510 and included a complete aero body package, F41 suspension and standard limited-slip axle. The 5.7-liter V-8 was $300 extra for the Trans Am and the mandatory QLC package was $385. The GTA-style interior featured leather appointments.

At the top of the line, the GTA continued to set the pace as one of America's finest high-performance cars. The 5.7-liter TPI V-8 was standard in this model (although you could order the 305-hp 5.0-liter TPI V-8 and get a credit). Inside, the GTA buyers found fancy cloth seats, leather-wrapped controls, a rear defogger, a standard cargo screen and a host of standard power accessories.

Model-year production of all Firebirds was 40,376, of which about 75 percent were base Firebirds, 16 percent were Formulas and 5 percent Trans Ams or GTA Tran Ams.

1990 PONTIAC TRANS AM 1LE

A little-known 1LE racing option was available for the 1990 Pontiac Firebird Trans Am.

Although a 5.7-liter Formula Firebird, Trans Am or GTA had some degree of muscle-car-enthusiast appeal, if you wanted even more power in your 1990 F-car there was another option. Buried deep in a factory-issued car distribution bulletin was the 1LE option that evolved out of the factory's racing program. It was a car that promised ultra-high performance to those interested in entering Firebirds or Camaros in Sports Car Club of America (SCCA) Showroom Stock racing, International Motor Sports Association (IMSA) Firehawk events or GM of Canada's Motorsports series.

To get a car with the 1EL option, the Trans Am buyer had to start by ordering a non-air-conditioned car with a special G92 rear axle and either the 5.0- or 5.7-liter TPI V-8. Then the 1LE option could be installed. It included the RPO G80 limited-slip differential, RPO J65 four-wheel disc brakes, RPO KC4 oil cooler, QLC 16-inch tires, the RPO N10 dual-converter exhaust system and the RPO C41 air conditioning delete package. Pontiac then automatically installed a 3.42:1 ratio rear axle, an aluminum driveshaft; an 18-gallon fuel tank with high-wall reservoir and special wide-strainer pickup, a WS6 suspension, Corvette heavy-duty front and rear disc brakes and specific shock-absorber valving.

The 1LE engines included special features, too. For instance, the 5.0-liter used a cast-iron block, cast-iron heads, a speed-density air/fuel metering system, a special idler pulley and 9.3:1 compression pistons. This produced 330 ft. lbs. of torque at 3200 rpm. This engine came linked to a close-ratio five-speed manual transmission.

Although meant for showroom stock racing, 1LE cars were fully street legal. They could be driven daily by anyone willing to put up with their harsh-riding characteristics. Performance was fantastic, though. The 5.0-liter 1LE could do the quarter mile in 14.47 seconds at 96.60 mph. It wasn't the fastest Trans Am ever built, but it was pretty close. The package was so difficult to order (most dealers did not know it existed) that cars with 1LE equipment are extremely rare.

1991 PONTIAC FIREBIRD SLP

In 1991, SLP Engineering, of Toms River, New Jersey, offered muscle-car maniacs a Firebird variation to write home about. The letters "SLP" in the company's name stood for "Street Legal Performance." The firm's SLP package was offered for all TPI-engined Firebirds and Trans Ams and was available through the General Motors Service Parts Organization. The option represented an emissions-legal, original equipment manufacturer (OEM)-quality, integrated group of go-fast goodies.

Designed for easy installation on a factory-supplied new Firebird—and requiring no major modifications—the SLP kit was available from Pontiac dealers through the *GM Performance Parts Catalog*. The complete package provided 50 more hp at approximately 5,500 rpm and pushed the torque peak above 2,800 rpm. It promised a 1-second-better 0 to 60-mph performance time and also improved quarter-mile performance by about 1 second or 6 mph.

The SLP hardware included cast-aluminum high-flow Siamesed intake runners, tri-Y stainless-steel tuned-length exhaust headers, a low-restriction stainless-steel exhaust system, revised engine calibration components (Cal-Pacs and PROMS) and a low-restriction cold-air-induction units.

High Performance Pontiac magazine checked out the Firebird SLP package in a 5.7-liter Trans Am with the same setup that was offered through Pontiac dealers. The author of the article drove the car for a week and gave a good summary of its new-for-1991 technology. It produced 290 hp at 5,000 rpm and 350 ft. lbs. of torque. He compared the car with its bolt-on and plug-in modifications to a Royal Bobcat GTO of the 1960s.

A second car tested had the special header system with 1.75-inch primary tubes and 3-inch wide collector pipes (dressed-up with styled tips), which changed the torque and horsepower peaks to provide even a bit more performance. *High Performance Pontiac* reported a 5.7-second 0-to-60 time for the slightly faster car with the special headers.

1992 PONTIAC FORMULA SLP FIREHAWK

In 1992, Pontiac Motor Division and SLP Engineering teamed up to make the hot new Formula Firehawk available through the factory dealer network as a special 1992 Firebird model-option. Representatives of Pontiac and SLP Engineering exhibited one of these cars at the Boston "World of Wheels" show during the first week of January 1992. They explained that Firehawks would be offered in "street" and "competition" versions. The street version produced 350 hp at 5,500 rpm and 390 ft. lbs. of torque at 4,400 rpm.

The factory-built Formula Firebird that served as the basis for SLP's Firehawk carried the 5.0-liter TPI V-8 and a four-speed automatic transmission (both upgraded to 1LE specs) plus air conditioning. Externally, the main difference from a stock Formula model was the use of five-spoke aluminum alloy wheels and a Firehawk decal on the right-hand side of the rear fascia.

The factory Formula had a $19,242 base price and the Firehawk street package was $20,753 for a total delivered price of $39,995. The Firehawk Competition package was $9,905 additional, raising the total bill to $49,990.

When a Firehawk was ordered, Pontiac shipped a new Formula from its Van Nuys, California, factory to SLP Engineering in Toms River, New Jersey. The aftermarket company then extracted the entire drive train and added a Corvette ZF six-speed gearbox with computer-aide gear selection (CAGS), a Dana 44 rear axle with 3.54:1 gears, a shortened input shaft and a 16-pound flywheel. A heavy-duty block fitted with four-bolt mains then got a forged steel crank, Gen II cast pistons, Ed Pink Racing con rods and a hydraulic roller cam. Bolted to this were aluminum heads with 2-inch intake and 1.56-inch stainless-steel exhaust valves.

A special downdraft port-injection manifold was also employed. Designed by Ray Falconer, it featured 11 1/2-inch runners, a 52-mm throttle body, high-flow dual filter system and stainless-steel exhaust headers and exhaust pipes with dual catalytic converters.

Firehawk suspension modifications included revised spring rates, a lowered ride height, new struts, new rear shocks, larger front and rear anti-roll bars, special bushings and Corvette 11.85-inch disc brakes. Firestone 275/40ZR17 Firehawk tires were mounted on the 17 x 9.5-inch Ronal wheels. Recaro seats were extra for $995 and the center console inside the cars was modified to give more space for shift throws.

The competition version of the Firehawk included the Recaro seats as standard equipment, plus 13-inch Brembo vented disc brakes with four-piston calipers, a roll cage and an aluminum hood. The rear seat was also left out.

High Performance Pontiac magazine reported that only 250 copies of what it called the "Quickest Street Pontiac Ever" were going to be made. The magazine found that its test car did 0 to 60 mph in 4.6 seconds and covered the quarter mile in 13.20 seconds at 107 mph.

SLP Engineering targeted production of five cars per week starting in July 1991, but only produced actual cars on a build-to-order basis. A preproduction version of the Competition Firehawk was entered in the Bridgestone Petenza Supercar Series at Lime Rock Race Course on May 27, 1991. It took third place and the company soon had orders for three or four additional competition models.

The SLP kit was also available through GM Service Parts Organization, but it was not shown in sales literature because there was some initial uncertainty about its 1992 EPA certification. In the end, SLP Engineering wound up building only 25 street versions at least one of which was a Trans Am convertible with serial No. 27. That could raise questions in the future, but the reason for the high number was that cars 18 and 25 were ordered but never built.

1993 PONTIAC FIREBIRD

Pontiac draws its cards for its Firebird from the same deck of parts, pieces and mechanicals as Chevrolet does for its F-body brother the Camaro. However, Pontiac always seems to play its hand with a bit more flare and adventure.

Such was the case when it came time for the fourth-generation Firebird to bow as a 1993 model. While Chevy followed GM's simplification program with just one performance model—the Z28—Pontiac had two on the board: The Formula and Trans Am. Both had long histories.

The Firebird (as well as the Camaro) drew heavy media attention when they were added to the 1993 lineups a few weeks after the rest of the cars came out. They kept all their pony-car equipment such as V-8 engines, rear-wheel drive, 2+2 seating, swoopy styling and good performance. While Pontiac wasn't as anxious as Chevrolet to call attention to the Corvette heritage of the 350-cid 275-hp V-8, it sure wanted you to know that the new Trans Am and Formula were worthy of their names. Both the Formula and Trans Am models came standard with the LT1 and a Borg-Warner T56 six-speed manual transmission. Both also got four-wheel, ventilated disc brakes and 16 x 8-inch cast aluminum wheels.

Base delivery price for the 1993 Formula was $18,485, while the Trans Am took $21,875 to open the cash register. Obviously, there must have been some differences.

To go on those wheels, the Formula's standard tires were Goodyear Eagle GA P235/55R16s. Getting them meant also getting a 110-mph governor so the tires wouldn't be overdriven. The Trans Am came with Z-rated Eagle GS-C P245/50ZR16 tires and no governor. Theses tires were a $144 option for the Formula.

The Formula's standard 2.73:1 limited-slip differential also meant that the wide-ratio M28 version of the T56 manual transmission was used. The Trans Am packed high-performance 3.23 gearing, a close-ratio M29 T56 transmission and an engine oil cooler, which was a $110 Formula option.

While all body panels from the beltline down were different from the Camaro, there were also differences between the Formula and Trans Am. Basically, the Formula and base coupe shared body panels and a low rear spoiler. There were simulated air intakes in front. The Trans Am came with a longer nose with fog lights built in, but no air intakes.

Not all of the differences were mechanical or visual. The Trans Am interior made up the rest of the price difference with standard leather appointments, power windows, door locks and cruise control.

When it came time to meet the press, the V-8-powered Firebirds and Camaros were back to sharing, as the testers loved them and went fast (which probably had something to do with the former). "The Trans Am and Z28 models won't disappoint their confirmed and patient fans," said *Road and Track*, which ran a six-speed Trans Am 0-to-60 mph in 6.3 seconds. *Car & Driver* had an even heavier foot in a Formula and got 5.4 with a quarter-mile run of 14.2 seconds and 99 mph and a top speed of 153 mph.

1994 PONTIAC FORMULA FIREBIRD

The 1994 Formula Firebird had the same grille as the base model, but lacked any lettering on the side of the body. It had body-color sport mirrors standard and neutral-density tail-lamp lenses at the rear. New-for-1994 Firebird features included a dark aqua metallic color, flood-lit interior door-lock switches, visor straps, a Delco 2001 Series radio family, a compact-disc player without equalizer, a 5.7-liter sequential-port-fuel-injection V-8; a Mass-Airflow control systemc a four-speed electronically controlled automatic transmission, driver-selectable automatic-transmission controls, a six-speed manual transmission, a 1-to-4 gear-skip feature, traction control (released at midyear for cars with a V-8 and automatic transmission only) and two-component clearcoat exterior finish.

The Formula was the first of three models to come standard with the new 5.7-liter SFI V-8 and six-speed manual transmission. This 275-hp LT1 V-8 was optionally available with the four-speed automatic. With a V-8, the driver-transmission-select switch offered "normal" and "performance" modes. Formulas also got wider P235/55R16 base tires, 16 x 8-inch sport cast-aluminum wheels, standard air conditioning, four-wheel disc brakes, and a performance ride & handling suspension.

Again, the Formula had no body-side lettering, but "Formula V8" identification appeared on the left-hand headlamp cover and right-hand side of the rear bumper. The Formula retained body-color sport mirrors, and smoothly contoured tail lamps with neutral-density lenses (also used on Trans Ams and Trans Am GTs).

The Formula model was actually much the same, in a technical sense, as the Trans Am, except that it did not have speed-rated, high-performance P245/50ZR16 Goodyear Eagle GSC tires. A Firebird convertible was released in the spring. The Formula coupe was base priced at $16.982 and the ragtop was $22,499.

1994 PONTIAC TRANS AM

(Jerry Heasley photo)

The 1994 Pontiac Trans Am featured a redesigned front end.

Pontiac said the 1994 Trans Am had "the power to change minds" and suggested that it represented a mature approach to power, because its performance capabilities were "properly managed." It was much the same as the Formula, except for its speed-rated, high-performance P245/50ZR16 Goodyear Eagle GSC tires.

Externally, the "TA" gained a new, uniquely styled front end without Pontiac's traditional twin-air-slot grille. Instead, the nose had a blunter look, broken by round, sunken running lights on each side of center. The Trans Am name appeared on the body sides, and between the tail lamps (along with a "screaming-chicken" emblem).

A new Trans Am GT was added to the top of the Trans Am lineup. It featured body-color side moldings as standard equipment, plus a special GT spoiler (it looked more like an air foil than the other spoiler). Also standard on this car was an electric rear-window defogger, a remote keyless-entry system, rear carpet mats, a Delco 2001 Series sound system, a four-way manual driver's seat, and a leather-wrapped steering wheel, shift knob and parking-brake handle.

On Feb. 4, 1994, at the Chicago Auto Show, PMD announced that it was introducing a Firebird convertible in the spring. A press kit indicated that the ragtop would be available "on Firebird, Formula and Trans Am models," but only the Trans AM GT came in the open-air-driving style.

All convertibles featured a flush-folding power top that could be stored beneath an easily assembled three-piece tonneau cover. They included a glass rear window and electric rear-window defogger. "These Firebird convertibles weren't an afterthought," revealed Pontiac chief engineer Byron Warner. Warner said that 13 structural parts were added to the Firebird, and front cross member structural stiffness was increased. Structural adhesive was also utilized on 15 key areas, such as the cowl, pillar and rocker reinforcements. Convertibles were built on the St. Therese assembly line, to ensure high quality. Warner said that ragtop drivers "will think they're driving one of our coupes when the top is up."

1994 PONTIAC 25TH ANNIVERSARY TRANS AM

The attractive 25th Anniversary Trans Am special edition came out in 1994.

(Jerry Heasley photo)

Pontiac doesn't do much to mark milestones for its Firebird brand of pony cars, which started life in 1967, but it sure is faithful about marking anniversaries of its Trans Am model, which first became available midyear in 1969. There had been 10th (1979), 15th (1984) and 20th (1989) anniversary editions. All were built in fairly limited numbers. When model year 1994 came along, Pontiac watchers just knew something would go up the flagpole.

The 25th Anniversary Trans Am arrived on January 7, 1989. At first it was only announced for the Trans Am GT coupe. A month later at the Chicago Auto Show the Firebird convertible was introduced and a 25th Anniversary Trans Am GT convertible was put on display.

The theme was obviously taken from the original 1969 1/2 Trans Am, since the car's bright white exterior was decorated with a bright blue stripe down the center. There were also anniversary logos and door badges. Special 16-inch aluminum wheels were done in white, as were the Prado leather seating surfaces with blue embroidery logos that matched those on the door panels. Owners also got a special portfolio commemorating their purchase.

The price for all of this was only $995. Of course, you had to come up with the base price $22,309 for the GT coupe or $27,279 for the GT convertible. "The result is a white-on-white stunner of a car, with the highest profile in traffic this side of a presidential motorcade," said *Car & Driver*.

Despite its 3,668-lb. curb weight and automatic transmission, the 25th Anniversary convertible was good for a 0-to-60 run in 6.1 seconds.

While certainly not as rare as the first Trans Am convertible (only eight of those were made), the 1994 ragtop is certainly a keeper. Its production was low. Seeing that it is part of a set of special editions, its collector value is still fairly high.

1995 PONTIAC/SLP FORMULA FIREHAWK

To Firebird muscle model fans, the letters "SLP" stand for "Street Legal Performance." That was the goal of SLP Engineering. This Toms River, New Jersey, firm was what General Motors called an "aftermarket partner company." It converted new Firebirds that Pontiac shipped to its Garden State shop into super high-performance cars.

Promoted as "an irresistible force that moves you," the 1995 Formula Firehawk version of the Firebird offered 300- and 315-hp versions of the 5.7-liter LT1 V-8, plus all-new features like optional chrome wheels. In addition, Ed Hamburger and his SLP engineers added a Hurst six-speed gear shifter. About 750 Formula Firehawks were sold this year.

Twin air scoops on the Formula Firehawk's snout were part of a special air-induction system that added 25 to 35 hp. The suspension was upgraded from Formula specifications to increase handling limits. Coupes benefited from bigger, better-handling Firestone 275/40/17 tires and 17-inch wide wheels. Firehawk convertibles, however, came only with Firestone 16-inch tires and closed-lug 16-inch-wide alloy wheels. Other Formula Firehawk features included megaphone-style polished stainless-steel tailpipe tips, special exterior graphics and a sequentially numbered dash plaque. A sport suspension and performance exhaust system were optional.

A six-speed Firehawk coupe with the performance exhaust system went from 0 to 60 mph in 4.9 seconds and did the quarter mile

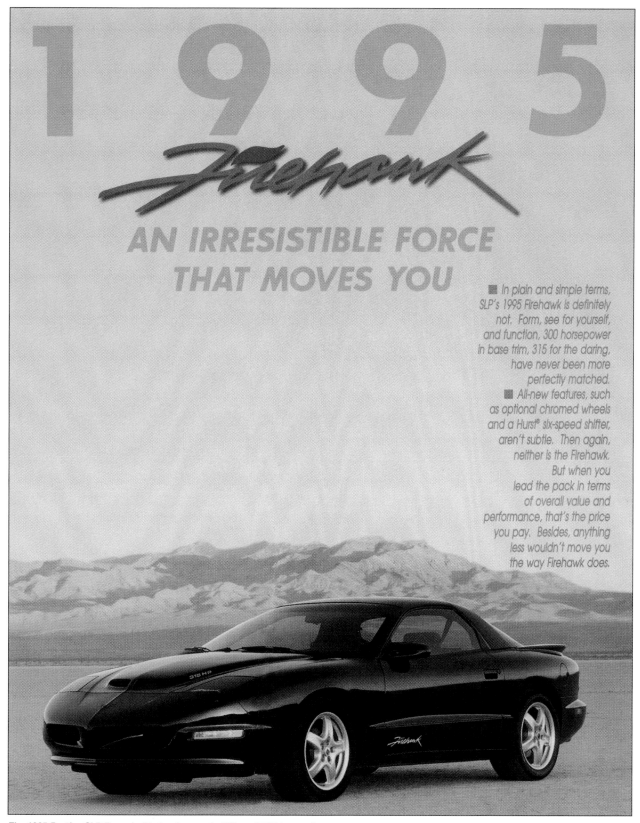

1995 Firehawk
AN IRRESISTIBLE FORCE THAT MOVES YOU

■ In plain and simple terms, SLP's 1995 Firehawk is definitely not. Form, see for yourself, and function, 300 horsepower in base trim, 315 for the daring, have never been more perfectly matched.

■ All-new features, such as optional chromed wheels and a Hurst® six-speed shifter, aren't subtle. Then again, neither is the Firehawk. But when you lead the pack in terms of overall value and performance, that's the price you pay. Besides, anything less wouldn't move you the way Firehawk does.

The 1995 Pontiac SLP Formula Firehawk came in 300- and 315-hp versions.

in 13.5 seconds at 103.5 mph. Its top speed was 160 mph. The Formula Firehawk was available as an SLP alteration on '95 Formulas, which buyers had to order through Pontiac dealers. The Firehawks came with a three-year, 36,000-mile limited warranty. The base price for the alteration was $6,495, an increase of $500 over the 1993 and 1994 versions.

Since the six-speed Hurst shifter was a new accessory for the high-performance 1995 Formula Firehawk model, SLP Engineering promoted this feature by photographing a Firehawk coupe alongside a 1965 Pontiac Catalina 2 + 2—an earlier high-performance Pontiac that also came with a Hurst shifter.

1995 PONTIAC TRANS AM

The 1995 Pontiac Trans Am coupe came with a suggested retail price of $21,184.

(Jerry Heasley photo)

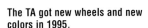

The TA got new wheels and new colors in 1995.

(Jerry Heasley photo)

"Firebird is styled to be noticed, equipped for outstanding performance and handling, and priced to be accessible," said general manager John Middlebrook at the Chicago Auto Show. "A lot of people are taking notice, because for the 1994 model year, Firebird sales were up 143 percent over the previous year. We look for the exciting lineup of 1995 Firebirds to continue a hot sales pace."

The top-of-the-line Trans Am had a number added or replacement standard features over those included with Formulas. They were: fog lamps, body-color body-side moldings, P245/50ZR16 speed-rated all-weather tires, cruise control, automatic power door locks, and an upgraded Delco sound system. Rear-seat courtesy lamps and a trunk lamp were deleted, however.

The 1995 Trans Am coupe had a suggested retail price of $21,184, while the convertible listed for $27,239 in standard equipment form. Both models were powered by the Chevrolet-built 5.7-liter LT1 V-8 with sequential fuel injection. Traction control was now offered for Firebird V-8 models equipped with a four-speed automatic or six-speed manual transmission.

Three new exterior colors were introduced: blue green chameleon, medium dark purple metallic, and bright silver metallic. Inside, a new bright red leather interior option was offered for all models, while a bright white leather interior was an extra limited to convertibles.

Other new features included 16-inch five-spoke wheels for V-8 models, all-weather speed-rated P245/50Z16 tires, a power antenna, and a four-spoke sport steering wheel. Firebird models with optional up-level sound systems were factory pre-wired to receive a Delco 12-disk CD changer, which was available as a new dealer-installed option. All 1995 Firebirds also had maintenance-free lower control-arm ball joints and "lubed-for-life" front-end components. Because Pontiac wheels were designed to show the wheel-and-brake mechanical parts, all Firebird models got a special coating to keep the brake rotors looking new. A new 16-inch, five-spoke wheel was available in chrome for Trans Ams.

1996 PONTIAC FORMULA FIREBIRD

The sleek 1996 Pontiac Formula Firebird coupe had a high-end engine option that produced 305 hp.

Firebird offerings for 1996 included base Firebird, Formula and Trans Am models. All came in coupe and convertible body styles. Formula shared the new WS6 Ram Air performance-and-handling package with the Trans Am.

The Model V87S Formula coupe had a base price of $19,464, while prices for the Model V67S Formula convertible started at $23,135. As on the Trans Am, exhaust system improvements boosted the output of the Formula Firebird's standard 5.7-liter LT1 V-8 to 285 hp—or 305 hp at 5400 rpm with the WS6 option, which produced 335 ft. lbs. of torque at 3200 rpm.

Pontiac said that the hairy-looking WS6 Formula, with its twin-nostril hood, "bridged the gap between the raw power of the Muscle Car Era and today's sophisticated performance and safety technology." The business department of the WS6-equipped Formula was under the hood, where the LT1 engine featured sequential-port fuel injection and an Opti-Spark ignition system. While providing 1960s-like acceleration, it could run smoothly on 91-octane gas.

The 1996 Formula Firebird with the WS6 option came with fat 17-inch Goodyear Eagle GS-C tires. The front and rear springs were both stiffened. The WS6 suspension upgrades included 32-mm/19-mm rear sway bars unique shock valving; stiffer transmission mounts and stiffer Panhard-bar bushings.

The 1996 Formula's V-8 was OBD II compliant (meaning that it met stage II on-board-diagnostic system regulations to assure proper emission controls). OBD II was designed to monitor the EGR valve, oxygen sensor, and crankshaft- and camshaft-position sensors to detect misfiring. Also new for the year was a theft-deterrent system with a personal security key fob available; a new Taupe interior color; a new front seat belt buckle for improved child safety; the availability of steering-wheel-mounted radio controls for all but the W51 sound system; the availability of a power antenna on all Firebirds; a new coaxial four-speaker system option; a new red-orange metallic body color; and zinc brake-corrosion protection on all models.

Pontiac said of the 1996 Firebird, "If it were in your blood, it'd be adrenaline; If it were more advanced, it'd be from NASA; If it came from Italy, it'd be way too expensive!"

1996 PONTIAC TRANS AM

The Pontiac Firebird roared into 1996 with more excitement and more powerful engines. There were several new high-performance packages for V-8 models. Trans Am coupes had a new WS6 Pontiac Ram Air performance-and-handling option that was instantly desirable and appealed to late-model muscle car collectors. The Ram Air-equipped Trans Ams were promoted almost as if they were separate models.

The 1996 Trans Am convertible was the high-priced Firebird this model year. Designated as the Model V67S + Y82 Trans Am, the ragtop retailed for $27,364. Structural adhesives were again used on 15 key areas of every convertible body that Pontiac built, including the cowl, windshield pillar and rocker reinforcements. The Model V87S + Y82 Trans Am Coupe had a base price of $21,414.

The horsepower of the LT1 V-8 (again sourced from the Corvette) was increased to 285, thanks to exhaust-system improvements. With the WS6 Ram Air option, this leaped to 305 hp at 5400 rpm, while torque was 335 ft. lbs. at 3200 rpm. The WS6 package also included a special twin-port hood scoop with Ram Air logos below each "nostril," 17 x 9-inch-wide cast-aluminum five-spoke wheels, P275/40ZR17 tires, a dual-pump catalytic converter system,

The 1996 Trans Am was another Pontiac speed demon with 305 hp.

aluminum exhaust tips and specific suspension tuning.

On the Trans Am, the twin-snout hood was combined with the twin-fog-lamp front fascia. The WS6 Performance & Handling package could not be ordered for the Trans Am convertible. PMD described the WS6 Trans Am as an "open-snouted, fire-breathing dragon made for serious driving enthusiasts who want the response of an I-Ain't-Kiddin' 305-hp V-8 when they press on the accelerator."

1997 PONTIAC FORMULA FIREBIRD

The Formula Firebirds were again characterized by the "twin-nostril" hood in 1997.

(Jerry Heasley photo)

New-for-1997 Firebird features included a redesigned center console with an auxiliary power outlet for cell phones and other electronic devices. The console came with a pull-out side cup holder and a revised storage area. Dark pewter interior finish was newly added, along with Cartagena cloth upholstery. HVAC (heating, ventilation and air-conditioning) control knobs were backlit for better nighttime visibility. Also new inside was a 500-watt Monsoon sound system.

Ragtops included a flush-folding power top, an easily assembled three-piece hard tonneau cover, a rear glass window with electric defogger, and a fully trimmed headliner for a quieter ride. Starting this year, all Firebird convertibles—even this base model—came with power mirrors, power windows, power door locks, cruise control, and rear-seat courtesy lamps.

The Formula was basically a V-8-powered Firebird with a fatter rear stabilizer bar, a quicker steering ratio and four-wheel disc brakes. The Model V87S Formula coupe retailed for $20,724. The V67S Formula convertible was $26,524.

The Formula's 5.7-liter V-8 produced 285 hp at 5000 rpm and 325 ft. lbs. of torque at 2400 rpm. With the WS6 Ram Air Package, these ratings changed to 305 hp at 5400 rpm and 335 ft. lbs. of torque at 3200 rpm. WS6-equipped Formulas were again characterized by the use of a twin-nostril hood with a Ram Air logo on each air-inlet opening.

Body-side moldings were standard on all models now. At midyear, all Firebirds got windshield wipers that went better with their sleek design. Bright green metallic was one new exterior paint choice and bright purple metallic was added at midyear. The other colors were: bright white, bright silver metallic, black, dark green metallic, blue-green chameleon, bright blue metallic, bright red, and red-orange metallic.

Daytime running lamps were made standard equipment on all Firebirds, including Formulas. Unlike conventional DRLs, which use low-intensity regular headlamps, the Firebirds used special high-intensity elements in the parking-signal lamps.

Pontiac expanded availability of the WS6 Performance & Handling package to V-8-powered Formula convertibles. This instantly created one of the year's most collectible cars, as the rapid ragtops seemed to have it all from looks to go-power and rarity.

1997 PONTIAC FIREBIRD
SPECIAL PERFORMANCE MODELS

The 1997 Firebird looked much the same as the 1996 model, but it was treated to a number of equipment upgrades for 1997. One was the optional Sport Appearance Package that made the low-end base Firebird look Trans Am-like.

The standard engine for the 1997 base Firebird was a 3.8-liter V-6 that had a new vibration dampener to reduce vibrations in the engine compartment at high rpms. It produced 200 hp. Available again was a 3800 V-6 Performance Package that included four-wheel disc brakes, a limited-slip differential, dual-outlet exhausts, five-spoke cast aluminum wheels (also available in chrome), P235/55R16 tires, a 14.4:1 steering ratio, and 3.42:1 axle with automatic transmission. There was also a W68 Sport Appearance Package for V-6s, which added or substituted body ground-effects components, specific fog lamps, and dual-outlet exhausts with cast-aluminum extensions.

With the emphasis on V-6 models, it was pretty obvious that gas-price-conscious buyers filled a market niche that Pontiac Motor Division had decided to focus on. In fact, PMD actually built an intriguing prototype car in its engineering garage during 1997. It was a hatch-roof coupe with silver paint, a special ASC (American Sunroof Corp.) graphics package and a *Ram Air* version of the 3800 Series II V-6. *High Performance Pontiac* magazine reported positively on the car's performance in its August 1997 issue, but said that Pontiac was not saying whether it had plans to do a production version.

At the same time, Ed Hamburger's crew at SLP (Street Legal Performance), in Toms River, New Jersey, planned to build about 8,000 cars with Firehawk-type performance conversions. However, SLP—an approved aftermarket converter—had started doing conversions on both Firebirds and Camaros in 1996, which meant that not all of the 1997 Firehawks were Formula Firebirds. Nevertheless, GM continued to farm out specialty work to companies like ASC and SLP, which resulted in some very interesting late-model muscle cars with instant collector-car status.

1997 PONTIAC TRANS AM

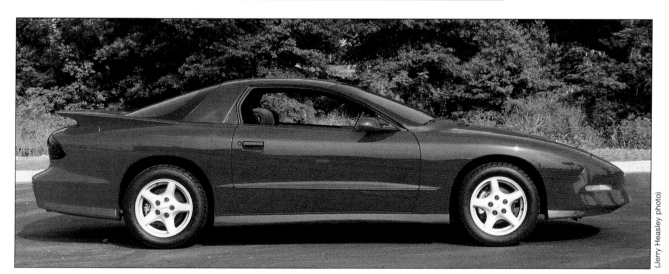

(Jerry Heasley photo)

The 1997 Pontiac Trans Am coupe could be ordered with different engines to fit in different price ranges.

"Either you get it or you don't," was one of the slogans used to sell 1997 Firebirds. The simple message was blunt and clear. You could get a Firebird in a variety of flavors, from affordable to expensive, from economical to guzzler, and from sports car to muscle car—but you couldn't get a Firebird that would please everyone.

The typical buyer of a V-6 Firebird coupe was a 36-year-old person making $55,000 a year. Just over half were married and just below half were male college graduates working in a professional field. At the other end of the Firebird spectrum, Trans Am buyer demographics indicated a median age of 40, average household

(Jerry Heasley photo)

The 1997 Pontiac Trans Am convertible began at $28,444.

income of $75,000 and that slightly over 50 percent of buyers were married males with a college degree and professional occupation.

Air conditioning and the PASS-Key II theft-deterrent system became standard equipment for all 1997 Firebirds, including Trans Ams. Also standard was a four-way seat adjuster located on the left-hand side of the driver's seat.

Starting this year, all Trans Am convertibles incorporated a number of standard features, including power mirrors, power windows, power door locks, cruise control and rear-seat courtesy lamps. The ragtops included a flush-folding power top that stored beneath an easily assembled three-piece hard tonneau cover. When the top was raised, the standard rear-glass window with electric defogger helped give a clear view out the back of the car. A fully trimmed headliner contributed to a quieter ride.

The Trans Am featured a distinctive fog-lamp front fascia that added 1.4 inches to its overall length and 1.2 inches to its front over-hang. It also had slightly more overhang at the rear. The standard 5.7-liter V-8 produced 285 hp at 5000 rpm and 325 ft. lbs. of torque at 2400 rpm. With the WS6 Ram Air Package, these ratings changed to 305 hp at 5400 rpm and 335 ft. lbs. at 3200 rpm. Cars with the $3,000 WS6 option were again characterized by the use of a twin-nostril hood with a Ram Air logo on each air-inlet opening.

The Trans Am coupe, Model V87S + Y82, now had a suggested retail price of $22,884 and prices for the Model V67S + Y82 Trans Am convertible began at $28,444. Trans Am coupes included power sport mirrors, cruise control, power door locks, an electric rear-window defogger, leather-wrapped interior and power windows. Trans Am convertibles also had a power antenna, P245/50ZR16 all-weather speed-rated tires, a Delco 2001 series stereo, remote-keyless entry and a leather-wrapped interior with steering wheel radio controls.

1998 PONTIAC FORMULA FIREBIRD

For 1998, Pontiac Motor Division's stable of aggressively styled cars included a bold new Firebird. In addition to a new appearance guaranteed to continue its legendary status among sports car enthusiasts, the 1998 Formula Firebird had numerous functional improvements, including more V-8 horsepower and torque.

The Formula Firebird model now shared its front fascia design with the base Firebird. The front-end design incorporated twin center ports below the hood and restyled, round, outboard-mounted fog lamps. Two new paint colors, navy metallic and sport gold metallic were available. The Formula Firebird also had new rear-end styling. Inside were gauges with clear white characters on black analog faces to help keep drivers informed of what was going on with their cars.

The 1998 Formula Firebird received a few additional creature comforts, some new colors, and 20 more hp.

In addition to standard Firebird features, the Formula models added or substituted: a power antenna, power door locks, dual power sport type mirrors with blue glass, a 500-watt peak-power "Monsoon" radio with CD and seven-band graphic equalizer (including a clock, touch control, seek up/down, search-and-replay, Delco theft lock and a high-performance 10-speaker system—only six speakers were used in convertibles). The sound system included 6.5-inch HSS speakers and tweeters in the doors, 6.5-inch subwoofers in the sail panels and a sub-woofer amp and 4-inch speakers and tweeters in the rear quarter panels (except on convertibles.)

The sound system option required power windows and door locks, a a leather appointments group, P234.50ZR16 speed-rated all-weather tires and power windows with an express-down feature (which required power windows and door locks).

A beefed-up LS1 5.7-liter V-8 generated 305 hp at 5200 rpm and 335 ft. lbs. of torque at 4000 rpm for enhanced mid-range responsiveness. That was 20 more hp and 10 more ft. lbs. of torque than the previous Firebird V-8 delivered. The WS6-equipped Ram Air LS1 V-8 boasted 320 hp. Pontiac Motor Division called it "a modern muscle car."

1998 PONTIAC TRANS AM

The 1998 Trans Am had a distinctive front-end design. Like Firebirds and Formulas, the Trans Am had center twin ports below the hood and round fog lamps. However, on Trans Ams, the fog lamps were located near the center, while the Firebird and Formula fog lamps were located further outboard.

The aggressive-looking hood design provided smoother contours and also improved underhood airflow. The standard hood had two openings with a Ram Air look that were actually non-functional. A revised 320-hp Ram Air (WS6) package did arrive at midyear. The Ram Air nose had two large "anteater" air scoops that were divided, in front, by a horizontal fin or blade. This was a very, very racy-looking design. Small "Ram Air" lettering appeared on the

sides of the scoops.

New pop-up head lamps had a "mini-quad" design that enhanced the appearance of the car when they were in use and also provided significantly improved road lighting. GM wanted Pontiac to drop flip-up headlights, because they're costly, but market researchers determined that they were a trademark of the Firebird, so they stayed.

An aggressive new fender design, with extractors (or brake-cooling ducts), was common to all Firebird models. A new 16-inch wheel was used on cars with the base V-8. Optional chrome wheels were carried over from 1997, as were the 17-inch wheels on Ram Air cars. Trans Am models also had new rear-end styling.

The 1998 Pontiac Trans Am received a redesigned hood and front end.

Mechanical upgrades included larger brakes all around. Up front, dual-piston aluminum calipers replace the old cast-iron jobs with single-piston bores. The parking brake was reworked, too. Organic pads replaced the previous "semi-mets" and the ABS hardware was also improved with a new Bosch solenoid.

Trans Ams came with all Formula equipment, plus an audible theft-deterrent system, remote keyless entry and a six-way power front driver's seat.

The 5.7-liter 305-hp V-8 was the same used in Formulas. The WS6-equipped Ram Air LS1 V-8 boasted 320 hp. In October 1997, *High Performance Pontiac* magazine featured the 1988 Firebird on its cover and in a story titled "Perfecting Excellence." It explained the LS1 engine improvements in great detail and gave a positive, seat-of-the-pants impression of the performance of the '98 over the already-hot '97.

1999 PONTIAC TRANS AM FIREHAWK

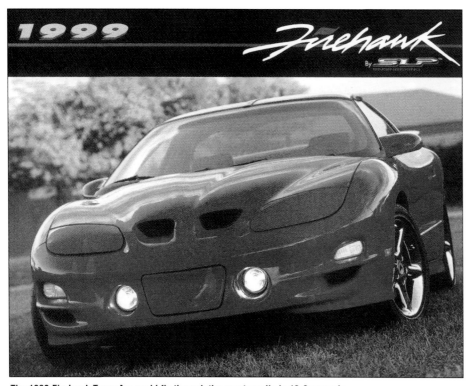

The 1999 Firehawk Trans Am could fly through the quarter mile in 13.6 seconds.

Motor Trend's Jack Keebler (April 1999) described his bright red SLP Trans Am Firehawk as "All Detroit muscle all the time." The "Street Legal Performance" Firebird's 16-valve 5.7-liter V-8 produced 327 hp at 5200 rpm and 345 ft. lbs. of torque at 4400 rpm. The car could do 0 to 60 mph in 5.3 seconds and covered the quarter mile in 13.6 seconds at 105.6 mph.

Keebler was comparing the $31,000 heated-up Firebird to nine other super cars, including the $140,000 Mercedes Benz CL600 and the $299,900 Bentley Continental R. It was the lowest-priced car in the pack, but was right up there with the top performing models.

The reworked 346-cid LS1 block was attached to a Borg-Warner T-56 six-speed manual transmission. A set of meaty P275/40ZR17 Firestone tires "attached" it to the road and helped it slide through a slalom course at 66 mph while pulling a strong 0.89 Gs on a skid pad. The car built by SLP Engineering could still be ordered directly through Pontiac factory dealers.

2000 PONTIAC TRANS AM
10TH ANNIVERSARY FIREHAWK

Pontiac made sure the SLP Trans Am 10th Anniversary Firehawk was again one of the fastest things on the road in 2000.

By 2000, ex-Mopar drag racer Ed Hamburger's SLP Engineering had become a success story. Started in Red Bank, New Jersey, to provide "street legal performance" to muscle car lovers, the firm's futures took off when it struck a deal with Pontiac to convert Firebirds into world-class supercars for the street and sell the SLP package as a factory-approved option through Pontiac dealerships. In 1991, this conversion evolved into the fabulous SLP Trans Am Firehawk, which became a Pontiac dealer option in 1992 and then seemed to get better and faster each year.

Early SLP Firebirds had been more or less based on the image of the black Trans Am that appeared in Burt Reynolds' "Smokey and the Bandit" flicks. The 2000 SLP Trans Am 10th Anniversary Firehawk was based on a car used in the more current *X-Man* movie, but the overall look of a mean black machine with gold trim was the same. It had gold-painted alloy wheels and gold body stripes.

Pontiac dealer order sheets listed the $3,999 Firehawk package as option No. WU6. The $1,999 anniversary package was an add-on that the buyer had to specifically request. It came only in black and only on coupes and included gold stripe decals down the center of the body; gold alloy wheels; Firestone Firehawk radial tires (275/40ZR-17) and 10th anniversary logos.

The Firehawk relied on the Trans Am's LS1 V-8 fitted with a Ram Air induction system designed by SLP (not the WS6 system). The composite hood, which was also designed by SLP and had smaller "nostrils" than the factory version, directed cold air to the hot engine. Other performance upgrades included a freer-flowing exhaust system with special gold, Siamese exhaust tips.

The 346-cid V-8 was tuned for 335 hp at 5200 rpm and 350 ft. lbs. of torque at 4000 rpm. It came mated to a six-speed manual gearbox. It took the $37,658 Firehawk about 5 seconds to zip from 0 to 60 mph. It could cover the quarter mile in 13.6 seconds at 106 mph.

2001 PONTIAC FIREHAWK

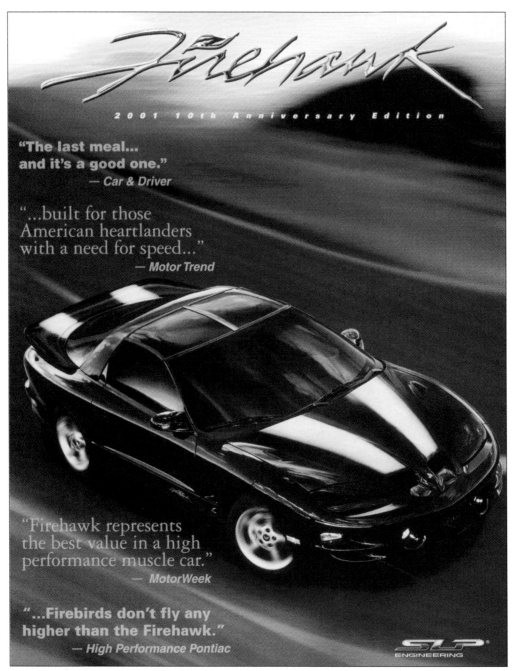

Performance-car fans could have their own Firehawk for $30,000 to $36,000 in 2001.

Pontiac Motor Division and SLP Engineering have had a long-term, muscle car-oriented relationship since the early 1980s and the fruit of their romance for 2001 was another sleek black, modified Firebird created as a modern interpretation of the car from *Smokey and the Bandit*. Like those movies, the Firehawk concept is over 20 years old and it's beginning to show its gray hair, but what a great way to age!

The 2001 Firehawk was based on the Pontiac Trans Am with the 5.7-liter Corvette LS1 V-8. It had a base price of just under $30,000, though most cars hit about $36,000 in total when delivered with a standard assortment of options.

After reworking the 346-cid block a bit, the SLP shop was able to wring 335 hp and 345 ft. lbs. of torque out of the TPI V-8, which is linked to a five-speed manual transmission.

The Firehawk had a 101.1-inch wheelbase and tipped the scales at 3,487 lbs. The car's suspension featured long and short control arms, coil springs all around, a solid rear axle and fat front and rear anti-roll bars. The ABS brakes are vented discs 11.9 inches in diameter up front and 12 inches in diameter at the rear. The five-spoke cast aluminum wheels carried P275/40ZR17 Firestone Firehawk tires front and rear.

Motor Trend (November 2000) liked the Firehawk's great value and strong power train, but criticized its huge, heavy doors, the tiny rear seats and the lack of storage space. The magazine also felt that the heated-up Pontiac had a "teen machine" image. It also mentioned a "hip hopping" rear live axle as a problem on curvy roads. In a straight line, however, the 2001 Firehawk had no problem making it from 0 to 60 mph in 5.16 seconds.

2002 PONTIAC FIREHAWK

Pontiac made sure the SLP Trans Am 10th Anniversary Firehawk was again one of the fastest things on the road in 2000.

SLP Engineering, of Troy, Michigan, produces the Firehawk version of the Pontiac Firebird at is special assembly facility in Montreal, Canada. It is 20 minutes away from the General Motors F-Car assembly plant in Ste. Therese, Canada, where these cars are built. GM ships the cars to SLP for the performance modifications and they are then returned to the GM factory and shipped to Pontiac dealerships.

SLP promotes its 2002 Firehawk with the slogan "It doesn't get any better" and few could argue that claim. The 11th edition of this modern muscle car offers more muscle and more excitement. With up to 345 hp, the 2002 Firehawk can pull up to .90 gs on a skidpad.

New for the 2002 model is the heated-up version of the LSI V-8 engine that develops 350 ft. lbs. of torque. It is coupled to an SLP (Steet Legal Performance) high-flow induction system, as well as the company's proprietary Dual-Dual Performance Exhaust system. To handle the added power, the cars can be shod with new and improved 17-inch Firestone SZ50 extended performance tires.

Special Firehawk features include: an optional IROC-inspired deck-lid spoiler, a super-wide composite hood with scoops and heat extractors, a Firehawk front fascia badge, Firehawk graphics and the extra-cost 17 x 9-inch five-spoke, painted aluminum wheels.

To build a Firehawk, a customer must order a V87X Trans Am coupe, a V67X Trans Am convertible, or a V87X Firebird coupled with the W66 Formula option from the dealer. Then check option WU6, which adds a GM RPO V12 power-steering cooler, plus the QLC tires and 16-inch wheels required for a basic Firehawk.

You can get the Firehawk package in a 330-hp version for $3,999, or the 345-hp version for $4,299. Available options include the all-new rear deck lid spoiler for $699, 17-inch wheels for $799, a Bilstein performance suspension for $1,099, 1LE performance suspension for $1,899, an Auburn high-torque performance differential with AAM cast-aluminum cooling cover for $899, premium front floor mats embroidered with the Firehawk logo for $99, a custom rear deck mat with embroidered logo for $99, a commemorative portfolio for $59 and a custom-fitted car cover with a locking cable and tote bag for $159.

SHELBY

2000 SHELBY SERIES 1

Carroll Shelby's $174,975 Series 1 roadster took a long time to come to market, but when it finally arrived, many people thought it was worth the wait. Others weren't quite convinced until they heard about the supercharged version of the Series 1 roadster released in model year 2000.

The Vortec supercharger was actually merchandised as a dealer-installed extra. The system included special camshafts, a larger-than-stock throttle body and tweaked engine control system software. It brought the Series 1 roadster's price up to around $195,000.

With the supercharger and related goodies installed, the 244-cid Oldsmobile Aurora V-8 produced 450 hp at 6800 rpm and 400 ft. lbs. at 5300 rpm. The engine sported double overhead camshafts and four valves per cylinder. It was linked to a six-speed manual gearbox. It took the lightweight (2,650 lbs.) Series 1 from 0 to 60 mph in an amazing 3.71 seconds. The quarter mile required 12.14 seconds and the car was traveling 120.03 mph by the time the fun ended.

Underneath the Series 1's sleek, race-car-style body was a competition-style suspension with upper and lower control arms, coil springs and front and rear anti-roll bars. Vented disc brakes were used front and rear with 13-inch vented discs up front and 12-inchers at the rear. In front the car wore 18 x 10-inch cast-aluminum rims, with 18 x 12-inch wheels in the rear. The tires were Goodyear Eagle F1 Supercar models, 265/40ZR18 in front and P315/40ZR18 in the rear. Production of the Series 1 was limited to 500 cars.

(Drew Phillips photo)

(Drew Phillips photo)

Not many American production cars could hang with the exotic 2000 Shelby Series 1, which could do the quarter mile in just over 12 seconds.

A Shelby Series 1 with a Vortec supercharger would run you about $195,000 in 2000.

Shelby paid plenty of attention to detail with its 2000 masterpiece.

STUDEBAKER

1963 STUDEBAKER R2 AVANTI

In many ways, the 1963 Studebaker Avanti R2 was ahead of its time.

As a symbol of change and fresh thinking, the Studebaker Avanti was intended as a prime factor in an effort to save Studebaker from oblivion by shaking it loose from its rather musty and stodgy image. Although this effort ended in failure, the Avanti has gained recognition as an outstanding example both of styling excellence and performance competence.

Three engine alternatives were offered for the 1963 Avanti: the base R1 power plant, the supercharged R2 and the seldom-seen and expensive R3. The R1 was a nice, if somewhat unexciting, 280-cid 240-hp V-8. The R3, although garnering a great deal of publicity, was an extremely rare commodity. The R2 was readily available and (at $210) not terribly expensive. It offered a brand of performance rather different from that of the 400-plus-cid V-8s generally available in the mid-1960s.

While the R2 lacked the brute force of other muscle cars, the use of a supercharged and relatively small V-8, along with clever and resourceful use of existing Studebaker components, resulted in an American car that needed no apologies or alibis for either its acceleration or handling.

Officially listed as a 1963 model, the Avanti received a tremendous publicity boost through the successful assault upon existing American records by an R3-engineered Avanti in August. Among the new marks established was a two-way Flying Mile mark of 168.15 mph. Early in 1963, a four-speed-equipped R2 Avanti that was almost completely stock, except for its exhaust system, averaged 158.15 mph through the measured mile.

The R2 Avanti engine was based on Studebaker's V-8, which had entered production in 1951 with a displacement of 232 cid and 120 hp. By 1963, this V-8 had evolved through several displacement changes and for the R2 had reached 289 cid. A sealed Carter AFB four-barrel carburetor was used in conjunction with a Paxton SN-60 centrifugal supercharger. Due to the supercharger, the compression ratio of the R2 was at 9.0:1—lower than the R1's 10.25:1. Output of the R2 was impressive: 289 hp at 5200 rpm and 330 ft. lbs. of torque at 3600 rpm.

Aside from having an engine that developed 1 hp per cubic inch, the Avanti was the first full-size American car to be endowed with front caliper disc brakes. These 11.5-inch units were supplied by Bendix and were produced under license from Dunlop. In their basic design they were similar to those used by Jaguar. Finned drums were used at the rear.

Neither the Avanti's standard three-speed manual transmission nor its optional air conditioning were available with the R2 engine. Instead, customers selected either a four-speed Warner Gear T-10 all-synchromesh gearbox or a three-speed "power-shift" automatic produced by Borg-Warner, which permitted manual shifting if desired. Overall length of the Avanti was 192.4 inches and curb weight was approximately 3,400 lbs.

The performance and top-speed capability of the R2 was superb. *Road and Track*, October 1962, reported a 0-to-60 time for the four-speed model of 7.3 seconds. *Motor Trend,* July 1962, noted that a power-shift model needed 8 seconds for the same run.

With a total 1963 model year run of just 3,834 units, the Avanti was truly a limited-edition vehicle. The subsequent output of an additional 809 units in 1964—as well as the regeneration of the Avanti in its various Avanti II permutations—has not diluted the appeal of the 1963 R2 Avanti.

1963 STUDEBAKER R2 SUPER HAWK

A supercharged engined helped turn the 1963 Studebaker Hawk into the R2 Super Hawk.

The 1963 Studebaker Super Hawk—billed in some publications of the time as a 1963 1/2 model—was the last, wonderful gasp of the Raymond Loewy coupe. The Hawk's basic style stemmed from that 10-year-old design with some handsome updating done by Brooks Stevens in late 1962.

The R2 Super Hawks featured the supercharged Avanti engine. The idea for the Super Hawk was born on the Utah salt flats at Bonneville in January of 1963 when Andy Granatelli, then Studebaker Corp.'s vice president in charge of Paxton Products Division, drove an R2-powered GT Hawk in a series of high-speed runs. These runs netted a top speed mark of 140.23 mph for the Flying Mile. All subsequent Super Hawks with the R2 engine are replicas of that Bonneville car.

The Bonneville-bred Super Hawk package carried a price tag of $581.70 back in 1963. That included an R2 engine with a Paxton-McCulloch supercharger, power-assisted disc brakes, front and rear heavy-duty shocks and springs, rear-axle radius rods (traction bars), a rear anti-roll bar, a twin-traction rear axle, 6.70-15 four-ply tires, a tachometer and front-and-rear carpeting. And to show they were serious, Studebaker also included a 160-mph speedometer, a manifold pressure gauge and special identification badges.

With only 289 cid, the Studebaker V-8 was one of the smallest engines then offered in a full-sized American car. It was rated at 210 hp at 4500 rpm and had an 8.5:1 compression ratio in basic trim with a two-barrel carburetor. Studebaker was reluctant to give any horsepower figures above the basic, but *Motor Trend* estimated that its output was 300 hp at 5000-5200 rpm. This was brought about by a half-point rise in compression, a four-barrel carburetor, a slightly wilder camshaft and the Paxton SN-60 centrifugal supercharger. *Motor Trend* pulled two-way quarter-mile runs that averaged out at 85.2 mph and 16.8 seconds. The 0 to 60-mph run was accomplished in 8.5 seconds.

The Paxton supercharger was belt driven and had a boost ratio of 6:1. On the 289-cid Studebaker engine, the supercharger delivered a maximum of 4 lbs. of boost at 4,000 rpm and held this figure up to 5,500 rpm. Above 4,000 rpm, it delivered full-rated pressure any time the throttle was opened wide. *Motor Trend* found this meant an honest 118 mph at 5700 rpm on a backstretch of the old Riverside Raceway.

The Golden Hawk was one of the best-braking domestic cars of its day. It featured Dunlop-licensed Bendix disc brakes at the front, plus large, finned drum brakes in the rear. Power assist was considered a must by *Motor Trend* because of the high pedal pressure required.

Either a four-speed stick or a Power-Shift automatic had to be ordered with the Super Hawk package. The Power-Shift was a standard Borg-Warner automatic transmission with modifications. With the lever in the "1" position, first gear only was engaged and the transmission wouldn't upshift until the lever was moved manually. The "2" position was the same. With the lever in "D," the transmission would start in second and automatically upshift at 5000 rpm. Second was also available automatically as passing gear while cruising in D range below 65 mph. A passing gear was also available manually below 80 mph.

While the 1-2 and 2-3 shifts in the automatic transmission Studebaker supplied were accomplished with less slippage than the standard Borg-Warner, it still didn't equal the manual four-speed.

Another interesting option available in 1963 for the Golden Hawk was Halibrand magnesium wheels for $240 per set from Studebaker dealers. Finding these on a collector car today should increase its value.

1964 STUDEBAKER AVANTI

The stylish 1964 Studebaker Avanti came with four different engine options.

The Avanti had plenty going for it as a muscle car, but the model died an untimely death after 1964.

Why change something as great looking as the Avanti?

In 1964, Studebaker didn't have the reason or resources to tailor big alterations for its high-performance "last hurrah." Actually, there wasn't even a distinct point at which 1963 model production halted and assemblies of '64 Avantis began.

Changes were kind of phased in. A round heater, defroster and vent knobs were a characteristic of most, but not all, '64s. And the majority—some say all except the first 59 built—had square headlamp housings.

Performance options included R1, R2, R3 and R4 engines. The first was the base 289-cid 240-hp four-barrel V-8 with a 10.25:1 compression ratio. A lower 9.0:1 compression ratio accompanied the supercharged R2 engine with its 289 hp. With 304.5 cid, the supercharged R3 developed 335 hp and was used in only 10 cars. Even rarer was the 280-hp dual-quad carbureted R4, which was installed on only one car.

The R1 Avanti did the quarter mile in 17.2 seconds and sped from 0 to 60 mph in just over 9 seconds. With the R4, the figures were 15.8 seconds and 8 seconds, respectively. Faster yet was the R3, which hustled down a drag strip in 14.3 seconds and achieved 60 mph in 6.7 seconds.

To promote the '64s, Andy Granatelli returned to the Bonneville Salt Flats in Utah with a fleet of Avantis. There, he broke his own record by driving an R3-engined car 170.78 mph. Studebaker President Sherwood H. Egbert managed to turn in a 168-mph pass.

Unfortunately, Egbert was more successful at driving a racecar than he was at running an automobile company. In December 1963, the company closed its U.S. production facilities in South Bend, Indiana. Some Studebakers continued to be built in Canada for a while, but Avantis were not. When the last of the 809 models made in 1964 was constructed, the Studebaker Avanti was done for.

1964 STUDEBAKER DAYTONA

The long-lost 1964 Studebaker Daytona is a valuable, if largely forgotten, muscle car today.

Designer Brooks Stevens effected more than a facelift when he created the new Studebaker Daytona hardtop in 1964. The crisp, squared-off roof that Stevens grafted onto the now 4-year-old Lark body looked every bit as up to date as Chevy's equally angular Impala. Of course, the Daytona was narrower than a full-size Chevy (Studebaker's basic body stampings dated back to 1953 and most American cars had grown substantially wider over the intervening decade), but its size fit nicely with the new intermediates.

What really made the Daytona stand out were the performance options available. Lacking money for frequent styling changes, Studebaker had attempted to garner attention through performance with its Hawk coupes and the stunning Avanti. Studebaker's overhead-valve V-8, first introduced in 1951, had been a farsighted enough design that more than a dozen years later it was being boosted to outputs exceeding 1 hp per cubic inch.

Studebaker designated its high-output V-8s as the R-series engines. The "base" R1 engine developed 240 hp from a 289-cid displacement. Next came the R2, also a 289, but equipped with a supercharger for a rated 289 hp. The R3, also supercharged and with a slightly larger displacement of 304.5 cid, gave a power rating of 335 hp. The final engine in this series, dubbed the R4, ran two four-barrel carburetors without supercharging for a rated 280 hp. It was this engine that Studebaker selected to create a street "sleeper" from its

docile-looking Daytona hardtop.

With a top speed of 132 mph and 0-to-60 acceleration of 7.8 seconds, Studebaker's R4 Daytona could show its taillights to any production sedan. Its performance was rivaled only by that of the Pontiac GTO, which was also released in 1964. As might be expected, performance carried a mileage penalty. An R4 Daytona owner could expect little more than 12 to 14 mpg. With a total carburetor venturi area of 13 inches, the Daytona's 304.5-cid engine was capable of gulping plenty of fuel.

Performance cars of the 1950s and 1960s have a great reputation for going like lightning in a straight line, but come to a corner and watch out. To give the Daytona some measure of road-handling ability, Studebaker fit it with an Avanti suspension package that consisted of stiffer springs and shocks, anti-roll bars front and rear, and front disc brakes. To glue the engine's power to the pavement, these performance cars came standard with traction bars and a limited-slip differential. To put the R4's power to pleasurable use, Studebaker fitted its hot Daytona model with a Borg-Warner T-10 four-speed transmission.

Not many performance Daytonas were built (besides the R4, other R series engines could also be optioned) making them one of the least known and rarest of muscle cars—a real "sleeper" even today.

1964 STUDEBAKER HAWK GT

The 1964 Studebaker Hawk GT could handle and perform with the best cars of its era.

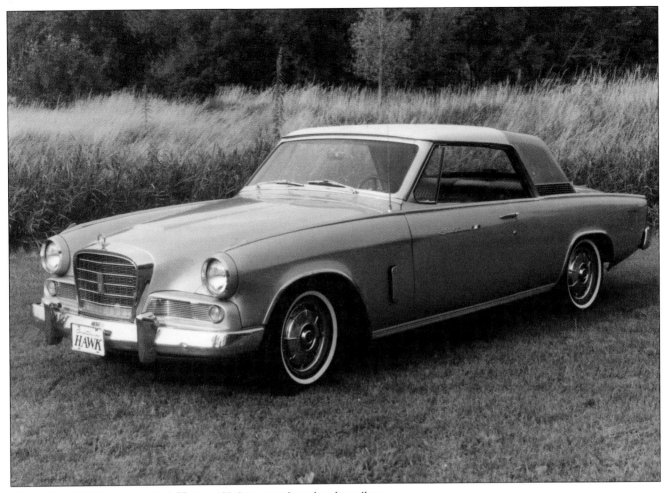

The shortlived 1964 Studebaker Hawk GT came with three supercharged engine options.

The 1964 Studebaker GT Hawk was the end of the line for Studebaker in many ways. It was the final model of the Raymond Loewy-inspired and Robert Bourke-designed hardtop body that debuted in 1953. In addition, all Studebaker production halted on December 20, 1964, after 1,767 Hawks were built. Studebaker kept making sedans and station wagons in Hamilton, Ontario, Canada, but production of Hawks, Avantis and trucks ceased forever.

The 1963 and 1964 Hawks benefited from the Avanti's options. The R-series engines offered in high-performance Avantis were made available in Hawks. The R1 option was a non-supercharged 289-cid, 240-hp V-8. The R2 was also a 289-cid engine, but had a Paxton supercharger puffing out an estimated 290 hp (Studebaker didn't advertise the horsepower ratings). Studebaker owned Paxton and had the services of its colorful vice president, Andy Granatelli.

An ultra-rare R3-optioned engine was truly a high-output job. It was bored out to 304.5 cid and built by race engine craftsmen at Paxton Products in California. They were estimated to have between 335 and 400 hp.

For a final hurrah, Granatelli took samples of the entire 1964 Studebaker line— Hawks, Avantis, Daytonas, even a six-cylinder Commander sedan—to Bonneville again in October 1963. The result was an astounding 337 new speed marks in United States Auto Club (USAC) record books. A 1964 R3-engined prototype Super Hawk was driven by Paula Murphy to a record 154 mph.

In spite of all this frenzied activity, Studebaker sales were dismal. The decision to cease production came shortly after President John Kennedy's assassination on November 22, 1963.

The '64 Studebaker GT was truly a "family sports car." With its optional Avanti engines, disc brakes, heavy-duty springs and sway bars, sporty interior and modern styling, the Grand Turismo Hawks could hold their own with the best Detroit and Europe offered.

A fully equipped GT, with R2 engine, four-speed transmission, limited-slip differential, disc brakes, heavy-duty suspension and numerous convenience items, cost about $4,500—a fairly hefty price then. However, when compared with similar performance cars of the era, the GT Hawk was competitive.

PRICE GUIDE

VEHICLE CONDITION SCALE

❶ Excellent: Restored to current maximum professional standards of quality in every area, or perfect original with components operating and appearing as new. A 95-plus point show car that is not driven.

❷ Fine: Well-restored or a combination of superior restoration and excellent original parts. Also, an extremely well-maintained original vehicle showing minimal wear.

❸ Very Good: Completely operable original or older restoration. Also, a good amateur restoration, all presentable and serviceable inside and out. Plus, a combination of well-done restoration and good operable components or a partially restored car with all parts necessary to complete and/or valuable NOS parts.

❹ Good: A driveable vehicle needing no or only minor work to be functional. Also, a deteriorated restoration or a very poor amateur restoration. All components may need restoration to be "excellent," but the car is mostly useable "as is."

❺ Restorable: Needs complete restoration of body, chassis and interior. May or may not be running, but isn't weathered, wrecked or stripped to the point of being useful only for parts.

❻ Parts car: May or may not be running, but is weathered, wrecked and/or stripped to the point of being useful primarily for parts.

Note: Prices taken from *Old Cars Price Guide* and include some models and years not covered in this book.

AMC

	6	5	4	3	2	1
1965 Marlin						
2d FBk	550	1,700	2,800	5,600	9,800	14,000

NOTE: Deduct 5 percent for 6-cyl.

	6	5	4	3	2	1
1967 Rambler Marlin						
2d FBk Cpe	550	1,600	2,700	5,400	9,450	13,500
1968 AMX						
2d FBk	800	2,400	4,000	8,000	14,000	20,000

NOTE: Add 25 percent for Craig Breedlove Edit.

	6	5	4	3	2	1
1968 Javelin SST						
2d FBk	660	1,980	3,300	6,600	11,550	16,500

NOTE: Add 20 percent for GO pkg. Add 30 percent for Big Bad pkg.

	6	5	4	3	2	1
1969 AMX						
2d FBk Cpe	800	2,400	4,000	8,000	14,000	20,000

NOTE: Add 25 percent for Big Bad Pkg.

	6	5	4	3	2	1
1969 Rambler Hurst S/C						
2d HT	720	2,160	3,600	7,200	12,600	18,000
1969 Javelin SST						
2d FBk Cpe	660	1,980	3,300	6,600	11,550	16,500

NOTE: Add 20 percent for GO Pkg. Add 30 percent for Big Bad pkg.

	6	5	4	3	2	1
1970 Rebel "Machine"						
2d HT	750	2,200	3,700	7,400	13,000	18,500
1970 AMX						
2d FBk Cpe	800	2,400	4,000	8,000	14,000	20,000
1970 Javelin SST						
2d FBk Cpe	576	1,728	2,880	5,760	10,080	14,400

NOTE: Add 20 percent for GO pkg. Add 30 percent for Big Bad pkg.

	6	5	4	3	2	1
1971 Javelin AMX						
2d HT	540	1,620	2,700	5,400	9,450	13,500

NOTE: Add 15 percent for GO Pkg.

	6	5	4	3	2	1
1971 Hornet SC/360						
2d HT	520	1,560	2,600	5,200	9,100	13,000
1972 Javelin						
2d SST	280	840	1,400	2,800	4,900	7,000
2d AMX	320	960	1,600	3,200	5,600	8,000
2d Go "360"	500	1,550	2,600	5,200	9,100	13,000
2d Go "401"	550	1,700	2,800	5,600	9,800	14,000
2d Cardin	520	1,560	2,600	5,200	9,100	13,000

NOTE: Add 20 percent for 401 V-8. Add 25 percent for 401 Police Special V-8. Add 30 percent for GO Pkg.

	6	5	4	3	2	1
1978 AMX						
2d HBk	144	432	720	1,440	2,520	3,600
1979 AMX, V-8						
2d HBk	148	444	740	1,480	2,590	3,700

NOTE: Deduct 7 percent for 6-cyl.

(Janet Kaufmann photo)

1970 AMC Rebel Machine

1970 Buick GS 455

BUICK

	6	5	4	3	2	1
1965 Riviera, V-8, 117" wb						
2d HT	760	2,280	3,800	7,600	13,300	19,000
2d HT GS	800	2,400	4,000	8,000	14,000	20,000

NOTE: Add 20 percent for 400.

1966 Skylark Gran Sport, V-8, 115" wb						
2d Cpe	640	1,920	3,200	6,400	11,200	16,000
2d HT	880	2,640	4,400	8,800	15,400	22,000
2d Conv	920	2,760	4,600	9,200	16,100	23,000

1967 Gran Sport 340, V-8, 115" wb						
2d HT	640	1,920	3,200	6,400	11,200	16,000

1967 Gran Sport 400, V-8, 115" wb						
2d Cpe	560	1,680	2,800	5,600	9,800	14,000
2d HT	660	1,980	3,300	6,600	11,550	16,500
2d Conv	840	2,520	4,200	8,400	14,700	21,000

1968 Gran Sport GS 400, V-8, 112" wb						
2d HT	680	2,040	3,400	6,800	11,900	17,000
2d Conv	800	2,400	4,000	8,000	14,000	20,000

NOTE: Add 15 percent for Skylark GS Calif. Spl.

1969 Gran Sport GS 400, V-8, 112" wb						
2d HT	720	2,160	3,600	7,200	12,600	18,000
2d Conv	880	2,640	4,400	8,800	15,400	22,000

NOTE: Add 30 percent for Stage I option.

1970 Gran Sport GS 455, V-8, 112" wb						
2d HT	720	2,160	3,600	7,200	12,600	18,000
2d Conv	920	2,760	4,600	9,200	16,100	23,000

NOTE: Add 40 percent for Stage I 455.

1987 Buick Gran National

(Jerry Heasley photo)

	6	5	4	3	2	1
1971-1972 Gran Sport, 350, V-8						
2d HT	680	2,040	3,400	6,800	11,900	17,000
2d Conv	880	2,640	4,400	8,800	15,400	22,000
2d HT GSX	960	2,880	4,800	9,600	16,800	24,000

NOTE: Add 40 percent for Stage I & 20 percent for GS-455 options. Add 15 percent for folding sunroof.

1986 Regal, V-6						
2d Cpe, V-8	188	564	940	1,880	3,290	4,700
2d Cpe Ltd, V-8	196	588	980	1,960	3,430	4,900
2d Cpe T-Type	400	1,200	2,000	4,000	7,000	10,000
2d T-Type Grand Natl	760	2,280	3,800	7,600	13,300	19,000

CHEVROLET

1961 Chevrolet Impala SS sports coupe

1961 Impala, V-8	6	5	4	3	2	1
2d Sed	520	1,560	2,600	5,200	9,100	13,000
4d Sed	524	1,572	2,620	5,240	9,170	13,100
4d HT	580	1,740	2,900	5,800	10,150	14,500
2d HT*	840	2,520	4,200	8,400	14,700	21,000
2d Conv*	1,320	3,960	6,600	13,200	23,100	33,000

1962 Bel Air, V-8						
2d Sed	424	1,272	2,120	4,240	7,420	10,600
4d Sed	428	1,284	2,140	4,280	7,490	10,700
2d HT	960	2,880	4,800	9,600	16,800	24,000
4d Sta Wag	600	1,800	3,000	6,000	10,500	15,000

NOTE: Add 10 percent for "Power-Pack" & dual exhaust on 283 V-8. Add 15 percent for A/C. Add 35 percent for 348 CID. Add 40 percent for Super Sport option. Add 50 percent for 409 V-8. Deduct 10 percent

	6	5	4	3	2	1

1962 Chevy II, 4 & 6-cyl.

	6	5	4	3	2	1
2d Sed	404	1,212	2,020	4,040	7,070	10,100
4d Sed	400	1,200	2,000	4,000	7,000	10,000
2d HT	720	2,160	3,600	7,200	12,600	18,000
2d Conv	880	2,640	4,400	8,800	15,400	22,000
4d Sta Wag	540	1,620	2,700	5,400	9,450	13,500

1963 Impala, V-8

	6	5	4	3	2	1
4d Sed	520	1,560	2,600	5,200	9,100	13,000
4d HT	600	1,800	3,000	6,000	10,500	15,000
2d HT*	1,040	3,120	5,200	10,400	18,200	26,000
2d Conv*	1,360	4,080	6,800	13,600	23,800	34,000
4d Sta Wag	600	1,800	3,000	6,000	10,500	15,000

NOTE: Add 15 percent for "Power-Pack" & dual exhaust. Add 15 percent for A/C. Add 35 percent for 409 CID. Add 15 percent for Super Sport option. Deduct 10 percent for 6-cyl. except Chevy II.

1964 Impala, V-8

	6	5	4	3	2	1
4d Sed	420	1,260	2,100	4,200	7,350	10,500
4d HT	580	1,740	2,900	5,800	10,150	14,500
2d HT*	960	2,880	4,800	9,600	16,800	24,000
2d Conv*	1,400	4,200	7,000	14,000	24,500	35,000
4d Sta Wag	640	1,920	3,200	6,400	11,200	16,000

NOTE: Add 15 percent for Super Sport option. Add 15 percent for Power-Pack & dual exhaust. Add 15 percent for A/C. Add 35 percent for 409 CID. Deduct 10 percent for 6-cyl.

1964 Malibu Series, V-8

	6	5	4	3	2	1
4d Sed	384	1,152	1,920	3,840	6,720	9,600
2d HT*	800	2,400	4,000	8,000	14,000	20,000
2d Conv*	1,240	3,720	6,200	12,400	21,700	31,000
4d Sta Wag	520	1,560	2,600	5,200	9,100	13,000

NOTE: Add 15 percent for Super Sport option. Deduct 10 percent for 6-cyl.

1965 Impala Super Sport, V-8

	6	5	4	3	2	1
2d HT	840	2,520	4,200	8,400	14,700	21,000
2d Conv	1,280	3,840	6,400	12,800	22,400	32,000

NOTE: Add 20 percent for "Power-Pack" & dual exhaust. Add 15 percent for A/C. Add 35 percent for 409 CID. Add 35 percent for 396 CID, 325 hp. Add 50 percent for 396 CID, 425 hp. Add 40 percent for 409

1966 Malibu, V-8

	6	5	4	3	2	1
4d Sed	392	1,176	1,960	3,920	6,860	9,800
4d HT	400	1,200	2,000	4,000	7,000	10,000
2d HT	840	2,520	4,200	8,400	14,700	21,000
2d Conv	1,120	3,360	5,600	11,200	19,600	28,000
4d Sta Wag	400	1,200	2,000	4,000	7,000	10,000

1966 Impala Super Sport, V-8

	6	5	4	3	2	1
2d HT	1,000	3,000	5,000	10,000	17,500	25,000
2d Conv	1,240	3,720	6,200	12,400	21,700	31,000

1966 Chevelle

	6	5	4	3	2	1
2d Sed	376	1,128	1,880	3,760	6,580	9,400
4d Sed	380	1,140	1,900	3,800	6,650	9,500
4d Sta Wag	388	1,164	1,940	3,880	6,790	9,700

1966 Nova Super Sport

	6	5	4	3	2	1
2d HT	800	2,400	4,000	8,000	14,000	20,000

NOTE: Add 60 percent for High Performance pkg.

1967 Chevelle Super Sport 396, 115" wb

	6	5	4	3	2	1
2d HT	1,200	3,600	6,000	12,000	21,000	30,000
2d Conv	1,360	4,080	6,800	13,600	23,800	34,000

NOTE: Add 10 percent for 396 CID, 350 hp. Add 30 percent for 396 CID, 375 hp.

1967 Chevy II Nova SS, V-8, 110" wb

	6	5	4	3	2	1
2d HT	700	2,100	3,500	7,000	12,250	17,500

NOTE: Add 60 percent for High Performance pkg.

1967 Camaro, V-8

	6	5	4	3	2	1
2d IPC	1,320	3,960	6,600	13,200	23,100	33,000
2d Cpe	880	2,640	4,400	8,800	15,400	22,000
2d Conv	1,120	3,360	5,600	11,200	19,600	28,000
2d Z28 Cpe	1,680	5,040	8,400	16,800	29,400	42,000
2d Yenko Cpe	3,120	9,360	15,600	31,200	54,600	78,000

NOTE: Deduct 5 percent for Six, (when available). Add 15 percent for Rally Sport Package, (when available; except incl. w/Indy Pace Car). Add 25 percent for SS 350 (when available; except incl. w/Indy

1968 Chevelle SS 396

	6	5	4	3	2	1
2d HT	1,040	3,120	5,200	10,400	18,200	26,000
2d Conv	1,320	3,960	6,600	13,200	23,100	33,000

1968 Camaro, V-8

	6	5	4	3	2	1
2d Cpe	760	2,280	3,800	7,600	13,300	19,000
2d Conv	920	2,760	4,600	9,200	16,100	23,000
2d Z28	1,040	3,120	5,200	10,400	18,200	26,000
2d Yenko Cpe	2,560	7,680	12,800	25,600	44,800	64,000

NOTE: Deduct 5 percent for Six (when available). Add 10 percent for A/C. Add 15 percent for Rally Sport Package (when available). Add 25 percent for SS package. Add 15 percent for SS-350 (when availab

1968 Nova 307 V8

	6	5	4	3	2	1
2d Cpe	392	1,176	1,960	3,920	6,860	9,800
4d Sed	360	1,080	1,800	3,600	6,300	9,000

NOTE: Deduct 5 percent for 4 or 6-cyl. Add 25 percent for SS package. Add 25 percent for 327 CID. Add 30 percent for 350 CID. Add 35 percent for 396 CID engine.

1969 Chevelle Malibu SS 396

	6	5	4	3	2	1
2d HT	920	2,760	4,600	9,200	16,100	23,000
2d Conv	1,160	3,480	5,800	11,600	20,300	29,000

NOTE: Add 60 percent for Yenko Hardtop.

(Mike Carbonella photo)

1970 Chevrolet Chevelle SS 455

1993 Chevrolet Camaro Z/28

(Jerry Heasley photo)

	6	5	4	3	2	1
1969 Camaro, V-8						
2d Spt Cpe	800	2,400	4,000	8,000	14,000	20,000
2d Conv	1,000	3,000	5,000	10,000	17,500	25,000
2d Z28	1,000	3,000	5,000	10,000	17,500	25,000
2d IPC	1,160	3,480	5,800	11,600	20,300	29,000
2d ZL-1*	3,040	9,120	15,200	30,400	53,200	76,000
2d Yenko	1,960	5,880	9,800	19,600	34,300	49,000

NOTE: Deduct 5 percent for Six, (when available). Add 10 percent for A/C. Add 10 percent for Rally Sport (except incl. w/Indy Pace Car). Add 25 percent for SS-350 (when avail.; except incl. w/Indy Pac

1969 Chevy II, Nova V-8

	6	5	4	3	2	1
2d Cpe	220	660	1,100	2,200	3,850	5,500
4d Sed	216	648	1,080	2,160	3,780	5,400
2d Yenko Cpe	2,400	7,200	12,000	24,000	42,000	60,000

NOTE: Add 25 percent for Nova SS. Add 30 percent for 350 CID. Add 35 percent for 396 CID. Add 10 percent for Impala "SS". Add 25 percent for other "SS" equipment pkgs.

1970 Nova, V-8

	6	5	4	3	2	1
2d Cpe	208	624	1,040	2,080	3,640	5,200
4d Sed	204	612	1,020	2,040	3,570	5,100
2d Yenko Cpe	2,240	6,720	11,200	22,400	39,200	56,000

NOTE: Add 25 percent for SS option.

1970 Monte Carlo

	6	5	4	3	2	1
2d HT	720	2,160	3,600	7,200	12,600	18,000

NOTE: Add 35 percent for SS 454.

1970 Camaro, V-8

	6	5	4	3	2	1
2d Cpe	600	1,800	3,000	6,000	10,500	15,000
2d Z28	760	2,280	3,800	7,600	13,300	19,000

NOTE: Deduct 5 percent for Six, (except Z28). Add 35 percent for the 375 horsepower 396, (L78 option). Add 35 percent for Rally Sport and/or Super Sport options.

1970 Chevelle Malibu SS 396

	6	5	4	3	2	1
2d HT	1,000	3,000	5,000	10,000	17,500	25,000
2d Conv	1,200	3,600	6,000	12,000	21,000	30,000

1970 Chevelle Malibu SS 454

	6	5	4	3	2	1
2d HT	1,160	3,480	5,800	11,600	20,300	29,000
2d Conv	1,360	4,080	6,800	13,600	23,800	34,000

NOTE: Add 30 percent for 396 CID, 375 hp. Add 50 percent for LS6 engine option.

	6	5	4	3	2	1
1971 Nova, V-8						
4d Sed	200	600	1,000	2,000	3,500	5,000
2d Sed	208	624	1,040	2,080	3,640	5,200
2d SS	272	816	1,360	2,720	4,760	6,800

1971 Monte Carlo

	6	5	4	3	2	1
2d HT	720	2,160	3,600	7,200	12,600	18,000

NOTE: Add 35 percent for SS 454. Add 25 percent for SS 402 engine option.

1971 Camaro, V-8

	6	5	4	3	2	1
2d Cpe	600	1,800	3,000	6,000	10,500	15,000
2d Z28	720	2,160	3,600	7,200	12,600	18,000

NOTE: Add 35 percent for Rally Sport and/or Super Sport options.

1971 Chevelle

	6	5	4	3	2	1
2d HT	600	1,800	3,000	6,000	10,500	15,000
2d Malibu HT	800	2,400	4,000	8,000	14,000	20,000
2d Malibu Conv	1,000	3,000	5,000	10,000	17,500	25,000
4d HT	400	1,200	2,000	4,000	7,000	10,000
4d Sed	220	660	1,100	2,200	3,850	5,500
4d Concours Est Wag	360	1,080	1,800	3,600	6,300	9,000

1972 Monte Carlo

	6	5	4	3	2	1
2d HT	720	2,160	3,600	7,200	12,600	18,000

NOTE: Add 35 percent for 454 CID engine. Add 25 percent for 402 engine option.

1972 Camaro, V-8

	6	5	4	3	2	1
2d Cpe	640	1,920	3,200	6,400	11,200	16,000
2d Z28	760	2,280	3,800	7,600	13,300	19,000

NOTE: Add 35 percent for Rally Sport and/or Super Sport options.

1972 Chevelle Malibu SS

	6	5	4	3	2	1
2d HT	840	2,520	4,200	8,400	14,700	21,000
2d Conv	1,080	3,240	5,400	10,800	18,900	27,000

1972 Chevelle Malibu SS 454

	6	5	4	3	2	1
2d HT	920	2,760	4,600	9,200	16,100	23,000
2d Conv	1,160	3,480	5,800	11,600	20,300	29,000

1975 Vega

	6	5	4	3	2	1
2d Cpe	200	600	1,000	2,000	3,500	5,000
2d HBk	204	612	1,020	2,040	3,570	5,100
2d Lux Cpe	204	612	1,020	2,040	3,570	5,100
4d Sta Wag	208	624	1,040	2,080	3,640	5,200
4d Est Wag	212	636	1,060	2,120	3,710	5,300
2d Cosworth	320	960	1,600	3,200	5,600	8,000

1977 Camaro, V-8

	6	5	4	3	2	1
2d Spt Cpe	400	1,200	2,000	4,000	7,000	10,000
2d Spt Cpe LT	420	1,260	2,100	4,200	7,350	10,500
2d Spt Cpe Z28	520	1,560	2,600	5,200	9,100	13,000

1978 Camaro, V-8

	6	5	4	3	2	1
2d Cpe	240	720	1,200	2,400	4,200	6,000
2d LT Cpe	260	780	1,300	2,600	4,550	6,500
2d Z28 Cpe	360	1,080	1,800	3,600	6,300	9,000

1979 Camaro, V-8

	6	5	4	3	2	1
2d Spt Cpe	232	696	1,160	2,320	4,060	5,800
2d Rally Cpe	256	768	1,280	2,560	4,480	6,400
2d Berlinetta Cpe	264	792	1,320	2,640	4,620	6,600
2d Z28 Cpe	276	828	1,380	2,760	4,830	6,900

NOTE: Deduct 20 percent for 6-cyl.

1980 Camaro, 6-cyl.

	6	5	4	3	2	1
2d Cpe Spt	244	732	1,220	2,440	4,270	6,100
2d Cpe RS	252	756	1,260	2,520	4,410	6,300
2d Cpe Berlinetta	256	768	1,280	2,560	4,480	6,400

1981 Camaro, V-8

	6	5	4	3	2	1
2d Cpe Spt	264	792	1,320	2,640	4,620	6,600
2d Cpe Berlinetta	272	816	1,360	2,720	4,760	6,800
2d Cpe Z28	368	1,104	1,840	3,680	6,440	9,200

1982 Camaro, V-8

	6	5	4	3	2	1
2d Cpe Spt	268	804	1,340	2,680	4,690	6,700
2d Cpe Berlinetta	276	828	1,380	2,760	4,830	6,900
2d Cpe Z28	376	1,128	1,880	3,760	6,580	9,400

NOTE: Add 20 percent for Indy pace car.

1983 Camaro, V-8

	6	5	4	3	2	1
2d Cpe Spt	272	816	1,360	2,720	4,760	6,800
2d Cpe Berlinetta	360	1,080	1,800	3,600	6,300	9,000
2d Cpe Z28	380	1,140	1,900	3,800	6,650	9,500

1984 Camaro, V-8

	6	5	4	3	2	1
2d Cpe	264	792	1,320	2,640	4,620	6,600
2d Cpe Berlinetta	272	816	1,360	2,720	4,760	6,800
2d Cpe Z28	364	1,092	1,820	3,640	6,370	9,100

NOTE: Deduct 10 percent for V-6 cyl.

1985 Camaro, V-8

	6	5	4	3	2	1
2d Cpe Spt	268	804	1,340	2,680	4,690	6,700
2d Cpe Berlinetta	276	828	1,380	2,760	4,830	6,900
2d Cpe Z28	368	1,104	1,840	3,680	6,440	9,200
2d Cpe IROC-Z	384	1,152	1,920	3,840	6,720	9,600

NOTE: Deduct 30 percent for 4-cyl. Deduct 20 percent for V-6.

1986 Camaro

	6	5	4	3	2	1
2d Cpe	272	816	1,360	2,720	4,760	6,800
2d Cpe Berlinetta	360	1,080	1,800	3,600	6,300	9,000
2d Cpe Z28	380	1,140	1,900	3,800	6,650	9,500
2d Cpe IROC-Z	400	1,200	2,000	4,000	7,000	10,000

1986 Monte Carlo SS

	6	5	4	3	2	1
2d Cpe	400	1,200	2,000	4,000	7,000	10,000
2d Cpe Aero	560	1,680	2,800	5,600	9,800	14,000

1987 Camaro

	6	5	4	3	2	1
2d Cpe V-6	276	828	1,380	2,760	4,830	6,900
2d Cpe LT V-6	360	1,080	1,800	3,600	6,300	9,000
2d Cpe V-8	368	1,104	1,840	3,680	6,440	9,200
2d Cpe LT V-8	372	1,116	1,860	3,720	6,510	9,300
2d Cpe Z28 V-8	388	1,164	1,940	3,880	6,790	9,700
2d Cpe IROC-Z V-8	408	1,224	2,040	4,080	7,140	10,200
2d Conv IROC-Z V-8	800	2,400	4,000	8,000	14,000	20,000

NOTE: Add 20 percent for 350 V-8 where available. Add 10 percent for Anniversary Edition.

1987 Monte Carlo

	6	5	4	3	2	1
2d Cpe LS V-6	264	792	1,320	2,640	4,620	6,600
2d Cpe LS V-8	272	816	1,360	2,720	4,760	6,800
2d Cpe SS V-8	400	1,200	2,000	4,000	7,000	10,000
2d Cpe Aero V-8	520	1,560	2,600	5,200	9,100	13,000

1988 Camaro, V-8

	6	5	4	3	2	1
2d Cpe	240	720	1,200	2,400	4,200	6,000
2d Conv	560	1,680	2,800	5,600	9,800	14,000
2d IROC-Z Cpe	420	1,260	2,100	4,200	7,350	10,500
2d IROC-Z Conv	700	2,150	3,600	7,200	12,600	18,000

1989 Camaro, V-8

	6	5	4	3	2	1
2d RS Cpe	260	780	1,300	2,600	4,550	6,500
2d RS Conv	640	1,920	3,200	6,400	11,200	16,000
2d IROC-Z Cpe	340	1,020	1,700	3,400	5,950	8,500
2d IROC-Z Conv	720	2,160	3,600	7,200	12,600	18,000

1990 Camaro V-6

	6	5	4	3	2	1
2d RS Cpe	240	720	1,200	2,400	4,200	6,000

1990 Camaro, V-8

	6	5	4	3	2	1
2d RS Cpe	264	792	1,320	2,640	4,620	6,600
2d RS Conv	600	1,800	3,000	6,000	10,500	15,000
2d IROC-Z Cpe	520	1,560	2,600	5,200	9,100	13,000
2d IROC-Z Conv	680	2,040	3,400	6,800	11,900	17,000

1991 Camaro, V-6

	6	5	4	3	2	1
2d Cpe	240	720	1,200	2,400	4,200	6,000
2d Conv	560	1,680	2,800	5,600	9,800	14,000

1991 Camaro, V-8

	6	5	4	3	2	1
2d RS Cpe	260	780	1,300	2,600	4,550	6,500
2d RS Conv	580	1,740	2,900	5,800	10,150	14,500
2d Z28 Cpe	420	1,260	2,100	4,200	7,350	10,500
2d Z28 Conv	660	1,980	3,300	6,600	11,550	16,500

1992 Camaro, V-6

	6	5	4	3	2	1
2d RS Cpe	400	1,200	2,000	4,000	7,000	10,000
2d RS Conv	600	1,800	3,000	6,000	10,500	15,000
2d Z28 Cpe	540	1,620	2,700	5,400	9,450	13,500
2d Z28 Conv	680	2,040	3,400	6,800	11,900	17,000

NOTE: Add 10 percent for V-8 where available.

1993 Camaro

	6	5	4	3	2	1
2d Cpe, V-6	420	1,260	2,100	4,200	7,350	10,500
2d Cpe Z28, V-8	540	1,620	2,700	5,400	9,450	13,500

1994 Camaro

	6	5	4	3	2	1
2d Cpe, V-6	340	1,020	1,700	3,400	5,950	8,500
2d Conv, V-6	380	1,140	1,900	3,800	6,650	9,500
2d Z28 Cpe, V-8	420	1,260	2,100	4,200	7,350	10,500
2d Z28 Conv, V-8	500	1,500	2,500	5,000	8,750	12,500

CORVETTE

1960

	6	5	4	3	2	1
Conv	2,450	7,300	12,200	24,400	42,700	61,000

NOTE: Add $1,800 for hardtop. Add 40 percent for F.I., 275 hp. Add 60 percent for F.I., 315 hp. Add 25 percent for two 4 barrel carbs, 245 hp. Add 35 percent for two 4 barrel carbs, 270 hp.

1961

	6	5	4	3	2	1
Conv	2,500	7,450	12,400	24,800	43,400	62,000

NOTE: Add $1,800 for hardtop. Add 40 percent for F.I., 275 hp. Add 60 percent for F.I., 315 hp. Add 25 percent for two 4 barrel carbs, 245 hp. Add 35 percent for two 4 barrel carbs, 270 hp.

1962

	6	5	4	3	2	1
Conv	2,500	7,550	12,600	25,200	44,100	63,000

NOTE: Add $1,800 for hardtop; 30 percent for F.I.

1963

	6	5	4	3	2	1
Spt Cpe	2,050	6,100	10,200	20,400	35,700	51,000
Conv	2,100	6,250	10,400	20,800	36,400	52,000
GS			value not estimable			

NOTE: Add 30 percent for F.I.; $4,500 for A/C. Add $1,800 for hardtop; $3,000 for knock off wheels. Z06 option, value not estimable.

1964

	6	5	4	3	2	1
Spt Cpe	1,900	5,650	9,400	18,800	32,900	47,000
Conv	2,100	6,250	10,400	20,800	36,400	52,000

NOTE: Add 30 percent for F.I.; $4,500 for A/C. Add 30 percent for 327 CID, 365 hp. Add $1,800 for hardtop; $3,000 for knock off wheels.

1965

	6	5	4	3	2	1
Spt Cpe	1,900	5,650	9,400	18,800	32,900	47,000
Conv	2,100	6,250	10,400	20,800	36,400	52,000

NOTE: Add 40 percent for F.I.; $4,500 for A/C. Add 60 percent for 396 CID. Add $3,000 for knock off wheels. Add $1,800 for hardtop.

1966

	6	5	4	3	2	1
Spt Cpe	1,900	5,650	9,400	18,800	32,900	47,000
Conv	2,100	6,250	10,400	20,800	36,400	52,000

NOTE: Add $4,500 for A/C.; 20 percent for 427 engine - 390 hp. Add 50 percent for 427 engine - 425 hp. Add $3,000 for knock off wheels; $1,800 for hardtop.

1999 C5 Corvette Hardtop Pace Car

	6	5	4	3	2	1
1967						
Spt Cpe	1,900	5,750	9,600	19,200	33,600	48,000
Conv	2,100	6,350	10,600	21,200	37,100	53,000

NOTE: Add $4,500 for A/C. L88 & L89 option not estimable, 30 percent for 427 engine - 390 hp. Add 50 percent for 427 engine - 400 hp, 70 percent for 427 engine - 435 hp; $4,000 for aluminum wheels.

	6	5	4	3	2	1
1968						
Spt Cpe	1,400	4,200	7,000	14,000	24,500	35,000
Conv	1,550	4,700	7,800	15,600	27,300	39,000

NOTE: Add 40 percent for L89 427 - 435 hp aluminum head option. L88 engine option not estimable. Add 40 percent for 427, 400 hp. Add 20 percent for L71 427-435 hp cast head.

	6	5	4	3	2	1
1969						
Spt Cpe	1,400	4,200	7,000	14,000	24,500	35,000
Conv	1,550	4,700	7,800	15,600	27,300	39,000

NOTE: Add 40 percent for 427 - 435 hp aluminum head option. L88 engine option not estimable. Add 40 percent for 427, 400 hp. Add 20 percent for L71 427-435 hp cast head.

	6	5	4	3	2	1
1970						
Spt Cpe	1,350	4,100	6,800	13,600	23,800	34,000
Conv	1,500	4,550	7,600	15,200	26,600	38,000

NOTE: Add 70 percent for LT-1 option. ZR1 option not estimable.

	6	5	4	3	2	1
1971						
Spt Cpe	1,300	3,950	6,600	13,200	23,100	33,000
Conv	1,500	4,450	7,400	14,800	25,900	37,000

NOTE: Add 50 percent for LT-1 option; 30 percent for LS 5 option; 75 percent for LS 6 option.

	6	5	4	3	2	1
1972						
Spt Cpe	1,300	3,950	6,600	13,200	23,100	33,000
Conv	1,500	4,450	7,400	14,800	25,900	37,000

NOTE: Add 50 percent for LT-1 option. Add 30 percent for LS 5 option. Add 25 percent for air on LT-1.

	6	5	4	3	2	1
1973						
Spt Cpe	1,250	3,700	6,200	12,400	21,700	31,000
Conv	1,400	4,200	7,000	14,000	24,500	35,000

NOTE: Add 10 percent for L82. Add 25 percent for LS4.

	6	5	4	3	2	1
1974						
Spt Cpe	1,100	3,350	5,600	11,200	19,600	28,000
Conv	1,300	3,950	6,600	13,200	23,100	33,000

NOTE: Add 10 percent for L82. Add 25 percent for LS4.

	6	5	4	3	2	1
1975						
Spt Cpe	1,150	3,500	5,800	11,600	20,300	29,000
Conv	1,400	4,200	7,000	14,000	24,500	35,000

NOTE: Add 10 percent for L82.

	6	5	4	3	2	1
1976						
Cpe	1,100	3,350	5,600	11,200	19,600	28,000

NOTE: Add 10 percent for L82.

	6	5	4	3	2	1
1977						
Cpe	1,100	3,350	5,600	11,200	19,600	28,000

NOTE: Add 10 percent for L82.

	6	5	4	3	2	1
1978						
Cpe	1,300	3,850	6,400	12,800	22,400	32,000

NOTE: Add 10 percent for anniversary model. Add 25 percent for pace car. Add 10 percent for L82 engine option.

	6	5	4	3	2	1
1979						
Cpe	1,150	3,500	5,800	11,600	20,300	29,000

NOTE: Add 10 percent for L82 engine option.

	6	5	4	3	2	1
1980						
Cpe	1,150	3,500	5,800	11,600	20,300	29,000

NOTE: Add 20 percent for L82 engine option.

	6	5	4	3	2	1
1981						
Cpe	1,150	3,500	5,800	11,600	20,300	29,000
1982						
2d HBK	1,200	3,600	6,000	12,000	21,000	30,000

NOTE: Add 20 percent for Collector Edition.

1983

NOTE: None manufactured.

	6	5	4	3	2	1
1984						
2d HBk	1,100	3,250	5,400	10,800	18,900	27,000
1985						
2d HBk	1,100	3,250	5,400	10,800	18,900	27,000
1986						
2d HBk	1,100	3,350	5,600	11,200	19,600	28,000
Conv	1,300	3,850	6,400	12,800	22,400	32,000

NOTE: Add 10 percent for pace car.

	6	5	4	3	2	1
1987						
2d HBk	1,100	3,350	5,600	11,200	19,600	28,000
Conv	1,300	3,850	6,400	12,800	22,400	32,000
1988						
2d Cpe	1,100	3,300	5,500	11,000	19,300	27,500
Conv	1,200	3,600	6,000	12,000	21,000	30,000
1989						
2d Cpe	1,100	3,350	5,600	11,200	19,600	28,000
Conv	1,250	3,700	6,200	12,400	21,700	31,000
1990						
2d HBk	1,100	3,250	5,400	10,800	18,900	27,000
Conv	1,250	3,700	6,200	12,400	21,700	31,000
2d HBk ZR1	1,950	5,900	9,800	19,600	34,300	49,000

	6	5	4	3	2	1
1991						
2d HBk	1,300	3,950	6,600	13,200	23,100	33,000
Conv	1,450	4,300	7,200	14,400	25,200	36,000
2d HBk ZR1	2,100	6,250	10,400	20,800	36,400	52,000
1992						
2d HBk Cpe	1,350	4,100	6,800	13,600	23,800	34,000
2d Conv	1,500	4,450	7,400	14,800	25,900	37,000
2d ZR1 Cpe	2,100	6,350	10,600	21,200	37,100	53,000
1993						
2d Cpe	1,400	4,200	7,000	14,000	24,500	35,000
2d ZR1 Cpe	2,150	6,500	10,800	21,600	37,800	54,000
2d Conv	1,500	4,550	7,600	15,200	26,600	38,000

NOTE: Add 10 percent for Anniversary model.

1994	6	5	4	3	2	1
2d Cpe	1,400	4,200	7,000	14,000	24,500	35,000
2d Conv	1,550	4,700	7,800	15,600	27,300	39,000
2d ZR1 Cpe	2,200	6,600	11,000	22,000	38,500	55,000

CHRYSLER

1960 300 Letter Series "F", V-8
	6	5	4	3	2	1
2d Conv	2,560	7,680	12,800	25,600	44,800	64,000
2d HT	2,080	6,240	10,400	20,800	36,400	52,000

NOTE: 300 Letter Series cars containing the Pont-A-Mousson 4-speed transmission, the value is not estimable.

1961 300 Letter Series "G", V-8
	6	5	4	3	2	1
2d Conv	2,000	6,000	10,000	20,000	35,000	50,000
2d HT	1,600	4,800	8,000	16,000	28,000	40,000

NOTE: Add 20 percent for 400HP engine.

1962 300 Letter Series "H", V-8
	6	5	4	3	2	1
2d Conv	1,960	5,880	9,800	19,600	34,300	49,000
2d HT	1,560	4,680	7,800	15,600	27,300	39,000

1963 300 Letter Series "J", "413" V-8
	6	5	4	3	2	1
2d HT	1,200	3,600	6,000	12,000	21,000	30,000

1964 300 Letter Series "K", V-8
	6	5	4	3	2	1
2d Conv	1,440	4,320	7,200	14,400	25,200	36,000
2d HT	1,200	3,600	6,000	12,000	21,000	30,000

NOTE: Add 10 percent for two 4-barrel carbs.

1965 300 Letter Series "L", V-8
	6	5	4	3	2	1
2d Conv	1,320	3,960	6,600	13,200	23,100	33,000
2d HT	1,160	3,480	5,800	11,600	20,300	29,000

1966 Chrysler 300, V-8
	6	5	4	3	2	1
2d Conv	960	2,880	4,800	9,600	16,800	24,000
2d HT	760	2,280	3,800	7,600	13,300	19,000
4d HT	640	1,920	3,200	6,400	11,200	16,000

1967 300, V-8, 124" wb
	6	5	4	3	2	1
2d Conv	880	2,640	4,400	8,800	15,400	22,000
2d HT	700	2,100	3,500	7,000	12,250	17,500
4d HT	640	1,920	3,200	6,400	11,200	16,000

1968 300, V-8, 124" wb
	6	5	4	3	2	1
2d Conv	920	2,760	4,600	9,200	16,100	23,000
2d HT	700	2,100	3,500	7,000	12,250	17,500
4d HT	640	1,920	3,200	6,400	11,200	16,000

1970 300, V-8, 124" wb
	6	5	4	3	2	1
2d Conv	800	2,400	4,000	8,000	14,000	20,000
2d HT Hurst	680	2,040	3,400	6,800	11,900	17,000
2d HT	520	1,560	2,600	5,200	9,100	13,000
4d HT	420	1,260	2,100	4,200	7,350	10,500

DODGE

1961 Lancer 770
NOTE: Add 10 percent for Hyper Pak 170-180 hp engine option, and 20 percent for Hyper Pak 225-200 hp.
	6	5	4	3	2	1
4d Sta Wag	400	1,200	2,000	4,000	7,000	10,000

1966 Coronet 500, V-8, 117" wb
	6	5	4	3	2	1
4d Sed	372	1,116	1,860	3,720	6,510	9,300
2d HT	580	1,740	2,900	5,800	10,150	14,500
2d Conv	950	2,900	4,800	9,600	16,800	24,000

1966 Charger, 117" wb
	6	5	4	3	2	1
2d HT	900	2,750	4,600	9,200	16,100	23,000

NOTE: Autos equipped with 426 Hemi, value inestimable.

1967 Charger, V-8, 117" wb
	6	5	4	3	2	1
2d HT	950	2,900	4,800	9,600	16,800	24,000

1967 Coronet 500, V-8, 117" wb
	6	5	4	3	2	1
4d Sed	376	1,128	1,880	3,760	6,580	9,400
2d HT	600	1,800	3,000	6,000	10,500	15,000
2d Conv	950	2,900	4,800	9,600	16,800	24,000

1970 Chrysler-Hurst 300-H two-door hardtop

1970 Dodge Coronet R/T

	6	5	4	3	2	1
1967 Coronet R/T, V-8, 117" wb						
2d HT	840	2,520	4,200	8,400	14,700	21,000
2d Conv	1,150	3,500	5,800	11,600	20,300	29,000
1967 Coronet 440, V-8, 117" wb						
4d Sed	372	1,116	1,860	3,720	6,510	9,300
2d HT	560	1,680	2,800	5,600	9,800	14,000
2d Conv	900	2,750	4,600	9,200	16,100	23,000
4d Sta Wag	388	1,164	1,940	3,880	6,790	9,700
1968 Coronet Super Bee, V-8, 117" wb						
2d Sed	1,300	3,850	6,400	12,800	22,400	32,000
1968 Coronet R/T						
2d HT	1,500	4,550	7,600	15,200	26,600	38,000
2d Conv	1,650	4,900	8,200	16,400	28,700	41,000
1968 Dart GT Sport 340, 111" wb						
2d HT	760	2,280	3,800	7,600	13,300	19,000
2d Conv	1,100	3,350	5,600	11,200	19,600	28,000
1968 Dart GT Sport 383, 111" wb						
2d HT	840	2,520	4,200	8,400	14,700	21,000
2d Conv	1,150	3,500	5,800	11,600	20,300	29,000
1968 Charger R/T						
2d HT	1,450	4,300	7,200	14,400	25,200	36,000
1969 Dart Swinger 340						
2d HT	780	2,340	3,900	7,800	13,650	19,500
1969 Dart GT Sport 383, 111" wb						
2d HT (383 hp)	1,150	3,500	5,800	11,600	20,300	29,000
2d Conv (330 hp)	1,250	3,700	6,200	12,400	21,700	31,000
1969 Charger R/T						
2d HT	1,250	3,700	6,200	12,400	21,700	31,000
1969 Charger Daytona						
2d HT	2,500	7,550	12,600	25,200	44,100	63,000
1969 Charger 500						
2d HT	1,500	4,450	7,400	14,800	25,900	37,000
1969 Coronet R/T						
2d HT	1,300	3,950	6,600	13,200	23,100	33,000
2d Conv	1,550	4,700	7,800	15,600	27,300	39,000
1969 Coronet Super Bee, V-8						
2d HT	1,250	3,700	6,200	12,400	21,700	31,000
2d Cpe (base 440/375)		1,200	3,600	6,000	12,000	21,000
30,000						

NOTE: Add 75 percent for Super Bee six pack.

	6	5	4	3	2	1
1970 Coronet R/T						
2d HT	1,350	4,100	6,800	13,600	23,800	34,000
2d Conv	1,700	5,050	8,400	16,800	29,400	42,000
1970 Coronet Super Bee						
2d HT	1,150	3,500	5,800	11,600	20,300	29,000
2d Cpe	1,100	3,250	5,400	10,800	18,900	27,000
1970 Dart Swinger 340						
2d HT	650	2,000	3,300	6,650	11,600	16,600
1970 Charger						
2d HT	1,150	3,500	5,800	11,600	20,300	29,000
2d HT 500	1,300	3,850	6,400	12,800	22,400	32,000
2d HT R/T	1,450	4,300	7,200	14,400	25,200	36,000
2d HT	950	2,900	4,800	9,600	16,800	24,000
2d HT Fml	1,000	3,000	5,000	10,000	17,500	25,000
2d Conv	1,150	3,500	5,800	11,600	20,300	29,000
1970 Challenger R/T						
2d HT	1,050	3,100	5,200	10,400	18,200	26,000
2d HT Fml	1,100	3,250	5,400	10,800	18,900	27,000
2d Conv	1,300	3,850	6,400	12,800	22,400	32,000
1970 Challenger T/A						
2d Cpe	1,650	4,900	8,200	16,400	28,700	41,000
1971 Demon						
2d Cpe	220	660	1,100	2,200	3,850	5,500
2d 340 Cpe	260	780	1,300	2,600	4,550	6,500
1971 Charger						
2d HT 500	1,000	3,000	5,000	10,000	17,500	25,000
2d HT	900	2,750	4,600	9,200	16,100	23,000
2d Super Bee HT	1,050	3,100	5,200	10,400	18,200	26,000
2d HT R/T	1,100	3,350	5,600	11,200	19,600	28,000
2d HT SE	1,100	3,250	5,400	10,800	18,900	27,000
1978 Magnum XE						
2d Cpe	212	636	1,060	2,120	3,710	5,300
1979 Magnum XE, V-8						
2d Cpe	220	660	1,100	2,200	3,850	5,500

FORD

	6	5	4	3	2	1
1960 Galaxie Special, V-8, 119" wb						
2d HT	840	2,520	4,200	8,400	14,700	21,000
2d Sun Conv	1,160	3,480	5,800	11,600	20,300	29,000

	6	5	4	3	2	1
1961 Galaxie, V-8, 119" wb						
2d Sed	276	828	1,380	2,760	4,830	6,900
4d Sed	360	1,080	1,800	3,600	6,300	9,000
4d Vic HT	420	1,260	2,100	4,200	7,350	10,500
2d Vic HT	720	2,160	3,600	7,200	12,600	18,000
2d Star HT	760	2,280	3,800	7,600	13,300	19,000
2d Sun Conv	880	2,640	4,400	8,800	15,400	22,000
1962 Galaxie 500, V-8, 119" wb						
4d Sed	232	696	1,160	2,320	4,060	5,800
4d HT	380	1,140	1,900	3,800	6,650	9,500
2d Sed	228	684	1,140	2,280	3,990	5,700
2d HT	600	1,800	3,000	6,000	10,500	15,000
2d Conv	760	2,280	3,800	7,600	13,300	19,000
1962 Galaxie 500 XL, V-8, 119" wb						
2d HT	680	2,040	3,400	6,800	11,900	17,000
2d Conv	880	2,640	4,400	8,800	15,400	22,000
1963 Galaxie 500, V-8, 119" wb						
4d Sed	224	672	1,120	2,240	3,920	5,600
4d HT	360	1,080	1,800	3,600	6,300	9,000
2d Sed	220	660	1,100	2,200	3,850	5,500
2d HT	680	2,040	3,400	6,800	11,900	17,000
2d FBk	760	2,280	3,800	7,600	13,300	19,000
2d Conv	840	2,520	4,200	8,400	14,700	21,000
1963 Galaxie 500 XL, V-8, 119" wb						
4d HT	420	1,260	2,100	4,200	7,350	10,500
2d HT	720	2,160	3,600	7,200	12,600	18,000
2d FBk	800	2,400	4,000	8,000	14,000	20,000
2d Conv	920	2,760	4,600	9,200	16,100	23,000
1964 Galaxie 500XL, V-8, 119" wb						
4d HT	560	1,680	2,800	5,600	9,800	14,000
2d HT	800	2,400	4,000	8,000	14,000	20,000
2d Conv	1,040	3,120	5,200	10,400	18,200	26,000
1964 Sprint, V-8, 109.5" wb						
2d HT	620	1,860	3,100	6,200	10,850	15,500
2d Conv	680	2,040	3,400	6,800	11,900	17,000
1964 Fairlane Thunderbolt						
2d Sed			value not estimable			
1965 Galaxie 500 XL, V-8, 119" wb						
2d HT	600	1,800	3,000	6,000	10,500	15,000
2d Conv	680	2,040	3,400	6,800	11,900	17,000
1966 Galaxie 500, XL, V-8, 119" wb						
2d HT	540	1,620	2,700	5,400	9,450	13,500
2d Conv	680	2,040	3,400	6,800	11,900	17,000
1966 Fairlane 500 GT, V-8, 116" wb						
2d HT	600	1,800	3,000	6,000	10,500	15,000
2d Conv	880	2,640	4,400	8,800	15,400	22,000
1967 Galaxie 500 XL						
2d HT	580	1,740	2,900	5,800	10,150	14,500
2d Conv	720	2,160	3,600	7,200	12,600	18,000
1967 Fairlane 500 XL, V-8						
2d HT	400	1,200	2,000	4,000	7,000	10,000
2d Conv	680	2,040	3,400	6,800	11,900	17,000
2d HT GT	520	1,560	2,600	5,200	9,100	13,000
2d Conv GT	720	2,160	3,600	7,200	12,600	18,000
1968 Torino GT, V-8						
2d HT	520	1,560	2,600	5,200	9,100	13,000
2d FBk	600	1,800	3,000	6,000	10,500	15,000
2d Conv	680	2,040	3,400	6,800	11,900	17,000
1969 Torino GT, V-8						
2d HT	520	1,560	2,600	5,200	9,100	13,000
2d FBk	600	1,800	3,000	6,000	10,500	15,000
2d Conv	720	2,160	3,600	7,200	12,600	18,000
1970 Cobra, V-8, 117" wb						
2d HT	920	2,760	4,600	9,200	16,100	23,000

MUSTANG

1964	6	5	4	3	2	1
2d HT	940	2,820	4,700	9,400	16,450	23,500
Conv	1,320	3,960	6,600	13,200	23,100	33,000

NOTE: Deduct 20 percent for 6-cyl. Add 20 percent for Challenger Code "K" V-8.

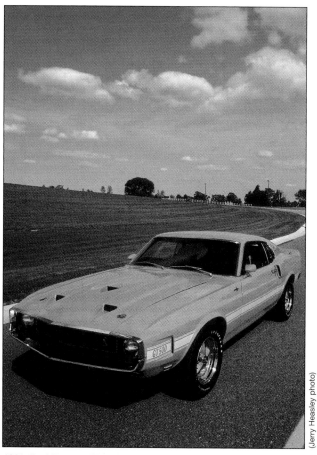

1969 Ford Mustang GT 500

(Jerry Heasley photo)

	6	5	4	3	2	1
1965						
2d HT	940	2,820	4,700	9,400	16,450	23,500
Conv	1,320	3,960	6,600	13,200	23,100	33,000
FBk	1,120	3,360	5,600	11,200	19,600	28,000

NOTE: Add 30 percent for 271 hp Hi-perf engine. Add 10 percent for "GT" Package. Add 10 percent for "original pony interior". Deduct 20 percent for 6-cyl.

1965 Shelby GT						
GT-350 FBk	2,320	6,960	11,600	23,200	40,600	58,000
1966						
2d HT	940	2,820	4,700	9,400	16,450	23,500
Conv	1,360	4,080	6,800	13,600	23,800	34,000
FBk	1,200	3,600	6,000	12,000	21,000	30,000

NOTE: Same as 1965.

1966 Shelby GT						
GT-350 FBk	2,120	6,360	10,600	21,200	37,100	53,000
GT-350H FBk	2,200	6,600	11,000	22,000	38,500	55,000
GT-350 Conv	3,040	9,120	15,200	30,400	53,200	76,000
1967						
2d HT	860	2,580	4,300	8,600	15,050	21,500
Conv	1,200	3,600	6,000	12,000	21,000	30,000
FBk	980	2,940	4,900	9,800	17,150	24,500

NOTE: Same as 1964-65 plus. Add 10 percent for 390 cid V-8 (code "S"). Deduct 15 percent for 6-cyl.

1967 Shelby GT						
GT-350 FBk	1,840	5,520	9,200	18,400	32,200	46,000
GT-500 FBk	2,040	6,120	10,200	20,400	35,700	51,000
1968						
2d HT	860	2,580	4,300	8,600	15,050	21,500
Conv	1,200	3,600	6,000	12,000	21,000	30,000
FBk	980	2,940	4,900	9,800	17,150	24,500

NOTE: Same as 1964-67 plus. Add 10 percent for GT-390. Add 50 percent for 427 cid V-8 (code "W"). Add 30 percent for 428 cid V-8 (code "R"). Add 15 percent for "California Special" trim.

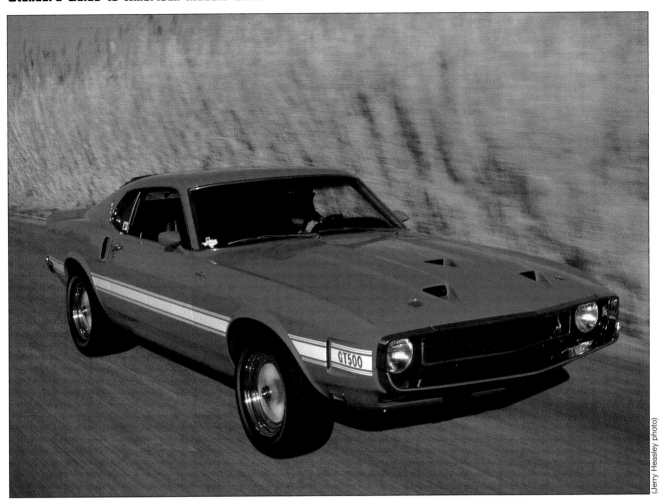

1969 Ford Mustang GT 500 Fastback

	6	5	4	3	2	1
1968 Shelby GT						
350 Conv	2,360	7,080	11,800	23,600	41,300	59,000
350 FBk	1,440	4,320	7,200	14,400	25,200	36,000
500 Conv	2,880	8,640	14,400	28,800	50,400	72,000
500 FBk	1,960	5,880	9,800	19,600	34,300	49,000

NOTE: Add 30 percent for KR models.

	6	5	4	3	2	1
1969						
2d HT	820	2,460	4,100	8,200	14,350	20,500
Conv	980	2,940	4,900	9,800	17,150	24,500
FBk	900	2,700	4,500	9,000	15,750	22,500

NOTE: Deduct 20 percent for 6-cyl.

	6	5	4	3	2	1
Mach 1	1,040	3,120	5,200	10,400	18,200	26,000
Boss 302	1,600	4,800	8,000	16,000	28,000	40,000
Boss 429	2,480	7,440	12,400	24,800	43,400	62,000
Grande	860	2,580	4,300	8,600	15,050	21,500

NOTE: Same as 1968; plus. Add 40 percent for "R" Code. Add 30 percent for Cobra Jet V-8. Add 40 percent for "Super Cobra Jet" engine.

	6	5	4	3	2	1
1969 Shelby GT						
350 Conv	2,320	6,960	11,600	23,200	40,600	58,000
350 FBk	1,680	5,040	8,400	16,800	29,400	42,000
500 Conv	2,640	7,920	13,200	26,400	46,200	66,000
500 FBk	1,800	5,400	9,000	18,000	31,500	45,000

	6	5	4	3	2	1
1970						
2d HT	820	2,460	4,100	8,200	14,350	20,500
Conv	960	2,880	4,800	9,600	16,800	24,000
FBk	880	2,640	4,400	8,800	15,400	22,000
Mach 1	960	2,880	4,800	9,600	16,800	24,000
Boss 302	1,520	4,560	7,600	15,200	26,600	38,000

	6	5	4	3	2	1
Boss 429	2,400	7,200	12,000	24,000	42,000	60,000
Grande	860	2,580	4,300	8,600	15,050	21,500

NOTE: Add 30 percent for Cobra Jet V-8. Add 40 percent for "Super Cobra Jet". Deduct 20 percent for 6-cyl.

	6	5	4	3	2	1
1970 Shelby GT						
350 Conv	2,240	6,720	11,200	22,400	39,200	56,000
350 FBk	1,680	5,040	8,400	16,800	29,400	42,000
500 Conv	2,640	7,920	13,200	26,400	46,200	66,000
500 FBk	1,800	5,400	9,000	18,000	31,500	45,000

	6	5	4	3	2	1
1971						
2d HT	640	1,920	3,200	6,400	11,200	16,000
Grande	660	1,980	3,300	6,600	11,550	16,500
Conv	960	2,880	4,800	9,600	16,800	24,000
FBk	880	2,640	4,400	8,800	15,400	22,000
Mach 1	960	2,880	4,800	9,600	16,800	24,000
Boss 351	1,600	4,800	8,000	16,000	28,000	40,000

NOTE: Same as 1970. Deduct 20 percent for 6-cyl. Add 20 percent for HO option where available.

	6	5	4	3	2	1
1972						
2d HT	640	1,920	3,200	6,400	11,200	16,000
Grande	660	1,980	3,300	6,600	11,550	16,500
FBk	800	2,400	4,000	8,000	14,000	20,000
Mach 1	880	2,640	4,400	8,800	15,400	22,000
Conv	920	2,760	4,600	9,200	16,100	23,000

NOTE: Deduct 20 percent for 6-cyl. Add 20 percent for HO option where available.

	6	5	4	3	2	1
1973						
2d HT	620	1,860	3,100	6,200	10,850	15,500
Grande	660	1,980	3,300	6,600	11,550	16,500
FBk	760	2,280	3,800	7,600	13,300	19,000
Mach 1	880	2,640	4,400	8,800	15,400	22,000
Conv	960	2,880	4,800	9,600	16,800	24,000

1974 Mustang II, Mustang Four

	6	5	4	3	2	1
HT Cpe	240	720	1,200	2,400	4,200	6,000
FBk	252	756	1,260	2,520	4,410	6,300
Ghia	252	756	1,260	2,520	4,410	6,300

1974 Mustang Six

	6	5	4	3	2	1
HT Cpe	240	720	1,200	2,400	4,200	6,000
FBk	256	768	1,280	2,560	4,480	6,400
Ghia	256	768	1,280	2,560	4,480	6,400

1974 Mach 1 Six

	6	5	4	3	2	1
FBk	380	1,140	1,900	3,800	6,650	9,500

1975 Mustang

	6	5	4	3	2	1
HT Cpe	240	720	1,200	2,400	4,200	6,000
FBk	252	756	1,260	2,520	4,410	6,300
Ghia	252	756	1,260	2,520	4,410	6,300

1975 Mustang Six

	6	5	4	3	2	1
HT Cpe	244	732	1,220	2,440	4,270	6,100
FBk	256	768	1,280	2,560	4,480	6,400
Ghia	256	768	1,280	2,560	4,480	6,400
Mach 1	380	1,140	1,900	3,800	6,650	9,500

1975 Mustang, V-8

	6	5	4	3	2	1
HT Cpe	364	1,092	1,820	3,640	6,370	9,100
FBk Cpe	368	1,104	1,840	3,680	6,440	9,200
Ghia	380	1,140	1,900	3,800	6,650	9,500
Mach 1	420	1,260	2,100	4,200	7,350	10,500

1976 Mustang II, V-6

	6	5	4	3	2	1
2d	252	756	1,260	2,520	4,410	6,300
3d 2 plus 2	256	768	1,280	2,560	4,480	6,400
2d Ghia	268	804	1,340	2,680	4,690	6,700

NOTE: Deduct 20 percent for 4-cyl. Add 20 percent for V-8. Add 20 percent for Cobra II.

1976 Mach 1, V-6

	6	5	4	3	2	1
3d	360	1,080	1,800	3,600	6,300	9,000

1977 Mustang II, V-6

	6	5	4	3	2	1
2d	260	780	1,300	2,600	4,550	6,500
3d 2 plus 2	268	804	1,340	2,680	4,690	6,700
2d Ghia	276	828	1,380	2,760	4,830	6,900

NOTE: Deduct 20 percent for 4-cyl. Add 30 percent for Cobra II option. Add 20 percent for V-8.

1977 Mach 1, V-6

	6	5	4	3	2	1
2d	368	1,104	1,840	3,680	6,440	9,200

1978 Mustang II

	6	5	4	3	2	1
Cpe	244	732	1,220	2,440	4,270	6,100
3d 2 plus 2	252	756	1,260	2,520	4,410	6,300
Ghia Cpe	256	768	1,280	2,560	4,480	6,400

1978 Mach 1, V-6

	6	5	4	3	2	1
Cpe	360	1,080	1,800	3,600	6,300	9,000

NOTE: Add 20 percent for V-8. Add 30 percent for Cobra II option. Add 50 percent for King Cobra option. Deduct 20 percent for 4-cyl.

1979 V-6

	6	5	4	3	2	1
2d Cpe	248	744	1,240	2,480	4,340	6,200
3d Cpe	252	756	1,260	2,520	4,410	6,300
2d Ghia Cpe	260	780	1,300	2,600	4,550	6,500

1979 V-6

	6	5	4	3	2	1
3d Ghia Cpe	264	792	1,320	2,640	4,620	6,600

NOTE: Add 30 percent for Pace Car package. Add 30 percent for Cobra option.

1980 6-cyl.

	6	5	4	3	2	1
2d Cpe	212	636	1,060	2,120	3,710	5,300
2d HBk	216	648	1,080	2,160	3,780	5,400
2d Ghia Cpe	224	672	1,120	2,240	3,920	5,600
2d Ghia HBk	228	684	1,140	2,280	3,990	5,700

NOTE: Deduct 20 percent for 4-cyl. Add 30 percent for V-8.

1981 6-cyl.

	6	5	4	3	2	1
2d S Cpe	196	588	980	1,960	3,430	4,900
2d Cpe	204	612	1,020	2,040	3,570	5,100
2d HBk	208	624	1,040	2,080	3,640	5,200
2d Ghia Cpe	208	624	1,040	2,080	3,640	5,200
2d Ghia HBk	212	636	1,060	2,120	3,710	5,300

NOTE: Deduct 20 percent for 4-cyl. Add 35 percent for V-8.

1982 4-cyl.

	6	5	4	3	2	1
2d L Cpe	180	540	900	1,800	3,150	4,500
2d GL Cpe	184	552	920	1,840	3,220	4,600
2d GL HBk	188	564	940	1,880	3,290	4,700
2d GLX Cpe	196	588	980	1,960	3,430	4,900
2d GLX HBk	200	600	1,000	2,000	3,500	5,000

1982 6-cyl.

	6	5	4	3	2	1
2d L Cpe	196	588	980	1,960	3,430	4,900
2d GL Cpe	200	600	1,000	2,000	3,500	5,000
2d GL HBk	204	612	1,020	2,040	3,570	5,100
2d GLX Cpe	212	636	1,060	2,120	3,710	5,300
2d GLX HBk	216	648	1,080	2,160	3,780	5,400

1982 V-8

	6	5	4	3	2	1
2d GT HBk	256	768	1,280	2,560	4,480	6,400

1983 4-cyl.

	6	5	4	3	2	1
2d L Cpe	184	552	920	1,840	3,220	4,600
2d GL Cpe	188	564	940	1,880	3,290	4,700
2d GL HBk	196	588	980	1,960	3,430	4,900
2d GLX Cpe	200	600	1,000	2,000	3,500	5,000
2d GLX HBk	204	612	1,020	2,040	3,570	5,100

1983 6-cyl.

	6	5	4	3	2	1
2d GL Cpe	204	612	1,020	2,040	3,570	5,100
2d GL HBk	208	624	1,040	2,080	3,640	5,200
2d GLX HBk	216	648	1,080	2,160	3,780	5,400
2d GLX HBk	220	660	1,100	2,200	3,850	5,500
2d GLX Conv	240	720	1,200	2,400	4,200	6,000

1983 V-8

	6	5	4	3	2	1
2d GT HBk	360	1,080	1,800	3,600	6,300	9,000
2d GT Conv	400	1,200	2,000	4,000	7,000	10,000

1984 4-cyl.

	6	5	4	3	2	1
2d L Cpe	188	564	940	1,880	3,290	4,700
2d L HBk	192	576	960	1,920	3,360	4,800
2d LX Cpe	192	576	960	1,920	3,360	4,800
2d LX HBk	196	588	980	1,960	3,430	4,900
2d GT Turbo HBk	212	636	1,060	2,120	3,710	5,300
2d GT Turbo Conv	260	780	1,300	2,600	4,550	6,500

1984 V-6

	6	5	4	3	2	1
2d L Cpe	192	576	960	1,920	3,360	4,800
2d L HBk	196	588	980	1,960	3,430	4,900
2d LX Cpe	196	588	980	1,960	3,430	4,900
2d LX HBk	200	600	1,000	2,000	3,500	5,000
LX 2d Conv	280	840	1,400	2,800	4,900	7,000

1984 V-8

	6	5	4	3	2	1
2d L HBk	200	600	1,000	2,000	3,500	5,000
2d LX Cpe	204	612	1,020	2,040	3,570	5,100
2d LX HBk	204	612	1,020	2,040	3,570	5,100
2d LX Conv	320	960	1,600	3,200	5,600	8,000
2d GT HBk	212	636	1,060	2,120	3,710	5,300
2d GT Conv	340	1,020	1,700	3,400	5,950	8,500

NOTE: Add 20 percent for 20th Anniversary Edition. Add 40 percent for SVO Model.

1985 4-cyl.

	6	5	4	3	2	1
2d LX	196	588	980	1,960	3,430	4,900
2d LX HBk	200	600	1,000	2,000	3,500	5,000
2d SVO Turbo	240	720	1,200	2,400	4,200	6,000

1985 V-6

	6	5	4	3	2	1
2d LX	204	612	1,020	2,040	3,570	5,100
2d LX HBk	208	624	1,040	2,080	3,640	5,200
2d LX Conv	396	1,188	1,980	3,960	6,930	9,900

1985 V-8

	6	5	4	3	2	1
2d LX	220	660	1,100	2,200	3,850	5,500
2d LX HBk	224	672	1,120	2,240	3,920	5,600
2d LX Conv	420	1,260	2,100	4,200	7,350	10,500
2d GT HBk	400	1,200	2,000	4,000	7,000	10,000
2d GT Conv	560	1,680	2,800	5,600	9,800	14,000

NOTE: Add 40 percent for SVO Model.

1986 Mustang

	6	5	4	3	2	1
2d Cpe	200	600	1,000	2,000	3,500	5,000
2d HBk	200	600	1,000	2,000	3,500	5,000
2d Conv	380	1,140	1,900	3,800	6,650	9,500
2d Turbo HBk	240	720	1,200	2,400	4,200	6,000

1986 V-8

	6	5	4	3	2	1
2d HBk	240	720	1,200	2,400	4,200	6,000
2d Conv	420	1,260	2,100	4,200	7,350	10,500
2d GT HBk	400	1,200	2,000	4,000	7,000	10,000
2d GT Conv	560	1,680	2,800	5,600	9,800	14,000

NOTE: Add 40 percent for SVO Model.

	6	5	4	3	2	1
1987 4-cyl.						
2d LX Sed	200	600	1,000	2,000	3,500	5,000
2d LX HBk	204	612	1,020	2,040	3,570	5,100
2d LX Conv	360	1,080	1,800	3,600	6,300	9,000
1987 V-8						
2d LX Sed	200	600	1,000	2,000	3,500	5,000
2d LX HBk	204	612	1,020	2,040	3,570	5,100
2d LX Conv	424	1,272	2,120	4,240	7,420	10,600
2d GT HBk	220	660	1,100	2,200	3,850	5,500
2d GT Conv	400	1,200	2,000	4,000	7,000	10,000
1988 V-6						
2d LX Sed	160	480	800	1,600	2,800	4,000
2d LX HBk	168	504	840	1,680	2,940	4,200
2d LX Conv	360	1,080	1,800	3,600	6,300	9,000
1988 V-8						
2d LX Sed	200	600	1,000	2,000	3,500	5,000
2d LX HBk	220	660	1,100	2,200	3,850	5,500
2d LX Conv	400	1,200	2,000	4,000	7,000	10,000
2d GT HBk	380	1,140	1,900	3,800	6,650	9,500
2d GT Conv	560	1,680	2,800	5,600	9,800	14,000
1989 4-cyl.						
2d LX Cpe	180	540	900	1,800	3,150	4,500
2d LX HBk	188	564	940	1,880	3,290	4,700
2d LX Conv	420	1,260	2,100	4,200	7,350	10,500
1989 V-8						
2d LX Spt Cpe	236	708	1,180	2,360	4,130	5,900
2d LX Spt HBk	240	720	1,200	2,400	4,200	6,000
2d LX Spt Conv	560	1,680	2,800	5,600	9,800	14,000
2d GT HBk	388	1,164	1,940	3,880	6,790	9,700
2d GT Conv	680	2,040	3,400	6,800	11,900	17,000
1990 4-cyl.						
2d LX	184	552	920	1,840	3,220	4,600
2d LX HBk	192	576	960	1,920	3,360	4,800
2d LX Conv	380	1,140	1,900	3,800	6,650	9,500
1990 V-8						
2d LX Spt	240	720	1,200	2,400	4,200	6,000
2d LX HBk Spt	248	744	1,240	2,480	4,340	6,200
2d LX Conv Spt	520	1,560	2,600	5,200	9,100	13,000
2d GT HBk	400	1,200	2,000	4,000	7,000	10,000
2d GT Conv	560	1,680	2,800	5,600	9,800	14,000
1991 4-cyl.						
2d LX Cpe	180	540	900	1,800	3,150	4,500
2d LX HBk	200	600	1,000	2,000	3,500	5,000
2d LX Conv	360	1,080	1,800	3,600	6,300	9,000
1991 V-8						
2d LX Cpe	220	660	1,100	2,200	3,850	5,500
2d LX HBk	240	720	1,200	2,400	4,200	6,000
2d LX Conv	400	1,200	2,000	4,000	7,000	10,000
2d GT HBk	380	1,140	1,900	3,800	6,650	9,500
2d GT Conv	540	1,620	2,700	5,400	9,450	13,500
1992 V-8, 4-cyl.						
2d LX Cpe	200	600	1,000	2,000	3,500	5,000
2d LX HBk	220	660	1,100	2,200	3,850	5,500
2d LX Conv	400	1,200	2,000	4,000	7,000	10,000
1992 V-8						
2d LX Sed	360	1,080	1,800	3,600	6,300	9,000
2d LX HBk	380	1,140	1,900	3,800	6,650	9,500
2d LX Conv	520	1,560	2,600	5,200	9,100	13,000
2d GT HBk	420	1,260	2,100	4,200	7,350	10,500
2d GT Conv	600	1,800	3,000	6,000	10,500	15,000
1993 4-cyl.						
2d LX Cpe	220	660	1,100	2,200	3,850	5,500
2d LX HBk	224	672	1,120	2,240	3,920	5,600
2d LX Conv	408	1,224	2,040	4,080	7,140	10,200
1993 V-8						
2d LX Cpe	360	1,080	1,800	3,600	6,300	9,000
2d LX HBk	368	1,104	1,840	3,680	6,440	9,200
2d LX Conv	552	1,656	2,760	5,520	9,660	13,800
2d GT HBk	400	1,200	2,000	4,000	7,000	10,000
2d GT Conv	620	1,860	3,100	6,200	10,850	15,500
1993 Cobra						
2d HBk	700	2,100	3,500	7,000	12,250	17,500

NOTE: Add 40 percent for Code R.

	6	5	4	3	2	1
1994 V-6						
2d Cpe	320	960	1,600	3,200	5,600	8,000
2d Conv	440	1,320	2,200	4,400	7,700	11,000
1994 GT, V-8						
2d GT Cpe	420	1,260	2,100	4,200	7,350	10,500
2d GT Conv	480	1,440	2,400	4,800	8,400	12,000
1994 Cobra, V-8						
2d Cpe	560	1,680	2,800	5,600	9,800	14,000
2d Conv	640	1,920	3,200	6,400	11,200	16,000

MERCURY

	6	5	4	3	2	1
1964 Comet Cyclone, V-8, 114" wb						
2d HT	640	1,920	3,200	6,400	11,200	16,000

NOTE: Deduct 25 percent for 6-cyl. Caliente.

	6	5	4	3	2	1
1965 Comet Cyclone, V-8, 114" wb						
2d HT	640	1,920	3,200	6,400	11,200	16,000
1966 Comet Cyclone, V-8, 116" wb						
2d HT	560	1,680	2,800	5,600	9,800	14,000
2d Conv	800	2,400	4,000	8,000	14,000	20,000
1966 Comet Cyclone GT/GTA, V-8, 116" wb						
2d HT	640	1,920	3,200	6,400	11,200	16,000
2d Conv	920	2,760	4,600	9,200	16,100	23,000
1967 Cyclone, V-8, 116" wb						
2d HT	600	1,800	3,000	6,000	10,500	15,000
2d Conv	720	2,160	3,600	7,200	12,600	18,000
1967 Cougar, V-8, 111" wb						
2d HT	680	2,040	3,400	6,800	11,900	17,000
2d XR-7 HT	720	2,160	3,600	7,200	12,600	18,000
1968 Cyclone GT 427, V-8						
2d FBk Cpe	920	2,760	4,600	9,200	16,100	23,000
2d HT	880	2,640	4,400	8,800	15,400	22,000
1968 Cyclone GT 428, V-8						
2d FBk Cpe	720	2,160	3,600	7,200	12,600	18,000
1968 Cougar, V-8						
2d HT Cpe	600	1,800	3,000	6,000	10,500	15,000
2d XR-7 Cpe	680	2,040	3,400	6,800	11,900	17,000

NOTE: Add 10 percent for GTE package. Add 5 percent for XR-7G.

	6	5	4	3	2	1
1969 Cyclone, V-8						
2d HT	520	1,560	2,600	5,200	9,100	13,000
1969 Cyclone CJ, V-8						
2d HT	568	1,704	2,840	5,680	9,940	14,200
1969 Cougar, V-8						
2d HT	560	1,680	2,800	5,600	9,800	14,000
2d Conv	620	1,860	3,100	6,200	10,850	15,500
2d XR-7	600	1,800	3,000	6,000	10,500	15,000
2d XR-7 Conv	660	1,980	3,300	6,600	11,550	16,500
2d HT	720	2,160	3,600	7,200	12,600	18,000

NOTE: Add 30 percent for Boss 302. Add 50 percent for 428 CJ.

	6	5	4	3	2	1
1969 Marauder, V-8						
2d HT	380	1,140	1,900	3,800	6,650	9,500
2d X-100 HT	560	1,680	2,800	5,600	9,800	14,000
1970 Cyclone GT, V-8						
2d HT	620	1,860	3,100	6,200	10,850	15,500
1970 Cyclone Spoiler, V-8						
2d HT	660	1,980	3,300	6,600	11,550	16,500

NOTE: Add 40 percent for 429 V-8 GT and Spoiler.

	6	5	4	3	2	1
1970 Cougar, V-8						
2d HT	580	1,740	2,900	5,800	10,150	14,500
2d Conv	640	1,920	3,200	6,400	11,200	16,000
1970 Cougar XR-7, V-8						
2d HT	640	1,920	3,200	6,400	11,200	16,000
2d Conv	760	2,280	3,800	7,600	13,300	19,000
2d HT	720	2,160	3,600	7,200	12,600	18,000

NOTE: Add 30 percent for Boss 302. Add 50 percent for 428 CJ.

	6	5	4	3	2	1
1970 Marauder, V-8						
2d HT	400	1,200	2,000	4,000	7,000	10,000
2d X-100 HT	560	1,680	2,800	5,600	9,800	14,000
1971 Cyclone GT, V-8						
2d HT	560	1,680	2,800	5,600	9,800	14,000
1971 Cyclone Spoiler, V-8						
2d HT	580	1,740	2,900	5,800	10,150	14,500

NOTE: Add 40 percent for 429 V-8 GT and Spoiler.

OLDSMOBILE

	6	5	4	3	2	1
1962 Jetfire Turbo-charged, V-8, 112" wb						
2d HT	640	1,920	3,200	6,400	11,200	16,000
1963 Jetfire Series, V-8, 112" wb						
2d HT	640	1,920	3,200	6,400	11,200	16,000
1964 Cutlass 4-4-2						
2d Sed	584	1,752	2,920	5,840	10,220	14,600
2d HT	660	1,980	3,300	6,600	11,550	16,500
2d Conv	800	2,400	4,000	8,000	14,000	20,000
1965 Cutlass 4-4-2						
2d Sed	552	1,656	2,760	5,520	9,660	13,800
2d HT	640	1,920	3,200	6,400	11,200	16,000
2d Conv	760	2,280	3,800	7,600	13,300	19,000
1966 Cutlass 4-4-2						
2d Sed	680	2,040	3,400	6,800	11,900	17,000
2d HT	760	2,280	3,800	7,600	13,300	19,000
2d Conv	880	2,640	4,400	8,800	15,400	22,000

NOTE: Add 30 percent for triple two-barrel carbs. Add 90 percent for W-30.

	6	5	4	3	2	1
4d 3S Sta Wag	420	1,260	2,100	4,200	7,350	10,500
4d 2S Sta Wag	412	1,236	2,060	4,120	7,210	10,300
4d 3S Cus Sta Wag	428	1,284	2,140	4,280	7,490	10,700
4d Cus Sta Wag 2S	420	1,260	2,100	4,200	7,350	10,500
1967 Cutlass 4-4-2						
2d Sed	680	2,040	3,400	6,800	11,900	17,000
2d HT	800	2,400	4,000	8,000	14,000	20,000
2d Conv	920	2,760	4,600	9,200	16,100	23,000

NOTE: Add 70 percent for W-30.

	6	5	4	3	2	1
1968 4-4-2, V-8, 112" wb						
2d Cpe	680	2,040	3,400	6,800	11,900	17,000
2d HT	760	2,280	3,800	7,600	13,300	19,000
2d Conv	920	2,760	4,600	9,200	16,100	23,000
1968 Hurst/Olds						
2d HT	880	2,640	4,400	8,800	15,400	22,000
2d Sed	800	2,400	4,000	8,000	14,000	20,000
1969 4-4-2, V-8, 112" wb						
2d Cpe	680	2,040	3,400	6,800	11,900	17,000
2d HT	760	2,280	3,800	7,600	13,300	19,000
2d Conv	920	2,760	4,600	9,200	16,100	23,000
1969 Hurst/Olds						
2d HT	920	2,760	4,600	9,200	16,100	23,000
1970 4-4-2, V-8, 112" wb						
2d Cpe	760	2,280	3,800	7,600	13,300	19,000
2d HT	920	2,760	4,600	9,200	16,100	23,000
2d Conv	1,040	3,120	5,200	10,400	18,200	26,000
1970 Rallye 350, 112" wb						
2d HT	880	2,640	4,400	8,800	15,400	22,000
1971 4-4-2, V-8, 112" wb						
2d HT	880	2,640	4,400	8,800	15,400	22,000
2d Conv	1,040	3,120	5,200	10,400	18,200	26,000

PLYMOUTH

	6	5	4	3	2	1
1965 Satellite, V-8, 116"wb						
2d HT	750	2,300	3,800	7,600	13,300	19,000
2d Conv	1,150	3,500	5,800	11,600	20,300	29,000
1966 Satellite, V-8, 116" wb						
2d HT	900	2,650	4,400	8,800	15,400	22,000
2d Conv	1,150	3,500	5,800	11,600	20,300	29,000

	6	5	4	3	2	1
1967 Barracuda, V-8, 108" wb						
2d HT	850	2,500	4,200	8,400	14,700	21,000
2d FBk	900	2,650	4,400	8,800	15,400	22,000
2d Conv	1,150	3,500	5,800	11,600	20,300	29,000

NOTE: Add 10 percent for Formula S and 40 percent for 383 CID.

	6	5	4	3	2	1
1967 GTX, V-8, 116" wb						
2d HT	1,100	3,250	5,400	10,800	18,900	27,000
2d Conv	1,350	4,100	6,800	13,600	23,800	34,000
1968 Belvedere, V-8, 116" wb						
4d Sed	296	888	1,480	2,960	5,180	7,400
2d Sed	292	876	1,460	2,920	5,110	7,300
4d 6P Sta Wag	300	900	1,500	3,000	5,250	7,500
1968 Road Runner, V-8, 116" wb						
2d Cpe	1,200	3,600	6,000	12,000	21,000	30,000
2d HT	1,300	3,850	6,400	12,800	22,400	32,000
1969 Belvedere, V-8, 117" wb						
4d Sed	288	864	1,440	2,880	5,040	7,200
2d Sed	284	852	1,420	2,840	4,970	7,100
4d 6P Sta Wag	288	864	1,440	2,880	5,040	7,200
1969 Road Runner, V-8, 116" wb						
2d Sed	1,150	3,500	5,800	11,600	20,300	29,000
2d HT	1,300	3,850	6,400	12,800	22,400	32,000
2d Conv	1,550	4,700	7,800	15,600	27,300	39,000
1969 GTX, V-8, 116" wb						
2d HT	1,200	3,600	6,000	12,000	21,000	30,000
2d Conv	1,550	4,700	7,800	15,600	27,300	39,000
1970 GTX						
2d HT	1,150	3,500	5,800	11,600	20,300	29,000
1970 'Cuda						
2d HT	1,300	3,850	6,400	12,800	22,400	32,000
2d Conv	1,550	4,700	7,800	15,600	27,300	39,000
2d Hemi Cuda Conv		value not estimable				
1970 Duster "340"						
2d Cpe	650	1,900	3,200	6,400	11,200	16,000
1970 Fury GT						
2d HT	850	2,500	4,200	8,400	14,700	21,000

NOTE: Add 60 percent for 440 6 pack. Autos equipped with 426 Hemi, value inestimable. Add 10 percent for 'Cuda 340 package. Add 40 percent for 'Cuda 383 (not avail. on conv.).

	6	5	4	3	2	1
1970 Road Runner						
2d Cpe	1,050	3,100	5,200	10,400	18,200	26,000
2d HT	1,150	3,500	5,800	11,600	20,300	29,000
2d Superbird	2,600	7,800	13,000	26,000	45,500	65,000
2d Conv	1,550	4,700	7,800	15,600	27,300	39,000
1971 Sport Fury "GT"						
2d HT	650	2,000	3,300	6,600	11,600	16,500

NOTE: Add 40 percent for 440 engine. Deduct 10 percent for 'Cuda 340 package. Add 70 percent for 440 6 pack. Autos equipped with 426 Hemi, value inestimable.

	6	5	4	3	2	1
1971 Road Runner						
2d HT	880	2,640	4,400	8,800	15,400	22,000
1971 Satellite Sebring						
2d HT	660	1,980	3,300	6,600	11,550	16,500
1971 'Cuda						
2d HT	1,000	3,000	5,000	10,000	17,500	25,000
2d Conv	1,120	3,360	5,600	11,200	19,600	28,000
1972 'Cuda						
2d HT	760	2,280	3,800	7,600	13,300	19,000
1972 Road Runner						
2d HT	840	2,520	4,200	8,400	14,700	21,000

PONTIAC

	6	5	4	3	2	1
1964 LeMans, V-8, 115" wb						
2d HT	640	1,920	3,200	6,400	11,200	16,000
2d Cpe	580	1,740	2,900	5,800	10,150	14,500
2d Conv	680	2,040	3,400	6,800	11,900	17,000
2d GTO Cpe	800	2,400	4,000	8,000	14,000	20,000
2d GTO Conv	1,040	3,120	5,200	10,400	18,200	26,000
2d GTO HT	880	2,640	4,400	8,800	15,400	22,000

NOTE: Deduct 20 percent for Tempest 6-cyl.

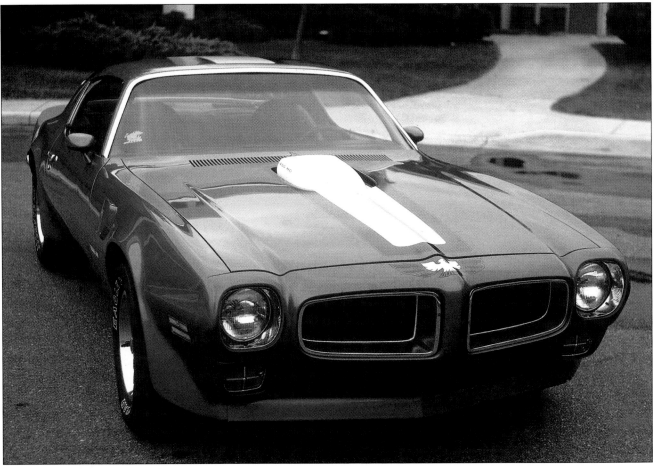

1970 Pontiac Trans Am

	6	5	4	3	2	1
1965 LeMans, V-8, 115" wb						
4d Sed	360	1,080	1,800	3,600	6,300	9,000
2d Cpe	420	1,260	2,100	4,200	7,350	10,500
2d HT	580	1,740	2,900	5,800	10,150	14,500
2d Conv	760	2,280	3,800	7,600	13,300	19,000
2d GTO Conv	1,120	3,360	5,600	11,200	19,600	28,000
2d GTO HT	960	2,880	4,800	9,600	16,800	24,000
2d GTO Cpe	880	2,640	4,400	8,800	15,400	22,000

NOTE: Deduct 20 percent for 6-cyl. where available. Add 5 percent for 4-speed.

	6	5	4	3	2	1
1965 Catalina, V-8, 121" wb						
4d Sed	312	936	1,560	3,120	5,460	7,800
4d HT	400	1,200	2,000	4,000	7,000	10,000
2d Sed	380	1,140	1,900	3,800	6,650	9,500
2d HT	580	1,740	2,900	5,800	10,150	14,500
2d Conv	680	2,040	3,400	6,800	11,900	17,000
4d Sta Wag	580	1,740	2,900	5,800	10,150	14,500

	6	5	4	3	2	1
1966 2 Plus 2, V-8, 121" wb						
2d HT	660	1,980	3,300	6,600	11,550	16,500
2d Conv	760	2,280	3,800	7,600	13,300	19,000

	6	5	4	3	2	1
1966 Tempest Custom, OHC-6, 115" wb						
4d Sed	304	912	1,520	3,040	5,320	7,600
4d HT	308	924	1,540	3,080	5,390	7,700
2d HT	532	1,596	2,660	5,320	9,310	13,300
2d Cpe	400	1,200	2,000	4,000	7,000	10,000
2d Conv	560	1,680	2,800	5,600	9,800	14,000
4d Sta Wag	300	900	1,500	3,000	5,250	7,500

NOTE: Add 20 percent for V-8.

	6	5	4	3	2	1
1966 GTO, V-8, 115" wb						
2d HT	840	2,520	4,200	8,400	14,700	21,000
2d Cpe	760	2,280	3,800	7,600	13,300	19,000

	6	5	4	3	2	1
2d Conv	1,000	3,000	5,000	10,000	17,500	25,000

NOTE: Add 5 percent for 4-speed.

	6	5	4	3	2	1
1967 GTO, V-8, 115" wb						
2d Cpe	680	2,040	3,400	6,800	11,900	17,000
2d HT	800	2,400	4,000	8,000	14,000	20,000
2d Conv	920	2,760	4,600	9,200	16,100	23,000

	6	5	4	3	2	1
1967 Firebird, V-8, 108" wb						
2d Cpe	720	2,160	3,600	7,200	12,600	18,000
2d Conv	880	2,640	4,400	8,800	15,400	22,000

NOTE: Deduct 25 percent for 6-cyl. Add 15 percent for 350 HO. Add 10 percent for 4-speed. Add 30 percent for the Ram Air 400 Firebird.

	6	5	4	3	2	1
1967 2 Plus 2, V-8, 121" Wb						
2d HT	660	1,980	3,300	6,600	11,550	16,500
2d Conv	880	2,640	4,400	8,800	15,400	22,000
4d 3S Sta Wag	520	1,560	2,600	5,200	9,100	13,000

	6	5	4	3	2	1
1967 Grand Prix, V-8, 121" wb						
2d HT	640	1,920	3,200	6,400	11,200	16,000
Conv	840	2,520	4,200	8,400	14,700	21,000

NOTE: Add 30 percent for 428. Add 10 percent for Sprint option. Add 15 percent for 2 plus 2 option. Add 10 percent for Ventura Custom trim option.

	6	5	4	3	2	1
1968 Grand Prix, V-8, 118" wb						
2d HT	640	1,920	3,200	6,400	11,200	16,000

NOTE: Add 10 percent for Sprint option. Add 30 percent for 428. Add 25 percent for Ram Air I, 40 percent for Ram Air II. Add 10 percent for Ventura Custom trim option.

	6	5	4	3	2	1
1968 GTO, V-8, 112" wb						
2d HT	760	2,280	3,800	7,600	13,300	19,000
2d Conv	920	2,760	4,600	9,200	16,100	23,000

NOTE: Add 25 percent for Ram Air I, 40 percent for Ram Air II.

1969 GTO, V-8, 112" wb

	6	5	4	3	2	1
2d HT	840	2,520	4,200	8,400	14,700	21,000
2d Conv	1,000	3,000	5,000	10,000	17,500	25,000

1969 Firebird, V-8, 108" wb

	6	5	4	3	2	1
2d Cpe	720	2,160	3,600	7,200	12,600	18,000
2d Conv	880	2,640	4,400	8,800	15,400	22,000
2d Trans Am Cpe	760	2,280	3,800	7,600	13,300	19,000
2d Trans Am Conv	1,040	3,120	5,200	10,400	18,200	26,000

NOTE: Deduct 25 percent for 6-cyl. Add 15 percent for "HO" 400 Firebird. Add 10 percent for 4-speed. Add 20 percent for Ram Air IV Firebird. Add 50 percent for '303' V-8 SCCA race engine.

1970 LeMans GT 37, V-8, 112" wb

	6	5	4	3	2	1
2d Cpe	520	1,560	2,600	5,200	9,100	13,000
2d HT	580	1,740	2,900	5,800	10,150	14,500

1970 GTO, V-8, 112" wb

	6	5	4	3	2	1
2d HT	880	2,640	4,400	8,800	15,400	22,000
2d Conv	1,040	3,120	5,200	10,400	18,200	26,000

1970 Grand Prix, V-8, 118" wb

	6	5	4	3	2	1
2d Hurst "SSJ" HT	620	1,860	3,100	6,200	10,850	15,500
2d HT	580	1,740	2,900	5,800	10,150	14,500

NOTE: Add 10 percent for V-8 LeMans Rally Pkg. Add 40 percent for GTO Judge. Add 40 percent for 455 HO V-8. Add 10 percent for Grand Prix S.J. Add 25 percent for Ram Air III. Add 40 percent for Ram Ai

1970 Firebird, V-8, 108" wb

	6	5	4	3	2	1
2d Firebird	600	1,800	3,000	6,000	10,500	15,000
2d Esprit	620	1,860	3,100	6,200	10,850	15,500
2d Formula 400	640	1,920	3,200	6,400	11,200	16,000
2d Trans Am	760	2,280	3,800	7,600	13,300	19,000

1971 LeMans GT 37, V-8, 112" wb

	6	5	4	3	2	1
2d HT	600	1,800	3,000	6,000	10,500	15,000

1971 GTO

	6	5	4	3	2	1
2d HT	800	2,400	4,000	8,000	14,000	20,000
2d Conv	1,100	3,350	5,600	11,200	19,600	28,000

NOTE: Add 40 percent for GTO Judge option.

1971 Firebird, V-8, 108" wb

	6	5	4	3	2	1
2d Firebird	620	1,860	3,100	6,200	10,850	15,500
2d Esprit	600	1,800	3,000	6,000	10,500	15,000
2d Formula	640	1,920	3,200	6,400	11,200	16,000
2d Trans Am	760	2,280	3,800	7,600	13,300	19,000

NOTE: Add 25 percent for Formula 455. Deduct 25 percent for 6-cyl. Add 40 percent for 455 HO V-8. Add 10 percent for 4-speed. (Formula Series - 350, 400, 455).

1971 Grand Prix

	6	5	4	3	2	1
2d HT	600	1,800	3,000	6,000	10,500	15,000
2d Hurst "SSJ" Cpe	660	1,980	3,300	6,600	11,550	16,500

1972 GTO

	6	5	4	3	2	1
2d HT	680	2,040	3,400	6,800	11,900	17,000
2d Sed	560	1,680	2,800	5,600	9,800	14,000

1972 Grand Prix

	6	5	4	3	2	1
2d HT	568	1,704	2,840	5,680	9,940	14,200
2d Hurst "SSJ" HT	620	1,860	3,100	6,200	10,850	15,500

1972 Firebird, V-8, 108" wb

	6	5	4	3	2	1
2d Firebird	580	1,740	2,900	5,800	10,150	14,500
2d Esprit	560	1,680	2,800	5,600	9,800	14,000
2d Formula	600	1,800	3,000	6,000	10,500	15,000
2d Trans Am	720	2,160	3,600	7,200	12,600	18,000

NOTE: Add 10 percent for Trans Am with 4-speed. Deduct 25 percent for 6-cyl. Add 40 percent for 455 HO V-8.

1973 Firebird, V-8, 108" wb

	6	5	4	3	2	1
2d Cpe	560	1,680	2,800	5,600	9,800	14,000
2d Esprit	580	1,740	2,900	5,800	10,150	14,500
2d Formula	600	1,800	3,000	6,000	10,500	15,000
2d Trans Am	620	1,860	3,100	6,200	10,850	15,500

NOTE: Add 50 percent for 455 SD V-8 (Formula & Trans Am only). Deduct 25 percent for 6-cyl. Add 10 percent for 4-speed.

1973 Grand AM

	6	5	4	3	2	1
2d HT	520	1,560	2,600	5,200	9,100	13,000
4d HT	300	900	1,500	3,000	5,250	7,500
2d GTO Spt Cpe	520	1,560	2,600	5,200	9,100	13,000

NOTE: Deduct 5 percent for 6-cyl.

1974 Firebird, V-8, 108" wb

	6	5	4	3	2	1
2d Firebird	340	1,020	1,700	3,400	5,950	8,500
2d Esprit	520	1,560	2,600	5,200	9,100	13,000
2d Formula	580	1,740	2,900	5,800	10,150	14,500
2d Trans Am	600	1,800	3,000	6,000	10,500	15,000

NOTE: Add 40 percent for 455-SD V-8 (Formula & Trans Am only). Deduct 25 percent for 6-cyl. Add 10 percent for 4-speed.

1974 Ventura Custom

	6	5	4	3	2	1
4d Sed	192	576	960	1,920	3,360	4,800
2d Cpe	180	540	900	1,800	3,150	4,500
2d HBk	196	588	980	1,960	3,430	4,900
2d GTO	260	780	1,300	2,600	4,550	6,500

NOTE: Deduct 4 percent for 6-cyl.

(Justin Barsalov photo)

(Justin Barsalov photo)

(Justin Barsalov photo)

1987 Pontiac GTA

1975 Firebird, V-8, 108" wb

	6	5	4	3	2	1
2d Cpe	300	900	1,500	3,000	5,250	7,500
2d Esprit	340	1,020	1,700	3,400	5,950	8,500
2d Formula	340	1,020	1,700	3,400	5,950	8,500
Trans Am	540	1,620	2,700	5,400	9,450	13,500

NOTE: Add 18 percent for 455 HO V-8. Deduct 25 percent for 6-cyl. Add 10 percent for 4-speed. Add $150 for Honeycomb wheels.

1976 Firebird, V-8

	6	5	4	3	2	1
2d Cpe	248	744	1,240	2,480	4,340	6,200
2d Esprit Cpe	260	780	1,300	2,600	4,550	6,500
2d Formula Cpe	268	804	1,340	2,680	4,690	6,700
2d Trans Am Cpe	276	828	1,380	2,760	4,830	6,900

NOTE: Add 20 percent for 455 HO V-8. Deduct 25 percent for 6-cyl. Add 10 percent for 4-speed. Add $150 for Honeycomb wheels. Add 20 percent for Limited Edition.

1986 1/2 Grand Prix 2 plus 2

	6	5	4	3	2	1
2d Aero Cpe	560	1,680	2,800	5,600	9,800	14,000

NOTE: Deduct 5 percent for smaller engines.

1989 1/2 Firebird Trans Am Pace Car, V-6 Turbo

	6	5	4	3	2	1
Cpe	760	2,280	3,800	7,600	13,300	19,000

1990 Firebird, V-8

	6	5	4	3	2	1
2d Cpe	300	900	1,500	3,000	5,250	7,500
2d Formula Cpe	320	960	1,600	3,200	5,600	8,000
2d Trans Am Cpe	520	1,560	2,600	5,200	9,100	13,000
2d GTA Cpe	600	1,800	3,000	6,000	10,500	15,000

1991 Firebird, V-8

	6	5	4	3	2	1
2d Cpe	300	900	1,500	3,000	5,250	7,500
2d Conv	600	1,800	3,000	6,000	10,500	15,000
2d Formula Cpe	320	960	1,600	3,200	5,600	8,000
2d Trans Am Cpe	520	1,560	2,600	5,200	9,100	13,000
2d Trans Am Conv	660	1,980	3,300	6,600	11,550	16,500
2d GTA Cpe	600	1,800	3,000	6,000	10,500	15,000

1992 Firebird, V-8

	6	5	4	3	2	1
2d Cpe	320	960	1,600	3,200	5,600	8,000
2d Conv	600	1,800	3,000	6,000	10,500	15,000
2d Formula Cpe	340	1,020	1,700	3,400	5,950	8,500
2d Trans Am Cpe	540	1,620	2,700	5,400	9,450	13,500
2d Trans Am Conv	620	1,860	3,100	6,200	10,850	15,500
2d GTA Cpe	580	1,740	2,900	5,800	10,150	14,500

NOTE: Deduct 10 percent for V-6.

1993 Firebird

	6	5	4	3	2	1
2d Cpe, V-6	320	960	1,600	3,200	5,600	8,000
2d Formula Cpe, V-8	520	1,560	2,600	5,200	9,100	13,000
2d Trans Am Cpe, V-8	540	1,620	2,700	5,400	9,450	13,500

1994 Firebird

	6	5	4	3	2	1
2d Cpe, V-6	420	1,260	2,100	4,200	7,350	10,500
2d Conv, V-6	540	1,620	2,700	5,400	9,450	13,500
2d Formula Cpe, V-8	480	1,440	2,400	4,800	8,400	12,000
2d Formula Conv, V-8	580	1,740	2,900	5,800	10,150	14,500
2d Trans Am Cpe, V-8	540	1,620	2,700	5,400	9,450	13,500
2d Trans Am GT Cpe, V-8	580	1,740	2,900	5,800	10,150	14,500
2d Trans Am GT Conv, V-8	620	1,860	3,100	6,200	10,850	15,500

VIPER

1993 Viper, V-10

	6	5	4	3	2	1
2d Rds	3,000	9,000	15,000	30,000	52,500	75,000

1994 Viper, V-10

	6	5	4	3	2	1
2d Rds	3,000	9,000	15,000	30,000	52,500	75,000

1996 Dodge Viper GTS Official Pace Car

BURN RUBBER
with these hot books

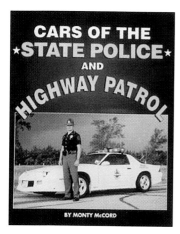

Cars of the State Police and Highway Patrol
by Monty McCord

Arm yourself with an in-depth photographic look at the vehicles, past and present, used by America's state police agencies. Monty McCord shows you close-up photos of door markings and license plates.

Softcover • 8-1/2 x 11
304 pages
500 b&w photos
Item# CSP01 • $16.95

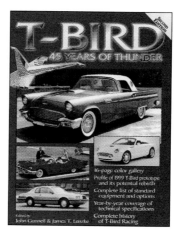

T-Bird 45 Years of Thunder
Second Edition
edited by John Gunnell & James T. Lenzke

You know it's fast. You know it's smooth. You know it's well built. Just like the all new T-bird: 45 Years of Thunder. Get a complete list of standard equipment and options for T-birds from 1955 through 1998 and coverage of the new concept T-birds and the soon-to-come 2001 production model. Plus, Vehicle Identification Number explanations, paint codes and technical specifications for all T-birds. And you'll glean through more than 45 years of literature written on the Thunderbird. Find out exactly what the famous Thunderbirds of the past looked like for your restoration purposes. Includes complete T-bird racing coverage, too.

Softcover • 8-1/2 x 11 • 352 pages
500 b&w photos • 16-page color section
Item# ATH02 • $21.95

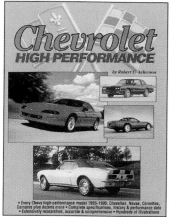

Chevrolet High Performance
by Robert Ackerson

From their exhilarating beginnings, the Chevrolet performance cars are expertly examined and explained by Robert Ackerson. Includes Corvettes, Chevelles, Camaros, and more. Highlights the star performer in NASCAR and NHRA drag races.

Softcover • 8-1/2 x 11
608 pages
200+ b&w photos
Item# CH01 • $24.95

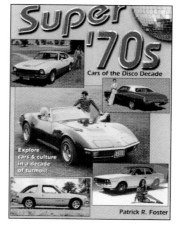

Super '70s Cars of the Disco Decade
by Patrick R. Foster

Patrick R. Foster guides readers on a trip through a tumultuous decade in automotive history. Witness the demise of big block gas-guzzlers and convertibles and the near-demise of the Chrysler Corporation. Relive the birth of the American subcompact, custom vans, t-tops and a new aesthetic. To put it all into perspective, Foster stops along the way to sample the music, movies and manias that made the 70s sensational.

Softcover • 8-1/2 x 11 • 304 pages
500 b&w photos
16-page color section, 44 color photos
Item# SSEV • $21.95

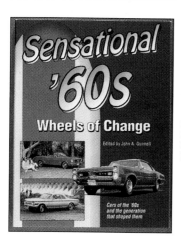

Sensational '60s
by John A. Gunnell

Cruise through the history of how the automobile helped shape America's history from 1960-1969 with more than 600 photos. Informative captions give you the facts, fads and philosophies of those turbulent years.

Softcover • 8-1/2 x 11
304 pages
600+ b&w photos
Item# SX01 • $16.95

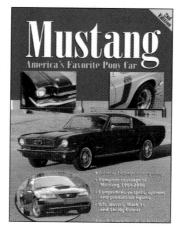

Mustang America's Favorite Pony Car
2nd Edition
by John A. Gunnell & Brad Bowling

GTs. Shelby-Cobras. Mach 1s. From the first steed to bolt off the production line to today, get a supercharged look at the most successful new car in automotive history. Go beyond the cloak of secrecy surrounding the pony car's early development and explore the prototypes and specials. See the legend in action at the track. Indy Pace Cars. And the 5.0 "litre of the street pack." Your complete 'Stang reference with up to date coverage showcases six more years than the last edition, plus an all-new 16-page color section-and helpful buying tips!

Softcover • 8-1/4 x 10-7/8 • 336 pages
300+ b&w photos
16-page color section, 36 color photos
Item# MS02 • $21.95

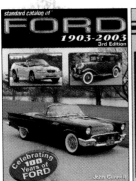
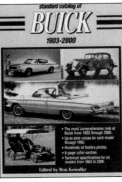

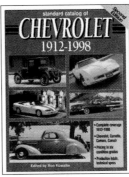
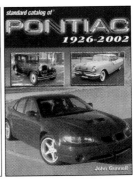
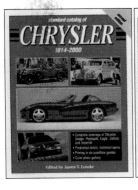
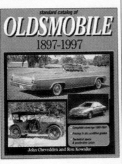
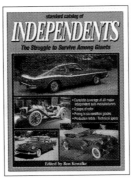

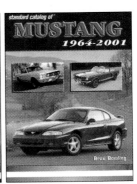